MICROSOFT®

WORD 2002

FOR LAW FIRMS

Check the Web for Updates

To check for updates or corrections relevant to this book and/or CD-ROM visit our updates page on the Web at **http://www.prima-tech.com/support/**.

Send Us Your Comments

To comment on this book or any other PRIMA TECH title, visit our reader response page on the Web at **http://www.prima-tech.com/comments**.

How to Order

For information on quantity discounts, contact the publisher: Prima Publishing, P.O. Box 1260BK, Rocklin, CA 95677-1260; (916) 787-7000. On your letterhead, include information concerning the intended use of the books and the number of books you want to purchase. For individual orders, turn to the back of this book for more information.

MICROSOFT®

WORD 2002

FOR LAW FIRMS

Payne Consulting Group, Inc.

A DIVISION OF PRIMA PUBLISHING

A Division of Prima Publishing

Publisher: Stacy L. Hiquet

Associate Marketing Manager: Heather Buzzingham

Managing Editor: Sandy Doell

Acquisitions Editor: Debbie Abshier

Project Editor: Elizabeth A. Agostinelli

Technical Reviewer: Randi Mayes

Copy Editor: Hilary Powers

Interior Layout: Marian Hartsough

Cover Design: Prima Design Team

Indexer: Sherry Massey

Proofreader: Jeannie Smith

ISBN: 076153394X
Library of Congress Catalog Card Number: 2001086712
Printed in the United States of America

00 01 02 03 04 DD 10 9 8 7 6 5 4 3 2 1

ACKNOWLEDGMENTS

Many people contributed to this book. To everyone who purchased this book—and our earlier books—you've shown the publishing industry at large that this is not a niche market. You supported these books and that's why we are able to write new ones. To our clients, we learn from you every day. As you tell us what you need software to do, express concerns about functionality, and allow us to come into your firms and work side by side, thank you.

Without Cory Linton from Microsoft, it's likely that we wouldn't have a lot to write about in this book. Cory led the entire initiative from the Microsoft end on discovering what law firms wanted, leading the Legal Advisory Council, and following through on delivering a product of which Microsoft can be proud. Thank you, Cory, for your dedication to the cause, unending patience, and hard work.

To the rest of the developers, product planners, and marketing and sales people at Microsoft, thank you for your work in building a great product. Special thanks to David Jaffe, Mark Eshom, Horacio Gutierrez, Kathleen Melle, Michael Mercieca, Greg Nicholson, Gretchen Rivas, Jan Roycraft, Steve Sinofsky, Lisa Swei, and John Vail at Microsoft.

The original Legal Advisory Council included twenty primary representatives and their designates, who were all instrumental in communicating the needs of law firms and getting Microsoft to listen. These individuals include:

Timothy Armstrong (Vinson & Elkins), Ed Castro (SAFECO Insurance Companies), Karen Cerri (Jones Day Reavis & Pogue), Scott Dugan (Bingham Dana), John Esvelt, Esq. (Fraser Milner), Linda Fisher, Esq. (formerly with Dechert), Judith Flournoy (Kelley Drye & Warren), Jeffrey Franchetti (Cravath, Swaine & Moore), Sally Gonzalez (formerly with Akin Gump Strauss Hauer & Feld), Jo Haraf (Morrison & Forester), Joseph Hartley, Esq. (Hartley & Hartley), Joy Heath-Porter (Sidley & Austin), Edward Jorczyk (Morrison & Forester), Andrew Jurczyk (Sonnenschein Nath & Rosenthal), Carol Landry (Kelley Drye & Warren), Robert Meadows (Heller Ehrman White & McAuliffe), Suellen Miller (Sonnenschein Nath & Rosenthal), Donna Payne (Payne Consulting Group), Richard Rodgers (Campbell University Law School), John Rogers (Herbert Smith), Len Rubin (Pfizer Legal Division), Kenneth Schultz (Greenberg Traurig), Carole

Sivertsen (Perkins Coie), Duncan Sutherland (formerly with Wilmer, Cutler & Pickering), Kathryne Valentine (Covington &Burling), Jeff Ward (Fulbright & Jaworski), Julius Welby (Linklaters and Paines), Cory Linton (Microsoft).

Some of the groups and people that we would like to individually recognize for their help and encouragement are American Bar Association, American Lawyer Media, Andrew Adkins, Siraj Al Hasan, Carol Anthony, John Allison, Andrea Ballard, Monica Bay, Kim Baker (at iManage), Frank Bayley, Len Bernstein, Tim Blevins, David Briscoe, Nadya Britton, Sheryn Bruehl, Azure Campbell, Pamela Campos, Center for Continuing Education, Amanda Clifford, Robert Craig, Kelli Crump, Arla Dillman, Denise Doyle, Farhad Farhad, Suzie Feld, Belinda Fernandez, Marsha Flowers, Gwen Foster, Jeff Franchetti, Pete Gaioni, George & George Douglas Gorman, Erica Greathouse, Sandy Hagman, Ethel Harding, Scott Harris, Mary Hilpert, Anne-Marie Istafanous, Anita Jaffee, Sherry Kappel, Chris Kitterman, Ross "friends don't let friends word-process without Reveal Codes" Kodner, Kelli Kohout, Kristi Lea Master, LawNet, *Law Office Computing, Law Technology News,* Soline Leng, Kristen Dana Collins Lewis, Vicki Leigh Lewis, George M. Lewis Sr., Hannah Caroline Lewis, Janet MacFarlane, Mal Mead, Karen Nickerson, Patricia O'Hara, Dean Olsen, Anne Palmer, Peter Parsons (attorney extraordinaire), Robyn Pascale, Pearl Payne, Alma Perez, Dora Pontow, Scott Randall, Jeffrey Roach, Glenn Rogers, Jim Rosenthal, Michele Rollins, Erik Ruthruff, Linda Sackett, Bonnie Speer-McGrath, Neil Squillante, Eugene Stein, Kelley Stennet, TechnoLawyer, Daryl Teshima, Charlene Traynor, the Washington Bar Association, Peggy Weschler, and Jill Windwere.

Last but not least, this book would not be possible without the people doing all the work behind the scenes, who often don't receive the credit they deserve. To Randi Mayes, our technical editor and *amazing* LawNet Executive Director: when Prima asked whom we wanted for technical editor, you were the first choice. Thank you for reading every word of the book, for your tireless effort in making sure all the steps work, and for your long-standing support. You are one of our favorite people! To Estelle Manticas, who tolerated what seemed like thousands of figure reshoots, frantic telephone calls and e-mail notes, and who *never* showed her frustration. We've been fortunate enough to work with Hilary Powers, probably the best copyeditor around, for the past two books. You make us look good and it's always a pleasure to work with you. Debbie Abshier has supported and believed in Payne Consulting Group—even before we were called Payne Consulting Group. Thanks for signing our books, Debbie. We will always consider you a friend. Sincere thanks and appreciation to Stacy Hiquet, who is one of the big bosses at Prima who is in charge of the book, to Elizabeth

Agostinelli, who stepped in at the last minute and took on the large and often unthanked role of project editor. You did a great job and it was a pleasure working with you. To Jennifer Breece, who created great posters and flyers and works hard to publicize our books—you all have great style.

I realize this is a long thank-you section but the book wouldn't be complete without thanking everyone who purchases this and other Payne Consulting Group books. We've received hundreds of e-mail messages about what you like, and suggestions for how to make the books even better. Without you there would be no Word for Law Firms books.

About the Authors

Payne Consulting Group, Inc., is a world leader in software training and development with a specialization in migrating law firms and government legal departments to Microsoft products. We are members of the original Microsoft Legal Advisory Council and because of this, have worked with Word 2002 and Office XP—every step of the way.

The company has authored 10 books on Microsoft products—three of which are for the legal community including Payne's *Word 97, Word 2000,* and now *Word 2002 for Law Firms.*

Payne developers offer a bevy of legal-specific products that make working with Microsoft Office software easier. One such product, the Metadata Assistant cleans confidential and residual information from documents was featured on the front page of the Wall Street Journal.

We are considered expert by Microsoft, law firms, and clients, and our goal is to transfer the knowledge that we have about software—making the transition to each product as seamless as possible. Payne Consulting Group is a Microsoft Certified Solution Provider. The company Web address is www.payneconsulting.com/. For information, send e-mail to info@payneconsulting.com.

MAIN AUTHORS

Donna Payne is president and founder of Payne Consulting Group. As an original member of the Microsoft Legal Advisory Council, Donna worked closely with Microsoft and the other council members to make Word 2002 and Office XP better suited for the legal community. Recently Payne embarked on a 20-city tour of the U.S. and Canada showing the legal features of Office XP. She continues to be a featured speaker for Microsoft, legal and technical conferences and is considered an expert on technology.

Donna is a member of the American Bar Association, and is a five-time recipient of the Microsoft Most Valuable Professional (MVP) award. She is a featured columnist for computer and law magazines and has been the subject of syndicated articles on leading women in technology.

Bruce Lewis is a high-end technical trainer and project manager for Payne Consulting Group. Bruce got his start in the legal industry as the in-house training manager for the Boston-based firm of Peabody & Arnold LLP. While there he managed the firm's WordPerfect to Word conversion. Prior to joining Payne, Bruce worked as a consultant for a well-known integrator in the Northeast, providing legal clients with everything from courseware development and high-end training to strategic consulting and project management.

Tara Byers is vice president of training for Payne Consulting Group. She is an iManage Certified Application Trainer and a Microsoft Expert in Word, Excel, and PowerPoint. Tara has been project manager for many law firm migrations from WordPerfect to Word, including an international firm of almost 2,000 users. As a speaker for Law Seminars International, she presents ways to master Word's features useful in a law office. Previous experience included regional management in a large retail environment as well as training and facility management for an international training company.

Shirley Gorman is director of client relations with Payne Consulting Group. She has over 20 years' experience in the trenches of law firms, first starting as word processing supervisor and later as training and development manager at Davis Wright Tremaine. Shirley has extensive software migration experience starting back in the "old days" when Wang ruled the law firm word processing arena. Next, she migrated the firm to WordPerfect and then to Word. She is a speaker at technical conferences and was asked to address the Microsoft developers regarding the specific needs of the legal industry.

CONTRIBUTORS

Susan Horiuchi is a trainer and project manager with Payne Consulting Group. She is a Microsoft Certified Expert in Microsoft Word and an iManage Certified Trainer. Susan has over 10 years' legal experience, starting out as a legal assistant and moving on to applications support specialist, trainer, and project manager. Susan has served as a member of a technology committee to improve technology in the law firm environment.

Other Contributors from Payne Consulting Group: *Leah Matthews,* ace developer and VBA trainer, contributed to the discussion of forms and fields as well as the VBA chapter. *Colette Crawford* worked on the bullets and numbering chapter, took many screen shots and tested the exercise files. *Jason Tank* added his Web expertise to the integration chapter. *Karen Walker*—a brilliant developer—was a great subject matter expert for designing useable and user-friendly forms found in the book. *Jane Krogman* made valuable contributions to the appendices of this book. Finally, *Robert Affleck,* one of the best developers in the business and a person who lives and breathes technology, served as a subject matter expert on several chapters.

Contents at a Glance

CONTENTS

CHAPTER 4 BUILDING A LEGAL DOCUMENT 87

CHAPTER 5 FORMATTING TEXT 121

CHAPTER 6
FORMATTING A PARAGRAPH 149

CHAPTER 7
FORMATTING A DOCUMENT 181

CHAPTER 10 TEMPLATES 285

CHAPTER 11 USING WORD TOOLS IN A LEGAL ENVIRONMENT 315

CHAPTER 14 AGREEMENTS, BRIEFS, AND OTHER LONG DOCUMENTS.... 435

INTRODUCTION

HOW MICROSOFT AND LAW FIRMS BUILT WORD 2002

The evolutionary process behind Word 2002 has been an exciting one. It all started on December 8, 1998, in Redmond, Washington, when Microsoft—along with Payne Consulting Group, Hummingbird, and Lexis-Nexis—held the first-ever Microsoft Legal Executive Summit. More than 100 law firms from around the world sent representatives to meet with the developers and product planners at Microsoft to discuss whether or not Microsoft Word adequately met the needs of law firms.

Within minutes of the start of the meeting, it was clear that law firms had a lot to say to Microsoft— not all of it good. In no uncertain terms, they let Microsoft know that their needs were not being met, that they didn't feel Microsoft understood the needs of law firms, and that they seriously questioned whether or not Microsoft actually cared about the legal community.

To the credit of Microsoft, the company responded not by glossing over the situation but by forming the Legal Advisory Council to work with the company to identify and prioritize the issues law firms had with the software. Among the most important issues were document corruption and problems with conversion, numbering, styles, track changes, ODMA integration, footnotes, mail merge, the integration between Excel and Word, fields, tables of contents, and security. The law firms also asked for a multi-selection feature, and the always-requested "Reveal Codes."

Upon seeing Word 2002 for the first time, the Legal Advisory Council was at first quiet, and then erupted into a round of applause. Microsoft listened to our complaints, suggestions, and feedback—and then created a product that we all can use.

Word 2002 is the first version of the product designed specifically for the legal industry. But make no mistake, Microsoft has not released a legal version of Word. Instead, the legal industry has collaborated with Microsoft to make the standard product much better.

This book explains the new and improved features of Word 2002 as well as information for how to successfully use Word in a legal environment.

Donna Payne
Member of the Legal Advisory Counsel and President of Payne Consulting Group

WHO SHOULD USE THIS BOOK

The simple answer is, everyone who uses or plans to use Microsoft Word. New Word users will find everything needed to get started and to master the use of Word in a law firm, government, or corporate legal environment. For those who have used previous versions of Word, *Word 2002 for Law Firms* covers the new and improved features of Word along with typical areas in which legal users have problems. We give you practical solutions to increase your productivity and decrease the amount of time that you'll need to get up and running as you make the transition to Word 2002.

The book is written for anyone from the beginning Word user to the more advanced. This book provides more hands-on exercises than our earlier books, plus an accompanying CD-ROM with even more exercises, macro examples, and information.

We think you'll find that this book is packed with ideas and effective approaches for using Word 2002 in your firm.

HOW TO READ THIS BOOK

Each chapter in the book provides an abundance of practical, hands-on exercises. These exercises have been designed to walk you through the steps to accomplish the tasks that you need to get the job done. In fact, you may find it tempting to skip the chapter text and go straight to the exercises—especially if you have documents to finish that were due yesterday. We recommend that you read through the text as much as possible, however. We've supplemented it with many notes and tips explaining aspects of Word's features that following the steps may not make entirely clear.

You don't have to use the book in any particular order; in fact, we think that you'll find it useful again and again as a reference source as issues come up. But if you're new to Word, you should spend some time with the first several chapters before you go on to other areas. The early chapters provide a foundation for using both Word's basic features and the more advanced ones that we cover as the book progresses.

If you are not new to Word, make sure to read Chapter 1 first. This chapter describes many of the new and improved features in Word 2002.

CONVENTIONS USED IN THIS BOOK

Before you skip over this section, let me explain that the conventions used in this book are important to understand. There are more conventions than just those that apply to Windows applications. This book has conventions of its own to make it easier to use.

KEYBOARD SHORTCUTS

Keyboard shortcuts are a combination of keys that you must press to access commands within Word 2002. You will see keyboard shortcuts listed in two ways:

- **Underlined Letters**. Underlined letters are used to denote hot keys—that is, the keys that allow you to access menus, items on menus, and items in dialog boxes. To access a menu, hold down the Alt key, and then press the underlined letter. Once a menu is open, you no longer need to depress the Alt key. For example, to access the New dialog box in Word, you would press Alt+F (to open the File menu), and then press N for the New command. To access commands in a dialog box, you always hold down the Alt key and press the underlined letter.
- **Keyboard Combinations**. Keyboard combinations are keys you must hold down simultaneously to get them to work. For example, pressing Ctrl+N is the shortcut to create a new blank document in Word. Some key combinations require pressing more than two keys. For example, Ctrl+Shift+K is the shortcut for turning on and off SMALL CAPITALS. When you see a keyboard combination, you must hold down all of its keys at the same time for it to work. If you are new to Windows, the easiest way to do this is to first press and hold down the Ctrl, Alt, or Shift key (or whatever combination you need), and then press the specified letter key. Trying to press them all simultaneously is difficult.

OTHER CONVENTIONS

- **Bold Text**. Bold text has been used to indicate text you must type to complete an exercise. For example, if we ask you to name a document **mybrief.doc**, it means to type "mybrief.doc" (with no quotes, of course) into the File Name box.
- **Extra Capital Letters**. The names of items that appear on menus, dialog boxes, and buttons have initial capital letters on all words, even though the

screen elements themselves often have only one initial capital—or none at all. This makes it easier to sort out the narrative text from the screen labels.

- **Button Names**. When you see a direction like "Click OK," it means that there is a button on the screen with "OK" printed on it. When you see a direction like "Click the Show/Hide button," it means that the button will not actually have "Show/Hide" printed on it. When you need to know what a button looks like to know what to press, we often provide a picture of the button for you to look for. The directions for using screen elements such as buttons always indicate that they should be clicked or chosen, never pressed.
- **Click and Alternate-Click**. These commands relate to the left and right mouse buttons. If you have set up your mouse for right-handed use (according to the Mouse settings in the Windows Control Panel), the primary button—the one you "normally" click (with your index finger)—is the left button, and the alternate button is the right button. If you have set up your mouse for left-handed use, the primary mouse button is the right button, and the alternate button is the left button. The alternate-click button is very handy and has many uses in Word 2002.
- **Programming Conventions**. If you venture into the chapter on Visual Basic for Applications, you should know that if a line of code continues from the previous line, we use the (mark. In other words, don't press the Enter key until the entire line of code has been entered.
- **Toolbar Conventions**. Word 2002 has many toolbars that make your life easier as you work, but generally only two are present when you first open Word. At first glance they may look like one because the default in Word 2002 is for them to share the same row. The first of these default toolbars contains buttons for basic tasks such as opening and printing a file; it is called the Standard toolbar. The second is the Formatting toolbar, which contains buttons for style and font settings and other tools used in formatting a document. Other toolbars can be turned on, usually by choosing Toolbars from the View menu, and you can turn off the option for the toolbars to share one row by clicking the drop-down arrow next to the last button on the toolbar and choosing Show Buttons On Two Rows. You can also choose Customize from the Tools menu and select Show Standard And Formatting Toolbars On Two Rows from the Options tab.
- **Key Conventions**. When referring to keys on the keyboard, not in Word, those keys are given the names printed on them whenever possible. The most common are Shift, Ctrl, Alt, Enter, and Spacebar. They all have initial capital letters, and the directions indicate that they should be pressed, not clicked.

SPECIAL ELEMENTS

You will see the following items used throughout this book:

This is a Tip. Tips are used to show you shortcuts and alternate methods for accomplishing tasks.

This is a Note. Notes are used when we need to give you more information about a task or feature. We might also use Notes to help you troubleshoot mishaps.

This is a Caution. Cautions are used when we need to alert you to a potential problem or misunderstanding.

NEW FEATURE!

This is a Sidebar. A Sidebar is an area of text that provides a discussion on how to best use a particular feature in Word 2002.

ON THE CD-ROM

A CD-ROM has been added to the book by popular request. This disc includes all exercises within the book plus extra exercise files that cover topics not extensively covered in the book. For example, there is an in-depth exercise on creating and working with financial tables on the CD-ROM. Macro code examples and information have been added to the CD-ROM as well to provide an array of resources — even if you do not have access to the Internet when reading the book.

Chapter 1

In Brief: What's New

IN THIS CHAPTER

- New Features in Word 2002
- Improved in Word 2002

Be prepared, Word has changed a lot from previous versions. The good news is that Microsoft worked closely with the Legal Advisory Council and law firms to find out what law firms need to be more productive using the software. The bad news is that there are many new or revised features (some of which may not be obvious) that would take you some time to discover on your own.

This chapter focuses on new and improved features of Word. It lists and summarizes each feature, and gives you a few simple steps to let you try it out. Subsequent chapters provide more detailed explanation and exercises to help you get comfortable with using Word 2002.

NEW FEATURES IN WORD 2002

At least 25 new features have been added to Word. The most important ones for law firms are probably the document stability and recovery, security, Smart Tags, ODMA support, Mail Merge, and collaboration improvements. Each new feature is listed in the following sections.

APPLICATION AND DATA RECOVERY

What good is an application if it keeps crashing? Not much, you will probably say. That's why one of Microsoft's primary focuses in this release was document and application stability. The Application and Data Recovery feature helps to eliminate loss of documents caused by General Protection Faults (GPFs, for short) by reporting errors as they occur and then saving documents before shutting down the application. When Word is restarted, Word recovers the document automatically. This feature saves documents, eliminates frustration, and exits an application process as gently as possible when it experiences problems.

Most times Word can correct a problem and shut down properly, but if Word is not responding, click Start, Programs and select Microsoft Office Tools. Choose Microsoft Office Application Recovery and then restart or end the Word session. Figure 1.1 shows the Microsoft Office Application Recovery dialog box.

If you choose to restart Word, a Document Recovery Pane like the one shown in Figure 1.2 appears, which allows you to recover documents that were saved automatically.

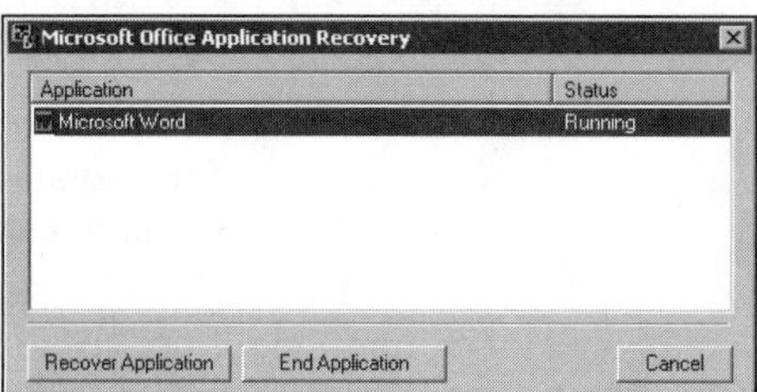

FIGURE 1.1

The top priority for law firms and Microsoft was better document and application stability.

APPLICATION ERROR REPORTING

When an error occurs, Word can automatically send a report directly to Microsoft that includes just the data on the error necessary to diagnose and correct the problem. Law firm IT departments concerned about security can set these errors to be stored on a staging server so they can review the information prior to sending it to Microsoft.

Figure 1.3 shows the Application Error Reporting dialog box.

This feature occurs automatically. Click Send Error Report from the dialog box or choose not to notify Microsoft of the error.

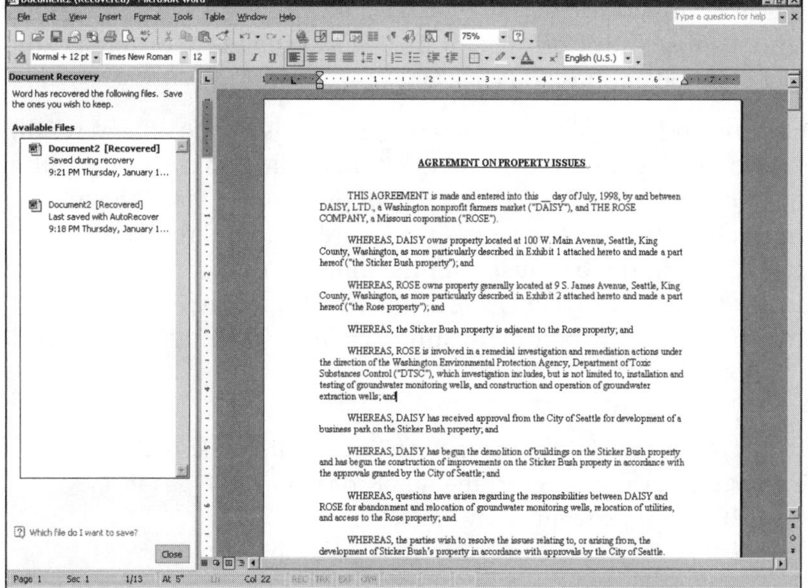

FIGURE 1.2

The Document Recovery Pane displays a list of all documents that were open at the time of the application crash. If a document is unstable and needs to be repaired, [Repaired] displays next to the document name.

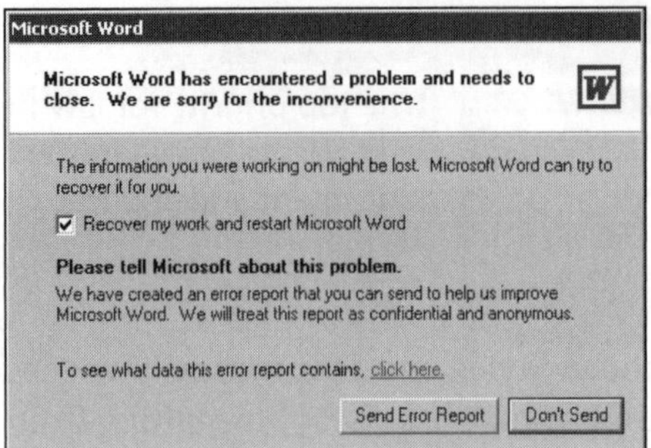

FIGURE 1.3

Application Error Reporting gives Microsoft immediate feedback if something is not working correctly.

ASK A QUESTION

There has been a lot of uproar over whether Clippit (the main character of the Office Assistant) should be retired. For those who do not like the Office Assistant, you no longer have to go through the Help dialog box or use the Office Assistant to get help on a feature in Word. The new Ask a Question feature places a box next to the Document Close control (upper-right corner of the document window) where you can click and type any question. The answer is displayed in an Answer Wizard balloon.

Click in the Ask a Question box and type a question or a word that you want to search the help files for information on. Press Enter to start the search.

AUTOCORRECT OPTIONS BUTTONS

Word automatically corrects text as you type. To control what is corrected, from the Tools menu, choose AutoCorrect Options. Select the AutoFormat as You Type tab. Select required options and click OK.

AutoCorrect Options buttons allow you to control what is corrected and when, without having to display the AutoCorrect Options dialog box. To trigger the AutoCorrect Options button, type **The 1st day of the month**. Place the mouse pointer without clicking over the words that were changed to superscript, in this case, "1st." Position the mouse over the blue bar that appears beneath the text and click the AutoCorrect Options button drop-down arrow. Select Undo Superscript, Stop Automatically Superscripting Ordinals, or Control AutoCorrect Options.

NOTE

If the text "1st" did not change into a superscripted ordinal, from the Tools menu, choose AutoCorrect Options. Select the AutoFormat As You Type tab and enable Ordinals (1st) With Superscript.

CLEAR FORMATTING

Not everyone uses styles or is an advanced Word user. When people use trial-and-error to get the effects they want, formatting can be modified extensively until you don't know what the text is supposed to look like. Word now provides a method for stripping all formatting and returning text to the Normal document style, but without removing hyperlinks.

From the Format menu, choose Styles and Formatting. Select the text that you want to remove the formatting from. Click Clear Formatting from the Styles And Formatting Task Pane.

DIGITAL SIGNATURES

Word documents can now have digital signatures attached verifying that the document is valid and comes from the original sender—without being tampered with. From the Tools menu, choose Options, and select the Security tab. Click Digital Signatures.

DOCUMENT RECOVERY

When a document is corrupt and cannot be opened, it is too late to solve its problems. Word includes document recovery that automatically displays a message box when a file-corrupting error occurs, which allows you to Repair or Save the file before it gets out of reach. This eliminates the need to recreate documents.

DRAWING CANVAS

The name *drawing canvas* conjures an image of a surface where a painting is created. The Word drawing canvas is quite similar to this but is an electronic drawing area that holds one or more objects and gives them an absolute position. This feature makes positioning text and graphics that must appear together easy.

Type several paragraphs of text in a document. Display the Drawing toolbar and insert an AutoShape. Click on the diagonal hash lines surrounding the object. Click Text Wrapping on the Drawing Canvas toolbar and select Tight. Click Text Wrapping again and select Edit Wrap Points. Drag any point around the object to change the text wrap position for the object.

HANDWRITING

Handwriting Recognition isn't as flashy as its spoken counterpart, but it is impressive. It can be used to insert cursive or printed text into documents as is (referred to as Ink), or as typeface characters (Text). This feature is excellent for quickly jotting down notes or creating to-do lists. The Drawing Pad component will even allow you to insert handwritten drawings or diagrams right into documents as inline graphics. From the Tools menu, choose Speech. Click Handwriting and select what type of handwriting to use.

LIST STYLES

The List Styles feature allows you to create and name a style for bulleted and numbered lists, and then apply the same style to other lists.

From the Format menu, choose Bullets And Numbering. Select the List Styles tab shown in Figure 1.4.

Click Add to create a new list style. To apply the list style to another list, select the unformatted list. From the Format menu, choose Styles And Formatting if necessary to display the Task Pane. Click the list style that you previously created, and the new list is formatted exactly like the other list in the document.

MARKUP AND TRACK CHANGES

The new Markup feature shows changes to the document by displaying callouts in the margin reflecting insertions or deletions when working in Print or Web Layout view. This makes viewing text easier by placing the edit marks off to the side.

From the Tools menu, choose Track Changes to turn the feature on. The Reviewing toolbar opens. Make a change to the document. Verify that Display For Review on the Reviewing Toolbar is set to Final Showing Markup. Figure 1.5 shows a document showing the Markup feature.

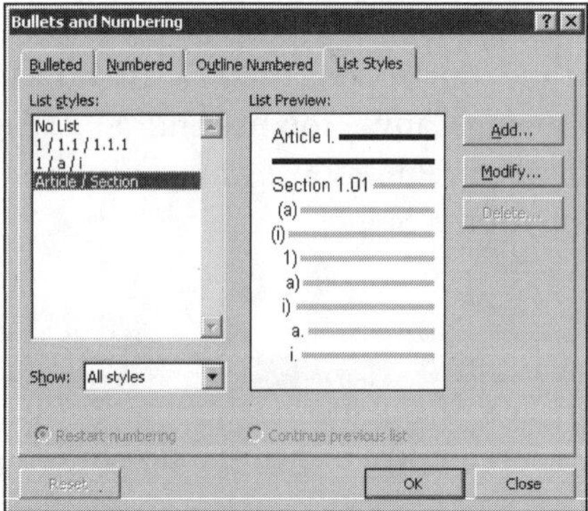

FIGURE 1.4

List styles are a type of numbered list that can be created, named, saved, and modified.

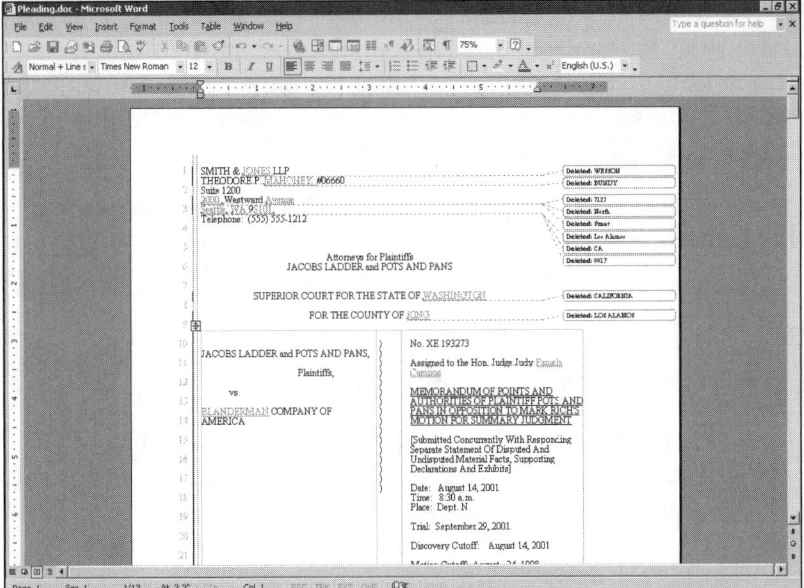

FIGURE 1.5

Word's new way of marking tracking changes is similar to proofreader marks. The Markup balloons can be set to appear in the left or right margin of the document, or not at all.

MULTI-SELECTION

The new Word Multi-selection feature allows you to select different areas of a document, even if they are not contiguous, by holding the Ctrl key as you click and drag the mouse. Select text in one paragraph, hold the Ctrl key, and select additional, nonadjoining text. Click the Bold, Underline, and Italic buttons. All selected text is formatted.

To take this feature one step further, use the new Find And Replace feature to select all text that meets a specific criterion. Once text is selected, formatting can be applied to the selection.

MULTI-USER DOCUMENTS

Word 2000 introduced Single Document Interface, which created a separate button on the Taskbar representing each open document. Not all Word users appreciated this behavior, so Microsoft added the ability to turn the feature off. From the Tools menu, choose Options and select the View tab. Clear the Windows In Taskbar option and click OK.

NAME, ADDRESS, AND DATE SMART TAGS

Previous versions of Word recognized Internet address and MailTo formatting to automatically add a hyperlink as the information was typed. Word now recognizes names, addresses, dates, telephone numbers, and more, and provides smart tag options for controlling each. Names typed in list format receive a smart tag with options to Send Mail, Schedule a Meeting, Open Contact, Add to Contacts, Insert Address, Remove this Smart Tag, or Smart Tag Options. Figure 1.6 shows the smart tag for names.

Address smart tag options include Add to Contacts, Display Map, Display Driving Directions, Remove this Smart Tag, Smart Tag Options. Dates Smart Tag Options include Schedule a Meeting, Show My Calendar, Remove This Smart Tag, and Smart Tag Options.

NEW DOCUMENT TASK PANE

Creating and opening documents has never been easier. Microsoft has added a New Document Task Pane that allows you to open a recently edited document, create a new document from a template, or search the Internet for additional templates.

From the File menu, choose New. The New Document Task Pane appears. To display the standard Templates dialog box, click General Templates in the New From Template section of the Task Pane.

OPEN AND REPAIR

There is nothing more frustrating than attempting to open a document and getting a message that the file cannot be opened and may be corrupt. Word now includes an Open And Repair feature that attempts to open and repair the damaged file. Unlike the Recover Text From Any File import filter available in previous versions of Word, the formatting is not stripped from the document when it is opened.

From the File menu, choose Open. Select the file name. Click the drop-down arrow on the Open button and select Open And Repair.

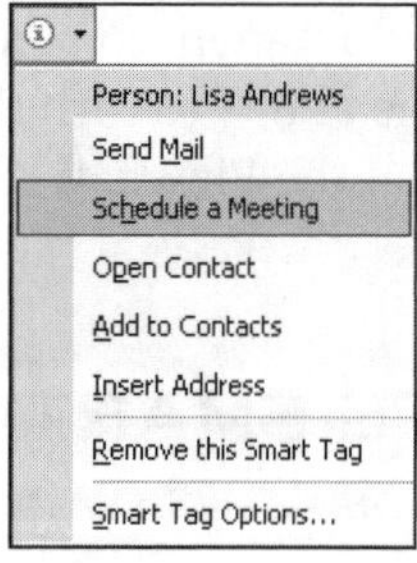

FIGURE 1.6

Word comes with several smart tag add-ins and more are available. West Group has smart tags that recognize citations. You can also build smart tags of your own.

OPEN DOCUMENT MANAGEMENT API (ODMA SUPPORT)

Firms that use a document management system will appreciate the work that Microsoft has put into making Word integrate more seamlessly with these products. Word now supports ODMA with the following features: Mail Merge, Insert File, Insert Picture, Information (such as document name in fields), Save As, and Compare And Merge.

PASTE OPTIONS BUTTON

When information is copied and then pasted, a Paste Options button appears. The options when copying to and from Word include Keep Source Formatting, Match Destination Formatting, and Keep Text Only (which is the same as Edit, Paste Special, Unformatted Text).

Select information to be copied. Press Ctrl+C or Edit, Copy to copy the text. Press Ctrl+V or Edit, Paste to paste the information. The Paste Options button appears as a Clipboard symbol below the copied text. Click the drop-down arrow and choose an option. If text is copied from another application, different Paste Options appear.

REVEAL FORMATTING TASK PANE

WordPerfect users have asked for reveal codes for years and Word now provides the ability to see—or reveal—information about how text and the entire document are formatted. From the Format menu, choose Reveal Formatting to display the Reveal Formatting Task Pane shown in Figure 1.7.

The Font section of the Task Pane lists the name of the font used and the font size. The Paragraph section lists the alignment, indentation, and spacing for the active paragraph. Section lists margins, layout, and paper size. If the active paragraph contains bullets or numbering, or if you are in a table, additional options appear in the task pane. Other options include Distinguish Style Source. Text can also be compared to other text by selecting text and clicking the Compare To Another Selection option at the top of the Reveal Formatting Task Pane and then selecting the text to be compared.

SAVE AS FILTERED WEB PAGE

The Save As Filtered Web Page option strips out XML tags when saving the document, producing clean HTML files. The option strips out much of the formatting that is specific to Word HTML and style markup used when reading the file in Word. If a file must be returned to Word for making edits, do not use Save As

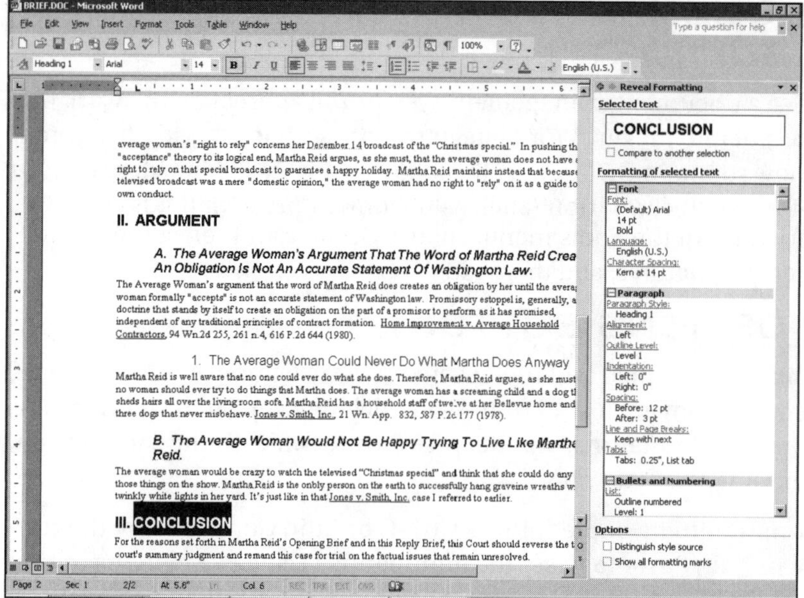

FIGURE 1.7

Click the hyperlinks in the Reveal Formatting Task Pane to display the dialog box specific to the formatting that needs to be changed.

Filtered Web Page; use Save As Web Page instead to preserve Word formatting and XML tags.

From the File menu, choose Save As Web Page. Click the drop-down arrow next to Save As Type and select Web Page, Filtered. Click Save.

SEARCH TASK PANE

The Search Task Pane provides an easy way to stay within Word and search for text within a document, e-mail message, or other Office application file. Using the Search Task Pane, you can also search for folders in addition to files. Files can be indexed for faster searching as well.

From the File menu, choose Search, or click Search on the Standard toolbar.

SECURITY

When you create, open, or save a Microsoft Word document, the document may include information that contains data that you may not want others outside of your organization to discover. Microsoft refers to this information as *metadata*, used to enhance editing, viewing, filing, and retrieving Microsoft Office documents. There is new security in Microsoft Word that helps with these issues.

From the Tools menu, choose Options. Select the Security tab. In the Privacy Options section, check Remove Personal Information From This File On Save, or Warn Before Printing Or Saving Or Sending A File That Contains Tracked Changes Or Comments. Test this option carefully to make sure all confidential information is removed from the file.

Digital signatures can also be added to sign the entire document to add a measure of security. From the Tools menu, choose Options and select the Security tab. Click Digital Signatures, and then Add.

SEND FOR REVIEW

When documents are shared with others, it is often necessary to send a document to someone else for review, then see changes made, and merge them to the original file. Send For Review makes this easy. From the File menu, choose Send To, Mail Recipient for Review. An Outlook e-mail message is created and the file attached. When the attachment is received and the file opened, the Reviewing toolbar appears. Click Reply With Changes to return the document as an e-mail attachment to the original sender. When the original sender receives the file and opens it, a message appears asking if they would like to merge the attachment into the original file.

SHOW DOCUMENT FORMAT

It's often difficult to tell what software and version a document was originally created in. These facts are important because if you plan to send the document back to the author and they used a different file format, they may have difficulty accessing the file, or it may be unreadable in some instances. For example, the file format for Word 95 is different from the one used for Word 97 and later.

The Show Document Format feature shows you what type of file format the document is in. Open the document. From the File menu, choose Properties. Select the General tab. The Type section shows the file format for the document. Since Word versions 97 and higher use the same file format, these versions are combined to show Word97 to 2002.

SPEECH

If you prefer dictating to typing, you can do this using the new Speech feature in Word. If this feature is installed, you can dictate text, format text and change text formatting, and expand menus just by speaking. The feature is currently limited to U.S. English, Simplified Chinese, and Japanese. To access the Speech feature in Word (and all of Office), install the feature on your computer. Train the computer on your speaking patterns with the training program that is included upon installation. From the Tools menu, choose Speech. Select Dictation mode or Command mode from the Speech toolbar.

STYLES AND FORMATTING TASK PANE

Everything in Word has a style, whether the Normal default style or a manually applied style. Since styles and formatting are instrumental in using Word correctly, it makes sense that they should be easy to access. The Styles And Formatting Task Pane shown in Figure 1.8 makes applying styles and recognizing formatting easy.

From the Format menu, choose Styles And Formatting to display the Styles And Formatting Task Pane. Click the Show drop-down arrow and select All Styles. This shows all styles available in Word. Change Show to Formatting In Use. Select text and then click the appropriate style or formatting on the task pane. Create a new style by clicking New Style. Select everything formatted with a particular style in the document by clicking Select All. As formatting changes, it appears in the task pane.

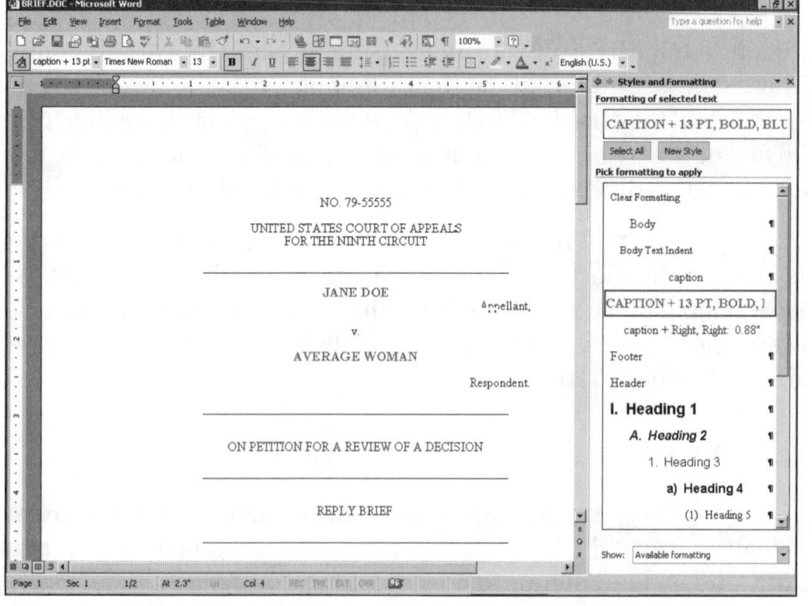

FIGURE 1.8

The Styles And Formatting Task Pane organizes all things that have to do with styles in one location.

STYLE SEPARATOR AND TABLE OF CONTENTS

When information to be included in the table of contents must appear on the same line as text not to be included, use the new Style Separator feature. This feature is not available through any toolbar or menu command so you will need to go through a few steps to make this command accessible.

From the View menu, choose Toolbars, and Customize. Select the Commands tab. From the Categories list, select All Commands. From the Commands section, locate and select InsertStyleSeparator. Figure 1.9 shows this new command.

Drag the button to an existing toolbar and release the mouse, and then close the Customize dialog box. Create a new document and type **Agreement**. Format this with Heading 1 style by pressing Ctrl+Alt+1. Click anywhere within the word Agreement, then click the Style Separator button. At the end of the word Agreement, click and begin typing text that should not be in the table of contents. Agreement in this example is formatted with Heading 1 style, whereas the additional text is formatted with Normal style. The two styles are separated.

TABLE STYLE

Table Style allows you to create and name a style for tables, and then apply this format to other tables. Insert a table and select the entire table. From the Table menu, choose Table AutoFormat. Click New to create a new table style or Modify to work with an existing table style. Name the table style and apply any formatting. Insert a new table in the document. From the Format menu, choose Styles And Formatting to display the Styles And Formatting Task Pane. Click within the new table and then click the style that you just created in the Table AutoFormat dialog box.

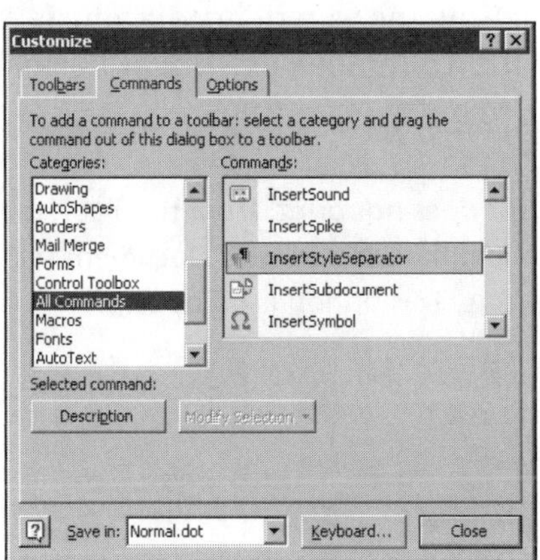

FIGURE 1.9

When adding the button to the toolbar, look for InsertStyleSeparator. Once added, however, the ScreenTip on the button reads Style Separator.

TEMPLATE GALLERY

Have you ever needed an arbitration agreement, affidavit of no creditors, or certificate as to minutes of a meeting of directors? Microsoft has added hundreds of templates to its Web site, and these are fully editable from within Word. To access these forms, from the File menu, choose New. In the New From Template section, click Templates on Microsoft.com. Click Legal and select a form.

TRANSLATE

Historically, law firms worked with clients who spoke the same language as they did. Aside from the requisite Latin phrases, the need to communicate in different languages was minimal. This has all changed. Many law firms have offices in several countries and share documents between these offices. Firms also represent clients who speak multiple languages, which makes the ability to translate text essential.

Word includes a Translation feature that translates text to other languages. The language dictionaries installed determine available languages, but you can also access a translation through the Web. From the Tools menu, choose Language and select Translate. The Translate Task Pane opens. The result is displayed in the Results box. If no translation is available, click Go in the Translate Via The Web section of the Translate Task Pane.

WATERMARKS

A *watermark* is text or pictures that appear behind text in a document to convey a message. Most often in legal documents, the text that appears is the word DRAFT or CONFIDENTIAL.

From the Format menu, choose Background and then Printed Watermark. Select Text Watermark and an item from the drop-down list, or type a custom watermark. Choose whether to lay out the watermark diagonally or horizontally. Click OK to insert the watermark. To remove existing watermarks, select No Watermark.

NOTE

If a watermark appears onscreen but does not print, from the Tools menu, choose Options. Select the Print tab. In the Include with Document section of the dialog box, check Drawing Objects. This option is on by default.

WHITE SPACE BETWEEN PAGES

Print Layout view displays a document as it will print, which makes it easy to tell what you're doing but also wastes a lot of real estate taken up by blank white space between page breaks. The White Space Between Pages feature hides unused space so you see more of the document onscreen.

Open a document with several pages of text or create a new multi-page document. From the View menu, choose Print Layout. Hover the mouse pointer over the top or bottom edge of the page and click when the two-arrow symbol appears. This hides the space between pages. Hover and click over the line that separates the two pages to show space between pages.

NOTE

If you are working in Print Layout view but this option is not available, from the Tools menu, choose Options. Select the View tab and check White Space Between Pages (Print View Only).

WORD COUNT

Word now includes a Word Count toolbar that lets you update the word count in a document and see the result without having to display the Word Count dialog box.

From the View menu, choose Toolbars and turn on the Word Count toolbar. Click the Word Count Statistics drop-down arrow and select Words. The number of words in the document appears in the box until you type or perform a different count. Click the drop-down arrow again and view the number of words, characters with no spaces, characters with spaces, lines, paragraphs, or pages.

IMPROVED IN WORD 2002

In addition to the numerous new features, Word has made significant improvement to many existing features.

AUTOCOMPLETE

AutoComplete now displays help when a word is recognized. Type **January**. After you type the "u," the AutoComplete tip appears followed by the help text, "Press ENTER to insert."

BULLETS AND NUMBERING

Applying bullets and complex numbering has always been a chore for legal users. Microsoft has made the process easier with this version. Once a bullet or number is applied to a list, you can double-click it to display the Bullets And Numbering dialog box. From there apply customizations to the format. Word also allows you to alternate-click a list and either continue or restart numbering without having to display the Bullets And Numbering dialog box.

The best change to Bullets and Numbering is the elimination of the "Jason" tab. See the Bullets and Numbering chapter for more information.

CHECK FORMAT

The Check Format feature scans for inconsistencies in how a document is formatted and allows you to quickly locate and fix the problem. These inconsistencies are marked with a wavy underline. This feature works automatically, or from the Format menu, choose AutoFormat.

COMPARE AND MERGE DOCUMENTS

It's not uncommon to create multiple versions of a document (each saved with a unique document name such as My Document v.1). These versions can be compared to one another with changes displayed onscreen. From the Tools menu, choose Compare and Merge Documents. The Legal Blackline option in the Compare and Merge Documents dialog box compares the two documents and creates a third, yet unnamed document with the changes marked.

DOCUMENT CONVERSION

Microsoft has made improvements to the way WordPerfect 5.x and 6.x documents are converted to Word. Some conversion issues addressed include: Numbering, Compatibility Settings, Language, Negative Tabs, Font, {PRIVATE} field codes, Window/Orphan control, Styles, and Advance codes.

FIELD DIALOG BOX

The Field dialog box has been improved to make inserting and formatting fields in Word documents easier. Instead of using complex field switches for formatting, select options from drop-down lists, and boxes. From the Insert menu, choose Field. Select from the list of Field Names, and specify formatting options. If you prefer viewing field codes to plain text, click the Field Codes button.

FOOTNOTE AND ENDNOTE

Word documents can now contain multiple footnote and endnote numbering schemes. Insert a section break, click within the section to include the footnote or endnote, and from the Insert menu, choose Reference, Footnote. Specify formatting options and whether to apply the formatting to the whole document, or a particular section.

LANGUAGE SUPPORT

Word now includes support for editing more languages than was available in Word 2000. The new languages include Armenian, Georgian, Hindi, Persian, Tamil, Thai, Vietnamese, and Urdu.

MAIL MERGE

Mail Merge now takes place in a Mail Merge Task Pane. A wizard walks you through steps required to create customized letters, e-mail messages, envelopes, labels, or a directory. Figure 1.10 shows Step 1 of the new Mail Merge Wizard.

To start the Mail Merge Wizard, from the Tools menu, choose Letters and Mailings, Mail Merge Wizard.

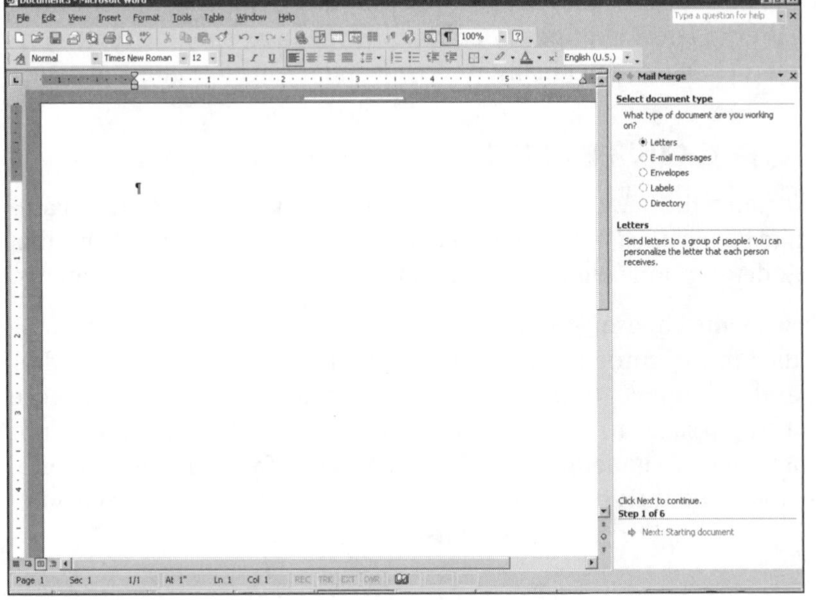

FIGURE 1.10

A Directory mail merge is the same as the Word 2000 Category merge.

OFFICE CLIPBOARD

Office 2000 introduced the Office Clipboard that allowed you to store up to 12 pieces of information from different applications, and then paste them one at a time, or all at once. Word has improved this feature by expanding the maximum number of pieces copied to 24. The Clipboard also appears as a separate task pane showing an icon (if available) identifying the application the data was copied from, and as much of the information as possible.

From any Office application, copy at least two pieces of information. This opens the Clipboard Task Pane. If you prefer to open the task pane manually, from the View menu, choose Task Pane. Click the drop-down arrow at the top of the task pane and select Clipboard.

PICTURE BULLETS

Word now allows for different picture bullets for different levels in a list. From the Format menu, choose Bullets and Numbering, and select the Bulleted tab. Select a bullet style and click Customize. Click Picture and select a Picture bullet. Click OK. Type text and press Enter. Press Tab to indent the bullet under the first one. From the Format menu, choose Bullets and Numbering and click Customize. Click Picture and select a different type of bullet.

REVIEWING TOOLBAR

The Reviewing toolbar now provides more options for viewing and editing a document. Filter to show changes or comments made by specific reviewers, accept and reject changes individually, or accept and reject all changes at once.

TABLE OF CONTENTS

If you haven't gotten the hang of using styles yet and don't want to have to manually mark text to be included in the table of contents, you'll be happy to learn that Word can now detect nonheading style text and include it in the table of contents.

From the View menu, choose Toolbars and select Outlining. Select the text to be included in the table of contents. Click the Level drop-down list on the Outlining toolbar and pick a level to be assigned to the selected text. Follow these steps for all text passages to be included in the table of contents that do not have styles assigned. To generate the table of contents, from the Insert menu, choose Reference, and then Index And Tables. Select the Table Of Contents tab and click OK.

CHAPTER 2

WORD 101

IN THIS CHAPTER

- Starting Word 2002
- The Word application window
- Creating and saving documents
- Opening existing legal documents
- Working with Word in a document management environment
- Protecting documents
- Exiting Word

If you're new to Word or have limited experience with previous versions of Word then this chapter is for you. Word 101 covers those features of Word that you need to become familiar with to create, save, open and close documents in a Word or Word and document management system environment.

If you are already an experienced Word user, you may want to skim through this chapter to find out more about what's new in the Word 2002 environment. If you're completely new to Word, get ready for your formal (OK—not that formal) introduction to Word 2002.

STARTING WORD 2002

Before you can begin creating documents in Word you have to start the application. This can be accomplished in a number of different ways depending on the way Word is set up for your environment. Here's a look at two of the most common methods.

STARTING WORD 2002

1. Click Start and then choose Programs, Microsoft Word.
2. Alternatively, double-click the Word icon on your Desktop.

NOTE

If you work with Word in an integrated document management environment such as iManage, DOCS Open, or WORLDDOX®, the steps for starting Word will be different from the ones used in a nonintegrated environment. Using Word in a document management environment is covered later in this chapter.

TIP

If your law firm hasn't removed the Run command from the Start menu, you have another method for starting Word. Click the Start button and choose Run. Type **WinWord** in the Open box and press Enter.

If you are using Word in a document management environment, open the document management software before you start Word. Document management software manufacturers include iManage, Hummingbird, WORLDOX®, and even Microsoft, which is a newcomer to this market with SharePoint Portal Services.

THE WORD APPLICATION WINDOW

The Word application window is made up of parts that make working in Word easier. Menus, toolbar buttons, task panes, and more are all designed to provide instant access to all of the tools and features that make up Microsoft Word.

Word 2002 comes with a sleek, more refined look than its predecessors. Although many of the menus and toolbars look the same, there are some new features worth noting. Figure 2.1 shows the Word application window.

Minimize Application Window
Restore Application Window
Close Application Window
Menu Bar
Formatting Toolbar
Title Bar
Standard Toolbar
Ask A Question
Close (Document) Window
View Buttons
Vertical Ruler
Active Cursor
Tab Alignment Box
Horizontal Ruler
Select Browse Object
Status Bar
Horizontal Scroll Bar
Vertical Scroll Bar

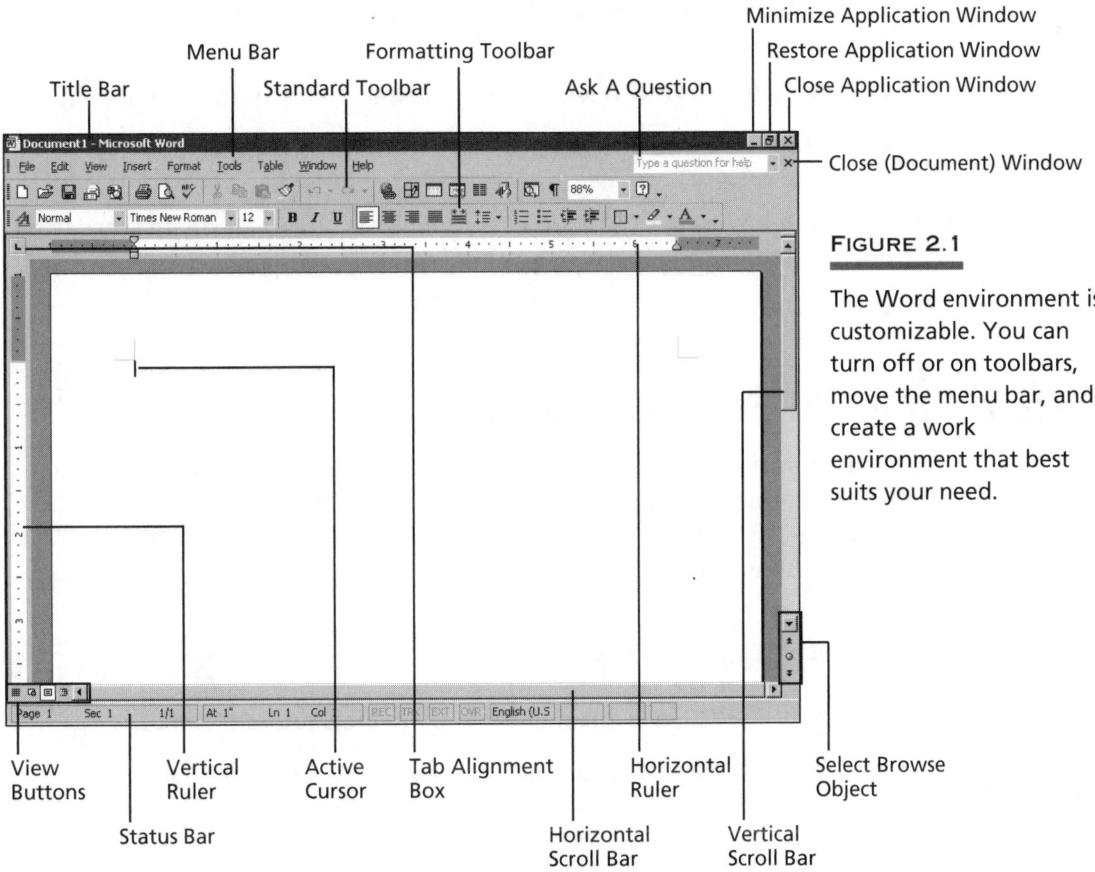

FIGURE 2.1

The Word environment is customizable. You can turn off or on toolbars, move the menu bar, and create a work environment that best suits your need.

The following list of terms will provide you with a brief description of each of the main components of the Word application window.

- **Title Bar**. Lists the title of your document and of the application itself.
- **Menu Bar**. Offers a set of nine different menus, each of which opens up when clicked to give you a menu list of associated commands.
- **Standard Toolbar**. Contains the set of buttons that allow you to quickly perform many different application commands.
- **Formatting Toolbar**. Contains the set of buttons that allow you to, among other things, apply different types of formatting to your document.
- **Minimize/Restore/Close Buttons**. Allow you to manipulate the Word application and Word document window.
- **Browse Object**. Allows you to browse through your document using different document objects—page, section, footnote, endnote, and others.
- **Status Bar**. Provides important document information.
- **Vertical Scroll Bar**. Allows you to move through a document vertically by page, screen, or line.
- **Horizontal Ruler**. Lets you set indents, tabs, and margins for your document.
- **Horizontal Scroll Bar**. Allows you to scroll horizontally through your document if necessary.
- **Application Window**. Contains everything else—this is the main Word window, and it stays open while one or more documents are active.
- **Document Window**. Displays the active document.

CREATING NEW DOCUMENTS

Creating new documents with Word is easy. As with most Windows-based applications, there is always more than one way to accomplish a specific task. The following list provides three of the most common methods used for creating new documents in Word.

CREATE A NEW DOCUMENT

1. Click the New Blank Document button on the Standard toolbar.
2. Use the keyboard shortcut Ctrl+N.

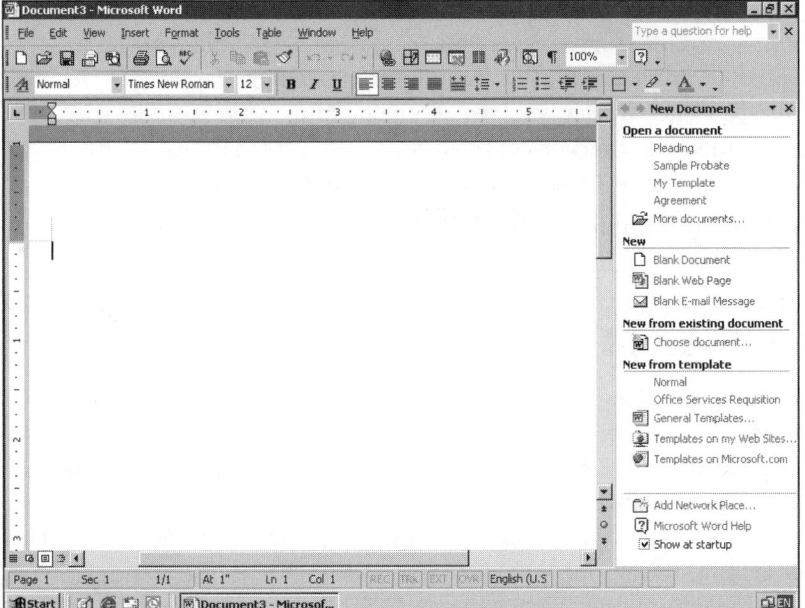

FIGURE 2.2

The New Document Task Pane lists most recently opened documents and makes it easy to create new documents based on other documents or templates.

3. From the File menu, choose New and then select Blank Document from the New Document Task Pane that appears on the right side of the document window. Figure 2.2 shows the New Document Task Pane, which is new to Word 2002.

If you don't want to use the New Document Task Pane instead add a button to the toolbar that provides choices for creating new documents. From the View menu, choose Toolbars, Customize. Select the Commands tab and select File under Categories, and New (with the arrow) under Commands. Drag the button to any toolbar and release the mouse. Close the Customize dialog box.

Click the drop-down arrow on the New button and choose what type of document to create.

NEW FEATURE!

The New Document Task Pane is a new feature in Word 2002. It allows you to open existing documents, create new documents, Web pages, and e-mail messages, or look for additional Word templates.

With Word you can have multiple documents open at once. You can choose to have each document reside in its own window so you can access it directly from the Windows taskbar. (In "Word speak," this is known as SDI, or Single Document Interface.) Alternatively, you can use the multiple-window approach found in Word 97 and earlier versions of the program. To set the option that's appropriate for you, from the Tools menu, choose Options and select the View tab. Check or uncheck the option Windows In Taskbar.

SAVING DOCUMENTS

After you start Word and begin creating new documents, you need to save your files. It's important that you get in the habit of saving your documents right away and at frequent intervals thereafter to avoid loss of data resulting from an unexpected crash or power failure. When you save a document for the first time, Word prompts you to choose a folder in which to save your document. The default folder is My Documents. You can save your file there, use standard Windows file-browsing techniques to choose another folder, or create a new folder.

The terms *directory* and *folder* are interchangeable; both refer to a place where you can store documents.

When you save a document for the first time, you will also have to choose a file name. Word supports file names of up to 255 characters in length but you'll probably want to limit it to something less than that (maybe 245 or so . . . just kidding). Keep the document name brief yet descriptive. Word documents are identified by the file extension *.doc.* You won't have to add this extension to the document name when saving—Word automatically does it for you.

You cannot include the following characters in a document name: { } / \ > < * ? " , | : ; .

SAVE A DOCUMENT TO MY DOCUMENTS DIRECTORY

1. From the Standard toolbar, click New Blank Document to create a new document.
2. Click Save.
3. In the Save As dialog box shown in Figure 2.3, choose the default folder My Documents to save your document in.
4. In the File Name box, type the name **Loan Agreement**.

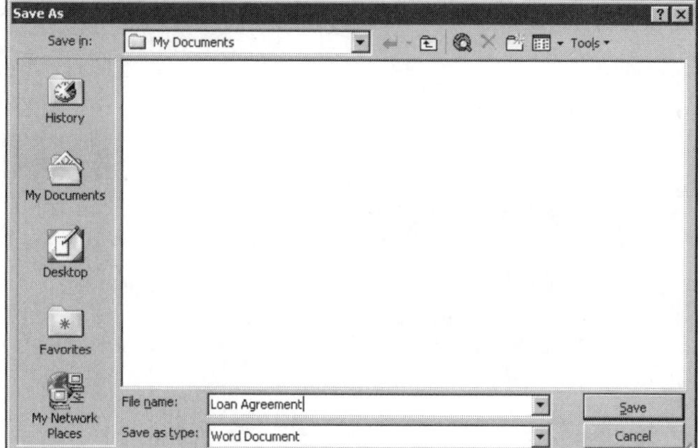

FIGURE 2.3

When a document is saved for the first time, the Save As dialog box opens prompting you to give the file a name and specify a location for the document to be saved.

5. Click Save.
6. Do not close the document yet.

That's it! Now each time you click Save while working in the current document, Loan Agreement, Word will save the changes you've made. The following exercise will lead you through the process of saving a document to a Matter folder using Windows' folder-management techniques. You'll use this same document later when practicing opening existing documents.

Remember to save frequently while working on documents to avoid loss of data!

Use the keyboard shortcut Ctrl+S to save documents quickly. The keyboard shortcut to display the Save As dialog box is F12 (function key).

SAVING A DOCUMENT TO A SPECIFIC MATTER DIRECTORY

1. From the Standard toolbar, click New Blank Document.
2. Click Save.
3. From the Save As dialog box, click the drop-down arrow next to Save In and choose (C:).
4. Next, from within the Save As dialog box, click the Create New Folder button (or press Alt+5) and type in the name **Matter 123456**. The resulting dialog box is shown in Figure 2.4.

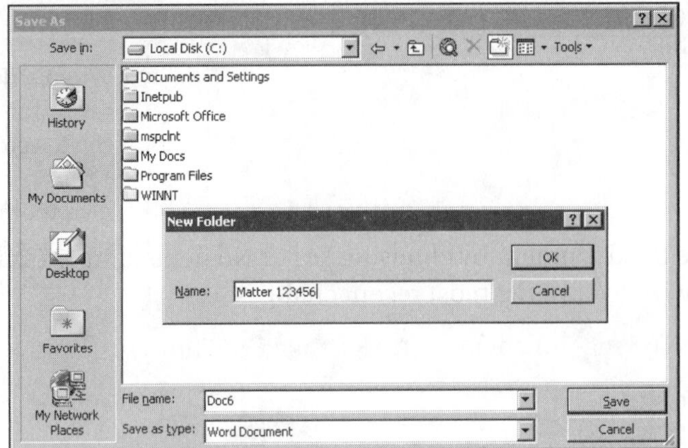

FIGURE 2.4

No matter how your firm organizes files, you can create as many folders as necessary to get the file structure you need.

5. Click OK.
6. In the File Name box, type **McDonald & Elliot Trust**.
7. Click Save.

You've just created a new Matter folder that contains the document **McDonald & Elliot Trust**. Never mind that there's nothing in it now—you'll come back to this document later when you get to the process of opening existing legal documents.

CLOSING DOCUMENTS

Now that you've practiced naming and saving documents, it's time to go over the last step in the process—closing documents.

CLOSING A DOCUMENT

1. Using the Windows Taskbar, select the document you first created, Loan Agreement. (You should have two open documents, the other being McDonald & Elliot Trust.)
2. From the File menu, choose Close.
3. If you've saved everything you've done to the file, Word will automatically close the document.
4. If you've done anything to change the file since the last time you saved it, you'll see the message box shown in Figure 2.5.

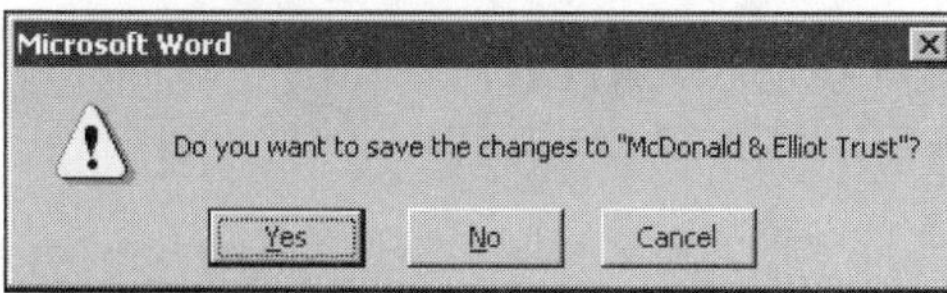

FIGURE 2.5

If any changes have been made to the document, you are prompted to save the document.

5. Close the document by choosing Yes or No depending on whether or not you wish to save the most recent changes.
6. Close the second document, McDonald & Elliot Trust, in the same manner.

You can also alternate-click on a document icon on the Windows Taskbar and close a document.

If you have several documents open and wish to close them all at once, hold down the Shift key while simultaneously selecting the File menu and choose Close All —this command is only available when you hold down the Shift key.

OPENING EXISTING LEGAL DOCUMENTS

Now that you're becoming more familiar with the basics of the Word environment, including creating, naming, saving, and closing documents, it's time to learn how to get back into documents.

To open an existing document, you have to know where to look for it. If you normally save to the default My Documents folder, then finding and opening your documents will be a breeze—until you get so many documents that they get lost in the clutter, which happens surprisingly fast. If you're a bit more organized and go through the process of setting up specific folders, then finding and opening your documents takes a little more digging but it will save you time and trouble in the long run.

Follow the next exercise to open the document Loan Agreement created in the preceding exercise.

OPEN AN EXISTING DOCUMENT FROM THE MY DOCUMENTS FOLDER

1. Start Word.
2. From the Standard toolbar, click Open or, from the File menu, choose Open. Keyboard users can press Ctrl+O to display the Open dialog box.
3. From the Open dialog box, locate the document Loan Agreement in the default My Documents folder, as shown in Figure 2.6.
4. Select Loan Agreement and click Open or double-click Loan Agreement to open the file. That's all there is to it!

NOTE

If you don't see your document, make sure the Files Of Type drop-down list in the Open dialog box is set to All Files (*.*) or Word Documents (*.doc).

The following exercise takes you through the process of finding and opening the document McDonald & Elliot you saved to the folder titled Matter 123456.

OPEN A DOCUMENT FROM A SPECIFIC MATTER FOLDER

1. From the Standard toolbar, click Open or, from the File menu, choose Open.

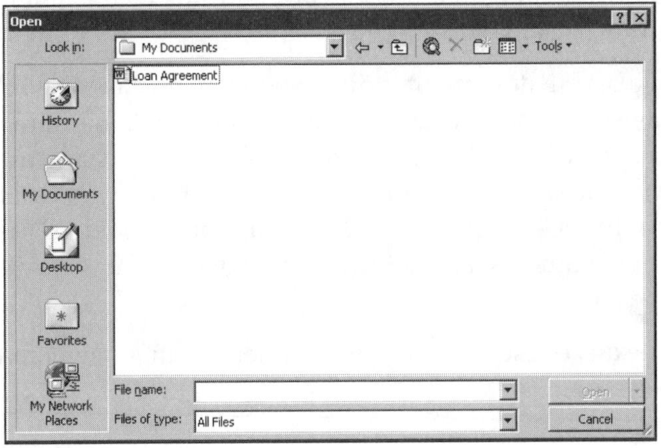

FIGURE 2.6

If the Open dialog box is set to have files appear as icons, documents can sometimes be difficult to find. Click the Views button on the Open dialog box to change the way files are viewed.

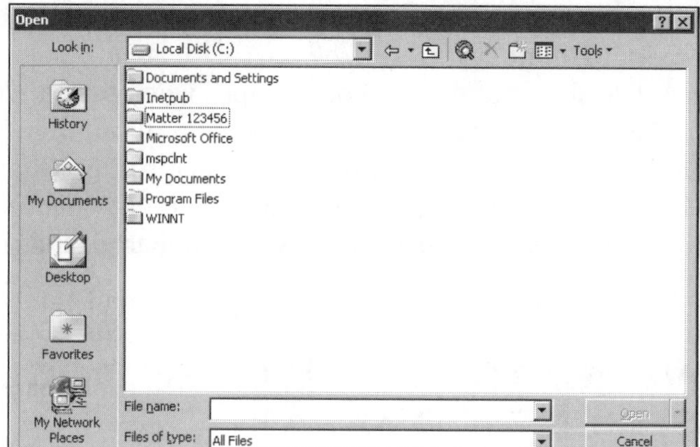

FIGURE 2.7

Matter Folder 123456.

2. From the Open dialog box, click the drop-down arrow at the top of the screen next to Look In and choose (C:) from the list of menu options.
3. Locate the folder named Matter 123456, as in Figure 2.7.
4. Double-click Matter 123456. Notice that it now shows up in the Look In field.
5. From within Matter 123456, select McDonald & Elliot Trust and click Open.
6. Alternatively, double-click McDonald & Elliot Trust to open the file.

USING WORD IN A DOCUMENT MANAGEMENT SYSTEM ENVIRONMENT

Most midsize to large law firms use document management software as a means of creating a secure repository for their documents. The three leading document management systems on the market today are DOCS Open, iManage, and WORLDOX®. These systems help law firms maintain, organize, and protect hundreds of thousands (and even millions!) of documents in a secure, searchable database. After all, documents are the lifeblood of every law firm.

The first part of this chapter introduces you to working with Word in a nonintegrated (that is, no document management system) environment. Now it's time to shift gears to see how using Word with document management is different.

The rules of the road change a bit if you work in an integrated environment. Document management systems take control of certain native Word commands such as File, Open, and Save. For example, when saving Word files using one of the document management systems, you fill out document *profiles* containing a number of predefined, searchable fields rather than naming and saving to a local folder. These fields contain document-specific information including document description, author, client and matter, and so on, and help to make documents unique.

IMPROVEMENTS TO THE OPEN DOCUMENT MANAGEMENT (ODMA) API

In previous versions of Word, when you chose certain menu commands such as File, Save As, you were presented with Word's native dialog box. The following dialog boxes now support ODMA:

- Compare And Merge Documents
- Insert File
- Insert Picture
- Open
- Save
- Save Address List—Mail Merge Wizard
- Save As
- Select Recipients—Mail Merge Wizard

In addition to integrating better with document management system dialog boxes, Microsoft has added two properties that can be used by inserting a field or through VBA automation to tie information from the document management system and Word together. These are Author and Doc ID.

Let's look at using Word in the context of a document management environment where certain native Word commands have been replaced with document management–specific commands:

- Starting Word
- Creating New Documents
- Saving Documents
- Finding Documents
- Closing Word

The following sections look at three different systems, DOCS Open, iManage, and WORLDOX®. The figures and versions of document management systems described in this book may not match what you have installed at your firm and should only be used as a reference for using Word and a document management system.

DOCS OPEN AND WORD

DOCS Open is one of the leading document management systems on the market today and is widely used within the legal community. Each DOCS Open database can store hundreds of thousands and even millions of documents. Users can search for documents within the database using profile or textual information. Searches can be saved and documents can be grouped into projects.

NOTE

The examples used in this book may not accurately reflect your environment. Contact your system administrator with any questions you may have regarding DOCS Open setup.

STARTING WORD FROM WITHIN DOCS OPEN

1. Click Start and then choose Programs, DOCS Open.
2. Alternatively, double-click the DOCS Open icon on your Desktop.
3. Once DOCS Open has loaded, double-click the Word icon located in the Applications window (Figure 2.8) to start Word.

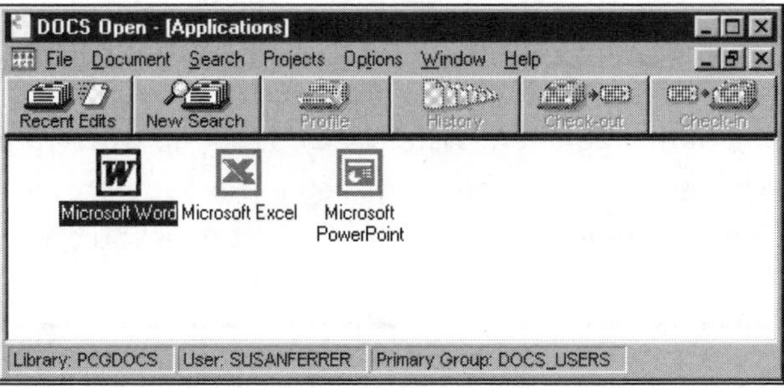

FIGURE 2.8

The DOCS Open Applications window shows icons for each application that can be started from within the document management system.

CREATING NEW DOCUMENTS

Once you've started Word from within DOCS Open, the process of creating new documents is pretty much the same as when working in a nonintegrated environment.

CREATE A NEW WORD DOCUMENT

Use any one of these techniques:

1. From the Standard toolbar, click New Blank Document.
2. Use the keyboard shortcut Ctrl+N.
3. Choose File, New and select Blank Document from the list of templates and click OK.

SAVING WORD DOCUMENTS WITH DOCS OPEN

Now you come to the part where things change dramatically. The first time you click Save in a new document, you'll find yourself looking at a Profile window instead of Word's Save As dialog box. Every document profile contains a number of fields that you will be required to fill in before you can save your document to the DOCS Open database. These fields are searchable and help to create a unique identity for each document.

NOTE

Your profile fields may be different from the ones used in this example. Contact your system administrator with any questions about your DOCS Open environment.

FRONT END PROFILING

Your document management system may be set up with *front end* profiling, which means you will be prompted to fill out a profile when first creating a new document rather than the first time you click Save.

SAVE A NEW DOCUMENT AND FILL OUT A DOCUMENT PROFILE

1. Start DOCS Open.
2. Start Word from the Applications window.
3. From the Standard toolbar click Save or choose File, Save.
4. Fill out the Profile by entering information into each of the required profile fields, as shown in Figure 2.9. Use the Tab key to move from one field to the next.
5. Click OK to complete the profile.

FINDING WORD DOCUMENTS IN DOCS OPEN

One of the main benefits of using a document management system is that it allows you to find documents easily. You can search for your own documents or those created by others. This section shows you a few of the different ways you can search for documents using DOCS Open.

- Recent Edits
- Profile Searching
- Full Text Searching

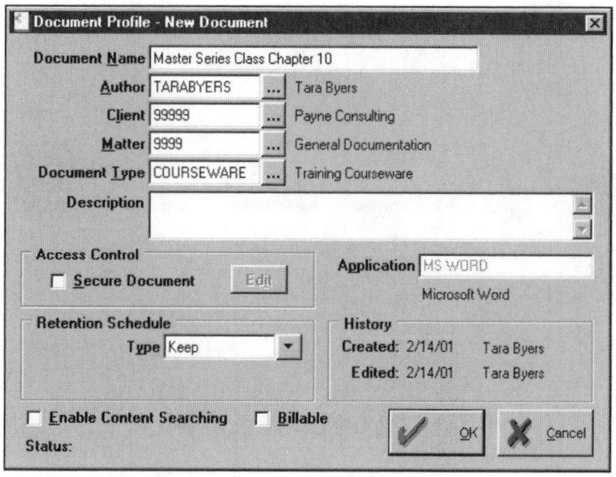

FIGURE 2.9

Information that you enter into the document profile makes searching for and retrieving documents easier.

RECENT EDITS

If you need to find a document you've created or have worked on lately, you can use the Recent Edits feature of DOCS Open to quickly see a list of your 30 most recently edited documents.

SEARCH FOR AND OPEN A DOCUMENT USING RECENT EDITS

1. Start DOCS Open.
2. Start Word.
3. From the Standard toolbar, click Open or choose File, Open to activate the Quick Retrieve (Recent Edits) window shown in Figure 2.10.
4. Select the document you wish to open and click OK.
5. Alternatively, double-click the document to open the selected file.

You can also access the Quick Retrieve window directly from DOCS Open by clicking the Recent Edits button.

PROFILE SEARCHING

Another way you can find documents in DOCS Open is by searching on specific profile fields. This is particularly useful if you need to find documents located under a specific client or matter, or documents created by another person. You can narrow or broaden your search by the number of fields you search on.

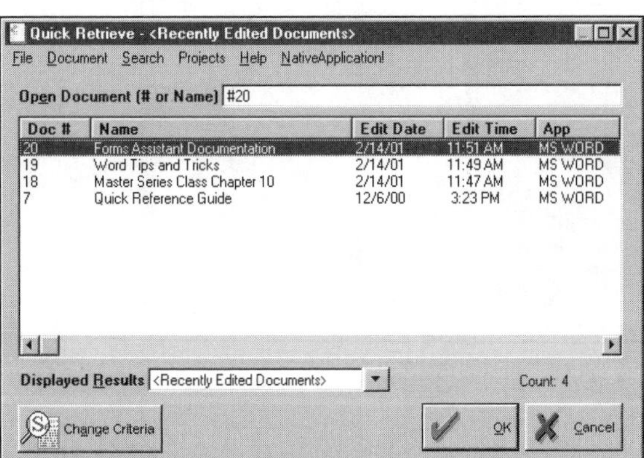

FIGURE 2.10

Files that have been opened recently appear in the Quick Retrieve Recent Edits window. By double-clicking a file from this list, opening documents takes only seconds.

FIND A WORD DOCUMENT BY PROFILE SEARCHING

1. Start DOCS Open, if necessary.
2. From the DOCS Open toolbar, click New Search.
3. Search using a combination of any of the fields shown in Figure 2.11. For example, if you're looking for a specific document created by another user under a known client and matter, fill in the author, client, and matter fields with the necessary information.
4. Or, if you're looking to find all known documents associated with a particular client and matter, you would fill in only the client and matter fields with the correct information.
5. Click OK to generate the list.
6. Practice more by experimenting with filling in different profile fields.

Click the Browse button at the end of each field to generate a lookup table. Lookup tables show a list of all possible entries associated with each field.

CLOSING WORD FROM DOCS OPEN

Once you finish working with Word, close all open documents and exit the program before closing DOCS Open. If you attempt to close DOCS Open before closing Word, you may receive a warning message.

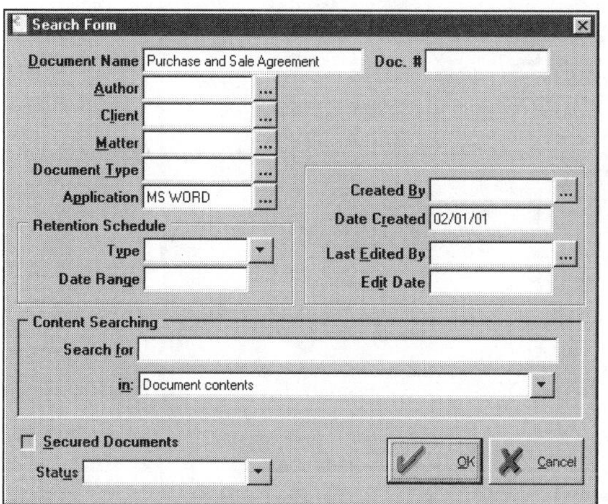

FIGURE 2.11

By entering more information into the Search Form fields, you can narrow your search criteria.

IMANAGE AND WORD

Well known for its three-tier architecture, scalability, and reliability, iManage is another leading document management system available to legal and corporate users. iManage's "Explorer-wlike" interface is popular and allows users to find documents, create projects and even jump right out to the Web.

NOTE

The examples used in this book may not accurately reflect your document management system environment. Contact your system administrator with any questions you may have regarding iManage setup and configuration.

STARTING WORD IN THE IMANAGE ENVIRONMENT

STARTING WORD

1. Click Start, Programs, iManage InfoRite.
2. Alternatively, double-click the iManage icon on your Desktop.
3. From the iManage Desktop (Figure 2.12), double-click a document located in the Worklist to launch Word.

NOTE

The Worklist shows a list of the last 40 documents you have opened or edited.

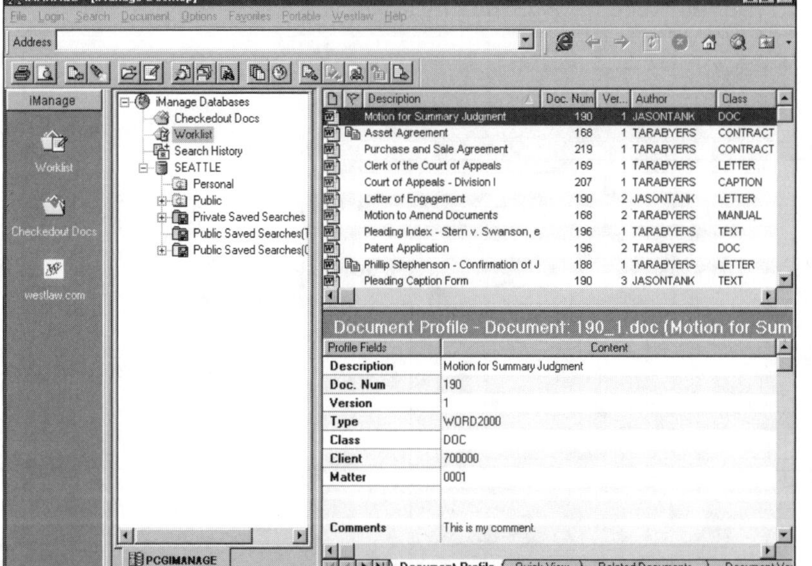

FIGURE 2.12

Many options are available when working in the iManage Desktop environment.

Creating New Documents

The process of creating new documents with Word when working in an iManage environment is the same as when working in a nonintegrated environment.

Create a New Word Document

Use any one of these techniques:

- From the Standard toolbar, click New Blank Document.
- Use the keyboard shortcut Ctrl+N.
- Choose File, New and select Blank Document from the list of templates and click OK.

Saving Word Documents with iManage

iManage uses document profiles to create unique identities for each document in the iManage database. Every time you save a new document in iManage, you have to fill out a document profile. Each profile contains a number of searchable fields that help make the associated document unique and easy to find.

NOTE

The profile fields used at your firm may be different from the ones used in this example. Contact your system administrator with any questions about your iManage environment.

Save a New Document and Fill Out a Document Profile

1. Start iManage.
2. Open an existing document from the Worklist to launch Word.
3. Create a new document.
4. From the Standard toolbar, click Save or, from the File menu, choose Save.
5. Enter information into each of the required profile fields to complete the document profile. Use the Tab key to move from one field to the next.
6. Click OK.

NOTE

You can start Word before launching iManage. The first time you choose File, Save or File, Open from within Word, iManage will open and take over. But instead of the full-featured iManage Desktop, you'll have the more limited Integrated Desktop from which to work.

FINDING WORD DOCUMENTS IN IMANAGE

One of the primary benefits of using a document management system is that it helps you find documents quickly. iManage allows you to search for documents in a number of different ways. Here are a few methods you can use to locate documents from within iManage:

- iManage Worklist
- Opening from Word
- Profile Searching

WORKLIST

The iManage Worklist contains a list of the last 40 documents you've created, opened, or edited. The Worklist is a convenient way to open those documents you most frequently use.

OPEN WORD DOCUMENTS FROM THE WORKLIST

1. Start iManage.
2. From the iManage Desktop, locate the Worklist pane (Figure 2.13).
3. Scroll through the list of your 40 most recently used documents.
4. Double-click a document to open it from the Worklist.

OPENING FROM WORD

iManage replaces some of Word's native commands, such as Save and Open. You can open a document located in the iManage database directly from Word.

OPEN DOCUMENTS IN DATABASES FROM WORD

1. Start Word.
2. From the Standard toolbar, click Open or, from the File menu, choose Open—the iManage Integrated Desktop shown in Figure 2.14 will appear.

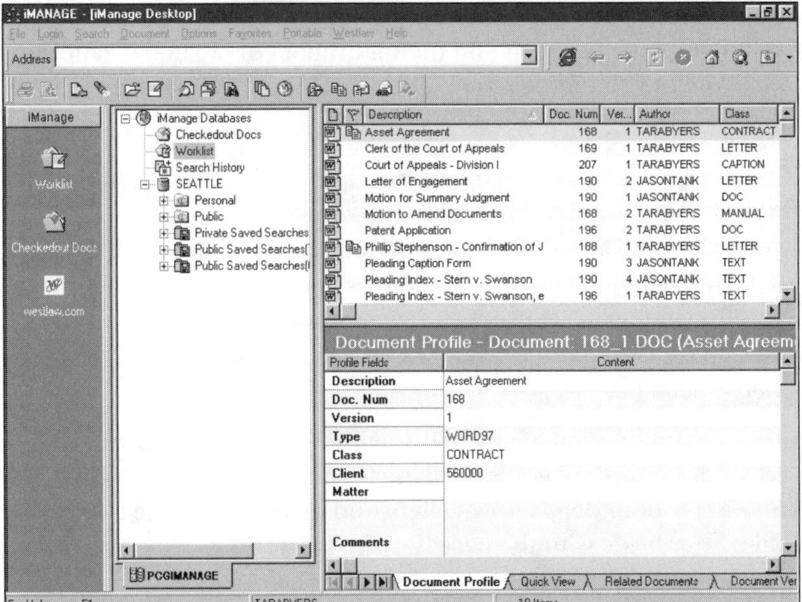

FIGURE 2.13

The iManage Worklist provides quick access to files that you use often.

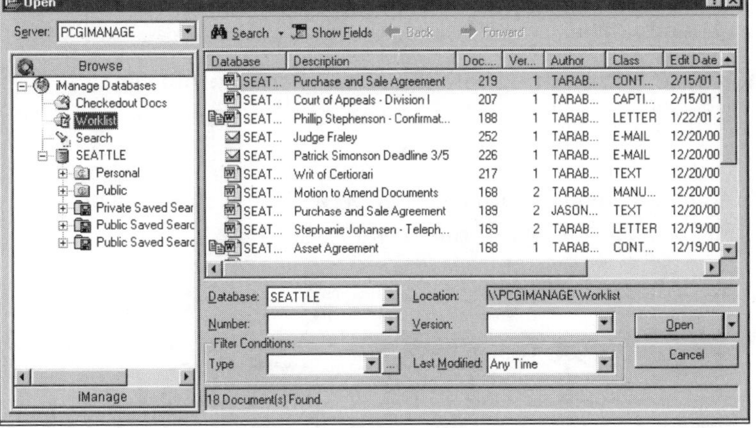

FIGURE 2.14

iManage Integrated Desktop.

3. Double-click a document from the Worklist or perform a Profile search to locate a document not found in the Worklist. The next section discusses Profile Searching.

PROFILE SEARCHING

There may be times when you need to find a document that's not in your Worklist. Profile Searching allows you to search for documents using one or more document profile fields. It can be particularly useful if you need to find documents grouped under a specific client and matter number or created by another user. You can narrow or broaden each profile search by the number of fields you search on.

FIND A DOCUMENT IN IMANAGE USING PROFILE SEARCHING

1. Start iManage.
2. From the iManage Desktop toolbar, click Search or, from the Search menu, choose Search.
3. Search using a combination of any of the available fields, as shown in Figure 2.15. For example, if you're looking for a specific document created by another user under a known client and matter, fill in the author, client, and matter fields with the necessary information.
4. Or, if you're looking to find all known documents associated with a particular client and matter, you would fill in only the client and matter fields with the pertinent information.
5. Click OK to generate the list.
6. Practice more by experimenting with filling in different profile fields.

Click the Browse button at the end of each field to view a lookup table. Lookup tables show a list of all possible entries associated with each field.

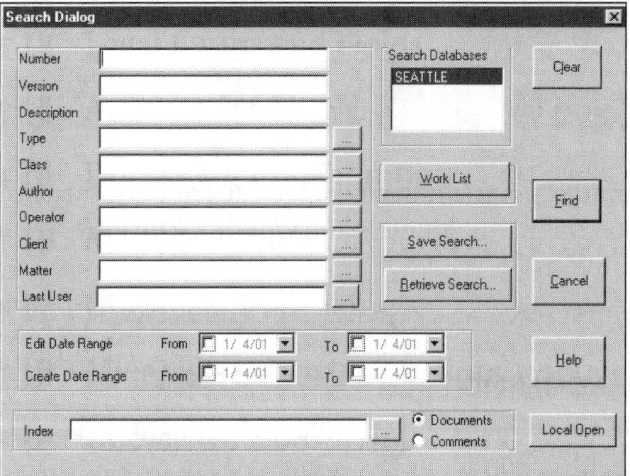

FIGURE 2.15

iManage Profile Search dialog box.

CLOSING WORD AND IMANAGE

Once you finish working with Word, close all open documents and exit the program before closing iManage. If you attempt to close iManage before closing Word, you may receive a warning message.

WORLDOX® AND WORD

The following section looks at using Word with WORLDOX® in the following ways:

- Starting Word
- Saving documents
- Finding documents

STARTING WORD WITH WORLDOX®

Opening WORLDOX® can be as easy as opening Word. WORLDOX® may already be set up to automatically open when you log onto your computer for the first time. Check with your system administrator to see if this feature has been activated or if you have any questions about the WORLDDOX® configuration.

SAVING WORD DOCUMENTS WITH WORLDOX®

Certain native Word commands such as Save and Open are replaced by WORLDOX® when the two programs are run in an integrated environment. Instead of seeing the familiar Save As dialog box every time you click Save in a new Word document, you will see a Profile window containing a number of fields that you will be required to fill in.

SAVE A NEW DOCUMENT AND FILL OUT A DOCUMENT PROFILE

1. Start Word.
2. From the Standard toolbar, click Save or choose File, Save.
3. Fill out the document profile by entering information into each of the required profile fields. Use the Tab key to move from one field to the next.
4. Click OK to complete the profile.

FINDING WORD DOCUMENTS IN WORLDOX®

The key feature in using a document management system is being able to find documents quickly. WORLDOX® uses a feature called Quick Pick to locate documents.

FIND AND OPEN DOCUMENTS USING QUICK PICK

1. Start Word.
2. From the Standard toolbar, click Open or choose File, Open.
3. Click Find Menu.
4. Type in your author identification and click OK.
5. A list will appear containing all the documents associated with your author identification.

Figure 2.16 shows the Quick Pick dialog box.

PROTECTING DOCUMENTS

Imagine this—you've just spent hours working on a long, complex agreement and have taken some time off to reward yourself with a double tall latte. Upon your return you find, to your horror, that someone has opened your document and changed it completely. Worse still, you don't have a backup of the original!

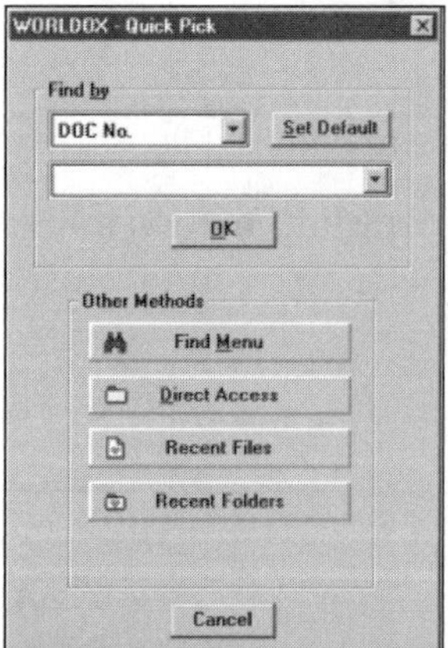

FIGURE 2.16

Quick Pick dialog box.

Believe it or not, the scenario just described happens. You can avoid finding yourself in a similar situation by using Word's document protection feature, which includes:

- Requiring a password to open a document (High Security)
- Requiring a password to modify a document (Medium Security)
- Recommending that documents be opened as Read-Only (Low Security)

In this section, Word's protection options are examined. Each document management system has its own method of security. Refer to your firm's system administrator for more information.

PASSWORD REQUIRED TO OPEN A DOCUMENT

If you're working on a confidential deal that is for your eyes only, or you don't want to worry about someone accidentally (or intentionally, for that matter!) changing your document, you can use Word's Password Required To Open protection feature and password-protect the file. This is the highest level of document protection available from within Word and it assures that only you, or those you may have given password information to, can open the document.

Don't forget the password, or you won't be able to open the document! Make it something you're likely to remember, and note that passwords are case-sensitive.

Follow the steps in the next exercise to save a document with the Password Required To Open level of security.

PASSWORD REQUIRED TO OPEN

1. Create or open an existing document.
2. From the File menu, choose Save As.
3. Click Tools and choose Security Options from the drop-down list. The dialog box shown in Figure 2.17 appears.

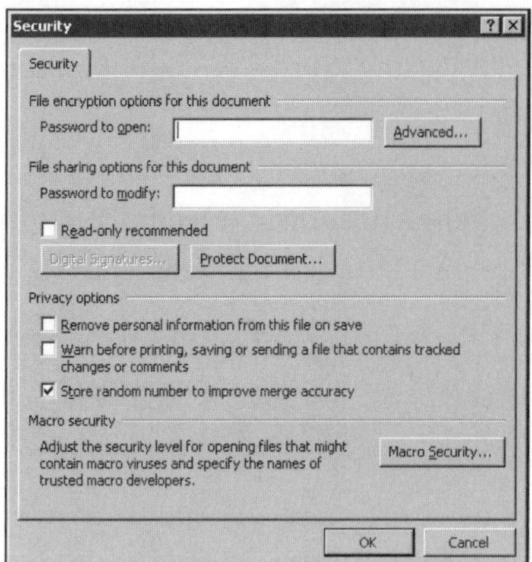

FIGURE 2.17

The Security tab is new to Word 2002 and includes options for protecting a document, embedded information, and the ability to digitally sign documents.

4. In the Security Options dialog box, type a password in the Password To Open box. The chosen characters will be replaced with asterisks, as shown in Figure 2.18.
5. Click OK, reenter the password in the Confirm Password dialog box shown in Figure 2.19, and click OK.
6. Type a name in the File Name box and click Save.
7. The next time you attempt to open the document, you will be prompted to enter the password when you open the file.

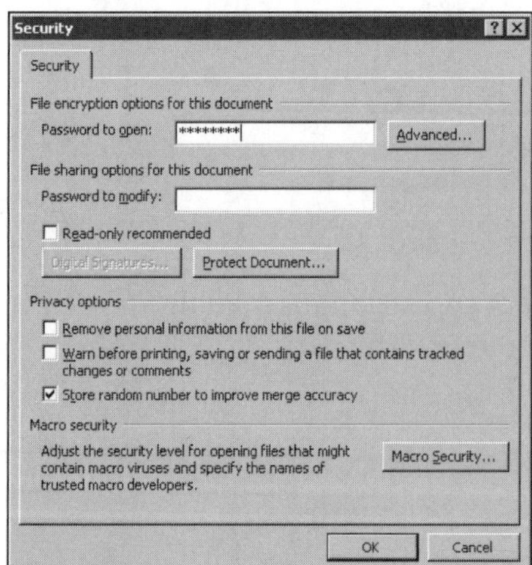

FIGURE 2.18

While it's possible to buy a password-cracker program, it's not an easy task to open password-protected files without knowing the password. Create a list of used passwords and remember that they are case-sensitive.

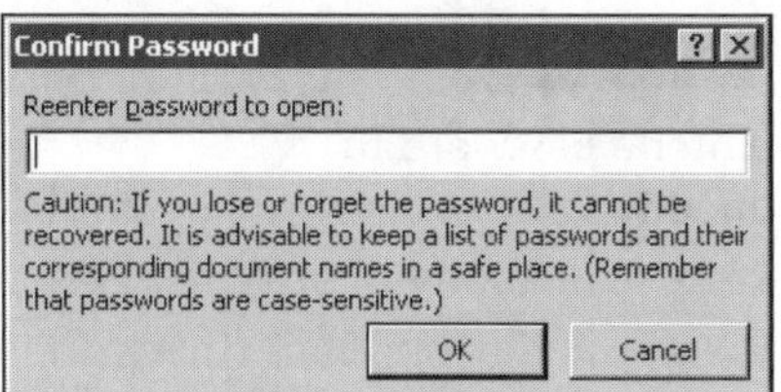

FIGURE 2.19

You will be prompted to input the password twice, and the password must match exactly.

TIP

To remove password protection from the document, go back to the Security Options dialog box, clear the password, and click OK. You can get to the Security settings from the Options dialog box as well. From the Tools menu, choose Options and select the Security tab. Set or remove protection and click OK.

PASSWORD REQUIRED TO MODIFY A DOCUMENT

The next lower level of security is requiring a password to modify the contents of a document. While not as secure as the top level of protection, this can be useful if you don't want someone else making changes to your document but you do want to make it available for viewing or copying. An example of this might be a master agreement or contract that others use as a template. If someone attempting to open the document does not know the password, they can open it as read-only and save it as a new document under a different name while the original document remains unchanged. Follow the steps in the next exercise to set the Password Required To Modify level of security to a document.

SETTING A PASSWORD TO MODIFY A DOCUMENT

1. From the File menu, choose Save As.
2. Click Tools and choose Security Options from the drop-down list.
3. Enter a password in the Password To Modify box.
4. Click OK and reenter the password when prompted.
5. Click OK.
6. Name the file, if necessary, and click Save.

The next time you or anyone else attempts to open the document, the dialog box shown in Figure 2.20 will appear.

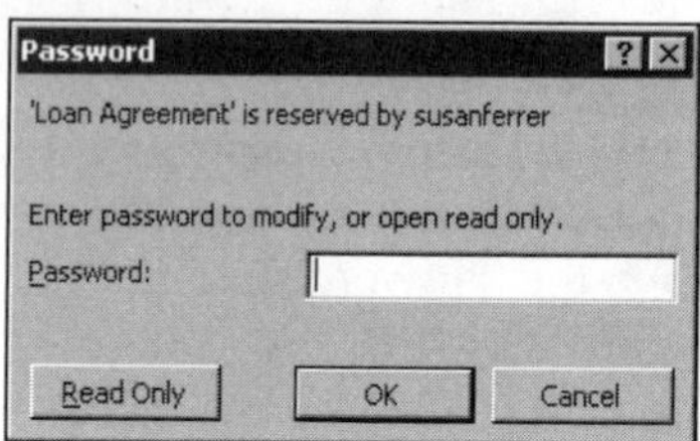

FIGURE 2.20

Enter a password to modify.

Enter the password if you want to modify the document; otherwise, click Read Only.

NOTE

You can create a new document from a read-only file by opening the document as read-only and then choosing File, Save As and providing the new name. The original file will not be affected.

READ-ONLY RECOMMENDED PROTECTION

Read-Only Recommended is the lowest level of document protection available. This option suggests that users open the document as read-only—but remember, it's only a suggestion. Other users can choose not to accept it, open your document normally, and then make changes to it, so use this option sparingly. Follow the steps in the next exercise to set Read-Only Recommended protection.

SETTING A DOCUMENT FOR READ-ONLY RECOMMENDED PROTECTION

1. From the File menu, choose Save As.
2. Click Tools and choose Security Options from the drop-down list.
3. In the Security Options dialog box, place a check in the Read-Only Recommended box (shown in Figure 2.21) and click OK.

The next time you or anyone else opens the document, you'll see the message shown in Figure 2.22.

CAUTION

This level of protection is not secure. Users can choose No and make changes to the original file.

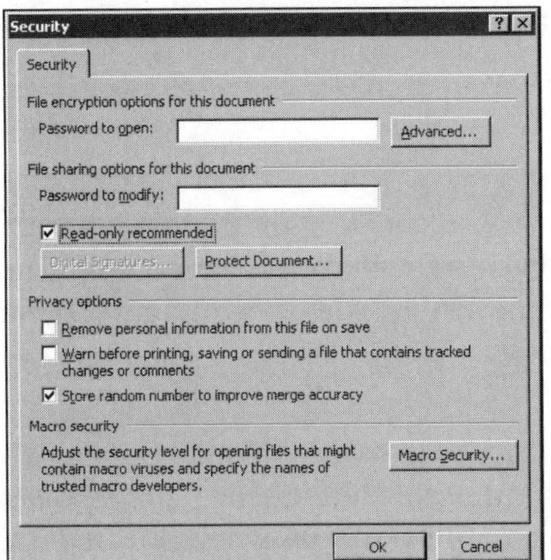

FIGURE 2.21

Read-Only Recommended protection.

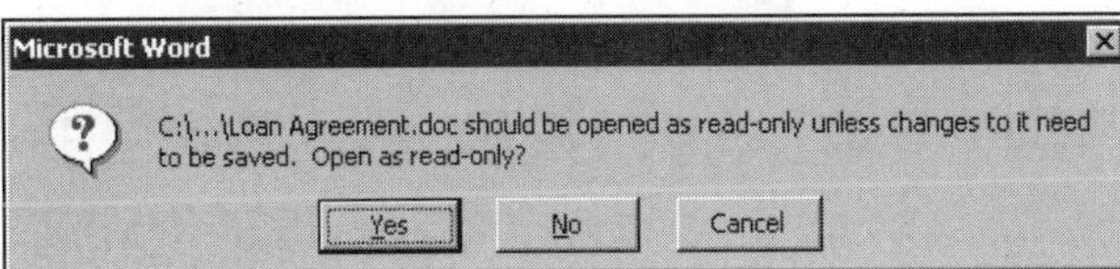

FIGURE 2.22

Message displayed for Read-Only Recommended protection.

EXITING WORD

Closing Word is the last step in the process of mastering the basics of the application. If you have several documents open, you can save and close them prior to exiting Word or just exit and let Word do the closing for you. Follow the steps in the next exercise to close Word.

EXITING WORD

1. From the File menu, choose Exit.
2. If you have one or more open documents and haven't saved the most recent changes, you will see the message shown in Figure 2.23 before Word will close out altogether.

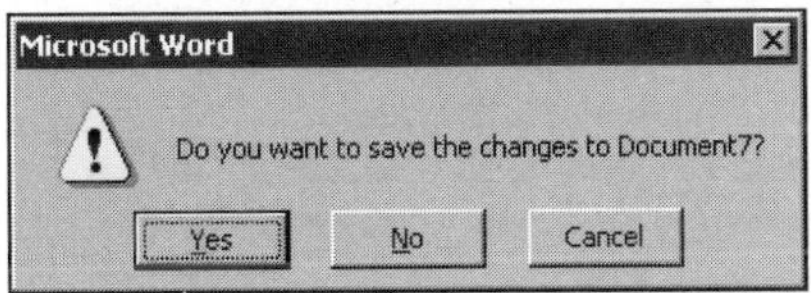

FIGURE 2.23

If any changes have been made to a document, when you close the file, Word prompts you to save changes.

3. Choose Yes or No if prompted to save changes for any open documents.

SUMMARY

Congratulations! You've made it through Word 101 and should now be familiar enough with the basics of the Word 2002 environment to get around quite comfortably. This chapter has covered a lot of ground, but you're now ready to move forward and explore Word in greater detail and substance.

If you've read this chapter from head to toe and followed along with the exercises, then you should be comfortable identifying the key components in the Word Application window, creating and saving new documents, opening and closing existing documents, applying password protection, and finding your way around using Word in a document management setting.

TROUBLESHOOTING WORD BASICS

I have several documents open and want to save them all at once; is there any way to do this?

Hold the Shift key and from the File menu, choose Save All. The Save All command only appears when you have more than one document open and hold down the Shift key when clicking File.

If I'm working with a document management system, what's the best way to keep others from getting into my documents?

Most document management systems provide profile-level security that allows you to set document security options when filling out the document profile. This type of security can not only prevent others from opening a document, it can also prevent them from even seeing it in the database. If you're using document management, it's a good idea to set document security at the profile level rather than using Word's password protection.

I'm trying to open a file that is password protected. I know I'm typing the correct password but it won't open. What am I doing wrong?

Check to make sure you don't have Caps Lock turned on. Passwords in Word, and all of Microsoft Office, are case-sensitive.

Chapter 3

The Word Environment

IN THIS CHAPTER

- Components of the Word window
- Changes to single document interface
- Document views and other features
- Introduction to the new task pane
- File properties
- Help

Word is a highly flexible and customizable application, which makes it an invaluable tool in the legal environment. If you were to visit a dozen people at your firm, you'd most likely see a dozen different ways of using Word. There is no right or wrong way to use any of the components found in the Word environment. The key to successfully working with Word is to identify how you can best take advantage of the many tools at your disposal.

This chapter focuses on helping you understand the various aspects of the Word environment.

COMPONENTS OF THE WORD WINDOW

The Word 2002 environment is made up of many components and features that allow you to take advantage of Word's powerful word processing capabilities. If you've used any Windows-based software before, you will recognize some of the elements that are covered in this section. Other components, such as the task pane, are new.

TITLE BAR

The title bar appears at the top of the Word window and contains the icon for the application that you are working in, the name of the document, and the application name—in this case, Microsoft Word. The title bar also contains three buttons that help to close or size the entire Word window. These are the Minimize, Restore Down/Maximize, and Close buttons.

MENU BAR

The menu bar appears by default just below the title bar at the top of the Word application window. The menu bar contains nine menus that, when selected, expand to reveal sets of related commands. The default menu items in Word 2002 are File, Edit, View, Insert, Format, Tools, Table, Window, and Help. By default, the menu bar is docked immediately below the title bar and above any toolbars, but you don't have to keep it there. The menu bar can be in a docked or floating wherever you wish, as in Figure 3.1.

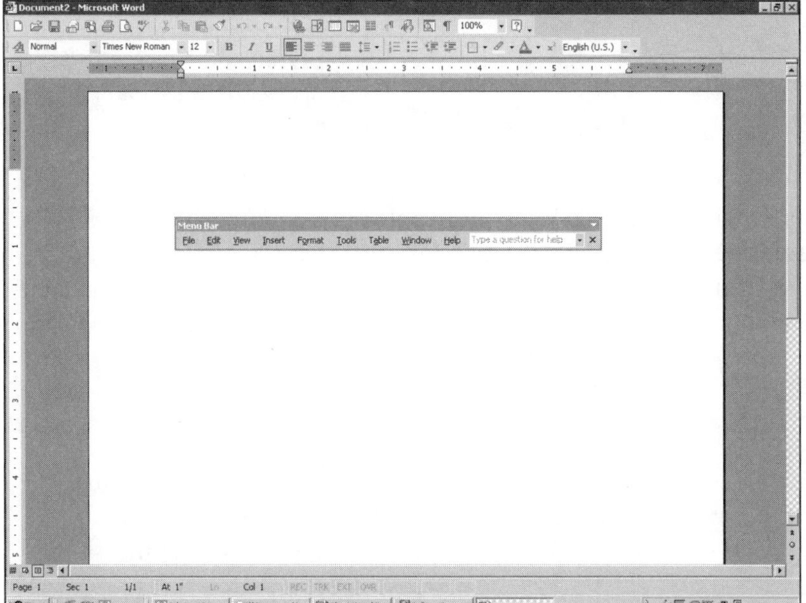

FIGURE 3.1

The components of the Word environment are flexible. The menu bar can be docked or floating.

The term *docked* refers to a menu bar or toolbar that is attached to any part of the document window. By contrast, a *floating* menu bar or toolbar hovers over the active document.

You can reposition the menu bar by grabbing and dragging the move handle to a new location. The *move handle* is the line to the left of the menu bar. Toolbars also have a move handle. You can return a floating menu bar or toolbar to its original position by dragging it back into place or double-clicking on the title bar that appears when the item is floating instead of docked.

MENU COMMANDS

Each item on the menu bar contains a list of related commands that allow you to perform specific actions while working in Word. For example, the Save command is located under the File menu, as is the Print command. You'll find commands for viewing the document in various ways and gaining access to elements such as headers and footers on the View menu. Likewise, if you need help, reach for the Help menu, as in Figure 3.2.

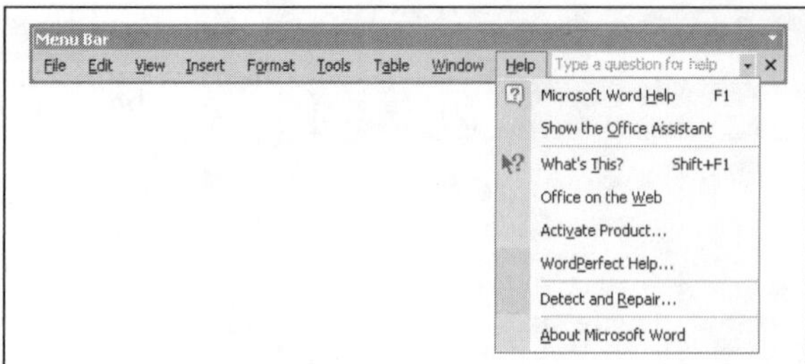

FIGURE 3.2

The Help menu with its commands on a floating menu.

Use hotkeys, also called shortcut keys, to expand any of the menus by pressing the Alt key and then the underlined letter associated with the menu command you want to use. For example, Alt+F opens the File menu. Once a menu is expanded, type the underlined letter of the next related command you wish to select from the expanded menu list. To continue with the example, Alt+F+O would expand the File menu, then select the Open command, displaying the Open dialog box.

Table 3.1 lists the changes that have been made to each menu from Word 2000.

PERSONALIZED MENUS

Many people feel overwhelmed the first time they expand some of the menus because there are so many commands from which to choose. In Word 2000, Microsoft introduced a feature that allowed the application to show a personalized list of commands that temporarily hides commands not frequently used, by adapting to the way you use Word. This feature can be turned on or off but it's quite useful if you don't like long or cluttered menus.

If the option for personalized or adaptive menus is enabled, you will see a set of double arrows called *chevrons* at the bottom of the menu list. If you don't see the chevrons, either this feature is turned off or you are already viewing the entire list of commands.

As you work, Word remembers the commands most recently selected from the menu and will show these the next time you expand the menu. This allows you to quickly see and access the commands you use most frequently without having to wade through rarely used commands.

You can automatically expand a menu by double-clicking on the specific menu bar item. For example, double-click Table to see the entire Table menu.

TABLE 3.1 MENU CHANGES FROM WORD 2000

MENU	COMMAND CHANGES
File	Search, and Send To: Mail Recipient (For Review) added. If using Microsoft SharePoint Porter Server as a document management system, Check-in, Checkout, and Publish are added to the File menu.
Edit	Office Clipboard, and cascading Clear menu with the following options: Formats, Contents, have been added.
View	Task Pane and Markup commands have been added. If you have an East Asian language installed, you will also have Show Paragraph Marks and Gridlines on the View menu. The Comments command has been removed from the View menu.
Insert	Several menu commands have been consolidated to become a submenu of Reference. These commands include: Footnote, Caption, Cross-Reference, and Index and Tables. Picture also contains a submenu including the following commands: Clip Art, From File, From Scanner or Camera, Organization Chart, New Drawing, AutoShapes, WordArt, Chart. The Insert menu now contains the Diagram command, which inserts Organizational, Cycle, Radial, Pyramid, Venn, and Target diagrams.
Format	The submenu for Background includes Printed Watermark. The Theme command is how you now access the Style Gallery. Styles and Formatting replaces the Styles command, and a Reveal Formatting command has been added to the Format menu.
Tools	The Language submenu now includes the Translate command. New commands include Speech (not available if running Word from Windows Terminal Server), Tools On The Web, Letters and Mailing (formerly Mail Merge) with a submenu that includes: Mail Merge Wizard, Show Mail Merge Toolbar, Show Japanese Greetings Toolbar (if installed), Envelopes and Labels, Letter Wizard. AutoCorrect Options replaces the AutoCorrect command, and Compare And Merge Documents replaces Merge Documents.
Table	No high-level menu command changes have been made to this menu.
Window	No changes have been made to the Window menu.
Help	The command Activate Product is added to the Help menu. This command starts the Activation Wizard.

NAVIGATE THROUGH MENUS

1. Place your mouse pointer over the move handle, the thin line at the beginning of the menu bar, and drag the menu bar to a new location. Notice that the pointer turns into a four-sided arrow when you place it over the move handle.

2. Drag the menu bar back into place.
3. Click once on the Insert menu and note that there are approximately six commands visible. Don't worry if you have a few more or less. Word tracks and displays the commands that get used.
4. Click the chevrons at the bottom of the list to expand the Insert menu and note the difference in the number of menu commands.
5. Click the Tools menu once and note the number of commands that appear. Click away from the menu to close the Tools menu.
6. Double-click Tools to see the full list of commands on the Tools menu.

TIP

If you prefer to see the entire list of commands associated with each menu item, turn off Word's personalized menu feature. From the Tools menu, choose Customize and select the Options tab. Check the box next to Always Show Full Menus, as in Figure 3.3.

CREATING NEW MENUS

Once you become comfortable working with Word, you may find yourself using a similar set of menu commands repeatedly. You can create a personal menu that places all your favorite and most frequently used commands in one convenient location. The following exercise walks you through creating a menu, and the one after that adds the commands.

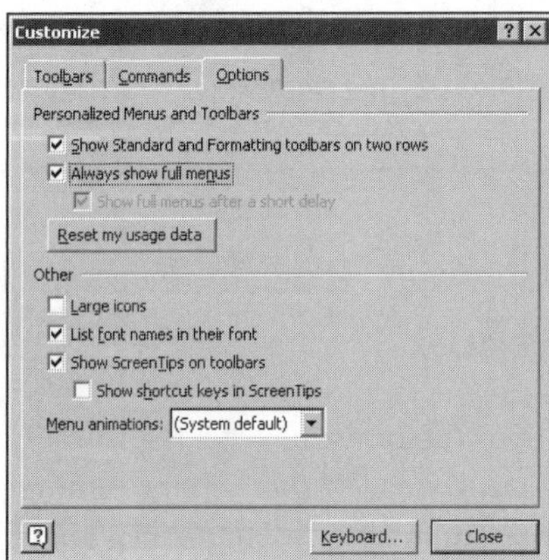

FIGURE 3.3

If you prefer to see all menu commands instead of the personalized menu, you can set the option to always show full menus.

CREATE A NEW MENU

1. From the Tools menu, choose Customize.
2. Select the Commands tab. The Commands tab has two sections, Categories and Commands.
3. Scroll through the Categories list and select New Menu, as in Figure 3.4.
4. From the Commands list, select New Menu.
5. Click and drag New Menu up to the menu bar, releasing the mouse button once the New Menu command is just to the right of the Help menu.
6. With the Customize dialog box still open, alternate-click the New Menu command just added to the menu bar. In the box to the right of Name, type **My Menu** and then press Enter.
7. Alternate-click on the text you just typed, add an ampersand in front of the first M, and then press Enter. The text in the Name box should look like this: &My Menu. This assigns the shortcut key M to the menu command. Figure 3.5 shows the customized menu.
8. Close the Customize dialog box.

Place an ampersand (&) in front of one letter in the menu name to assign it a shortcut key. It's a good idea to look at all other menu items before assigning shortcut keys. Word will allow you to create duplicate shortcut keys without warning. If you press the shortcut key once, the first menu item is activated. Pressing the shortcut key again then activates the second item.

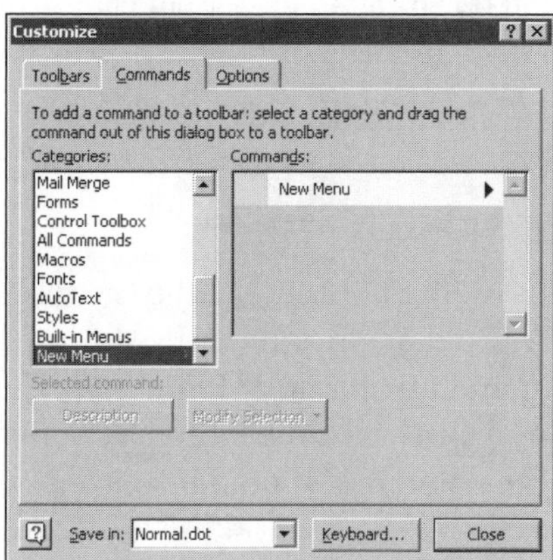

FIGURE 3.4

You don't have to be satisfied with the nine default menu items—you can create your own and add commands that are most useful to your working environment.

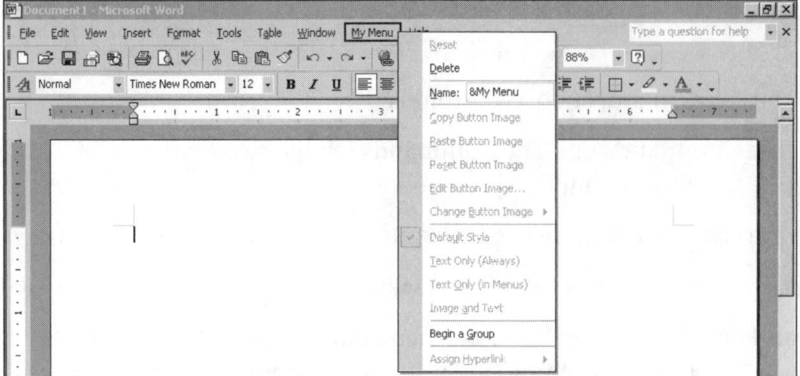

FIGURE 3.5

The ampersand indicates to Word that the character immediately to the right is to be used as the shortcut key.

You've just added a menu item to the menu bar. The next section will walk you through the process of adding commands under the new menu.

ADDING LEGAL MENU COMMANDS

You can add menu commands to a new or an existing menu. This exercise adds a few legal-specific commands to the menu created in the preceding exercise.

ADDING MENU COMMANDS

1. From the Tools menu, choose Customize to open the Customize dialog box.

TIP

You can access the Customize dialog box by alternate-clicking any active toolbar and choosing Customize from the shortcut menu.

2. Select the Commands tab.
3. Select All Commands from the list of Categories.
4. From the list of Commands on the right side of the Customize dialog box, select InsertStyleSeparator. Hold down your mouse button and drag the InsertStyleSeparator command up onto My Menu. Once the command is over the menu, a small empty box will appear directly beneath the menu command. This is where the command should be placed.

5. Release the InsertStyleSeparator command when it appears over the empty box below My Menu.

Once the mouse pointer is released, the command name changes from InsertStyleSeparator to Style Separator.

6. From the Categories list, select File.
7. From the Commands list, select Close All.
8. Hold down your mouse button and drag the Close All command to My Menu. Release your mouse button when Close All appears above Style Separator. The result is shown in Figure 3.6.
9. Practice adding more commands to My Menu by searching through each of the categories to find the commands you most frequently use and dragging them onto the customized menu.
10. Close the Customize dialog box.

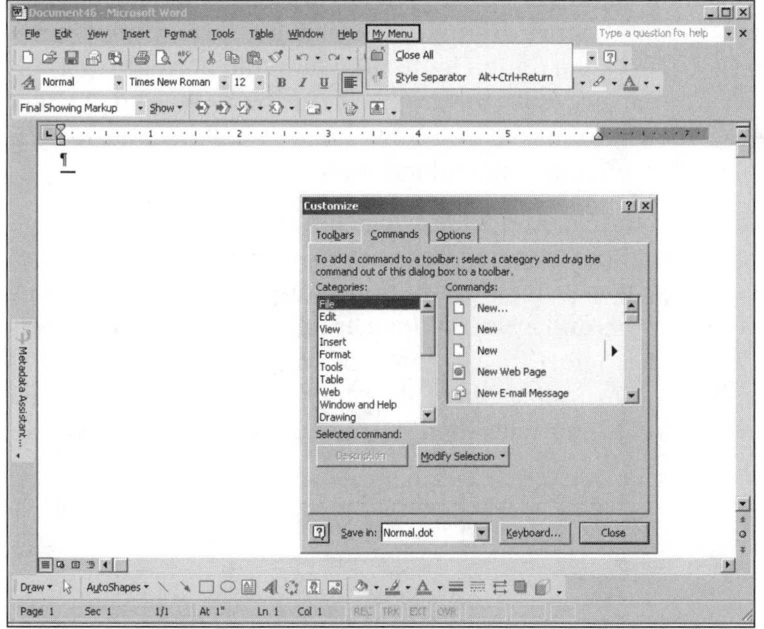

FIGURE 3.6

Adding commands to a new menu item makes them more readily available. Style Separator by default does not appear on any menu or toolbar.

NOTE

Word 2002 has more than 1,000 commands that can be added to menus or toolbars. The exact number and purpose varies depending on the options you have installed.

NOTE

You can remove a menu command from any menu while the Customize dialog box is open. To remove a command, just click and drag the command off the expanded menu. To remove the entire menu command, it is not necessary to have the Customize dialog box open. Just hold down the Alt key while dragging the menu command off the menu bar.

TOOLBARS

Toolbars contain buttons that are shortcuts to performing frequently used commands. Word 2002 has 30 different toolbars, each with its own unique set of commands. Just like the menu bar, toolbars can either be docked or floating, on or off.

STANDARD AND FORMATTING TOOLBARS

The two most commonly used toolbars, Standard and Formatting (Figures 3.7 and 3.8) initially share the same row. If you prefer to have the Standard and Formatting toolbars on separate rows, from the Tools menu, choose Customize. From the Options tab, check the option Show Standard And Formatting Toolbars On Two Rows. You can also click the drop-down arrow at the end of either toolbar and choose Show Buttons On Two Rows. This new Word 2002 feature acts as a toggle depending on how your toolbars are set up.

With over 1,000 toolbar button commands available, it would be fairly difficult to know what each button does without a little help. You can hover your mouse pointer, without clicking, over each toolbar button to display the button's name in a ScreenTip. If you try this and a ScreenTip does not appear, from the Tools menu, choose Customize. Select the Options tab and check the box next to Show ScreenTips On Toolbars. Select Show Shortcut Keys in ScreenTips to display the associated keyboard shortcut when the mouse pointer is hovered over the toolbar button.

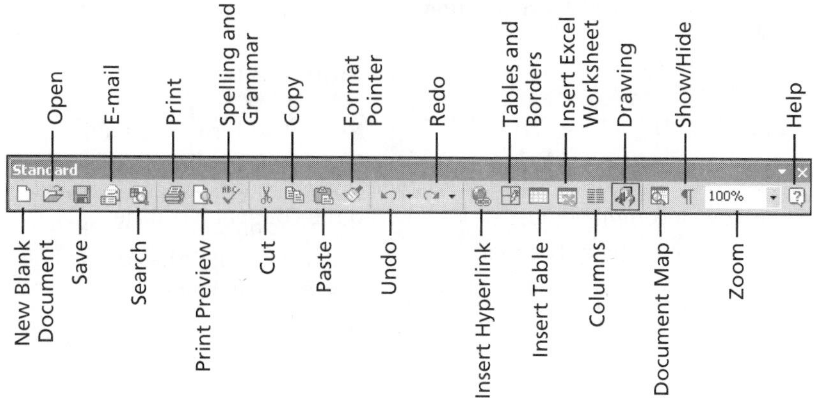

FIGURE 3.7

The Standard toolbar includes buttons to create a new document, open, save, search, print and work with documents.

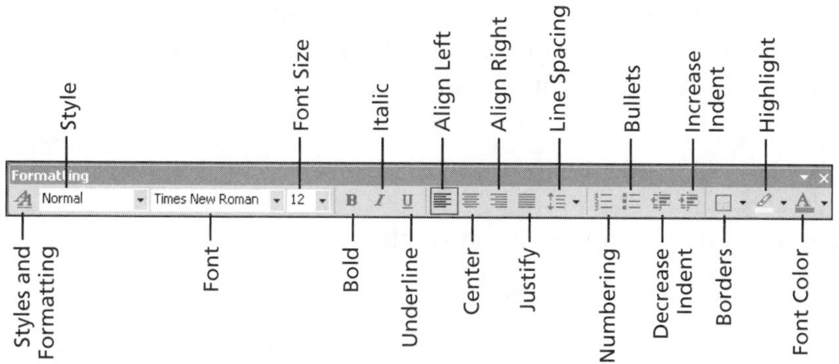

FIGURE 3.8

The Formatting toolbar includes buttons that change the way text in your document looks and includes buttons to change the font, size, and more.

NEW FEATURE!

Three new buttons have been added to the Standard and Formatting toolbars. The Standard toolbar includes a Search button and a Styles and Formatting button that opens the respective Task Pane. The Formatting toolbar includes a Line Spacing button that was requested by law firms. The Line Spacing button has a drop-down arrow that, when clicked, reveals options for 1.0, 1.5, 2.0, 3.0, and More line spacing. When More is chosen, the Paragraph dialog box opens. Figure 3.9 shows the new Line Spacing button.

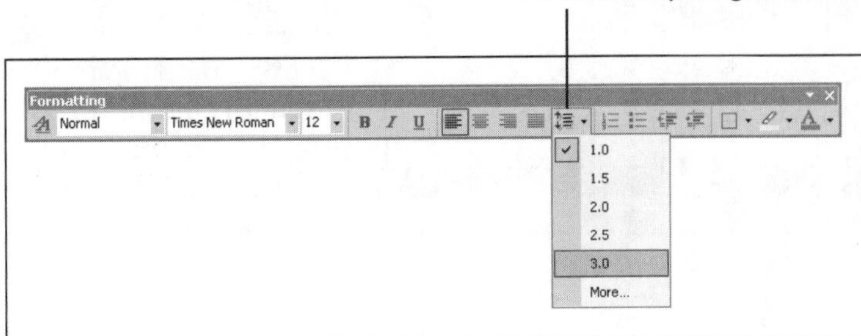

FIGURE 3.9

You asked for it – you got it! The Formatting toolbar now includes a button for controlling line spacing. Select the text, click the button, and the correct line spacing is applied.

ADDING AND REMOVING TOOLBAR BUTTONS

You may find that you rarely or never use some of the default buttons on the Standard and Formatting toolbars. Or you might wish to add a button that doesn't appear. You can prevent your toolbars from becoming overly cluttered by displaying only those buttons you actually use.

ADD AND REMOVE TOOLBAR BUTTONS

1. Click the drop-down arrow at the end of the Standard toolbar.
2. Click Show Buttons On Two Rows.
3. At the end of the Standard toolbar, click the drop-down arrow and choose Add Or Remove Buttons, Standard. You'll see a menu expand with all the buttons available for the Standard toolbar, as shown in Figure 3.10. Active buttons have a check mark next to them. To activate any button, click the area to the left of the command name to place a check mark in the box.
4. Uncheck both the Columns and Hyperlink buttons.
5. Check the options for the Close and Find buttons.
6. Click outside the expanded menu and note the changes made to the Standard toolbar.
7. Practice adding and removing buttons on the Formatting toolbar.

To restore the toolbars' default settings, click the drop-down arrow at the end of each toolbar, choose Add Or Remove Buttons, Standard or Formatting, and select Reset Toolbar at the bottom of the expanded menu.

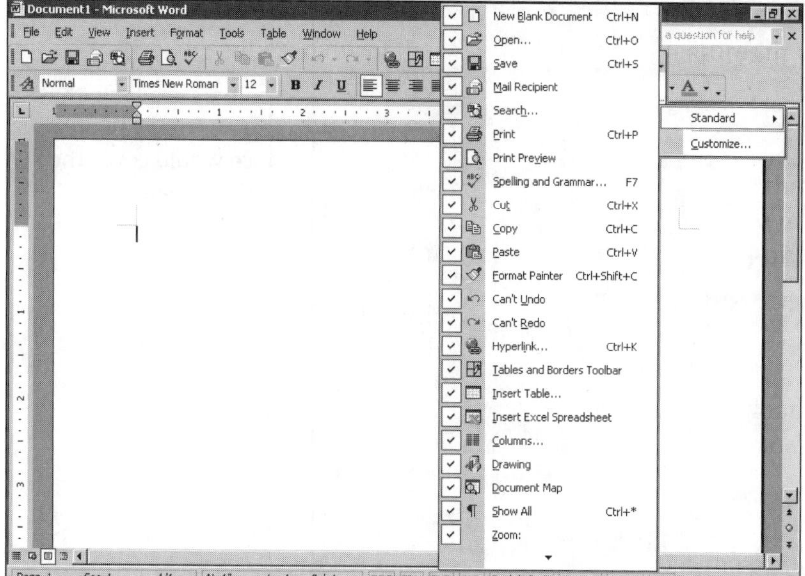

FIGURE 3.10

Buttons that you use most often can be added to the toolbar while buttons that are seldom used can be removed.

NEW AND IMPROVED FEATURE!

Word 2000 introduced the ability to add buttons to the toolbar without going through the Customize dialog box. Word 2002 takes this much further by providing a menu that allows you to control the placement of the Standard and Formatting toolbars as well as allowing you to select multiple buttons to be added to a toolbar at one time instead of having to close the menu and return to it each time you want to turn on or off a button.

OTHER TOOLBARS

Other toolbars can appear automatically when you activate related features. For example, if you select a picture, the Picture toolbar automatically appears. When the picture is deselected, the toolbar disappears. Figure 3.11 shows many of the toolbars available in Word on one screen. Of course it would be nearly impossible to work with this many toolbars on at once.

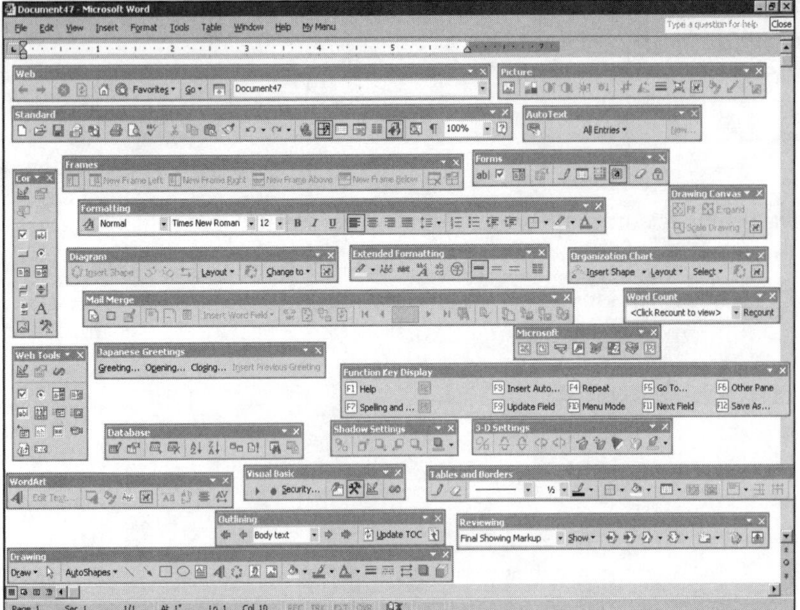

FIGURE 3.11

Word has so many toolbars available that turning them all on at once would cover the entire screen.

You can activate any of Word's default toolbars by alternate-clicking a visible toolbar and selecting from the drop-down list of available toolbars. To see a complete list of Word toolbars, from the Tools menu, choose Customize and then select the Toolbars tab. Place a check mark next to the toolbar you wish to activate. Figure 3.12 shows the Toolbars tab in the Customize dialog box.

The following list contains a brief description of some of the more common toolbars available in Word. Some toolbars can be displayed by alternate-

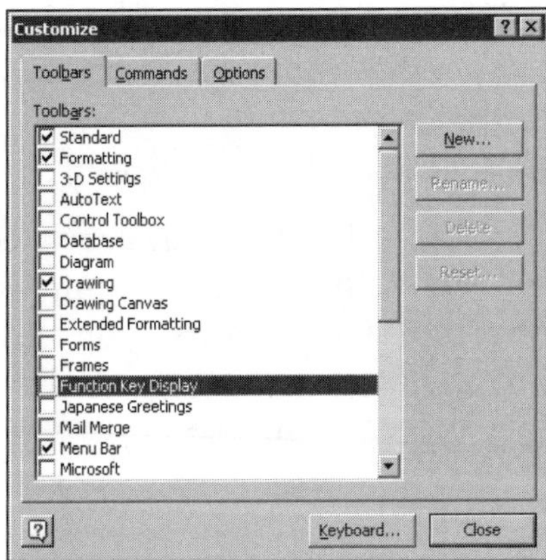

FIGURE 3.12

Some toolbars are not listed when you alternate-click on a toolbar button and only appear by displaying the Customize dialog box. One such toolbar is Function Key Display.

clicking on a toolbar button while others are only visible from within the Customize dialog box.

- **Standard**. Contains common Word commands including New, Open, Save, E-mail, Search, Print, Copy, and more.
- **Formatting**. Contains commands for applying different types of formatting.
- **AutoText**. Provides commands that help you create and insert AutoText entries.
- **Control Toolbox**. Provides a set of tools for creating user forms, which are used in conjunction with the Visual Basic Editor.
- **Database**. Provides tools for working with lists including adding, deleting, and sorting records.
- **Drawing**. Provides tools for creating and formatting Word AutoShapes, drawing objects, text boxes, and more.
- **Extended Formatting**. Provides tools for working with Japanese text.
- **Forms**. Provides commands and controls for creating and editing online forms.
- **Frames**. Provides tools for creating frame-based Web pages.
- **Function Key Display**. Provides a list of function keys F1 through F12 and their associated commands.
- **Japanese Greetings**. Provides a list of common Japanese greetings, openings, and closings.
- **Mail Merge**. Provides commands for working with Word's Mail Merge feature.
- **Outlining**. Provides tools for working with Outline view and Table of Contents.
- **Picture**. Provides commands for editing bitmaps and other graphics files.
- **Reviewing**. Provides commands for working with Comments and Track Changes.
- **Tables and Borders**. Provides tools to help create, format, and edit Word tables.
- **Task Pane**. Toggles the new Word Task Pane on and off.
- **Visual Basic**. Provides tools to record new macros and access the Visual Basic Editor.
- **Web**. Provides commands for navigating through documents containing hyperlinks, as well as allowing you to jump directly to the Internet.
- **Web Tools**. Provides tools and controls for creating Web pages.
- **Word Count**. Allows you to quickly count the number of words in a document using different criteria.
- **Word Art**. Provides useful commands for creating and formatting Word Art.

PRACTICE TURNING TOOLBARS ON AND OFF

1. Alternate-click any active toolbar.
2. Select the Drawing toolbar from the list. Note that it automatically docks to the lower portion of the document window.
3. Grab the move handle and drag the Drawing toolbar until it floats over the active document, then release the mouse button.
4. Alternate-click the Drawing toolbar and turn it off by selecting it from the list of toolbars.
5. From the Tools menu, choose Customize and select the Toolbars tab.
6. Place a check mark next to the Picture and Organization Chart toolbars. Are the toolbars floating or docked?
7. Practice activating and deactivating other toolbars by using both methods.

CREATE A LEGAL TOOLBAR

Even with 30 different toolbars available to choose from in Word, you may find that creating a customized legal toolbar with your most frequently used buttons is the best way to maximize Word's power. Figure 3.13 illustrates the process.

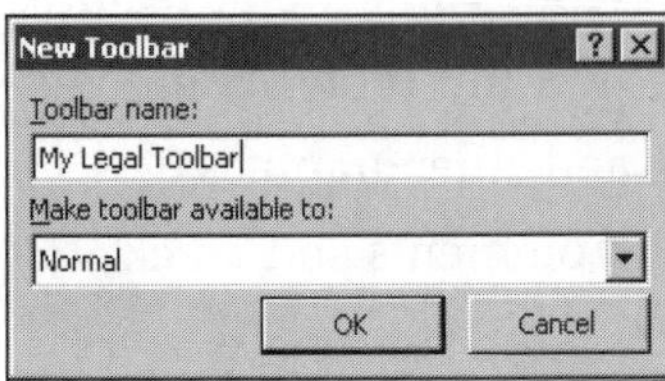

FIGURE 3.13

Just like menu bars, you are not stuck with the defaults that Microsoft provides. You can create custom toolbars and add the buttons that are most useful to you.

CREATE A CUSTOM LEGAL TOOLBAR

1. From the Tools menu, choose Customize and select the Toolbars tab. Or, if you prefer, alternate-click any active toolbar and choose Customize, Toolbars.

2. Click New.
3. In the Toolbar Name box, type **My Legal Toolbar** and click OK.
4. From the Customize dialog box, select the Commands tab. Note that it contains two sections, Categories and Commands.
5. From the list of Categories, select Insert, and then find Symbol on the Commands list.
6. While holding your mouse button down, click and drag the Symbol button to My Legal Toolbar. Release the mouse button when the Symbol button appears as an I-beam on the toolbar palette.
7. Go back to the Commands section in the Customize dialog box, then locate and select Mark Citation. Add this command to the toolbar in the same fashion.
8. From Categories, select Format, then from Commands, locate and select Double-Spacing. Add it to the toolbar.
9. Finally, go back to Categories and select File. Look under Commands until you locate Close All and add it to the toolbar.
10. Add any additional commands you frequently use at your firm.
11. Close the Customize dialog box. Your toolbar should resemble the one shown in Figure 3.14.

Your new toolbar will now be available in Word's default list of toolbars. Toggle the toolbar on or off by alternate-clicking any visible toolbar and checking or un-checking it from the list.

NOTE

You can rename or delete your custom toolbar by selecting it from the list of toolbars on the Toolbars tab of the Customize dialog box, then choosing Rename or Delete.

FIGURE 3.14

Buttons have been added to this custom toolbar to add faster access to tasks that are common in legal documents.

CHANGES TO SINGLE DOCUMENT INTERFACE

SDI, or Single Document Interface, was introduced as a new feature in Word 2000. The principle of this feature is to provide a separate button on the taskbar for each open document. Each document still appears in a list under the Window menu; however, SDI provides an alternative method for navigating between open documents.

One of the great things about Microsoft is that its people realize not everyone works the same way so, in Word 2002, they made SDI an option. In Word 2002, you can either turn SDI on or off depending on your preferences.

TURN SINGLE DOCUMENT INTERFACE OFF AND ON

1. From the Tools menu, choose Options.
2. Select the View tab. The View tab is shown in Figure 3.15.
3. Uncheck the box next to Windows In Taskbar and click OK.
4. From the Standard toolbar, click New Blank Document three times to create three new documents. How many document buttons appear on the Windows taskbar?
5. From the Window menu, switch to Document 3 by selecting it from the list of Window commands.
6. From the Tools menu, choose Options. Select the View tab and place a check mark next to Windows In Taskbar to turn SDI back on.

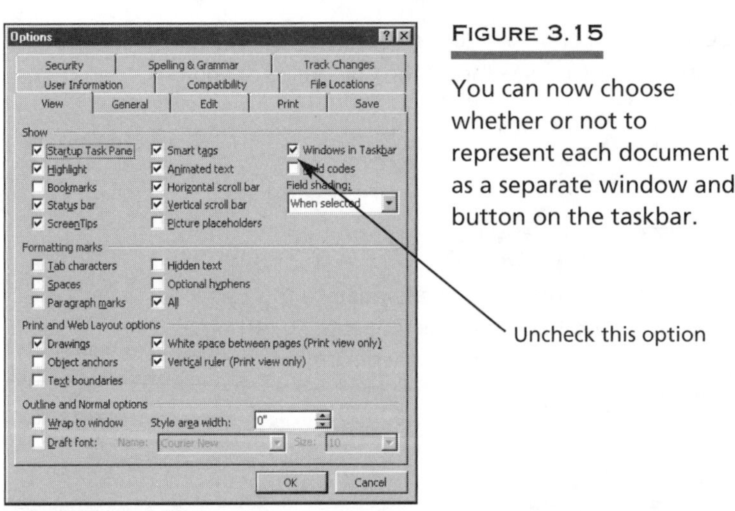

FIGURE 3.15

You can now choose whether or not to represent each document as a separate window and button on the taskbar.

VIEWS

Word provides a number of different ways to look at a document. Although each view can be useful depending on the task at hand, you'll probably end up working with one particular view most of the time and occasionally using the others.

You can switch between the four main views by clicking one of the view buttons on the lower-left side of the document window (above the status bar, as shown in Figure 3.16), or by choosing Normal, Web Layout, Print Layout, or Outline from the View menu.

The four primary views in Word are

- Normal
- Print Layout
- Web Layout
- Outline

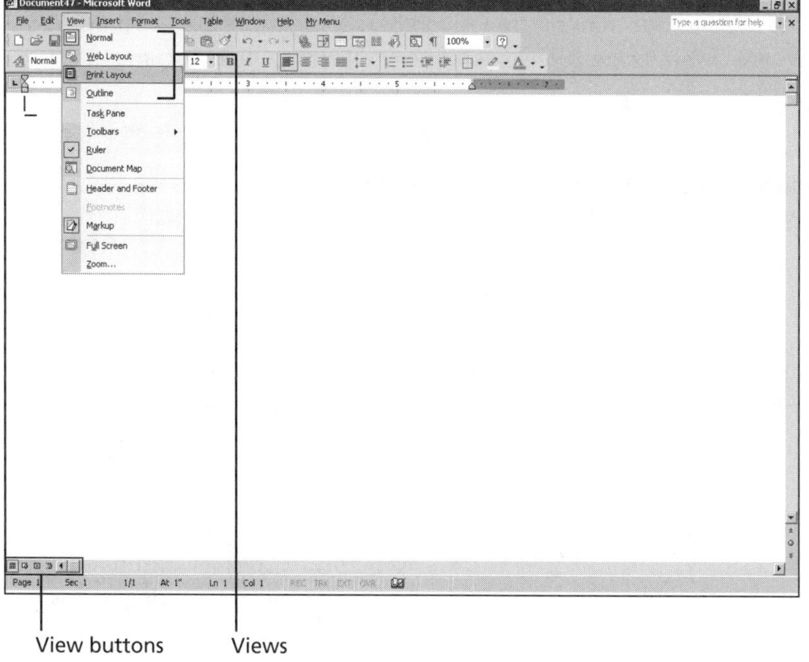

FIGURE 3.16

There are two ways to switch between the various views in Word: Click one of the View buttons that appear at the bottom-left corner of the screen, or from the View menu, choose how you want to view the document.

NORMAL VIEW

If you're a fast typist, work with lengthy documents, and don't care if things do not appear onscreen the way they will print, then Normal will probably be your view of choice. The Normal view allows you to move quickly through long documents without having to constantly repaginate. Many power typists work in Normal view, then switch to Print Layout view to check things over prior to printing.

In Normal view (Figure 3.17), soft page breaks appear as horizontal dotted lines. Hard page breaks are shown with the words Page Break in the middle of the horizontal line. Section breaks appear as double dotted lines. One disadvantage of working in Normal view is that you can't see headers and footers, columns, text boxes, and drawing objects. But if your primary objective is adding and editing text in a document as quickly as possible, Normal view is a good choice.

A soft page break occurs naturally when the maximum amount of information is placed on a page. Hard page breaks are inserted manually when you want to force new information onto the next page. A section break is a manually inserted break that is used when different formatting, such as page number formats or changing the page layout from portrait to landscape, is required. All of these types of breaks are covered extensively in Chapter 7, "Formatting a Document."

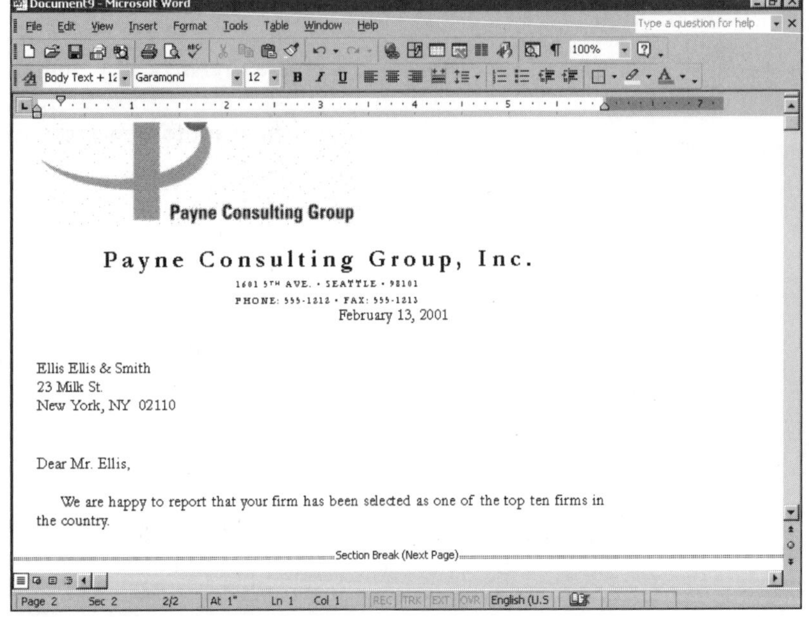

FIGURE 3.17

When a fast typist enters text into a document, often it takes a few seconds for Word to catch up because it repaginates the document as new pages are added. Normal view does not force a repagination. Therefore, extremely fast typists prefer working in this view.

PRINT LAYOUT

Print Layout view (Figure 3.18) provides a view of the document as it will appear on the printed page. In this view, you can see and work directly with headers and footers, graphics, columns, and drawing objects. Print Layout view also allows you to see where you might need to make adjustments to lay out a presentation prior to printing. One downside to working in Print Layout view is the time it takes Word to repaginate as you scroll through large documents or edit documents containing graphics.

NOTE

In Word 97 and earlier versions, Print Layout view was referred to as Page Layout view.

HIDE WHITE SPACE IN PRINT LAYOUT VIEW

One reason why some people choose to work in Normal instead of Print Layout view is the wasted space between the bottom of one page and the top of the next. Word now includes a Hide White Space option to hide all unused areas of a page quickly.

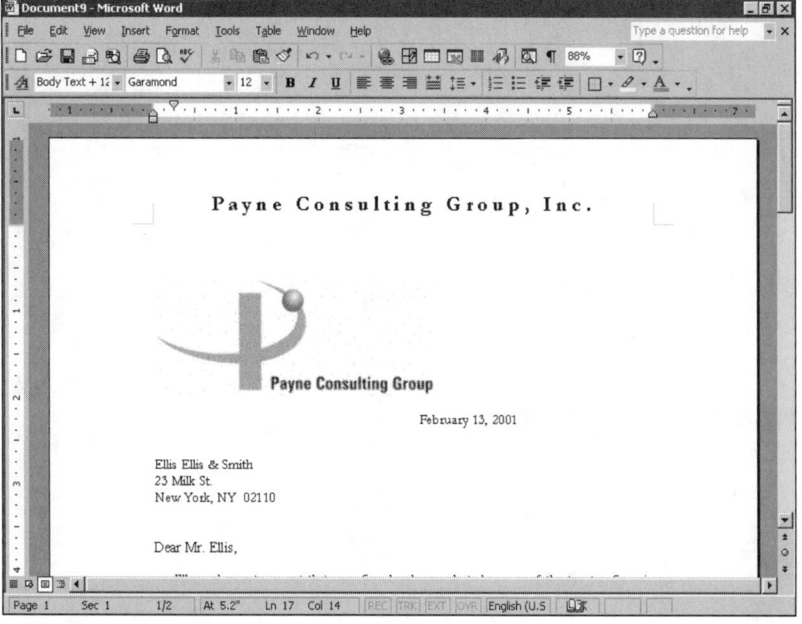

FIGURE 3.18

People who tend to be more visual often prefer Print Layout view since in this view you are able to see what the document will look like when it is printed.

SHOW/HIDE WHITE SPACE

1. Create a new document.
2. Type =**rand**() and press Enter. This generates random text in the document.
3. Click after each paragraph and press Ctrl+Enter to insert a page break.
4. Switch to Print Layout view, if necessary.
5. Scroll to the bottom of the first page. Place your mouse pointer over the area that separates the two pages.
6. The mouse pointer changes to two arrows and the Hide White Space ScreenTip appears (Figure 3.19). Click, and the white space between pages in the document is hidden (Figure 3.20).
7. Place the mouse pointer over the line that now divides the page, and the ScreenTip toggles to Show White Space. Click on any of the divider lines to remove the option.

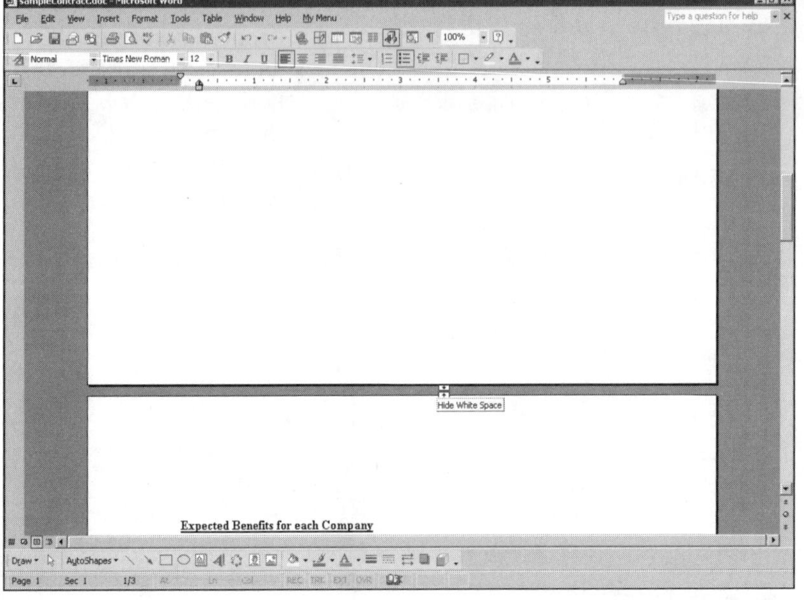

FIGURE 3.19

The mouse pointer changes to two arrows when held over the space between two pages.

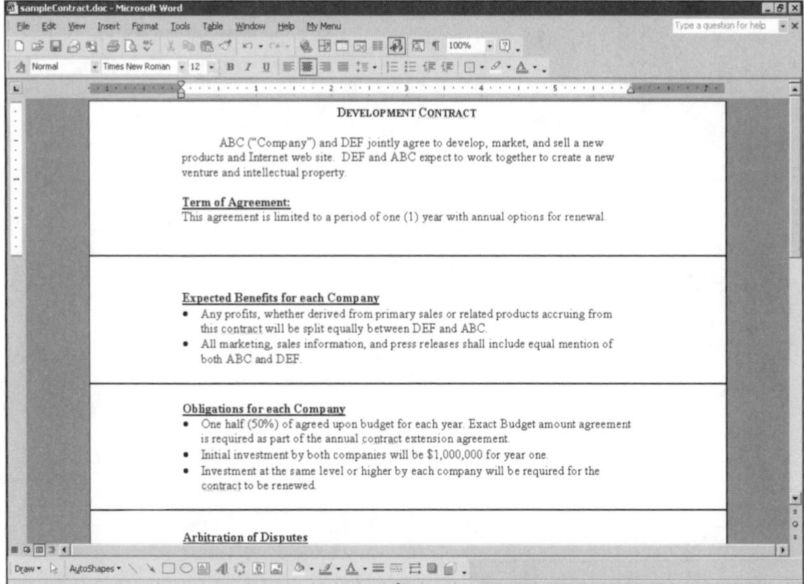

FIGURE 3.20

Although headers and footers are hidden when Hide White Space is turned on, footnotes and endnotes are not affected.

WEB LAYOUT

Web Layout view (Figure 3.21) is useful if you're creating Web pages in Word or if you want to see how a document will appear when opened in a browser such as Internet Explorer or Netscape. Text is wrapped to fit the document window, and graphics that appear in the document will be positioned just as they would be online. Certain document objects such as headers and footers, page numbers, and columns are not visible in Web Layout view.

In Word 97 and earlier versions, Web Layout view was referred to as Online Layout view.

OUTLINE VIEW

Outline view (Figure 3.22) uses Word's heading styles to create document outlines. It provides you with a way of electronically organizing your ideas into a logical, coherent outline before creating a lengthy document. In Outline view, you create the outline first and add the text afterwards. While working with documents in Outline view, you can promote, demote, expand, and collapse heading levels to change the structure of the document. When you are ready to add text to each of the various headings, switch back to Print Layout or Normal view to insert the information.

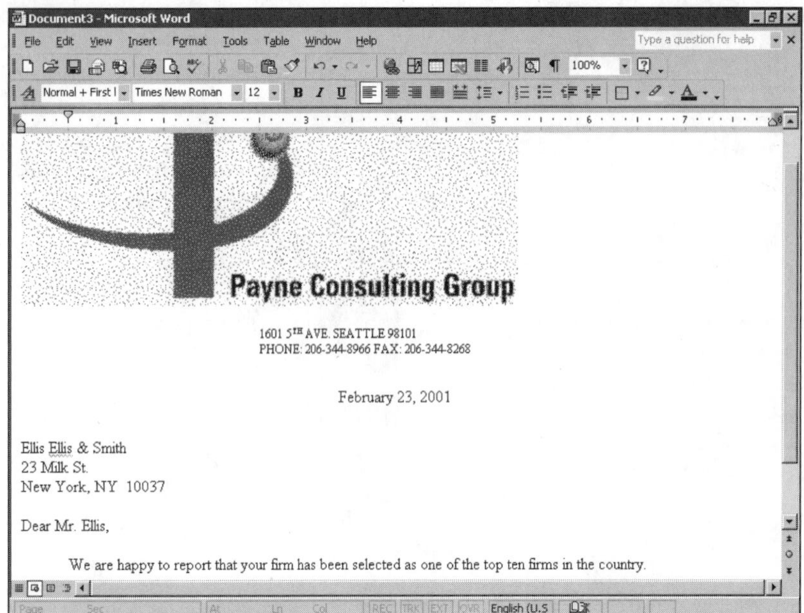

FIGURE 3.21

Web Layout view.

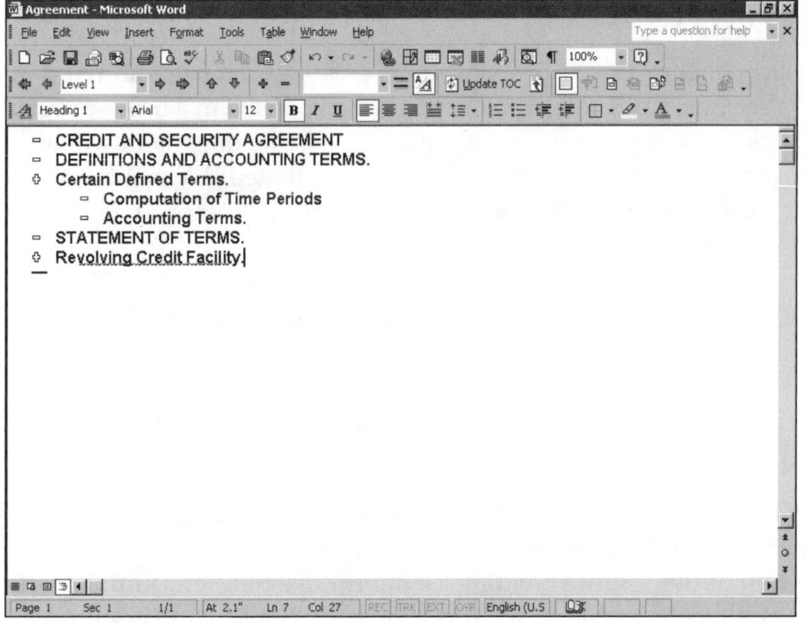

FIGURE 3.22

A great use for Outline view is when drafting presentation or speech notes, or when documents will be sent to PowerPoint, which uses heading and subtext for slides.

Paragraph formatting such as alignment and indents is not accurately reflected in Outline view.

DOCUMENT MAP

The Document Map (Figure 3.23) is a feature that is great for law firms. When you turn on the feature from the View menu or click the Document Map toolbar button, a separate pane appears to the left of the document that contains all items formatted with a heading or outline style. When you click on an item within the Document Map, Word takes you directly to the location in the document where that heading appears, even if it's Section 13.4 on page 217 or page 2027. Document Map is very useful for working with briefs, trust agreements, or other lengthy documents.

USE DOCUMENT MAP

1. Create a new document.
2. Type your firm name and press Ctrl+Alt+1. Press Enter to move to the next line.
3. Type several cities on separate lines.
4. Select the list of cities and press Ctrl+Alt+2.
5. From the View menu, choose Document Map.
6. Click any topic within the Document Map to move to that exact location. Imagine how useful this could be if working with a 500-page agreement.

You can expand or collapse the headings in the Document Map pane by clicking on the + or – signs next to each heading.

In the preceding exercise, heading styles were applied to the text to have them appear in the Document Map. You can also add text not associated with a specific heading style to the Document Map pane by first selecting the text, choosing Format, Paragraph, and selecting an outline level from the drop-down list next to Outline Level on the Indents And Spacing tab. Word has also added an Outlining toolbar to make marking text with an associated outline level easier.

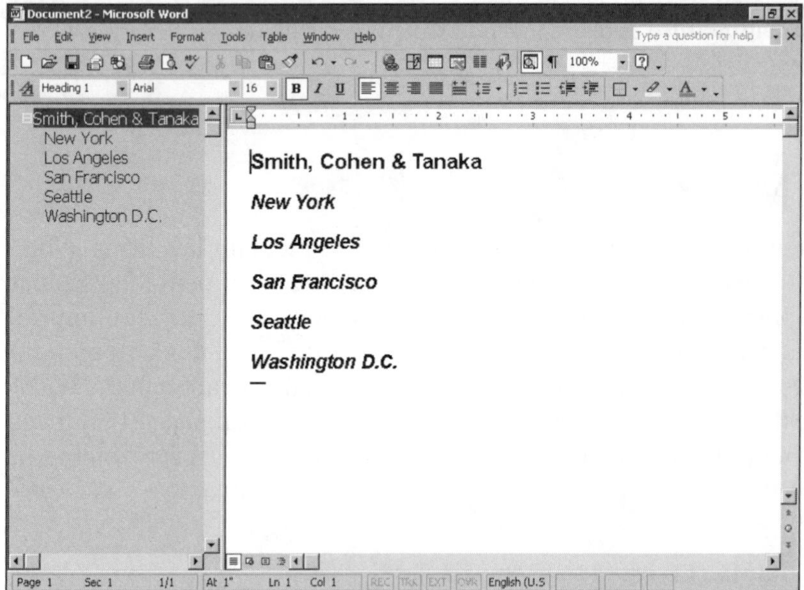

FIGURE 3.23

The Document Map allows you to navigate to a specific location in the document with one mouse click.

ZOOM

Although the Zoom feature is not exactly a view, it does change how the document looks onscreen by adjusting the percentage that is visible or by showing page width or other predefined zoom sizes. The Zoom feature can be accessed on the Standard toolbar (look for the button that has a value followed by a percent sign and a drop-down list with various zoom percentages) or by choosing Zoom from the View menu.

You can choose from one of several preset percentages from the drop-down list or type a different percentage directly into the Zoom box and press Enter. The percentage you choose will determine whether or not you see more or less readable text. The higher the percentage, the larger the text. Most people prefer to work in the range of 75% to 100%. Some of the zoom options will vary depending on your current view. If you want to see how your document will look when printed, choose a very low percentage, such as 25%, while in Print Layout view. If you want the text of your document to wrap to the document window, choose Page Width Zoom while in Normal view. The Zoom box is shown in Figure 3.24.

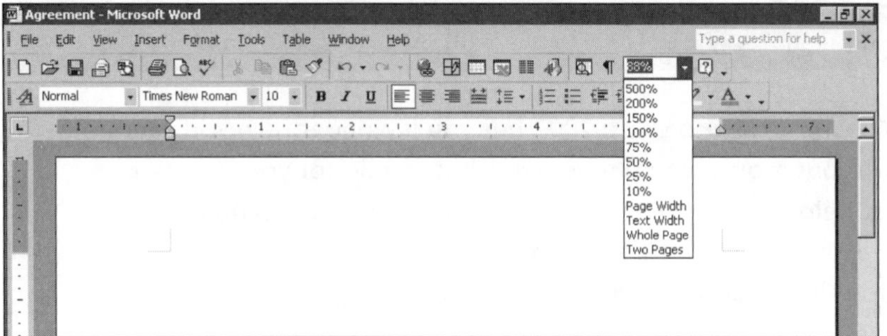

FIGURE 3.24

The Zoom box changes how the document is shown onscreen.

TASK PANE

The Task Pane command is located on the View menu, but this new Word 2002 feature does more than just adjust the view of a document. Depending on what type of work you are doing, the task pane changes so as to help you with the process. Once activated, the task pane appears on the right side of the document window and contains one or more of the following help options: New From Existing Document, Clipboard, Search (which will search by text as well as location), Search (ClipArt and Media Files), Styles And Formatting, Reveal Formatting, Mail Merge, and Translate. Figure 3.25 shows one view of the task pane.

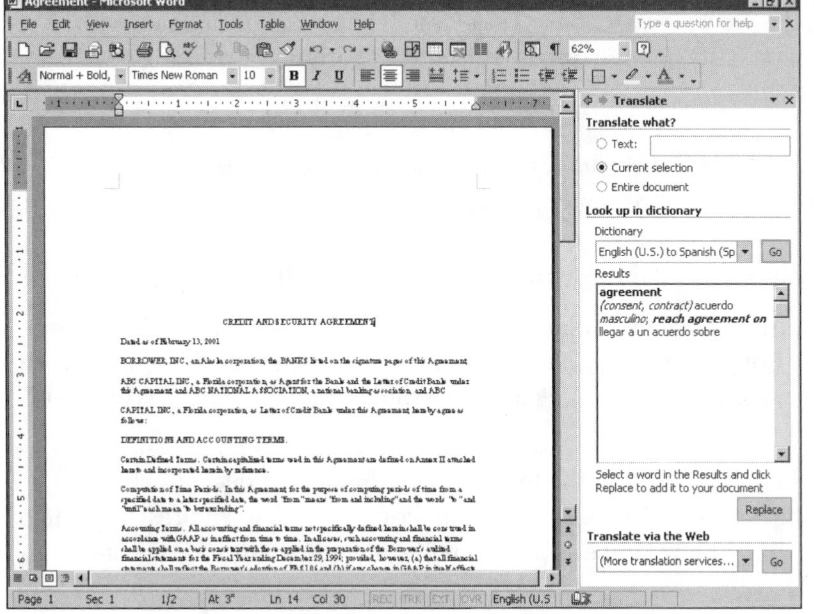

FIGURE 3.25

The task pane provides quick access to many commands and features that were hidden in previous versions of Word.

NEW FEATURE!

The task pane is new to Word 2002 but you'll wonder how you ever got along without it once you see how much it can do for you. The task pane can help you create and find documents, view all items on the improved Office Clipboard, search for files by text or location, and search for ClipArt or media files. If that isn't enough, you can see all styles and formatting in the task pane and quickly create or apply styles in the document, reveal formatting, distinguish style source, and show all formatting marks. The task pane also walks you through the new and improved Mail Merge feature. Finally, it provides help with the new Word Translate feature.

Although the task pane looks a little like Document Map in the way it uses the real estate of the screen, you will quickly realize the value of this feature and won't want to work without it.

DISPLAY AND VIEW THE TASK PANE

1. Create a new document.
2. From the View menu, choose Task Pane. The task pane appears with a list of recently opened documents and a shortcut for creating new documents.

The Task Pane command in the View menu is a toggle. If you do not see the task pane after you select the option, select it again.

3. Type your name in the document and then select the text.
4. Press Ctrl+C twice to display the Office Clipboard, or from the Edit menu, choose Copy. The task pane now changes to display the Clipboard, which stores copied information. Figure 3.26 shows the Clipboard Task Pane in action.
5. Click the down-arrow at the top of the task pane and select the first instance of Search. The task pane changes as shown in Figure 3.27 to help you search for any Office application file, including e-mail messages.

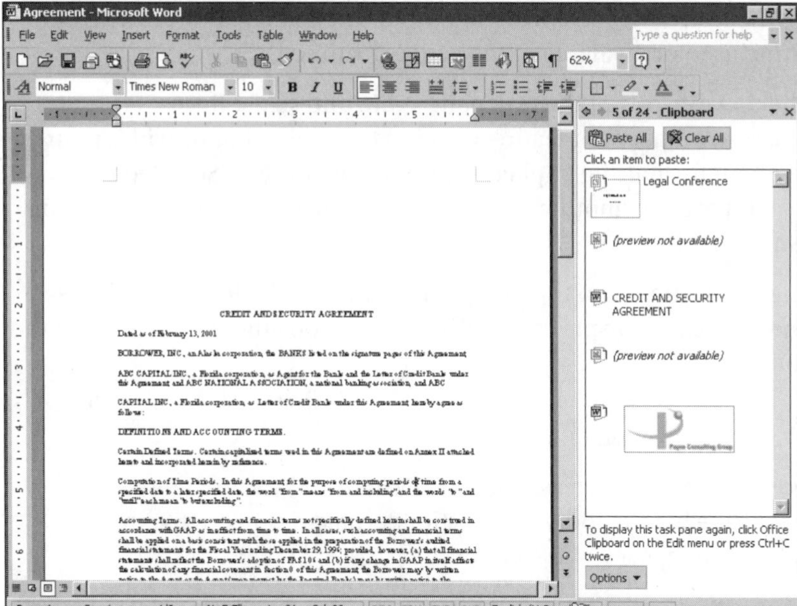

FIGURE 3.26

The Clipboard Task Pane is much improved over previous versions. Graphics are displayed as well as text without having to hover the mouse over a toolbar button.

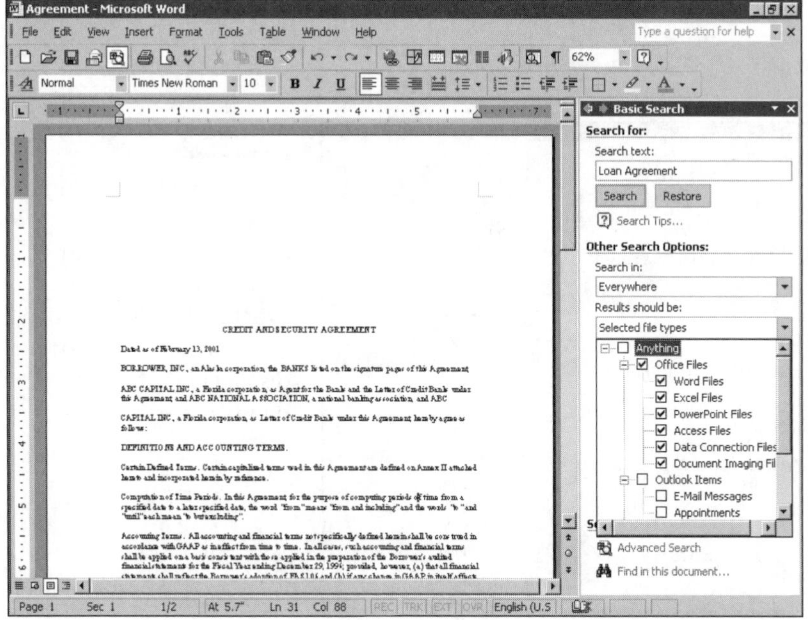

FIGURE 3.27

Search Word, Excel, Access, PowerPoint, even Outlook e-mail messages and appointments.

6. Change the task pane to Styles And Formatting to display any styles and formatting used or available in the active document.
7. Click the down-arrow of the task pane again and select Reveal Formatting. The result (shown in Figure 3.28) is a task pane that provides information about formatting applied within the document. Selected text can also be compared to another selection in the document as well using this task pane.
8. Click the "X" at the top of the task pane to turn off the feature and close the pane. You can redisplay the task pane by choosing Tas<u>k</u> Pane from the <u>V</u>iew menu.

NOTE Keyboard shortcuts have not been assigned to any item in the various task panes. If the task pane has the focus in the active document, you can use the Tab key to move through many of the options.

NOTE The rest of this book discusses the task pane whenever it's relevant to the matter at hand. This chapter just gives you an introduction to the feature.

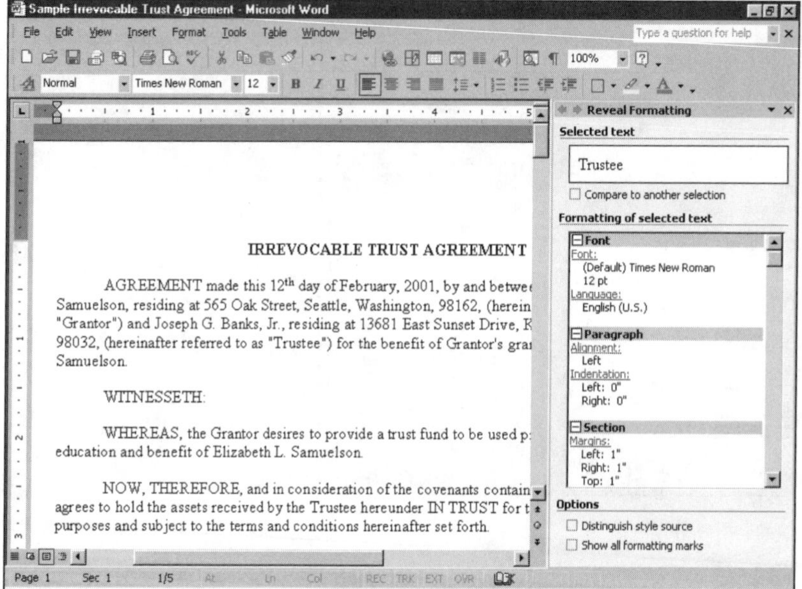

FIGURE 3.28

The Reveal Formatting task pane includes hyperlinks that when clicked take you to the exact dialog box option that controls each setting displayed in the task pane.

FILE PROPERTIES

Every document you create in Word contains pieces of information that help identify it and make it unique. These collections of information are known as *document properties.* Document title, size, location, and date created are just a few of the many properties that, taken as a whole, help create a complete identity for your Word documents.

From the File menu, choose Properties to view the properties for the active document. Each tab in the dialog box contains important information that is being tracked about your document. Some of the tabs store information automatically and others require user input. Here's a look at each of the five tabs that make up the Properties dialog box, shown in Figure 3.29.

Some document management systems, such as DOCS Open, take over the Properties command and display the document profile instead. Word's document properties still exist for these documents but can only be viewed when the document is saved locally (outside of the DMS). See your system administrator for more information.

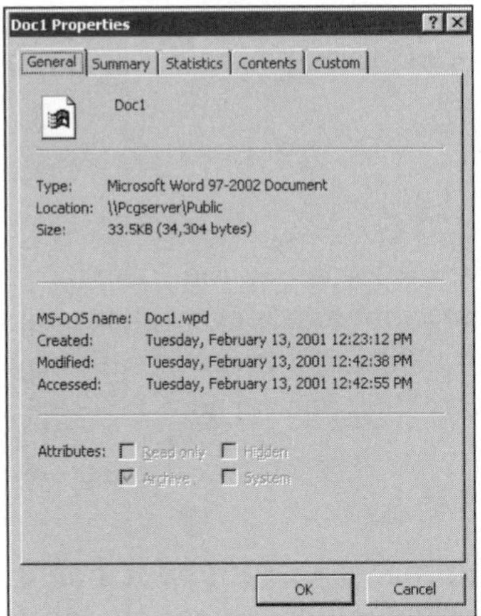

FIGURE 3.29

The Document Properties dialog box, showing the tabs and the contents of the General tab.

GENERAL TAB

The General tab automatically provides the following document information:

- **Title**. Title of the document
- **Type**. File type (such as Word document)
- **Location**. Where the document currently resides
- **Size**. File size
- **MS-DOS Name**. Truncated eight-character DOS file name
- **Created**. Date and time the document was created
- **Modified**. Date and time the document was last modified
- **Access**. Date and time the document was last accessed

SUMMARY TAB

The Summary tab contains a number of fields that allow you to input specific information about your document. Some of the information is automatically filled in for you. The Document Title automatically comes from the first line of text in the document. The author and company fields contain information gathered from the User Information tab in the Tools, Options dialog box.

The remaining fields can be used to add additional information about the specifics of your document, including keywords, comments, category, and subject. These fields are searchable and can help assist in locating hard-to-find documents.

STATISTICS TAB

The Statistics tab repeats some of the information found on the General tab and also includes statistics such as the number of pages, characters, paragraphs, lines, and more. It also shows total editing time, last saved by, and revision number if you are working with more than one version.

CONTENTS TAB

The Contents tab provides an outline view of your document based on any heading styles contained in the document. To see the outline, go to the Summary tab, click the Save Preview Picture check box, and then save the document.

CUSTOM TAB

The Custom tab of the File Properties dialog box (Figure 3.30) allows you to create custom file properties to make your document even easier to identify. You can use Word's built-in list of custom fields or create your own. For example, if you wanted to associate your document with a specific client-matter number, you could create custom client-matter fields.

CREATE CUSTOM CLIENT AND MATTER FILE PROPERTIES

1. Create a new document, and from the File menu, choose Properties. Select the Custom tab.
2. From the list below the Name box, select Client.
3. Leave the Type field as Text.
4. In the Value field, type **McDonald & Elliot**.
5. Click Add.
6. From the list below the Name field, scroll down and select Matter.
7. In the Value field, type **123456**.
8. Click Add.
9. Click OK.

That's it! You've just created a custom client-matter number that will help uniquely identify your document.

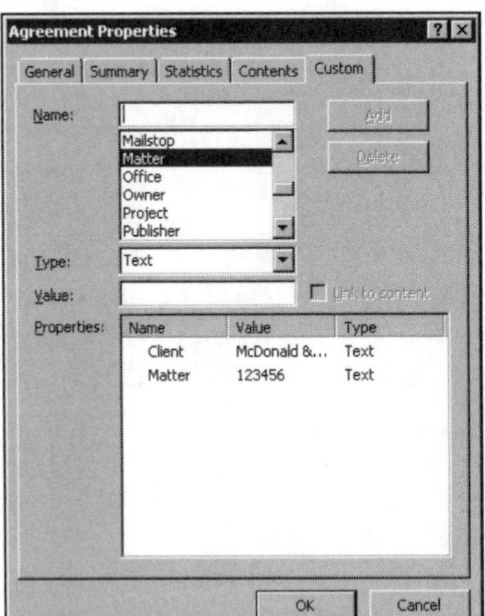

FIGURE 3.30

Some firms that choose not to use a commercial document management system often use custom document properties to manage documents.

WORD HELP

Word provides a number of online help resources for those times when you need important questions answered. From the ever-helpful Office Assistant to ScreenTips to Office On The Web, Microsoft provides an extensive online Word knowledge base.

OFFICE ASSISTANT

The Office Assistant can provide a great deal of value—or can be more a hindrance than help. The Office Assistant attempts to anticipate your need for help by popping up with tips and suggestions during the execution of certain commands. For example, if you begin a document with "Dear John," the Assistant will appear and ask if you need help writing a letter. Some users find this level of assistance a bit intrusive; others find it extremely helpful. Depending on your work style, you can choose to keep the Office Assistant turned on or off or modify the option settings to better control the assistance you receive.

> **NEW FEATURE!**
>
> One of the new help features in Word 2002 is the Type A Question For Help box located at the end of the menu bar, as shown in Figure 3.31. You can type a word or phrase into the box (such as limitation to view all of the limits for Word), press Enter, and get a list of possible answers or help topics.

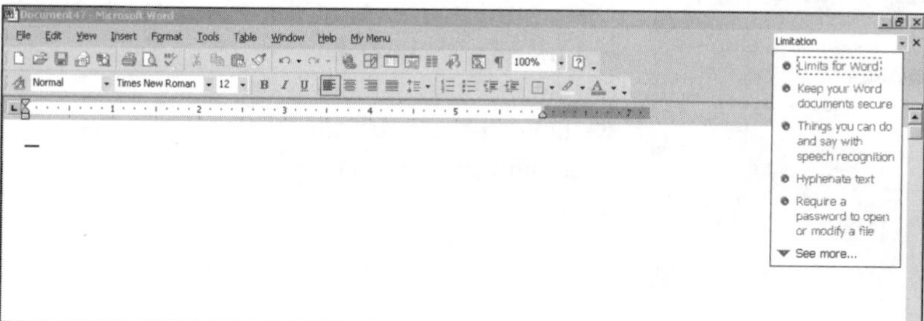

FIGURE 3.31

The Ask A Question box provides help from the active document screen and eliminates the need for heavy usage of the Office Assistant.

WORK WITH THE OFFICE ASSISTANT

1. From the Help menu, choose Microsoft Word Help, or press F1.
2. When the Office Assistant appears, type the word **number** in the question box and click Search.
3. Click a suggested topic to see the full answer.
4. Close the Help window.
5. From the Help menu, choose Show The Office Assistant.
6. Alternate-click the Office Assistant and click Options.
7. Uncheck Use The Office Assistant to turn the Assistant off.
8. Select the Gallery tab to choose a different Assistant. Click OK when completed.
9. Alternate-click the Office Assistant and select Hide from the drop-down list.

MICROSOFT WORD HELP

If you want access to a more visible, complete online help directory, you can turn off the Office Assistant and use standard Microsoft Word Help. The Help window contains three tabbed sections, Contents, Answer Wizard, and Index. Each section provides a different method for getting the information you need.

MICROSOFT WORD HELP

1. Turn off the Office Assistant.
2. Press F1 and maximize the Microsoft Word Help window.
3. Select the Contents tab. Double-click Getting Started. How many subtopics are associated with Getting Started?

NOTE

The tabs may not show the first time F1 is pressed. If this happens, click the Show Tabs icon.

4. Select the Answer Wizard tab.
5. In the question box, type **legal** and click Search. How many topics do you see? Click a topic to display more information.
6. Select the Index tab.
7. In the Type Keywords box, type **template** and click Search. How many topics are associated with that keyword?
8. From under Choose A Topic, click any topic to display more information.

NOTE

The first time you select the Index tab, Word has to build the index. This may take a few minutes.

WHAT'S THIS?

If you need information about a specific toolbar button, menu command, or paragraph format, use the What's This? feature. From the Help menu, choose What's This? and a question mark appears next to your mouse pointer. Click on the screen item you want to learn more about and the Reveal Formatting Task Pane opens. You can also use the keyboard shortcut Shift+F1 to activate the What's This? pointer.

WORDPERFECT HELP

WordPerfect help is available to assist those who are making the transition from WordPerfect to Word. From the Help menu, choose WordPerfect Help to see a listing of WordPerfect commands and their Word equivalents.

OFFICE ON THE WEB

Office on the Web is an online help resource that transports you directly to the Office portion of Microsoft's Web site. From the Help menu, choose Office On The Web. Once there, you can choose from a number of Word help topics including articles, tips and tricks, newsgroups, and much more.

DETECT AND REPAIR

Detect and Repair is a help feature that uses the Microsoft Windows Installer to check for and repair problems you may be having with Word (or any other installed Office application) related to missing program files or registry settings.

Detect and Repair does not fix corrupt or missing documents, but it's great if your spelling or thesaurus file develops a problem and you receive errors each time you attempt to check the spelling in a document.

From the Help menu, choose Detect And Repair, Start to run the Windows Installer.

SUMMARY

This chapter is dedicated to familiarizing you with the Word environment. It shows how to use some of the features that will help you work more efficiently in Word, including menu bars, toolbars, SDI, views, file properties, and help.

Word contains many components and features that allow you to create a customized, flexible working environment. It's useful to take the time to look at some of those tools so as to be able to use Word's tremendous power to your advantage. Word is much more than a simple word processor; it's a sophisticated, powerful program that provides you with the resources you need to be productive and efficient in today's legal environment.

TROUBLESHOOTING THE WORD ENVIRONMENT

I created a custom toolbar but when I open a new document it's not there—where did it go?

You probably saved it to a custom template. If you want to make a personal toolbar available to all new documents, make sure you save it to Word's global template, Normal.dot. When naming your new toolbar, make sure the Make Toolbar Available To drop-down list shows Normal.dot. You'll learn more about templates and the Normal.dot file in Chapter 10, "Templates."

I accidentally removed a menu from the menu bar—how can I get it back?

Restoring a lost menu is easy. From the Tools menu, choose Customize and then select the Toolbars tab. Select Menu Bar and click Reset.

If you have customized other menu commands, you may not want to reset the entire menu bar. In this case, display the Customize dialog box and select the Commands tab. Scroll through the list of Categories to locate and select Built-In Menus. From the Commands list, click and drag the missing menu back up to the menu bar.

I've tried every possible Help resource, including Office on the Web, and still can't find the answer to my question. Are there any other resources available?

If you're really having difficulty finding the answer to a Word question, go to http://search.support.microsoft.com. You can search Microsoft's Knowledge Base, which contains articles that provide assistance for difficult or known issues related to the software.

Chapter 4

Building a Legal Document

IN THIS CHAPTER

- Getting around
- Typing, selecting, and deleting text
- Moving text
- Office Clipboard
- AutoCorrect Options—AutoCorrect, AutoFormat, AutoText, and the Smart Tag feature

Legal users often need to work quickly and efficiently under trying circumstances and get documents out the door in time to meet filing deadlines, closings, and client requests. What good is a word processing application if it doesn't automate some of the tasks that once caused major delays and hours of frustration? With Word you can put away the correction fluid and set aside the scissors and glue. From click-and-drag to drag-and-drop, AutoText to AutoCorrect, Word contains many powerful editing and automation tools that will help make the job of building legal documents easier and less time consuming.

GETTING AROUND

Being able to move around in a document can oftentimes be just as important as getting the words down in the first place. How many times have you needed to make last-minute changes to a long, complex brief while under pressure to meet a filing deadline? Legal users depend on their ability to move quickly and easily through long documents. With Word, you can use both the keyboard and the mouse to navigate by character, word, line, paragraph, screen, and page.

NAVIGATING WITH THE KEYBOARD

Use the shortcut keys shown in Table 4.1 to move quickly through documents without lifting your hands from the keyboard.

TIP

Press F5 or Ctrl+G to activate the Find And Replace dialog box as shown in Figure 4.1. Make sure Page is selected under Go To What, enter a specific page number, and click Go To or press Enter.

NAVIGATING WITH THE MOUSE

If you'd rather not have to remember all those keystroke commands, Word provides several methods for navigating through long documents by using the mouse.

To move from one place to another on the active screen, position your mouse pointer in the appropriate spot, click, and begin typing—it's that simple. If you

TABLE 4.1 NAVIGATION SHORTCUT KEYS

KEYBOARD COMMAND	RESULT
Up-Arrow	Moves insertion point up one line at a time.
Down-Arrow	Moves insertion point down one line at a time.
Left-Arrow	Moves insertion point one character to the left.
Right-Arrow	Moves insertion point one character to the right.
Ctrl+Up-Arrow	Moves insertion point up one paragraph at a time.
Ctrl+Down-Arrow	Moves insertion point down one paragraph at a time.
Ctrl+Left-Arrow	Moves insertion point one word to the left.
Ctrl+Right-Arrow	Moves insertion point one word to the right.
Page Up	Moves insertion point up one screen.
Page Down	Moves insertion point down one screen.
Ctrl+Page Up	Moves insertion point up one full page.
Ctrl+Page Down	Moves insertion point down one full page.
Home	Moves insertion point to the beginning of the current line.
End	Moves insertion point to the end of the current line.
Ctrl+Home	Moves insertion point to the beginning of the document.
Ctrl+End	Moves insertion point to the end of the document.

need to move to another page or section within a document, use the vertical scroll bar as shown in Figure 4.2.

You can scroll by line, active screen, or page with the vertical scroll bar. Click the single arrows located at the top and bottom of the scroll bar to move through the document one line at a time. Hold the mouse button down on either of the arrows while clicking to scroll continuously up or down through the document.

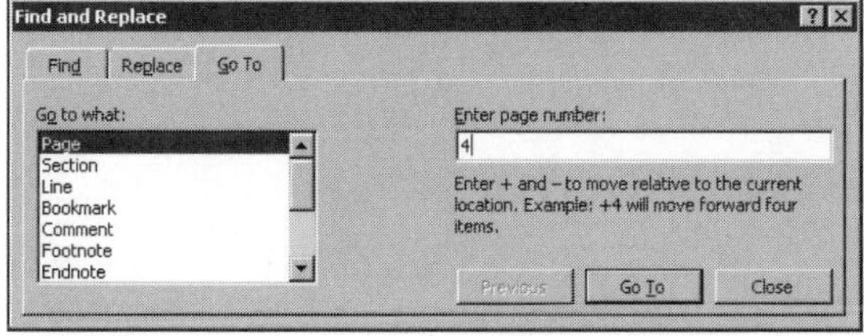

FIGURE 4.1

Use the Go To command to move to pages, sections, bookmarks, graphics, tables, and more.

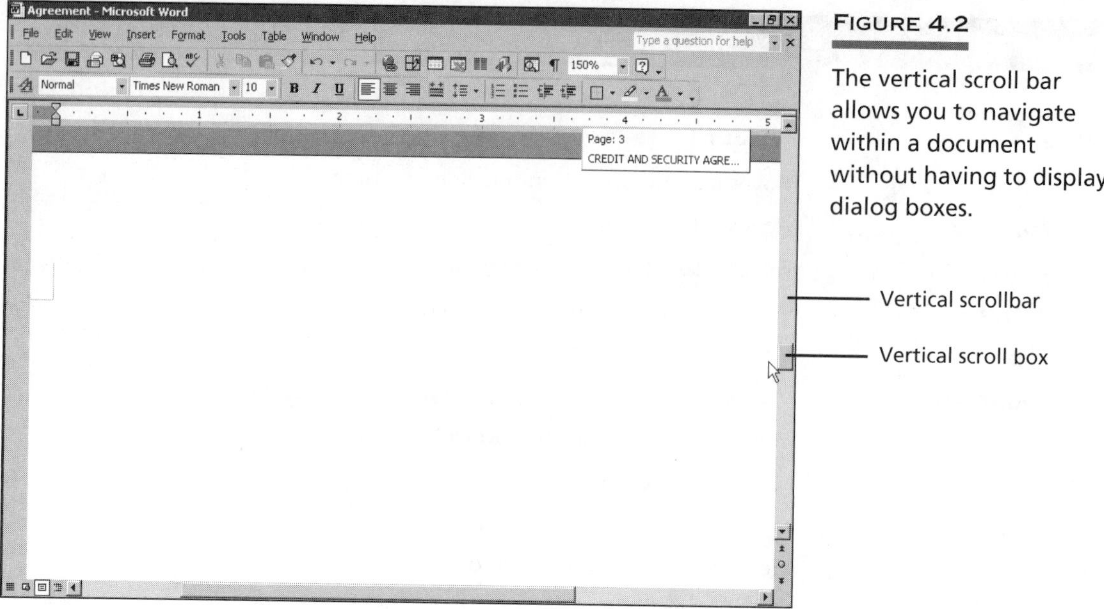

FIGURE 4.2

The vertical scroll bar allows you to navigate within a document without having to display dialog boxes.

The double arrows above and below the Select Browse Object allow you to scroll through the document one full page at a time.

Click the Select Browse Object button and click Browse By Page as shown in Figure 4.3 to set the double arrows to browse by page.

If you browse by any object other than page, the double arrows above and below the Select Browse Object button turn blue.

If it's speed you require, click and drag the vertical scroll box up or down to quickly find a specific section or paragraph in a long document. As you drag the scroll box, a ScreenTip will display the current page number along with heading information associated with that page so you won't have to guess where to stop.

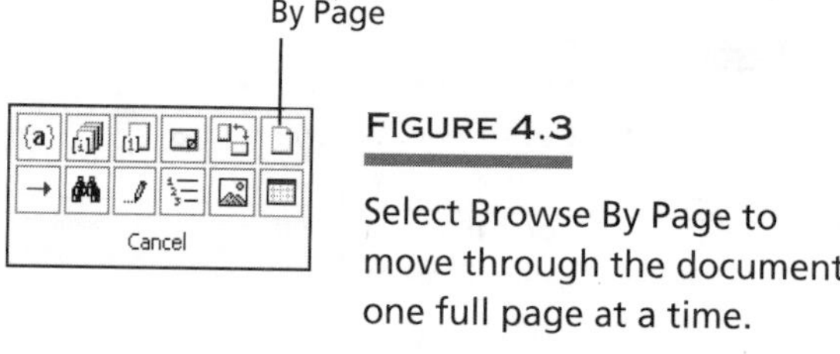

FIGURE 4.3

Select Browse By Page to move through the document one full page at a time.

TYPING, SELECTING, AND DELETING TEXT

Entering text into a document is easy. Place your hands on the keyboard and let your fingers do the rest. The more difficult aspect of document creation is knowing how to manipulate the text you've entered in the document. Legal documents by nature require a fair amount of formatting and editing. For example, agreements often go through numerous revisions before the final version goes out the door. You may also need to copy text from a master document and place it into the contract you're working on. From toolbar buttons and menu commands to shortcut keys and mouse actions, Word offers a number of different ways for you to select and edit the text.

NOTE

One of the rules to remember in Word (and it will be repeated often throughout this book!) is "select to affect." Select the text you wish to affect prior to applying the editing commands. Read Chapter 5, "Formatting Text," to learn all about applying character formatting.

USING THE KEYBOARD TO SELECT TEXT

Using assorted shortcut key combinations, you can select characters, words, phrases, paragraphs, and even whole documents without ever removing your fingers from the keyboard.

Table 4.2 provides a list of keystroke commands that can be used to select text.

PRACTICE SELECTING TEXT USING THE KEYBOARD

1. Create a new document.
2. Type **Section 1. The right of the citizens of the United States to vote shall not be denied or abridged by the United States or by any State on account of sex.** Press Enter twice.
3. Type **Section 2. Congress shall have power to enforce this article by appropriate legislation.**
4. Press Ctrl+Home to move to the beginning of the document.
5. Press Ctrl+Shift+Right-Arrow to select the first word in the first paragraph.

TABLE 4.2 SELECTION SHORTCUT KEYS

SHORTCUT KEY	RESULT
Shift+Right-Arrow	Selects character to the right of the insertion point.
Shift+Left-Arrow	Selects character to the left of the insertion point.
Shift+Up-Arrow	Selects next line up.
Shift+Down-Arrow	Selects next line down.
Ctrl+Shift+Right-Arrow	Selects to the end of a word.
Ctrl+Shift+Left-Arrow	Selects to the beginning of a word.
Ctrl+Shift+Up-Arrow	Selects to the beginning of a paragraph.
Ctrl+Shift+Down-Arrow	Selects to the end of a paragraph.
Shift+End	Selects to the end of the line.
Shift+Home	Selects to the beginning of the line.
Shift+Page Up	Selects one screen up.
Shift+Page Down	Selects one screen down.
Ctrl+Shift+Home	Selects from insertion point position to the beginning of the document.
Ctrl+Shift+End	Selects from insertion point position to the end of the document.
Ctrl+Shift+F8	Selects a vertical block of text (use the arrow keys to make the selection after applying the keyboard command).
F8+Arrow keys	Selects blocks of text. Press Esc key to turn off selection command, and then click off the selection to deselect text.
F8 twice	Selects whole word. Press Esc key to turn off selection command, and then click off the selection to deselect text.
F8 three times	Selects entire sentence. Press Esc key to turn off selection command, and then click off the selection to deselect text.
F8 four times	Selects entire paragraph. Press Esc key to turn off selection command, and then click off the selection to deselect text.
F8 five times	Selects entire document. Press Esc key to turn off selection command, and then click off the selection to deselect text.
Ctrl+A	Selects entire document.

6. Press Shift+End to select to the end of the first line.
7. Press Shift+Down-Arrow to select the next line down.
8. Press Ctrl+Shift+Left-Arrow several times to deselect words to the left of the insertion point.
9. Press Ctrl+A to select the entire document.
10. Press any of the arrow keys to remove the selection.

USING THE MOUSE TO SELECT TEXT

If the thought of remembering all those keyboard commands makes your head spin, you might want to consider using the mouse instead. As with the keyboard, you can use the mouse to select characters, words, lines, paragraphs, and even whole documents.

Use the following mouse actions to select text:

- **Click and drag.** Select individual characters, words, lines, or paragraphs using click and drag. Place your mouse pointer at the point where you want to start, click, and while holding down the mouse button, drag in the appropriate direction.

If you're trying to select individual characters and can't keep the entire word from getting selected, Word is being helpful again. To regain control, from the Tools menu, choose Options, select the Edit tab, and uncheck the option When Selecting, Automatically Select Entire Word.

- **Double-click.** Selects the entire word where the mouse pointer is positioned.
- **Triple-click.** Selects entire paragraph where the mouse pointer is positioned.

SELECTION ARROW

The Selection Bar area is the section of the document to the left of where text is typed. When the mouse pointer is in this area it turns into an arrow, and you can click to quickly select large amounts of text as shown in Table 4.3.

NEW FEATURE!

Word contains a new feature called Smart Paragraph Selection. This option automatically selects the paragraph mark when all the words within a paragraph are selected. In Word, the paragraph mark contains formatting attributes for each paragraph, so you may find this option a benefit or a curse depending on what you're trying to do. Read Chapter 6, "Formatting a Paragraph," to learn more about paragraph formatting. To turn this feature on or off, from the Tools menu, choose Options, select the Edit tab, and check or uncheck Use Smart Paragraph Selection.

TABLE 4.3 SELECTION ARROW BEHAVIOR

MOUSE ACTION PERFORMED WITH SELECTION ARROW	RESULT
Single-click	Selects entire line.
Double-click	Selects entire paragraph.
Triple-click	Selects entire document.
Click and drag up or down	Selects lines of text in the direction of the drag.

USE THE SELECTION ARROW TO SELECT TEXT

1. Create a new document.
2. Type **Section 1. The right of citizens of the United States, who are eighteen years of age or older, to vote shall not be denied or abridged by the United States or by any State on account of age.** Press Enter twice.
3. Type **Section 2. The Congress shall have power to enforce this article by appropriate legislation.**
4. Place your mouse pointer in the left margin area until it turns into a right-pointing arrow.

NEW FEATURE!

In Word you can now select noncontiguous sections of text. To do so, hold down the Ctrl key while selecting words, phrases, sentences, and paragraphs. Once you've selected the appropriate passages of noncontiguous text, apply formatting such as bold, italics, and underline.

5. Move the arrow up so it's even with the top of the first paragraph. Click once. Notice the entire first line is selected.
6. With the first line still selected, hold down the mouse button and drag the arrow downward until the entire first paragraph is selected.
7. Move your mouse pointer over the paragraph and click to deselect. Practice more by using the commands from Table 4.3.

USING THE KEYBOARD AND MOUSE TO SELECT TEXT

In addition to the various selection methods described previously, you can also use a combination of the mouse and keyboard to select text.

- To select one complete sentence, place your mouse pointer in the sentence, hold down the Ctrl key, and click.
- To select a large contiguous block of text, place your mouse pointer at the beginning of the selection, scroll to the end of the desired selection, hold down the Shift key, and click.
- To select text vertically, hold the Alt key and drag the mouse to the left or right and then down. This is useful for selecting and formatting text that is in columns but not within a table.

DELETING TEXT

Getting rid of unwanted text is easy with Word. For starters, you can use the Backspace and Delete keys, respectively, to remove text to the left and right of the insertion point. Or you can select the appropriate text and press any of the following keys: Enter, Backspace, and Delete. You can even type over and replace selected text when the appropriate option is set.

If you want to be able to type over and replace selected text, from the Tools menu, choose Options, select the Edit tab, and check the option Typing Replaces Selection.

Press the Insert key or double-click OVR on the status bar to activate Overtype mode. When this feature is in use, you can remove existing text by typing over it without selecting it first.

Use the Overtype option carefully. You may end up accidentally deleting more text than intended.

MOVING TEXT

Most legal documents rarely end up looking anything like the first draft. Agreements, contracts, and other similar documents often require extensive revision. Now that you've learned how to select text, you're ready to find out how to use Word's editing commands to reposition text within or between documents.

CUT, COPY, AND PASTE

Three of the most commonly used editing commands in any word processing application are Cut, Copy, and Paste. You can apply any of these commands to selected text from a number of locations in Word.

EDIT MENU

You can cut, copy, or paste text using the commands from the Edit menu. Select the text you wish to edit and choose the appropriate command. Cut removes selected text from the document and places it on the Office Clipboard.

The Office Clipboard is covered later in this chapter.

The Copy command copies selected text to the Clipboard, leaving the original text as is. Paste inserts the cut or copied information from the Clipboard to a new location in the same document, a different Word document, or even a document in a different application.

FORMATTING TOOLBAR

You can access the Cut, Copy, and Paste commands from the Formatting toolbar as shown in Figure 4.4. Select the text you wish to edit and click the appropriate toolbar button.

SHORTCUT MENU

You can even use shortcut menus to apply the Cut, Copy, and Paste commands. Select the text you wish to cut or copy, alternate-click, and choose the appropriate command from the shortcut menu. Move your mouse pointer to the position where you wish to insert the cut or copied text, alternate-click, and choose Paste from the shortcut menu as shown in Figure 4.5.

The keystroke commands for Cut, Copy, and Paste are Ctrl+X, Ctrl+C, and Ctrl+V, respectively.

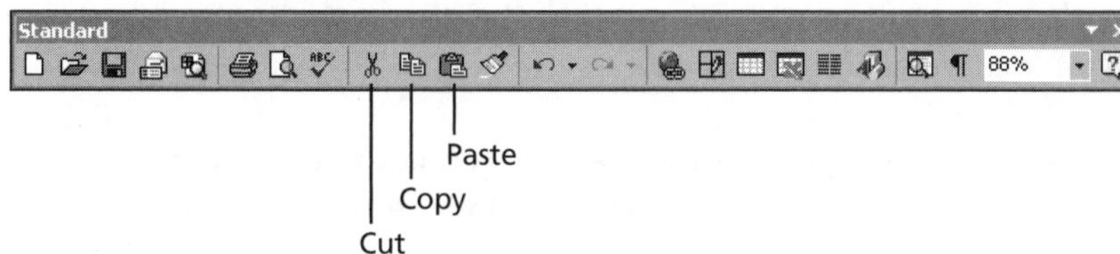

FIGURE 4.4

Cut, Copy, and Paste commands are quickly accessible from the Formatting toolbar.

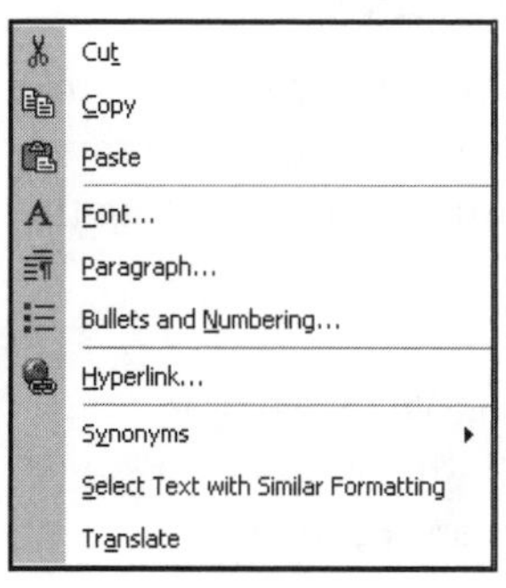

FIGURE 4.5

The shortcut menu offers faster methods for performing frequent actions. Included are the Cut, Copy, and Paste commands.

PRACTICE USING THE CUT, COPY, AND PASTE COMMANDS

1. Create a new document.
2. Type **The Vice President of the United States shall be President of the Senate but shall have no Vote, unless they be equally divided.**
3. Select the entire paragraph. From the Edit menu, choose Copy.
4. Press Enter twice. Alternate-click and choose Paste from the shortcut menu.
5. Select Vice President from the second copied paragraph.
6. Press Ctrl+X to cut the selected text.
7. Create a new document. Press Ctrl+V to paste the selection into the new document.

NOTE

Word has a feature called Smart Cut and Paste. When this option is activated, Word automatically adjusts the spacing for deleted or inserted text. From the Tools menu, choose Options, select the Edit tab, and place a check next to Smart Cut And Paste. You can specify paste options further by clicking the Settings button. These settings are new to Word 2002.

TIP

If the appropriate option is set, you can also use the Insert key to paste text from the Clipboard. From the Tools menu, choose Options, select the Edit tab, and check Use The INS Key for Paste.

MOVING TEXT USING DRAG AND DROP

Drag and drop is an aptly named Word feature that lets you move selected text within or between documents using the mouse. Select the words or paragraphs you wish to move, click, and while holding down the mouse button, drag the selection to the desired location and drop.

TIP

You can also drag and drop using the alternate mouse button. When you drag and release the mouse button (drop), a drop-down menu with the options Move Here, Copy Here, Link Here, Create Hyperlink Here appears. For most legal documents, you'll choose Move or Copy.

PRACTICE USING DRAG AND DROP

1. Create a new document.
2. Type **(i) information necessary to establish the identity of the person, including name, address, and taxpayer identification number.** Press Enter twice and type **(ii) the amount, status, and history of the claim; and.**
3. From the first paragraph, select the word *information.* Click and hold down the primary mouse button, and then drag the selection down to the second paragraph. Release the mouse before the word *amount.* Use the dotted insertion point that follows the mouse pointer when dragging as a marker for positioning the selected text.
4. Select the word *status* from the second paragraph. Alternate-click and drag it to the first paragraph. Drop it after the word *name* and choose Copy Here from the shortcut menu.

TIP

You can also copy selected text by holding down the Ctrl key while you drag and drop.

OFFICE CLIPBOARD

The Office Clipboard is a feature that allows you to collect items from various Office and non-Office applications and paste them into your documents. Text, graphics, Excel tables, and even PowerPoint slides can all be cut and copied from and pasted to different Microsoft Office applications by using the Office Clipboard.

The latest version of Microsoft Office expands the Clipboard so that it can now collect and paste up to 24 items at one time (up from 12 in Word 2000). To open the Clipboard Task Pane, choose Office Clipboard from the Edit menu. The Clipboard Task Pane is shown in Figure 4.6.

TIP

Press Ctrl+C twice to open the Clipboard Task Pane.

NOTE

The actual number of items the Clipboard can hold varies depending on the amount of available PC memory.

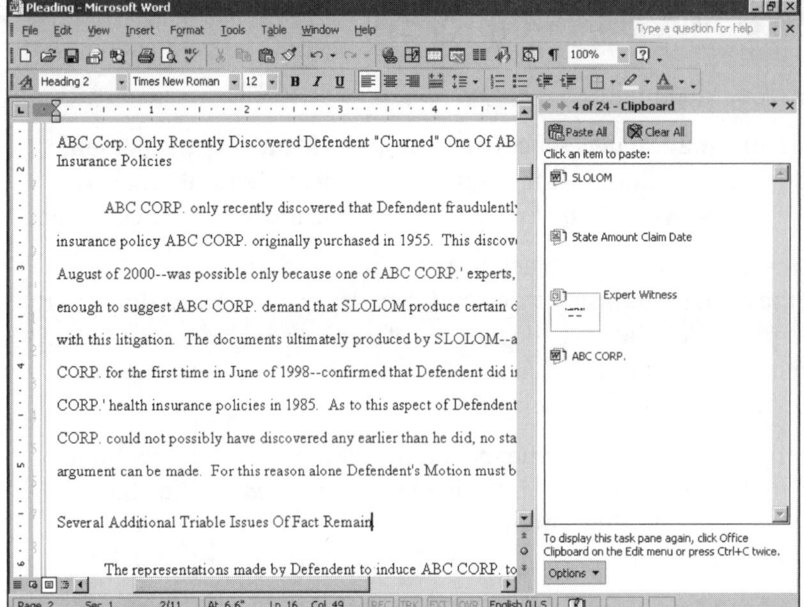

FIGURE 4.6

The Clipboard Task Pane can show actual graphic objects that have been copied.

The top of the Clipboard Task Pane provides a reference for the number of items that currently reside on the Clipboard, that is, 4 of 24 and so forth. The top of the list also reflects the most recently cut or copied item in descending order. Each item in the Clipboard Task Pane is represented by the specific application or graphics logo used to create it. You can paste each item separately or all at once depending on the requirements of your document. To remove specific selections, click the drop-down arrow next to each item and choose Delete. Alternatively, you can choose Clear All to clear the entire contents of the Clipboard.

PRACTICE USING THE OFFICE CLIPBOARD

1. Create a new document. From the Edit menu choose Office Clipboard to open the Clipboard Task Pane.
2. Type the following list of names. Press Enter after each name. **William Rehnquist**, **Sandra Day O'Connor**, **Ruth Bader Ginsburg**, **John Paul Stevens**, **Antonin Scalia**, **Clarence Thomas**, **Anthony Kennedy**, **Steven Bryer**, **David Souter**.
3. Select each name individually and press Ctrl+C. When you've finished, the Clipboard should contain nine items.

4. Create a new document. Open the Clipboard Task Pane. Notice that the copied items appear.
5. Click any of the copied items in the Clipboard Task Pane to paste the item into the new document.
6. Click Clear All at the top of the Task Pane to clear the Office Clipboard.

NEW FEATURE!

The Paste Options button appears at the lower right-hand side of pasted text in documents as shown in Figure 4.7. If you've pasted a formatted item or style, click the Paste Options button and choose one of three options—Keep Source Formatting (pasted text is same as the original), Match Destination Formatting (pasted text matches formatting of the current paragraph), or Keep Text Only (removes formatting and pastes unformatted text). If you don't want to see the Paste Options button, from the Tools menu, choose Options, select the Edit tab, and uncheck Show Paste Options Buttons. When information is pasted from different applications such as Microsoft Excel, additional options appear.

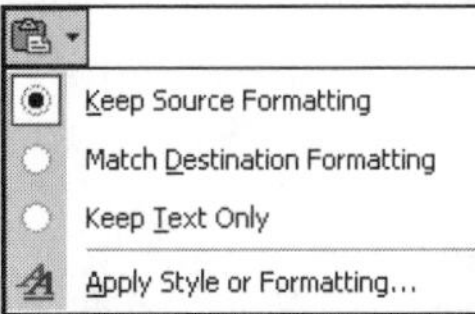

FIGURE 4.7

The Paste Options button replaces the need to choose Edit, Paste Special, Unformatted Text.

PRACTICE USING THE PASTE OPTIONS BUTTON

1. Create a new blank document.
2. Type at least one paragraph of text and apply formatting such as bold, underline, or other formatting.
3. Select the text. Press Ctrl+C to copy the text. Press Enter.
4. Create a new document. Press Ctrl+V to paste the copied text.

5. Click the Paste Options button that appears next to the pasted text and choose Keep Source Formatting. The text retains the original formatting.
6. Click the Paste Options button again and choose Keep Text Only. This removes formatting and pastes the text only.
7. Close the document without saving.

AUTOCORRECT OPTIONS

Do you find yourself spending time correcting the same spelling mistakes over and over? Have you ever wondered if there was a faster, easier way to create signature blocks? Are there specific lists, phrases, or blocks of text you repeatedly enter into your legal documents? If you answered yes to any of those questions, you'll be interested to know that Word contains a number of automated features that can be used to help make routine tasks less time consuming. These features are controlled from the five tabbed sections of the AutoCorrect dialog box (shown in Figure 4.8), which can be accessed by choosing AutoCorrect Options from the Tools menu.

Each of the five sections—AutoCorrect, AutoFormat As You Type, AutoFormat, AutoText, and Smart Tags—contains options that can be used to make working with Word more productive and even more fun.

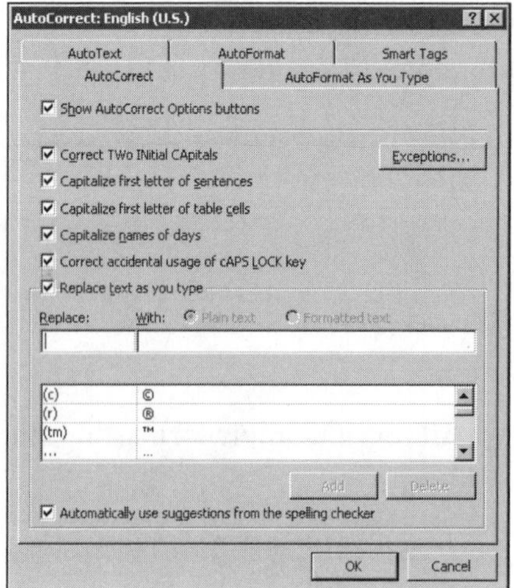

FIGURE 4.8

The AutoCorrect dialog box includes many useful features that automate formatting in Word.

AUTOCORRECT

If too much of your time goes into correcting the same spelling mistakes, AutoCorrect is for you. This powerful Word feature automatically replaces incorrectly spelled words with correctly spelled words as you type. The lower portion of the dialog box contains a long list of commonly misspelled words along with their correctly spelled replacements. For example, if you accidentally type *acheive*, Word replaces it with *achieve*. Scroll through the list to see if some of the words you frequently misspell are represented. The AutoCorrect dialog box was shown on the tab at the front of Figure 4.8.

While the default set of AutoCorrect entries provides a good starting point for correcting common mistakes, most legal documents contain words that aren't on the list. If the words you always misspell don't appear, Word lets you create your own entries. You can even create AutoCorrect abbreviations for commonly used phrases or blocks of text, such as the name of your firm.

When selected, the check box options automatically correct specific spelling errors. Table 4.4 provides an explanation of each AutoCorrect option.

NEW FEATURE!

The AutoCorrect Options button is new to this version of Word and is shown in Figure 4.9. Automatically corrected words are underlined with a small blue box. When you place your mouse pointer on the box, an Options button appears. The Options button contains a drop-down menu with choices specifically related to the automatically corrected word. You can also click Control AutoCorrect Options to open the AutoCorrect dialog box.

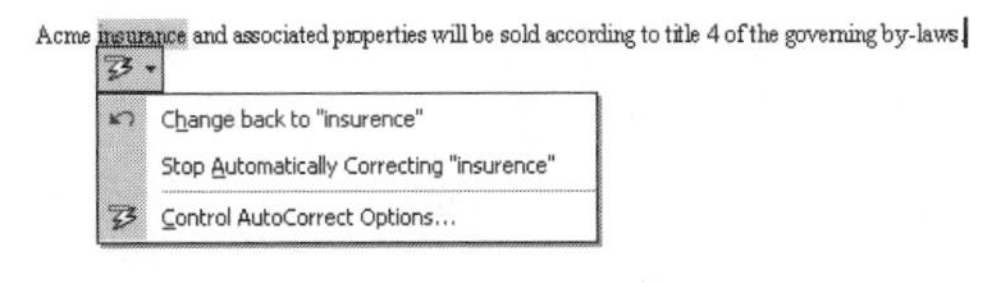

FIGURE 4.9

Pick what you want from the AutoCorrect Options menu.

TABLE 4.4 MAIN AUTOCORRECT OPTIONS DIALOG BOX

AUTOCORRECT OPTION	AUTOCORRECT RESULT
Show AutoCorrect Options buttons	Displays AutoCorrect Options button for automatically corrected words.
Correct TWo INitial CApitals	Automatically lowercases the second letter in words entered with two initial capital letters.
Capitalize first letter of sentences	Always capitalizes the first letter of a sentence.
Capitalize first letter of table cells	Always capitalizes the first letter of text in a table cell.
Capitalize names of days	Automatically capitalizes the first letter of the days of the week.
Correct accidental usage of cAPS LOCK key	Automatically detects and turns off the Caps Lock key when a word is typed with an initial lowercase letter and the rest in all caps.
Replace text as you type	Automatically corrects misspelled words labeled as AutoCorrect entries.

CREATE AN AUTOCORRECT ENTRY FOR YOUR FIRM'S NAME

1. Create a blank document.
2. Type **Ellis Johnson Young & Howard LLP** (or type the name of your firm).
3. Select the text.
4. From the Tools menu, choose AutoCorrect Options and select the Auto-Correct tab.
5. In the Replace field type **ejy** (Ellis Johnson Young & Howard LLP should already be in the With field).

NOTE

If the AutoCorrect entry you're creating requires formatting, select the formatting options, create the entry, and click the Formatted Text button. Otherwise, choose the default option, Plain Text.

6. Click Add to complete the AutoCorrect entry, and then click Close.
7. Create a new document. Type **ejy** and press the Spacebar.

Don't create an AutoCorrect entry with a real word that you would ever use. Every time you type the entry and press the Spacebar, Word will insert the AutoCorrect equivalent into the document—which would be a disaster if you used something like *the* as the entry.

CREATE AN AUTOCORRECT ENTRY FOR A FREQUENTLY MISSPELLED WORD

1. Create a new document.
2. Type **litgitation** and press the Spacebar. You should see a wavy red line below the misspelled word.

If you don't see the red line, choose Options from the Tools menu, select the Spelling & Grammar tab, and check the option Check Spelling As You Type.

3. Alternate-click the misspelled word.
4. Choose AutoCorrect from the shortcut menu and select **litigation**.
5. Every time you misspell litigation in the same manner, Word will automatically correct it for you.
6. Create a new document. Type **litgitation** and press the Spacebar.

Word is particular in regard to case when adding words to AutoCorrect. If you add a word that contains an initial cap, Word will only correct it when it contains an initial cap. This applies to words typed in uppercase as well. But if you add the word all in lowercase, Word will correct all instances regardless of the case used.

EXCEPTIONS

The Exceptions button on the AutoCorrect tab allows you to create a list of exceptions for the options Correct TWo INitial CApitals and Capitalize First Letter Of Sentences. For example, suppose you use the word *IDs* regularly. If the option Correct TWo INitial CApitals is checked, Word will automatically change the word to *Ids*. To get around this you can create an exception. You can also add exceptions to the Other Corrections tab that do not fall under the other exception lists. The AutoCorrect Exceptions dialog box is shown in Figure 4.10.

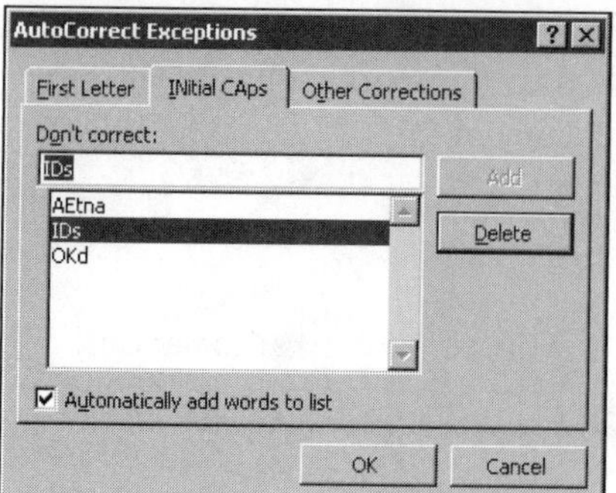

FIGURE 4.10

If AutoCorrect works most of the time the way you want it to, just create an exceptions list for things you don't want it to change instead of turning off the feature.

CREATE AN AUTOCORRECT EXCEPTION FOR TWO INITIAL CAPS

1. Create a new document.

NOTE

Make sure the option Correct TWo INitial CApitals is turned on for this exercise. From the Tools menu, choose AutoCorrect Options, select the AutoCorrect tab, and check the second option.

2. Type **IDs** and press the Spacebar. Notice that Word automatically changes the capitalization.
3. From the Tools menu, choose AutoCorrect Options, select the AutoCorrect tab, click Exceptions, and then INitial CAps.
4. Under Don't Correct, type **IDs** and click Add.
5. Click OK twice.
6. Type **IDs** and press the Spacebar. If the word has been successfully added to the Exceptions list, you will see the capitalization is unchanged.

AUTOFORMAT AS YOU TYPE

AutoFormat As You Type is a feature that automatically applies certain types of formatting to your documents based on the options you choose from the AutoFormat As You Type dialog box, as shown in Figure 4.11. Each of the three sections—Replace As You Type, Apply As You Type, and Automatically As You

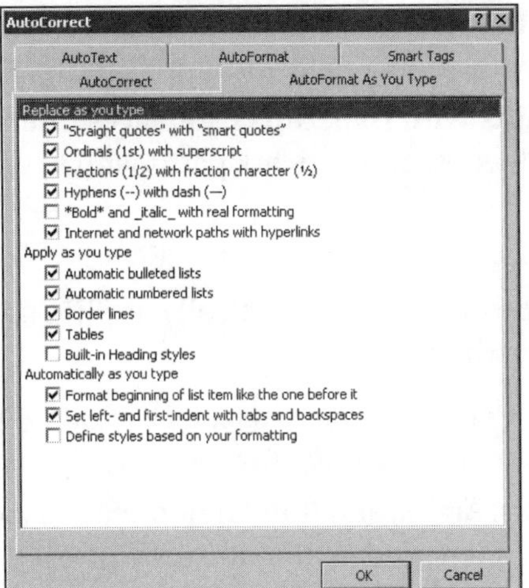

FIGURE 4.11

As you type text, AutoFormat As You Type watches for specific patterns of text and formatting and applies additional formatting automatically.

Type—contains a number of options that apply specific types of formatting to your documents. This can be very helpful or somewhat of a nuisance depending on your work style.

Many users new to Word often wonder why Word seems to take over when they least expect it or want it to. The options on the AutoFormat As You Type tab do a lot to determine how much control you have when working with Word—check there first if the program seems to be getting too helpful.

REPLACE AS YOU TYPE

When activated, each of the following options automatically replaces certain types of formatting.

- **Straight Quotes With Smart Quotes**. Automatically replaces straight quotes (" ") with the more fashionable curly or smart quotes (“ ”).
- **Ordinals (1st) With Superscript**. Replaces ordinals such as 1st, 2nd, and 3rd with 1st, 2nd, and 3rd.
- **Fractions (1/2) With Fraction Character** (_). Replaces the common fractions 1/2, 3/4, and 1/4 with the fraction characters ½, ¾, and ¼.
- **Hyphens** (--) **With Dash** (–). Replaces two hyphens with a single en dash. (Watch out for this one if you routinely use two hyphens for the longer em dash.)

- ***Bold* And _Italic_ With Real Formatting.** Replaces words enclosed with asterisks or underscores with bold or italic formatting.
- **Internet And Network Paths With Hyperlinks.** Replaces Internet and intranet URLs, e-mail addresses, and network paths with hyperlinks.

APPLY AS YOU TYPE

Each of the Apply As You Type options automatically applies specific types of formatting to your documents while you type.

- **Automatic Bulleted Lists.** Certain characters (such as * or =>) followed by a space or tab, text, and Enter are converted to bullets.
- **Automatic Numbered Lists.** Arabic and Roman numerals, as well as alphabetic characters followed by a period, automatically convert to numbered lists when followed by a space or tab, text, and Enter.
- **Border Lines.** Three dashes (---), equal signs (===), asterisk characters (***), underscores (___), pound signs (###), or tildes (~~~), followed by Enter, automatically create border lines.
- **Tables.** Type +-----+-----+ to automatically create a table. The plus (+) sign marks the column border. The number of dashes (-) determines the width of the column.
- **Built-In Heading Styles.** Automatically applies heading styles to specific types of formatting.

AUTOMATICALLY AS YOU TYPE

Each of the Automatically As You Type options adjusts the formatting of your documents when you do specific things to them.

- **Format Beginning Of List Item Like One Before It.** Automatically repeats character formatting that you apply to the beginning of a list item. For example, if the first word or phrase of a list item is bold, Word automatically applies bold formatting to the first word or phrase of the next list item.
- **Set Left And First Indent With Tabs And Backspaces.** Increases and decreases left indents when you press Tab or Backspace. You can also use the Tab and Backspace keys to move between levels in outline numbered lists.
- **Define Styles Based On Your Formatting.** Word automatically creates defined paragraph styles based on the formatting you choose.

Be careful about choosing the Define Styles Based On Your Formatting option! Word can take over and create styles you may not want in your documents. For example, if text at the top of a page is formatted as centered, bold, and a larger font size than other text, when you press Enter, a Title style is often applied automatically.

AUTOFORMAT

AutoFormat is a feature that closely resembles AutoFormat As You Type. The difference between the two is the way in which formatting is applied. Based on the options you select, AutoFormat As You Type automatically applies formatting as you enter text into the document. AutoFormat, on the other hand, applies selected options to your completed documents when you choose the AutoFormat command from the Format menu. Figure 4.12 illustrates the AutoFormat dialog box.

Be careful about using the AutoFormat feature with legal documents. AutoFormat can apply formatting that you may not expect or want, such as unneeded styles or lists. This can be in direct conflict with court-specified rules.

With AutoFormat, Word looks at each paragraph in your document and applies formatting to those parts of your document that match the options in the AutoFormat dialog box.

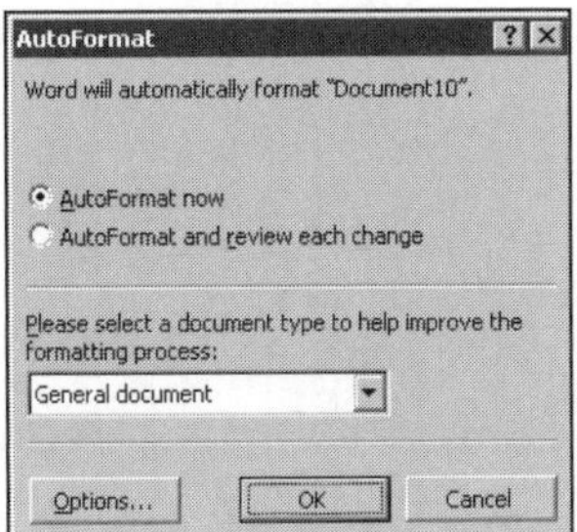

Figure 4.12

AutoFormat is useful for applying formatting rules to existing text.

AUTOTEXT

For legal users, AutoText can be one of Word's most powerful and useful features. AutoText lets you create entries for frequently used words, phrases, paragraphs, and even whole documents! You can insert captions, tables, signature blocks and letterhead, and automatically number interrogatories and answers with just a few keystrokes.

Word contains a built-in list of AutoText entries that include salutations, closings, reference lines, and mailing instructions. Figure 4.13 shows the AutoText tab. AutoText can be inserted into documents in a number of ways—via the AutoText dialog box and AutoText menu, with shortcut keys, or by accepting the AutoComplete ScreenTips.

NOTE

AutoComplete is a feature that launches a ScreenTip whenever you type the first four letters of a named AutoText entry. Once the ScreenTip appears you can press Enter or F3 to insert the AutoText entry or continue typing to bypass it.

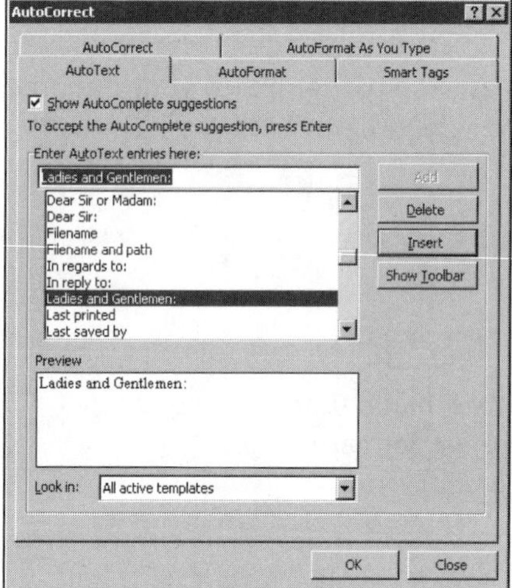

FIGURE 4.13

Imagine creating long legal phrases once, and being able to use AutoText to insert these same phrases without having to retype them.

INSERT A BUILT-IN AUTOTEXT ENTRY

1. Create a new document.
2. Type **ladi**. Notice the AutoComplete tip that appears above the text.

Make sure AutoComplete is enabled. Choose AutoText from the Insert menu, select AutoText, and check Show AutoComplete Suggestions.

3. Press Enter to insert the AutoText *Ladies and Gentlemen:*
4. Practice inserting AutoText with days of the week and months of the year.

CREATE A CUSTOM AUTOTEXT ENTRY

One of the primary benefits of using AutoText is the time it saves you in entering frequently used phrases, addresses, and large blocks of text. Each of these items can be created as an AutoText entry and quickly inserted into your documents. You can create as many AutoText entries as you need. AutoText entries are stored in document templates. If you create a large number of AutoText entries, it might be useful (and safe) to save them to a custom template so they don't get lost if Normal.dot (Word's global template) becomes corrupted. As with other template features, you can use the Organizer to copy AutoText entries between templates.

Read Chapter 10, "Templates," to learn more about how Word handles templates, and how to use the Organizer to copy styles, toolbars, macros, and AutoText entries between documents and templates.

CREATE AN AUTOTEXT ENTRY

1. Create a new document.
2. Type **Mr. James R. Doe** and press Enter. Type **Levit, Young, Howard & Phillips LLP** and press Enter. Type **1515 Madison Avenue** and press Enter. Type **New York, NY 10005** and press Enter.
3. Select the entire block of text.
4. From the Insert menu, choose AutoText and select New.

5. Create a name for your entry. Make it something short and easy to remember. In this example, choose the default, **Mr. James R**.

NOTE

Make sure the name you choose for the AutoText entry is at least four characters. Otherwise Word will not provide an AutoComplete tip and you'll have to press F3 to insert the AutoText entry.

6. Create a new document.
7. Type **Mr. Ja**—you should see an AutoComplete tip referencing your AutoText entry. Press Enter to insert the address block.

REMOVING AUTOTEXT ENTRIES

You may find that at some point in the future you no longer need one or more of the AutoText entries you've used in the past. To delete an entry, do the following: From the Insert menu, choose AutoText, and select AutoText again from the expanded submenu. Scroll through the list of AutoText entries. Select the entry you wish to remove and click Delete.

REDEFINING AN AUTOTEXT ENTRY

You can add or remove information from an existing AutoText entry without having to create a new entry. Word allows you to redefine an AutoText entry by renaming the modified entry with the same name as the original.

REDEFINE AN AUTOTEXT ENTRY

1. Create a new document.
2. Insert the AutoText entry from the preceding exercise.
3. Change **LLP** to **LLC**.
4. Select the entire block of text.
5. From the Insert menu choose AutoText and select New.
6. Use the same name for the redefined entry. Type **Mr. James R.**

TIP

In order to redefine an AutoText entry, you must enter the exact name of the original entry. If you are not sure what you named your original entry, select AutoText instead of New from the AutoText menu. The AutoText dialog box will open and you can scroll through the list of AutoText entries. Select the correct entry and click Add.

7. Word will ask whether or not you wish to redefine the AutoText entry, as shown in Figure 4.14.
8. Click Yes.
9. Create a new document.
10. Type **Mr. Ja** and press F3 to insert the redefined AutoText entry.

SMART TAGS

If asked to list the best new features in Word 2002, smart tags would be at the top of the list. Smart tags are built into Word and Excel, and make using the software easier. Imagine typing a name and letting Word pull address information from Outlook Contacts automatically. Smart tags offer this functionality and more. Without going into too much technical detail, here's an overview of the smart tag process.

When smart tags are installed and enabled (Tools, AutoCorrect, Smart Tags) Word scans the document paragraph by paragraph looking for text strings that it recognizes as a smart tag type. Once a type is identified, a smart tag indicator appears along with a button that displays a shortcut menu listing all actions available for the type of smart tag. Smart tag indicators display as thin purple lines underneath specific text in your documents. When you place your mouse pointer over a smart tag indicator, a Smart Tag Actions button appears. Click the Action button and choose an option from the menu shown in Figure 4.15.

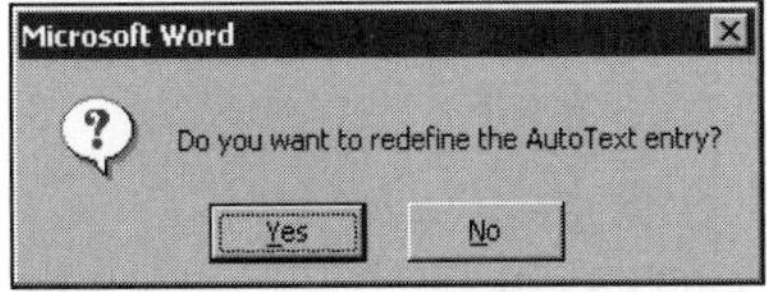

FIGURE 4.14

Name an AutoText with the same name as an existing entry and you will replace the original.

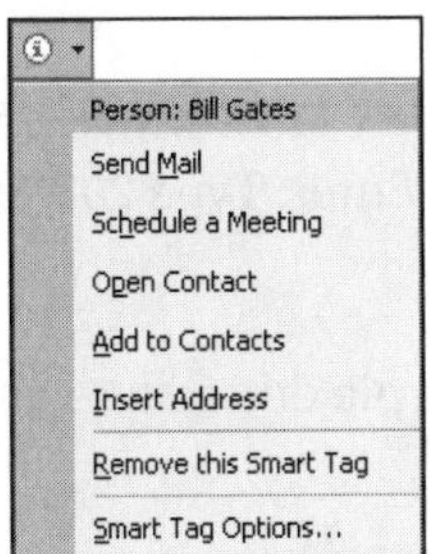

FIGURE 4.15

An action associated with the type of smart tag entered becomes available in the Smart Tag Actions menu. Send an e-mail, schedule an appointment, insert an address, and more.

RECOGNIZED SMART TAG TYPES

Smart tag types that are recognized by Word depend on the options you have selected on the Smart Tags tab of the AutoCorrect dialog box, and the add-ins (also called plug-ins in Installation Wizard) installed on your computer. The following are default types recognized by Word:

- Person names
- Dates
- Times
- Addresses
- Places
- Telephone numbers
- Recent Outlook e-mail recipients
- Smart Tag lists (MSN MoneyCentral Financial Symbols)—an add-in recognizer for stock symbols listed on the United States Stock Exchanges.

NAME TYPE SMART TAG The Name type smart tag will be useful to law firms that use both Word and Outlook 2002. You can automatically create a contact in Outlook from a person's name and address information found in a Word document, or insert the person's address that is stored in Contacts. Place your mouse pointer over the smart tag indicator, click the Smart Tag Actions button, and select the action to be performed from the smart tag menu—no more copying and pasting between Word and Outlook!

NOTE

The Insert Address action inserts the person's address if found in Outlook Contacts but not the company name.

USE A SMART TAG TO ADD A CONTACT TO AN OUTLOOK CONTACTS FOLDER

1. Create a new document.
2. Type **Mr. John P. Doe** and press Enter. Type **1313 Smith St.** and press Enter. Type **Hoboken, NJ 10023** and press Enter. Type **201-555-1212**.
3. Press Enter twice.
4. Place your mouse pointer over the thin purple dotted line under Mr. John P. Doe.

If you don't see Smart Tag indicators, from the Tools menu, choose Options, select the View tab, and check Smart Tags in the Show section of the dialog box. Also, from the Tools menu, choose AutoCorrect Options and select the Smart Tags tab to make sure smart tags are enabled.

5. Click the Smart Tag Action button.
6. Choose Add To Contacts from the list of actions.
7. Fill in any additional information in the Outlook New Contact dialog box.
8. Click Save and Close.

Name smart tag actions include

- Send Mail opens an Outlook e-mail message and inserts the person's e-mail address as the Recipient.
- Schedule A Meeting creates a Meeting Request e-mail message.
- Open Contact opens the associated Outlook Contact record if one exists.
- Add To Contacts creates a new Outlook Contact record for the name. If you attempt to add a contact that already exists, the Duplicate Contact Detected dialog box will open.
- Insert Address extracts the address matching the recognized name and places it into the document. If a duplicate entry is found for this action, the Insert Address dialog box displays, prompting you to choose the correct entry to insert into the document.

ADDRESS TYPE SMART TAG When an Address type smart tag is recognized, the actions available are Add to Contacts, Display Map, Display Driving Directions, Remove This Smart Tag, and Smart Tag Options. The Display Map and Display Driving Directions actions require connection to the Internet.

Display Map starts Internet Explorer and goes to Find A Map on www.expedia.com.

USE A SMART TAG TO MAP AN ADDRESS OR DISPLAY DRIVING DIRECTIONS

1. Type **1601 5th Avenue, Seattle, WA 98101** and press Enter.
2. Place your mouse pointer over the thin purple dotted line for the address.

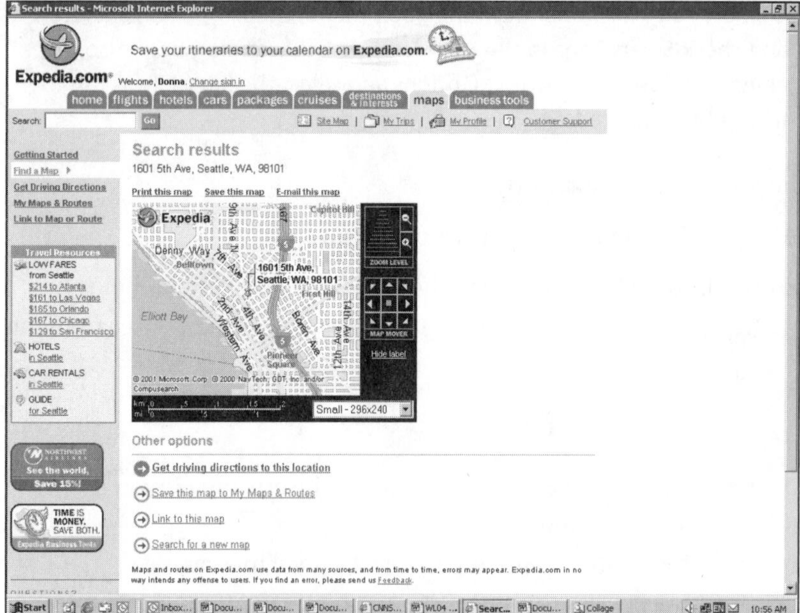

FIGURE 4.16

You may need to add additional information for locating an exact location on Expedia maps.

3. If you have Internet connectivity and use Internet Explorer, click the Smart Tag Action button and choose Display Map. The result is shown in Figure 4.16.
4. Close Internet Explorer.

MSN MONEYCENTRAL FINANCIAL SYMBOLS SMART TAG If the MSN MoneyCentral Financial Symbols smart tag is installed and enabled, you can type a stock symbol in your Word document and it will be recognized as a smart tag.

USE A SMART TAG TO GET STOCK QUOTES

1. From the Tools menu, choose AutoCorrect Options and select the Smart Tags tab.
2. Make sure MSN MoneyCentral Financial Symbols is enabled. If it does not appear in the list of available smart tags, the feature may not have been installed. Click OK to close the AutoCorrect dialog box.

3. Type **MSFT** and press the Spacebar. A smart tag should appear under the stock symbol for Microsoft.
4. Place your mouse pointer over the thin purple dotted line for the address and choose Stock Quote On MSN MoneyCentral from the Smart Tag Action menu. A Web browser window opens and navigates to the MSN Web site, which displays the stock price.

LEGAL SPECIFIC SMART TAGS Smart tags can be developed to meet specific business needs. West Group has developed a great set of smart tag add-ins that include actions to find a referenced citation in Westlaw's database, view Keycites and citation references, insert a hyperlink to Westlaw, or mark the citation for a table of authorities. This Smart Tag component is available in West Group's CiteLink software, which will identify and mark for table of authorities all cites and references in a document. Figure 4.17 shows the Smart Tag Action menu that West Group built. For more information on this smart tag add-in visit the company Web site at www.westgroup.com.

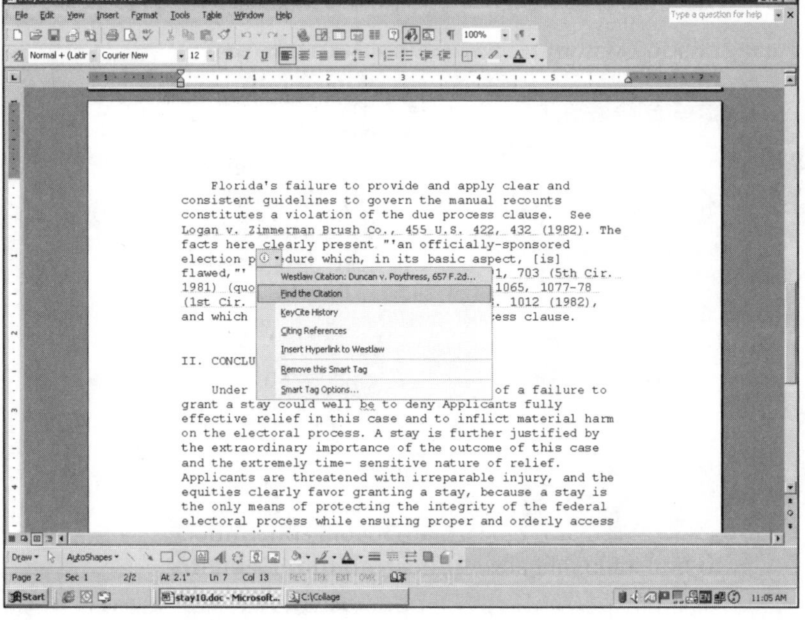

FIGURE 4.17

West Group's smart tags use Blue Book format as a text string recognizer. When the citation is detected, a smart tag indicator is added to the citation.

NOTE

If you would like to learn how to create smart tags of your own, go to **www.microsoft.com**, type the keyword Smart Tag, and click Search. The Microsoft Office XP Smart Tag SDK (Software Development Kit) is particularly useful.

CONTROLLING SMART TAGS

You can turn the smart tag feature on or off. All settings for smart tags are displayed in the AutoCorrect and Options dialog boxes. The Smart Tags tab in the AutoCorrect dialog box is shown in Figure 4.18.

In addition to the recognizers for Smart Tags, there are a few more options to be aware of:

- **Label Text With Smart Tags**—Turns off recognition of new smart tags. If smart tags already exist in a document they are not affected.
- **Recheck Document**—Rechecks the current document for smart tags.
- **Remove Smart Tags**—Clears all smart tags from the document.
- **More Smart Tags**—Opens a Web browser and looks for new smart tags that have been developed and made available.
- **Save Options**—Opens the Save tab on the Options dialog box (Tools, Options) that includes the settings Embed Smart Tags, and Save Smart Tags as XML Properties In Web Pages.

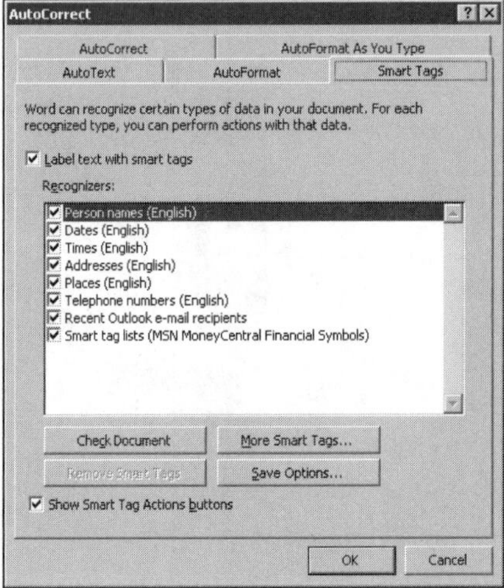

FIGURE 4.18

If Smart Tags are not being recognized by Word, the option to recognize the type may have been deselected.

- **Show Smart Tag Action Buttons**—Controls whether or not Smart Tag Action buttons are displayed with smart tags. This disables the feature for all Word documents.

NOTE

Embedded smart tags increase the file size slightly but not enough to cause the file to become much larger than the original.

SUMMARY

This chapter opened with a discussion of the various ways to navigate and select text in Word documents using either the mouse or keyboard. That was followed by a detailed look at each of the components found in the AutoCorrect Options dialog box. Chapter 4 concluded with an examination of a new Word feature, Smart Tags.

TROUBLESHOOTING BUILDING A LEGAL DOCUMENT

I just created an AutoText entry for the paragraph symbol (¶) with the letter p and named it P. Why doesn't the ScreenTip (yellow box) appear with the AutoText entry when I type P?

For the ScreenTip associated with an AutoText entry to appear, the name of the AutoText entry must be at least four characters long. Since you named your AutoText entry P (one character), you'll have to type **P** and press F3 to insert the paragraph symbol into your document.

Each time I click in my document, text is selected. What's going on?

You may have pressed the F8 key, which activates extended selection mode. Double-click EXT on the status bar or press Esc to turn off extended selection.

Every time I type a Web or e-mail address in a document, it turns into a colored, underlined hyperlink. I don't want the printed copy of my documents to contain these hyperlinks. What can I do?

From the AutoCorrect tab of the AutoCorrect Options dialog box (Tools, AutoCorrect Options, AutoCorrect), uncheck the option Internet And Network Paths With Hyperlinks under Replace As You Type. To remove an existing hyperlink from a document, alternate-click on the hyperlinked text and then choose Remove Hyperlink from the shortcut menu.

I notice that Word automatically turns the fractions ½, ¼, and ¾ into appropriate fraction characters. Are there any other fraction characters available, and if so, how can I create them?

Open the Symbol dialog box (Insert, Symbol) and select the Symbols tab. Click the drop-down arrow next to Font and choose Normal Text or a standard font such as Times New Roman. Next, click the drop-down arrow next to Subset and choose Mathematical Operators from the list. You should see the fraction characters ⅓, ⅔, ⅛, ⅜, ⅝, and ⅞. Select the appropriate fraction and click AutoCorrect to create an AutoCorrect entry. If you need more fraction characters you can purchase a mathematical font set separately.

I've turned off the Define Styles Based On Your Formatting option (Tools, AutoCorrect Options, AutoFormat As You Type, Automatically As You Type); however, whenever I apply certain formats to the text in my documents, Word applies the style Heading 1. Why is this happening?

Word is automatically applying Heading styles to your text because there's another option you need to turn off as well. Go back to the same dialog box (Tools, AutoCorrect Options, AutoFormat As You Type) and, under Apply As You Type, uncheck the option Built-In Heading Styles.

CHAPTER 5

FORMATTING TEXT

IN THIS CHAPTER

- Using the Formatting toolbar to format text
- Fonts: True Type vs. Printer
- Using the Font dialog box to format text
- Inserting legal symbols
- Copying formatting with the Format Painter
- Reveal Formatting feature
- Styles And Formatting feature

Whether it's a 1-page memo, a 90-page brief, or the daily bulletin posted to your firm's intranet, the documents you create rely on formatting to emphasize key points, ideas, and arguments. Character formatting includes everything from making sure that font size and style meet court requirements to inserting legal symbols into a complex patent application. In addition to all the formatting options found in past versions of Word, Microsoft introduces some great new features that are specifically designed to address the needs of the legal community. Reveal Formatting and Styles And Formatting, two features that open the lid on character, paragraph, and document formatting, will impress even the most diehard WordPerfect users who have been grieving over the loss of Reveal Codes.

FORMATTING TOOLBAR

The Formatting toolbar contains the set of buttons used most frequently when adjusting the look of the text in your legal documents. The commands on the Formatting toolbar can be used to modify font style and size as well as apply bold, italic, underline, highlight, and color to selected text. Figure 5.1 shows the Formatting toolbar.

The rule to remember with Word is "select to affect." Before applying any of the formatting commands, first select the text you wish to change.

The following formatting commands are available on the Formatting toolbar:

- **Font List**. This drop-down contains a list of available fonts. Select a font from the list or type the name of a specific font directly into the Font box and press Enter. The keyboard shortcut for this button is Ctrl+Shift+F.

If you are starting a document, or just inserting a new paragraph, you can choose formatting options before you start typing the text.

A *font* is a set of characters of a particular typeface. Times New Roman, Courier New, and Bookman Old Style are just a few examples of the many different fonts that exist. Fonts are generally separated into two categories—True Type and Printer. Each one will be discussed later in the chapter.

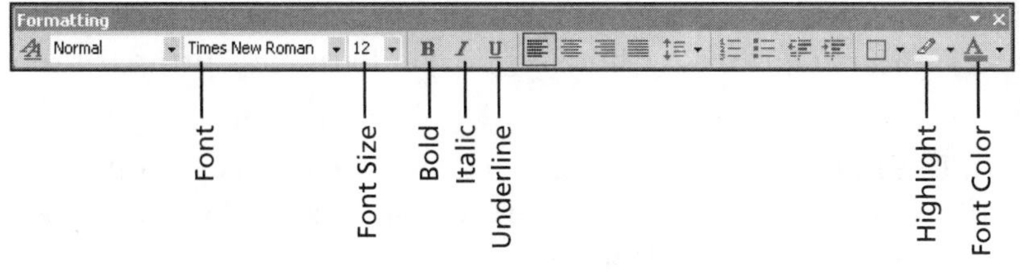

FIGURE 5.1

Buttons on the Formatting toolbar make applying formatting to text easy. Select text to be affected and click Bold, Italic, Underline, or any other Formatting toolbar button.

- **Font Size**. You can choose from a list of fixed font sizes or type a number directly into the Font Size box. Fonts are measured in point size, with 72 points equal to one inch. Font size for most legal documents is 12 points, or one-sixth of an inch. The keyboard shortcut for this button is Ctrl+Shift+P.

Note that point size measures the height of the font, from the top of the tallest ascending stroke to the bottom of the lowest descender, rather than the width of the letters. As a result, two fonts of the same point size can take up very different amounts of space for a given passage of text.

- **Bold**. This button applies bold formatting to selected text. The keyboard shortcut is Ctrl+B.
- **Italic**. This button applies italic formatting to selected text. The keyboard shortcut is Ctrl+I.
- **Underline**. This button applies single underline formatting to selected text. The keyboard shortcut is Ctrl+U.
- **Highlight**. You can select from a number of different colors to highlight text onscreen. This feature is great for marking text as you review a document. Highlighted color prints as a light shade of gray on most black-and-white printers.
- **Font Color**. You can emphasize key parts of a document by changing the color of the letters themselves (as opposed to changing the background color with highlighting). This works best for online collaboration. To print with color, you must have access to a color printer.

Not all available buttons appear on the toolbar by default. If they did, there would be little room for the document on the screen. To add additional buttons to the Formatting toolbar, click the drop-down arrow at the end of the Formatting toolbar (Toolbar Options). Choose Add Or Remove Buttons, then Formatting.

- **Grow Font.** This button increases the selected font size. The keyboard shortcut to grow the font by one point size is Ctrl+]. To grow the font to the next available point size, use Ctrl+Shift+>.
- **Shrink Font.** This button decreases font size. The keyboard shortcut to shrink the font by one point size is Ctrl+[. To shrink the font by previous two-point size, use Ctrl+Shift+<.
- **Superscript.** This button shrinks the text and raises the text to a position above the text. This formatting is common for footnotes and endnotes references. The keyboard shortcut for superscript formatting is Ctrl+Shift+= (that is, Ctrl and the plus sign on the regular keyboard, which is at Shift+=).
- **Subscript.** This button shrinks the text and lowers the formatting to a position below normal text. Subscript formatting is used in scientific formulas. The keyboard shortcut for subscript is Ctrl+=.
- **Language.** If you are working with a document in another language, Word can detect this automatically once you specify what language you are using. For example, if you are typing a Spanish word such as *Hola*, you will likely not want this flagged as a spelling error. By selecting the word *Hola* and applying a different language, you instruct Word to use Spanish language rules for spelling and grammar.

NOTE

Word allows you to apply any of the formats available on the Formatting toolbar to new or existing text. To affect existing text, select the text prior to applying formatting. To affect new text, select the appropriate formatting commands first and then begin typing.

FORMAT TEXT USING THE FORMATTING TOOLBAR

1. Create a new document.
2. Type **APPEAL FROM THE UNITED STATES COURT OF APPEALS FOR THE DISTRICT OF COLUMBIA CIRCUIT**.
3. Select the text.
4. From the Formatting toolbar, click the drop-down arrow to the right of the Font button and select Arial.

5. Click the drop-down arrow next to Font Size and change the font size to 16.
6. Click the Bold button or press Ctrl+B.
7. Click outside the paragraph to deselect the text.
8. Select UNITED STATES and click the Italic button or press Ctrl+I.

The shortcut keys for **Bold**, *Italic*, and Underline are Ctrl+B, Ctrl+I, and Ctrl+U, respectively.

The Highlight and Color buttons can be useful for emphasizing key sections of a document. For example, an agreement under review might contain important information relevant to both parties. That information could be highlighted to attract the attention of all interested reviewers.

Emphasize Text Using the Highlight and Color Buttons

1. Create a new document.
2. Type **All legislative powers herein granted shall be vested in a Congress of the United States, which shall consist of a Senate and House of Representatives.**
3. Select all of the text. The keyboard shortcut to do this is Ctrl+A.
4. Click the drop-down arrow next to the Highlight button and select Yellow from the list of available highlight colors, as shown in Figure 5.2.
5. Select the text again, click the drop-down arrow next to the Highlight button, and select None.
6. Click once to deselect the text.

FIGURE 5.2

Don't forget to remove document highlighting from the document when it is ready to go final.

7. Select **Congress of the United States.**
8. Click the drop-down arrow next to Font Color and choose Red.

To remove manually applied character formatting (also known as direct formatting), select the appropriate words, phrases, or paragraphs and press Ctrl+Spacebar.

Any formatting that you manually apply to the text in the document, such as font style, size, bold, underline, or other formatting, is referred to as *direct formatting.*

FONTS: TRUE TYPE VS. PRINTER

Fonts are divided into two main categories—True Type and Printer. True Type fonts are installed directly into the software of the computer, are scalable (sizeable), and look the same in the printed document as they do onscreen. True Type technology was originally developed by Apple and later incorporated into Microsoft's Windows operating system. As a result, True Type fonts are device, or hardware, independent. A document constructed using True Type fonts can be sent to any printer as long as the fonts themselves are installed on the computer sending the document to print. Most of the fonts used in the legal environment are True Type.

The Font list contains a combination of True Type and Printer fonts. True Type fonts are identified by a bolded and offset T, while Printer fonts are represented by a small printer icon appearing next to the font name in the list.

Printer fonts, sometimes referred to as *Resident* or *Internal* fonts, are installed directly on the printer. Printer fonts are generally designed with a specific size and resolution for a specific model of printer. Some printer fonts are scalable while others are not. As a result, there are often discrepancies between what you see onscreen and what you get on the printed page.

To install a new font, go to the Windows Control Panel (Start, Settings, Control Panel) and double-click the Fonts folder. From the File menu, choose Install New Font; From Folders, navigate to the drive and folder containing the font you wish to install. Open the folder, select the font, and click OK. The font will be installed to C:\Windows\Fonts and will be available for use. (You can do this for several fonts at the same time.)

NOTE

True Type fonts are identified by the file extension .ttf.

FONT DIALOG BOX

Although the Formatting toolbar is convenient for quickly applying formatting to the text in your documents, the Font dialog box contains an even greater number of formatting features and options. You can apply the options contained in the Font dialog box to selected text or choose the formatting options first and then begin typing. From the Format menu, choose Font to open the Font dialog box, which is shown in Figure 5.3.

TIP

The shortcut key to display the Font dialog box is Ctrl+D.

The Font dialog box includes three tabs: Font, Character Spacing, and Text Effects. Each tab contains specific commands that allow you to change the appearance of the text in the document. The Font tab is visible in Figure 5.3.

FONT TAB

The Font tab is the most commonly accessed tab in this dialog box. It offers additional commands to those offered on the Formatting toolbar. The Font tab includes options and settings that change how the font is formatted. For

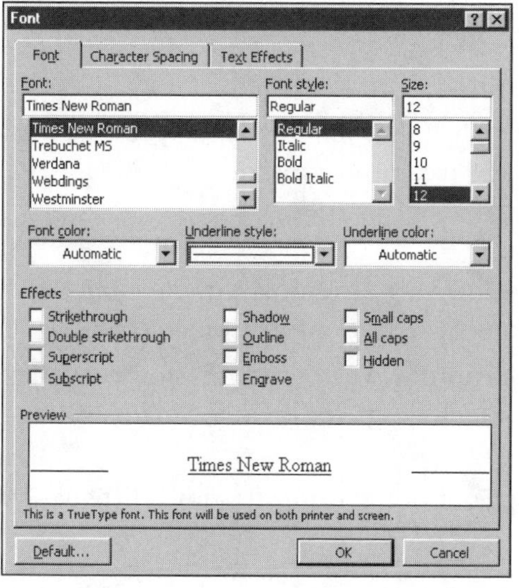

FIGURE 5.3

As you select options in the Font dialog box, a preview is displayed to show what effect the option will have on the text.

The Font, Font Style, and Size boxes are referred to as a *combo box* because there is a combination of text box and list boxes used for the control. To take this one step farther, if you are permitted to select an option from a list or type into the box, this is referred to as an *unrestricted combo box*.

example, you can apply a single underline from the Formatting toolbar, but the Font tab offers a variety of underline styles and colors.

- **Font.** This drop-down combo box features the same list of fonts as the Formatting toolbar. Click the drop-down arrow and select an appropriate font.

To change the default font, font size, or any other options from the Font dialog box, select the appropriate feature and click Default. Click Yes to make the changes applicable to the current document and all future documents.

- **Font Style**. This drop-down combo box includes four options for applying emphasis to the text in a document: Regular, Italic, Bold, and Bold Italic. Select words, sentences, or paragraphs and apply one of the formatting commands.
- **Size**. This drop-down combo box provides a list of fixed font sizes. Select a size from the list or type a different number, such as 44 or 44.5, directly into the box—True Type fonts are fully scalable, so you can have almost anything you want.

Word only recognizes full and half sizes for Font Size. If you type a value other than a full or half size, you will receive an error that the entry is not a valid number.

- **Font Color**. The drop-down arrow reveals a menu choice of 40 different colors, as shown in Figure 5.4. Click More Colors to see even more!
- **Underline Style**. The drop-down arrow on this box lets you choose from a list of underline styles, including Words Only, Single, Double, or Dotted Underline.
- **Underline Color**. Like Font Color, this drop-down list gives you a choice of underline colors.

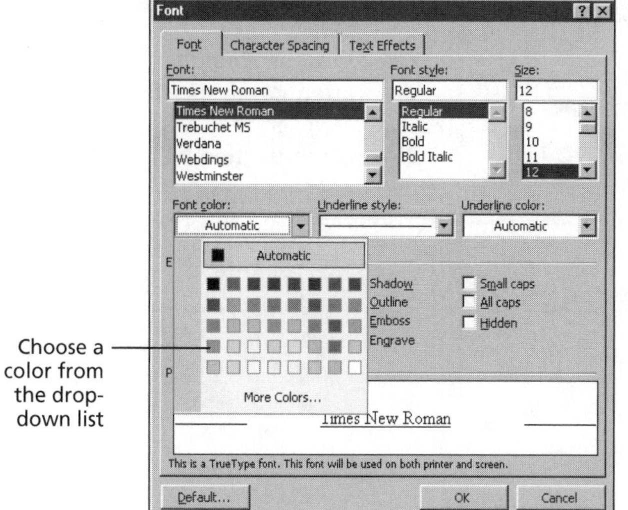

FIGURE 5.4

Select a font color from Word's palette of colors.

USE OPTIONS IN THE FONT DIALOG BOX TO APPLY CHARACTER FORMATTING

1. Create a new document.
2. Type **The Act does not violate separation of powers principles by impermissibly interfering with the functions of the Executive Branch. pp. 685-696.**
3. Select Executive Branch.
4. From the Format menu, choose Font to open the Font dialog box. Select Bold from the Font Style list.
5. Click the drop-down arrow beneath Underline Style and choose Words Only from the list. Look in the Preview Pane at the bottom of the dialog box to see how the selected text will appear in the document.
6. Click OK.

From All Caps to Emboss, the Effects section of the Font tab, as shown in Figure 5.5, contains a series of formatting check boxes that can be used to apply emphasis or add creativity to the text in your documents.

- **Strikethrough**. Checking this box makes selected text appear with a line drawn across it.

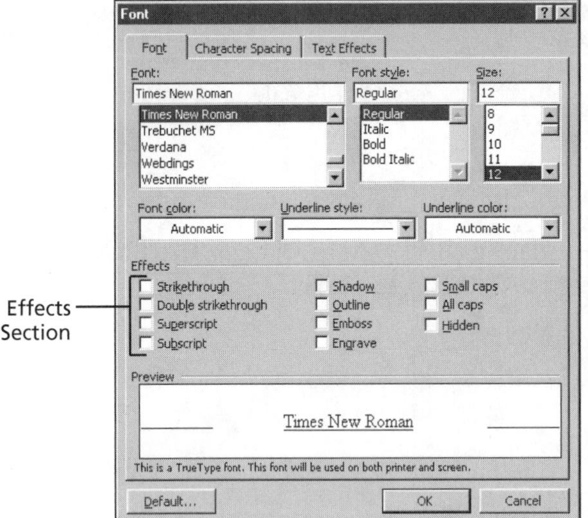

FIGURE 5.5

Effects can be added to draw attention to specific text; however, they can also be a distraction if overused.

- **Double Strikethrough**. Checking this box makes selected text appear with two lines drawn across it.
- **Superscript**. Checking this box pushes selected text higher and smaller than other text on the line. In the example 10^2, the 2 appears as a superscript.
- **Subscript**. Checking this box pushes selected text lower and smaller than other text on the line. In the example H_20, the 2 appears as a subscript.
- **Shadow**. Checking this box applies a shadow to selected text.
- **Outline**. Checking this box makes selected text appear as a hollow outline.
- **Emboss**. Checking this box applies an embossed or raised effect to selected text.
- **Engrave**. Checking this box makes selected text appear to be etched into the document.
- **Small Caps**. Checking this box makes selected lowercase text appear as small capital letters. It has no effect on uppercase text.
- **All Caps**. Checking this box makes selected text appear as normal size capital letters. It does not actually change the case of the letters, just the way they look on the screen.
- **Hidden**. Checking this box assigns the hidden attribute and makes selected text disappear unless Show/Hide is turned on. Hidden text does not print with the document by default but can be printed if the option to include hidden text is checked in the Print Options dialog box.

APPLY VARIOUS EFFECTS TO SELECTED TEXT

1. Create a new document.
2. Type **U.S. Supreme Court** and select the text.
3. From the Format menu, choose Font and select the Font tab.
4. In the Effects section, place a check next to All Caps. Use the Preview pane to see how the selected text will appear in the document.
5. Check Emboss, then check Engrave.
6. Uncheck Engrave and check Strikethrough.
7. Click OK.

CHARACTER SPACING

There may be times when specific words or phrases within legal documents require spacing or positioning that falls outside the realm of Word's default settings. The Character Spacing tab, shown in Figure 5.6, contains all the options you will need to make any spacing, scaling, or positioning changes.

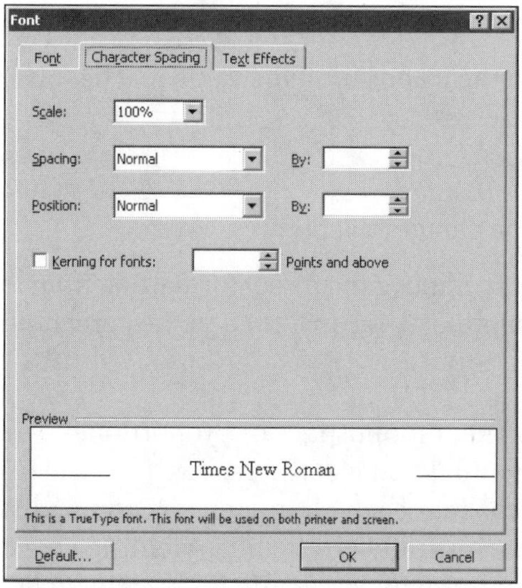

FIGURE 5.6

Control the spacing of text and characters on the Character Spacing tab.

Each Character Spacing option is described in the following list:

- **Scale**. Increases or decreases the proportion of selected text. Click the drop-down arrow and choose a fixed percentage or type a number directly into the list box, say, **125%**.
- **Spacing**. Expands or condenses the space between characters of selected text. Click the drop-down arrow and choose the appropriate option. Set the amount in the By scroll box using the spinners or type a number. The default is 1 point.
- **Position**. Raises or lowers selected text relative to the position of the current line. Click the drop-down arrow and choose the appropriate option and then set an amount in the By scroll box. The default is 3 points.
- **Kerning For Fonts**. Provides further control of the spacing of specified font sizes. See the discussion following the next exercise.

INCREASE THE SPACE BETWEEN CHARACTERS TO CREATE A LEGAL MEMORANDUM

1. Create a new document.
2. Press Ctrl+E to center the first paragraph.
3. Type **Memorandum**. Double-click the word to select it.
4. From the Format menu, choose Font and select the Font tab.
5. Place a check next to All Caps. Select the Character Spacing tab.
6. Click the drop-down arrow next to Spacing and choose Expanded.
7. Click the spinners in the By box until the value reaches 10 or type **10** directly into the box.
8. Click OK.
9. Click at the end of the paragraph and press Enter.
10. Press Ctrl+Spacebar to remove the direct formatting from the current paragraph, and then press Ctrl+L to left-align the paragraph.

Fonts can be classified as either monospace or proportional. Monospace fonts, such as those found on manual and electric typewriters, use fixed spacing for each character. This means that each character, say an I or a W, takes up the same amount of space horizontally on the line, yielding an exact number of characters per inch no matter which specific letters are typed. Proportional fonts, found on most word processors and PCs, use variable spacing. This means that the amount of space a character takes on the horizontal line is based on the width of that character. In the same example, an I takes up less space than a W, so the number of characters per inch will vary depending on which letters are typed.

Kerning tightens the space between proportional font characters to achieve a more visually appealing look for the document text. When the size of the font is relatively small, up to about 12 points, it's difficult to spot the variable space between characters of a proportional font. However, when the font size is larger, say 36 points, the difference is more obvious. The Kerning For Fonts option automatically applies kerning to text above a specified point size.

To apply kerning, check the box and then select a minimum point size. For example, if you choose 16 Points And Above, Word will automatically apply kerning to any text in your document that is at least 16 points.

TEXT EFFECTS: ANIMATION

Although the options contained in the Animations section of the Font dialog box may not be particularly useful for legal documents (see Figure 5.7), they can spice up documents submitted to the firm intranet or add life to an online bulletin. But beware—a little animation can go a long way!

Las Vegas Lights, Marching Red Ants, and Sparkle Text are just a few of the available animations.

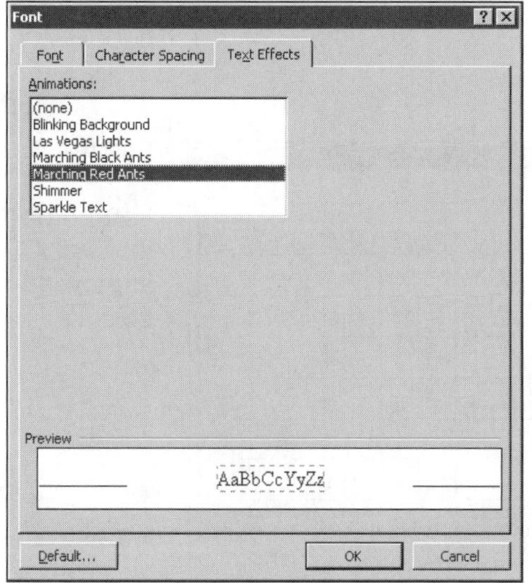

FIGURE 5.7

Add Las Vegas Lights or Marching Ants to your text in the Text Effects tab.

NOTE

Animations do not print—they are only viewable online.

ADD ZIP TO THOSE NON-LEGAL DOCUMENTS

1. Create a new document.
2. Type **Firm Picnic**. Select the text.
3. From the Format menu, choose Font and select the Font tab. Change the font size to 36 points.
4. Select the Text Effects tab.
5. Select Marching Ants.
6. Click OK.

LEGAL SYMBOLS

Agreements, patent applications, and contracts often require the use of specific legal symbols. Word provides several different methods for applying the appropriate symbols to your legal documents: the Symbol dialog box, keyboard shortcuts, and AutoCorrect. You can open the Symbol dialog box, shown in Figure 5.8, by choosing Symbol from the Insert menu.

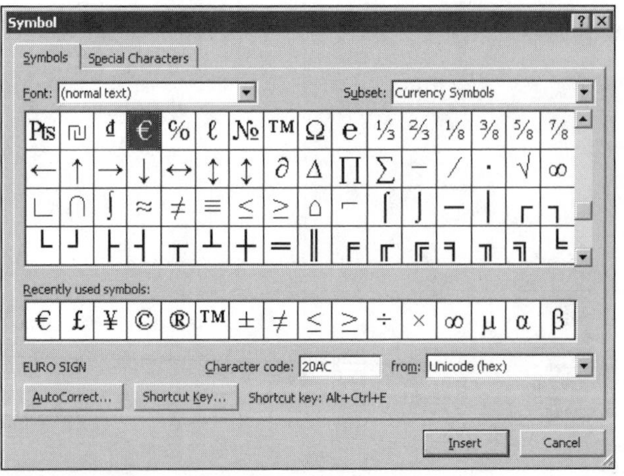

FIGURE 5.8

Inserting symbols is easy in Word 2002's new and improved Symbol dialog box.

USING THE SYMBOL DIALOG BOX TO INSERT SYMBOLS

Separated into two tabbed sections, the Symbol dialog box contains an enormous collection of symbols ranging from the obvious to obscure. From here you can insert the commonly used Register, Trademark, and Copyright symbols as well as European and Asian currency symbols. The dialog box even maintains a list of the 16 most recently used symbols.

INSERT LEGAL SYMBOLS INTO YOUR DOCUMENTS

1. Create a new document.
2. Type **Section 13.25**.
3. Select the word *Section*.
4. From the Insert menu, choose Symbol, then select the Special Characters tab.
5. Select the Section symbol (§) from the list of special characters. Click Insert and then click Close.

USING KEYBOARD SHORTCUTS TO INSERT LEGAL SYMBOLS

If you prefer, you can also use keyboard shortcuts to insert symbols. For example, the Copyright symbol (©) can be applied by typing Alt+Ctrl+C. The Special Characters section on the Symbol dialog box provides a list of the most commonly used legal symbols along with their corresponding keyboard shortcuts. Notice that the Section and Paragraph symbols do not have shortcuts assigned to them by default. You can assign your own shortcut key to these symbols—and to any others you use frequently.

NOTE

Follow these steps to assign keyboard shortcuts to the Section and Paragraph symbols: Select either symbol from the Special Characters list and click Shortcut Key. This takes you to the Customize Keyboard dialog box shown in Figure 5.9. Enter an appropriate keystroke combination in the Press New Shortcut Key box. If the keystroke combination that you've chosen is currently unassigned, click Assign; otherwise, try another combination. For example, try Ctrl+Shift+Alt+P for the Paragraph symbol and Ctrl+Shift+Alt+S for the Section symbol.

CAUTION

Before assigning keyboard shortcuts, take a look at the menu bar to see if any that you wish to create are being used to expand the menus. For example, Alt+F displays the File menu, Alt+E the Edit menu, and so forth.

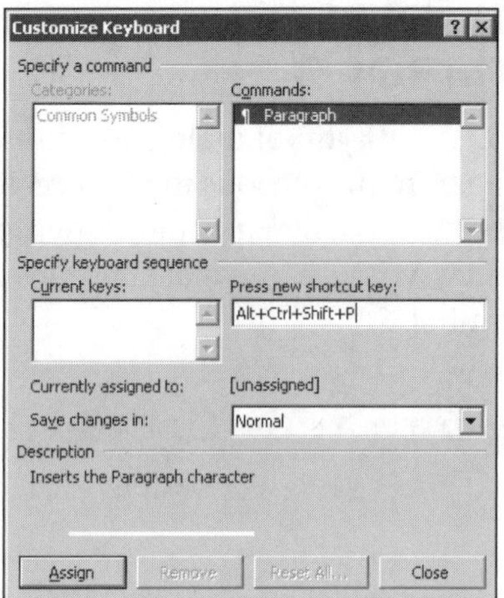

FIGURE 5.9

Most symbols have shortcut keys assigned by default, but for those that do not, use the Customize Keyboard dialog box to assign them.

Avoid overriding Word's built-in list of assigned keyboard shortcuts. Other users sharing your computer may end up frustrated when the assigned shortcut no longer applies the default command.

USING AUTOCORRECT TO INSERT LEGAL SYMBOLS

Use Word's AutoCorrect feature to quickly insert symbols into your documents. The Copyright, Registered Trademark, and Trademark Pending symbols exist as AutoCorrect entries. Type **(c)**, **(r)**, and **(tm)**, respectively, and Word will automatically convert the text to the corresponding symbol. You can even create new AutoCorrect entries for symbols you frequently use.

If these entries do not work for you, check with your system administrator, as many firms choose to disable the (c), (r), and (tm) AutoCorrect entries when installing Word.

CREATE AN AUTOCORRECT ENTRY FOR A FREQUENTLY USED SYMBOL

1. Create a new document.
2. From the Insert menu, choose Symbol, and then select the Symbols tab.

3. Click the drop-down arrow next to Font and select Times New Roman. Click the drop-down arrow next to Subset and select Currency Symbols from the list.
4. Select the Euro symbol and click AutoCorrect. The AutoCorrect dialog box shown in Figure 5.10 opens.
5. In the Replace field type **e$** and click Add. Click OK.
6. Close the Symbol dialog box and type **e$** to automatically insert the Euro symbol.

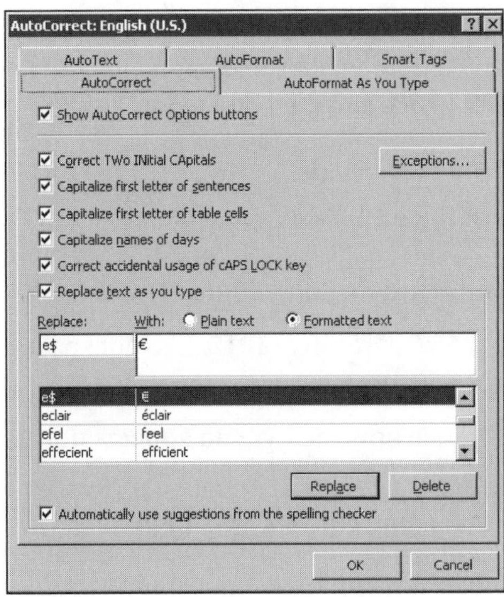

FIGURE 5.10

Create an AutoCorrect entry for the Euro currency symbol.

NONBREAKING SPACES AND HYPHENS

Oftentimes it is important that certain pieces of information remain together in legal documents. Firm name, telephone number, address, and client matter number are just a few items that might be difficult to identify should they break across lines. Word provides two types of formatting options for keeping selected text together: nonbreaking spaces and hyphens.

Before applying either option, turn on Show/Hide so you can view the formatting marks that will identify both types of nonbreaking spaces.

NOTE

If you don't see all the nonprinting characters onscreen, from the Tools menu, choose Options, select the View tab, and check All under Formatting Marks.

If text already exists within the document, place your mouse pointer between the words where you wish to apply the nonbreaking space, select the space mark, and press the appropriate shortcut key combination. Ctrl+Shift+Spacebar inserts a nonbreaking space, Ctrl+Shift+- (that is, Ctrl plus the underscore, which is at Shift+-) inserts a nonbreaking hyphen. Otherwise, type the shortcut key combination between words as you add text.

NOTE

You can also use the Symbol dialog box to insert nonbreaking spaces and hyphens. From the Insert menu, choose Symbol, and select either option from the Special Characters tab. Click Insert, and then click Close.

INSERT A NONBREAKING HYPHEN

1. Create a new document. Turn on Show/Hide.
2. Type **212** Ctrl+Shift+- **555** Ctrl+Shift+- **1212**. (Do not space between the numbers and the keyboard shortcuts.)
3. Turn off Show/Hide. Notice how the hyphen appears normal size. Press Enter.
4. Turn on Show/Hide. Type **Ellis Ellis & Smith LLP**.
5. Select the space between Ellis and the ampersand (&).
6. From the Insert menu, choose Symbol. Select the Special Characters tab, then select Nonbreaking Space.
7. Click Insert, and then click Close.

NOTE

When Show/Hide is turned on, nonbreaking hyphens appear as longer hyphens and nonbreaking spaces appear as degree signs that make it easier to identify them in the document.

FORMAT PAINTER

Have you ever spent too much time manually formatting the same words or phrases within a long document and wondered if there was an easier way to get the job done? Well, there is—the Format Painter allows you to copy applied character (or paragraph) formatting to selected text or paragraphs within your documents. For example, suppose you are working on an agreement that contains the word *article* in several places. Each occurrence of the word might require bold, 14-point italic type. Rather than having to manually apply the same format repeatedly, you can use the Format Painter to do all the work.

USE FORMAT PAINTER TO APPLY FORMATTING

1. Create a new document.
2. Type **The Electors shall meet in their respective states and vote by ballot for President and Vice-President, one of whom, at least, shall not be an inhabitant of the same state with themselves.**
3. Double-click the word *Electors* to select it. From the Formatting toolbar, apply bold and italic. Change the font size to 14 points.
4. With the text still selected, double-click the Format Painter on the Standard toolbar (shown in Figure 5.11). Notice how the mouse pointer changes to a paintbrush.

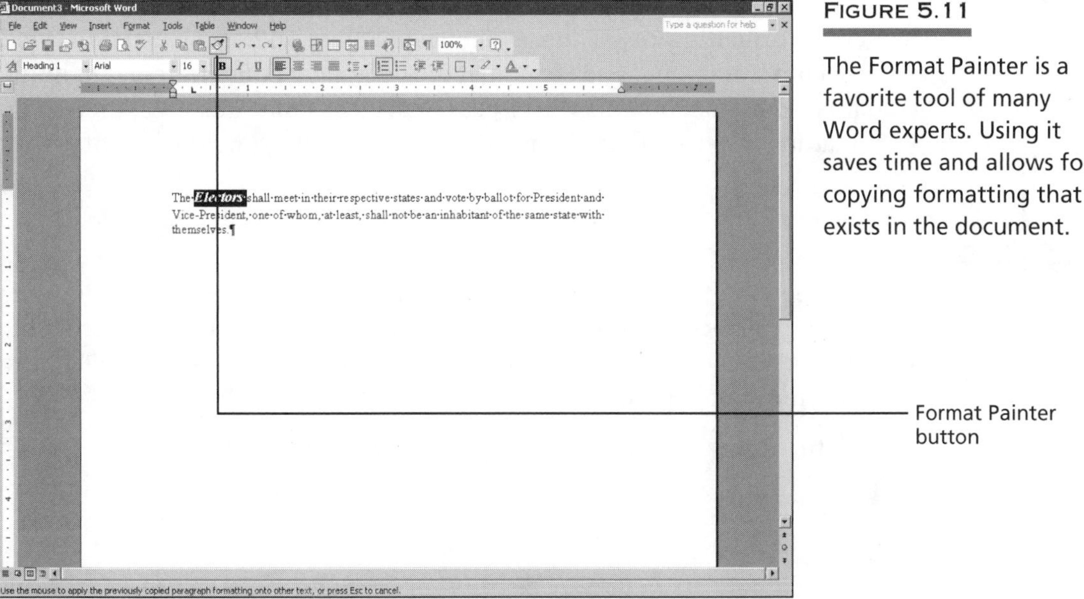

FIGURE 5.11

The Format Painter is a favorite tool of many Word experts. Using it saves time and allows for copying formatting that exists in the document.

Double-clicking the Format Painter allows you to apply formatting to multiple words, phrases, or sections. Single-click the Format Painter to apply formatting only once.

5. Move the paintbrush mouse pointer over the word *President* and click. Do the same for *Vice-President.*
6. Click and drag to select the words *shall not be an inhabitant.*
7. Release the mouse. Notice how all the words received the formatting. Click the Format Painter or press the Esc key to deactivate the Format Painter.

The keyboard shortcut to access the Format Painter is Ctrl+Shift+C.

REVEAL FORMATTING

You asked for it and now you've got it! Frustrated WordPerfect users the world over will be thrilled to see the addition of Reveal Formatting to the latest version of Word. Longtime WordPerfect users, accustomed to working with Reveal Codes, were often baffled and confused with Word's method of dealing with formatting. Reveal Formatting clears up the mystery behind formatting in Word and allows you to see the formatting for each part of the Word document.

The Reveal Formatting Task Pane, as shown in Figure 5.12, is divided into three sections: Font, Paragraph, and Section. If the document contains tables or numbered lists, additional options will appear in the task pane. Each section reveals the formatting associated with that particular part of the Word document.

Read Chapters 6 and 7 to learn all about Paragraph and Document formatting.

The Font section of the Reveal Formatting Task Pane displays font style, size, and other character attributes for selected words, phrases, or paragraphs. You can even open the Font dialog box to make formatting changes to selected text by clicking the Font hyperlink.

To open the Reveal Formatting Task Pane from the Format menu, choose Reveal Formatting.

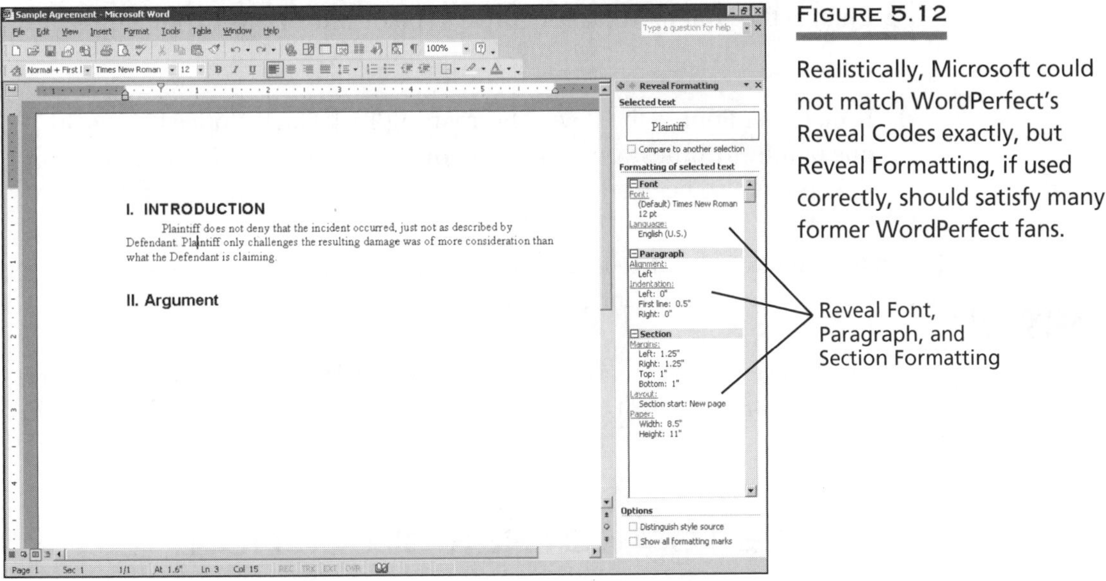

FIGURE 5.12

Realistically, Microsoft could not match WordPerfect's Reveal Codes exactly, but Reveal Formatting, if used correctly, should satisfy many former WordPerfect fans.

TIP

You can press Shift+F1 and click on text in the document to open the Reveal Formatting Task Pane. Likewise, from the Help menu, choose What's This? for the same result.

USE REVEAL FORMATTING TO APPLY CHARACTER FORMATTING

1. Create a new document.
2. Type **Morrison, Independent Counsel v. Olsen, et al.**
3. From the Format menu, choose Reveal Formatting. Notice the font name and size appear under Font.
4. Select the text.
5. Click the blue hyperlink in the Font section of the Reveal Formatting Task Pane to open the Font dialog box.
6. Place a check in the All Caps check box.

7. Change the Font to Arial, Font Style to bold, and Size to 14 points.
8. Click OK.
9. Look under Font in the Reveal Formatting Task Pane. Notice that each one of the attributes you applied is now visible. A new section called Effects has also been added.

NOTE

Depending on the speed of your computer, the task pane may take a few seconds to update to reflect recent changes.

10. Close the Reveal Formatting Task Pane by clicking the (X) Close button on the upper-right side of the pane.

COMPARE TO ANOTHER SELECTION

Text can appear to be formatted similarly but may, in fact, be very different. Even small differences in font size, color, or character spacing can make documents look and print incorrectly. Word 2002 solves this problem by providing an option to compare two selections. The differences are displayed in the Reveal Formatting Task Pane.

NOTE

Text formatting, numbered and bulleted lists, and tables can all be compared to show differences within the task pane.

COMPARE SELECTED TEXT TO ANOTHER SELECTION

1. Create a new document.
2. Type **Johnson Littler & Hawkins**. Select and center the text, make it bold, italic and a different size and color. Click after the last word and press Enter.
3. Press Ctrl+Shift+N to reset the next paragraph to the default Normal style.
4. Type **Stanton Burdette and Westerdahl**. Do not apply any additional formatting to this text.
5. Open the Reveal Formatting Task Pane. Select the first paragraph of text (Johnson Littler & Hawkins).

6. Click Compare To Another Selection on the task pane.
7. With the first paragraph still selected, hold the Ctrl key and select the second paragraph of text. The Reveal Formatting Task Pane shown in Figure 5.13 displays formatting differences for selected text.

APPLY AND CLEAR FORMATTING OPTIONS

The Reveal Formatting Task Pane offers a quick method to detect and apply formatting of surrounding text to the selection, or to clear formatting altogether.

If text is selected or if the active cursor is within a word, the Selected Text box shows the first few words of text for the selection. If a paragraph mark is selected or active, the preview displays the words *Sample Text.*

When the mouse pointer is hovered over the Preview box, a drop-down arrow appears with three options:

- **Select All Text With Similar Formatting.** Selects all text in the document with the same font and paragraph formatting.
- **Apply Formatting Of Surrounding Text.** Detects and formats selected text formatting of the text to the left of the first character in the selection.

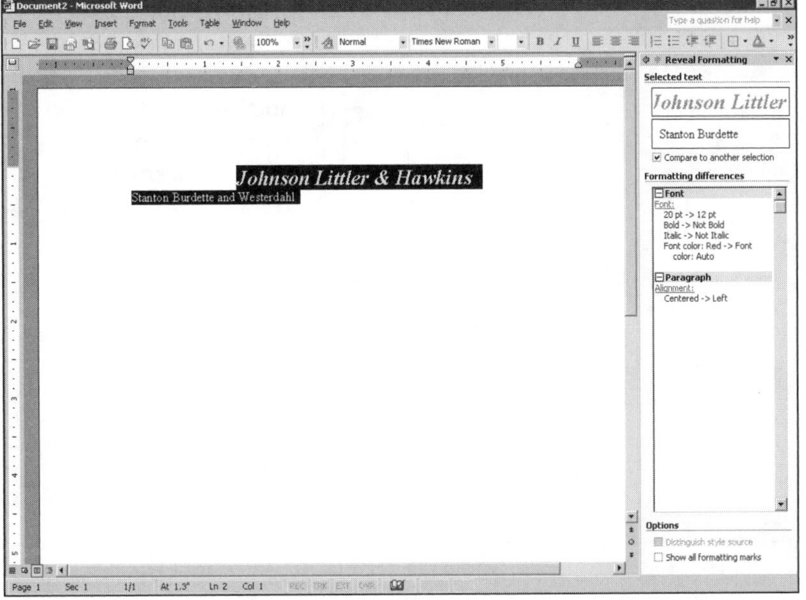

FIGURE 5.13

Compare To Another Selection is a great tool for troubleshooting why text prints or appears differently than it should.

- **Clear Formatting**. Strips direct character and paragraph formatting and then resets the selected text to Normal style.

TIP

The Edit menu also contains an option to clear formats. From the Edit menu, choose Clear, Formats. You can also use the Customize dialog box to assign a shortcut key to Clear Formatting.

APPLY AND CLEAR FORMATTING

1. On a blank line, type **This text is bold, italic, and underlined**. Select the text and apply bold, italic, and underline formatting.
2. Click after the last word.
3. Type **Non-format** and select this text.
4. From the Format menu, choose Reveal Formatting to open the task pane if necessary.
5. Position the mouse pointer over the Selected Text box (Figure 5.14) in the task pane and click the drop-down arrow.

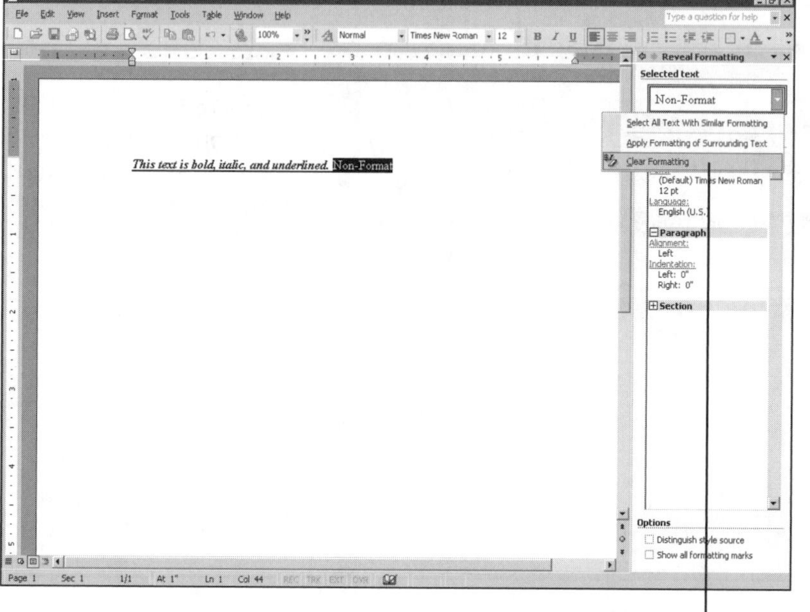

FIGURE 5.14

The drop-down arrow options on the various task panes offer additional options and quick access to performing common tasks.

6. Select Clear Formatting.

STYLES AND FORMATTING

Just when you thought Word couldn't possibly come up with any more ways of working with text, along comes Styles And Formatting. This powerful new Word feature is great for quickly applying direct formatting to selected words, phrases, and paragraphs in your legal documents, or clearing it from them. You can even use the Styles And Formatting Task Pane to apply styles.

TIP

Read Chapter 9, "Styles," to learn all about this important Word feature.

The Styles And Formatting Task Pane, shown in Figure 5.15, can be opened by choosing Styles And Formatting from the Format menu or by clicking the Styles And Formatting button on the Formatting toolbar.

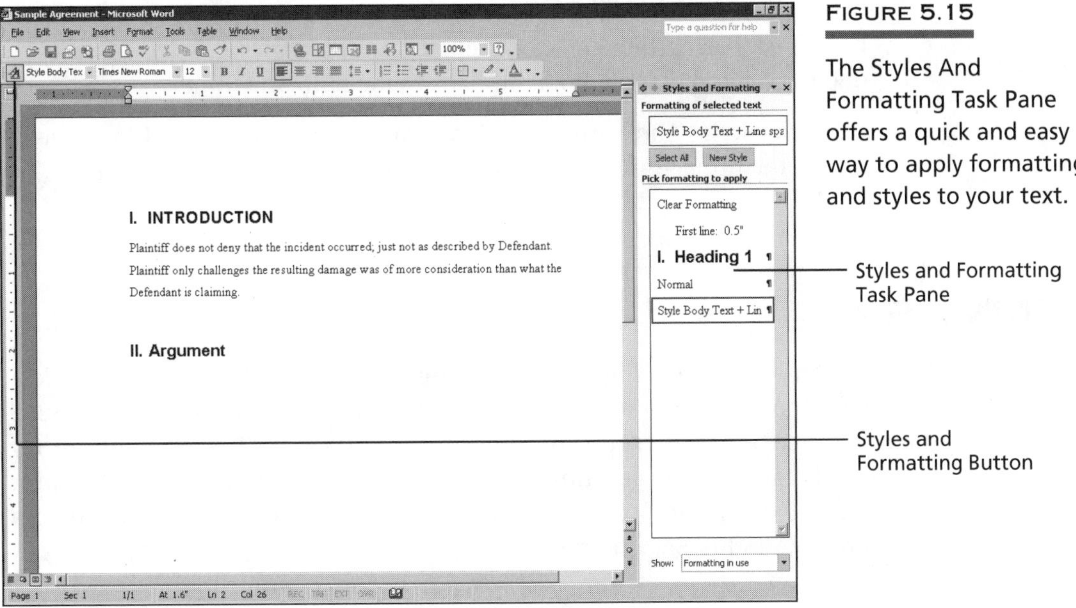

FIGURE 5.15

The Styles And Formatting Task Pane offers a quick and easy way to apply formatting and styles to your text.

USE THE STYLES AND FORMATTING PANE TO APPLY AND CLEAR DIRECT FORMATTING

1. Create a new document.
2. From the Format menu, choose Styles And Formatting.
3 Type **Amendment Text**. Press Enter twice.
4. Type **The powers not delegated to the United States by the Constitution, nor prohibited by it to the States, are reserved to the States respectively, or to the people.**
5. Select *Amendment Text.* From the Format menu, choose Font and select the Font tab. Choose Bold for the Font Style and place a check next to All Caps. Click OK.
6. From the Styles And Formatting Task Pane, look under Formatting Of Selected Text—it should be Bold, All Caps.
7. Move to the next paragraph and select *United States.* From under Pick Formatting To Apply in the Styles And Formatting Task Pane, select Bold, All Caps.
8. Press Ctrl+A to select all text.
9. From Pick Formatting To Apply, select Clear Formatting. Select all text once again and reapply Bold, All Caps to the entire document.
10. Close the Styles And Formatting Task Pane by clicking the (X) Close button on the upper-right side of the task pane.

SUMMARY

This chapter looked at using the Formatting toolbar, Font dialog box, and Format Painter to apply character formatting to legal documents. It also discussed the difference between True Type and Printer fonts as well as the methods for inserting legal symbols and nonbreaking spaces and hyphens. The chapter ended with a discussion of Word's newest features—Reveal Formatting and Compare To Another Selection.

TROUBLESHOOTING FORMATTING TEXT

I applied bold and underlining from the Formatting toolbar but none of the text in my document was affected—why not?

To apply character formatting to existing text, select the text first and then make the formatting choices.

My font list is too long. Is there any way I can reduce the number of fonts?

There are a couple of things you can do. First, open the Fonts folder from the Windows Control Panel (Start, Settings, Control Panel). From the Tools menu, choose Folder Options and select the True Type Fonts tab. Check the box Show Only True Type Fonts In The Programs On My Computer. You may have to restart your computer for the settings to take effect.

Alternatively, from the View menu of the Fonts folder, select the option Hide Variations (Bold, Italic, Etc.) to remove duplicate fonts from the list. Of course, you could simply use the Windows Control Panel to uninstall some fonts you never use. However, this means no one else can use them either, so the decision should be made for the firm as a whole rather than by each individual.

A document I'm sending to a client contains a font they don't have on their PC. Is there any way they can view the document without the font?

Yes. You can embed the font in the document. That way, the person on the other end can view and even edit the document, even though they do not have the specific font. To embed a True Type font, follow these instructions: From the Tools menu, choose Options and select the Save tab. Check the option Embed True Type Fonts. Note: Embedding fonts increases the size of the file.

Some text in my document prints lighter than other text. I'm using the same font; what could be the cause of this?

The problem likely is caused by Automatic versus Black color having been applied to text. Type text in the document and click the Font Color drop-down arrow and click Automatic. Select different text and click the drop-down arrow next to Font Color and select Black. From the Format menu, choose Reveal Formatting to open the task pane. Select the first text, which has automatic color applied. Click Compare To Another Selection. Hold the Ctrl key and select text formatted as black. The task pane shows the formatting differences, including color.

Since codes cannot be viewed or edited in the Reveal Formatting Task Pane, how can I change the formatting easily?

When Microsoft developed this feature, they consulted with the Legal Advisory Council. WordPerfect users wanted reveal codes–like functionality, but some members had never used WordPerfect or the feature reveal codes and didn't want to have to start, since they had used Word for years. The compromise that Microsoft came up with was to provide easy access to make adjustments to text and formatting but to do so by offering hyperlinks to dialog boxes where these changes could be made. Selecting text, clicking the specific hyperlink in the Reveal Formatting Task Pane and making even complex adjustments take only seconds.

Chapter 6

Formatting a Paragraph

IN THIS CHAPTER

- Paragraph marks
- Formatting toolbar
- Ruler
- Components of the Paragraph dialog box
- The new Reveal Formatting feature

Paragraph formatting includes alignment, indentation, line spacing, tabs, and much more. Each paragraph contains numerous formatting options. Word stores document formatting in the paragraph mark—which means that each paragraph can be formatted differently. For longtime WordPerfect users, this concept may seem a bit strange, but after reading through this chapter, you'll have a better understanding of how Word handles paragraph formatting.

PARAGRAPH MARKS

Before you can understand how Word deals with paragraph formatting, you need to learn how and where Word stores the different formats you will be applying. Unlike WordPerfect, which uses codes to turn on and off formatting, Word stores all the formatting for each paragraph in the paragraph mark. This is often the most difficult concept for new Word users to grasp.

The formats contained within each paragraph mark include indentation, alignment, line spacing, space after, tabs, and more. Every time you press the Enter key, you create a new paragraph that inherits all the formatting found in the preceding paragraph. If you accidentally delete a paragraph mark but not the text associated with it, the paragraph below the deleted paragraph mark becomes part of the one above it. This may sound confusing, but it will become clearer as you work through the chapter.

TIP

To see the paragraph marks in a document, click the Show/Hide (paragraph mark) button on the Standard toolbar (Figure 6.1). Keyboard users can press Ctrl+Shift+8 to enable the feature.

The ability to see paragraph marks while working can help you make more sense of what's going on in a document.

Word allows you to change the format of any one paragraph in a document without affecting the format of other paragraphs, or you can build an initial format and let all the paragraphs you create from that point on share the same formatting.

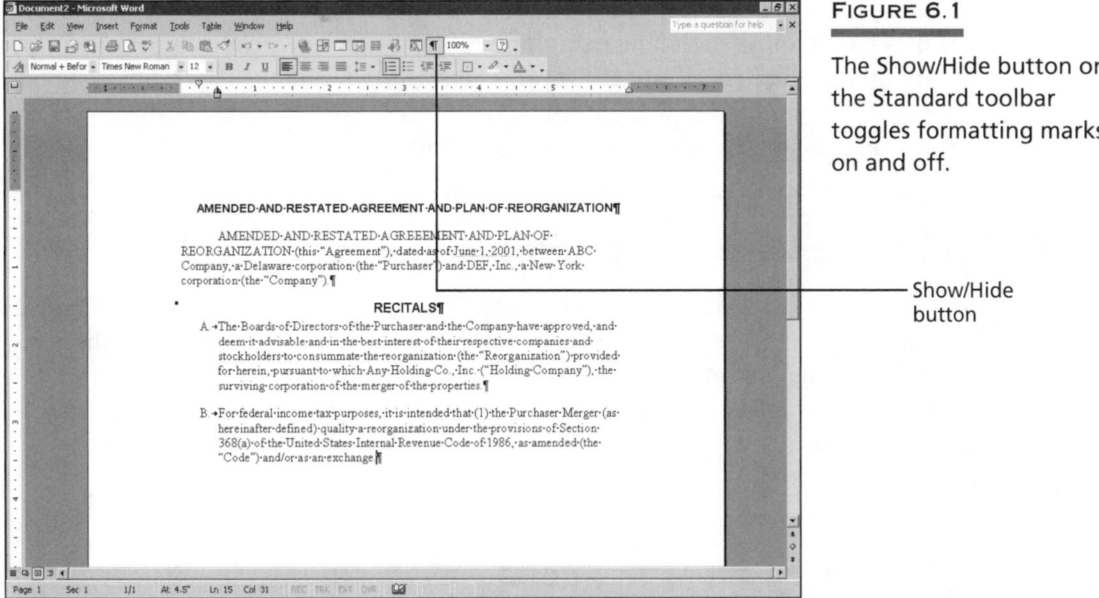

FIGURE 6.1

The Show/Hide button on the Standard toolbar toggles formatting marks on and off.

SEE HOW FORMATTING DIFFERENT PARAGRAPHS WORKS

1. Create a new document.
2. Turn on Show/Hide.
3. Type **This Is My First Paragraph** and press Enter. Do you see the new paragraph mark?
4. In the second paragraph, type **This Is My Second Paragraph**. With your insertion point still in the second paragraph, press Ctrl+E to center the paragraph. Press Enter to create another paragraph.
5. In the third paragraph, type **This Is My Third Paragraph**. Is the third paragraph centered?
6. Place the insertion point in the third paragraph and press Ctrl+L to left-align the text.
7. Select all three paragraphs and press Ctrl+R to right-align the text. Notice how each paragraph is affected.

The preceding exercise illustrates in a very simple fashion the way Word handles paragraphs. Each new paragraph takes on the formatting characteristics of the preceding paragraph. However, you can make changes to individual paragraphs without affecting an entire document or you can select entire groups of paragraphs and apply uniform changes to all.

APPLYING PARAGRAPH FORMATTING

Word provides several methods for applying paragraph formatting. The three main tools used to apply the formatting are the Formatting toolbar, the Paragraph dialog box, and, in some cases, the horizontal ruler. While the Formatting toolbar and ruler allow you to apply certain types of paragraph formatting more quickly, both are less flexible and contain far fewer options than the Paragraph dialog box itself.

FORMATTING TOOLBAR

The Formatting toolbar (Figure 6.2) contains a series of commands that allow you to apply different types of formatting to your document. For now, let's focus on just those buttons that affect paragraph formatting.

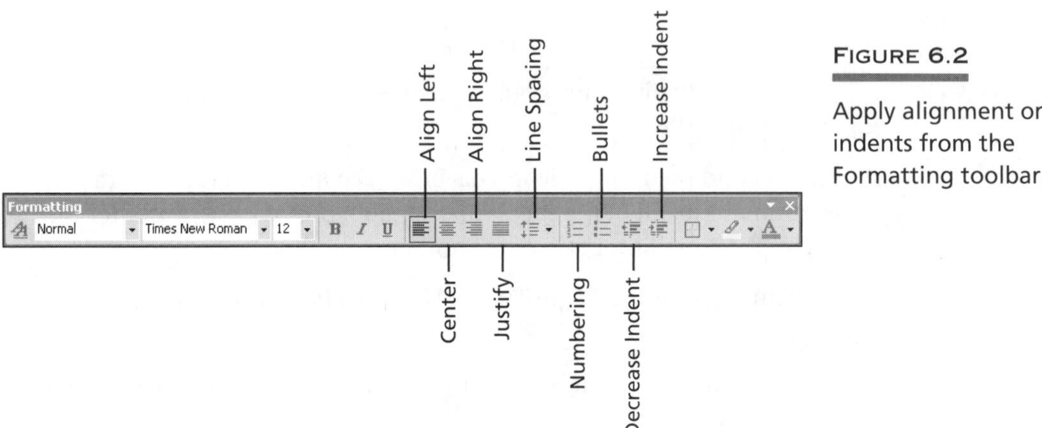

FIGURE 6.2

Apply alignment or indents from the Formatting toolbar.

ALIGNMENT BUTTONS

Horizontal alignment determines the look and direction of the edges of the paragraph. The alignment buttons on the Formatting toolbar (Figure 6.3) allow you to quickly set the horizontal alignment for one or more paragraphs.

- **Align Left**. Aligns selected paragraphs to the left margin or indent and is sometimes referred to as *flush left.*
- **Center**. Centers selected paragraphs between the margins or indents of a paragraph.
- **Align Right**. Aligns selected paragraphs of text, numbers, or graphics to the right margin or indent and is sometimes referred to as *flush right.*
- **Justify**. Aligns selected paragraphs to both the left and right margins or indents, presenting a more even (or squared-off) look, like the page of a printed book or magazine.

USE THE FORMATTING TOOLBAR FOR PARAGRAPH ALIGNMENT

1. Create a new document.
2. Type the following: **The issue is factual and to be resolved from all the evidence and is, in great part, a question of judgment rather than mathematics.** Press Enter to create a new paragraph.

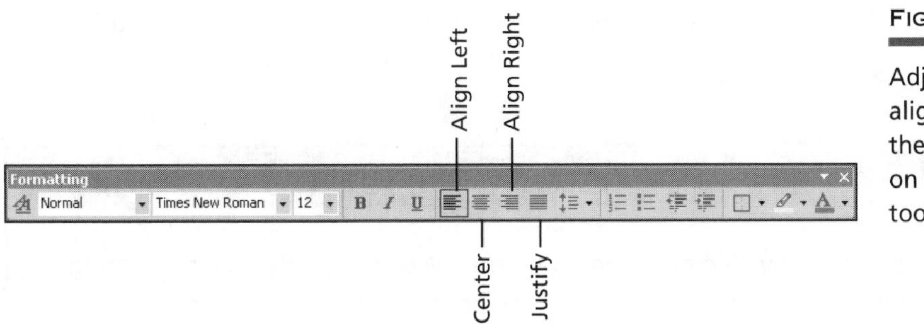

FIGURE 6.3

Adjust paragraph alignment with one of the Alignment buttons on the Formatting toolbar.

3. In the next paragraph, type **In making our determination, we may embrace or reject expert testimony if, in our judgment, either approach is appropriate.**
4. Click anywhere in the first paragraph and click the Center alignment button. What effect did that have on the second paragraph?
5. Click anywhere in the second paragraph and click the Align Right button. Move your insertion point to the end of the sentence and press Enter to create a third paragraph. Type in some more text.
6. How is the third paragraph aligned? With your insertion point in the third paragraph, click the Justify button.
7. Keep this document open for the next exercise.

NOTE

To adjust horizontal alignment for a single paragraph, click anywhere in the paragraph and choose one of four alignment commands. To adjust multiple paragraphs, select all of the desired paragraphs simultaneously and then choose the horizontal alignment command you wish to apply to the selected paragraphs.

LINE SPACING

Line spacing determines the amount of vertical space between lines of text within a paragraph. Although most documents are single-spaced by default, certain types of legal documents such as pleadings, agreements, and trusts often require double-spacing. The Line Spacing command on the Formatting toolbar allows you to quickly apply line spacing to one or more paragraphs.

NEW FEATURE!

Due to popular demand from law firms, Microsoft added a Line Spacing button to the Formatting toolbar. Select the paragraphs to affect. Click the drop-down arrow on the Line Spacing button and select 1.0, 1.5, 2.0, 2.5, 3.0, or More. Clicking More displays the Paragraph dialog box.

SET LINE SPACING

1. Place your insertion point anywhere in the first paragraph.

To apply paragraph formatting to one paragraph, click anywhere in the paragraph and click the appropriate formatting command from the Formatting toolbar. To affect multiple paragraphs, you must select each paragraph prior to executing the formatting command.

2. Click the drop-down arrow next to the Line Spacing button and choose 2.0 from the list.
3. Place your insertion point in the second paragraph and choose 1.5 from the drop-down list on the Line Spacing button.
4. Select both paragraphs and choose 1.0.

Keyboard users can press Ctrl+1 for single line spacing, Ctrl+2 for double line spacing, and Ctrl+5 for 1.5 line spacing.

INDENTATION

Indentation determines the distance of the paragraph from either the left or right margins. The last two buttons on the Formatting toolbar associated with paragraph formatting are the Increase Indent and Decrease Indent buttons (Figure 6.4). Each button allows you to select a paragraph or paragraphs and make left-indentation changes quickly.

- **Decrease Indent**. When clicked, this button moves the selected paragraphs back (to the left) 0.5" on the ruler.
- **Increase Indent**. When clicked, this button moves the selected paragraphs forward (to the right) 0.5" on the ruler.

FIGURE 6.4

Increase or decrease paragraph indents from indent buttons on the Formatting toolbar.

USE THE FORMATTING TOOLBAR TO SET INDENTS

1. Create a new document.
2. Type **The first question before the Court must be one of jurisprudence. Any intelligent examination of legal issues requires the use of reason and rational thought.** Press Enter to create a new paragraph.
3. In the second paragraph, type **If the premise from which the examination begins is faulty, the conclusion to the problem will be even more so.**
4. Place your insertion point anywhere in the first paragraph and click the Increase Indent button twice. Look at the Left Indent marker on the horizontal ruler to see how much the indentation has changed (Figure 6.5).
5. Place your insertion point in the second paragraph and click the Increase Indent button three times. Click the Decrease Indent button twice.

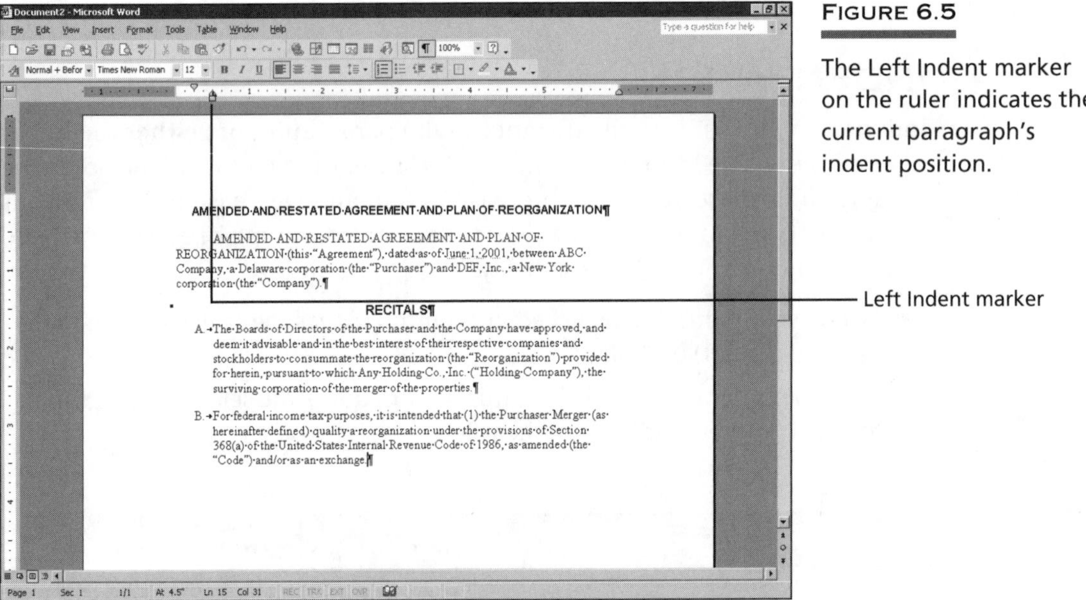

FIGURE 6.5

The Left Indent marker on the ruler indicates the current paragraph's indent position.

PARAGRAPH DIALOG BOX

When it comes to applying paragraph formatting, the Paragraph dialog box provides far more formatting options than the Formatting toolbar. To activate the Paragraph dialog box, place your insertion point in the paragraph you wish to format and, from the Format menu, choose Paragraph. To apply specific formatting to more than one paragraph, simultaneously select all the paragraphs you want to affect prior to activating the dialog box. The Paragraph dialog box is shown in Figure 6.6.

TIP

To quickly activate the Paragraph dialog box, alternate-click in the paragraph you wish to format, or select multiple paragraphs, alternate-click, and choose Paragraph. The keyboard shortcut for displaying the Paragraph dialog box is Alt+O, P.

The Paragraph dialog box has two tabs, Indents And Spacing and Line And Page Breaks. Each tab is broken down into distinct sections divided by separator lines, and each contains different options related to paragraph formatting.

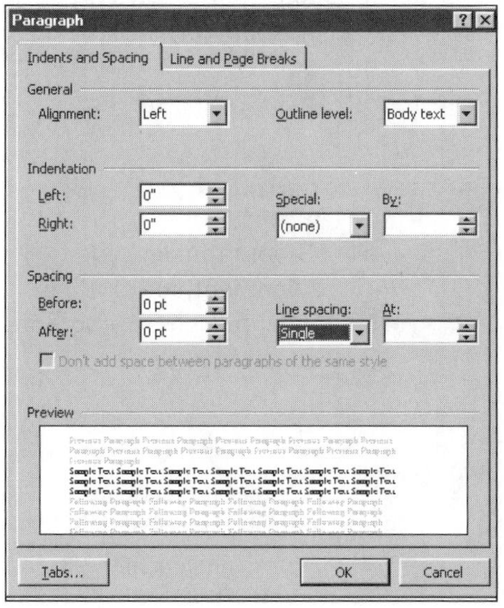

FIGURE 6.6

Select alignment, indents, spacing, and more from the Paragraph dialog box.

INDENTS AND SPACING TAB

The Indents And Spacing tab contains a number of formatting commands that allow you to set paragraph alignment, indentation, space before and after a paragraph, line spacing, and tabs. When you apply formatting options to any paragraph in Word, each subsequent, new paragraph inherits the same set of options. You can, however, apply formatting changes to any paragraph within a document without affecting any of the other existing paragraphs.

GENERAL

The General section of the Indents And Spacing tab (Figure 6.7) contains two options that allow you to set paragraph alignment and outline levels for one or more paragraphs.

The Alignment option includes a drop-down list with the same set of paragraph alignment commands found on the Formatting toolbar. You can select from one of the four available commands to set paragraph alignment:

- **Left.** Aligns to the left margin or indent.
- **Centered.** Centers between the margins or indents of a document.
- **Right.** Aligns to the right margin or indent.
- **Justified.** Aligns selected paragraphs to both the left and right margins or indents, presenting a more even (or squared-off) look.

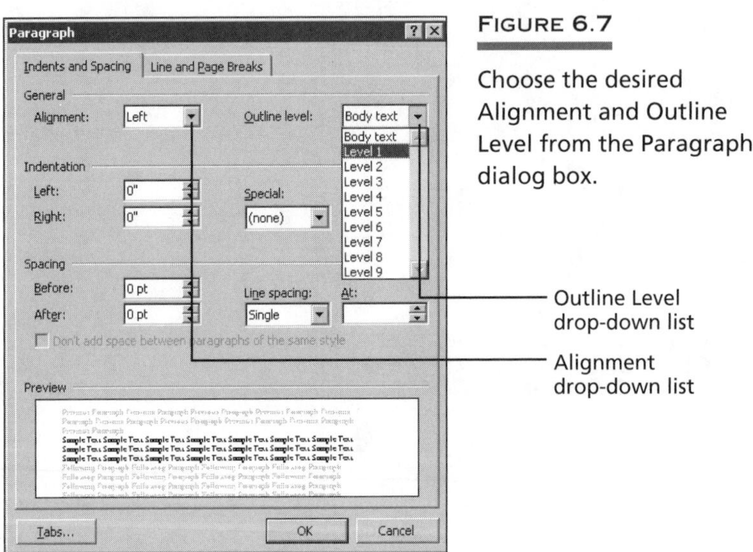

FIGURE 6.7

Choose the desired Alignment and Outline Level from the Paragraph dialog box.

The Outline Level option allows you to associate one or more paragraphs with one of Word's nine outline levels. Assigning an outline level gives you access to two great features in Word:

- **Document Map.** The Document Map is a feature that uses text formatted with Word's heading styles or an outline level to navigate quickly through long documents. For more information, see Chapter 3, "The Word Environment."
- **Table of Contents.** Word 2002 can generate a table of contents easily using heading styles 1 through 9. You can get the same result with user-defined styles in conjunction with outline levels. Chapter 14, "Agreements, Briefs, and Other Long Documents," explores the Table of Contents feature in depth.

If a paragraph is already formatted with headings 1 through 9, then the Outline Level option will be unavailable.

SET PARAGRAPH ALIGNMENT AND OUTLINE LEVEL

1. Create a new document and type the following: **This case is not about any diminution in the value of the Plaintiff's copyrights; none has occurred or is reasonably foreseeable as a result of ABC Corp.**
2. From the View menu, choose Document Map. The Document Map pane appears on the left side of your screen. Notice that no paragraphs are listed in the Document Map pane.
3. Alternate-click the paragraph and choose Paragraph from the shortcut menu. Select the Indents And Spacing tab from the Paragraph dialog box.
4. In the General section, click the drop-down arrow next to Alignment and choose Centered from the list of available commands.
5. Click the drop-down arrow next to Outline Level and select Level 1 from the list of Outline Levels.
6. Click OK. Notice that the paragraph now appears in the Document Map.

INDENTATION

Indentation determines the distance of the paragraph from either the left or right margins. The Indentation section of the Indents And Spacing tab contains a set of commands that allow you to apply different types and amounts of indentation to one or more paragraphs. Using the options available in this section (shown in Figure 6.8), you can either increase or decrease left and right paragraph indentation, set first-line indents, or even create hanging indents.

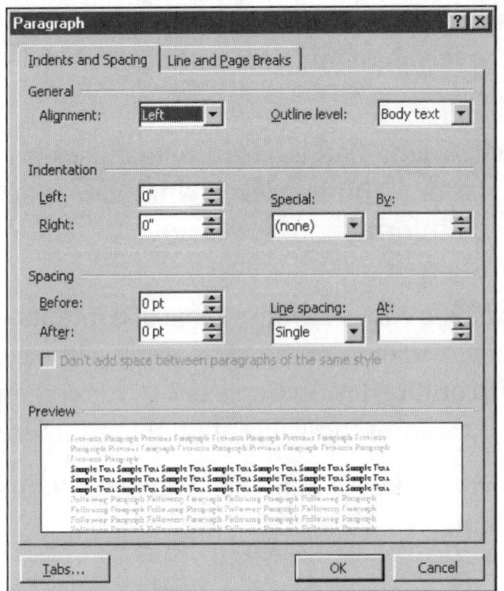

FIGURE 6.8

Paragraphs can be indented in the Paragraph dialog box, as shown here, using the ruler or keyboard shortcuts. The keyboard shortcuts for a hanging and left indent are Ctrl+T and Ctrl+M respectively.

NOTE

As you apply various formatting options, use the Preview pane at the bottom of the dialog box to see how your document will be affected by applying the formatting.

You can apply paragraph formatting to one or more paragraphs depending on what you need to do within the document. The indentation you set for one paragraph will automatically carry down to each new paragraph you create thereafter—but will not affect existing paragraphs. To apply indentation (or any other type of paragraph formatting, for that matter) to more than one paragraph, you'll need to select all the paragraphs to be formatted and then apply the formatting changes. The key rule to remember with Word is "select to affect."

PRACTICE CHANGING PARAGRAPH INDENTATION

1. Create a new document and type the following: **Answers and Deposition of John W. Smith, produced as a witness on behalf of the Plaintiff, taken in the above styled and numbered cause on the 15th of August, 2000.**
2. From the Format menu, choose Paragraph. Select the Indents And Spacing tab.
3. From the Indentation section, click the up-arrow at the end of the Left indentation box until it reaches .5". (You can also type **.5** directly into the box.)

4. Do the same for the Right indentation option and click OK.
5. Press the Enter key to create a new paragraph and type the following: **Question: Based on the amounts that were reported by the estate, what would you assess the new taxes to be?** Press the Tab key after the colon.
6. Notice that the new paragraph has the same indentation as the preceding paragraph.
7. Keep this document open.

In addition to providing you with the ability to alter left and right paragraph indentation, the Indents And Spacing tab of the Paragraph dialog box also contains commands that allow you to create first-line and hanging indents.

A first-line indent is one where only the first line of the paragraph is indented. A hanging indent is just the opposite—the first line of the paragraph is not indented but all subsequent lines in the paragraph are.

CREATE A FIRST-LINE INDENT USING THE PARAGRAPH DIALOG BOX

1. Using the document from the preceding exercise, place your insertion point in the first paragraph.
2. Alternate-click on the paragraph text and choose Paragraph from the shortcut menu. Select the Indents And Spacing tab.
3. From the Indentation section, click the drop-down arrow under Special and choose First Line (Figure 6.9). Notice that By automatically changes to .5"—which is the default for most legal documents. You can change this amount by typing the exact number into the box or by using the spinners to increase or decrease the size of the first-line indent.

> *Spinner* is the control must often found in dialog boxes with arrows that can be clicked in the up or down direction to set a value.

4. Click OK. You've created a paragraph with a first-line indent of .5".
5. Keep this document open for the next exercise.

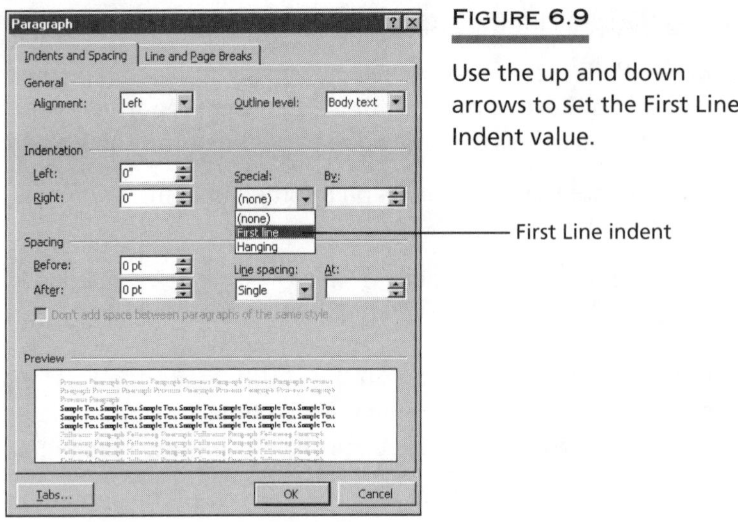

FIGURE 6.9

Use the up and down arrows to set the First Line Indent value.

CREATE A HANGING INDENT USING THE PARAGRAPH DIALOG BOX

1. Using the document from the preceding exercise, place your insertion point in the second paragraph and, from the Format menu, choose Paragraph. Select the Indents And Spacing tab.
2. From the Indentation section, click the drop-down arrow under Special and choose Hanging (Figure 6.10).

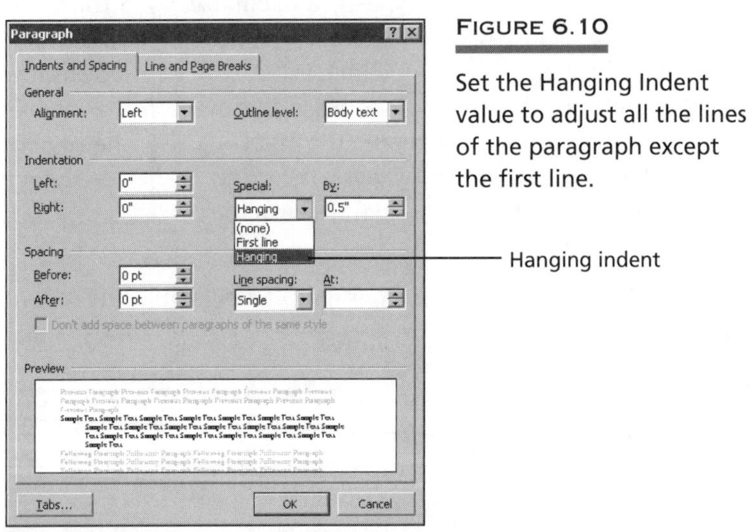

FIGURE 6.10

Set the Hanging Indent value to adjust all the lines of the paragraph except the first line.

3. Press the Tab key to move to the By field and type **1**.
4. Click OK. Notice how the indentation changes for the second paragraph.
5. Select both paragraphs and press Ctrl+Q to remove the applied indents.

Direct formatting is any type of font or paragraph formatting you apply to text in a document rather than formatting with styles.

TIP

The keyboard shortcut Ctrl+Q removes any direct paragraph formatting from selected paragraphs.

USING THE RULER TO CHANGE INDENTATION

The horizontal ruler allows you to quickly apply the same types of indents that you just accessed through the Paragraph dialog box. The various markers on the horizontal ruler are identified in Figure 6.11.

The markers on the ruler display indentation settings for the paragraph that contains the insertion point.

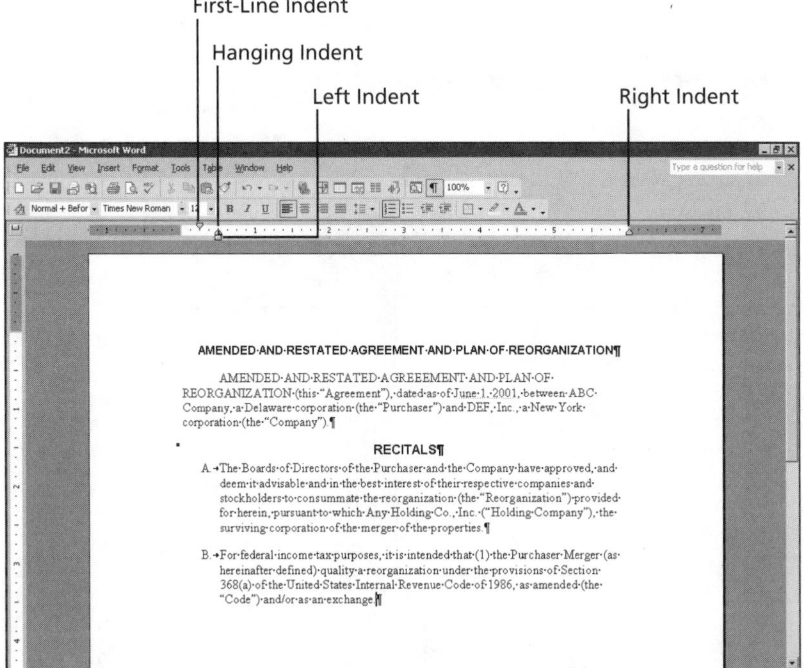

FIGURE 6.11

Each type of indent is represented with an indent marker on the Horizontal ruler.

NOTE

If you select multiple paragraphs with varying indentations, one or more of the marker buttons may be grayed out.

The ruler is most useful when you want to quickly make indentation changes to one paragraph. Using the ruler, you can change the left and right indents and also create hanging or first-line indents.

SET INDENTS USING THE RULER

1. Create a new document. Make sure the horizontal ruler is visible. If it's not, from the View menu, choose Ruler.
2. Type the following: **Plaintiffs represent a broad range of individuals and entities who are speakers, content providers, and users of the Web.**
3. Place your mouse pointer on the Left indent marker and drag it to .5".

TIP

It is very easy to grab the wrong indent marker on the ruler. Use ScreenTips to reveal the indent marker's name before you start to drag the marker (as shown in Figure 6.12). To access ScreenTips, let your mouse pointer hover over the indent marker. If you don't see the ScreenTip, from the Tools menu, choose Customize, select the Options tab, and check the option Show ScreenTips On Toolbars.

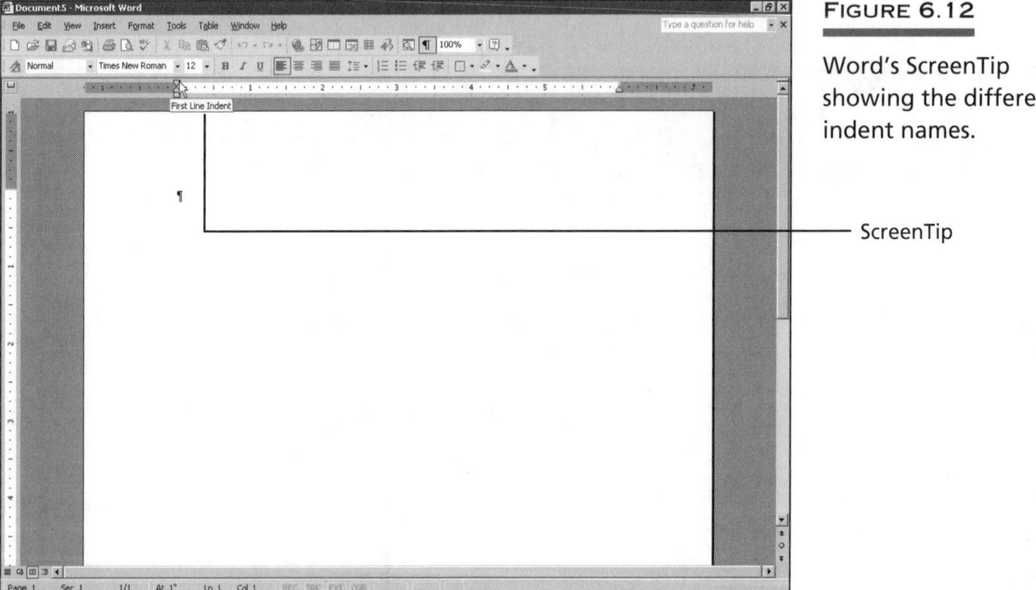

FIGURE 6.12

Word's ScreenTip showing the different indent names.

4. Place your mouse pointer over the Right indent marker and drag it to the 5" position on the ruler.
5. Create a first-line indent by placing your mouse pointer over the First Line indent marker and dragging it to the 1" position on the ruler.
6. Create a hanging indent by placing your mouse pointer over the Hanging indent marker and dragging it to the 1.5" position on the ruler.
7. Press Ctrl+Q to remove the applied indents.
8. Practice using different indentation settings.

TIP

If you are a keyboard person, try the following shortcut keys to apply indents:

Type of Indent	Increase	Decrease
Left	Ctrl+M	Ctrl+Shift+M
Hanging	Ctrl+T	Ctrl+Shift+T

NOTE

Indents can also be set from the Tab Alignment box on the far-left end of the horizontal ruler. Click the Tab Alignment box until First Line Indent appears and then click the position on the ruler for the first line indent. The Tab Alignment box also contains a shortcut to creating a hanging indent.

USE TAB TO SET INDENTS

Word has an option to set left and first-line indents with tabs and backspaces. When this AutoFormat As You Type option is turned on in AutoCorrect Options, you can apply indents as you are typing by using the Tab and Backspace keys.

USE TAB AND BACKSPACE TO SET INDENTS

1. Create a new document.
2. Type =**rand**() and press Enter. This will insert some generic text into your document.
3. Click at the beginning of the first paragraph and press Tab. What happened?
4. Click at the beginning of the second paragraph and press Tab twice.
5. Leave your mouse pointer in the same place and press Backspace to decrease your indents.

Pressing Tab once will apply a first-line indent. Pressing Tab twice will apply a first-line indent as well as a left indent.

NOTE

Your insertion point must be at the beginning of a paragraph of text for the Tab and Backspace key to increase and decrease indents.

If pressing Tab and Backspace does not change indents, from the Tools menu, choose AutoCorrect Options and select the AutoFormat As You Type tab. Select the option to Set Left- And First-Indent With Tabs And Backspaces.

SPACING

The Spacing section on the Indents And Spacing tab in the Paragraph dialog box contains commands that allow you to set line spacing as well as space between paragraphs. Line spacing is the vertical space between lines within a paragraph. Space Before/After is the space between paragraphs.

SPACE BEFORE/AFTER

As mentioned earlier in this chapter, Word stores all the formatting for each paragraph in the paragraph mark. Every time you press Enter, you're actually creating a new paragraph—even if that new paragraph doesn't contain any text. Most typists are used to pressing the Enter key twice to create space between single-spaced paragraphs. This is not a desirable way of working in Word because it creates a lot of unused, unnecessary paragraph marks.

You can create space between paragraphs by using the Spacing Before or Spacing After commands in the Spacing section of the Indents And Spacing tab. This will help you create cleaner Word documents.

CREATE SPACE BETWEEN PARAGRAPHS

1. Create a new document. Turn on Show/Hide.
2. Type the following: **OPINION** (with no period at the end).
3. Press Enter and type the following in the next paragraph: **This case involves the valuation of real property for tax purposes. We must decide the value of decedent's one-half interest in the subject property.**
4. Select both paragraphs. Alternate-click and choose Paragraph. Select the Indents And Spacing tab.

5. From the Spacing section, click the spinner (the upward-pointing arrow) next to After until it shows 12 pt (that is, 12 points of space—equal to one line of regular text). Click OK. The results should resemble Figure 6.13.
6. Place your insertion point at the end of the second paragraph and press Enter to create a new paragraph.
7. Type the following: **The estate's valuation was predicted on the assumption that residential development is the highest and best use for the property.**
8. Notice that the second and third paragraphs are also separated by 12 points of space.

NOTE

You can create more space before or after each paragraph depending on the type of document you're working with. Each new paragraph will inherit the Space Before/After attributes of the preceding paragraph.

TIP

Choosing whether to use Space Before or Space After is definitely a personal preference. Be careful not to use a combination of both in the same document as this could cause too much space between paragraphs.

The keyboard shortcut for adding 12 points of space before the paragraph or removing it is Ctrl+0 (zero), which acts as a toggle.

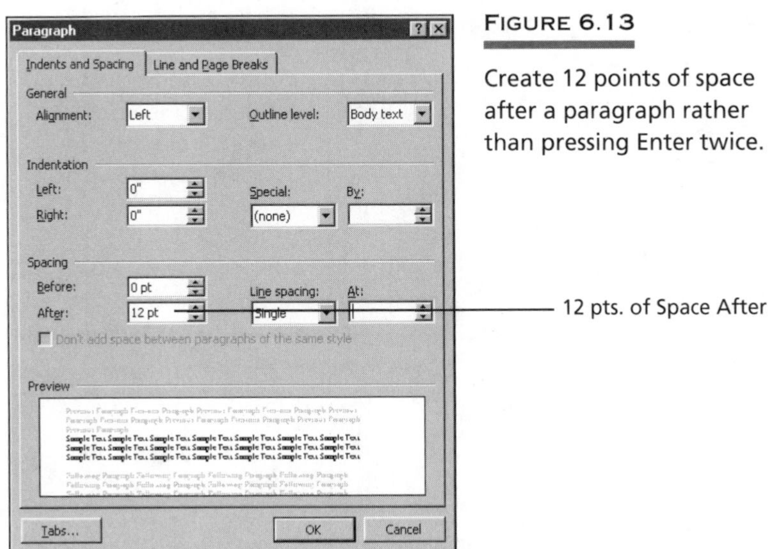

FIGURE 6.13

Create 12 points of space after a paragraph rather than pressing Enter twice.

Using Space Before or Space After also gives you the ability to easily reduce the amount of space between paragraphs, which can help fit more text on each page. For example, instead of using 12 points of Space After, try 9 points or even 6 points. This is a great trick for keeping documents under a specific page count. It also eliminates the possibility of a page starting with a paragraph mark at the top, since you want the text to start at the same place on all pages.

LINE SPACING

Line spacing determines the amount of vertical space between lines of text within a paragraph. Most simple documents such as letters and memos are single-spaced. Pleadings, briefs, agreements, and trusts, as well as other legal documents, often require double-spacing. Word provides a number of different line spacing options for you to work with from within the Paragraph dialog box, as shown in Figure 6.14.

- **Single**. Single line spacing sets the amount of spacing needed for the largest font on that line plus additional space to separate it from the other lines.
- **1.5 Lines**. One and a half times that of single line spacing. For example, 12 points single-spaced would be equal to 18 points with 1.5 line spacing.
- **Double**. Double that of single line spacing. Used in pleadings, briefs, and many agreements.
- **At Least**. Sets the minimum value of line spacing but gives Word the option to adjust if needed to accommodate larger font sizes or graphics that would not otherwise fit within the specified spacing.

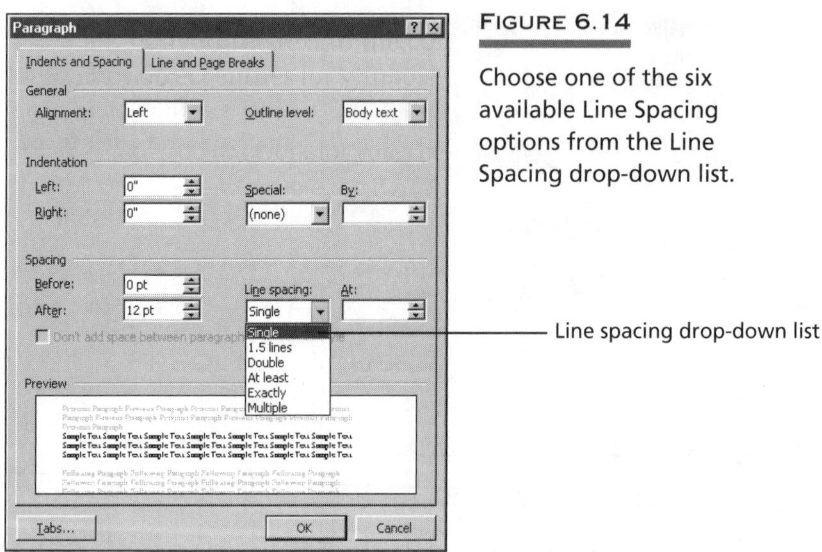

FIGURE 6.14

Choose one of the six available Line Spacing options from the Line Spacing drop-down list.

- **Exactly**. Fixed line spacing that spaces all lines evenly regardless of font sizes.

If you increase the font size of text in a paragraph formatted with Exactly line spacing, you take the chance that the top part of the text may be cut off.

- **Multiple**. Line spacing that is increased or decreased by the number of lines that you specify in the At box. For example, if you set line spacing to Multiple and enter 3 in the At box, the line spacing will be triple line spacing.

SET LINE SPACING

1. Create a new document and type the following: **The parties disagree about how to handle the fact that approval for residential development had not been obtained. The agreement calls for payments at closing that would occur as much as two and four years into the future.**
2. From the Format menu, choose Paragraph. Select the Indents And Spacing tab.
3. From the Spacing section, click the drop-down arrow next to Line Spacing and choose 1.5 lines (as in Figure 6.15). Notice how the line spacing has changed in the Preview pane.
4. Click the drop-down arrow again and choose Double.
5. Click OK.

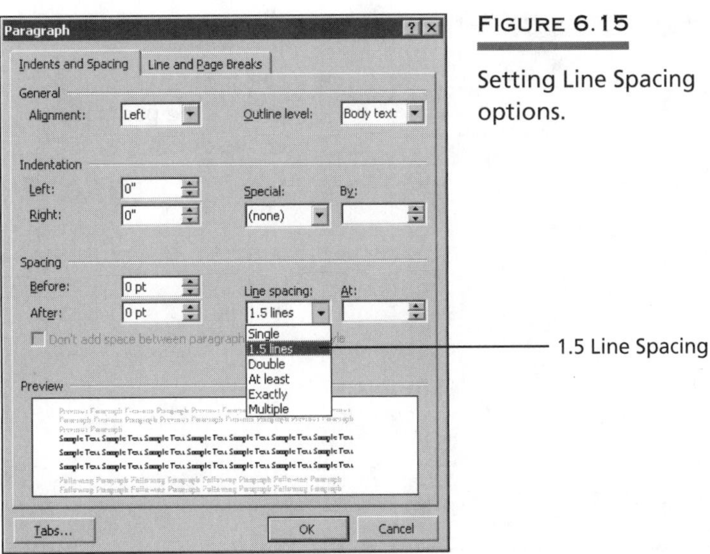

FIGURE 6.15

Setting Line Spacing options.

The following keyboard commands offer shortcuts to line spacing formats:

Single	Ctrl+1
Double	Ctrl+2
1.5 lines	Ctrl+5

LINE AND PAGE BREAKS

The second tab on the Paragraph dialog box, Line And Page Breaks, contains a series of check boxes that deal primarily with pagination and text flow. Like the Indents And Spacing tab, Line And Page Breaks is broken into two sections divided by separator lines (Figure 6.16).

To apply any of the options found in Line And Page Breaks to one or more paragraphs, from the Format menu, choose Paragraph, select the Line And Page Breaks tab, and check or uncheck each option as necessary. As is the case with all other aspects of paragraph formatting, you can apply any of the commands found on this tab to one or more paragraphs.

- **Widow/Orphan Control**. This option is turned on by default to prevent occurrences of widows or orphans in the document. A *widow* is when the last line of a paragraph is left by itself at the top of a page. An *orphan* is the first line of a paragraph left by itself at the bottom of a page.

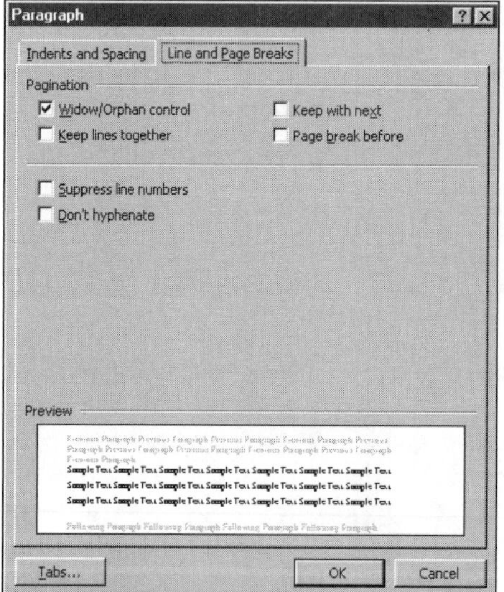

FIGURE 6.16

Select options to control the pagination of the document.

- **Keep With Next**. If you want to keep one or more paragraphs together on the same page, select this option. For example, if you want to prevent a heading and the paragraph that follows it from being separated by a page break, apply Keep With Next to the heading paragraph.

It is a very common mistake to select too many paragraphs when applying Keep With Next, especially if you are familiar with WordPerfect's Block Protect command. If Keep With Next is applied to consecutive paragraphs, there is a chance that the document will print incorrectly, and you could end up with large amounts of blank space on a page.

- **Keep Lines Together**. If you want to keep all of the lines in one paragraph together on the same page, select the appropriate paragraph and check this option.

Keep Lines Together applies to the lines in an individual paragraph only. Word does not have a feature to keep lines of separate paragraphs together.

- **Page Break Before**. When this option is selected, the paragraph is preceded by a hard page break.
- **Suppress Line Numbers**. Apply this option to one or more paragraphs that contain line numbering where numbering should not appear.
- **Don't Hyphenate**. Apply this option to paragraphs that you do not want to be automatically hyphenated. (To turn on automatic hyphenation, from the Tools menu, choose Language, Hyphenation and check the Automatically Hyphenate Document option.)

PARAGRAPH POSITION MARKS

Paragraph Position marks, as shown in Figure 6.17, indicate that Keep Lines Together, Keep With Next, Page Break Before, or Suppress Line Numbers have been turned on. You can double-click on this mark to access the Paragraph dialog box. To see the paragraph position marks onscreen, you must have Show/Hide turned on.

TABS

Tabs allow you to evenly align text to the left, right, center, decimal, or even a bar character at a specified tab stop. By default, tab stops are .5" apart. This means that each time you press Tab on the keyboard, the tab character advances one-half inch. To see the tab characters onscreen, you must have Show/Hide turned on.

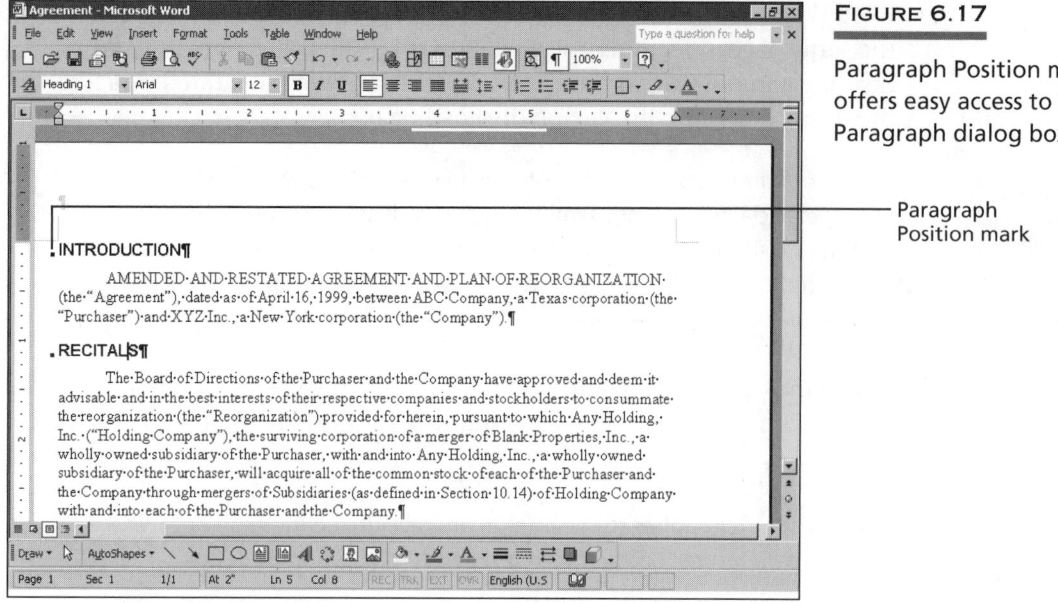

FIGURE 6.17

Paragraph Position mark offers easy access to the Paragraph dialog box.

TIP

If you still don't see the tab characters after turning on Show/Hide, from the Tools menu, choose Options, select the View tab, and check All in the Formatting marks section.

While the default tab settings can be useful in some cases, more likely than not you're going to want to set specific tab stops when working with legal documents. You can do this a couple of different ways—either from within the Tabs dialog box or using the horizontal ruler. The Tabs dialog box also allows you to set tab leaders.

NOTE

Tab leaders are characters, normally dotted or dashed lines, that fill the space used by the tab character. For example, a table of contents normally contains tab leaders between the text and the page number.

SETTING TABS USING THE PARAGRAPH DIALOG BOX

Word includes five types of tab stops:

- **Left.** Left text extends to the right from the tab stop.

- **Center**. Center text is centered on the tab stop.
- **Right**. Right text extends to the left from the tab stop until the tab's space is filled, and then the text extends to the right.
- **Decimal**. Used mostly with numbers—text before the decimal point extends to the left, and text after the decimal point extends to the right.
- **Bar**. Creates a separator line at the specified tab stop. The bar tab is useful when working with Asian languages.

SET TABS AND LEADERS USING THE TABS DIALOG BOX

1. Create a new document.
2. From the Format menu, choose Tabs. The dialog box shown in Figure 6.18 appears.
3. Type **2.5** in the Tab Stop Position, select Center from the Alignment section, choose 2 from the Leader section, and click Set.
4. Type **5.5** in the Tab Stop Position, choose Decimal from the Alignment section, choose 2 from the Leader section, and click Set. Click OK.
5. Type **John W. Smith**. Press Tab.
6. Type **212-555-1212**. Press Tab.
7. Type **$150.25** and press Enter.
8. Add more names, numbers, and dollar figures to the list.

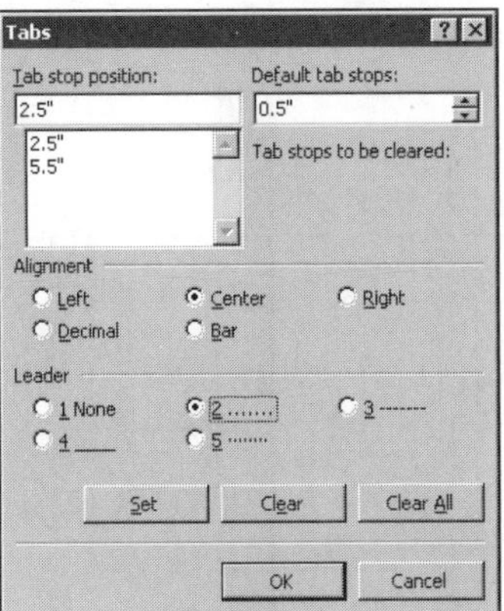

FIGURE 6.18

Create, view, and modify tabs in the Tabs dialog box.

NOTE

To remove tab stops that have been set, select the paragraph or paragraphs you wish to affect, go to the Tabs dialog box, and click Clear All. If you only want to remove a specific stop, then select it from the list and click Clear.

SETTING TABS USING THE HORIZONTAL RULER

You can use the horizontal ruler to quickly set tabs. The main difference between using the ruler and the Tabs dialog box is that you can't set tab leaders with the ruler.

Tab markers reside on the far-left end of the horizontal ruler. Each of the five available tab stops can be accessed by clicking the Tab Alignment box (Figure 6.19).

You can use the ruler to set tabs by selecting the appropriate tab and then clicking the spot on the horizontal ruler where you wish to set the tab.

NOTE

You can quickly set a tab on the ruler and bring up the Tab dialog box to add dot leaders by double-clicking on the ruler where you want to set the tab.

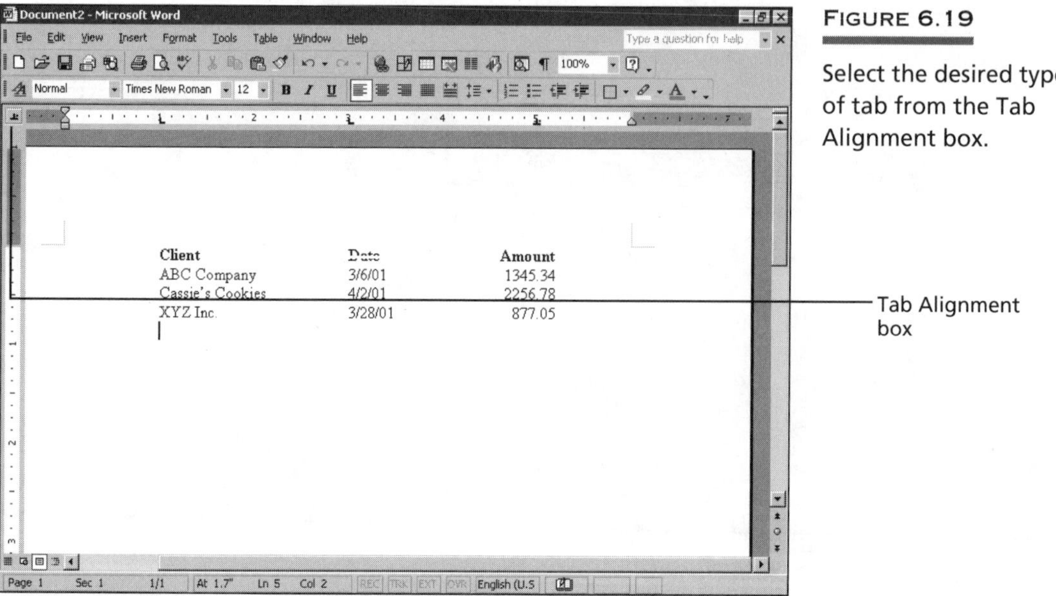

FIGURE 6.19

Select the desired type of tab from the Tab Alignment box.

A good example of using the ruler to set tabs might be for a signature block at the end of a letter or agreement. Rather than pressing the Tab key seven times to create the right amount of indented space, you can set a left tab at 3.5" and then create the signature block by pressing tab once.

SET TABS FOR A SIGNATURE BLOCK

1. Create a new document. Make sure the ruler is visible—if it's not, from the View menu, choose Ruler.
2. On the horizontal ruler, the Tab Alignment button should have the Left Tab marker showing (as in Figure 6.20). If not, click the Tab Alignment button until the left tab is shown.
3. Place your mouse pointer at 3.5" on the ruler and click to set the left tab.
4. Press Tab and type **Susan B. Anderson**. Press Enter.
5. Press Tab and type **Attorney At Law**. Press Enter.
6. Press Tab and type **Jones & Murphy, LLP**.

You can adjust a tab stop by clicking and dragging it to a new position on the

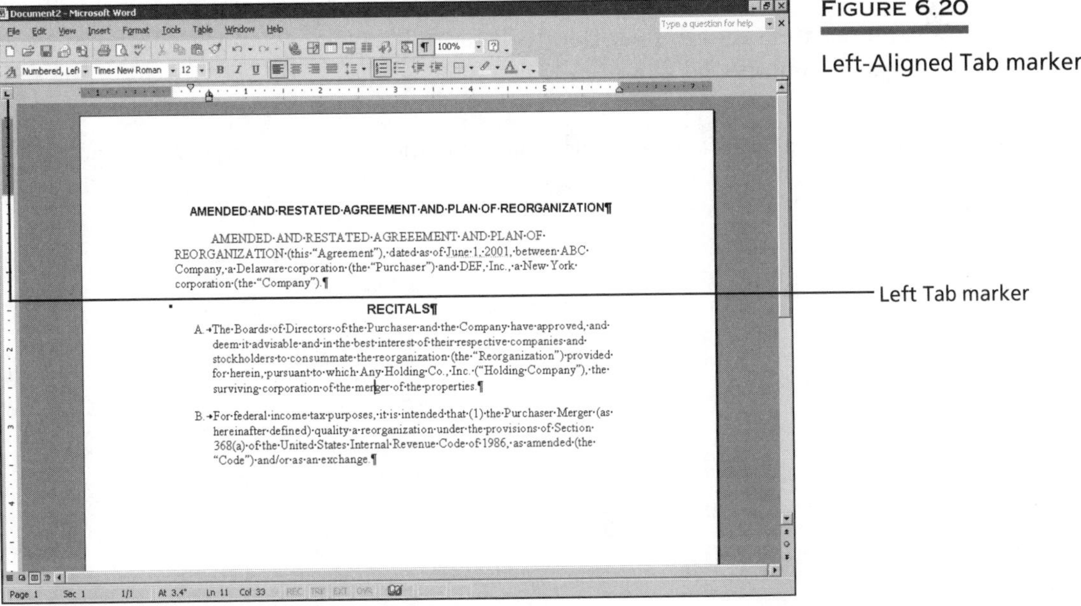

FIGURE 6.20

Left-Aligned Tab marker

ruler. To adjust the tab stop position for a single paragraph, click anywhere in the paragraph and then move the tab stop. To adjust multiple paragraphs, select them all simultaneously and then move the tab stop on the ruler.

To remove a tab stop, simply click and drag it off the ruler.

NOTE

If you select multiple paragraphs with different tab stops, the tab stops will appear grayed out on the horizontal ruler; however, you can still move or remove the tab.

CLICK AND TYPE

Introduced in Word 2000, the Click And Type feature makes it easy to start typing at any point in the document. This feature eliminates the need to press Enter multiple times to center text on a page, or press Tab to place text where you want at the rightmost portion of the page. With Click And Type, you position your cursor where you would like to type and just double-click. Word will insert the correct alignment, indents, tabs, and text wrapping as well as any paragraph marks needed to begin typing at the desired location.

This feature is especially helpful when trying to replicate the Flush Right command of WordPerfect. After typing the text on the left side of the page, use Click And Type to move the cursor to the right side of the page and insert the desired text.

The type of formatting that will be applied is visible from the type of Click And Type pointers that appear before you double-click. Table 6.1 illustrates the types of pointers that may appear when using Click And Type.

NOTE

The Click And Type feature is only available in the Print Layout and Web Layout views.

TABLE 6.1 CLICK AND TYPE POINTERS

POINTER	DESCRIPTION	RESULT
	Align Left	Creates a left-aligned paragraph with tab stop positioned as needed.
	Center	Creates a centered paragraph or inserts a Center tab.
	Align Right	Creates a right-aligned paragraph or inserts a Right tab at the right margin.
	Left Indent	Creates a First-line indent.
	Left Text Wrap	Inserts a text-wrapping break on the left of side of the object and sets the object's text wrapping to square.
	Right Text Wrap	Inserts a text-wrapping break on the right side of the object and sets the object's text wrapping to square.

NOTE

To ensure Click And Type is available, from the Tools menu, choose Options. In the Edit tab, select Enable Click And Type and click OK.

USE CLICK AND TYPE

1. Create a new document.
2. Type **Draft**.
3. Place your mouse pointer at the right margin adjacent to the text that you just typed.
4. Double-click to activate Click And Type.
5. Type **For Discussion Only**.

NOTE

Click And Type is not active outside of left and right indents or margins, in areas that have columns, bulleted or numbered lists, and with objects that are floating or contain top and bottom text wrapping.

REVEAL FORMATTING

In previous versions of Word you could press Shift+F1, click any text, and see a pop-up tip with paragraph formatting information about the text being examined. This was what Microsoft called Reveal Formatting. Word 2002 takes Reveal Formatting to a new level by displaying the Reveal Formatting Task Pane. The task pane displays the parts of the document (such as the header, footer, or paragraph) you happen to be working in and all of its formatting attributes. Since Word allows you to format paragraphs differently, the Reveal Formatting Task Pane will show the formatting specific to the paragraph your insertion point is placed in.

You can open the Reveal Formatting Task Pane shown in Figure 6.21 by pressing Shift+F1 and clicking the text you're interested in. Alternatively, from the Format menu, choose Reveal Formatting.

The Reveal Formatting Task Pane is divided into sections. The Paragraph section provides information related to paragraph formatting, such as alignment, indentation, outline level, and tab settings. You can click the hyperlink associated with each of the visible paragraph formats to quickly jump to the corresponding dialog box where you can make any necessary formatting changes.

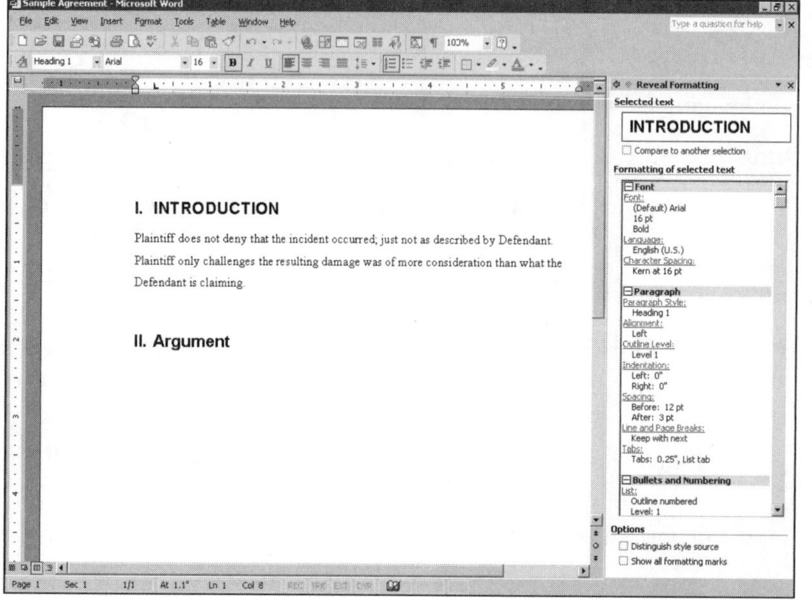

FIGURE 6.21

Discover and change formats in the Reveal Formatting Task Pane.

MAKE FORMATTING CHANGES IN THE REVEAL FORMATTING PANE

1. Create a new document.
2. From the Format menu, choose Reveal Formatting.
3. Type **OPINION** and press Enter.
4. Type **Based on the amounts that were reported by the estate, respondent assessed $100,000 in new taxes.** and press Enter.
5. Place your insertion point in the first paragraph. From the Reveal Formatting Task Pane, click the Alignment hyperlink under Paragraph—this will take you directly to the Paragraph dialog box.
6. From the drop-down list in the Alignment section, choose Centered. Click OK.
7. Select both paragraphs including the third empty paragraph mark.
8. From the Reveal Formatting Task Pane, click the Alignment hyperlink under Paragraph.
9. Change the Spacing After to 12 points. Click OK.
10. Notice that the Spacing format appears in the Paragraph section of the Reveal Formatting Task Pane.
11. Click the Close button on the Reveal Formatting Task Pane.

SUMMARY

It all comes back to those paragraph marks! This chapter has been packed full of all types of formats that you can apply to your paragraphs. All this formatting is stored in the paragraph marks. Keep this in mind when using Delete, Cut, Copy, or Paste. If you want to cut or copy text with the formatting intact, select the paragraph mark along with the text. If you just want the text and not the paragraph formatting, do not select the paragraph mark. Keep Show/Hide turned on while you work to be aware of the paragraph marks.

TROUBLESHOOTING PARAGRAPH FORMATTING

How can I prevent my signature block from splitting across pages?

Remember that each line is actually its own separate paragraph. Select each paragraph in the signature block and apply Keep With Next. If the signature block is created with soft breaks (Shift+Enter), apply Keep Lines Together instead of Keep With Next.

I just received a single-spaced document from a client, and every time I add a new paragraph and press Enter, it ends up two spaces below the preceding paragraph. What should I do?

The line spacing within the document is not actually becoming double-spaced when you press Enter. The user on the other end applied Space After to the paragraphs you're working with, so you don't have to press Enter twice to create the necessary space between paragraphs.

When I open the Document Map, I only see text associated with the headings in my document—is there any way to include other parts of the document in that view?

Yes—select the paragraph or paragraphs that you also want to be available in the Document Map. From the Format menu, choose Paragraph and select the Indents And Spacing tab. Click the drop-down arrow at the end of the Outline Level list box and choose the appropriate level for that text. When you open Document Map, the selected paragraphs will be viewable.

In the middle of my document, there is an odd break that leaves a large white space on one page. When I look at it in Normal view, it looks like a page break, but I cannot delete it.

It sounds like Page Break Before has been turned on in a paragraph. To check this, click in the paragraph directly below the break. From the Format menu, choose Paragraph. On the Line And Page Breaks tab, uncheck Page Break Before.

The text in a couple of paragraphs seems to have the top of the letters cut off.

Check the line spacing in the Paragraph dialog box. Change the setting from Exactly to Single line spacing.

When my document prints, the text seems to only print on half the page, causing a lot of wasted space.

The Keep With Next feature has probably been applied to multiple paragraphs. Look for Paragraph Position marks on paragraphs. If these appear, select the offending paragraphs and turn off Keep With Next.

Chapter 7

Formatting a Document

In This Chapter

- Page setup
- Margins
- Page and section breaks
- Headers and footers
- Print Preview feature
- Printing the document

As anyone can testify who has had a pleading or brief rejected by a court because it did not comply with the court mandated formatting requirements, document formatting is more than adding "frills" to the look of a document. As a general rule, Word users within law firms need to know more about document formatting than any other Word user. One might easily say that law firms push Word features to the extreme. In no place is this more evident than in lengthy legal documents. Even documents such as contracts and agreements, which are not necessarily filed with the court, require complex formatting. Therefore, understanding how Word handles items such as margins, page orientation, paper size, and line and page numbering is critical for the legal user.

PAGE SETUP

Margins, paper size, page orientation, and line numbering are just a few of the items included in the overall format of a document. Word makes it easy to set up documents with the Page Setup dialog box—a one-stop shop, if you will, for document formatting.

The Page Setup dialog box, which can be accessed by choosing Page Setup from the File menu, is divided into three tabbed sections—Margins, Paper, and Layout—each containing a number of specific options that will determine how the document looks, flows, and prints. This section looks at each of the tabs found in the Page Setup dialog box, starting with the Margins tab shown in Figure 7.1.

MARGINS TAB

The Margins tab is actually made up of four distinct sections—Margins, Orientation, Pages, and Preview.

MARGINS

Page margins are the white space between the text and edges of a document. Every document contains top, bottom, left, and right margins. The first tab found under the Page Setup dialog box is where the margins are set for the document.

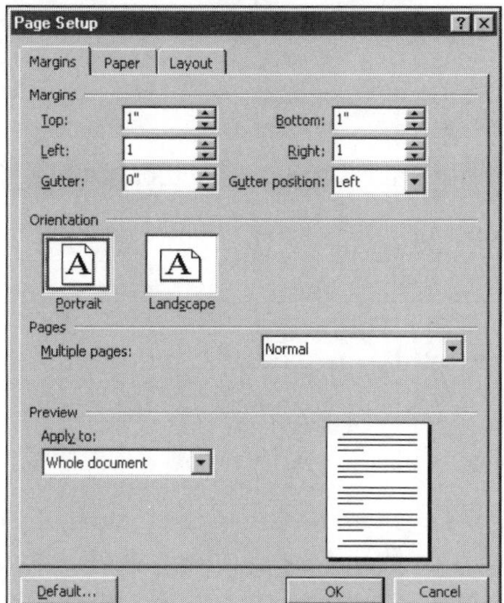

FIGURE 7.1

Page Setup provides margin, page orientation, and select multiple page setting options. Look at the preview as you make selections.

By default, Word sets the top and bottom margins at 1" while the left and right margins are set to 1.25". Most legal documents require that all four margins be evenly set at 1". The margins can be increased or decreased by either typing the desired margin size directly into the box next to the specific margin or by clicking the up or down spinners to achieve the desired result. You probably won't want to change this setting each time you create a new document—and you don't have to. Word allows you to change the default margin size.

IMPROVED FEATURE

In previous versions of Word, the Page Setup dialog box contained four tabs: Margins, Paper Size, Paper Source, and Layout. Word 2002 consolidated the dialog box to just three tabs: Margins, Paper, and Layout. If an East Asian language is enabled, a fourth tab, Document Grid, is displayed with these options: Text Flow, Grid, Characters, Lines, Preview, Drawing Grid, Set Font, and Default.

CHANGE MARGINS TO 1"

1. Create a new document.
2. From the File menu, choose Page Setup and select the Margins tab.
3. Click the downward-pointing spinner in the Left box until it reaches 1". Do the same thing for the Right box.

Click Default and then click Yes to set the margins to 1" for all future documents.

If you are changing the margin settings somewhere in the middle of a document, be careful not to choose the This Point Forward option from the Apply To drop-down list in the Preview section unless you are comfortable working with section breaks. If you are not at the beginning of a document, Word automatically creates a Next Page section break when you choose This Point Forward. Section breaks are covered later in this chapter.

In the Margins section, a top or left gutter margin can be set for documents requiring additional margin space.

A *gutter margin* adds space to the top or left side of a document. Gutter margins are used predominantly with reports or other bound documents. The gutter margin includes extra space to help make certain that none of the text is hidden when the document is bound.

CHANGING MARGINS FROM THE RULER

The margin settings for a document can also be modified by using the horizontal and vertical rulers. To do so, switch to Print Layout view (make sure the rulers are visible), place your mouse pointer where the gray and white margin areas meet on the ruler (the pointer turns into a double-sided arrow), and drag the margin to the setting, as shown in Figure 7.2. Hold the Alt key as you drag the margin to show the measurements on the ruler.

ORIENTATION

The next section on the Margins tab, Orientation, sets the page orientation for a document. Most legal documents are set to Portrait orientation by default—that is, with the long side vertical—but there may be times when you are working with a wide table or report that requires the extra width that Landscape

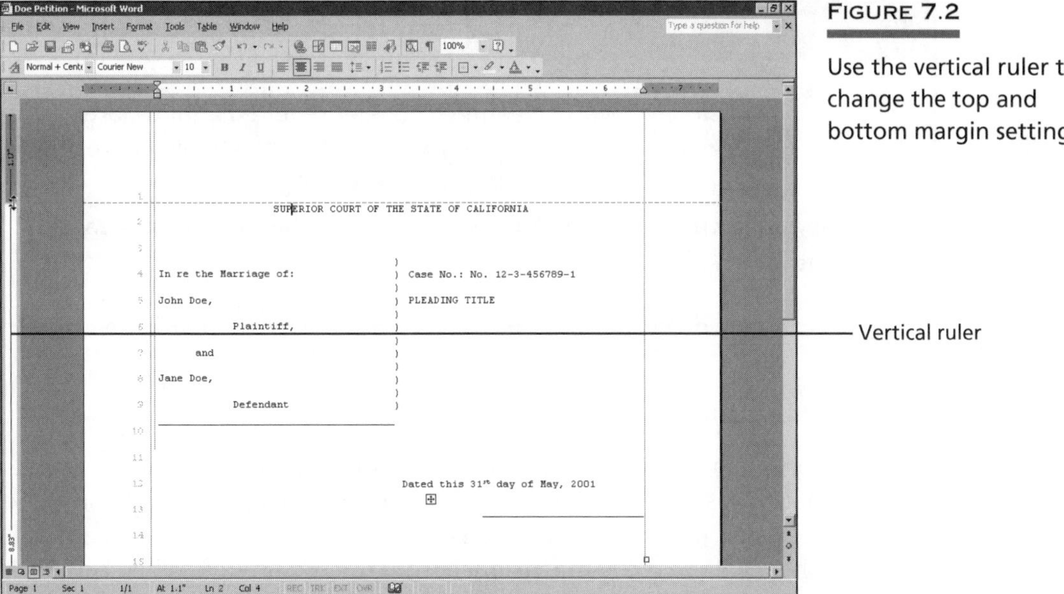

FIGURE 7.2

Use the vertical ruler to change the top and bottom margin settings.

orientation provides. Click either option to set the page orientation for the document or a section of the document.

PAGES

The Pages section on the Margins tab contains a drop-down list of page setup options that you can choose from depending on the type of document needed. Each option in the Multiple Pages drop-down list will affect the layout of your document differently.

- **Normal**. Selected by default, this is the normal page layout used for most legal documents.
- **Mirror Margins**. Creates margins on the left and right page that mirror each other with equal margins. Used for double-sided documents such as books or magazines.
- **2 Pages Per Sheet**. Prints two pages on one sheet of paper. This option is useful for creating folded place cards or handouts.
- **Book Fold**. Use this option to create a folded booklet. Word prints two pages on one side of the paper and automatically sets the page orientation to landscape. When selecting this option, you can choose the amount of pages to print per booklet in the Sheets Per Booklet drop-down list.

> **CREATING BOOKLETS**
>
> In previous versions of Word, creating a booklet required a third-party solution or a lot of creative formatting and printing. The Book Fold option in Word 2002 makes this previously difficult task easier. Just create your document as usual and select Book Fold when you are ready to print.

MIRROR MARGINS

Another type of margin, commonly used with double-sided documents such as books or magazines, is the mirror margin. Mirror margins are set up to have the margins on the left page mirror those on the right page, so that the text on both sides of a sheet will be the same distance from the outer edge. When selected, the Page Setup dialog box shows Inside and Outside margins in place of left and right margins. You can create Mirror Margins from the Page Setup dialog box by clicking the drop-down arrow at the end of Multiple pages and choosing Mirror Margins from the list. Once this option has been set, you can choose the appropriate top, bottom, inside, and outside Mirror Margin settings in the Margins section, as shown in Figure 7.3.

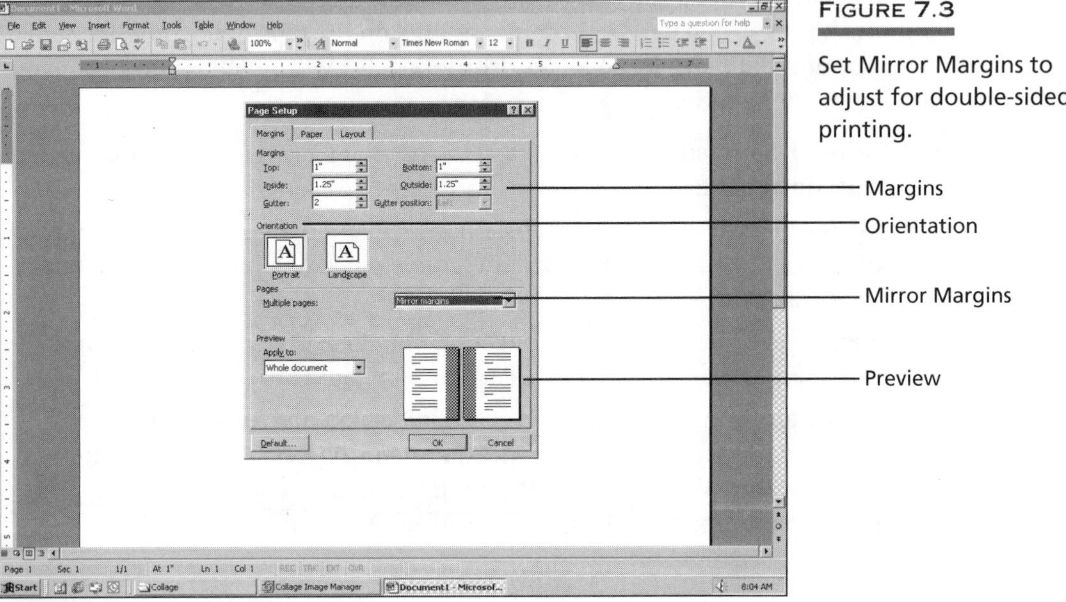

FIGURE 7.3

Set Mirror Margins to adjust for double-sided printing.

In Print Preview, mirror margins are shown as a turquoise "binding" connecting mirrored pages.

PREVIEW

The Preview section on the Margins tab contains a pane that visually reflects the options selected from the Page Setup dialog box. The Apply To drop-down list has two options, Whole Document and This Point Forward.

- **Whole Document**. Any changes you make in the Page Setup dialog box will affect the entire document.
- **This Point Forward**. Changes will only affect the rest of the document, starting with the place where the insertion point is currently located. Be careful; choosing this option in the middle of a document can create a section break, which may lead to unintended consequences.

PAPER TAB

The Paper tab contains several options for choosing paper type, size, and even paper source for printers with more than one tray. Print options can also be set from this location, as shown in Figure 7.4.

Click the Paper Size drop-down arrow to view a list of different types of paper, including A4, Legal, Executive, and more—with the default being Letter (that is, 8.5"x11") in the U.S. English version of Word. The Width and Height boxes

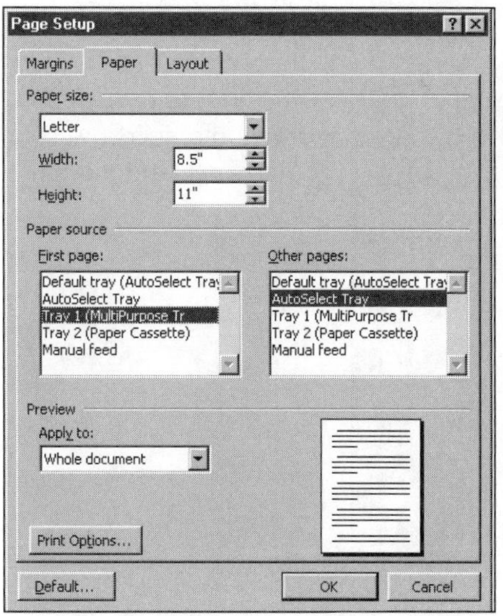

FIGURE 7.4

Select the Paper Size and Paper Source. Click the Print Options button for more options.

adjust automatically depending on the type of paper selected from the list. Custom paper type can even be created by selecting Custom Size from the list and setting the Width and Height to the necessary specifications.

Paper Source determines where specific pages of a document will print from for printers with more than one tray. For example, many firms print the first page of a letter on preprinted letterhead with the firm logo and the remaining pages of the letter on plain bond paper. When the firm letter template is created, First Page is set to the tray containing the letterhead and the Other Pages field is set to the tray containing the plain paper.

Once again, it is easy to see how your document will look before it is printed since the Preview section changes along with the options selected.

Click the Default button to retain the changes made in the Page Setup dialog box for future documents.

PRINT OPTIONS

When clicked, the Print Options button opens up a separate dialog box that allows you to choose specific options related to the printed document. Figure 7.5 shows the available print options.

You'll get a closer look at each of the print options later in the chapter as part of the discussion on printing documents.

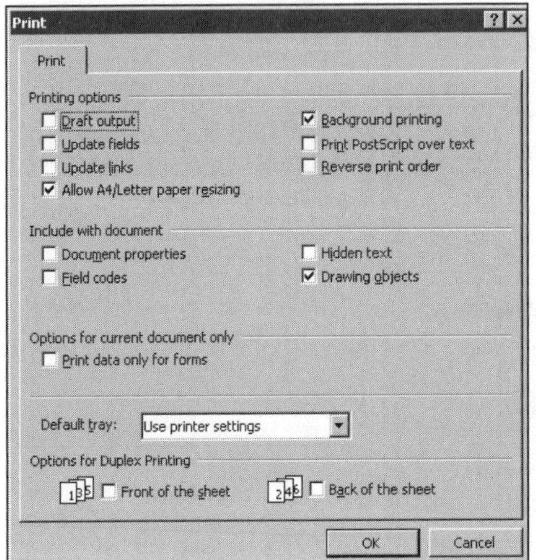

FIGURE 7.5

Choose what to print by selecting items such as drawing objects, comments, and hidden text.

LAYOUT TAB

The Layout tab contains options for different types of breaks, headers and footers, vertical alignment, line numbering, and borders, as shown in Figure 7.6. Some of the features found in this section of the Page Setup dialog box will be discussed in greater detail later in the chapter—for the time being, here is a brief introduction to each selection.

SECTION

Section indicates the type of section break for Word to use. This is a fairly advanced Word feature, which is discussed in great detail in the "Sections and the Word Document" section of this chapter—and again throughout the book.

HEADERS AND FOOTERS

The Headers And Footers section contains options for manipulating and creating different types of headers and footers of the document. It also allows you to specify how far the header and footer print from the edge of the paper. These features are discussed in greater detail in the "Using Headers and Footers" section of this chapter.

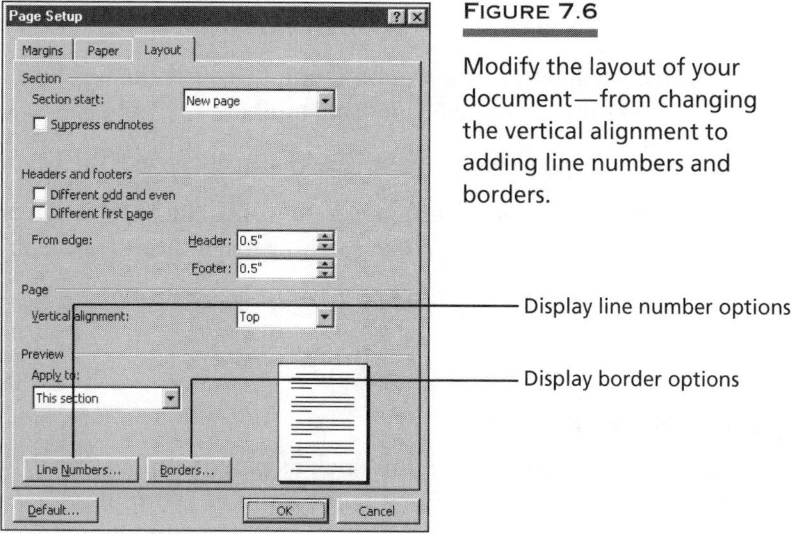

FIGURE 7.6

Modify the layout of your document—from changing the vertical alignment to adding line numbers and borders.

PAGE

The Vertical Alignment drop-down list contains different options for positioning text vertically on the page. This feature is most useful when you need to create a centered title page.

- **Top**. Positions text at the top of the page so text flows from top to bottom. This is the default setting for legal documents.
- **Center**. Centers text vertically on the page. This is often used with title pages.
- **Justified**. Justifies text vertically between the top and bottom margins.
- **Bottom**. Positions text at the bottom of the page.

NOTE

If the Vertical Alignment is set to Bottom or Center, Word actually uses the header to create the vertical white space between the body of the text and the top of the page.

CREATE A TITLE PAGE BY SETTING THE VERTICAL ALIGNMENT

1. Create a new document. Turn on Show/Hide from the Standard toolbar and switch to Print Layout view.
2. Type **United States District Court** and press Enter.
3. Type **No. D93-231R** and press Enter.
4. Type **Western District of Washington**.
5. Select each paragraph and horizontally center the text by clicking the Center button on the Formatting toolbar.
6. From the File menu, choose Page Setup and select the Layout tab.
7. From the Vertical Alignment section, click the drop-down arrow and choose Center. Figure 7.7 shows how to center text vertically.
8. Click OK. Notice how the text is centered vertically.

LINE NUMBERING

Certain types of legal documents, such as patent applications, may require line numbering, depending on filing requirements. Word provides an easy-to-use dialog box for times when you need to apply line numbering to a document.

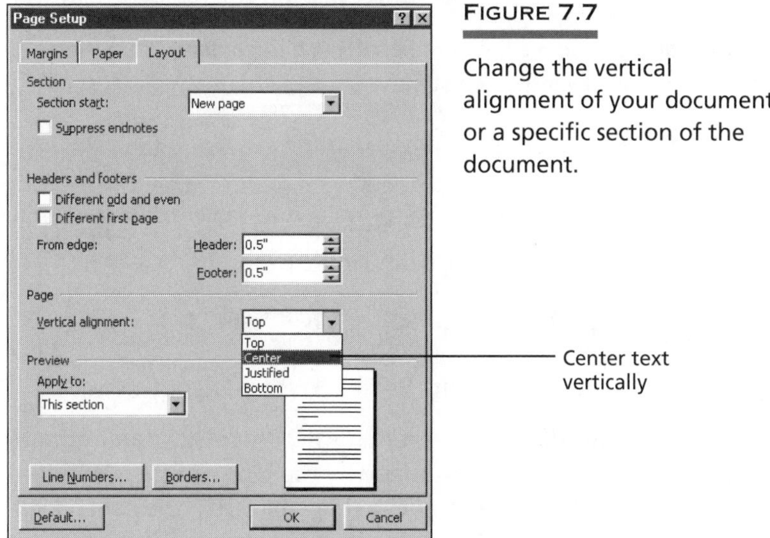

FIGURE 7.7

Change the vertical alignment of your document or a specific section of the document.

Select Line Numbers from the bottom left portion of the Layout tab and choose the appropriate options for your document, as shown in Figure 7.8.

NOTE

This feature is not meant to be used for numbered pleading paper, as required by certain courts such as in California. Pleading paper requires a set number of lines per page and is best accomplished by setting up a template with the preset line numbers stored in the header layer. See Chapter 10, "Templates," for a more detailed explanation.

The Line Numbers dialog box contains a series of options, including where to start numbering, distance from text, what intervals to count by, and whether or not numbering should be continuous or restarted at each new page or section. Line numbers will appear in the left margin.

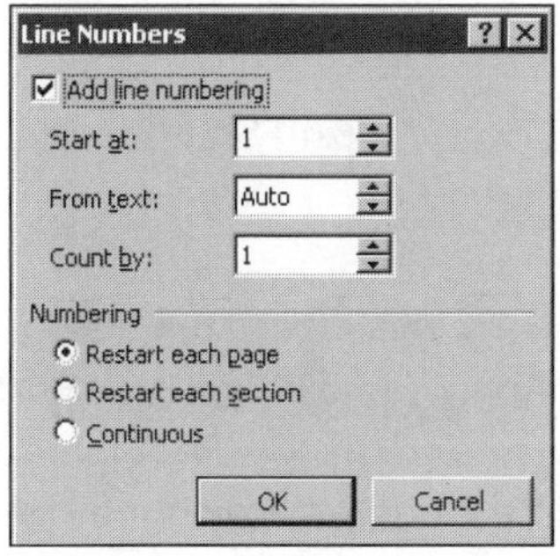

FIGURE 7.8

Many patent applications require line numbers. These line numbers are used as a reference to the page and exact line location of text discussed.

You can add or remove line numbers from a document at any time. To view line numbering, however, you must be in Print Layout view.

Line numbering will not display or print next to tables or floating graphics.

ADD LINE NUMBERS TO A DOCUMENT

1. Create a new document. Switch to Print Layout view.
2. Type **Plaintiffs also assert that ABC 9A.45.320 denies them equal protection of the law as guaranteed by the United States Constitution. As for the injunctive relief requested by plaintiffs, the court declines to enter an injunction barring defendants from enforcing ABC 9A.45.320.**
3. From the File menu, choose Page Setup, select the Layout tab, and click Line Numbers.
4. Check the Add Line Numbering box.
5. From the Numbering section, select Continuous.
6. Click OK twice. The line numbers should appear in the margin to the left of the text.
7. Place your insertion point anywhere in the paragraph. From the Formatting toolbar, click the Line Spacing button and choose 2.0.

Use Count By from the Line Numbers dialog box to count lines at specific intervals. For example, set Count By at 5 to show line numbers 5, 10, 15, and so on. (Patent application line numbers often appear in intervals of 5.)

BORDERS

The Borders button is a shortcut to the Borders And Shading dialog box shown in Figure 7.9.

If the document has been divided into sections, the Page Setup dialog box will reflect this by showing This Section in the Apply To field. The Page Border dialog box does not change automatically. Be sure to change the Apply To field so as to prevent the border from appearing in the entire document by mistake.

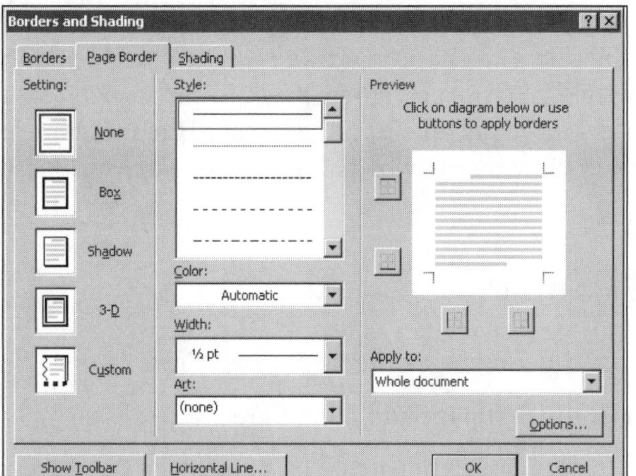

FIGURE 7.9

Apply a customized border to the document or to a section in the document.

PAGE BREAKS

Most people with word processing experience are familiar with the term *page break*. Page breaks occur most of the time without any user intervention or awareness whatsoever. Word automatically creates a page break as text reaches the end of one page and flows onto the next. This is called a *soft* page break—represented in Normal view by a continuous dotted line, as shown in Figure 7.10.

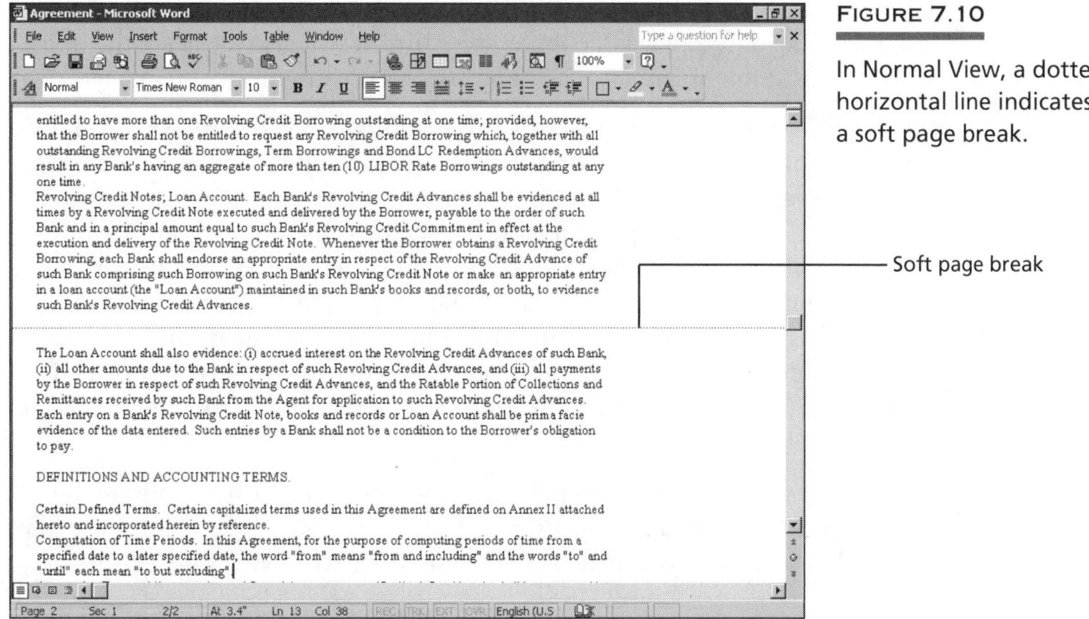

FIGURE 7.10

In Normal View, a dotted horizontal line indicates a soft page break.

There may be times when a logical part of a document ends in the middle of a page, such as the end of a chapter, a title page or a table of contents, and the text that follows needs to start on a new page. In cases such as these, you create or insert what is known as a *hard* page break. Hard page breaks are represented in Normal view by the words *Page Break* surrounded by continuous dotted lines.

CREATE A HARD PAGE BREAK

1. Create a new document. Switch to Normal view.
2. Type **This is my first page** and press Enter.
3. From the Insert menu, choose Break, select Page Break from the list that appears, and click OK.
4. On the second page, type **This is my second page** and press Enter.
5. Press Ctrl+Enter to create a hard page break. This takes you to a third page.
6. Switch to Print Layout view and scroll up to the first page.

SECTIONS AND THE WORD DOCUMENT

To grasp the concept of section breaks, you have to understand how Word defines a document. This part of the chapter will not only help solidify your understanding of the Word document structure, it will also illustrate the different types of section breaks you can apply to your documents.

Word treats every document as a series of sections. Each section in a Word document can have its own page orientation, margin settings, columns, headers and footers, and page numbers. For example, you may need to create a document that contains a title page, a table of contents, the body of the document, and an exhibits section. You obviously would not want page numbering on the title page, but you might want lowercase Roman numerals for the table of contents. Furthermore, you might want Arabic page numbering for the body of the document and a combination of numbers and lettering for the exhibits section. To satisfy the requirements of the document in question, you would need to create several different sections.

When you first create a document, it has only one section. Every time you insert a section break, Word adds another section to the document. The status bar shows what section of the document you are in at any given time, as shown in Figure 7.11.

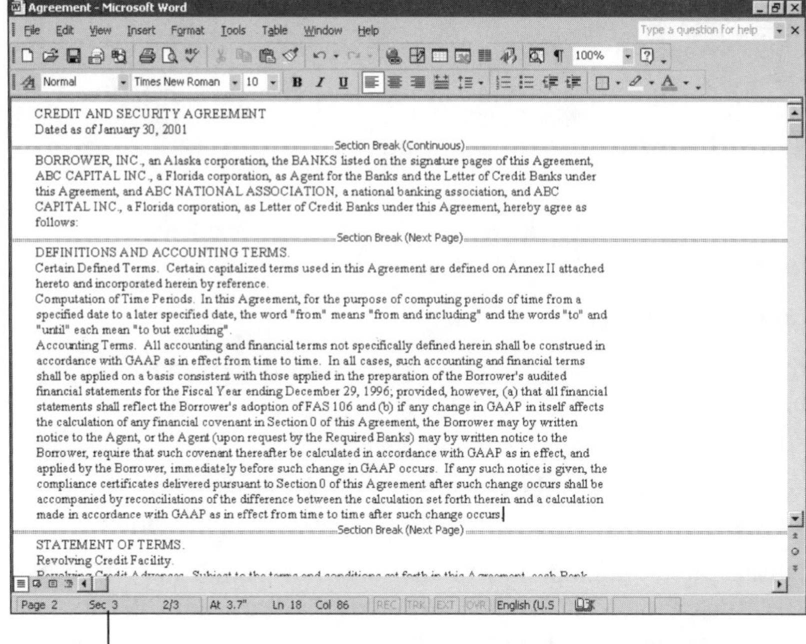

FIGURE 7.11

In Normal view, section breaks appear across the page as double horizontal lines. The status bar lists the section where the insertion point is currently located.

TYPES OF SECTION BREAKS

Word contains four types of section breaks covering the many needs for section formatting.

- **Next Page**. Inserts a section break that starts on a new page. This break appears in Normal view as double-dotted lines with the words *Section Break (Next Page)*. This type of break is commonly used in complex legal documents that require a separate section for different parts of the document, such as title page, table of contents, document main body, and exhibits.
- **Continuous**. Creates a section break without moving text to another page, so you can have multiple sections on the same page. This break is often used to create newspaper-style columns in the middle of a page. Appears in Normal view as double-dotted lines with the words *Section Break (Continuous)*.
- **Even page**. Creates a section break at the beginning of the next even-numbered page in a document. Appears in Normal view as double-dotted lines with the words *Section Break (Even Page)*.
- **Odd page**. Creates a section break at the beginning of the next odd-numbered page. This could be used in a bound document where all the chapter titles begin on an odd-numbered page. Appears in Normal view as a double-dotted line with the words *Section Break (Odd Page)*.

CREATE SECTION BREAKS FOR LEGAL DOCUMENTS

1. Create a new document. Switch to Normal view. Turn on Show/Hide.
2. Type **United States Court of Appeals Ninth Circuit**. Press Ctrl+E to center the text and press Enter.
3. From the Insert menu, choose Break and then select Next Page from the list of break types that appear. Click OK.
4. Type **Table of Contents** and press Enter.
5. From the Insert menu, choose Break and then select Next Page from the list of break types that appear. Click OK.
6. Type **The eighth article of this Treaty shall be in force for five years from the date of the exchange of the ratifications, and afterwards until one or the other Party shall signify a wish to terminate it.** and press Enter.
7. You've just created a document with three sections—a title page, a table of contents, and a main body. Scroll up and down through the document and observe how the status bar changes.

Use the status bar to identify which section of the document you are working in. It will say Sec 1, Sec 2, etc. , next to the page number of the document.

8. Switch to Print Layout view.
9. Press Ctrl+Home to move your insertion point to the top of the document.
10. From the File menu, choose Page Setup. Select the Layout tab, click the drop-down arrow next to Vertical Alignment, and choose Center. In the Apply To drop-down list, select This Section and click OK.
11. Save this exercise as **Practice Sections** for use in the section titled "Using Headers and Footers."

To remove or delete a section break, place your insertion point on the break itself and press the Delete key.

Be careful when deleting section breaks. The section containing the deleted break will inherit all the section formatting from the section *below*—not the one above.

OTHER BREAKS

A Text Wrapping break controls the way text wraps around a graphic or drawing object. A Column break forces the beginning of a new column in those sections that contain columns.

USING HEADERS AND FOOTERS

Headers and footers are located at the top and bottom of every document and, depending on the requirements of the document, contain information such as graphics, page numbers, chapter title, document number, or date that repeats on every page. The information in headers and footers can vary from section to section and can be set up differently for odd and even pages.

You must be in Print Layout view to enter information or edit a header or footer. Select Header And Footer from the View menu. When working in the header or footer, the text layer of the document is grayed out.

Notice that the headers and footers both contain two preset tab markers—a Center tab stop at 3" and a Right tab stop at 6". These two tab positions align text to allow three different types of information to appear on the same line in the header or footer. For example, you may have the document path flush left, page number centered, and date on the right.

NOTE

If the left and right margins are changed from the default 1.25", these default tab positions will need to be adjusted accordingly. The tabs are part of the Header and Footer style. For more information, see Chapter 9, "Styles."

HEADER AND FOOTER TOOLBAR

When you access the header or footer, the Header And Footer toolbar appears, as shown in Figure 7.12. The toolbar contains a number of commands that allow you to place specific information within the header or footer in one or more sections of a document.

The following list provides an explanation of each button on the Header And Footer toolbar, moving from left to right.

- **Insert AutoText**. Contains a number of AutoText entries that can be placed into either the header or footer. Some of the information contained in the AutoText entries are fields that automatically update, such as date and filename.
- **Insert Page Number**. Inserts the current page number as a field.

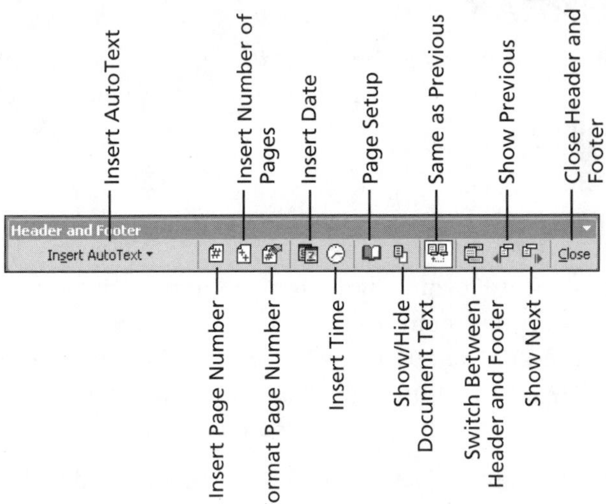

FIGURE 7.12

Insert page numbers, date and time, and more using the Header And Footer toolbar.

- **Insert Number Of Pages**. Inserts the total number of pages in the document as a field.
- **Format Page Number**. Opens up a dialog box that allows you to choose formatting options for page numbers, such as Roman and Arabic.
- **Insert Date**. Inserts the current date as an updating field.
- **Insert Time**. Inserts the current time as an updating field.
- **Page Setup**. Displays the Layout tab of the Page Setup dialog box. Make choices such as header and footer distance from the edge of the page, different first page, and more.
- **Show/Hide Document Text**. Works as a toggle to either show or hide the text of the document while working in the header and footer layer.
- **Same As Previous**. Allows you to either keep or break the link between headers and footers in different sections.
- **Switch Between Header And Footer**. Toggles between the header and footer of the document.
- **Show Previous**. Moves to the previous header or footer in the document.
- **Show Next**. Moves to the next header or footer in the document.

NOTE

The Show Previous and Show Next buttons do not necessarily move to the previous or next section in a document. Depending on the setup of the document, the button could move from a section's first page header to the same section header when a different first page option is selected, or from an odd to even header when that option is selected.

- **Close.** Closes the Header And Footer toolbar and returns to the document.

CREATE A HEADER AND FOOTER

1. Create a new document. Turn on Show/Hide.
2. Type **Title Page**, press Enter, and then press Ctrl+Enter to insert a hard page break.
3. Type **This is the first page of the document**, press Enter, then press Ctrl+Enter to insert a hard page break.
4. Type **This is the second page of the document**.
5. Place your insertion point back at the beginning of the document (Ctrl+Home) and, from the View menu, choose Header And Footer. You are in the header of the document.
6. Press the Tab key twice to move the insertion point to the right tab mark.
7. Type **DRAFT**.
8. From the Header And Footer toolbar, click Switch Between Header And Footer to move to the footer. Click Insert AutoText and choose Filename And Path from the menu.
9. Press the Tab key to move to the center tab.
10. From the Header And Footer toolbar, click Insert Page Number (the first button to the right of AutoText).
11. Click Close on the Header And Footer toolbar to return to the text layer of the document.
12. Scroll down through the document. Notice that the header and footer information shows on every page.
13. Leave this document open for the next exercise.

There is also a Page Number command available from the Insert menu. When inserted through the menu, the page number is placed in a frame, which can cause frustration if the page number needs to be modified in any way. Using the Insert Page Number button on the Header And Footer toolbar is the preferred method for inserting page numbers.

PAGE SETUP

When selected, the Page Setup button on the Header And Footer toolbar opens the Layout tab of the Page Setup dialog box. From here you can make a number of decisions related to the formatting of the header and footer in your document, as shown in Figure 7.13.

Choose Different Odd And Even for a document such as a book or manuscript that requires different headers and footers for odd- and even-numbered pages. For example, the title of this book appears on all the even pages while the chapter number and title appear on the odd pages.

You can increase or decrease the distance of the header or footer from the edge of the page by using the spinners next to the Header or Footer box. You can also type a number directly into the box.

The From Edge measurements for the header and footer set the boundary of where the header should start and where the footer should end in relation to the edge of the page. The size of the header and footer is controlled by the contents of each.

Some printers may not print the text or graphics contained in the header or footer if the distance from the edge of the page is less than their allowable printing area. Many printers allow for .3" as the minimum gap—but you can't count on that. If you want to maximize the space used on a page, check your printer's configuration and requirements.

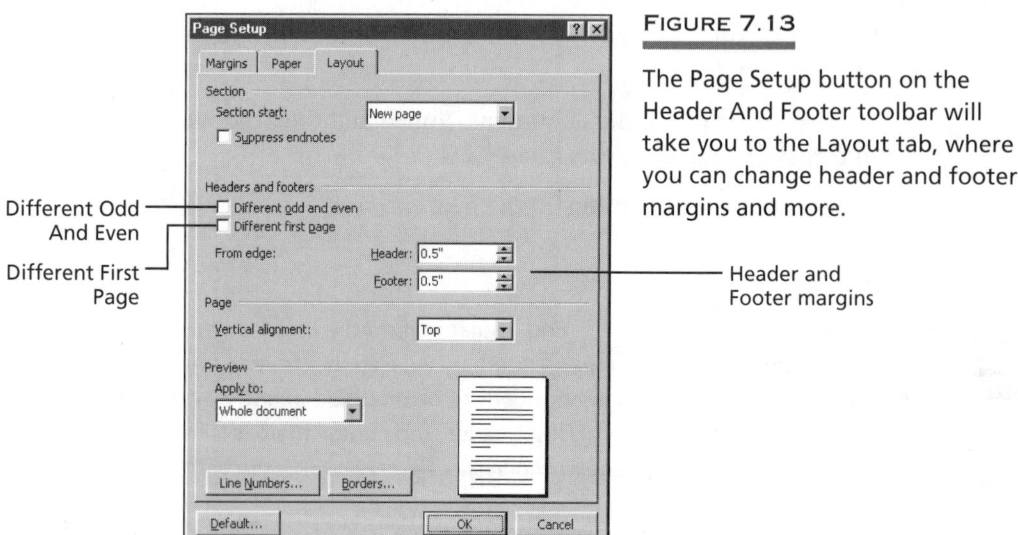

FIGURE 7.13

The Page Setup button on the Header And Footer toolbar will take you to the Layout tab, where you can change header and footer margins and more.

DIFFERENT FIRST PAGE

Many documents eliminate all header and footer information, including page numbering, on the first page. Select Different First Page when you don't want any of the header or footer information to appear on the first page of a document. Or you can select Different First Page to format the header or footer on the first page of the section differently from the rest of the section. This option is commonly used when setting up letter templates so that the first page header contains the firm's electronic letterhead, and subsequent page headers contain only the addressee name, date, and page number information.

The next exercise turns off the page number for the title page.

EXPERIMENT WITH DIFFERENT FIRST PAGE

1. The document from the previous exercise should still be open. Open or re-create it, if necessary.
2. Press Ctrl+Home to position the insertion point at the beginning of the document.
3. Double-click on the word *Draft* in the header area. The Header And Footer toolbar appears.

Double-clicking on text in the header or footer will open the Header And Footer layer. When in the header and footer, double-click on the text layer to return to the text.

4. Click Page Setup on the Header And Footer toolbar.
5. Select Different First Page. Click OK.
6. Notice the header now says First Page Header—Section 1.
7. Click Close on the Header And Footer toolbar. Notice the first page does not have any information in the header and footer, but the rest of the document still contains the information from the previous exercise.

If the document did not originate with you, there is a chance that when you select Different First Page, the information in the header or footer will not disappear. If this should happen and the footer or header says First Page Header or First Page Footer, you can delete the undesired text.

CREATING HEADERS AND FOOTERS IN A MULTI-SECTION DOCUMENT

Now that you've had the chance to work with headers and footers in a document that contains only one section, it's time to move on to something a bit more complex—headers and footers in a multi-section document. Some legal documents such as loan agreements often require different types of page numbering—the table of contents typically contains lowercase Roman numerals, the main body Arabic, and the exhibits section a combination of letters and numbers, such as A-1.

Word can individually format the header and footer for each section of a document. This is a powerful feature. For example, rather than having to manually type different styles of page numbers throughout a document, you can create sections and then insert automatic page numbering into the header or footer of each section.

As discussed earlier in this chapter, section breaks divide the document so you can format different areas of a document individually, including their headers and footers. But even when a document is divided into sections, Same As Previous is turned on by default. This feature links one section to the next. It is important to turn off Same As Previous in each section so you can format the section you are in without affecting previous sections.

FORMATTING HEADERS AND FOOTERS IN A MULTI-SECTION DOCUMENT

1. Open the exercise document titled Practice Sections. Position your cursor at the beginning of the document.
2. From the View menu, choose Header And Footer.
3. From the Header And Footer toolbar, click Switch Between Header And Footer. You should see Footer—Section 1.
4. Click Show Next to move to Footer—Section 2. This is the Table of Contents section of the document.
5. Remove the link between the Section 1 and Section 2 footer by clicking Same As Previous on the Header And Footer toolbar.

NOTE

The Same As Previous button works as a toggle. Once it has been turned off, if the button is clicked again, you will be asked if you want to delete the current header/footer and replace it with the previous one.

6. Press Tab to move to the center of the footer.
7. Click the Format Page Number button and click the drop-down arrow for Number Format, as shown in Figure 7.14.
8. From the drop-down list, select the lowercase Roman numerals (i, ii, iii).
9. From the Page Numbering section of the dialog box, select Start At and choose i. Click OK.

Each section should be set to start at 1 (in whatever format); otherwise the page numbering will continue from the preceding section, even though Same As Previous has been turned off.

10. From the Header And Footer toolbar, click Insert Page Number and then click Show Next to move to the Section 3 footer.
11. From the Header And Footer toolbar, click Same As Previous to break the link between the Section 2 and Section 3 footer, and then click Format Page Number.
12. Confirm the Number Format is Arabic numbering (1, 2, 3) and choose Start At 1 from the Page Numbering section of the dialog box.
13. Close the Header And Footer toolbar. Switch to Print Layout view. Scroll down through the document to see how each section is numbered correctly.

If you don't want the first page number in the main body of the document to appear, open the Header And Footer, move to the main body's section, click Page Setup, and choose Different First Page.

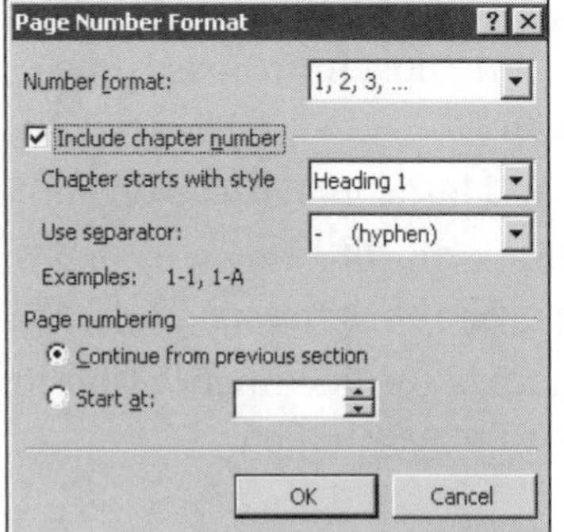

FIGURE 7.14

You can change the number format and have it start at a specific number.

PRINT PREVIEW

Print Preview is a feature in Word that allows you to see what your document will look like on the printed page before you actually send it to the printer. This can save you the time and trouble of having to reprint your document repeatedly to get it just right. With Print Preview, you can make any necessary edits before sending the final copy off—saving both you and your colleagues paper and time.

From the Standard toolbar, click Print Preview to switch to that view or, from the File menu, choose Print Preview.

The Print Preview window, shown in Figure 7.15, actually contains a separate Print Preview toolbar that is docked directly below the menu bar, replacing the Standard and Formatting toolbars. The commands on this toolbar allow you to print, view, and even shrink your document.

Just like any of the other toolbars found in Word, you can reposition the Print Preview toolbar anywhere within the Print Preview window. The following list provides a more detailed explanation of each of the commands found on the Print Preview toolbar.

- **Print**. Sends the active document directly to your default printer.
- **Magnifier**. Toggles the magnifier on and off, showing more or less readable text when selected.

When the magnifier is toggled off, you can edit your document in Print Preview.

- **One Page**. Shows the page where your insertion point is currently located within the document.
- **Multiple Pages**. Shows up to 32 pages at one time. Select more pages by clicking and dragging across, or down, or both. This option is useful to see the overall layout of a document. Figure 7.16 shows a document in multiple-page view within Print Preview.
- **Zoom**. Allows you to adjust the percentage to view more or less readable text. Click the drop-down arrow and select from an existing option, or type a percentage in directly, such as **88%**.
- **View Ruler**. Toggles the vertical and horizontal rulers on and off.
- **Shrink To Fit**. This command shrinks the document by one page, if possible, to prevent text from spilling over onto a new page.
- **Full Screen**. Allows you to see more of the document by hiding all the window components except the Print Preview toolbar.
- **Close**. Closes Print Preview.

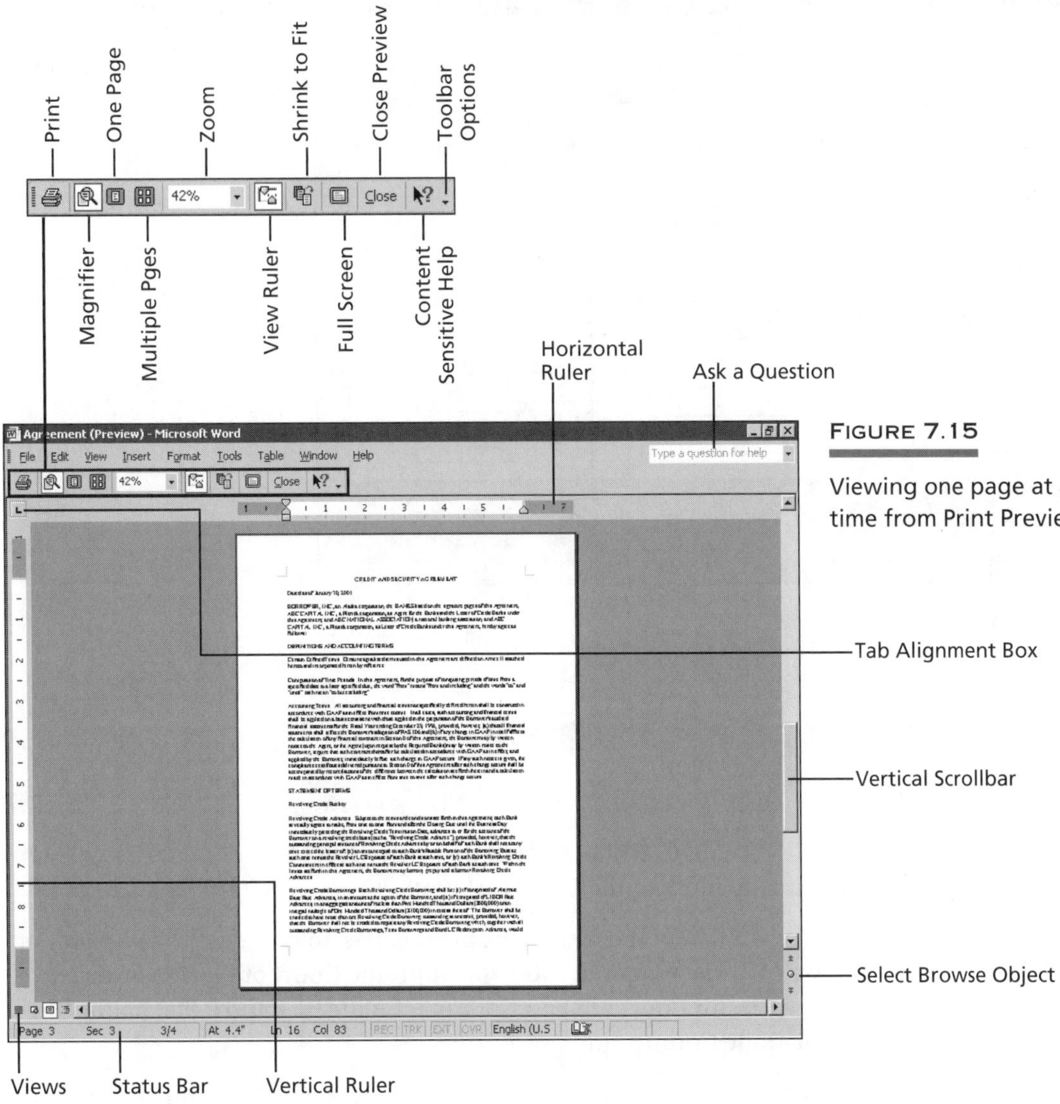

FIGURE 7.15

Viewing one page at a time from Print Preview.

- **What's This?** Provides content-sensitive help for a specific command or menu in the Print Preview window, as well as Reveal Formatting, for selected text in the document. Click this button and then click the text or control to see the associated information.

Do not use the Shrink To Fit option on documents that will be filed with courts that mandate certain formatting and spacing requirements.

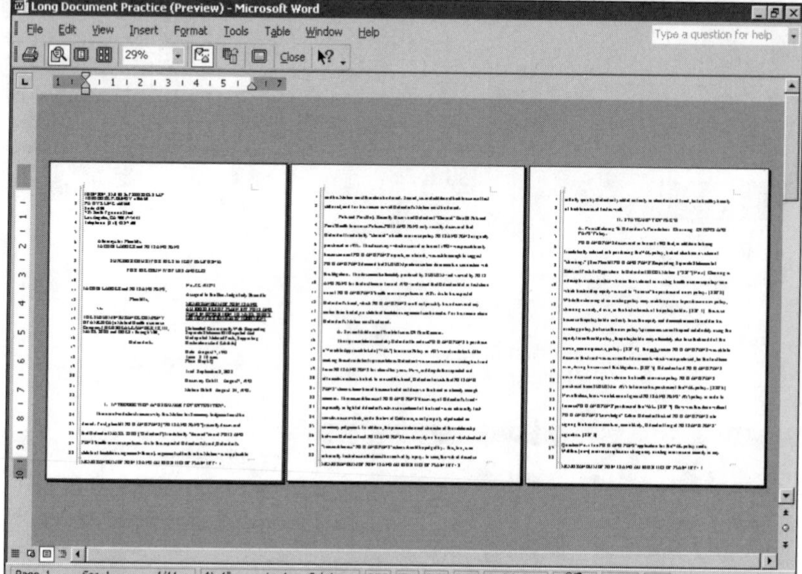

FIGURE 7.16

View multiple pages in Print Preview.

PRACTICE USING PRINT PREVIEW

1. Create a new document. Switch to Normal view.
2. Type **SUPREME COURT OF THE UNITED STATES**, press Ctrl+E to center the text, and press Enter. Press Ctrl+Enter to create a hard page break.
3. At the beginning of the next page, press Ctrl+L to left-align the paragraph, and type **On December 8, 2000, the Supreme Court of Florida ordered that the Circuit Court of Leon County tabulate by hand 9,000 ballots in Miami-Dade County.** and press Enter.
4. Click Print Preview. Click the drop-down arrow next to Zoom and change the percentage to 75%. Press Enter.
5. Click View Ruler to turn on the horizontal and vertical rulers.
6. Click Multiple Pages, choose 1 x 2 pages, and then click One Page.
7. From the horizontal ruler, drag the Left indent marker to 1" and set a right tab of 6".
8. Close Print Preview.

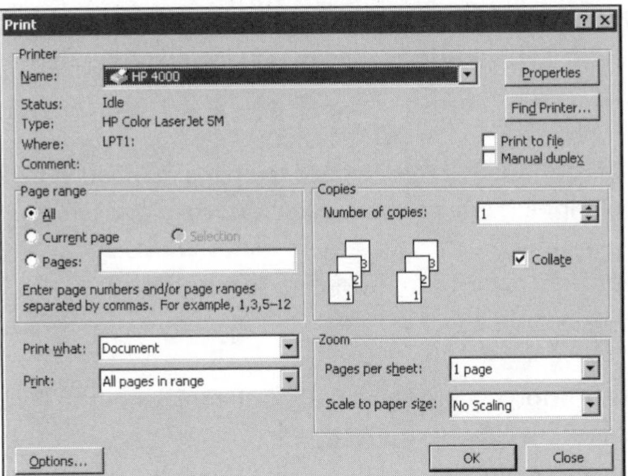

FIGURE 7.17

Select what part of the document to print, number of copies, and more from the Print dialog box.

PRINTING THE DOCUMENT

Once you've finished drafting, editing, reediting, and previewing your legal document, you may want to print a hard copy. Word lets you print a selection, the current page, a range of pages, or the entire document depending on your requirements. You can print one or more copies, document properties, odd or even pages, or even several pages per sheet.

If you have more than one printer, you can also select the closest or most appropriate printer for the job from a drop-down list of available printers. Figure 7.17 shows the Print dialog box, which contains all the options you need to print documents.

USE THE PRINT DIALOG BOX TO SET PRINT OPTIONS

1. Create a new document.
2. Type **The court further held that relief would require manual recounts in all Florida counties where so-called "undervotes" had not been subject to manual tabulation.** Select the paragraph.
3. From the File menu, choose Print to open the Print dialog box.
4. Click the Name drop-down arrow to see all available printers.
5. Click Properties to see a list of choices related to your specific printer. Click Cancel to return to the Print dialog box.

6. Look in the Page Range section of the Print dialog box to print All of the document, the Current Page, a Selection (selected text), or a Range Of Pages.

NOTE

To print a range of contiguous pages, type in the page numbers separated by a dash, say, 1-10. To print a range of noncontiguous pages, use commas to separate, that is, 1,3,5,22. If necessary, you can use both commas and dashes together: 1-4,6,9. To print from page 12 to the end of the document, type the page number followed by a dash, e.g., 12-.

7. Click the drop-down arrow to see a list of choices in the Print What drop-down list, as shown in Figure 7.18.
8. Click the Print drop-down arrow to choose whether or not to print All Pages In Range, Odd Pages, or Even Pages.
9. In the Copies section of the Print dialog box, choose the Number Of Copies you wish to print. The default is 1. Select Collate if you are printing multiple copies of a multipage document.
10. In the Zoom section, select the number of Pages Per Sheet and the Scale To Paper Size type. The default is No Scaling.
11. From the lower-left side of the Print dialog box, click Options to choose from a number of print-specific options. See the list in the following "Options" section for an explanation of each.
12. Click OK to send the document to the printer.

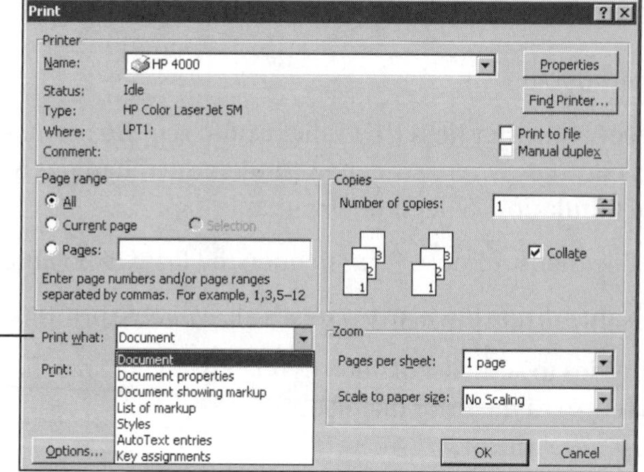

FIGURE 7.18

You can choose to print more than just the document.

Select Print To File if you want to save the document in a format that another printer can use. This is most commonly used for commercial printing services and PostScript printers. When printing to a file, Word will preserve font spacing, and line and page breaks.

PAGE RANGE

In the Print dialog box, the Page Range area prints specific areas of the document from one page to the entire document and everything in between. When text is selected, the Selection option becomes available to print only what is selected.

With most of this chapter devoted to sections, it is probably a good idea to explain how to print individual sections. To print an entire section, type **s** followed by the section number. For example, if you want to print Section 2, type **s2**. You can specify a page range within a section by using a combination of page number and section numbers. For example, **p3s4-p8s4** will print pages 3 through 8 of Section 4.

OPTIONS

The following list describes each of the print options available in the Options dialog box, as shown in Figure 7.19.

- **Draft Output**. Prints the document without most of the formatting. Used to speed up the printing process for draft copies of large documents.

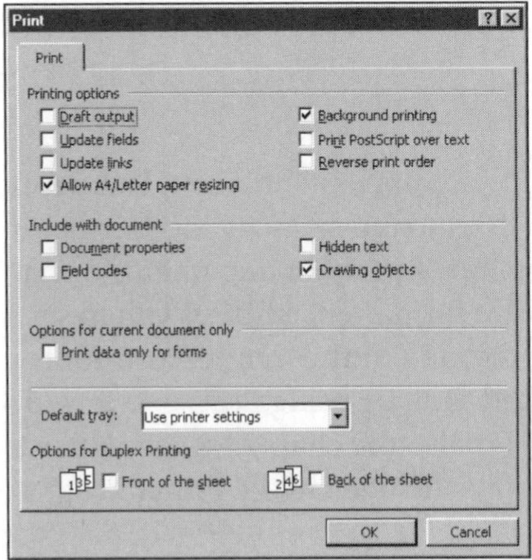

FIGURE 7.19

The Print Options dialog box allows you to define exactly what should print and whether or not it should be updated before printing, if applicable.

- **Update Fields**. Any fields contained within the document, such as dates, table of contents, or page numbers, will be updated prior to printing.
- **Update Links**. Any linked files are updated prior to printing.
- **Allow A4/Letter Paper Resizing**. Word adjusts the document formatted for A4 paper to print on 8.5" × 11" paper.
- **Background Printing**. Prints the document in the background, which allows you to continue to work, if necessary. This feature may be turned off to speed up the current print job.
- **Print PostScript Over Text**. Used when printing converted Macintosh documents.
- **Reverse Print Order**. Prints from the last page to first. Use this option to have pages print in the correct order on a printer that prints face up.
- **Document Properties**. Prints properties found in the Properties dialog box of the document.
- **Field Codes**. Prints the field codes rather than the field results for any fields contained within a document.
- **Hidden Text**. Prints text that has been formatted as hidden text.
- **Drawing Objects**. Prints any drawing objects contained within the document. If you use the Pleading Wizard to create pleadings, line numbers are placed in a text box in the header and footer layer and are considered a drawing object. If the Drawing Objects option is turned off, line numbers will appear onscreen but will not print.
- **Print Data Only For Forms**. Prints only the form fields contained in online forms.
- **Default Tray**. Choose a default tray to print from in a multi-tray printer.
- **Options For Duplex Printing**. Allows you to set options for documents that will be printed on both sides of the page.

SUMMARY

One of the most important things to understand about Word is how to lay out a document—from head to toe, start to finish. Most page formatting can be done through the Page Setup dialog box. But other document formatting, such as a change in how page numbers are formatted, requires you to set a section break and then turn off Same As Previous in the header and footer. The chapter looked at how to save paper and time by using Print Preview to view the way a document will print onscreen. Finally, the chapter covered how to print a document and talked about the options included in the Print dialog box.

TROUBLESHOOTING FORMATTING A DOCUMENT

Why can't I see the headers or footers in my document?

You're probably in Normal view. To see the headers and footers in your document, switch to Print Layout view.

My page number shows {PAGE} instead of the page numbers—what's going on?

Page numbers are actually fields. You're seeing the {PAGE} field itself instead of the result of the field, which is the numbers. Press Alt+F9 to see the numbers.

If you are seeing this in the printed document, click the Options button in the Print dialog box and ensure that Field Codes is not selected.

I inserted page numbers from the button on the Header And Footer toolbar and, in my three-page document, all the page numbers show 3.

Instead of clicking Insert Page Number, you accidentally selected the Insert Number Of Pages button. The Insert Number Of Pages field shows the total number of pages in the document, whereas the Insert Page Number field numbers each page sequentially.

Part of my document gets cut off each time I send it to the printer—why isn't all of the text showing up?

You've probably set your margins to a smaller measurement than the printer allows. Some of the text close to the edge of the paper in documents with small margins, .5" or less, may not print. Reset your margins to .5" or more.

There are only two paragraphs in my document but they are spread out over the entire page, top to bottom.

You may have inadvertently chosen a Justified Vertical Alignment. This command aligns the first line with the top margin and the last line with the bottom margin. From the File menu, choose Page Setup. Select the Layout tab and change the Vertical Alignment value to Top.

Is there a way to assign a keyboard shortcut to a Section break?

Alternate-click on any toolbar and choose Customize. Click the Keyboard button. Select Insert under Categories and InsertBreak from Commands. Press your keyboard shortcut (ALT+I will work), click Assign, and click Close twice. When you use the command, it will bring up the dialog box and allow you to select not only section breaks but also column and page breaks.

There is a "phantom" page break that I can't seem to make go away.

You may have formatted the paragraph to have a page break before it. It is probably best not to use that particular formatting until you are on the final edits of your document.

Why can't I get my document to print longways on the page after a landscape table? It was fine before the table.

You need to insert a Next Page section break after the table and change the Page Orientation of that section to Portrait.

Chapter 8

Bullets and Numbering

IN THIS CHAPTER

- Working with different types of bullets
- Simple numbered lists
- Complex outline numbering
- How styles and numbering work together
- New List Styles feature

So here it is, one the most important chapters in this book. Mastering numbering is an absolute necessity for most legal professionals. Numbering links to styles—another important feature in Word—works with the table of contents and is required in almost every legal document created. Microsoft has added some much-needed improvements to both bullets and numbering. Most notable for users of previous versions of Word is the fix of the dreaded "Jason tab."

BULLETS

When you see a list in a document, at least half the time bullets will appear next to each item. Most of the rest of the time, the list will have numbers. A bullet is a symbol that appears to the left of text and is designed to draw attention to the text that follows. Bullets can be square, round, arrow-shaped, check boxes, whatever you want; you can even use your firm's logo as a bullet.

Bullets can be started even before you have any text by just turning the feature on and typing. If you want to apply bullets to existing text, select the list first and then apply bullets. That's all there is to it. Any one of the following methods adds bullets:

- Click Bullets on the Formatting toolbar.
- From the Format menu, choose Bullets And Numbering and select the Bulleted tab.
- Type recognizable characters and let AutoFormat As You Type convert the text into automatic bullets.
- Use a keyboard shortcut.

Regardless of how the bullet is applied, the result is the same; you get a bulleted list.

FORMATTING TOOLBAR

Since bullets are actually formatting, the Bullets button is included on the Formatting toolbar. This button serves as a toggle to turn on and off bullets. The last bullet style used in a document will be the same bullet style used the next time you start bullet formatting.

NO MORE JASON TAB!

Previous versions of Word set a default tab of 0.25" between the end of an automatic paragraph number and the text of the paragraph. Even if you changed the value in the style with the ruler, the tab position would revert back to 0.25" whenever you clicked OK in the Customize dialog box. This created a lot of frustration for law firms, and the tab became known as the much-despised "Jason tab."

The term *Jason tab* was first coined by Tim Byrne of Microsystems when discussing major annoyances the product caused his law firm clients. "The tab," said Byrne, "was just like Jason in the *Friday the 13th* movies—it kept coming back to life, no matter what you did to it."

The Jason tab was finally put to rest in Word 2002.

APPLY BULLETS USING A TOOLBAR BUTTON

1. Create a new document. Type **Meeting Agenda** and press Enter. Type **Client Conference Call** and press Enter. Type **Review of Agreement** and press Enter. Type **Strategy** and press Enter. Type **New Items**.
2. Select Meeting Agenda and press Ctrl+E to center the text.
3. Select all the items beneath Meeting Agenda and click Bullets on the Formatting toolbar to apply bullet formatting to the list.
4. After New Items, press Enter and type **Questions**. As you can see, when you are in a bulleted list and press Enter, the paragraph formatting that contains the bullet is carried forward to the next paragraph.
5. Select the entire list and click Bullets to remove all bullets from the list.
6. Click Bullets again to toggle bullets back on.
7. Keep the document open for the next exercise.

BULLETS AND NUMBERING DIALOG BOX

The Formatting toolbar is great for applying bullets quickly, but often you need more control over the bullet style and formatting. For example, you may need to pick a different bullet type, or control the position of the bullet on the page or the distance between the bullet and the text. These things can be accomplished through the Bullets And Numbering dialog box shown in Figure 8.1.

APPLY BULLETS USING A MENU COMMAND

1. Select the list from the preceding exercise or create a new one.
2. From the Format menu, choose Bullets And Numbering and select the Bulleted tab. Notice that there are seven default bullet formats on the tab (in addition to None). Word refers to these bullet formats as *gallery positions.*
3. Click one of the bullet galleries to apply a different bullet type. Click OK to close the Bullets And Numbering dialog box. Notice that your list now uses the bullet format from the gallery position you selected.
4. Close the document without saving.

NEW FEATURE!

Now there's an easy way to get to the Bullets And Numbering dialog box. Just double-click any bullet or number in a document and the dialog box will open. This is a new enhancement to Word.

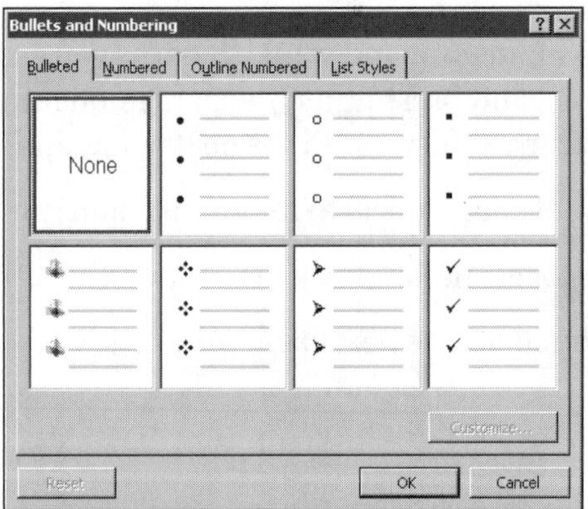

FIGURE 8.1

The Bullets And Numbering dialog box allows you to change the bullets and formatting associated with a bulleted list.

NEW FEATURE!

Word 2002 allows you to select a number or bullet and type over it. This makes changing the formatting of the list, restarting, or continuing a previous list easy. Just click on the number to select it, and type.

AUTOFORMAT BULLETS AS YOU TYPE

Fast typists often prefer to keep their hands on the keyboard, so Word provides keyboard equivalents that automatically convert to bullet symbols. Type any of the following characters: *, -, --, >, ->, =>, followed by a tab or space, type text, and press Enter. Voilà! You now have a bulleted list.

The ability to convert text to bullets on the fly is controlled by AutoCorrect. From the Tools menu, choose AutoCorrect Options. Select the AutoFormat As You Type tab and check the option for Automatic Bulleted Lists. Figure 8.2 shows the AutoFormat As You Type tab and the option that controls Automatic Bullets.

Table 8.1 shows a list of keyboard characters that AutoFormat As You Type recognizes, and the resulting bullet that it creates.

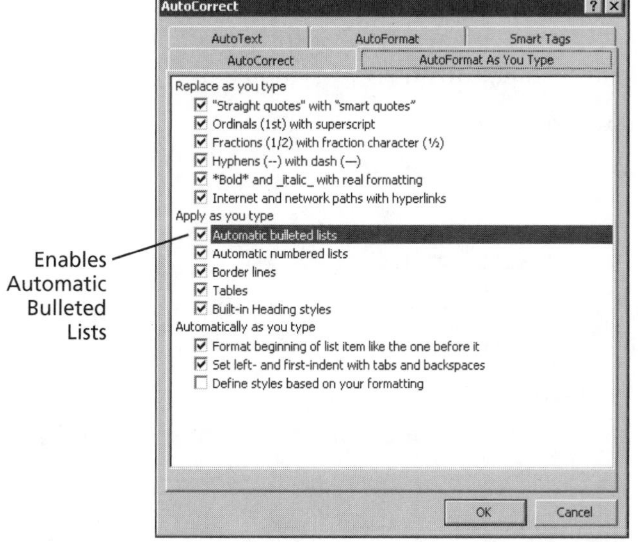

FIGURE 8.2

AutoFormat As You Type allows you to easily create bulleted lists.

TABLE 8.1 BULLET SYMBOLS USING AUTOFORMAT AS YOU TYPE

TYPE THIS SYMBOL	BULLET APPLIED
*	•
--	▪
>	➢
->	➔
=>	⇨

USE AUTOFORMAT AS YOU TYPE FOR BULLETED LISTS

1. Create a new document.
2. From the Tools menu, choose AutoCorrect Options, and select the AutoFormat As You Type tab. If necessary, turn on Automatic Bulleted Lists and click OK.
3. Type * (an asterisk).
4. Press Tab or the Spacebar and type **Litigation**.
5. Press Enter. Notice how the asterisk converts to a round bullet. Press Enter again to turn off bullets for the current paragraph.
6. Type -> and press Tab. Type **Trust and Estates** and press Enter. Notice how the typed characters change to an arrow symbol.
7. Close the document without saving.

TURNING OFF BULLETS

Bulleted lists are just as easy to turn off as they are to turn on. Use any of the following methods to turn off the Bullets feature:

- Press Enter twice at the end of a bulleted list.
- Click the Bullets button on the Formatting toolbar. (Remember, it works as a toggle.)

- From the Format menu, choose Bullets And Numbering and select None (the first gallery position), and then click OK.
- Press Backspace.

Even though Backspace removes the bullet, the insertion point is not returned to the left margin; it retains the indents of the bulleted list. For this reason, using Backspace to remove a bullet is not recommended.

CUSTOMIZING BULLETS

If your firm uses the same bullet symbol all the time, you may never need to customize the appearance of a bullet. However, there may be times when the default bullets are not sufficient. You may need to control the position of the bullet or of the following text, the bullet size, or even the color of the bullet. When you open the Bulleted tab and click Customize, you can adjust any bullet in Word to meet your exact needs.

SELECT A CUSTOM BULLET

1. Create a new document.
2. Type **Technology Committee Meeting Agenda:** and press Enter.
3. Click Bullets on the Formatting toolbar.
4. Type **Purchase of new printers.** and press Enter. Type **Installation of new comparison software.** and press Enter. Type **Update on status of remote access software.** and press Enter.
5. Select the bulleted paragraphs.
6. From the Format menu, choose Bullets And Numbering.
7. Select one of the bullet choices from the gallery and click Customize to open the Customize Bulleted List dialog box shown in Figure 8.3.
8. Click Character to open the Symbol dialog box shown in Figure 8.4. Any symbol can be used as a bullet.
9. Select any symbol and click OK.
10. Click Font to change the size, color, or font for the bullet. The Font dialog box is shown in Figure 8.5.
11. Click OK and close all open dialog boxes to apply the customized bullet.

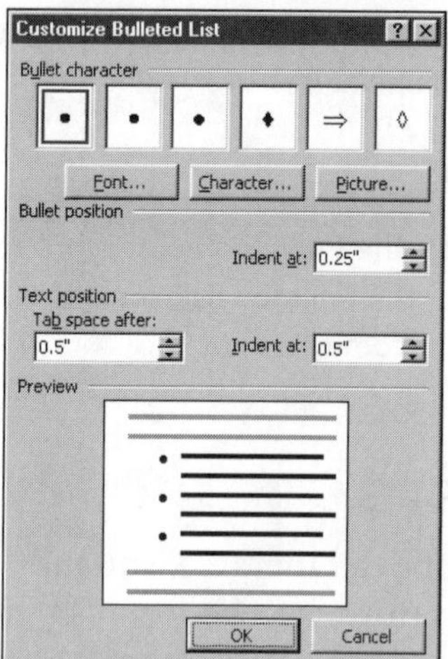

FIGURE 8.3

Select a different bullet symbol or picture, indent position, or font format in the Customize Bulleted List dialog box.

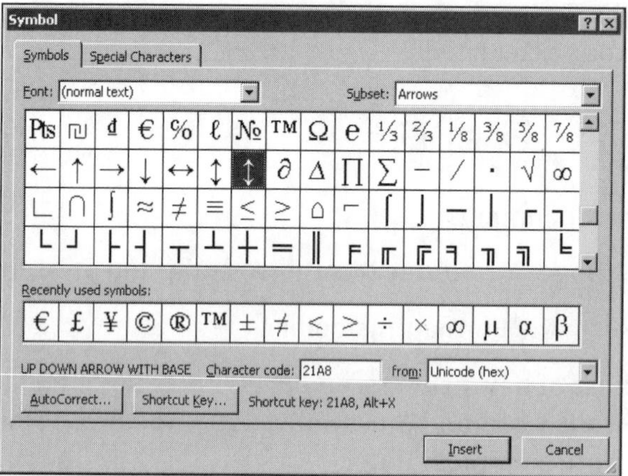

FIGURE 8.4

Select from a wide range of symbols to use as bullets in the Symbol dialog box.

NEW FEATURE!

The Symbol dialog box now includes a separate list of the recently used symbols, so you can get to the ones you use most frequently without scanning the whole list for them. The main list also has a new look—the symbol characters are larger and therefore easier to view.

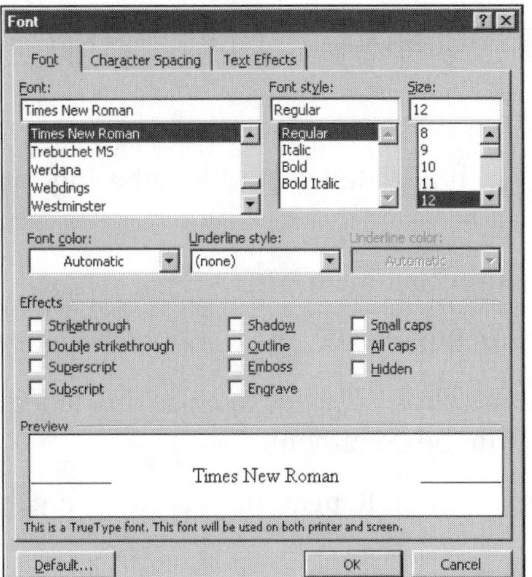

FIGURE 8.5

The Font dialog box changes the font of the bullet, not the following text.

PICTURE BULLETS

Legal documents rarely require fancy graphics or colorful bullets. However, not all documents created in a law firm go to clients or are filed with the court. On some occasions, you can add a bit more pizzazz to a document by applying a picture bullet.

Picture bullets are similar to regular bullets in Word except they have more formatting—usually with colors and shadows, but occasionally with animation. Use picture bullets for practice group flyers or online documents posted to an intranet.

When the picture bullet feature was introduced in Word 2000, it did not have all the functionalities of a regular, symbol bullet. This has been remedied in Word 2002.

Word includes a wide selection of picture bullets by default. You can also use picture file formats for these bullets, including .jpg, .bmp, or .gif.

The words *jpeg* and *gif* roll off of the tongue easily, but not too many people know what these abbreviations stand for. The file type .jpg (pronounced Jay-Peg) is short for Joint Photographic Experts Group, .gif is Graphics Interchange Format, and .bmp is bitmap file. Now you'll be ready for that graphics question on "Who Wants to Be a Millionaire!"

INSERT A PICTURE BULLET

1. Create a new document.
2. From the Format menu, choose Bullets And Numbering and select the Bulleted tab.
3. Select any bullet and click Customize.
4. Click Picture. The Picture Bullet dialog box, shown in Figure 8.6, appears.
5. Select a picture bullet and click OK twice to close the dialog boxes and place the picture bullet in the document.
6. Type some text and press Enter. Repeat the process to create a list with picture bullets.

Use the Picture Bullet dialog box to import additional graphics files, such as your firm's logo, into the picture gallery. Click Import to navigate to the appropriate network drive or folder where the file is stored. You can use any of the imported files as bullets.

BULLET POSITION

By default, bulleted lists in Word are indented .25" from the left margin and set with a .25" hanging indent. This setting may be adequate for a majority of lists, but you may sometimes need to adjust it. The Customize Bulleted List dialog

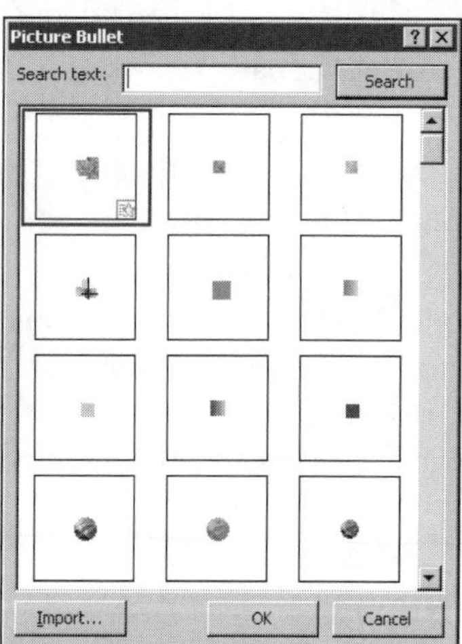

FIGURE 8.6

Picture bullets provide more choices for professional, and often lively, document formatting.

box has two sections that allow you to make changes to the relative position of both bullets and text.

- **Bullet Position**. Specifies the distance between the margin and the bullet. Click the appropriate spinner control for Indent At to increase or decrease the distance of the bullet from the margin. Alternatively, you can type a number into the box to set the distance.
- **Text Position**. Tab Space After specifies the distance between the bullet and text. The Indent At option sets the hanging indent.

CHANGE THE ALIGNMENT OF A BULLETED LIST

1. Create a new document. Type **Motion to Dismiss** and press Enter. Type **Certificate of Service** and press Enter. Type **Acceptance of Terms** and press Enter. Type **Letter to Opposing Counsel** and press Enter.
2. Select the list.
3. From the Format menu, choose Bullets And Numbering, and select the Bulleted tab.
4. Select any bullet and click Customize.
5. Set the Bullet Position Indent At to **0"**. This positions the bullet at the left margin.
6. Change Tab Space After to **.5"** and Indent to **.5"** in the Text Position section.
7. Click OK to return to the document.

BULLET STYLES

As mentioned in the introduction to this chapter, styles are an important part of Microsoft Word. Styles are fully explained in Chapter 9. However, since both the Bullets and Numbering features use styles, it's necessary to talk about styles briefly here as well as in the section on numbering later in this chapter.

A *style* in Word is a collection of formatting that is saved, named, and can be applied at any time thereafter. Imagine selecting a specific bullet, changing the position of the bullet and text, as well as the color and other attributes, and then having to repeat these steps each time you want to use this bullet format. Styles allow you to go through the formatting steps once and then save the information and apply it to other bulleted lists whenever necessary.

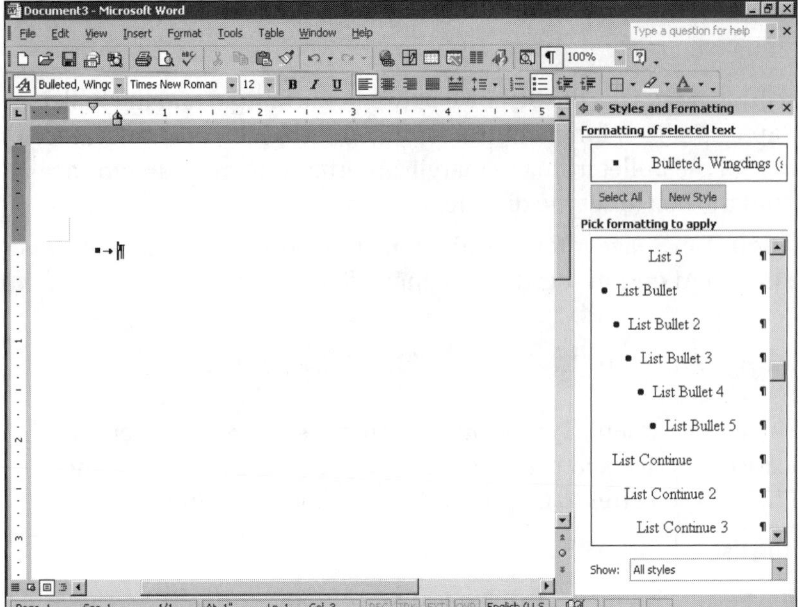

FIGURE 8.7

Select a List Bullet style from the Styles and Formatting Task Pane.

Word also contains five built-in bulleted list styles that can be applied to lists. These styles are available by choosing Styles And Formatting from the Format menu. Click the drop-down arrow next to Show and change the option to All Styles. Scroll through the list of Pick Formatting To Apply options and locate the List Bullet styles. The Styles and Formatting Task Pane and List Bullet styles are shown in Figure 8.7. Click any List Bullet style to apply the formatting to current or selected paragraphs.

The left-indent for each List Bullet style increases in .25" increments.

APPLY LIST BULLET STYLE

1. Create a new document. Type **Litigation** and press Enter. Type **Real Estate** and press Enter. Type **Banking** and press Enter. Type **IP** and press Enter.
2. Select the list. From the Format menu, choose Styles and Formatting.
3. At the bottom of the Styles and Formatting Task Pane, click the Show drop-down arrow and select All Styles.
4. Locate the List Bullet styles from the Pick Formatting To Apply section and select List Bullet 3.

5. Click the (X) Close button at the top-right corner of the Styles and Formatting Task Pane.

To apply a List Bullet style from the Style button on the Formatting toolbar, hold down the Shift key and click the drop-down arrow next to the Style button. Scroll through the list and select the appropriate List Bullet style. The keyboard shortcut to apply a List Bullet style is Ctrl+Shift+L.

BASIC NUMBERED LISTS

The most basic type of numbered list is 1, 2, 3 or A, B, C. Any one of the following methods adds numbers:

- Simply type items that begin with the basic numbers or letters followed by periods and allow AutoCorrect's AutoFormat As You Type to convert the text to a numbered list.
- Click the Numbering button on the Formatting toolbar.
- Open the Bullets And Numbering dialog box and select the Numbered tab.

Numbered lists can have different formats (for example, Roman, Arabic, Alphanumeric), as well as specific size and font choices. They can also be restarted at contiguous or noncontiguous locations within the document.

NUMBERING ON THE FORMATTING TOOLBAR

The Numbering button on the Formatting toolbar acts as a toggle to apply or remove numbering from selected paragraphs. If no text is selected, then numbering is toggled for the current paragraph only.

APPLY NUMBERING USING THE NUMBERING BUTTON

1. Create a new document.
2. Click Numbering on the Formatting toolbar.
3. Type **Definitions** and press Enter. Type **Introduction** and press Enter. Type **Argument** and press Enter. Type **Conclusion** and press Enter.
4. Leave the document open for the next exercise.

NUMBERING IN THE BULLETS AND NUMBERING DIALOG BOX

Although your numbering needs will probably be straightforward most of the time, you may sometimes need the extra control over numbering that you get by using the Numbering tab on the Bullets And Numbering dialog box. This tab contains a gallery of seven different default numbering formats (plus None) that can be applied with the click of a button.

From the Format menu, choose Bullets And Numbering and select the Numbered tab. Click to apply any of the available formats. Figure 8.8 shows the Numbered tab, gallery, and options for applying and controlling numbering.

USE THE NUMBERED TAB TO APPLY BASIC NUMBERING

1. The document from the preceding exercise should still be open. If not, create a simple numbered list with four paragraphs.
2. Select the four numbered paragraphs in the document.

The number can be selected, or the text next to the number, but not both when working with automatic bullets and numbering. Word considers the number to be part of the paragraph formatting. When copying or using Cut and Paste, make sure to select the text along with the paragraph mark that follows to ensure the number format is also included.

3. From the Format menu, choose Bullets And Numbering and select the Numbered tab.
4. Choose one of the default number formats and click OK.

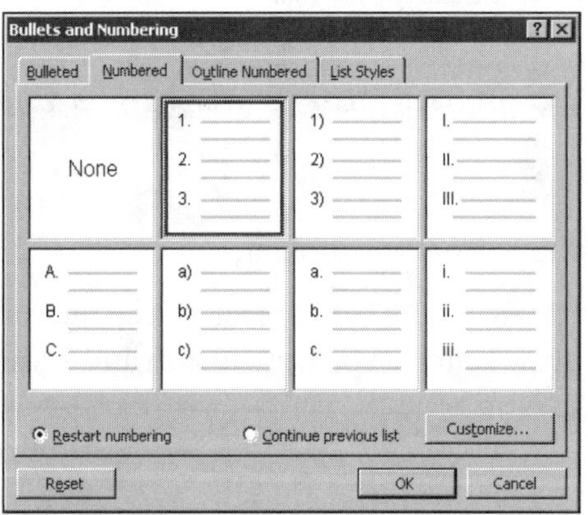

FIGURE 8.8

Select a number format for your list.

AUTOFORMAT AS YOU TYPE

Sometimes it's faster to manually type the list of numbers than it is to go into the Bullets And Numbering dialog box or click the Numbering button on the toolbar. If the Automatic Numbered Lists AutoCorrect setting is enabled, Word can convert the list as you type.

From the Tools menu, choose AutoCorrect Options and select the AutoFormat As You Type tab. Check Automatic Numbered Lists from the Apply As You Type section to have Word convert typed numbers to automatic numbered lists.

CREATE A NUMBERED LIST AUTOMATICALLY

1. Create a new document. Make sure that Automatic Numbered Lists is enabled.
2. Type **1.** (the number 1 followed by a period) and press Tab. Type some text and press Enter. The next consecutive number appears automatically for the next paragraph.
3. Press Enter twice to add new paragraphs and turn off automatic numbering.
4. Type **4.** and press the Spacebar. Type some text and press Enter. A space or tab can be used after the number's period to trigger the automatic-numbering feature.
5. Keep this document open for the next exercise.

TIP

Roman numerals (I, II, III) and letters (A, B, C) can be manually typed followed by a tab or space, and then the text. Word then converts the text to an automatic numbered list when Enter is pressed.

CUSTOMIZING NUMBERED LISTS

The Customize Numbered List dialog box contains several options that allow you to make changes to new or existing numbered lists. Figure 8.9 shows the Customize Numbered List dialog box. The number's font, format, style, and position in the document can all be modified.

Table 8.2 provides a brief description for each of the options in the Customize Numbered List dialog box.

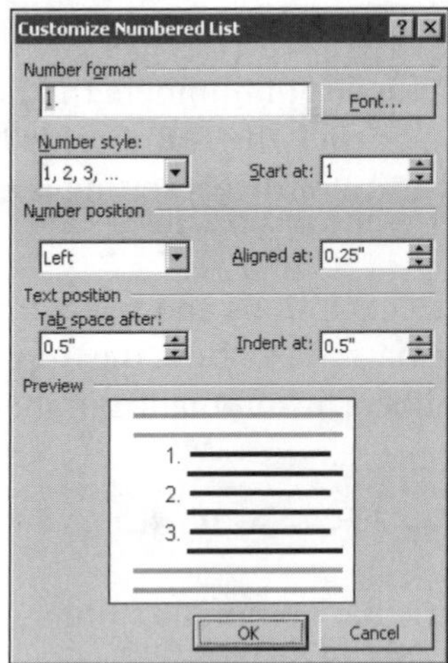

FIGURE 8.9

Use the Customize Numbered List dialog box to modify your numbered list.

The number and text formats are controlled separately. The Customize Numbered List dialog box only controls formatting of the number. To change the format of text, use the techniques described in Chapter 5, "Formatting Text."

CUSTOMIZE A NUMBERED LIST

1. Place the insertion point in the first paragraph of the numbered list from the preceding exercise.
2. From the Format menu, choose Bullets And Numbering. Notice that the current scheme of the document is selected in the gallery of the Numbered tab.

To quickly open the Bullets And Numbering dialog box without using a menu command, double-click the number next to the paragraph. This shortcut is new to Word 2002. Another method for quickly opening the dialog box is to alternate-click on a paragraph that contains a bullet or number and choose Bullets And Numbering.

3. Click Customize.
4. Click Font to open the Font dialog box. Set the Font and Font Style to Times New Roman and Bold.
5. Click OK to return to the Customize Numbered List dialog box.
6. From the Number Style drop-down list, select I, II, III.

TABLE 8.2 CUSTOMIZED NUMBERED LIST OPTIONS

OPTION	DESCRIPTION	NOTES
Number Format	Add text before or after the number in this box or encase the number in parentheses or brackets. For example, "Article 1" or "(a)". The shaded number in the Number Format box is actually a field code. If you type over or delete this code, the automatic number will not appear.	
Font	Choose the number font style, size, underline format, and color.	
Number Style	Select the style of numbering to use for the list including Arabic, Roman, alphabetic, or text numbers.	
Start At	Set the number starting level for the list.	Numbering can start from 0. through 32,767. or from A. through AAAAAA AAAAAAAAAAAAAAAAAAAAAAA.
Number Position	Choose to left, center, or right-align the numbers in the numbered list.	Number position is somewhat confusing. Remember that only the number format is controlled in the Customize Numbered Lists dialog box. Number Position aligns only the number—not the text.
Aligned At	Set the value where the number should be aligned from the left margin. For example, the value of 0" places the number at the left margin.	
Tab Space After	Use the spinner control to set the tab spacing between the number and text or type in the number manually.	This is new to this version of Word and eliminates a problem that is commonly known as the "Jason tab."
Indent At	Sets the hanging indent of a numbered list.	
Preview	Allows you to view the changes made.	The Preview section of the Customize Numbered List dialog box is not a true rendition of What You See Is What You Get or WYSWYG (pronounced whiz-e-wig) for short. So don't worry about trying to align number and text positions as shown in the graphic in the Preview section.

7. Set Aligned At to 0.5", Tab Space After to 0.5", and Indent At to 0".
8. Click OK to apply the customizations to the numbered list.

STOP, RESTART, AND CONTINUE A LIST

Most legal documents are a combination of numbered and unnumbered text. Numbered lists often begin, pause, and restart at different points in the document. Word makes it easy to control what number to use, anywhere and anytime, within the document.

PRACTICE RESTARTING A NUMBERED LIST

1. Create a list of several items and apply basic numbering.
2. Type a new paragraph of text that does not have a number applied.

There are a few different ways to end a numbered list: Click Numbering on the Formatting toolbar to toggle the feature off, or press Enter twice.

3. Type **The previous section can be modified if both the lessee and lessor agree to the terms in Appendix A** and press Enter.
4. Type **For specific details, see Appendix A** and press Enter.
5. Click Numbering to insert a number next to the current paragraph. Notice how Word assumes that the list should restart at 1. This occurs because there is text between the series of numbers. You can easily override this assumption.
6. Click the AutoCorrect Options button (the lightning bolt) that appears to the left of the newly inserted number and choose Continue Numbering.

The Restart and Continue Numbering commands are also available in the Bullets And Numbering dialog box or by alternate-clicking a numbered paragraph and choosing Restart or Continue Previous List from the shortcut menu.

7. From the Format menu, choose Bullets And Numbering. The Numbered List dialog box opens with the current scheme selected. Figure 8.10 shows the Restart Numbering and Continue Previous List options.
8. Select Restart Numbering at the bottom of the dialog box and click OK.

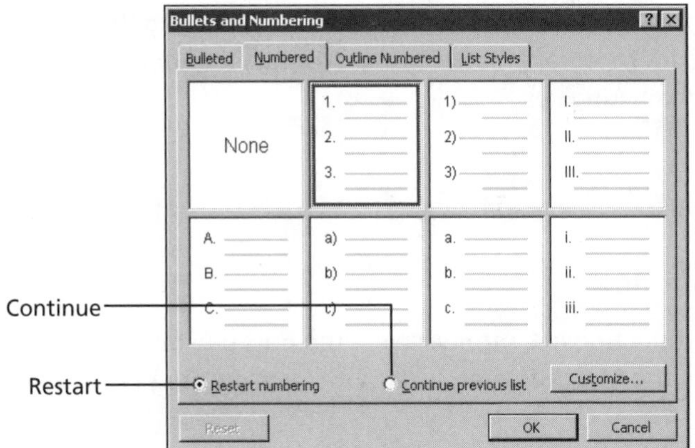

FIGURE 8.10

Choose to have your numbered list Restart Numbering or Continue Previous List.

The Standard toolbar includes a button that helps recognize formatting and will apply or "paint" this same formatting on other text. Format Painter can be used in conjunction with numbering to continue an earlier list in a document. Click an item formatted correctly and then click Format Painter once. Click the text where the next consecutive number should be applied, and Format Painter does all the formatting for you.

MERGING PASTED LISTS

Word contains a new feature called Merge Pasted Lists With Surrounded Lists. Essentially, this feature allows you combine numbered lists from two separate documents into one continuous list; even if the numbering is formatted differently. To ensure that this option is turned on, from the Tools menu, choose Options, select the Edit tab, and click Settings. The Merge Pasted Lists With Surrounding Lists option, shown in Figure 8.11, should be enabled.

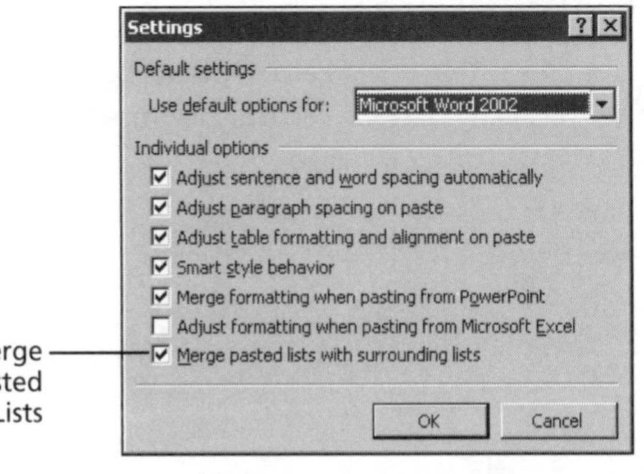

FIGURE 8.11

The Merge Pasted Lists With Surrounding Lists option makes it easier to join multiple lists together.

NOTE

Be sure to paste the list into an empty paragraph immediately following the existing list. If there's an extra paragraph between the existing list and the pasted list, Word restarts the numbering.

JOIN TWO LISTS

1. Create a new document.
2. From the Tools menu, choose Options, select the Edit tab, and click Settings. Make sure the Merge Pasted Lists With Surrounding Lists option is enabled.
3. Type **1. Computer** and then press Enter. Type **Printer** and press Enter. Type **PDA**. Each item should have an automatic number next to it (1., 2., 3).
4. Create a new document.
5. Type **A. Cellular** and press Enter. Type **Pager** and press Enter. Type **Wireless Modem**. Each items should have an automatic number next to it (A, B, C).
6. Select and copy the information that you typed in step 5.
7. Switch to the first document created in steps 1 and 3.
8. Move to the end of the list and paste the copied items. The list is joined and formatted consistently.
9. Close the document without saving.

NOTE

If Word detects a list in the preceding or following paragraph where information is being pasted, this same formatting is applied to your list.

NOTE

When information is pasted and joins an existing list, a Paste Options button appears with the choice to Merge With Existing List, or Paste List Without Merging.

OUTLINE NUMBERING

Pleadings, briefs, and agreements require more complex paragraph numbering than an agenda or simple memo. Complex numbering is applied and customized through the Bullets And Numbering dialog box located on the Outline Numbered tab. It is also possible to use the Numbering toolbar button—but you will have less control over the results.

Each outline contains nine levels of numbering, and each level can be modified to suit the needs of a particular document.

APPLY OUTLINE NUMBERING WITH THE NUMBERING BUTTON

The same Numbering toolbar button used to apply basic numbering can be used to apply outline numbering. Once an initial numbered list is created, press Tab or Backspace, or click the Increase or Decrease Indent buttons, to change levels. The Increase and Decrease Indent buttons, shown in Figure 8.12, are on the Formatting toolbar.

NOTE

Tab and Backspace to control different levels of numbering can only be used if the feature is enabled. From the Tools menu, choose AutoCorrect Options and select the AutoFormat As You Type tab. In the Automatically As You Type section, select Set Left- And First-Indent With Tabs And Backspaces and click OK.

USE INDENT, TAB, AND BACKSPACE TO CHANGE OUTLINE LEVEL

1. Create a new document.
2. Click Numbering on the Formatting toolbar to begin a numbered list.

FIGURE 8.12

Use the Increase and Decrease Indent Buttons on the Formatting toolbar to move between numbering levels.

3. Type **Statement of Terms** and press Enter.
4. Click Increase Indent to advance to the next level in an outline numbered list.
5. Type **Revolving Credit Facilities** and press Enter.
6. Press Tab to advance to the next outline number.
7. Type **Revolving Credit Borrowings** and press Enter.
8. Click Decrease Indent to move to the preceding level. You can also press Shift+Tab with the same result.
9. Leave this file open for the next exercise.

NOTE

Using the Increase and Decrease Indent buttons in conjunction with numbering gives the appearance of an outline numbered list. However, if you choose Bullets And Numbering from the Format menu, the Numbered, and not the Outline Numbered, tab is selected.

APPLY OUTLINE NUMBERING FROM A DIALOG BOX

Another way to apply outline numbering is through the Bullets And Numbering dialog box's Outline Numbered tab. The default outlines provide a good starting point for times when you need to incorporate multilevel numbering into your legal documents. Four of the seven outline number formats are linked to heading styles 1–9. Figure 8.13 shows the Outline Numbered tab in the Bullets And Numbering dialog box.

To apply outline numbering, choose from the Gallery list and click OK. Word then applies the first level of numbering to the current paragraph. Use Tab and Backspace keys or Increase and Decrease Indent buttons to promote or demote levels.

From the Format menu, choose Bullets And Numbering. Select the Outline Numbered tab, if necessary. Click any numbering scheme and then click OK. The outline numbering is applied to the current paragraph. Use Increase and Decrease Indent buttons on the Formatting toolbar, or press Tab and Shift+Tab, to promote or demote outline levels. Figure 8.14 shows a document with outline numbering applied.

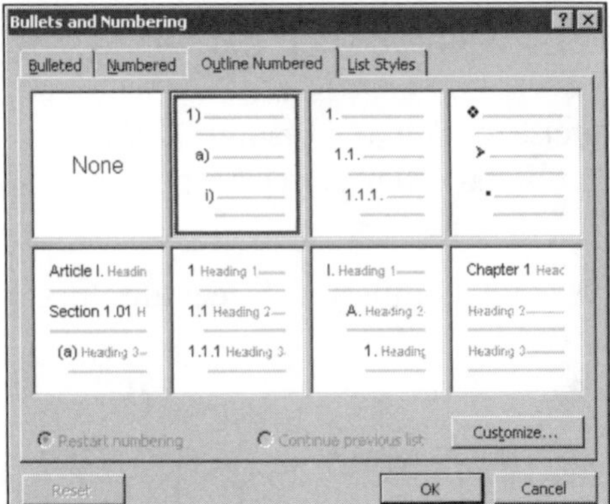

FIGURE 8.13

Outline numbering is popular in legal documents. The Outline Numbered tab allows for selection and customization of this style numbering.

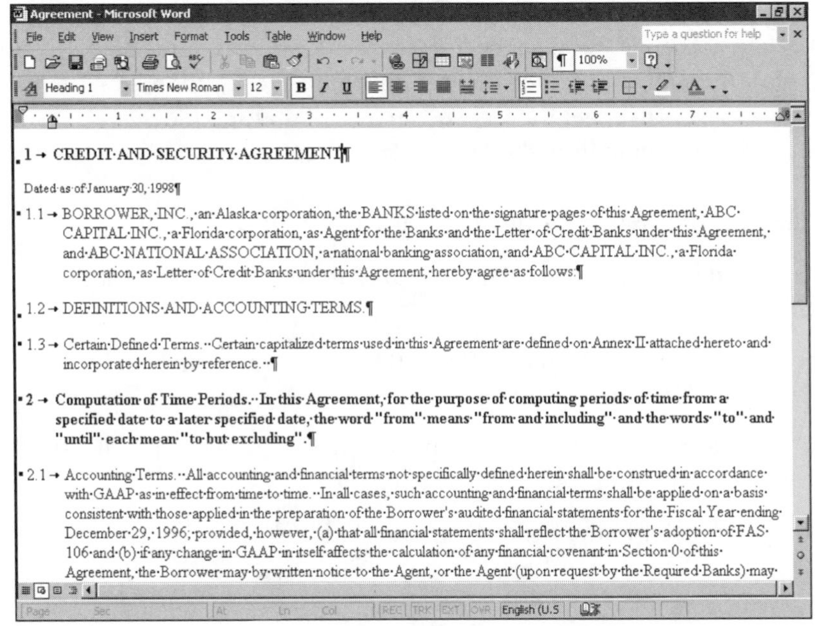

FIGURE 8.14

A document with outline numbering applied.

CUSTOMIZING OUTLINE NUMBERING

While the default outlines can be useful, you'll probably find that most documents require a more customized numbering scheme. The Customize Outline Numbered List dialog box contains a variety of options that can be used to modify each level of an outline. You can make changes to the number format, style, and position; adjust where text should be positioned; and choose the type of spacing to apply between number and text.

CUSTOMIZE AN OUTLINE-NUMBERING SCHEME

1. Using the file from the preceding exercise, click in the first numbered paragraph of the document. If you do not have that exercise, open Outline Numbering.doc on the CD-ROM.
2. From the Format menu, choose Bullets And Numbering. Select the Outline Numbered tab.
3. Click Customize.
4. Click More to view all available options. Level 1 should already be selected.

NOTE

The shaded number in the Number Format box is actually an updating field code. Do not delete or change this number. You can, however, add words or parentheses before, around, or after the number, changing a to (a), for example. The nonshaded text will repeat for every occurrence of that specific level. Change the style of the number from the Number Style drop-down list.

5. From the Number Style drop-down list, select I, II, III.
6. Start At should be set to **I**. Set Aligned At to **0"** to set the first level at the left margin.
7. Use the spinner to set Tab Space After to **0.5"**. This creates half an inch of space between the number and text.
8. Type **0"** for Indent At and text will wrap back to the left margin. Make sure (No Style) is selected in Link Level To Style.
9. Select Tab Character in the Follow Number With field.

TIP

Follow Number With determines which type of spacing separates the number and corresponding text. Choose from Tab, Space, or Nothing—the default for most outlines is Tab. Choose Nothing if you want to center the text under the number.

10. Select 2 under Level to format the next level. From the Number Style drop-down list, select 1,2,3.
11. In the Number Format box, click before the number code. Click the drop-down arrow under Previous Level Number and select Level 1. This inserts a Roman numeral I at the insertion point in Number Format.
12. Type a period between the two numbers. Set Aligned At to **0.5"**.

13. Use the spinner buttons to set the Tab Space After position to **1"**.
14. For Indent At, type **1"**.
15. Check the box next to Legal Style Numbering. This option will change any number to Arabic format. In this example, I.1 changes to 1.1.

Legal Style Numbering should be the last option applied, as it will gray out other options in the Number Style box.

16. Leave Restart Numbering After at Level 1. This ensures that Level 2 restarts numbering each time Level 1 numbering is applied.

You can choose to apply changes to the current paragraph only, from the insertion point forward, or to the whole list. By default, Whole List is selected.

17. Click OK to apply your changes.

It's a good rule of thumb to start at the top of the dialog box and work your way down for each level.

LINK STYLES TO OUTLINE NUMBERING

Word includes nine built-in Heading styles (Heading 1 through Heading 9) that can be linked together with outline numbering to create flexible multilevel schemes and automatically generate tables of contents. As shown in Figure 8.15, four of the seven outlines located in the Outline Numbered tab of the Bullets And Numbering dialog box link to heading styles.

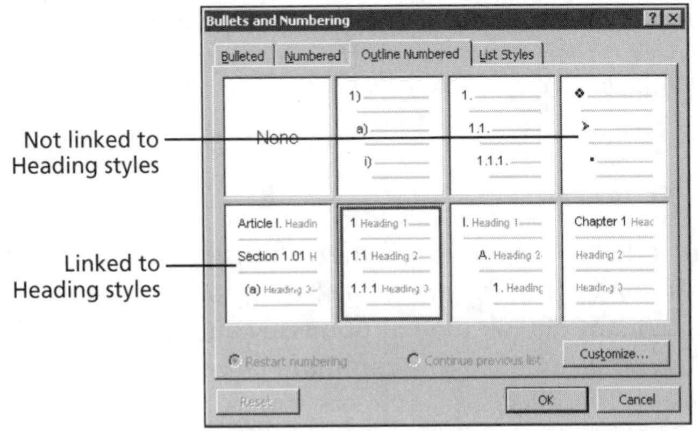

FIGURE 8.15

Use the outline-numbering schemes linked to heading styles when documents need tables of contents to include the numbered headings.

In addition to being able to quickly generate a table of contents, linking Heading styles to numbering allows you to make changes to any part of an outline by modifying the corresponding Heading style. The changes will affect all the numbering associated with the modified style.

APPLY OUTLINE NUMBERING LINKED TO HEADING STYLES

1. Create a new document.
2. From the Format menu choose Bullets And Numbering. Select the Outline Numbered tab and click one of the four outlines linked to Heading styles. Click OK. You can tell which outline-numbering schemes are linked to styles by the word *Heading* in the graphic next to the number.
3. Type **Definition of Terms** and press Enter.
4. Press Ctrl+Alt+2 to apply the next heading level in the outline.
5. Type **Concerned Parties** and press Enter.
6. Press Ctrl+Alt+1 and type **Deadlines**.
7. Click the drop-down arrow next to the Style box on the Formatting toolbar. Notice that each Heading style is linked to an outline level.
8. Press Enter twice and from the Insert menu, choose Reference. Select Index And Tables, and then Table Of Contents. Click OK. This inserts a table of contents in the document.

TIP

The best practice to customize outline numbered lists linked to styles is by modifying the first-level style. For example, to change the format of the number on Heading 3, choose to Modify Heading 1 in the Styles and Formatting Task Pane. Once the Modify Style dialog box opens, choose Numbering from the Format button. Click Customize and make the changes needed. This will ensure that all levels within the document remain linked.

STYLE SEPARATOR

When information to be included in the table of contents must appear on the same line as text not to be included, use the new Style Separator feature. This feature is not available through any default toolbar or menu command, so you will need to go through a few steps to make this command accessible. Figure

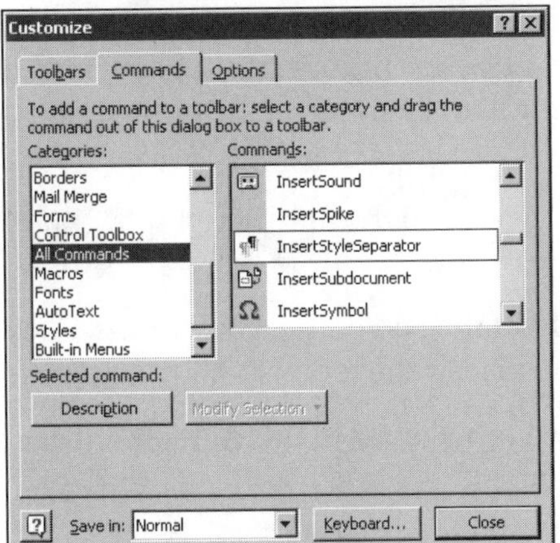

FIGURE 8.16

The New InsertStyleSeparator command assists with creating a table of contents.

8.16 shows this new command, and the following exercises illustrate how to install and use it.

ADD STYLE SEPARATOR TO A TOOLBAR

1. From the View menu, choose Toolbars, Customize.
2. Select the Commands tab.
3. From the Categories list, select All Commands.
4. From the Commands section, locate and select InsertStyleSeparator.
5. Drag the InsertStyleSeparator command to the Standard toolbar.
6. Close the Customize dialog box.

USE THE STYLE SEPARATOR FOR A TABLE OF CONTENTS

1. Create a new blank document. Press Ctrl+Shift+8, if necessary, to turn on Show/Hide.
2. Type **Table of Contents** and press Enter twice. This is where you will insert a table of contents.
3. Press Ctrl+Enter to create a page break. Place your insertion point at the top of page 2.

4. From the Format menu, choose Bullets And Numbering and select the Outline Numbered tab. Choose a numbering scheme linked to styles (locate the word *Heading* in the graphic of the outline numbering scheme).
5. Click OK. Word applies Level 1 to the first paragraph. Type **Certain Defined Terms**.
6. Place the insertion point at the end of the word *Terms*. Click the Style Separator button that was added to the toolbar.
7. Type **Certain capitalized terms used in this Agreement are defined on Annex II** and press Enter.
8. Press Ctrl+Alt+2 to apply Heading Level 2.
9. Type **Accounting Terms**. Place your insertion point at the end of *Terms* and click the Style Separator button.
10. Type **All accounting and financial terms not specifically defined herein shall be construed in accordance with** and press Enter.

NOTE

Use the keyboard shortcuts Ctrl+Alt+1 through Ctrl+Alt+3 to apply Headings 1 through 3.

11. Move back to the first page (Table of Contents) and place your insertion point in the empty paragraph mark below Table of Contents.
12. From the Insert menu, choose Reference, Index And Tables, and select the Table Of Contents tab. Figure 8.17 shows the Table Of Contents tab.

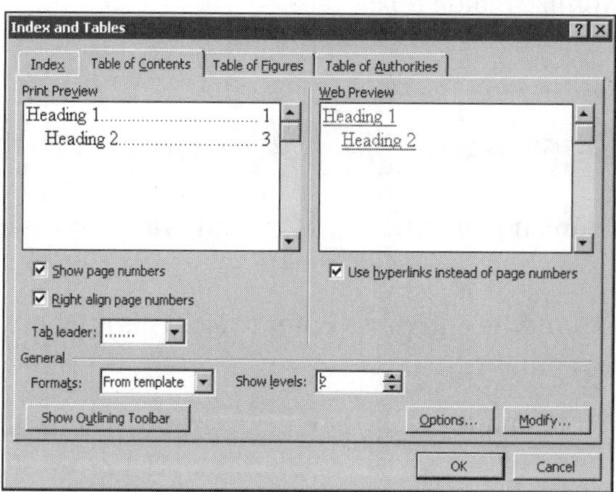

FIGURE 8.17

Select the number of levels and other options from the Table Of Contents dialog box.

13. Make sure that Show Levels is set to 2. Click OK to generate the table of contents. Notice that only the text entered prior to inserting the Style Separator command appears in the TOC.

If you try to use the Style Separator on a paragraph that already has the text typed, it removes the paragraph mark at the end of the paragraph, and the text in the following paragraph moves up.

LINKING USER-DEFINED STYLES TO OUTLINE NUMBERING

Once you have had the chance to truly discover the power and flexibility of styles, you'll want to start creating your own. Word lets you link both heading styles and user-defined styles to outline numbering. The Customize Outline Numbered List dialog box (Figure 8.18) contains the Link Level To Style drop-down list that allows you to link specific outline levels to any of Word's built-in or user-defined styles.

Each outline level must have a unique style linked to it. If you try to link the same style to more than one level, the style will only stay linked to the last level it was applied to; the other levels will show no style in the Link Level To Style field.

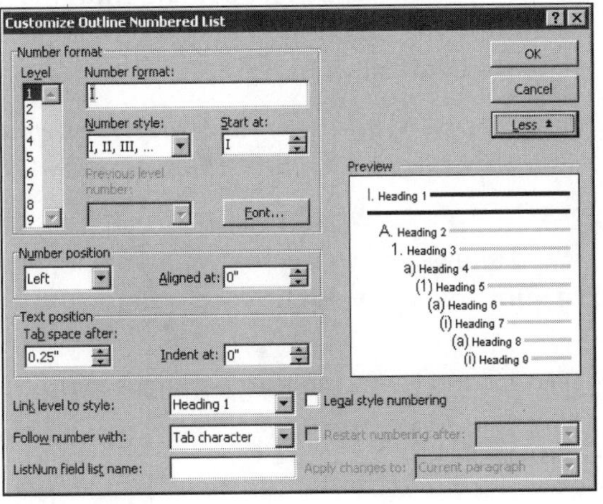

FIGURE 8.18

Link styles to each level of the outline numbered list in the Link Level To Style field.

RESETTING A GALLERY POSITION

Word retains any customization you apply to bulleted, numbered, or outline numbered lists. If you wish to return any of the lists to their default positions, select the appropriate scheme and click the Reset button in the Bullets And Numbering dialog box.

NOTE

If the Reset button is grayed out, the selected list or scheme has not been customized.

PRACTICE RESETTING A GALLERY LIST TO ITS DEFAULT POSITION

1. From the Format menu, choose Bullets and Numbering.
2. Select the Outline Numbered tab.
3. Select a gallery position.
4. Click Reset if the button is active.
5. Click Yes, when asked if you want to reset this gallery position to the default setting.
6. Repeat steps 3 through 5 for each gallery position.

NUMBERING INSIDE A PARAGRAPH

The preceding discussions have assumed that for each paragraph there exists only one number. What about paragraphs that contain multiple items requiring sequential, updateable numbering? The following paragraph provides an example where numbers are required within a paragraph:

Please bring the following items to the airport and present them upon check-in: 1) passport, 2) driver's license for rental car, 3) tickets, and 4) retreat agenda booklet.

The ListNum field in Word allows you to create dynamic, updateable lists within a single paragraph. ListNum fields can also be cross-referenced.

NOTE

Read Chapter 13, "Legal Forms and Fields," to learn all about Word fields.

INSERT NUMBERING INSIDE A PARAGRAPH

1. Create a new document.
2. Type **Please bring the following items to the airport and present them upon check in:** and press the Spacebar.
3. Press CTRL+ALT+L to insert a ListNum field and press the Spacebar.
4. Type **passport**, and press the Spacebar.
5. Press CTRL+ALT+L to insert the next number in the list and then press the Spacebar.

Copying and pasting the ListNum field is an alternative to using the shortcut keys.

6. Type **driver's license for rental car**, and press the Spacebar.
7. Repeat the preceding steps for the rest of the items in the list.

To increase or decrease the numbering level of a ListNum field, select the field and press any of the following keystroke combinations: Tab, Tab+Shift, Alt+Shift+Right-Arrow, or Alt+Shift+Left-Arrow. You can also use the Increase Indent or Decrease Indent buttons.

LIST STYLES

The pleadings, briefs, and agreements you create typically use the same outlines repeatedly. List Styles is a new feature in Word that allows you to create and save outline numbered lists for reuse in subsequent documents. List Styles also allows you to apply more than one outline numbering scheme to the same document. For example, if you regularly prepare agreements using two basic outlines, you can create two list styles and then apply either or both whenever the need arises.

List Styles is new to this version of Word and, as a result, doesn't quite match the flexibility found in some third-party numbering suites that are specifically geared for the legal market. Payne Consulting Group's Numbering Assistant, Legal MacPac, and Softwise MacroSuite all offer numbering solutions that meet the stringent demands of the legal community.

APPLYING A LIST STYLE

Word contains three default list styles. You can apply them directly or modify them as necessary. You can also create your own set of list styles.

APPLY A LIST STYLE

1. Create a new document.
2. From the Format menu, choose Bullets And Numbering.
3. Select the List Styles tab (Figure 8.19).
4. Make sure the Show drop-down menu has All Styles selected.
5. Select the 1/a/i list style and click OK.
6. The first number 1) is applied in the document.
7. Type some text and press Enter.
8. To move to the next level, press Tab or click the Increase Indent button on the Formatting toolbar.

NOTE

The Reset button is not available for list styles although it appears on the List Styles tab.

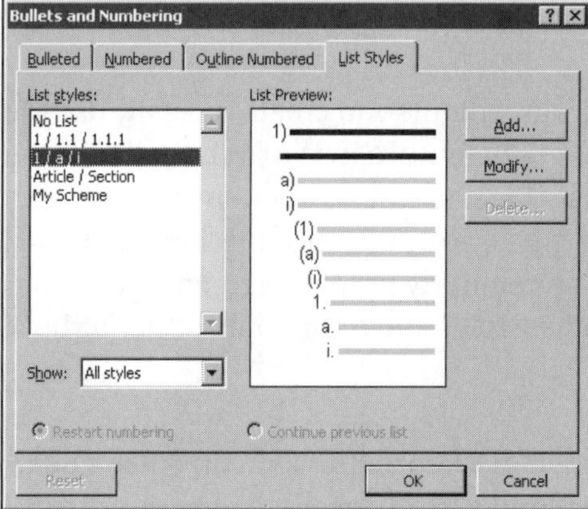

FIGURE 8.19

Add, modify, or delete list styles on the List Styles tab.

CREATE A NEW LIST STYLE

If the default List Styles do not meet your need, you can create a new list style by clicking Add to open the New Style dialog box. From here, you can choose, among other things, List Style name, number style, and indentation for each level in your custom List Style.

CREATE A NEW LIST STYLE

1. Create a new document.
2. From the Format menu choose Bullets And Numbering, select the List Styles tab, and click Add to open the New Style dialog box shown in Figure 8.20.
3. Type **Pleading** in the Name box.
4. Choose customization options for each level of the outline in the Apply Formatting To drop-down list.
5. Choose a Start At value for the first level. You'll probably want to leave the value set to 1.

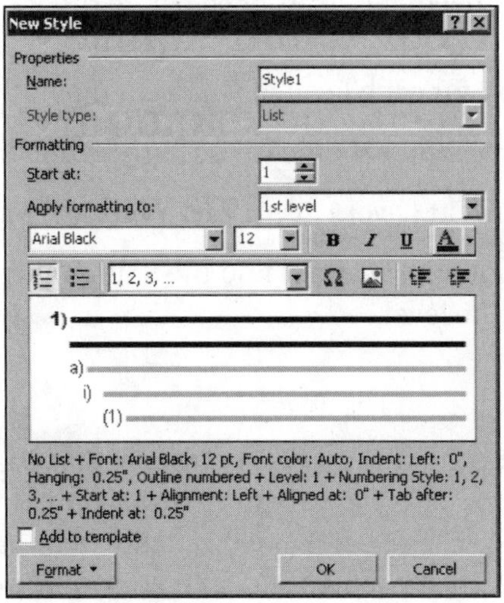

FIGURE 8.20

List styles can be named and customized in the New Style dialog box.

6. Select the font type, size, and style to format the number for the first level.

NOTE

Word will use the same font type, size, and style that is currently being used in the document if you don't make any changes.

TIP

For more options, choose Font from the Format button menu to access the complete Font dialog box.

7. Choose a number format from the drop-down list.

NOTE

You can also create a custom bullet list style. To do so, follow the same steps as for a numbered list but click the Bullet button instead and choose an appropriate option for each level in the bulleted list.

8. Click the Increase or Decrease Indent buttons, if needed.
9. Check the box next to Add To Template to make this list style available in all documents using the attached template.

TIP

Select Shortcut Key from the Format button menu to assign a keyboard shortcut to this list style.

CAUTION

Make sure you choose a shortcut key that is unassigned before clicking Assign.

10. Repeat steps 6 through 12 for each level of your scheme.
11. Click OK twice to apply the new scheme to the current document.
12. Word automatically begins at Level 1. Type text and press Enter.
13. Use the Tab key to promote the list level and the Shift+Tab key combination to demote the level.

NOTE

To delete a custom list style, go back to the Bullets And Numbering dialog box, select the List Styles tab, choose the style you wish to remove, and click Delete. This removes the list style from the current document. Use the Organizer to remove the list style from the attached template. Read Chapter 9, "Styles," to learn more about the Organizer.

Unlike previous versions of Word that stored custom numbering schemes in the registry, in Word 2002, list styles are stored in the document or saved to the template if the option to do so is selected.

Since list styles are new to Word 2002, you may wonder what happens if you use them in a document and then send the document to someone who uses Word 2000. Word 2000 users can still view and edit documents that contain list styles, however, when the document is saved in Word 2000, the list style's name is lost. If the file is later opened in Word 2002, the formatting is retained and works correctly, but the list style's name is lost and changes to display the name Current List1.

SUMMARY

All law firms use bullets and numbering, and few were completely satisfied by what Word had to offer in the past. Many firms resorted to purchasing third-party numbering products. While these products may still be a good idea, it's apparent that Microsoft has spent a great deal of time making Word's numbering feature work better in this version. At the top of the list is the elimination of the "Jason tab." This, Style Separator, and other improvements make applying and using simple and complex numbering much easier.

TROUBLESHOOTING BULLETS AND NUMBERING

I have a list of bulleted items and I need to leave a few bullets blank, but each time I press Enter after my bullet, it turns off bullets.

If you do not include any text after the bullet, Word assumes you are finished with the list. Once you have applied the bullet, press the Spacebar before you press the Enter key. This allows you to have a bullet with no text following it.

How do I use my firm's logo as a bullet in my documents?

All you have to do is click Customize in the Bullets And Numbering dialog box, click the Picture button, click Import, and navigate to your firm's logo picture file. Click the Import button once you find the file and then click OK.

I am using an outline numbering scheme attached to styles. I want my number to appear centered above my text, but when I try the format, the number line doesn't look centered on the screen. How do I fix this?

When using the Automatic Numbering feature, you have the option to have each number followed by a space, a tab, or nothing at all (this option is in the Customize Outline Numbered List dialog box). If you are trying to center the number on one line above the text below it, you will want to make sure to follow your number with nothing (rather than a tab). The tab setting adds .5" of spacing after the number and will therefore throw off center alignment.

When I use the shortcut key Ctrl+Alt+#, the style is applied to the paragraph but not the numbering. Why?

Check your settings in the Customize dialog box. Apply Heading 1 to a paragraph in the document. Leave the insertion point active in this paragraph (this ensures that the active numbering scheme will be chosen in your outline numbering gallery). From the Format menu, choose Bullets And Numbering and select the Outline Numbered tab. Look at the preview picture of the selected scheme. Does it show Heading styles? If not, you will need to add them.

My number is not incrementing. The scheme shows 1 on every paragraph.

Check the setting in the Customize dialog box to ensure that the number in the Number Format box is shaded. If it is not, the number has been typed in manually and is not a field. Delete that number and pick a number format from Number Style.

Chapter 9

Styles

In This Chapter

- Styles And Formatting Task Pane
- Applying existing styles
- Modifying a style
- Creating custom legal styles
- Organizing styles
- Creating a Style toolbar
- List and table styles

Styles are used in every document and for every character and paragraph typed. Understanding styles is not only vital to understanding how Word works, it will also allow you to leverage the true power behind the application and simplify the way you produce documents. Styles are linked to numbering and table of contents generation, and they are used to apply firm- and court-specified standard formats throughout documents. Styles are the backbone of Word.

Microsoft has completely redesigned the way styles work in Word 2002, so no matter how effectively you have used styles in previous versions—don't skip this chapter.

AN OVERVIEW OF STYLES

A *style* is a group of formatting commands that have been saved and named so they can be reused later. If you need to create a lengthy agreement where each article must be left-aligned, bold, in 14-point type, and underlined, the formatting alone could take hours if you had to manually apply it to each article. If this same formatting is applied once and saved as a style, you can recall it at any time and apply not one but all of these formatting options within seconds.

When a style format must change, you only need to make the change to the style once, and all other text formatted with the same style will update.

Styles also link to legal style numbering, the table of contents, and to the Document Map, a great navigational tool in Word.

If you learn to use and master styles, you can learn to use and master Microsoft Word.

WHY STYLES ARE VITAL TO LAW FIRMS

As mentioned previously, legal documents require precise formatting to meet court-specified rules. If these rules are not adhered to, you run the risk of documents being rejected by the courts. Even for documents not filed with the court, it's useful to have a consistent format that makes them easily recognizable as belonging to your firm—and creating a standardized look for your firm documents is made easy with styles. Document editing is just one benefit to using styles. The list of benefits includes:

- **Document Sharing**. It is rare that a legal document has only one editor. Since everyone works differently, if a firm and all reviewers use styles, it makes it easier to apply the appropriate formatting to each section of the document. Realistically, no one in the firm has time to call another reviewer of the document to ask how items such as footnotes, paragraph numbering, and headings should be formatted. If a style is created that holds these definitions, there is no chance for mistakes and no need to spend extensive time attempting to decipher formatting.
- **Court Rules**. Some documents require specific formats to meet court requirements. For years, firms have had some employees who were knowledgeable on those rules and to whom others went to for clarification. Styles can build these essential formats into the document so that all users can confidently create court documents quickly—even at 11 P.M. when the resident experts are not around and a document has to go out before midnight.
- **Consistency**. Many firms spend a tremendous amount of time and energy on branding an image. This effort becomes diluted if every attorney or secretary in the firm is distributing documents formatted based on individual preferences. When a firm creates its own consistent styles, its documents become recognizable through the use of consistent format and style (no pun intended).

> *Branding* is the term used to designate a unique image for the firm that includes firm logo, mission statement, standardized formats, and much more. This is also referred to as *branding an image*.

- **Table of Contents**. The Table of Contents feature is usually the biggest seller of styles. If a document is formatted using styles for the headings and numbered paragraphs, there is no need to mark text for inclusion in a table of contents. Just click where you want to insert the table of contents, choose the number of levels to appear, and Word generates the table of contents automatically. A table of contents can literally be created in five seconds if you use heading styles throughout the document.
- **Navigation**. When editing long, complex documents, much time can be wasted by scrolling through the document looking for the correct section to edit. A combination of styles and Word's Document Map feature provides one-click access to the exact page, section, even paragraph you want in the document. The Document Map feature (when enabled) appears on the left side of the screen and functions much like an index that takes you wherever you want to go.

TYPES OF STYLES

Word 2002 gives you four types of styles. This is two more than were available in previous versions of Word. The information you need to format will help you determine which type of style to create or apply. Here is a brief description of each type of style.

- **Paragraph**. Applies formatting to the entire paragraph, such as bullets, numbering, alignment, space before, and space after. Paragraph styles can be used to apply both character and paragraph formats to an entire paragraph.
- **Character**. Applies formatting that affects individual characters. Examples of character formatting include font, point size, and font style (bold, italic, and so on).
- **Table**. Applies border, shading, alignment, and character formats to tables. You can set up specific areas of a table with the appearance you want, save the formatting as a style, and then apply the style to other tables in the document. This helps you keep table formatting consistent throughout the file—or the firm.
- **List**. Applies outline number and bullet formats to lists. You can create and name your own choices and save them as a list style. For example, you might format a numbering scheme, name it "Client A Briefs," and use the numbering scheme when working on these types of documents for Client A.

UNCOVERING EXISTING STYLES

Each Word document contains styles. You can use one of Word's built-in styles or create your own; it is all up to you. Each document has default styles available but there are hundreds of styles that exist behind the scenes that you can display and then apply.

STYLES AND FORMATTING TASK PANE

The new home for styles is the Styles And Formatting Task Pane. Here you will find quick access to styles applied in the current document, user-defined styles, or all styles. The Styles And Formatting Task Pane is where you go to create, apply, and modify styles. To open the Styles And Formatting Task Pane, from the Format menu, choose Styles And Formatting or click the Styles And Formatting button on the Formatting toolbar.

The preview of the style in the Styles And Formatting Task Pane makes it easy to identify what style type is available and whether it's a paragraph, character, table, or list style. The symbol to the right of the style name distinguishes the type of style. Figure 9.1 shows each type of style and how it appears in the Styles And Formatting Task Pane.

The Styles And Formatting Task Pane is divided into sections: Formatting Of Selected Text, Pick Formatting To Apply, and Show.

SHOW LIST

The Show list provides greater control over what styles and formatting are displayed in the Styles And Formatting Task Pane. The Word 2000 Style dialog box included options for Styles In Use, All Styles, and User-Defined Styles. Word 2002 adds to this and includes the following options:

- **Available Formatting**. Lists the styles available in the document as well as any direct formats being used.

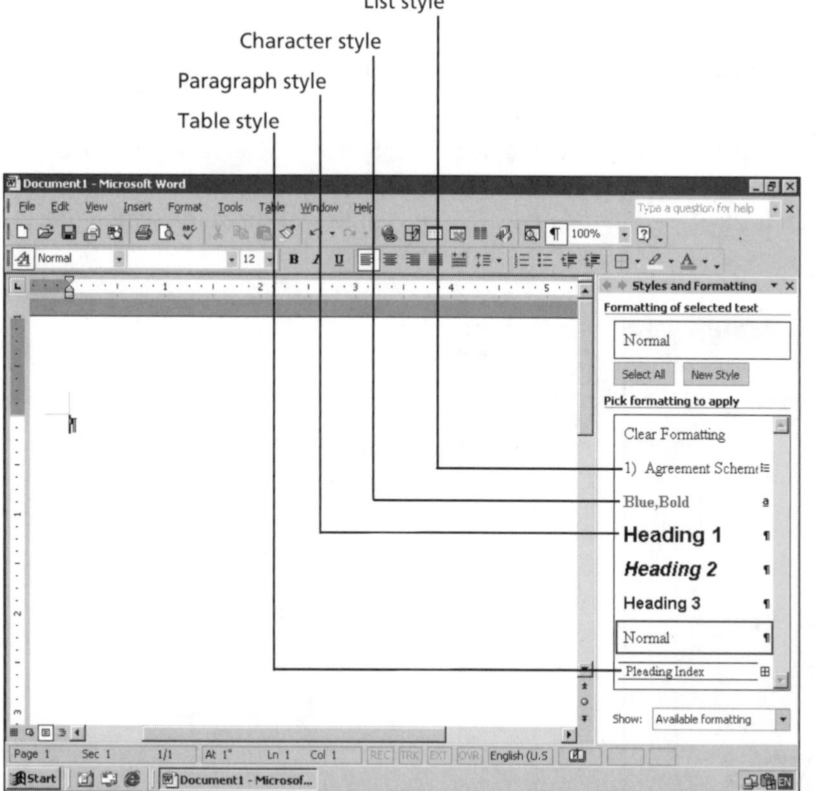

FIGURE 9.1

The Styles And Formatting Task Pane is one of the much improved features in Word 2002. The Task Pane allows you to quickly identify which styles are applied in the document, select all text formatted with a specific style, apply or modify styles, or create new styles.

- **Formatting In Use**. Lists just the styles and formats currently used in the document.
- **Available Styles**. Lists the styles available in the current document.
- **All Styles**. Lists all the custom styles in the document as well as in Word's extensive library of built-in styles.
- **Custom**. Allows you to select from the options of the Format Settings dialog box (shown in Figure 9.2) to create a view specific to your needs.

FORMAT SETTINGS OPTIONS

When Custom is selected from the Show drop-down list, the Format Settings dialog box displays and includes the following options for controlling what is visible in the Styles and Formatting Task Pane.

- **Show All**. Selects all check boxes in the dialog box except for Save Settings In Template. All styles and formatting will show in the Styles And Formatting Task Pane instead of the default styles Clear Formatting, Heading 1, Heading 2, Heading 3, and Normal.
- **Hide All**. Clears all boxes in the Format Settings dialog box and in the Styles And Formatting Task Pane.
- **Styles To Be Visible**. Options that appear in this section are controlled by what is selected for Category.
- **Category**. The list includes Available Styles, Styles In Use, All Styles, User-Defined Styles, and Do Not Show Styles. The Category drop-down list controls what is displayed in the Styles To Be Visible section of the dialog box.

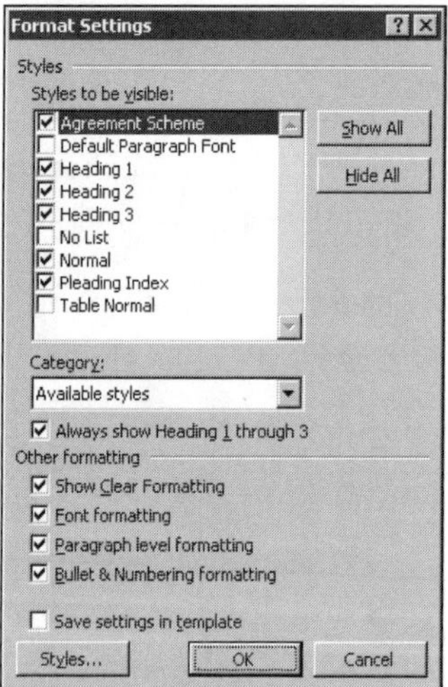

FIGURE 9.2

You can fine-tune what styles to show in the Format Settings dialog box.

- **Always Show Heading 1 Through 3**. Places Heading 1, Heading 2, and Heading 3 in the Styles To Be Visible section of the dialog box and in the Styles and Formatting Task Pane.
- **Show Clear Formatting**. Displays the Clear Formatting option in the Styles And Formatting Task Pane.
- **Font Formatting**. Allows direct formatting scheme to be added to the Pick Formatting To Apply list on the Styles And Formatting Task Pane.
- **Paragraph Level Formatting**. Allows direct paragraph formatting to be added to the Pick Formatting To Apply List on the Styles And Formatting Task Pane.
- **Bullet & Numbering Formatting**. Allows bullets and numbering formatting schemes to be added to the Pick Formatting To Apply List on the Styles And Formatting Task Pane.
- **Save Settings In Template**. Save all settings selected in the Format Settings dialog box to the active template.
- **Styles**. Displays the Style dialog box, which can be used to create, delete, modify, apply, and organize styles.

If no styles show in the Styles and Formatting Task Pane, the option to Hide All or not show styles may have been selected. Click the Show drop-down list arrow and choose Custom. Check Category to see if Do Not Show Styles is selected. Also, make sure Hide All hasn't been enabled. To view styles not shown by default in the Task Pane, check the option next to the desired style name.

USING THE FORMATTING TOOLBAR TO VIEW STYLES

The Formatting toolbar includes a Style button. This button lists the name of the style at the insertion point and includes a drop-down arrow that, when accessed, shows a list of styles available in the current document. By default, this list is short unless your firm has created a lot of styles of its own or has chosen to show additional styles. You can access all Word styles, however, by holding the Shift key while clicking the drop-down arrow.

VIEW STYLES FROM THE FORMATTING TOOLBAR

1. Create a new document.
2. Click the Style button's drop-down arrow. The styles currently available in the document appear, as shown in Figure 9.3.

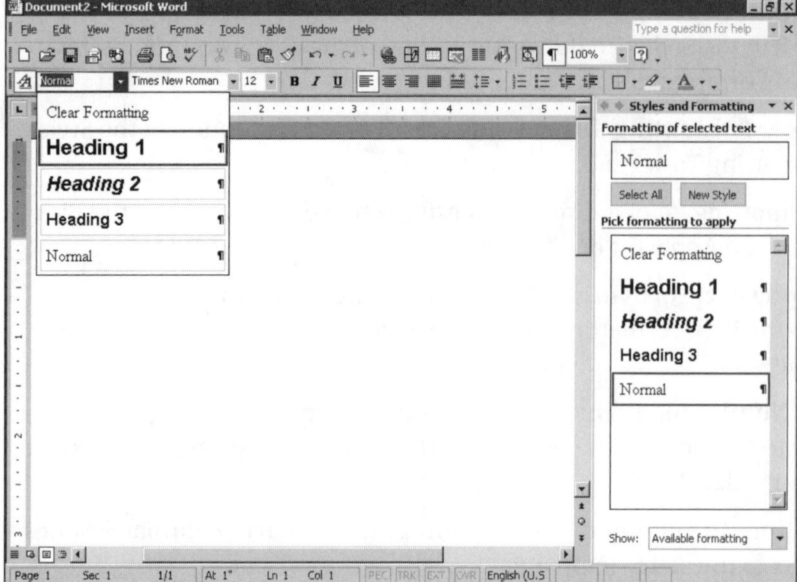

FIGURE 9.3

By default, few styles appear when you click the drop-down arrow on the Style button. Although the majority of styles are hidden from view, they can be displayed and applied quickly.

3. Press Esc to close the list of styles.
4. Hold the Shift key and click the Style drop-down arrow. All of Word's built-in styles appear in alphabetical order along with the ones specific to the document.
5. Press Esc or click in the contents of the document to close the Style drop-down list.

STYLE AREA WIDTH

The Styles And Formatting Task Pane lists the formatting of the selected paragraph as well as other available styles. However, there is another way to view applied paragraph styles as you work, and that's by opening up the Style Area on the left side of the document. This feature is only available when you work in Normal or Outline view, when it places the applied paragraph style name directly next to the text.

From the Tools menu, choose Options and select the View tab. Set Style Area Width to 1" or a desired size measurement and click OK. Make sure you are in Normal view and apply styles. The Style Area is shown in Figure 9.4.

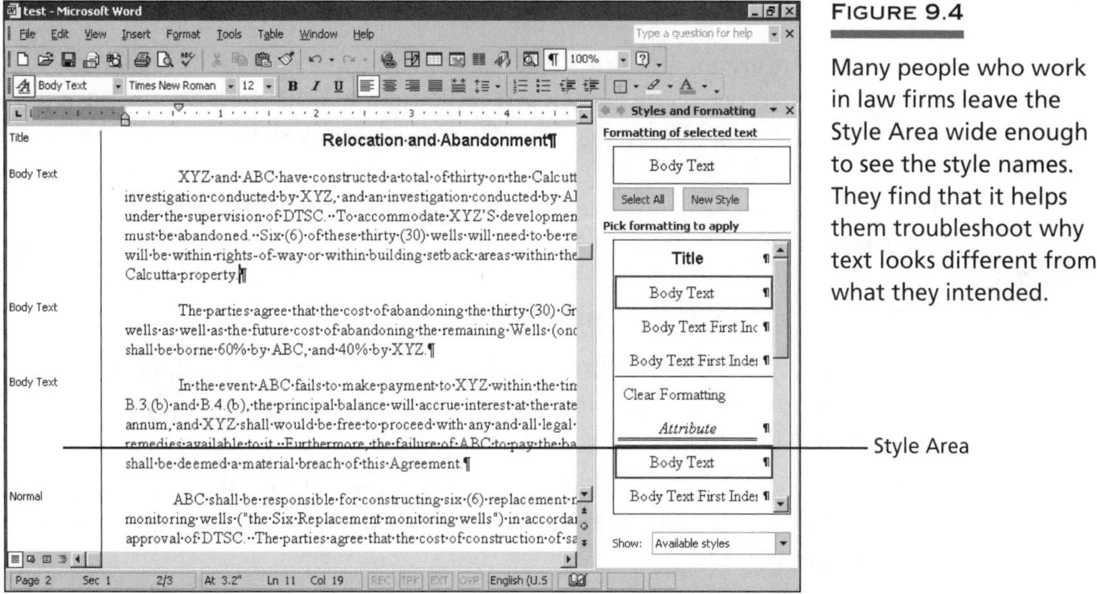

FIGURE 9.4

Many people who work in law firms leave the Style Area wide enough to see the style names. They find that it helps them troubleshoot why text looks different from what they intended.

TIP

A line divides the document window from the Style Area. This area can be resized by dragging the divider line with the mouse. If you move the divider line too far to the left, the feature is turned off. If this happens accidentally, return to the View tab on the Options dialog box and turn the setting back on by typing a number in the Style Area Width box.

APPLYING STYLES

Are you a keyboard person? Or do you prefer a mouse? When it comes to applying styles, you can use the method you find most comfortable. Click a style in the Pick Formatting To Apply section of the Styles And Formatting Task Pane, or just press a keyboard shortcut combination assigned to a style.

DIFFERENT WAYS TO APPLY A STYLE

1. Create a new document.
2. Type **Introduction.**
3. Using the Formatting toolbar, click the Style button's drop-down arrow and select Heading 1 from the list of available styles. You've applied Heading 1 style to the Introduction paragraph.

4. Place your insertion point after Introduction and press Enter.
5. Type **Argument** and press Ctrl+Alt+2 to apply Heading 2. You've just applied a style using a keyboard combination. Both methods are easy; it's a matter of preference which you use to apply styles.

Microsoft's built-in Heading 1, Heading 2, and Heading 3 styles have default shortcut keys assigned: Ctrl+Alt+1, Ctrl+Alt+2, and Ctrl+Alt+3, respectively.

6. Press Enter and type **Conclusion**.
7. If the Styles And Formatting Task Pane is not visible, from the Format menu, choose Styles And Formatting. Click Heading 3 to apply Heading 3 style to the current paragraph.
8. Leave your insertion point in that paragraph and click Heading 1 on the Styles And Formatting Task Pane. The paragraph is now formatted with Heading 1 style.

Notice how easy it is to apply a different style to a paragraph. Just click in the paragraph and apply the desired style.

9. Click at the end of the Introduction paragraph and press Enter.
10. Type **This paragraph introduces the subject of this brief**. Heading text by default is followed by Normal or Body Text style. If this was not the case, then press Ctrl+Shift+N to apply Normal style or click Normal on the Styles And Formatting Task Pane.
11. Select the word *introduces.*
12. Look for and click the Hyperlink style on the Styles And Formatting Task Pane.

If you do not see Hyperlink, change the Show drop-down list to display All Styles.

13. Leave this document open for the next exercise.

For paragraph styles, click anywhere in the paragraph. To apply character styles, you must first select the text.

CLEAR FORMATTING WITH STYLES

To remove a style from a paragraph, click Clear Formatting in the Pick Formatting To Apply section on the Styles And Formatting Task Pane. This will remove all formatting of the selected paragraph and apply Normal style. If you prefer a keyboard shortcut, press Ctrl+Shift+N to clear formatting and return the style to Normal.

NOTE

Clear Formatting is not available when the Styles And Formatting Task Pane is set to Show All Styles.

TIP

You can access the Clear Formatting command from the Edit menu. Select the text to remove the formatting from. From the Edit menu, choose Clear, Formats.

DEFINE STYLES BASED ON FORMATTING

If you find yourself applying the same formatting repeatedly, you can turn on the Define Styles Based On Formatting option. This applies a style to your text based on the format that you have applied. For example, format a paragraph with 14-point boldface type. Word will automatically apply Heading 1 style to that paragraph. This sounds great initially because it eliminates the step of having to apply a style.

But wait! Before you turn this feature on, here is the other side to what Define Styles Based On Formatting does. As you are formatting text, Word applies a style automatically—without your doing anything other than formatting. Sometimes Word guesses correctly, but oftentimes it does not. This relinquishes some control over what happens in your document. Define Styles Based On Formatting often leads to errors in the table of contents, and there are other problems that can occur.

Payne Consulting Group highly recommends avoiding the Define Styles Based On Formatting option. From the Tools menu, choose AutoCorrect Options. Select the AutoFormat As You Type tab and deselect Define Styles Based on Your Formatting.

OTHER OPTIONS THAT AUTOMATICALLY APPLY STYLES

Besides Define Styles Based On Your Formatting, Word contains three other options that will automatically apply a style to specific types of inserted text. We recommend that these options be turned off.

Choose AutoCorrect Options from the Tools menu and select the AutoFormat As You Type tab. These options are found in the Apply As You Type section.

- **Built-In Heading Styles**. This feature will apply Heading 1 through 9 to paragraphs formatted with similar formats.
- **Date Style**. When a date is inserted into the document, it will be formatted with the Date style if this option is turned on.
- **Closing Style To Letter Closings**. If checked, Word will apply the Closing style to closing text of a letter.

MODIFY A STYLE

One of the most common misconceptions about working with styles is that the formats are rigid. This is definitely not the case. As easily as you can apply a completely different style to a paragraph, you can reformat a style to match your changing needs. The style can be changed at any time, even after it has been applied.

There are a couple of different ways to modify a style. You can use the Modify Style dialog box. Or a simpler process would be to format the paragraph as you wish and then update the style and all related styles throughout the document.

MODIFY BY EXAMPLE

Think about how you change the format of text. Most people select the text and then apply the formats they wish to use. Changing a style follows the same logic. Once the style has been applied, change the format of the text to meet your needs.

As you apply direct formatting to a paragraph previously formatted with a style, the Styles And Formatting Task Pane reflects those changes by displaying the style name followed by a plus sign and the direct formats applied. For example, if text is formatted with Heading style 3 and you add underline formatting, the Styles And Formatting Task Pane will show "Heading 3 + Underline." The Styles And Formatting Task Pane with a modified style is shown in Figure 9.5.

> *Direct formatting* is formatting applied directly to the text after a style has been applied. For example, you might apply the Heading 1 style and then bold or italicize the text as direct formatting, making that heading different from others of the same level.

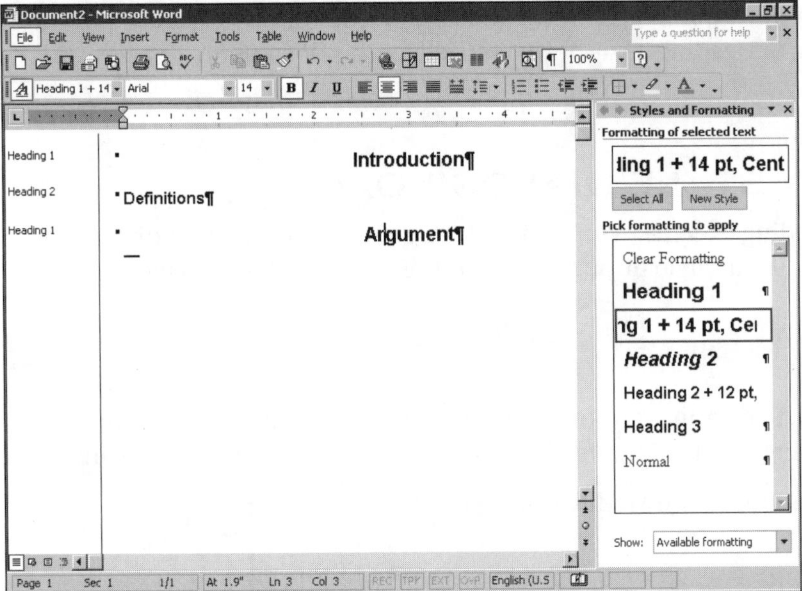

FIGURE 9.5

A style name followed by a plus sign indicates that direct formatting has been applied to the text over the original style. Sometimes direct formatting is necessary for a one-time use, but people who understand styles usually find it easier to manipulate the format of the document without direct formatting.

NOTE

If the Styles And Formatting Task Pane does not reflect direct formatting, from the Tools menu, choose Options. On the Edit tab, enable the Keep Track Of Formatting option.

USE THE TASK PANE TO MODIFY AND UPDATE STYLES

1. The document from the preceding exercise should still be open.
2. Select the Argument paragraph.
3. Format the paragraph to be centered and Small Caps.
4. Hover the mouse pointer over Heading 2 in the Styles And Formatting Task Pane until the drop-down arrow appears.
5. Select Update To Match Selection from the drop-down list next to the applied style name.

CAUTION

Be sure to click the drop-down arrow and not the style name. If you click the style name, that style will replace any direct formatting.

6. Add another paragraph of text and apply Heading 2 style. Notice how the format of Heading 2 has been changed for this document.

MODIFY STYLE DIALOG BOX

In the preceding exercise, you updated the style by modifying it directly. You can also modify the style through the Modify dialog box shown in Figure 9.6.

USE THE MODIFY STYLE DIALOG BOX

1. Using the document from the preceding exercise, click the drop-down arrow next to Heading 1 style in the Styles And Formatting Task Pane.
2. Select Modify. The Modify Style dialog box opens.

> **NEW LOCATION OF COMMAND**
>
> In previous versions of Word, you could access the Modify Style dialog box through the Format menu. In Word 2002, the Modify dialog box can only be accessed through the Styles And Formatting Task Pane.

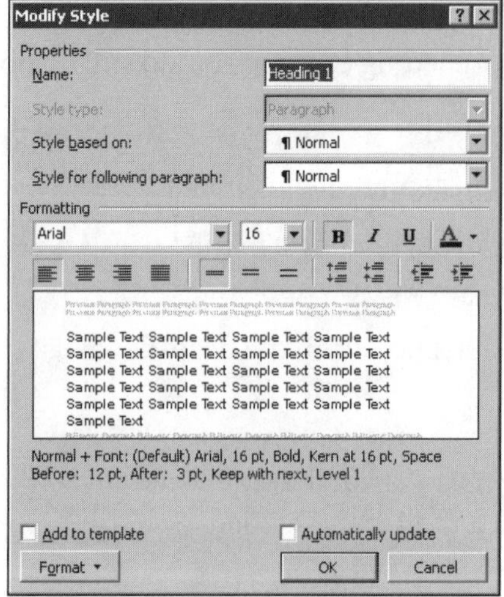

FIGURE 9.6

You can still modify styles—but now access is available only through the Styles And Formatting Task Pane.

3. Click Underline.
4. Click Format and choose Font. The Font dialog box opens.
5. Select All Caps and click OK.
6. Click OK to save changes to the style.

When you modify a style, whether by example or through the dialog box, that change is only applicable to the current document. However, there are two exceptions to this rule.

- **Exception 1**. Select Add To Template to save the modifications to the template the document was created from. Any new documents that are created from that same template will contain this modification, but old documents created from it will retain the original style unless you invoke the second exception.
- **Exception 2**. From the Tools menu, choose Templates and Add-Ins, and then choose Automatically Update Document Styles, which will "go back in time" and update any styles previously used in a document along with any modifications made to the template. This feature would need to be turned on in each document for this to occur.

Automatically Update Document Styles is not well known and can cause a lot of frustration because styles will change unexpectedly. Once a document has been created, the style formats are set and usually not changed, so we suggest not enabling this setting. If you do use it, turn it on to update the styles but be sure to turn it off when the task is complete.

IMPROVED FEATURE!

In previous versions of Word, there was confusion over whether to choose Apply or Close after modifying a style. In Word 2002, there is only an OK button to save changes and a Cancel button to exit without saving.

PROMPT TO UPDATE STYLE

Previous versions of Word allowed you to update a style by clicking directly on the Style button on the Formatting toolbar and pressing Enter. If the format had changed, a dialog box would appear with the choice of updating or reapplying the original style.

In Word 2002, this feature is no longer available. The prompt to Update Style option uses the same dialog box as in previous versions, but the dialog box does not work exactly as before.

USE PROMPT TO UPDATE STYLE

1. Open the file named Styles.doc from the accompanying CD-ROM. If you do not have access to the CD-ROM, create a document, apply a style, and then change the formatting.
2. From the Tools menu, choose Options. Select the Edit tab.
3. Enable Prompt To Update Style.
4. Click OK.
5. Select The Parties paragraph if you're using the file from the CD-ROM.
6. Format the paragraph to be Underlined and Not Bold.
7. In the Styles And Formatting Task Pane, click Heading 1. The Modify Style dialog box opens, as shown in Figure 9.7.
8. Select Update The Style To Reflect Recent Changes and click OK.

This message box will appear whether the format of the style has changed or not. This is different from the situation in previous versions of Word, where the prompt would only appear if direct formatting had been applied.

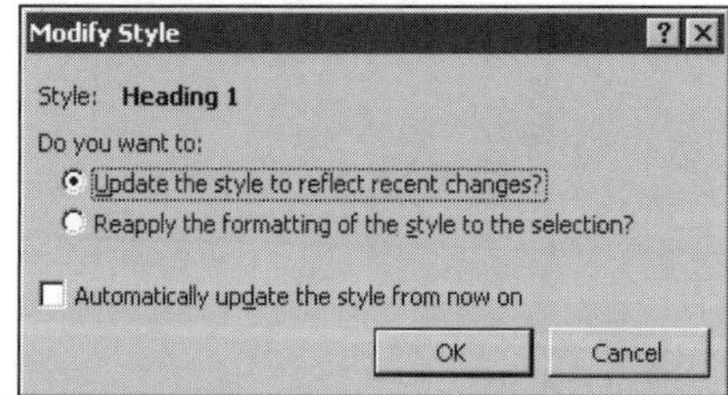

FIGURE 9.7

Seeing this dialog box will be comforting to people who have worked with styles in previous versions—it's familiar territory. Choose to Update or Reapply the style in the Modify Style dialog box.

NORMAL STYLE

The Normal style is the base style in all Word documents. For this reason, this style is treated differently from all other styles. You cannot use Modify By Example to change the Normal style; you must use the Modify Style dialog box instead.

Be very careful when changing the Normal style. Most styles are based on Normal—so if you change Normal, all the styles based on it will change as well.

REAPPLYING A STYLE

As shown in the preceding exercise, if the Prompt To Update Style option is enabled, you will be given an option to reapply the style, which removes any direct formatting.

If you do not have this option selected, you can click the style name in the Styles And Formatting Task Pane to achieve the same result.

Keyboard shortcuts can be used to remove directly applied formatting. The keyboard combination Ctrl+Q removes direct paragraph formatting such as indents, line spacing, bullets, and numbering. Ctrl+Spacebar removes direct character formatting such as bold, italic, underline, or other character formats applied over the style.

CREATING A STYLE OF YOUR OWN

Styles are not limited to Word's built-in choices. Word makes it easy to create your own styles. Creating a style is similar to modifying an existing one—whether you start from scratch using the New Style dialog box or use an existing format in the document, you can create a style suitable to your formatting needs.

CREATE A STYLE FROM SCRATCH

1. Create a new document.
2. Type **The electors of President and Vice President shall be appointed, in each State, on the Tuesday next after the first Monday in November, in every fourth year succeeding every election of a President and Vice President.** Press Enter.

3. Type **Whenever any State has held an election for the purpose of choosing electors, and has failed to make a choice on the day prescribed by law, the electors may be appointed on a subsequent day in such a manner as the legislature of such State may direct.**
4. Select this last paragraph.
5. Click New Style on the Styles And Formatting Task Pane. The New Style dialog box opens, as shown in Figure 9.8.
6. Type **My Style** in the Name box.
7. Set the Style Type to Paragraph.
8. Select Arial as the font, size 11, double-spaced.
9. Click OK.
10. Click My Style on the Styles And Formatting Task Pane to apply the newly created style.

CREATING A STYLE BASED ON AN EXAMPLE

The primary point to styles is to simplify formatting a document. If you've already formatted text the way you want it and you wish to store this formatting

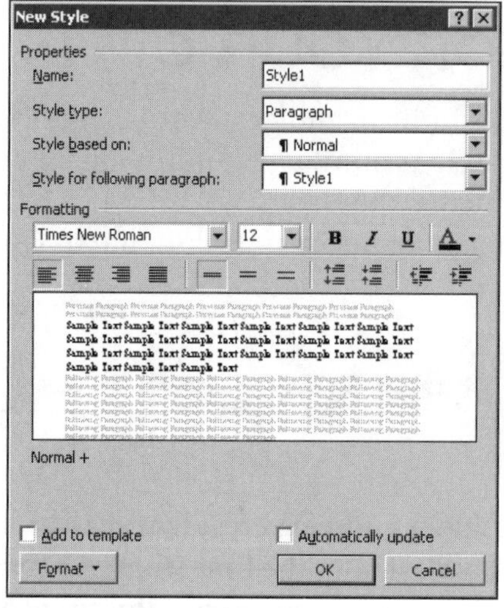

FIGURE 9.8

Most of the formatting that you will need to apply is on the face of the New Style dialog box. However, there are additional options available if you click the Format button on the dialog box.

as a style, you can base the style on the existing example. To define a style based on formatting, you only need to do one thing—name it. This makes it easy to take a document that comes from a client without styles and quickly convert it to a document containing styles without changing the formats.

THE NEW STYLE DIALOG BOX

1. Open No Styles.doc from the CD-ROM, or if you prefer, create a simple agreement without any styles applied.
2. Select the paragraph after the title that begins "THIS AGREEMENT"—or any paragraph of plain text, if you're using your own file.
3. Click on the Style button on the Formatting toolbar.
4. Type **Body** and press Enter. You've just created a style named Body.
5. Click in the next similar paragraph and apply this same style.
6. In the next paragraph, press F4. This repeats the last action.
7. Click in the paragraph headed "Relocation and Abandonment of Utilities"—or on any heading line in your own file.
8. Click New Style.
9. Type **My Heading** in the Name box and click OK.
10. Click Select All. This will select all paragraphs with similar formats.
11. Click My Heading to apply the new style.
12. Leave this document open for the next exercise.

TIP

To save time, format the paragraph and then click New Style. You will only have to give the style a name.

USING EXTRA STYLE FEATURES

Now that you can create styles, it's time to look at some of the options available for applying and working with them.

DON'T ADD SPACE BETWEEN PARAGRAPHS OF THE SAME STYLE

If you've displayed the Indents and Spacing tab on the Paragraph dialog box, you may have wondered about the Don't Add Space Between Paragraphs Of The Same Style option, which is grayed out. This is a new feature in Word 2002 and is a part of paragraph formatting; however, you can only access this command through the New or Modify Style dialog box, and only when creating or modifying a style that has a value set for Space Before and/or Space After for the paragraph style.

This option allows you to adjust spacing between paragraphs based on the surrounding paragraphs without having to create multiple styles that contain the same formatting except for paragraph spacing.

SHORTCUT KEY

Some of Word's built-in styles have shortcut keys associated with them, allowing you to apply the style without using the mouse. You can assign keyboard commands to any styles that you create or modify.

Open the Styles And Formatting Task Pane. Locate the style that you want to assign a keyboard shortcut. Click the drop-down arrow next to the style name and choose Modify. Click Format, Shortcut Key.

Figure 9.9 shows an example of how you can assign a keyboard shortcut when you first create a style.

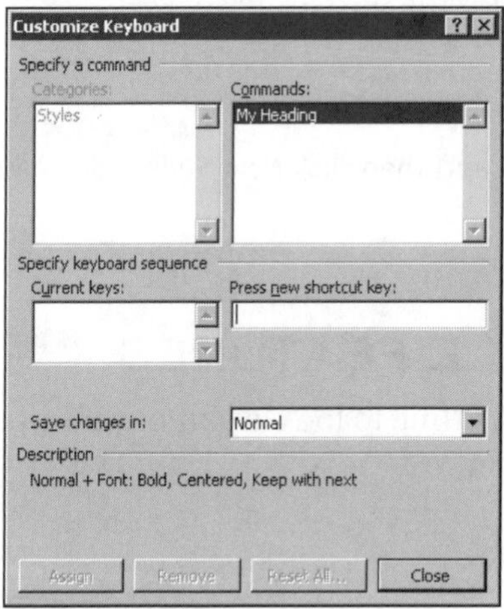

FIGURE 9.9

If you are creating a new style, you can assign a keyboard shortcut to a style from the New or Modify Style dialog boxes.

Be careful when assigning keyboard shortcuts to styles, since you do not want to overwrite an existing Word command. For example, if you assign Ctrl+S to a style, you are overwriting the default command associated with that shortcut (Save), which will be a shock to anyone else who happens to use the document or template where you stored the style.

Once you type or press the keyboard shortcut, check the Currently Assigned To area of the dialog box to ensure your choice is not currently assigned to something else. Word will use that area to tell you that you are overwriting an existing keyboard shortcut combination—but it won't argue with you if you go ahead.

Style for Following Paragraph

If you type something formatted with Heading 1 style and press Enter, typically you do not want to type another heading; instead, you will likely type a subheading or paragraph. When creating styles, you can specify what should follow the style by setting Style For Following Paragraph. It is good practice and protocol to set the style for the following paragraph so that inexperienced users are not "stuck" in an infinite loop of one style.

Set Up Style for Following Paragraph

1. The No Styles document should still be open from the preceding exercise.
2. Choose Modify from the drop-down arrow beside My Heading in the Styles And Formatting Task Pane.
3. Select Body from the Style For Following Paragraph section. Each time you press Enter after working in My Heading, the paragraph following will be styled as Body.
4. Click OK.
5. Go to the end of the document and press Enter.
6. Apply My Heading style.
7. Type **Appendix** and press Enter.
8. Type **The following table lists contact information**. Notice how the style changed automatically to Body after you pressed Enter.

ADD TO TEMPLATE

When a style is created, it is saved by default into the document where it was created. This is also the case when you modify an existing style. If you want to use the newly created or modified style in other documents, you can select the Add To Template option in the New Or Modify Style dialog box to save your style to the current template. This is especially useful for styles that you use firm-wide in pleading, letter, memo, fax, and agreement document types. Each time you choose File, New and base a document on a template that includes the style, the style will be available to you.

STYLE BASED ON

Most styles start from another style. For example, if you are creating a Subheading style, you might select the heading style that is similar to the way you want the style formatted, and then change the format to be exactly as you want. A style created for the first time most likely starts from the Normal style. The Style Based On option specified is the original style used before modifications were made.

Since most styles are based on Normal, it is easy to change the format of an entire document. Say you need to change the document to Arial from Times New Roman. If you change the Normal style to Arial, all styles based on it will change as well.

If a style is based on a style other than Normal, it will be a little more work to change the format of an entire document, since you will need to change multiple styles. Also, you may experience unexpected changes in the style, especially when you are not aware that the style is based on another.

If your Subheading is based on the Heading style and you change the Heading style to specify 24-point type, the subheading will also change to 24-point type if you have not already specified a particular point size for the subheading. Likewise, if you change the font color for the Heading style to purple but the subheading style's font color had already been changed to red, the subheading style will not change to purple when the Heading style is changed.

ALIASES

For all user-defined styles, the name of the style is flexible. A change of style name from Main Text to Body is accomplished through the Modify Style dialog box.

Word's built-in styles prevent name changes but allow aliases to be created. An alias is basically a nickname for a style. For applying styles through the Style button, you can type the alias name (which is usually shorter than the original name) to apply the style.

Aliases appear after the style name and are separated by a comma, as shown in Figure 9.10.

CREATE AN ALIAS

1. Create a new blank document.
2. In the Styles And Formatting Task Pane, select Modify from the drop-down menu next to Heading 1.
3. In the Name field, type **H1** and click OK.
4. Click the Style button on the Formatting toolbar.
5. Type **H1** and press Enter.
6. Type **This Is My Heading**.
7. Click on the Style drop-down arrow on the Formatting toolbar. Notice the alias beside Heading 1, as shown in Figure 9.10.

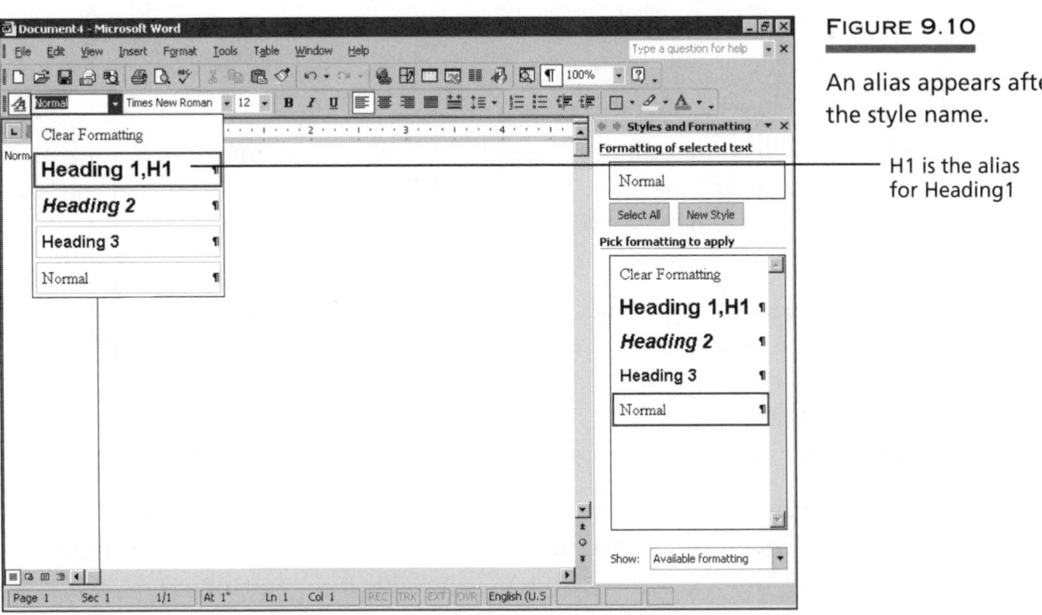

FIGURE 9.10

An alias appears after the style name.

AUTOMATICALLY UPDATE

Both the New Style and Modify dialog boxes allow you to set an Automatically Update option for the style. This changes the style on the fly as you apply formatting. For example, if you format a Heading 1 paragraph to be centered, every Heading 1 paragraph in the document will center itself to match this one—without notification of the change. The definition of the style changes as well (in this case, to centered), so all future Heading 1 lines will follow suit.

At first glance this feature may seem great. After all, you can eliminate one whole step (modify to match selection) with this option selected. However, if you are sharing this document with others who are not aware of this feature, it can be frustrating. As they apply formatting to text previously defined as a style, the actual formatting of the style and all text formatted with this style update automatically—and there's no record of what the style originally used to specify.

This frustration alone is enough to make someone refuse to use styles. For this reason, Payne Consulting Group strongly suggests not using this feature unless you are the only one working on the document.

Word's built-in TOC styles have Automatically Update turned on by default. Since TOC styles are not used in modifying a document, this is one style that actually benefits from having Automatically Update turned on. See Chapter 14, "Agreements, Briefs, and Other Long Documents," for more information.

ORGANIZING STYLES

Styles reside in a document or template. This means that when a document is sent to another party, the formatting will not change—and, even more important, the receiving party can continue to use the styles residing in that document.

If you create a style that is particularly useful, you will want to add it to a template so you can use it whenever you want. You will also want to do a little styles housecleaning and delete styles no longer used or required.

USING THE ORGANIZER TO COPY STYLES

Once you have created styles, you can use them in documents that were created previously, documents based on another template, or documents sent to you from a client. Word's Organizer allows you to do all of these things.

The Organizer is also discussed in the Templates chapter, since it can be used with macros, toolbars, and AutoText.

COPY STYLES USING THE ORGANIZER

1. Open Styles.doc.
2. From the Tools menu, choose Templates And Add-Ins.
3. Click Organizer. The Organizer dialog box opens, as shown in Figure 9.11.
4. Click Close File on the right side of the dialog box. Notice that the button instantly changes to Open File.
5. Navigate to where your exercise files are stored. Select Personal.dot or one of your existing templates, and click Open. The styles from that template are listed.
6. Select Delivery Method or another existing template and click Copy.

If the style name that you are trying to copy already exists in the document that you are attempting to copy it into, you will see a prompt asking if you want to overwrite the existing style.

7. Copy Firm Address as well.
8. Click Close.

When a style is based on another style, it is important to copy both styles so as to make sure the format of the style remains intact. For example, if you copy a Double Indent style but not the Indent style on which it is based, you may lose some formatting. The receiving document will change to base the style on Normal style, because it will not be able to find the style named Indent. Copy the style that another style is based on first, and then copy the other style.

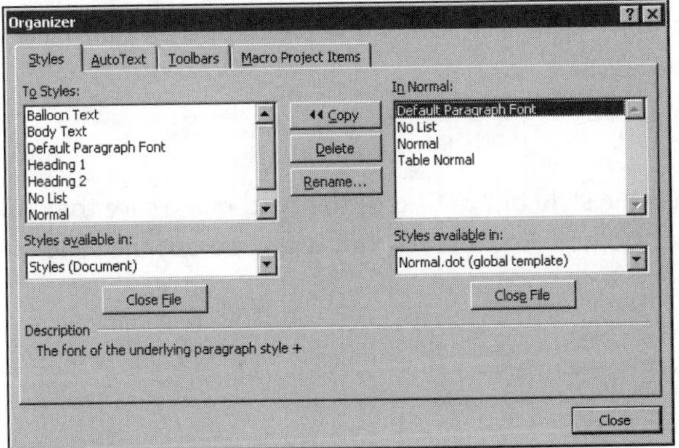

FIGURE 9.11

Copy, move, delete, and rename styles in the Organizer.

OTHER ORGANIZER COMMANDS

The Organizer also contains buttons to Delete and Rename styles. However, in Word 2002, the Styles And Formatting Task Pane offers these commands right at your fingertips. Since these commands are readily available, the primary use of the Organizer is to copy styles.

USING CUT, COPY, AND PASTE WITH STYLES

You can copy styles by copying a paragraph of text containing the style or by using the Format Painter. This is great when you want to copy a style from one document to another.

NOTE

When you're making a copy, be sure to include the paragraph mark at the end of the paragraph when you want to include the formatting—and to omit it when you don't want the formatting.

COPY STYLES BETWEEN DOCUMENTS

1. Open No Styles.doc.
2. Select the title at the top of the document. Be sure to select the paragraph mark that follows.
3. Click Copy or press Ctrl+C.
4. Create a new blank document.
5. Click Paste or press Ctrl+V.
6. Delete the newly inserted paragraph. The Centered Title style now appears in the Style drop-down list and the Styles And Formatting Task Pane. As soon as the paragraph is inserted into the document, the style is copied along with the text. Even if you delete the text of the paragraph, the style remains.

NOTE

If you want to keep the style but get rid of the text, make sure that you delete the paragraph text. Do not click Undo—that will wipe out the style as well.

If you paste the styled paragraph into a document that already contains a style with the same name, the existing style will not be overwritten. Use the Organizer to overwrite a style.

USING THE STYLE GALLERY

The Style Gallery command has been around in previous versions of Word. It offers a quick way to get all the styles from one template into your document. To access the Style Gallery, from the Format menu, choose Theme and click Style Gallery. Select a template that contains the styles you want to use from the Templates box. When you click OK, the styles from the selected template are copied into your document.

As mentioned in the Templates chapter, every document is created from a template. The styles available in a template are available in your new document. The Style Gallery (shown in Figure 9.12) allows you to take all the styles from another template and add them to your document.

In the last few versions of Word, the Style Gallery has been less than reliable. We have tested the feature in Word 2002, and it appears to function as intended.

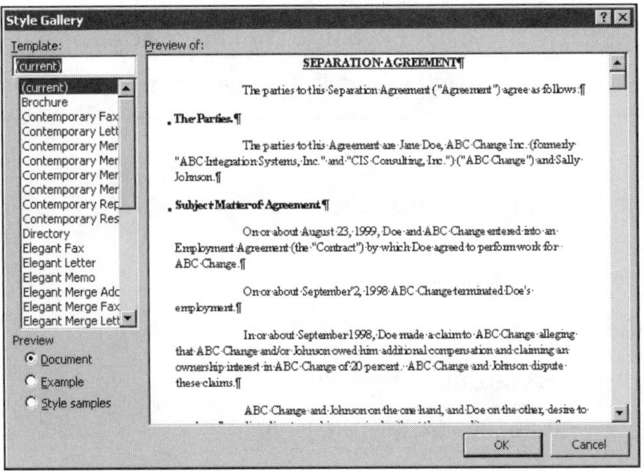

FIGURE 9.12

The Style Gallery also allows you to "try before you buy" if you want to see how your document will look with the selected group of styles applied.

DELETING STYLES

In previous versions of Word, deleting styles was difficult and often left to IT personnel or power users. In Word 2002, deleting styles is easy. Click the drop-down arrow next to the style name in the Styles And Formatting Task Pane, and choose Delete to delete the style from the current document. Or choose Delete from the Organizer to delete it from the template.

CREATING A STYLE TOOLBAR

Word 2002 introduces new style commands, which can be added to a toolbar to provide instant access to some of the more common style features. For example, the Style By Example command will automatically create a new style from the selected text, naming it Style1, Style2, and so forth.

Table 9.1 lists the new style buttons and the corresponding functionality.

TABLE 9.1 NEW STYLE BUTTONS

STYLE COMMAND	DESCRIPTION
Styles And Formatting	Toggles the Styles And Formatting Task Pane on and off.
Style By Example	Creates a new style from the selected paragraph using the naming convention of Style1, Style2, etc.
Rename Style	Opens a dialog box so you can insert a new name for the selected style.
Modify Style	Updates the style with the selected paragraph formatting.
Delete Style	Deletes the selected style from the current document.

CREATE A STYLE TOOLBAR

1. Create a new blank document.
2. From the Tools menu, choose Customize.
3. On the Toolbars tab, click New.
4. Name your toolbar **Styles** and click OK.
5. Select the Commands tab.

6. In the Categories section, select Format. This exposes all commands available for formatting.
7. Locate and drag the Style By Example button to the Styles toolbar.
8. Alternate-click the newly added command to make changes to the button's appearance.
9. Repeat steps 7 and 8 to add the following buttons:
   - Styles And Formatting
   - Redefine Style
   - Rename Style
   - Modify Style
   - Delete Style

   The Styles toolbar now contains buttons useful when working with styles. The result is shown in Figure 9.13.
10. Click Close to save your changes and close the Customize dialog box.

LIST STYLES

List styles—new in Word 2002—allow you to create and save outline numbering schemes and to apply the same formatting to your other lists quickly and without having to recreate the sometimes complex and time-consuming format. Word comes with three default list styles, which you can use or modify. You can also create list styles of your own.

List styles cannot be created by example.

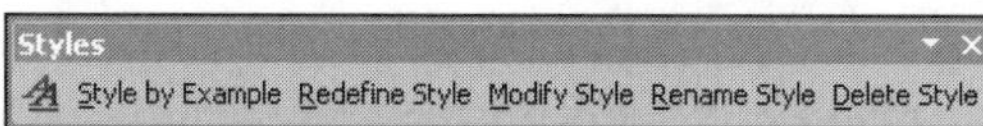

FIGURE 9.13

The purpose of toolbars is to make frequently used commands easier to access. By creating a Styles toolbar, you put the style controls at your fingertips.

CREATE A LIST STYLE

1. Create a new document.
2. Click New Style from the Styles And Formatting Task Pane.
3. Click the drop-down arrow next to Style Type, and choose List. The New Style dialog box shown in Figure 9.14 opens, giving you options to create a list style.
4. Type **Contract** in the Name field.
5. Click the Format button, and choose Numbering. The Bullets And Numbering dialog box opens.
6. Select the option on the top row—that is, 1, 1.1, 1.1.1—and click OK.

If this option is not available, select the third gallery position on the top row and click Reset. Click Yes, when prompted, to reset this gallery position.

7. Select 1st Level from the Apply Formatting To section.
8. Choose other formatting to apply for this level.

The font choices apply to the list number only, not the text of the list. To format the text, be sure to attach a style to your numbered list. See Chapter 8, "Bullets and Numbering," for more information on how to do this.

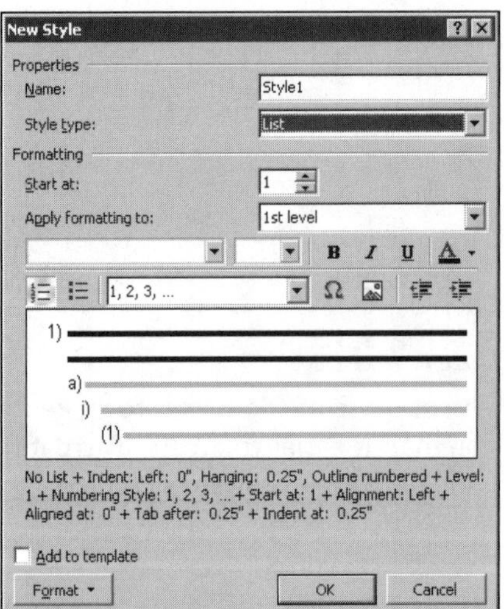

FIGURE 9.14

You have many formatting options when you create a list style.

9. Repeat steps 7 and 8 for the next two levels.
10. Check Add To Template to make this list style available in all documents based on this template.
11. Click OK.
12. Apply the Contract style. The level 1 number is inserted.
13. Type **Definitions** and press Enter.
14. Click Increase Indent on the Formatting toolbar to move to the next level.

NOTE

If you have the Style Area open, you will notice that "Normal" appears beside text formatted with the list style, rather than the list style name. Only paragraph styles appear in the Style Area. However, the Styles And Formatting Task Pane and the Style button will show the applied list style name.

TABLE STYLES

Table styles are another feature new to Word 2002. They allow users to specify and tweak how a table should appear with respect to borders, shading, and other formatting, and then quickly apply the saved table style to other tables in the document to give them the same format.

Not only can you control the overall table format, you can set specific formats for a header or end row, certain columns, and even for individual cells.

NOTE

As with list styles, table styles cannot be created by example and do not show up in the Style Area.

REQUEST GRANTED!

Were you one of the people asking to add your own formats to the Table AutoFormat dialog box? Many law firms asked for this feature and it is now available through the new table styles. When you create a table style, it will appear in the list of formats in the Table AutoFormat dialog box as well as the Styles And Formatting Task Pane.

CREATE A TABLE STYLE

1. Create a new document.
2. Click New Style on the Styles And Formatting Task Pane.
3. Name the style **Pleading Index**.
4. Click the Style Type drop-down arrow and select Table. The New Style dialog box opens, with options to create a table style, as shown in Figure 9.15.
5. Select a double-line format from the Line Style drop-down list.
6. Click the drop-down arrow next to the Borders button and choose Outside Borders.
7. Select a single line from Line Style.
8. Choose Inside Borders.
9. In the Apply Formatting To section, select Header Row.
10. From the Shading Color drop-down list, select a light gray fill color.
11. Select Table Properties from the Format button. The Table Properties dialog box opens, as shown in Figure 9.16.

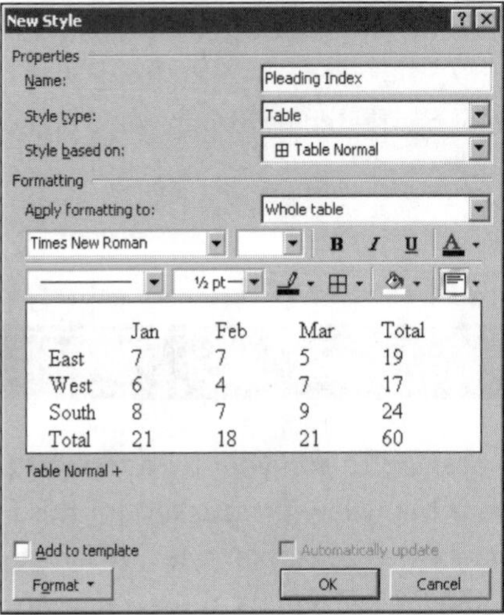

FIGURE 9.15

Apply font, color, borders, alignment, and other formatting to your table style.

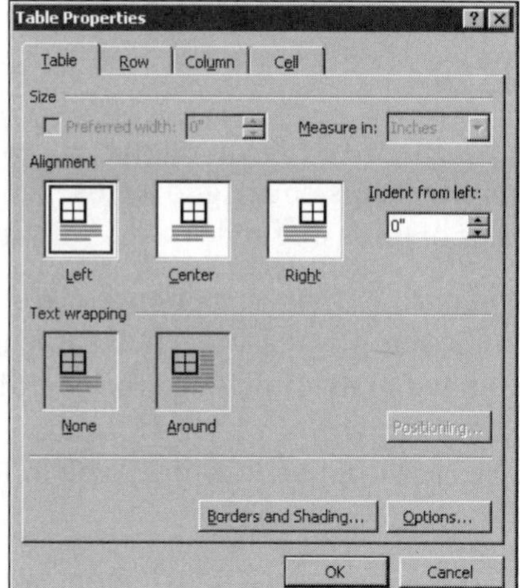

FIGURE 9.16

The Table Properties dialog box allows you to set properties for the Table, Row, Column, or Cell.

12. On the Row tab, select Repeat As Header Row At The Top of Each Page.
13. Click OK.
14. Select Add To Template to save this style in the attached template.
15. Click OK.
16. From the Table menu, choose Insert, Table.
17. Click AutoFormat to access Table AutoFormat styles.
18. Select Pleading Index from the list of styles and click OK.
19. Click OK again to insert the table formatted with your new Pleading Index style based on the Pleading Index AutoFormat.

TIP

If the table already exists in the document, click the Table style from the Style list or choose Table, Table AutoFormat to apply the style.

THE CONSEQUENCE OF NOT USING STYLES

In this chapter, after briefly explaining why you should use styles, we have discussed how to use styles. As this chapter is coming to a close, it is very important to reflect on the consequences of not using styles, especially in a law firm.

As you have read in this book, and perhaps have experienced, Word offers many different ways to get similar results. For this reason, when a document is being shared among many users, you have to acknowledge the possibility that the document itself could become a mishmash of varying formats—making it far more difficult to edit. When styles are not used, some of the following results could very well occur:

- **Wasted editing time**: Earlier in this chapter, it was demonstrated that format changes can be made globally in a document when styles are used. If styles have not been used, each paragraph must be changed individually. This alone can substantially increase editing time and reduce productivity.

  You have probably worked with a document where the format differs from one paragraph to the next, sometimes ever so slightly. Even more time will be wasted to try and figure out what format has been used and where. And, if one user is using styles and another user is not, someone must go through and uniformly apply styles or remove them. A combination of styles and direct formatting used with Normal style can cause all sorts of problems with operations ranging from inserting more text to generating a table of contents.
- **Automatic Paragraph Numbering**: Styles are intertwined with automatic paragraph numbering to obtain the consistency of the numbering format throughout the document. If styles have not been used to apply numbering, the document will contain a combination of automatic and manual numbers, outline and numbered lists, or different schemes in use so that the numbers are not continuous.
- **Cross-Referencing**: The strength of Word's cross-referencing feature is that it will update as paragraphs are added and removed. This strength is compromised if the paragraph numbering is not set up correctly. When incorrect paragraph numbering is used, incorrect cross-referencing occurs.
- **Table of Contents**: Using styles to generate a table of contents is effortless. Even better, when edits are made to the document, those changes are reflected accordingly in the table of contents.

Word does offer the ability to create a table of contents for documents that do not contain styles. This is discussed in Chapter 14. To do this, however, someone must go through and manually mark the document. Manually marked table of contents entries do not update when paragraphs are modified, inserted, or deleted. This causes a lot of extra work each time an edit is made to the document—and in the worst-case scenario, the table of contents is not correct.

- **Document Corruption**: The absence of styles would not in itself cause a document to become corrupt. However, if you have a complex document that many people have worked on and formatting has been applied using all sorts of methods, there is a good chance that some of the formatting (usually numbering) will become unstable. As your formatting becomes unstable, the document will show signs similar to a corrupt document or, in a very extreme circumstance where multiple poorly formatted pieces of documents are combined into one document, there is a chance that the document really will become corrupt.

SUMMARY

While the task of learning and understanding styles can be quite intensive, the benefits far outweigh the drawbacks. Styles can simplify the document creation and editing process. They create a standardized look to all your documents that project a professional image in keeping with law firms. With the new tools, such as the Styles And Formatting Task Pane, styles can be used by anyone.

TROUBLESHOOTING STYLES

The table style that I created is not appearing in the Table AutoFormat dialog box.

Table styles, like all styles, are available only in the document in which they were created unless the Add To Template option was checked. If the style is not listed, go back to the original document containing the table. Click Modify and select Add To Template. If this option was checked and the style is still not showing, the document you are currently working with could have a different template attached. In this case, use the Organizer to copy the style.

When I apply italics to a paragraph in my document, all the other paragraphs change to italics.

It sounds as though Automatically Update has been enabled. Choose Modify from the drop-down list beside the style name and uncheck Automatically Update.

When I choose Update To Match Selection, the formats that I have applied to my list style do not change.

List styles contain number formatting only, unless the numbering is attached to a paragraph style. You cannot include character or paragraph formatting in a list style except to format the number.

CHAPTER 10

TEMPLATES

IN THIS CHAPTER

- Word's built-in templates
- Normal, attached, and global templates
- Add-Ins
- Where templates live
- How to create your own legal template
- Using the Organizer
- Sharing templates with the rest of your firm
- Word's wizards

Whether it's a letter to a client, a memo to opposing counsel, or a brief to be filed with the Supreme Court, every new Word document you create is based on some type of template. Templates are the behind-the-scenes' players that make Word such a powerful word processing application. There are many different types of templates, but each serves a common purpose: to make your job of getting documents out the door less complicated.

In addition to examining template types and locations, this chapter looks at the many different ways your firm can use templates to create consistent documents and save time in the process.

TEMPLATES DEFINED

If you ask various people in your firm what a *template* is, it's likely that you will get different answers. To some, a template is an automated form that is filled out; to others it is a type of document that is created and used as boilerplate text for creating other documents. This is all true, but there's more to it. Templates, as defined in the word processing world, are files that are used as a basis for creating other documents. Think letter, memo, fax cover sheet, pleading, and agreement. Every Word document is based on some type of template. Some are elaborate and others simple.

Templates can contain everything from macros and AutoText entries to custom margins, specially formatted text, and graphics. Templates can even contain custom toolbars, menus, styles, and shortcut keys. Templates are incredibly powerful in the sense that they can be used to create consistently formatted documents with, for example, your firm's styles, toolbars, and macros. Templates also help standardize the look and feel of firm documents and assist in making sure that court-specified formatting requirements are met.

NOTE

Templates are identified by the .dot file extension, as opposed to the .doc extension associated with Word documents.

WORD'S BUILT-IN TEMPLATES

What's the easiest way to create a new document in Word? The answer is to click the New Blank Document button on the Standard toolbar. This (or pressing Ctrl+N) is standard procedure for most users. The resulting blank document that you see on the screen actually contains a number of fixed settings that you probably never even think about. Some of these settings include default margins, font style, font size, toolbar buttons, and menu commands—just to name a few. But what the document doesn't contain is probably even more important—no preset text, formatting, or graphics to help speed up the process of document creation.

NEW DOCUMENT TASK PANE

When Word starts, a New Document Task Pane opens that includes four sections for working with templates. These sections include: Open A Document, New, New From Existing Document, and New From Template.

NOTE

If the New Document Task Pane does not appear when you start Word, from the Tools menu, choose Options and select the View tab. Check the Startup Task Pane option and click OK.

- **Open A Document**—Displays a list of files that have recently been opened (MRU). Click More Documents to display the Open dialog box.

NEW FEATURE!

Word contains a new command to create a new blank document, Web page, e-mail message, or display the New dialog box. You can add this button by displaying the Customize dialog box and dragging the button to an existing toolbar. From the View menu, choose Toolbars, Customize. Select the Commands tab. Under Categories, select File. Select New (with the arrow) under Commands and drag the button next to the New Blank Document button on the Standard toolbar. Close the Customize dialog box. Click the drop-down arrow next to the button to choose what type of document to create. Select Other from the drop-down list and display the New dialog box.

- **New**—Click to create a new blank document, blank web page or blank e-mail message.
- **New From Existing Document**—Opens the New From Existing Document dialog box. Navigate to and select the file from which to base the document.
- **New From Template**—Under the New From Template sections are the following templates: The three most recently used templates, General Templates, which displays the Templates dialog box where you can choose a specific template; Templates wOn My Web Site, which opens the New From Templates On My Web Sites dialog box; and Templates On Microsoft.com, which opens a Web browser and takes you to a location on the Microsoft Web site that includes additional templates.

Word 2002 comes with many installed templates that can be used to quickly create all kinds of documents. To see the complete selection of built-in templates, open the New Document Task Pane shown in Figure 10.1 by choosing New from the File menu.

Once the New Document Task Pane is open, click General Templates to open the Templates dialog box. Word's built-in templates are divided into categories organized by tabs. Some of the categories include Letters & Faxes, Legal Pleadings, Memos, Reports, Publications, Web Pages, and Other Documents, as shown in Figure 10.2.

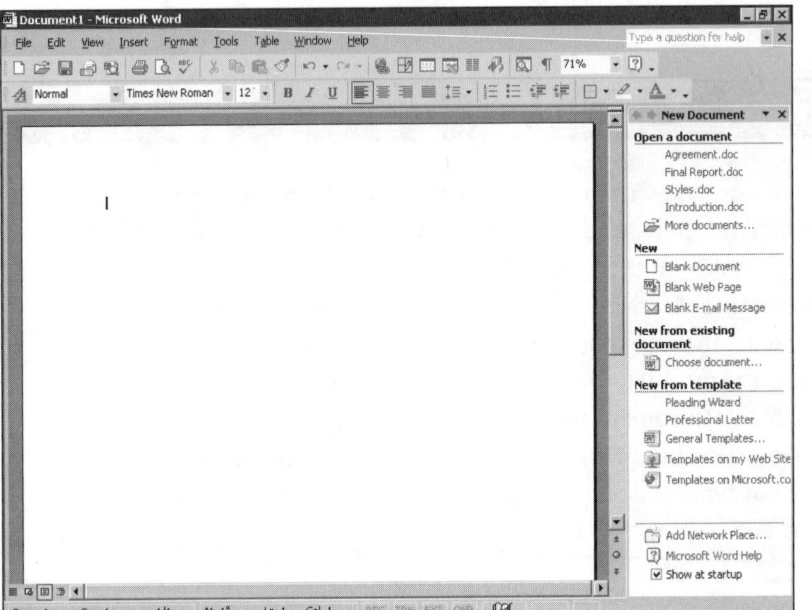

FIGURE 10.1

The New Document Task Pane is divided into different sections to allow you to quickly choose the type of document you wish to open or create.

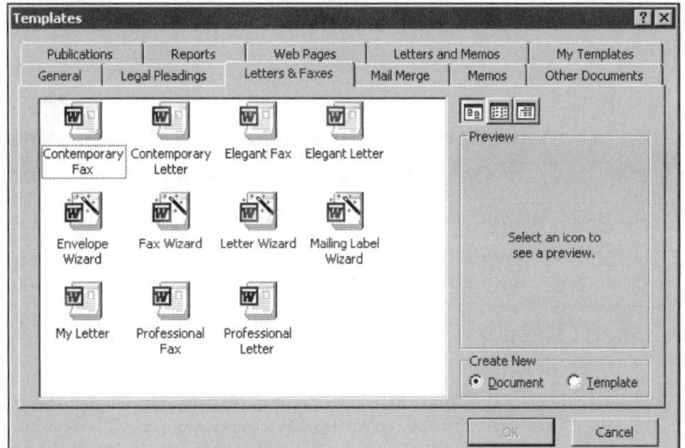

FIGURE 10.2

Click one of the three Preview buttons to change the way templates and wizards appear in the dialog box.

If you used Word 2000, most of the templates that you see in the Templates dialog box will look familiar. A new Mail Merge tab has been added, however, which includes 10 templates for creating mail merge documents.

Custom installation choices (installing or not installing certain templates) can result in your template folder not looking like the figures in this book. Also, some options may be disabled if your firm is using a document management system. For questions on the setup of your installation and configuration, consult your help desk or system administrator.

Also, if your firm has installed the MultiLanguage Pack, additional tabs may appear in the Templates dialog box. For example, if the Traditional Chinese MultiLanguage Pack has been installed, a Business Documents tab is created that contains templates such as Asset Checklist, Balance Sheet, Bill Statement, and more. The Japanese MultiLanguage Pack adds a PostCards tab, and the Korean MulitLanguage Pack creates a School tab.

One of the real benefits of using Word's built-in templates is that you can quickly create new documents *or* templates from the ones Word provides. For example, you can open the Templates dialog box and create a firm letter template using the Letter Wizard as an example—it's that easy.

Although these templates and wizards are useful for showing people how to get started, most firms quickly decide to create their own custom templates to include information and formatting specific to their firm. Third-party macro packages also offer additional solutions created specifically for law firms. For information on a third-party solution, see the "Resources" section in the Appendix.

NOTE

Most of the built-in templates have wizards associated with them. Wizards will be discussed in detail later in the chapter, but the primary purpose of this automation is to provide simplified steps for document creation.

CREATE A LETTER FROM A BUILT-IN TEMPLATE

1. From the File menu choose New to open the New Document Task Pane.
2. Click General Templates to open the Templates dialog box.
3. Select the Letters & Faxes tab.
4. Select Elegant Letter and click OK.

NOTE

Depending on your firm's installation choices, some built-in templates may only be what Word calls "advertised." This means they appear in the dialog box but are not installed until first use. When you try to use an "advertised" template, you will be prompted to install it. If you are connected to the server or have access to the installation files, this process should only take a minute or so. If you do not have access, when attempting to install on first use, contact your help desk or system administrator for assistance.

5. Click where it says Click Here And Type Recipient's Address and type the recipient's name and address.
6. Alternate-click the Dear Sir Or Madam field. Choose the desired salutation from the drop-down list.
7. Select the paragraph that starts with Type Your Letter Here and type the body of the letter.
8. Complete the rest of the letter by clicking in the appropriate places.
9. From the File menu, choose Save.

NOTE

If you do not see the type of template you need, click Templates On Microsoft.com in the New Document Task Pane. This connects you via the Internet to the Microsoft Office Template Gallery shown in Figure 10.3. Here, you can choose a Word template from a large selection of categories, including Legal.

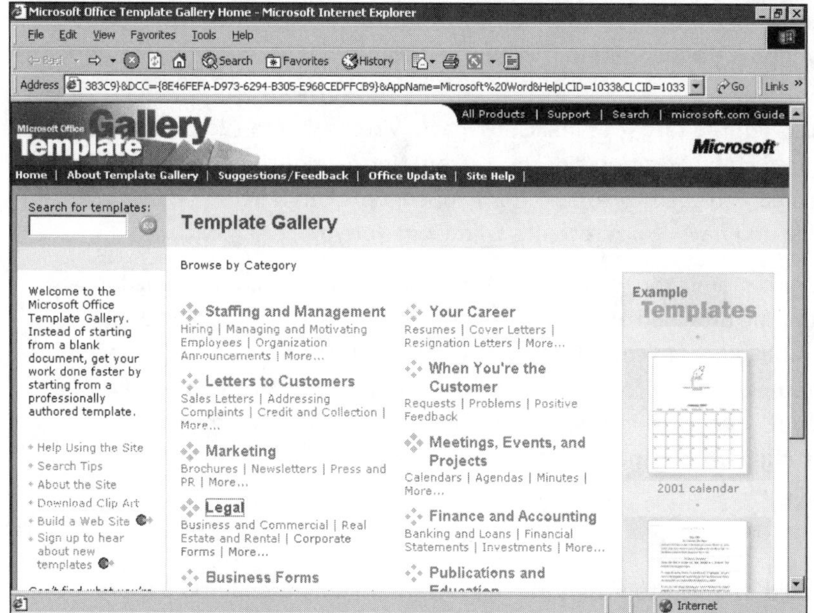

FIGURE 10.3

Legal templates include those for Business and Commercial, Real Estate and Rental, Corporate Forms, Pleadings, and Wills. Most of these templates use direct formatting instead of styles, but they will provide an example of how to set up your own templates for similar documents.

TYPES OF TEMPLATES

Some templates get used every time you start Word, some are available on demand, and others are used only occasionally. There are really four types of templates for Word: Normal, Attached, Global, and Add-In.

THE NORMAL TEMPLATE

Often called the mother of all templates, Normal.dot (pronounced normal-dot-dot) is Word's all-encompassing, ever-present master template. In fact, the Normal template is so vital to Word that if you delete it, Word will re-create it for you. Normal.dot contains settings that control everything from margins and toolbars to menus, shortcut keys, and just about anything else you can think of related to Word. Even if you don't have a blank document open in the application window, the Normal template is still running in the background. Here are just a few of the default settings you can change in the Normal template:

- Margins
- Font style
- Font size
- Toolbar buttons
- Menu commands
- Header & footer parameters
- Views
- Shortcut keys

When you make changes to the Normal template, each document created thereafter will pick up and retain the new settings.

Normal.dot is often the target of malicious macro viruses due to Word's reliance on it and its predictable location. For this reason, Normal.dot sometimes becomes infected and even corrupt. If this happens, you can delete the Normal.dot file and have Word recreate a new one for you.

Any changes or customizations that have been made to Normal.dot will be lost. For this reason, the attached and global templates discussed later in this chapter are preferable places to store firm customizations. It is also desirable to recommend that users make a copy of Normal.dot on their own machine—calling it "Normbak.dot" or something similarly recognizable—so they can recover their own settings without spending the time to recreate them if Normal.dot has to be replaced.

Law firms should avoid customizing the user's Normal template. If updates are made and Normal.dot needs to be replaced, all user customizations such as keyboard shortcuts, macros, and AutoText entries will be lost.

CHANGE THE DEFAULT FONT FOR THE NORMAL TEMPLATE

1. Create a new document.
2. From the Format menu choose Font.
3. Change the font to Arial, Bold, 10 points.
4. Click Default at the bottom of the Font dialog box. Figure 10.4 shows the message box that opens asking for confirmation of the change.
5. Click Yes. Every new document you create will have this font as the default.

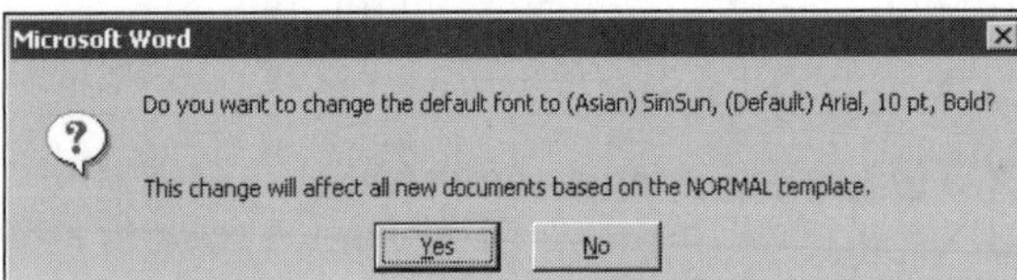

FIGURE 10.4

You can reset any changes made to Normal.dot by reopening the Font dialog box, making a change, and clicking Default.

DELETING THE NORMAL TEMPLATE

If for some reason Word begins to act strangely or crash with regularity, there's a good chance Normal.dot has become corrupted. When this happens the safest and fastest thing to do is to delete the Normal template. Deleting the Normal template may restore application stability. When you delete the Normal template Word automatically creates a new one the next time you start Word.

Remember—deleting Normal.dot will also delete any customizations you may have made including macros, styles, AutoText, toolbars, and others that may be stored in this location. If you have heavily customized Normal.dot, it's a good idea to create a backup copy of the template while it's still working and store it in a safe location!

To delete the Normal template, first close Word and then locate and delete the file. The default location is typically C:\Documents and Settings\UserName\Application Data\Microsoft\Templates. If you have a difficult time locating this template, click the Start button and choose Search, For Files Or Folders. Type **Normal.dot** in the Search For Files Or Folders Named box and click Search Now.

When your Normal.dot file appears in the Search Results window, delete the file. If others use your computer, however, make sure that you delete your own Normal.dot and not someone else's. Restart Word and the application will rebuild the file for you.

Once you've created a new Normal template you can use the Organizer to copy macros, AutoText, styles, and toolbars from your backup copy of the template. Using the Organizer is discussed later in the chapter. This is the preferred method over renaming the backup copy of Normal. If the template has become corrupt, using a copy of it is not generally a good idea.

When you create a new document by clicking the New Blank Document button on the Standard toolbar, the default is for this new document to be based on the Normal template. Some firms customize this feature so that clicking the New Blank Document button creates a document based on a firm-specific template such as a Blank.dot file. The benefit of this is that firm styles and AutoText are made available without having to customize the Normal template or rely on users' remembering one of the other options.

ATTACHED TEMPLATES

Every document is based on or attached to a template. If you create a letter using the Letter Wizard or a custom template, that template becomes the attached template. The document created from the attached template inherits any custom settings such as margins and font style and can use any of the styles, AutoText entries, and macros contained in the attached template.

There are two ways to attach a template to a document—by creating a new document based on a specific template such as the Letter or Memo template or by manually attaching a template to an existing document. To find out which template is attached to your current document, do the following—from the Tools menu, choose Templates And Add-Ins. Look under Document Template to see the attached template. Figure 10.5 shows an example of a document with Normal.dot attached.

ATTACH A DIFFERENT TEMPLATE TO A DOCUMENT

1. From the File menu choose New.
2. From the New Document Task Pane click General Templates and then select the Memos tab.
3. Double-click Contemporary Memo to generate a new memo. Notice the format of the memo.
4. From the Tools menu choose Templates And Add–Ins.
5. Click Attach.
6. Double-click Normal (or single-click and click Open).
7. In the Templates And Add-Ins dialog box check the Automatically Update Document Styles option, as shown in Figure 10.6.

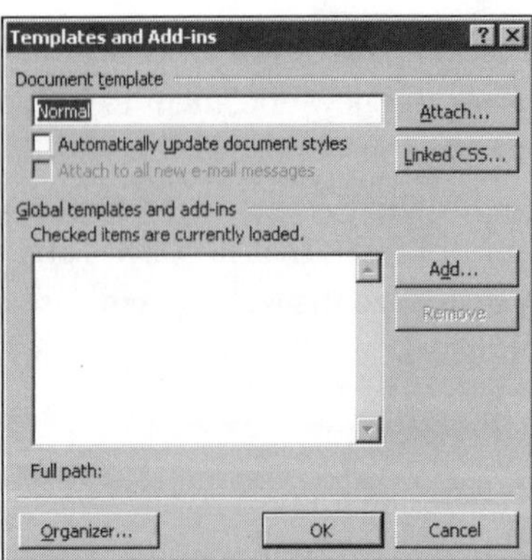

FIGURE 10.5

An attached template offers tools such as styles and toolbars to the document.

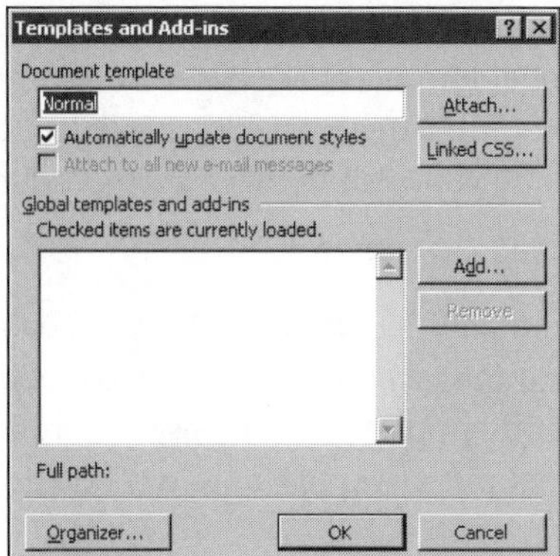

FIGURE 10.6

Checking the Automatically Update Document Styles option will copy over the styles from Normal.dot into the file, superseding the ones from Contemporary Memo.

8. Click OK. Can you see how certain formats of the memo change as a result of attaching a different template?
9. From the Tools menu choose Templates And Add–Ins and uncheck the option Automatically Update Document Styles.

NOTE

It's important to uncheck the option Automatically Update Document Styles once you've attached a new template. Otherwise, each time the document opens it will copy styles from the attached template. This can cause unexpected formatting changes on another computer where the template is set up differently, and can make it difficult to open the file on a computer that does not contain the attached template.

GLOBAL TEMPLATES

Attached templates usually contain custom settings specific to the particular document. A letter template, for example, may include the firm's logo, address, and telephone and fax numbers, as well as AutoText for its signature block. Some of these items may be required for documents other than letter types and can be stored in a global template to always make them available.

Global templates are templates that contain settings that are available to all files, independent of the attached template. These settings can include custom AutoText, toolbars, menus, and macros.

Global templates can be loaded automatically from Word's Startup folder or manually from the Templates And Add-Ins dialog box. Once a global template is loaded, all custom settings will be made available to every document you work on while the template is active.

Global templates stored in the Startup folder will automatically load each time you start Word. Manually loaded global templates are available for the individual Word session and unload when you turn them off, or when you close Word. They need to be reloaded the next time you wish to make them available.

The one thing that can't be stored in global templates is styles. Actually, they can be stored in a global template but they will not be available globally. Styles can only be accessed from the attached template. This is easy to forget and is a frequently asked question for most people trying to figure out how to set up and configure firm templates.

LOADING GLOBAL TEMPLATES AUTOMATICALLY

Global templates stored in the Word Startup folder load automatically every time you start Word. The location of the Startup folder is set and specified in the File Locations tab of the Options dialog box.

LOADING GLOBAL TEMPLATES MANUALLY

The method for loading global templates manually is very similar to the method for attaching templates. From the Tools menu, choose Templates And Add-Ins to open the Templates And Add-Ins dialog box.

Look under Global Templates And Add-Ins to see which, if any, global templates are already loaded. Click Add, and Word will open the User Templates file location specified in the File Location tab of the Options dialog box (Tools, Options, File Locations), as shown in Figure 10.7.

FIGURE 10.7

Load a template from this location or navigate to the appropriate folder or network directory.

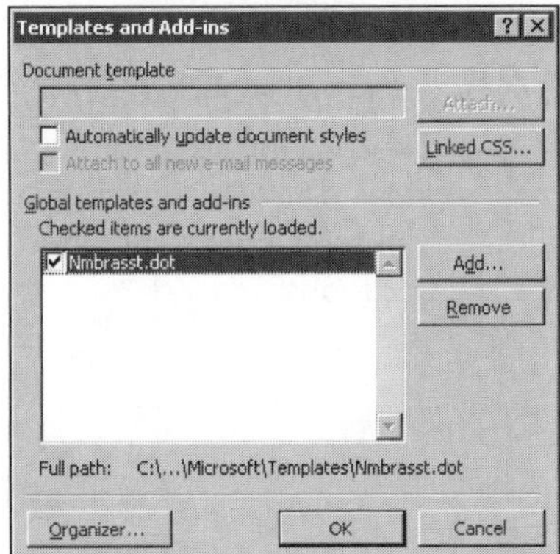

FIGURE 10.8

When you close Word, the manually loaded template will unload. To reload it, open the Templates And Add-Ins dialog box, place a check mark next to the template, and click OK.

Once you locate the appropriate template, select it and click OK. Notice that the template shows up in the Templates And Add-Ins dialog box, as shown in Figure 10.8.

ADD-INS

Add-ins are programs or utilities designed to work with Word in ways that either supplement existing features (such as a numbering add-in) or add new features (such as a legal dictionary). Add-ins generally make certain Word features less difficult to use. For example, several companies, including Payne Consulting Group, offer Numbering and Pleading Assistants, which help users to create complex documents much more quickly than they could with Word's native features.

WHERE TEMPLATES LIVE

The actual location of templates will vary depending on the operating system your firm uses. The locations of both user and workgroup templates as well as the location of Word's Startup folder can be found and even modified from the File Locations tab of the Options dialog box, as shown in Figure 10.9.

- **Global Templates**. Global templates that load automatically are stored in the Word Startup folder. The location of the Startup folder varies depending on the operating system your firm uses but can be found by tunneling through the File Locations tab on the Options dialog box. To quickly locate the Startup folder, from the Tools menu choose Options and select the File Locations tab. Under File Types, double-click Startup. Once the Modify Location dialog box opens, click the drop-down arrow next to Look In and you will see the correct path, as shown in Figure 10.10.

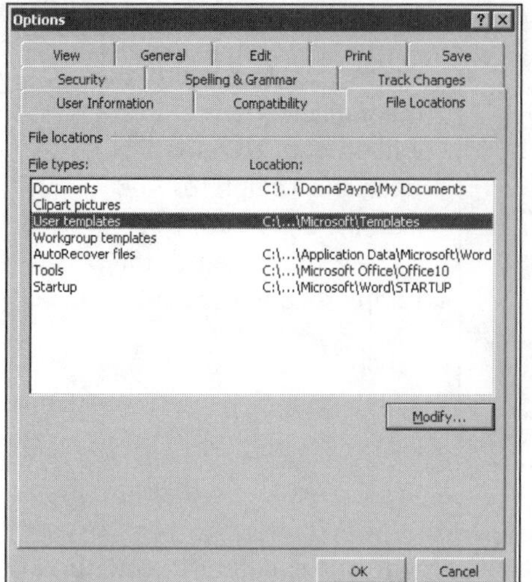

FIGURE 10.9

From the Tools menu, choose Options and select the File Locations tab to change template locations.

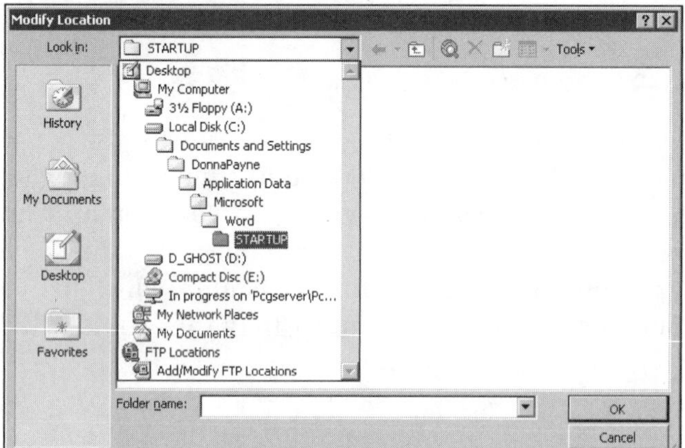

FIGURE 10.10

Templates stored in the Startup folder are loaded automatically every time Word starts.

- **User Templates**. User templates are custom templates that are created and stored in the location specified in the User Templates location on the File Locations tab of the Options dialog box. Whenever you create a custom template, the default is to save it to this location. To see the location of your User Template folder, follow the same steps as in the example for Global Templates. When you get to the File Locations tab, double-click User Templates and click the drop-down arrow next to Look In to see the full path, as shown in Figure 10.11.
- **Workgroup Templates**. Workgroup templates are meant to be shared among users or workgroups and therefore are generally stored on a network. The location is normally determined by a system administrator and is

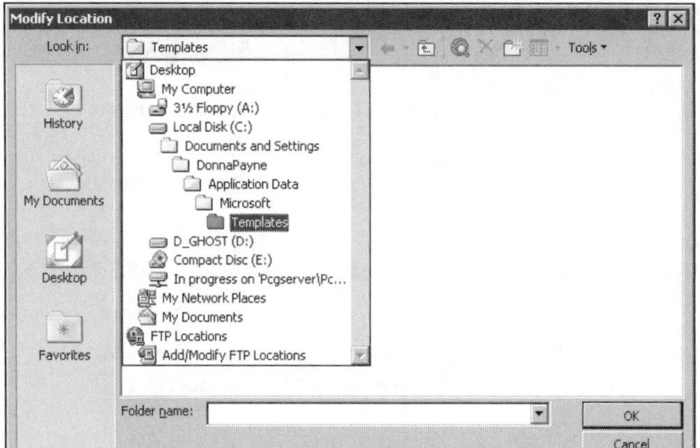

FIGURE 10.11

All the new templates you create are stored in this folder.

typically locked down. To see the location of your firm's workgroup templates, follow the same steps as in the preceding examples. Remember to double-click Workgroup Templates from the File Locations tab.

MORE ON FILE LOCATIONS

The default location for Office XP is C:\Program Files\Microsoft Office\Office10. This is the first Office Suite installed in a folder corresponding to its version number. The installed templates are found in this folder structure as well.

DEFAULT FILE LOCATIONS BY OPERATING SYSTEM

As mentioned throughout this chapter, the file locations for each type of template will vary by operating system. Table 10.1 lists each type of template and corresponding default file location for each operating system.

This table is intended as a general reference. Word file locations can also be modified or customized by the firm or individual, so the file locations on your computer may vary from these defaults.

CREATE YOUR OWN LEGAL TEMPLATE

Creating templates that contain information specific to your firm can help save a tremendous amount of time every time you generate a new document. Imagine a letter template defined with your firm name, address, logo, and signer

TABLE 10.1 WORD FILE LOCATIONS BY OPERATING SYSTEM

OPERATING SYSTEM	USER TEMPLATE LOCATION
Windows 2000	C:\Document Settings\<user name>\Application Data\Microsoft\Templates
Windows 98/NT 4.0 (with profiles) or Windows 2000 that has been upgraded from Windows 98/NT	C:\<Windows Folder>\Profiles\<username>\Application Data\Microsoft\Templates
Windows 98 (without profiles)	C:\<Windows Folder>\Application Data\Microsoft\Templates

OPERATING SYSTEM	STARTUP (GLOBAL TEMPLATE) LOCATION
Windows 2000	C:\Document Settings\<user name>\Application Data\Microsoft\Word\Startup
Windows 98/NT 4.0 (with profiles) or Windows 2000 that has been upgraded from Windows 98/NT	C:\<Windows Folder>\Profiles\<username>\Application Data\Microsoft\Word\Startup
Windows 98 (without profiles)	C:root>C;\<Windows Folder>\Application Data\Microsoft\Word\Startup

information. If the template is set up correctly, generating a new document from the template will take a fraction of the time it would take to create the document from scratch.

CREATING A TEMPLATE FROM AN EXISTING TEMPLATE

If your firm uses a simple format for a memo or letter, why reinvent the wheel by starting from scratch? Word offers the ability to create a new template from an existing one.

CREATE A FIRM MEMO FROM A BUILT-IN TEMPLATE

1. From the File menu choose New to open the New Document Task Pane.
2. Click General Templates to open the Templates dialog box.
3. Select the Memos tab and click once to select Professional Memo.
4. Choose Template from the Create New options, and click OK.

5. Type your firm's name where it says Company Name Here.
6. Click and type your name in the From field.
7. Customize the rest of the memo as needed.

TIP

Remember to enter information that is general enough to be used repeatedly. Avoid recipient or other information that is too specific.

8. From the File menu, choose Save. Word automatically directs the Save As dialog box to the User Template folder and sets the Save As Type setting to Document Template.

NOTE

The location of the User Templates folder is determined through settings on the File Locations tab (Tools, Options, File Locations).

9. Name the template **Firm Memo** and click Save.
10. Close the template.
11. From the File menu choose New. Click General Templates.
12. Select the General tab and locate the template (Firm Memo) that you just created.

CREATING A TEMPLATE FROM SCRATCH

Word's built-in templates can be useful for creating certain types of documents. But often, firms need to create templates that are task- or firm-specific and include customizations. You can easily create a template from scratch to include any type of information.

CREATE A FIRM INVOICE TEMPLATE FROM SCRATCH

1. Create a new blank document.
2. From the File menu, choose Page Setup.
3. Set the Left and Right margins to 1" and click OK.
4. From the View menu, choose Header And Footer.
5. In the header, type the firm name, address, and telephone number.
6. Select the text that you just typed. Format it as centered, 14-point type.

7. Click Switch Between Header And Footer on the Header And Footer toolbar to move to the footer.
8. Press Tab twice to move the insertion point to the right side of the footer.

NOTE

You may need to change the position of the tab stops to accommodate the margin changes.

9. Type **Tax Identification Number:** and type the firm's tax number. If you don't know what it is, type any number since this is only practice.
10. Click Close to leave the Header And Footer layer.
11. Create the body of the document, as shown in Figure 10.12.
12. From the File menu, choose Save.
13. Choose Document Template from the Save As Type drop-down list. Word directs the Save As dialog box to the Templates folder automatically.
14. Leave the Save As dialog box open for the next exercise.

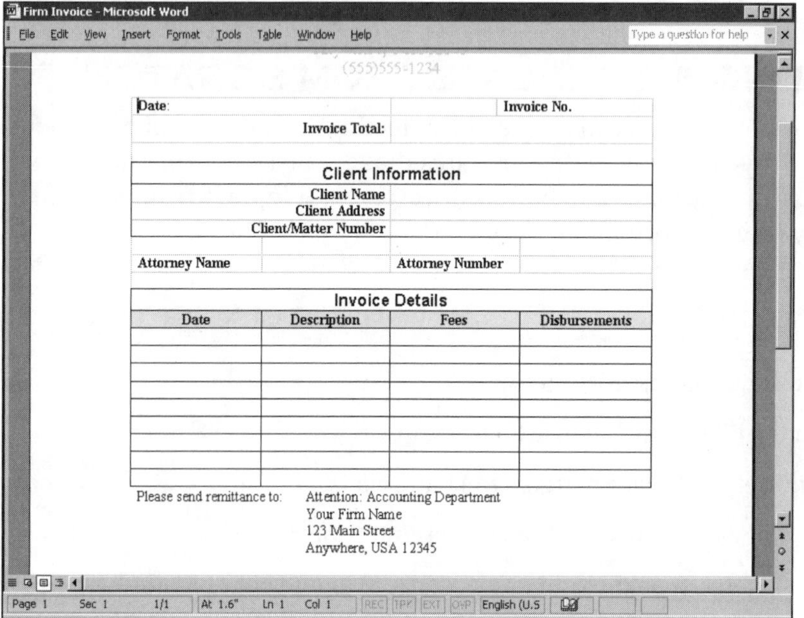

FIGURE 10.12

The body of a template should contain all the pertinent information needed in each document.

CREATE A NEW TAB FOR TEMPLATES

In the preceding exercises, when you saved the templates, Word automatically directed the Save As dialog box to the Templates folder. When the firm memo was saved, it appeared in the General tab of the Templates dialog box. If you want it to appear with the other memos or on a completely separate tab that just shows your customized templates, you can create a subfolder in the Templates folder.

CREATE A NEW TAB FOR CUSTOM TEMPLATES

1. The Save As dialog box should still be open from the preceding exercise.
2. Make sure that the Save As Type is set to Document Template.
3. Click the Create New Folder button. The New Folder dialog box opens, as shown in Figure 10.13.
4. Type **My Templates** and click OK. The folder is created and opens in the Save As dialog box.
5. Name your template **Firm Invoice** and click Save.
6. From the File menu, choose New to open the New Document Task Pane.
7. Click General Templates. The My Templates tab and Firm Invoice template should be visible.

To have a template appear on one of Word's built-in tabs, create a subfolder within the Templates folder and give it the same name as Word's tab.

8. Click Cancel to close the Templates dialog box.
9. Leave the Firm Invoice template open for the next exercise.

FIGURE 10.13

Creating a new folder will generate a separate tab in the Templates dialog box.

TEMPLATE ENHANCEMENTS

A template is not only a set of boilerplates for creating new documents, it's also a storage container for tools that are useful for creating specific types of documents—toolbars, stored AutoText, styles, and macros.

CREATE A TOOLBAR FOR THE TEMPLATE

When you work with a letter, toolbar buttons such as Envelopes and Labels are useful. Word has all sorts of toolbar buttons that make creation and formatting of pleadings easier. When working with specific templates such as these, it's a good idea to store custom toolbars with the templates so they are available for working with all documents based on these templates.

SAVE A TOOLBAR IN YOUR TEMPLATE

1. The template you created in the preceding exercise should still be open.
2. From the Tools menu, choose Customize. The Customize dialog box opens.
3. Select the Toolbars tab and click New. The New Toolbar dialog box opens.
4. Type **Invoice** as the Toolbar Name.
5. Ensure that Firm Invoice is listed in the Make Toolbar Available To field, as shown in Figure 10.14.
6. Click OK. The new toolbar is created.
7. Select the Commands tab.
8. From Categories, select Edit.
9. From the listed Commands, select and drag Paste Special to the new toolbar.

TIP

The plus sign beside the mouse pointer indicates that the command is on the toolbar. The X means that the button is not in an approved location yet. Do not release your mouse until you see the plus sign.

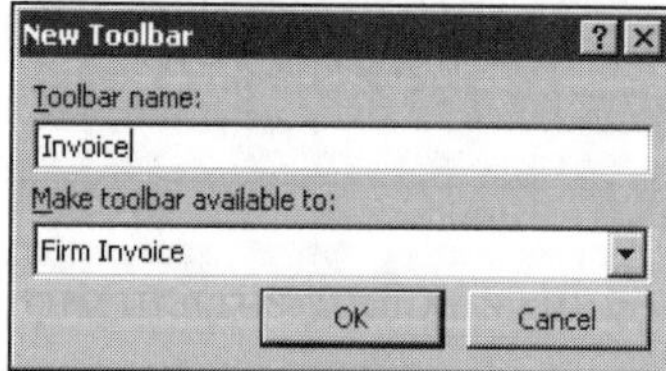

FIGURE 10.14

Choose the location in which to store your toolbar.

10. Add more buttons to your custom toolbar. Navigate through the Categories pane and select the appropriate Commands as listed below. Drag the following buttons to the custom toolbar:
    - View: Headers and Footers
    - Insert: Symbol
    - Insert: Footnote
    - Format: Change Case
    - Table: AutoSum
    - Table: Table and Borders Toolbar
    - All Commands: Update Fields
11. Click Close when the toolbar is complete.
12. Click Save. Leave this template open for the next exercise.

CREATE CUSTOM AUTOTEXT

As with toolbars, you'll have AutoText entries that are only used in certain document types. In these scenarios, storing the AutoText in the template used to create this type of document is a great idea.

STORE AUTOTEXT IN A FIRM TEMPLATE

1. The template from the preceding exercise should still be open.
2. Press Ctrl+End to move the insertion point to the bottom of the document.
3. Type **Terms: Net 30** and press Enter.
4. Select the text you just entered.
5. From the Insert menu, choose AutoText, AutoText.
6. The AutoText dialog box opens. Choose Firm Invoice (template) from the Look In drop-down list, as shown in Figure 10.15.
7. Type **Net 30** in Enter AutoText Entries Here and click Add.
8. Delete the Net 30 text from the document.
9. Repeat steps 3 through 8 to create an entry for **Net 60**.
10. Save and close the template. The AutoText entries have been stored in the template and will be available any time a document is created based on this particular template.

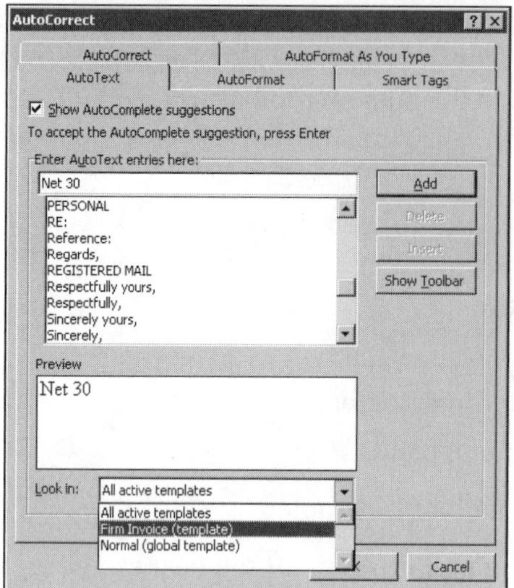

FIGURE 10.15

You can store AutoText entries in the template where they'll be most useful.

STYLES IN TEMPLATES

A lot of work goes into creating firm-specific styles. Once created, styles make applying consistent formatting a breeze. Since the template is the basis for all documents, firm styles should be added to the template.

Styles, toolbars, macros, and AutoText are easily transferred using the Organizer.

SAVING TEMPLATES AS OTHER FILE FORMATS

Word allows you to save templates as different file formats. This is new in Word 2002. From the File menu, choose Save As and change Save As Type to the preferred file format:

- Word document
- Web page
- Web page, filtered
- Web archive
- Document template
- Rich text format
- Plain text
- MS-DOS text with layout
- Text with layout
- Word 2.x for Windows
- Word 4.0 for Macintosh
- Word 5.0 for Macintosh
- Word 5.1 for Macintosh
- Word 6.0/95
- Word 97-2000 & 6.0/95 – RFT
- WordPerfect 5.0
- WordPerfect 5.0 Secondary File
- WordPerfect 5.1 for DOS
- WordPerfect 5.1 or 5.2 Secondary File
- WordPerfect 5.1 For Windows
- Works 2000
- Work 4.0 for Windows

If you save a template to a different file format, some features will be lost. Saving as a Word document retains the most formatting; however, when you do, you still lose AutoText stored in the template.

HOW THE ORGANIZER WORKS WITH TEMPLATES

The Organizer provides a relatively effortless way to copy custom toolbars or other tools between templates and documents.

COPY TEMPLATE INFORMATION WITH THE ORGANIZER

1. Open the Firm Memo template created earlier.
2. From the Tools menu, choose Templates And Add-Ins.
3. Click Organizer. The Organizer dialog box opens.
4. Click Close File on the right side of the dialog box. Notice that the button instantly changes to Open File.
5. Click Open File. The contents of the templates folder will be displayed. Open the My Templates folder.
6. Select Firm Invoice and click Open. The styles from that template are listed as shown in Figure 10.16.
7. Select the Toolbars tab.
8. Select the Invoice toolbar and click Copy. The toolbar is copied into the new template.

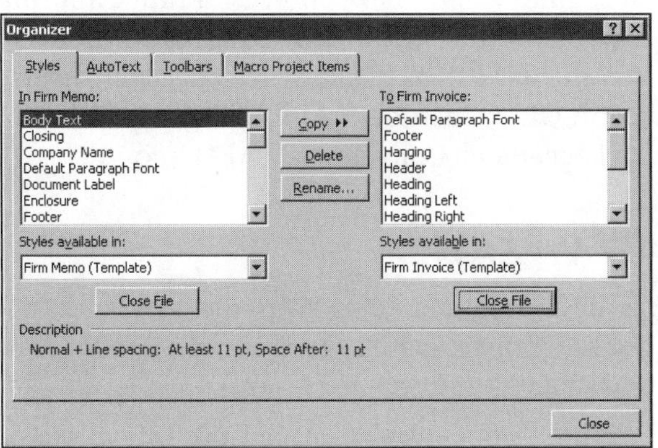

FIGURE 10.16

Use the Organizer to copy, delete, and rename styles, AutoText, toolbars, and macros.

9. Select the Styles and AutoText tabs and copy information if needed.
10. Click Close.

You can also delete and rename styles, AutoText, toolbars, and macros from within the Organizer.

SHARING TEMPLATES WITH THE REST OF YOUR FIRM

Sharing templates with others is a handy way to cut down on duplicate work. The sharer (you) can e-mail or give a floppy disk of the template to the sharee (the person you want to share with). The key to sharing is to know where to find the template and also where to put it (file location) on the sharee's computer.

Both the sharer and sharee can check their file locations by selecting Options from the Tools menu and selecting the File Locations tab. The file location listed for User Templates will be the place where you can both find the template and store it.

Some firms lock down access to certain folders and drives. If you cannot access this location, contact your help desk.

WIZARDS

A wizard is a step-by-step automated process used to assist you with some operation—in this case, creating a document. Typically, wizards consist of a series of steps that require you to make choices or input information along the way. Wizards can greatly reduce the amount of time it would normally take to set up complex documents such as pleadings or fax cover sheets. Some wizards available in Microsoft Office include Calendar, Agenda, Pleading, Letter, Fax, Mailing Label, Web Page, Batch Conversion, and Memo.

CALENDAR WIZARD

The Calendar Wizard is a favorite among Word users as it asks a few basic questions in a dialog box and finishes with a customized calendar document.

CREATE A CALENDAR DOCUMENT USING THE CALENDAR WIZARD

1. From the File menu choose New.
2. Click General Templates.
3. Double-click Calendar Wizard from the Other Documents tab. The wizard appears as shown in Figure 10.17.
4. Click Next to move to the first step.
5. Select the style of calendar you want and click Next.
6. Choose a page orientation for the calendar and whether to include room for a picture, and then click Next.
7. Pick the month range for the calendar, and then click Finish. A document opens with a calendar for each month displayed on a separate page.

PLEADING WIZARD

The Pleading Wizard helps create a custom pleading to match the wide spectrum of court requirements, including solutions for numbered pleading paper as required in California and some other states.

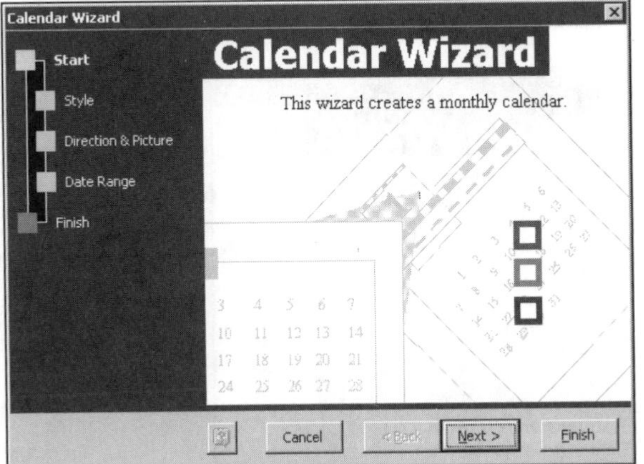

FIGURE 10.17

Follow the steps in the Calendar Wizard to create a custom calendar.

The Pleading Wizard controls three functions:

- Create a new pleading template for different courts.
- Modify an existing pleading template that was created with the Pleading Wizard.
- Create a pleading document from an existing template.

CREATE A PLEADING TEMPLATE

Court rules differ from state to state—not to mention court to court—so it is a good idea to have a copy of the pleading that you wish to create as well as the court rules for that jurisdiction before you attempt to create the pleading template. This will help create a useful and accurate pleading.

CREATE A PLEADING TEMPLATE USING THE PLEADING WIZARD

1. From the File menu choose New.
2. Click General Templates and select the Legal Pleadings tab.
3. Double-click the Pleading Wizard. The Legal Pleading Wizard dialog box opens, as shown in Figure 10.18.
4. Click Next to move to the first step of the Pleading Wizard.
5. Fill in the Court Name box and choose alignment options.
6. Follow each step in the wizard.
7. Select page layout options for the pleading.

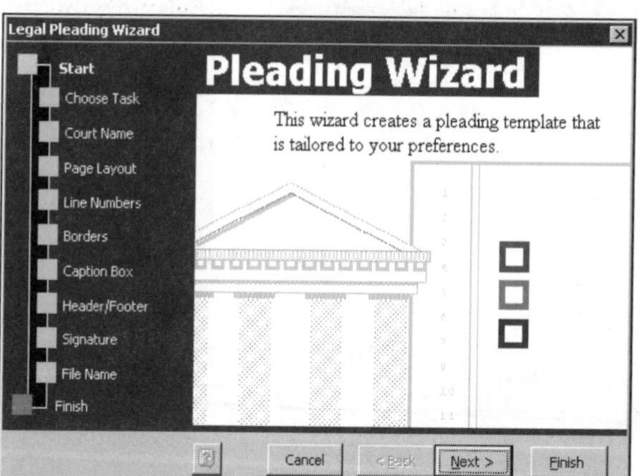

FIGURE 10.18

The template you create will be saved to the Legal Pleadings tab of the Templates dialog box.

8. Select line number options if your pleading requires numbered lines.
9. If necessary, set borders for the margins of the pleading.
10. Choose a caption style.
11. Select the appropriate options for the information contained in the header and footer.
12. Create a signature block if necessary.
13. Finally, name the template.

The name of the template will be used to access the template in the future, so use a specific name such as the court name—say, Municipal.dot—that way you'll be sure to recognize when you need it.

14. Click Finish. That's it—you can either proceed and create a pleading based on your template or click Cancel and come back later.
15. Click Cancel.

Create a Pleading Document

The complex page setup of the document is designed with the creation of the Pleading template. The next exercise lets you use that template to create a pleading document.

Create a Pleading Document Using the Pleading Wizard

1. From the File menu, choose New.
2. Click Pleading Wizard under New From Template.

If Pleading Wizard is not listed, click General Templates to open the Templates dialog box. Then select the Legal Pleadings tab and the desired pleading template.

3. Click Next to move to the Select Task step.
4. Choose Write A Pleading Document For The Court Selected Below.
5. Select the pleading created in the preceding exercise and click Next. The Legal Pleading Wizard dialog box opens, as shown in Figure 10.19.

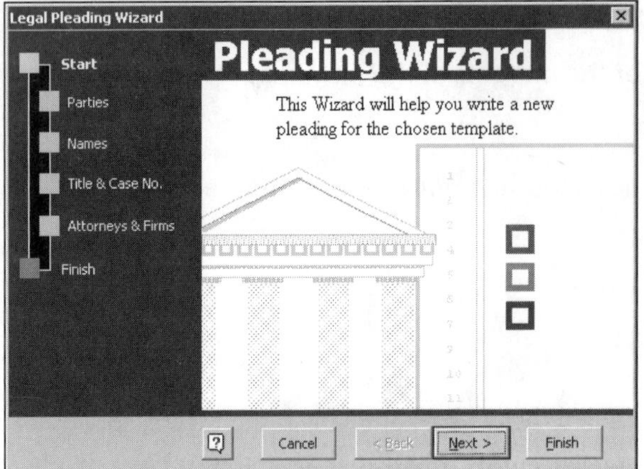

FIGURE 10.19

The Pleading Wizard assists in the creation of a pleading document based on the options selected in the pleading template previously created.

6. Click Next through the dialog boxes to fill out the applicable Party, Name, Case, Title, and Attorney information.
7. Click Finish to complete the document.
8. Save the document.

NOTE

Most law firms choose to skip the Pleading Wizard and deploy a third-party solution.

TIP

Occasionally, text in the document does not line up correctly with the line numbers on the pleading. If this happens, click in the paragraph with the misaligned text and press Ctrl+0 (zero). This adds 12 points of space before the paragraph.

PLEADING TOOLBAR

When you work with pleadings created through the Pleading Wizard, the Pleading toolbar opens automatically. This toolbar is shown in Figure 10.20.

The Pleading toolbar buttons function as follows:

- **Block Quotation**. Indents the selected paragraph .5" each time the button is clicked.
- **Single-Spacing**. Applies the correct single-spacing format in relation to line numbering, if applied.

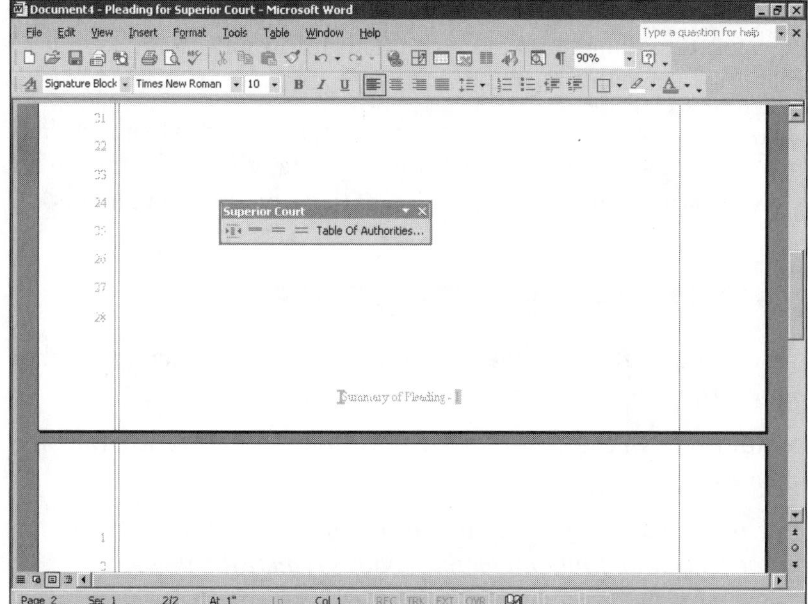

FIGURE 10.20

The Pleading toolbar offers access to commands that are unique to pleading documents.

- **1.5 Spacing**. Applies the correct line-and-a-half spacing format in relation to line numbering, if applied.
- **Double-Spacing**. Applies the correct double-spacing format in relation to line numbering if applied.
- **Table Of Authorities (TOA)**. Shortcut to the Table Of Authorities tab in the Index And Tables dialog box, which gives quick access to mark and insert a TOA when needed.

CAUTION

Each format button on the toolbar applies a corresponding style when applied. For example, the Double-Spacing button applies Double Space style. Block Quotation is the exception as it applies direct formatting for the left and right indents.

SUMMARY

Templates can save a tremendous amount of time and effort. Set up the template once, and then base all similar documents on the file. Letters, memos, faxes, pleadings, agreements, and briefs are good candidates for templates. To further make templates useful for law firms, styles, AutoText, macros, and even toolbars can be stored in most template types. This information can be shared between templates by using the Organizer.

Wizards usually contain step-by-step instructions on how to create a template or document. Word wizards such as Pleading, Agenda, and Calendar are all popular with law firms and simplify the creation of these types of documents.

TROUBLESHOOTING TEMPLATES

Whenever I create custom templates they always end up on the General tab of the Templates dialog box. Is there any way to sort them by type?

Create a subfolder within the Templates folder to create separate tabs for groups of templates.

When I was creating a letter template yesterday, I also made a toolbar containing my favorite buttons. I cannot find that toolbar today—where did it go?

If the toolbar was created when a template was open, it was most likely saved to that template. Open the Letter template you were working on and use the Organizer to copy the toolbar into Normal.dot. Toolbars stored in Normal.dot will be available to all documents.

When I opened a document, the formatting of the document completely changed.

From the Tools menu, choose Templates And Add-Ins. Check that the correct template is attached and that Automatically Update Document Styles is not enabled.

I do not see my new template in the Templates dialog box. Do I have to rebuild it?

If you can't find the template in any of tabs in the Templates dialog box, it was probably saved to the incorrect location. Check the File Locations listed for Template from Tools, Options and save your new template to that location.

I'm not totally satisfied with the Pleading Wizard. What else is there for me to use?

There are several companies that provide pleading template packages. Packages are available from Payne Consulting Group, Legal MacPac, Softwise, TechLaw, and KI Systems. Check the Resources appendix for contact information.

CHAPTER 11

USING WORD TOOLS IN A LEGAL ENVIRONMENT

IN THIS CHAPTER

- Find and replace
- Searching for files
- Spelling and grammar, including custom dictionaries
- Language tools, including the Thesaurus and Translator Features
- Word Count
- Speech and handwriting recognition

In the legal industry, time is literally money. Court filings, closings, and client demands all necessitate that you get things done efficiently and accurately. Word includes a wide selection of built-in tools designed to help you work smarter—not harder. Some of the better-known tools include spelling and grammar checking, a thesaurus, a word counter, and multi-language capability. In addition to these features, Word has enhanced the ever-popular and time-saving Find and Replace, and added some exciting new tools that include basic and advanced file searching, translation, and speech and handwriting recognition.

This chapter will help you become familiar with all the built-in features that make Word such an exciting and powerful tool for the legal industry.

FIND AND REPLACE

Have you ever finished working on a letter or a brief only to discover that you mistyped the client or company name throughout the document? With Word's Find And Replace dialog box, you can solve this problem within seconds. You can search for a word or a group of words, match case to find the word JONES instead of Jones, or you can use wildcards to search when you don't know exactly what you're looking for or would like to find multiple results.

In addition to finding text, Find And Replace can also locate and change special formatting such as bold, italic, styles, paragraph marks, tabs, section breaks, or graphics. Find And Replace is among the most powerful but underused features in Microsoft Word.

FIND TEXT IN A DOCUMENT

1. Create a new document. Type **We the People of the United States, in Order to form a more perfect Union, establish Justice, insure domestic Tranquility, provide for the common defense, promote the general Welfare.**

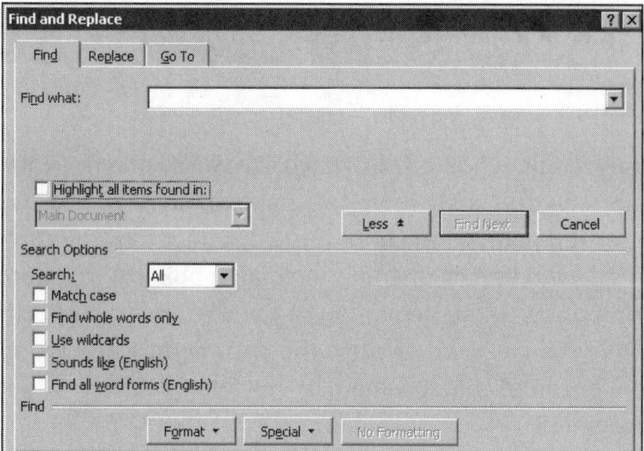

FIGURE 11.1

The Find And Replace dialog box provides many different ways to search for text.

2. From the Edit menu, choose Find, or press Ctrl+F to open the Find tab on the Find And Replace dialog box.
3. Click the More button, if it is available (it will say Less if it is not) to expand the dialog box to see additional check boxes, buttons, and options, as shown in Figure 11.1.
4. Type **the** in the Find What box.
5. Click Find Next several times and close the dialog box once Word has located all instances of the word *the.*
6. Leave this document open for the next exercise.

Table 11.1 describes each of the options that you can use to find text in your legal documents.

Operators and expressions can be used when finding or replacing text characters. An operator is a symbol that holds a position for a combination of characters. To use this feature, check Use Wildcards in the Find And Replace dialog box. Also, remember that searching with wildcards is always case-sensitive.

Table 11.2 lists the wildcards that can be used in Find And Replace operations.

TABLE 11.1 FIND AND REPLACE OPTIONS

OPTION	FUNCTION
Search	Controls the direction of the search. *All* will search the entire document or selection regardless of where the insertion point is. *Down* will search from the insertion point to the end of the document, or the current selection if text is selected before opening the dialog box. *Up* will search from the insertion point to the beginning of the document or selection. If you choose to search Down or Up in the document, when Word reaches the bottom or top of the document, it will ask if you wish to search the rest of the document.
Match Case	Specifies a case-sensitive search. For example, if you type **Law Firm** and check the Match Case option, Word will then ignore *law firm* (lowercase) or *LAW FIRM* (uppercase) and will only find *Law Firm* exactly as you typed it.
Find Whole Words Only	Searches only for whole-word instances of the text. For example, if you type **legal** and check this option, Word will not find *illegal, paralegal,* or *legally.*
Use Wildcards	Searches with *wildcards,* that is, characters or groups of characters that allow you to search without specifying exactly what you're looking for. For example, a question mark (?) finds any single letter, so if you type **p?t**, you find *pit, pat, pot,* and so forth. To find a string of characters, you will insert the asterisk (*) character instead. Using the above example, if you type **p*t**, you find *parent, poet, point,* and so forth. Word tries to help you use wildcards in the Find And Replace dialog box. Click the Wildcard check box and then click the Special button. Some of the more popular wildcards will appear in the Special list.
Sounds Like	Searches for words that sound the same but are spelled differently. For example, a search for **color** will find *color* and also *colour*, so you can make the text consistent.
Find All Word Forms	Searches for sets of words. For example, if you type **good** in the Find What box, Word will also report finding *better* and *best.* Typing **write** will find *writing, wrote, written,* and so on. You could even use it to replace *bad, worse,* and *worst* with *good, better,* and *best* in one operation.

TABLE 11.2 FIND OPTIONS

TYPE	TO FIND	EXAMPLE
?	Any single character	**s?t** finds *sat* and *set*
*	Any string of characters	**s*d** finds *said, sad,* and *started*
<	Beginning of a word	**<(inter)** finds *interrupt* and *intercept* but not *splinter*
>	End of a word	**>(in)** finds *in* and *spin* but not *interest*
[ ]	One of the specified characters	**w[io]n** finds *win* and *won* but not *wan*
[-]	Any single character within the range	**[l-o]ight** finds *light, might,* and *night*
[!-]	Any single character except the characters in the range in the brackets	**l[!a-m]ck** finds *lock* and *luck* but not *lick* and *lack*
{n}	Exactly *n* occurrences of the previous character	**be{2}t** will find *beet* but not *bet*
{n,}	At least *n* occurrences of the previous character	**be{1,}t** will find both *beet* and *bet*
{n,m}	From *n* to *m* occurrences of the previous character	**10{1,3}** finds *10, 100,* and *1000*
@	One or more occurrences of the previous character	**lo@t** finds *lot* and *loot*

NEW FIND AND REPLACE OPTIONS

If you've used Find and Replace in previous versions of Word, you'll be pleasantly surprised with the enhancements that have been made to 2002. You can now find and highlight all occurrences of a word simultaneously in either the document or the header and footer, allowing you to quickly make global replacements.

HIGHLIGHT ALL INSTANCES OF A WORD

1. Switch to the document used in the preceding exercise.
2. From the Edit menu, choose Find, or press Ctrl+F to open the Find And Replace dialog box. Click More, if necessary, to expand the dialog box to its full size.

3. In the Find What box, type **the.**
4. Select the option Highlight All Items Found In and select Main Document from the drop-down list.
5. Click Find All to highlight all instances of the word *the* within the active document. You can move the dialog box to the side to see the document better. You can even click in the document and make edits without having to first close the Find And Replace dialog box.
6. Select the Replace tab and click in the Replace With box.
7. Click the Format button and then Font to replace the selected text with specific formatting such as bold, italic, or a different font size or style, and then Click OK.

TIP

Use formatting shortcut keys in the Replace With box. For example, press Ctrl+B a few times—notice the keyboard shortcut combination toggles Bold formatting on and off.

8. Click Replace All to apply the special formatting, and then close the dialog box.

NOTE

If you do not select Highlight Items Found In, you must type **the** in the Replace With box. Failing to do this would remove the word from the document when you try to apply formatting to the word.

REPLACING SPECIAL CHARACTERS

Legal documents often contain special symbols such as paragraph marks and section symbols. In some cases, it might be more practical, or more suitable, to replace the symbols with text. With Word you can find and replace graphics or special characters as easily as text.

FIND AND REPLACE SPECIAL CHARACTERS

1. Create a new Word document.
2. Type the following paragraph: **The Court held that plaintiff was the employer of the installers' helpers under § 3401(d) and § 3401(e) and § 3402.** (From the Insert menu, choose Symbol, select Special Characters, click Section, and press Insert to insert the Section symbol.)

3. Select the Section symbol and press Ctrl+C to copy it. From the Edit menu, choose Replace, or press Ctrl+H. Delete any text in the Find What and Replace With boxes to begin a fresh Find And Replace and clear any residual formatting with the No Formatting button.

NOTE

Word remembers the criteria of the last search you performed during the session of Word. Therefore, if you have searched for a specifically formatted item in a recent Find or Replace, you must remove the formatting options manually before your next search. This is true for such formatting as a particular style, font size, or some other type of applied formatting, as well as Search options such as Match Case. To do this, place your insertion point in the Find What box, click No Formatting, deselect the Match Case option, and then move to the Replace With box and do the same.

4. Place your insertion point in the Find What box and then press Ctrl+V to paste the Section symbol.
5. Click in the Replace With box and type **Section**.
6. Click Replace All.
7. Close the Find And Replace dialog box.

SEARCHING FOR FILES

Have you ever saved a file locally and later forgotten where you put it or even the name you gave it? Perhaps you remember specific phrases of text or a client's name but can't seem to locate the shared network folder where you thought the document containing that information was stored. Word provides basic and advanced methods for searching and finding files, both locally and on the network. In addition, you can even search through Outlook e-mail messages and appointments directly from within Word.

BASIC SEARCH

Basic Search allows you to use a generalized set of search criteria to locate files, including such things as filename, file contents, file location, and file type.

Advanced Search—the topic of the next section—uses more specific criteria such as file properties, conditions, and Boolean operators (OR, AND), as well as file type and file location for those really difficult-to-find files.

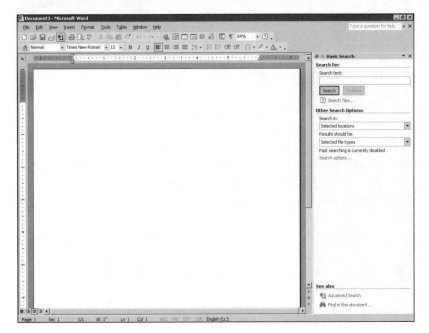

FIGURE 11.2

You can toggle between Basic and Advanced search by clicking the hyperlink at the bottom of the Search Task Pane—when one is currently selected, the other will appear as the link.

If your firm uses a document management system, you should use the search utilities specific to that system for locating files stored in the database.

To begin searching, open the Search Task Pane, as shown in Figure 11.2. From the File menu, choose Search.

FIND A FILE USING BASIC SEARCH

1. Create a new document. Type **The legal technicalities of this case make it impossible to accurately forecast an outcome.**
2. Press Ctrl+S to save the document. Save it to C:\My Documents (or your local default document directory) and name it **Legal Technicalities**. Close the document but keep Word open.
3. From the File menu, choose Search to open the Search Task Pane. If Basic Search isn't enabled, click the blue hyperlink that says "Basic Search" at the bottom of the task pane.
4. Move to the top of the task pane and type **technicalities** in the Search text box.

5. Click the drop-down arrow next to Selected locations in the Search In box and uncheck every location except My Computer.

From within the Search Task Pane, click Search Tips to generate a Word help file with hints for finding documents, Web pages, and e-mail messages.

6. Click the drop-down arrow next to Selected File Types in the Results Should Be section and check Word Files (uncheck everything else, if necessary).
7. Click Search at the top of the Search Task Pane.

To speed up the results of your search, you can enable the Indexing Service by clicking Search Options, as shown in Figure 11.3, and clicking Yes. Indexing occurs when your computer is idle.

8. Once Word locates the file, click the drop-down arrow next to the file name and choose Edit With Microsoft Word to open it.
9. To search for more documents, click Modify at the bottom of the task pane.

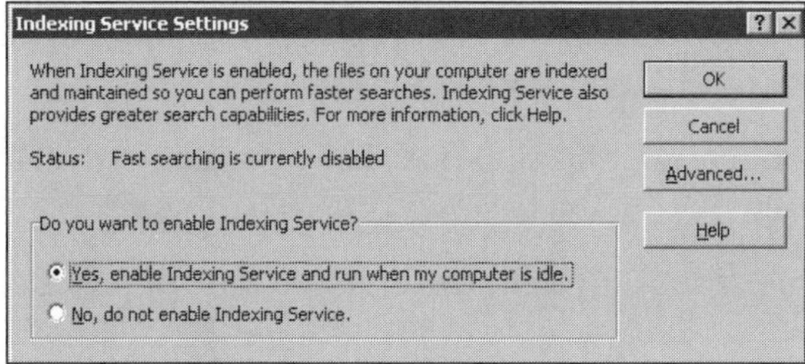

FIGURE 11.3

The Indexing Service indexes all the files on your computer, making searches more efficient and effective.

ADVANCED SEARCH

If you don't get the results you're looking for with Basic Search, click Advanced Search at the bottom of the task pane to begin expanding the search criteria. For example, you can search by author, file size, revision, number of pages, date created, keywords, notes, and much more. You can also use the Boolean operators AND and OR to restrict or broaden the search.

With Advanced Search, you can select as many (or as few) items as you need to return the exact result you're looking for. But be careful not to get too carried away—the more conditions you specify, the less likely you are to return a positive result.

NEW FEATURE!

Using the operator AND narrows the scope of a search because all conditions defined in the search must be met in order to generate a result. For example, searching for a document containing the words *litigation* AND *California* will only return documents that contain both words. The operator OR broadens the scope, as only one of the conditions must be met in order to generate a result. Searching for documents containing the words *litigation* OR *California* will bring back all documents that mention either litigation or California.

USE ADVANCED SEARCH TO LOCATE DOCUMENTS

1. From the File menu, choose Search, or click the Search button on the Standard toolbar.
2. Click Advanced Search on the Search Task Pane.
3. Click the drop-down arrow next to Property, and select a search property such as Author or Creation Date.
4. Click an option in the Condition box. The offerings here will vary with the Property chosen.
5. Enter the name of the author or the creation date of the document in the Value box.
6. If there is more than one criterion, click And or Or.
7. Click Add to populate the search criterion window. Repeat Step 6, as necessary, to define additional search conditions.
8. Select what locations to search in the Search In drop-down list. This limits the search, as shown in Figure 11.4.
9. Select what types of files and applications should be searched by clicking the drop-down arrow for Results Should Be.
10. Click Search.
11. Close the Search Task Pane.

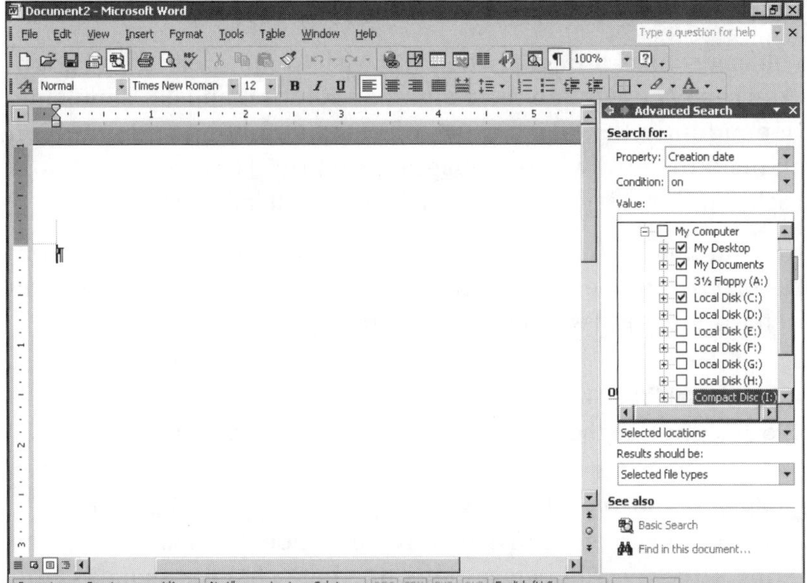

FIGURE 11.4

Click the plus (+) signs to expand each of the selected locations and check or uncheck each location, as necessary.

SPELLING AND GRAMMAR

If you are a notoriously poor speller or just not the world's greatest typist, you'll appreciate Word's spelling checker feature. The Spelling Checker can be used to reduce the amount of embarrassing errors that might otherwise show up in your documents. Some spelling corrections occur automatically, while others require you to manually start the process. When enabled, the Grammar Checker does much the same thing by looking for grammatically incorrect sentences and offering corrective suggestions. While Word's grammar feature can be useful for certain documents, you'll probably want to fine-tune it to meet the needs of your legal documents.

NEW FEATURE!

The Grammar Checker attempts to fix sentences that appear to be grammatically incorrect. When this feature is enabled, suspect sentences are identified by wavy green underlines. Legal documents typically contain long, run-on sentences and phrases that are often flagged as being grammatically incorrect by the Grammar Checker, and as a result, legal users often modify the options for this feature.

SPELLING AND GRAMMAR OPTIONS

With Word you can control how and when you wish to run spelling and grammar checks. You can choose to run them automatically or manually, simultaneously or independently. To take control of Word's spelling and grammar features, you need to know where to begin. From the Tools menu, choose Options and select the Spelling & Grammar tab, as shown in Figure 11.5.

The Spelling & Grammar tab, divided into two main sections, contains a series of check boxes that determine how and if spelling and grammar checking takes place. Each of the options is described in the following list.

Your firm may have established a default set of spelling and grammar checking options. If so, you may not see the same options selected as in Figure 11.5.

- **Check Spelling As You Type**. Enables automatic spelling checking. Errors are flagged in the document with a red wavy line under the detected spelling error. To see possible suggestions, alternate-click the marked word.
- **Hide Spelling Errors In This Document**. This option hides the red wavy line under detected spelling errors.
- **Always Suggest Corrections**. Controls whether Word offers suggestions for misspelled words when a spelling and grammar check is run manually. This only controls the use of spelling and grammar checking through the dialog box and does not affect background checking.

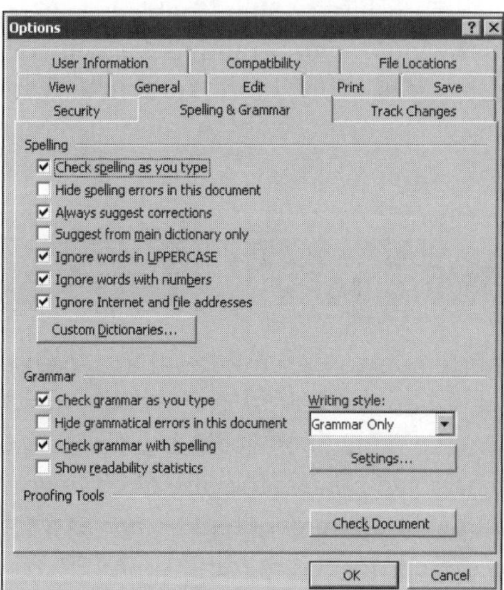

FIGURE 11.5

Some options become unavailable depending on which of the others are selected.

- **Suggest From Main Dictionary Only**. Suggests spelling corrections from the main dictionary only and not from any custom dictionaries you may have installed on your computer. Make sure to clear this option if you have a custom dictionary (legal, medical, engineering) and want to use it together with the main dictionary during spelling checking.
- **Ignore Words In UPPERCASE**. When this option is selected, the Spelling Checker does not detect words that are 100 percent uppercase.
- **Ignore Words With Numbers**. Check this, and the Spelling Checker will not detect words that contain numbers.
- **Ignore Internet And File Addresses**. Check this option to have Word skip Internet, e-mail, and file addresses during a spelling check.
- **Custom Dictionaries**. Word has a powerful built-in dictionary, but you will want to add familiar words to a custom dictionary of your own. This would include your name, the name of your firm, unusual street names, and possibly some legal and technical terms.
- **Check Grammar As You Type**. Enables automatic grammar checking as you type.
- **Hide Grammatical Errors In This Document**. Turns off the green flags on grammatical errors.
- **Check Grammar With Spelling**. To check spelling, but not grammar, clear this option.
- **Show Readability Statistics**. Readability statistics provide information such as the number of words, characters, paragraphs, and sentences in the document. Word also calculates the average number of sentences per paragraph, words per sentence, and characters per word. It also analyzes the percentage of passive sentences in the document and the grade level that can easily comprehend the text within the document.

CHECK SPELLING AND GRAMMAR AS YOU TYPE

The Check Spelling and Check Grammar As You Type options automatically mark what Word detects as misspelled words and grammatically incorrect sentences with red and green wavy underlines, respectively, while you type. Depending on your work style and time schedule, you can do one of two things: Correct each misspelled word and incorrect sentence as you go along, or run a manual spelling and grammar check when you finish with the document.

CORRECT SPELLING AND GRAMMAR ERRORS AS YOU TYPE

1. Create a new document. Type **We the Peiple of the United Stwtes, in Order to fourm a more perfec Union** (purposely misspell each misspelled word).

NOTE

This exercise assumes that the options Check Spelling As You Type and Check Grammar As You Type are enabled.

2. Press the Spacebar and note the red wavy line that appears under each misspelled word indicating a spelling error.
3. Alternate-click each misspelled word and select the correct spelling.

NOTE

To check grammatical errors at the same time as spelling errors, from the Tools menu, choose Options, and select the Spelling & Grammar tab. Check the option to Check Grammar With Spelling and click OK.

4. Create a new document. Type **The whole group are planning to meet in the hall at 7:00 p.m.** Press Enter. A wavy green line should appear beneath the grammatically incorrect phrase.
5. Alternate-click the flagged error and make the correction.

TIP

You can also double-click the Spelling And Grammar Status icon next to OVR on the status bar to move to the first detected spelling or grammar error and open the shortcut menu with potential correction suggestions.

TIP

To manually open the shortcut menu with spelling or grammar suggestions, click in the detected word or phrase and press Shift+F10. You can also alternate-click to open the shortcut menu and see the suggestions.

RUNNING A MANUAL SPELLING AND GRAMMAR CHECK

Sometimes it's easier and faster to get the words into a document without concerning yourself with correcting spelling or grammar mistakes as they occur. With Word, you can run a manual spelling and grammar check once you've finished working on a document. Even if you've corrected mistakes along the way, it's still good practice to run the spelling check before sending a document out the door.

Manually activate the Spelling and Grammar Checkers in one of the following ways: press F7, click the Spelling And Grammar button on the Standard toolbar, from the Tools menu, choose Spelling And Grammar, or alternate-click on a misspelled word to open the shortcut menu.

Figure 11.6 shows the Spelling And Grammar dialog box.

When you initiate a manual spelling or grammar check, Word begins at the point where your insertion point is located and works downward through the document.

If you choose Ignore or Ignore All on a particular word or phrase, this setting is stored with the document. As a result, when the Spelling Checker is run again, either by you or by another user, these words and phrases are skipped. To remove the Ignore "flag," you will have to reset the spelling and grammar checkers. Choose Options from the Tools menu and click Recheck Document in the Spelling And Grammar tab.

CHOOSING A GRAMMATICAL WRITING STYLE

The grammar checking feature in Word contains two default writing styles—Grammar ONLY and Grammar & Style. Each style allows you to pick and choose the grammar checking options that will work best for your documents. To choose a specific writing style, go to the Spelling & Grammar tab (Tools, Options, Spelling & Grammar), select a writing style from the drop-down menu, and click Settings to set specific options, as shown in Figure 11.7.

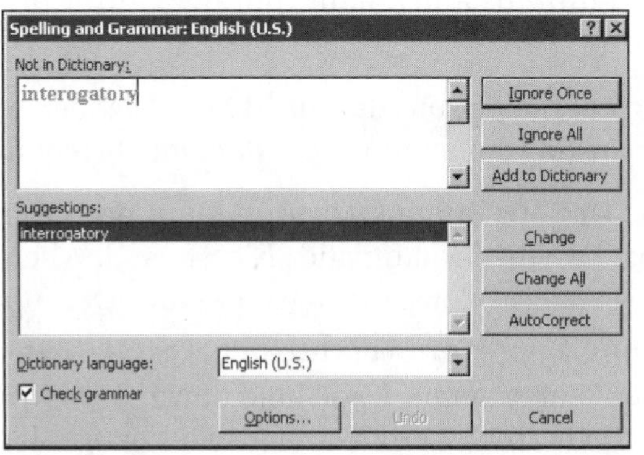

FIGURE 11.6

Ignore, add, change, or even create AutoCorrect entries from misspelled words using the Spelling And Grammar dialog box.

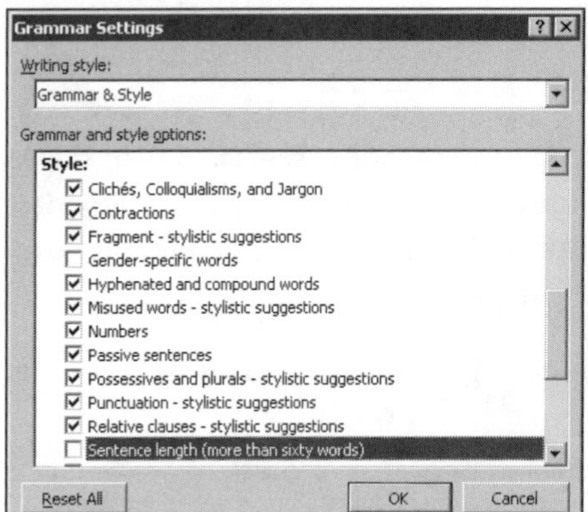

FIGURE 11.7

Fine-tuning some of the available options can make grammar checking a more useful tool for legal documents.

Scroll through the list of grammar checking options and select or deselect each of the check boxes, as necessary, to fit the requirements of your documents. For example, if you choose Grammar & Style, then you will probably want to deselect the Sentence Length option, or if you work in estate planning, you probably won't want to check the option for flagging gender-specific words as errors.

USING AUTOCORRECT WITH SPELLING

In addition to the spelling check features we've already examined, you can further eliminate the possibility of spelling errors through the use of AutoCorrect. AutoCorrect is a feature that automatically corrects spelling errors as you type. Word contains a long list of default AutoCorrect entries for commonly misspelled words. You can also create your own. For example, say you constantly misspell the word contract as conrtact—no problem, you can create an AutoCorrect entry that will automatically recognize the misspelled word and replace it with the correct spelling.

From the Tools menu, choose AutoCorrect Options and select the AutoCorrect tab to set AutoCorrect options and create your own AutoCorrect entries, as shown in Figure 11.8.

Check or uncheck each of the options described in the list below, as necessary, to control the level of spelling automation your documents require.

- **Show AutoCorrect Options Buttons**. Displays AutoCorrect Smart Tags beneath words that have been automatically corrected. When selected, the option buttons open a drop-down menu with AutoCorrect options.
- **Correct TWo INitial Capitals**. Corrects two initial capital letters at the beginning of a word. For example, if you hold down the Shift key just a bit too long and type *TOmorrow,* Word automatically changes it to *Tomorrow.*

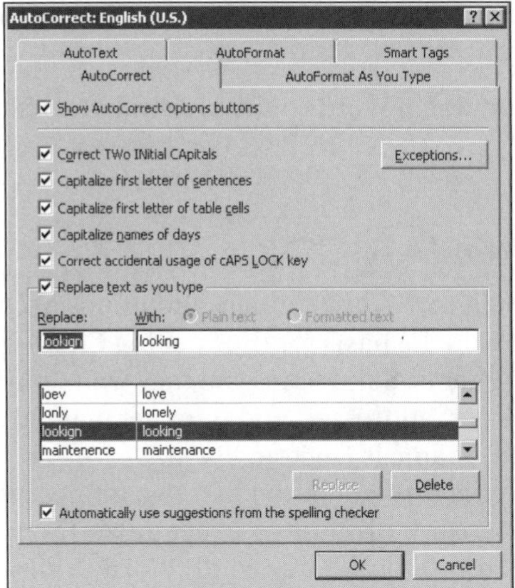

FIGURE 11.8

AutoCorrect is a powerful, time-saving feature that you can use to automatically correct misspelled words.

- **Capitalize First Letter Of Sentences**. Capitalizes the first word after a period. This setting sometimes causes capitalization to occur at incorrect times such as after Ltd. or similar words. If you use such words often, you can set each one as an exception on the AutoCorrect tab. For occasional problems, just press Ctrl+Z as soon as they occur to undo them.
- **Capitalize First Letter Of Table Cells**. Capitalizes the first word in each cell of a table.
- **Capitalize Names Of Days**. Corrects monday to Monday.
- **Correct Accidental Usage Of cAPS LOCK Key**. If you've accidentally pressed the Caps Lock key and then press the Shift key so only the first letter of a word is lowercase, Word corrects it by turning off Caps Lock.
- **Replace Text As You Type**. Corrects many common spelling errors as you type. If you type *beleive,* for example, Word corrects it to *believe.*

CREATE AUTOCORRECT ENTRIES FOR FREQUENTLY MISSPELLED WORDS

1. Type **The Esteat of Jane Doe**.
2. The word *Esteat* shows up with a red wavy underline. Alternate-click the word.
3. Select AutoCorrect from the shortcut menu.

4. Select the correct spelling, *Estate*, from the list to create an AutoCorrect entry.
5. Type **Esteat** again and watch Word automatically correct it for you.

CUSTOM DICTIONARIES

The standard dictionary built into Word contains thousands of commonly used words and terms that provide the basis for the Spelling Checker to accurately proof the text in your documents. Sometimes you may wonder what's going on when correctly spelled names, addresses, and titles get marked as misspelled. For example, say your firm's name is Leviton, Elkon, Kearney & Anderson LLP. When the Spelling Checker is turned on, the first two names get flagged with wavy red underlines because Word doesn't recognize them—they're not included in the standard dictionary. As a result, Word thinks they are misspelled. To prevent commonly used words from appearing as misspelled, you can add the words to the custom dictionary. The custom dictionary is actually an editable text file that contains all the words you manually add over time. Once a word has been added to the custom dictionary, it no longer gets flagged as incorrect.

ADD WORDS TO A CUSTOM DICTIONARY

NOTE

This exercise assumes the Check Spelling As You Type option is turned on.

1. Type **Leviton, Elkon, Kearney & Anderson LLP** and press Enter twice. Notice that Leviton and Elkon are marked as being misspelled.
2. Alternate-click *Leviton*.
3. Choose Add To Dictionary from the shortcut menu.
4. Do the same for Elkon.

Imagine you have a new client named Wickersham—or is it Wyckersham? You're pretty sure it's the former, so you add it to your custom dictionary. Then, oops! You find out it's the latter spelling. If you mistakenly add a misspelled word to the custom dictionary, you can quickly pull it out again or correct it.

EDIT THE CUSTOM DICTIONARY

1. Misspell the word *resources* by typing **resourses**.
2. Alternate-click the misspelled word and select Add To Dictionary from the shortcut menu.
3. From the Tools menu, choose Options and select the Spelling & Grammar tab.
4. Click the Custom Dictionaries button.
5. Choose Modify. The dialog box shown in Figure 11.9 will appear.
6. Select and delete the word *resourses.*
7. Click OK through each dialog box.

Good as Word's spelling and grammar checking abilities are, you need to remember that Word can't read. It can tell that *resourses* isn't in its dictionary, but it can't tell that *resources* should have been *resorts* in a particular sentence. Always proofread your own work by eye—or better yet, get someone else to do so—rather than relying on Word to tell you if anything is wrong.

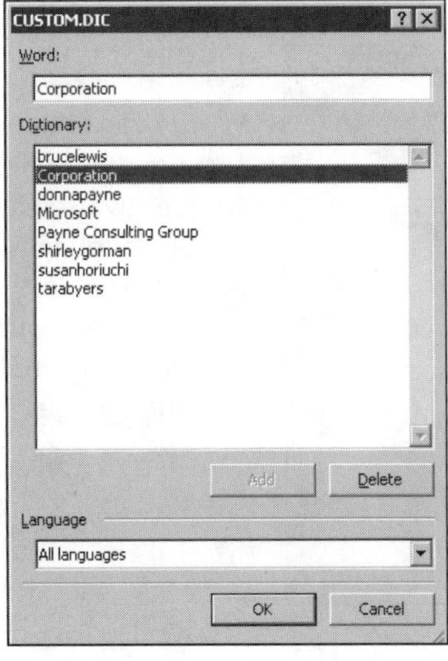

FIGURE 11.9

You can add or remove words in the custom dictionary. Some words to consider adding are your firm's name, your name, your address, the names of primary clients, and legal and medical phrases that are flagged as errors by default.

LANGUAGE

One of the real advantages to working with Word is the ability to create and proof documents in languages other than English. Legal documents in North America (as well as the United Kingdom and Australia, to name a few), are created in English, but some firms work with clients who speak other languages or have offices in other countries and need to accommodate differences in spelling. The English version of Word 2002 comes with built-in proofing tools for English, Spanish, and French. In addition to that, you can purchase (if necessary) the Office XP Multilingual User Interface Pack to work with Word in other languages by changing the language of the user interface and online help files. The Multilingual User Interface Pack also includes the Office XP Proofing Tools CD-ROM, which allows you to edit and proof documents in many different languages.

To purchase the Multilingual User Interface Pack, contact a certified reseller or go to www.microsoft.com/office/ and search on the keywords "Multilingual User Interface" to get more information.

To take advantage of Word's multilingual editing capabilities, you must first enable the specific languages from the Language Settings dialog box (Start, Programs, Microsoft Office Tools). Select the languages you want to enable in the Available Languages list and click Add, as shown in Figure 11.10.

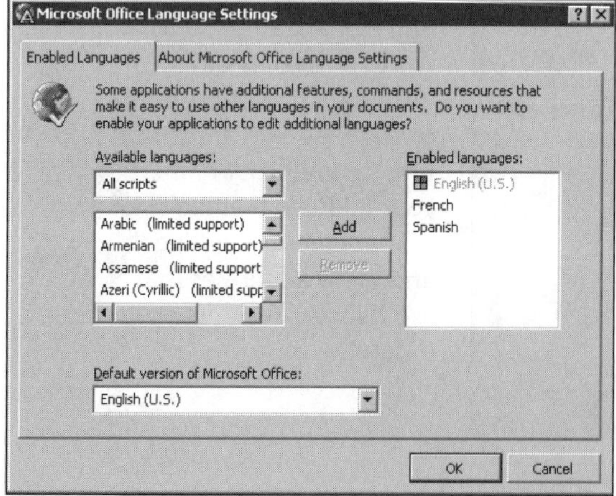

FIGURE 11.10

Word offers limited support for some of the less frequently used languages. Enable languages from the list of available choices in order to work with documents formatted in other languages.

NOTE

If a particular language is not supported by the system, the words *lin* *support* appear next to the language. In Figure 11.10, you can see th Available Languages set to All Scripts, the languages Arabic, Armeni Assamese, and Azeri all have limited support. If you see the words *li* *port* next to any of the available languages, then your firm may need to install the Multilingual User Interface Pack.

AUTOMATICALLY DETECT LANGUAGES

Once you've enabled the appropriate languages from the Language Settings dialog box, you may want to configure Word to automatically detect different languages as you type so it will check spelling against the appropriate dictionary. To do so, follow the steps in the following exercise.

AUTOMATICALLY DETECT A LANGUAGE AS YOU TYPE

1. From the Tools menu, choose Language, Set Language.
2. Select the option Detect Language Automatically, as shown in Figure 11.11.
3. You may have to restart Windows for the new settings to take effect.

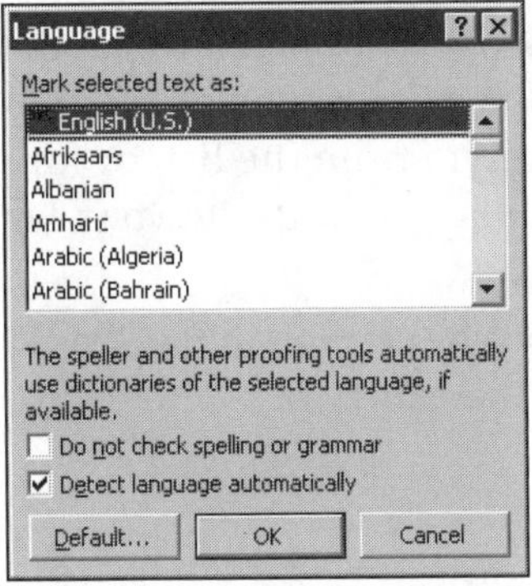

FIGURE 11.11

Automatically detecting languages enables you to proof documents that may contain sections or pages of foreign text.

CAUTION

If you do not use other languages on a frequent basis, you should not turn on Detect Language Automatically. This feature will change the language setting of an individual paragraph if it finds a word in the paragraph that is similar to a word in another language, such as French. This will cause Word's Spelling Checker to check the affected paragraph with an incorrect proofing language.

You are able to change the Language setting manually if you do not use the Detect Language Automatically feature. To do this, follow the steps in the next exercise.

SET THE LANGUAGE OF AN INDIVIDUAL PARAGRAPH

1. Create a new document.
2. Type in a paragraph of text and select it.
3. From the Tools menu, choose Language, Set Language.
4. Select the desired language under Mark Selected Text As and click OK.

THESAURUS

Finding the right word for the right occasion can sometimes be difficult, to say the least. And although most attorneys are rarely at a loss for words, Word's Thesaurus can be useful to even the most loquacious lawyer, legal assistant, or legal secretary by helping to quickly find an appropriate synonym for any word that requires a little spicing up. Synonyms generated from the Thesaurus can be accessed from a shortcut menu or directly from the Thesaurus dialog box.

The easiest way to use the Thesaurus is to alternate-click the word you wish to replace and choose Synonyms from the shortcut menu. Depending on the tense of the word and the word itself, a submenu with one or more suggestions will appear. Choose the appropriate synonym from the list, or for more choices, click Thesaurus to open the Thesaurus dialog box, as shown in Figure 11.12.

You can also open the Thesaurus dialog box by pressing Shift+F7, or from the Tools menu, choose Language and select Thesaurus.

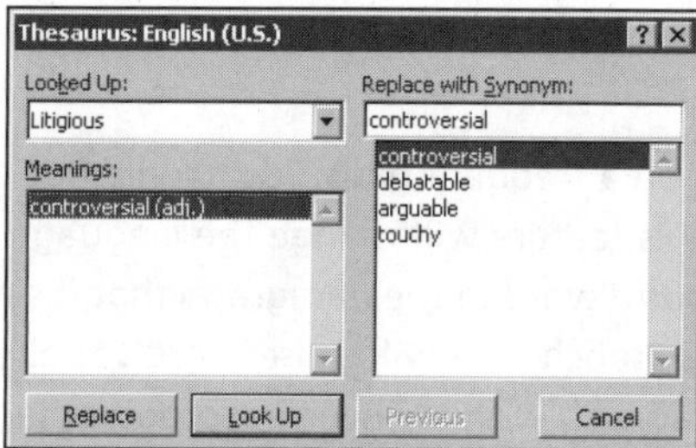

FIGURE 11.12

Replace words automatically, look up meanings, and improve the quality of your legal documents with the Thesaurus.

USE THE THESAURUS TO LOCATE SYNONYMS

1. Type **All legislative powers herein granted shall be vested**.
2. Alternate-click **granted** and choose a synonym from the list, or select Thesaurus to open the Thesaurus dialog box.
3. Choose a synonym to replace *granted.*
4. Alternate-click the replaced word and select Thesaurus to find even more choices.

TRANSLATION

Does your firm occasionally work with offices or clients in countries where French or Spanish is the spoken language? Word 2002 comes with a great new translation tool that lets you select words or phrases for translation. Basically, the language translation available is dependant on the version of Office XP installed. You can translate the following ways:

- English to French
- English to Spanish
- Spanish to English
- French to English

The Translation feature is designed to work with single words or short phrases, not complete sentences or whole documents. There is an option in the Translate Task Pane for Entire Document, but this is only activated in conjunction with the Translate Via The Web command. It cannot be done within Word. While a good idea in theory, the option Translate Entire Document may fall far short of providing accurate translation for more than just a few words.

USE THE TRANSLATION TOOL

1. Create a new document. Type **Agreement**.
2. From the Tools menu, choose Language and then choose Translate to open the Translate Task Pane, as shown in Figure 11.13.
3. Double-click Agreement to select it. Under Translate What, select Current Selection.

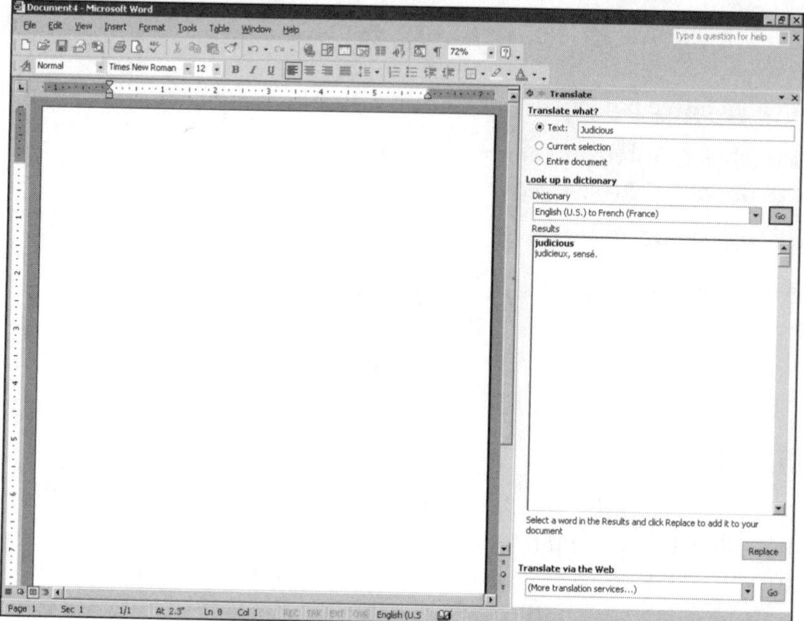

FIGURE 11.13

Translate from English to Spanish, or English to French, and vice versa.

4. Click the drop-down arrow under Dictionary and select the languages you wish to translate between. For this exercise, choose English (U.S.) To French (France).

5. Click Go.

6. The original word appears with the translated form beneath it, along with an example of the translated word in an actual sentence, in the Results box. If you want to replace your selected text with the translation, select the appropriate translation from the Results box and click Replace.

WORD COUNT

We are often asked to submit articles for various legal and technology publications. As a general rule, most publishers and editors will request that the size of the article fall between 1,200 and 2,400 words. Some courts require that legal documents not exceed a set number of words. Word Count is a feature that allows you to see not only how many words your document contains, but also other statistics such as number of pages, characters (with and without spaces), paragraphs, and lines. You can even choose whether or not to include text from footnotes and endnotes in the total count.

There are two ways to initiate a word count. From the Tools menu, choose Word Count. Through the Word Count dialog box, you can see how many words or characters are in the document, and you can choose whether or not to count text in the footnotes and endnotes. Alternatively, you can use the new Word Count toolbar—just alternate-click any toolbar and select Word Count.

USE WORD COUNT

1. Create a new document, type =**rand**(), and press Enter.
2. From the Tools menu, choose Word Count to open the dialog box shown in Figure 11.14.
3. Click Show Toolbar. Close the Word Count dialog box, but leave the toolbar open.
4. Place your insertion point at the end of the document, type =**rand**(), and press Enter.
5. From the Word Count toolbar, click the Recount button. Click the drop-down arrow to see the document statistics.

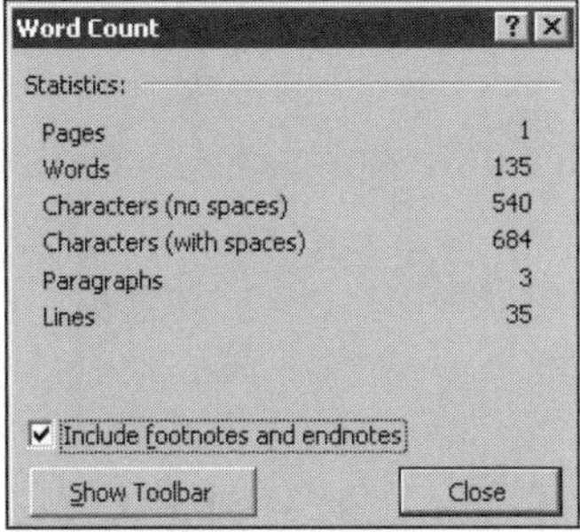

FIGURE 11.14

Click Show Toolbar to open the Word Count toolbar.

SPEECH RECOGNITION

Have you ever used Dragon NaturallySpeaking or other voice recognition software? If so, you'll be excited to know that Office XP now includes its own speech recognition utility. As the name implies, Speech Recognition lets you create letters, memos, and other documents by speaking directly into a microphone—like a dictation machine, but without the hassle of rewind. But to be fair, Speech Recognition does have its limitations, and Microsoft recommends that for best results you use it in conjunction with a mouse and the keyboard.

Speech Recognition can currently be used for three languages: U.S. English, Simplified Chinese, and Japanese.

To use Speech Recognition efficiently and correctly, you must speak clearly and slowly just as if using a recorder. Getting up to speed requires time and patience. You must train the speech recognition engine to recognize and distinguish the various patterns of your voice. So, if you want to just jump right in, this feature is not for you. Take 20 to 30 minutes, close the door, and practice with one of several training excerpts if you want to get the most out of this new feature.

Speech Recognition works with all Office XP programs and Internet Explorer 5.0 or greater.

Speech Recognition works in all Microsoft Office applications. Be aware of that when you move between Office applications. If you are dictating in Word and switch to Outlook without turning the microphone off, you may notice some strange things going on!

HARDWARE REQUIREMENTS

To use the Speech Recognition component in Word 2002, you'll need the following minimum system requirements:

- **Speech Input**: A high-quality close talk headset or microphone.
- **PC**: Minimum processing speed of 400MHz or greater with 128MB of RAM or greater.
- **Software**: Windows 98 or greater or Windows NT or higher and Internet Explorer 5.0 or higher.

INSTALLING SPEECH RECOGNITION

Before you can begin using Speech Recognition, you'll want to verify that it's installed on your computer.

INSTALL OR VERIFY SPEECH RECOGNITION INSTALLATION

1. From the Start menu, choose Settings, Control Panel.
2. Double-click Add/Remove Programs.
3. Click Change Or Remove Programs.

4. Scroll down the list of currently installed programs, select Microsoft Office, and click Change.
5. Select the top option, Add Or Remove Feature, and click Next.
6. Under Features To Install, click the plus (+) sign next to Office Shared Features to expand the menu.
7. Click the plus (+) sign next to Alternative User Input and click the drop-down arrow next to Speech.
8. Choose the option Run From My Computer or Run On First Use.
9. Click Update.

NOTE

Your firm may have elected to not install the Speech Recognition component. Check with your system administrator for more information if the installation exercise doesn't work.

INSTALLING SPEECH RECOGNITION FROM WITHIN WORD

Once you've performed a custom installation or verified that Speech Recognition is, in fact, available on your computer, you can quickly install it directly from within Word. To do so, open Word, and from the Tools menu, choose Speech. The first time you do so, you'll be prompted to go through a brief training exercise.

TIP

You'll know that Speech Recognition is installed by the identifying language icon (EN) located on the lower-right side (the System Tray) of the Taskbar.

SETTING UP AND CONFIGURING THE MICROPHONE

Before you begin training the speech recognition engine, it's very important that you configure the microphone properly. A microphone that is incorrectly configured will result in less accuracy and more frustration on your part when using the Speech Recognition tools.

NOTE

Get the best microphone you can find—preferably one with a headset. Some headsets on the market plug into not only your computer but also into your telephone, with a switch that lets you move from one to the other. However, try to first borrow one from a friend or co-worker to see how you like the feature before investing a lot of money in a microphone that you rarely use.

CONFIGURE THE MICROPHONE

1. Connect your microphone to your computer.
2. Position the microphone close to your mouth but slightly off to the side. (Not so close that you're breathing into it.)
3. From the Tools menu, choose Speech, or alternate-click the Language icon (EN) and choose Show The Language Bar.

If you don't see the Language icon, or if choosing Tools, Speech doesn't activate the Language bar, click Start, Settings, Control Panel. Double-click the Text Services icon. From the Text Services dialog box, select Language Bar. Check the Show The Language Bar On The Desktop option, as shown in Figure 11.15.

4. On the Language bar, click Speech Tools and select Options from the drop-down menu to open the Speech Properties dialog box.
5. On the Speech Recognition tab, click Configure Microphone. The Microphone Wizard dialog box opens, as shown in Figure 11.16.

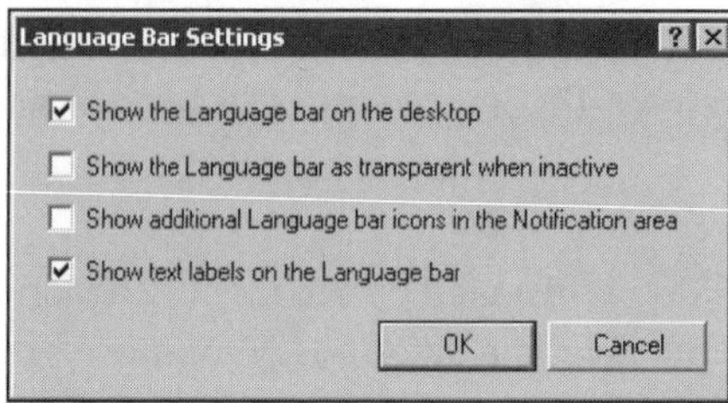

FIGURE 11.15

If you accidentally close the Language bar and can't activate it through normal means, use the Text Services dialog box to reopen it.

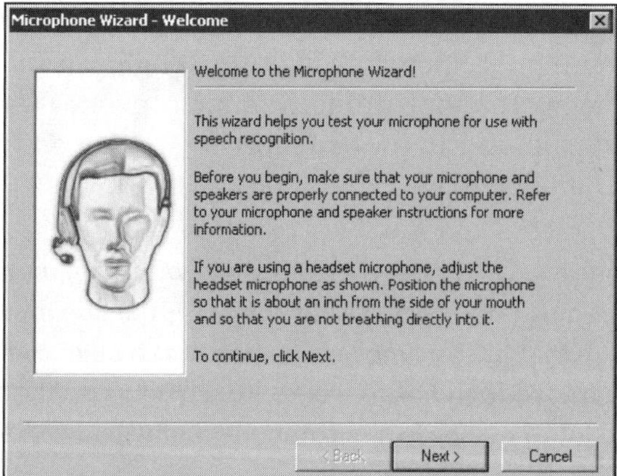

FIGURE 11.16

A properly configured microphone is essential to success with Speech Recognition.

6. Follow along with the Microphone Wizard to complete the configuration.

TIP

You can also configure the microphone directly from the Windows Control Panel. To do so, click Start, Settings, Control Panel. Double-click the Speech icon to open the Speech Properties dialog box. Click Configure Microphone and follow along with the wizard.

SPEECH RECOGNITION TRAINING

Once you've properly configured your microphone, you're ready to begin training the speech recognition engine. The first time you choose Speech from the Tools menu, you'll be presented with a training wizard that will identify patterns in the way you speak. The Voice Data Training Wizard interprets the words that you dictate into Office programs and is critical for speech recognition accuracy. So, before you begin training, retire to a quiet, secluded spot where you can avoid any interruptions for at least 20 minutes. Any time after you complete the initial training, you can go back to the training wizard and select a different training excerpt.

NOTE

It is important to note that Speech Recognition is not backward compatible. It can only be run using Word 2002 or another Office XP application. However, documents created with speech recognition can be opened and edited with previous versions of Word if the option Embed Linguistic Data is set in Word 2002. This option can be found on the Save tab of the Options dialog box (Tools, Options, Save).

FIRST-TIME SPEECH TRAINING

1. From the Tools menu, choose Speech. Word asks you to adjust your microphone and train speech.
2. Click Next and follow the wizard's instructions.
3. Speak clearly and in your normal voice.
4. Speak in a consistent, level tone.
5. Use a consistent rate.
6. Speak without pausing between words. Phrases are easier for the engine to interpret than single words.

NOTE

Additional training will result in higher accuracy. At any time after you complete the first training session, you can go back to the training wizard for more practice.

LANGUAGE BAR

The Language bar is an essential component of Speech Recognition and contains a set of buttons and commands that allow you to perform various speech-related actions. These include switching from Voice Command mode to Dictation mode, turning the microphone on and off, creating a new training profile, setting speech options, and much more. When Speech Recognition is turned off, you can activate the Language bar by selecting Speech from the Tools menu. You can also alternate-click the Language (EN) icon on the lower-right side of the Taskbar and choose Show The Language Bar. The Language bar option in the system tray is shown in Figure 11.17.

NOTE

The toolbar commands on the Language bar can be displayed as text or icons. To choose one or the other, alternate-click the toolbar and turn on or off the Text Labels option.

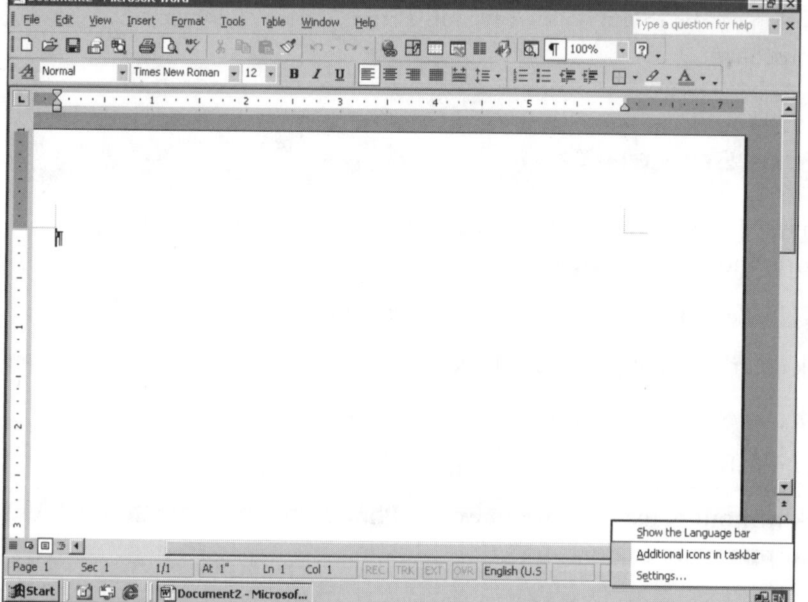

FIGURE 11.17

When selected, the option Additional Icons In Taskbar displays the keyboard and microphone icons in the System Tray. Click the keyboard icon to change the keyboard layout (if you have multiple layouts enabled) or click the microphone icon to turn on/off the microphone.

The following list provides more detailed information regarding the commands on the Language bar. To minimize or hide the Language bar, alternate-click the toolbar itself and choose Minimize. To restore the toolbar, alternate-click the Language (EN) icon on the lower-right side of the Taskbar and choose Show The Language Bar.

- **English (United States)**. Allows you to choose a language. The current choices are U.S. English, Japanese, and Chinese.
- **Correction**. Allows you to correct speech recognition errors.
- **Microphone**. Toggles the microphone on or off. When the microphone is turned on, you will see the Dictation, Voice Command, and Speech Command buttons.
- **Dictation**. Allows you to dictate text into the document. When the microphone is turned on, you can say "Dictation" to switch from Voice Command mode to Dictation mode—or simply click the Dictation button.
- **Voice Command**. Allows you to select menu, toolbar, and dialog box items by saying their names. To activate Voice Command, either click the button or say "Voice Command" when the microphone is turned on.
- **Speech Command**. Shows you what voice command you have spoken. It will also tell you if you're speaking too loudly or too softly.
- **Tools**. Presents you with the drop-down menu shown in Figure 11.18, containing the options listed in Table 11.3.

TABLE 11.3 SPEECH TOOLS OPTIONS

SPEECH TOOL	FUNCTIONS
Learn From Document	Add words that the speech recognition engine is not recognizing. If there is a word that is not recognized when you speak it, type the word, select it, and then click this button. The voice recognition system will process it and store it in memory.
Options	Add or remove speech recognition profiles.
Show Speech Messages	Turn on the display of voice commands as you speak.
Training	Give the voice recognition software further training so it will reflect your speech more accurately.
Add/Delete Words	Add new words, such as your company name or your own name, that do not appear in any of the readings. You can also delete words if they are appearing incorrectly.
Current User	Indicate which user profile to use. (Any number of users can train a given machine under their own names.)

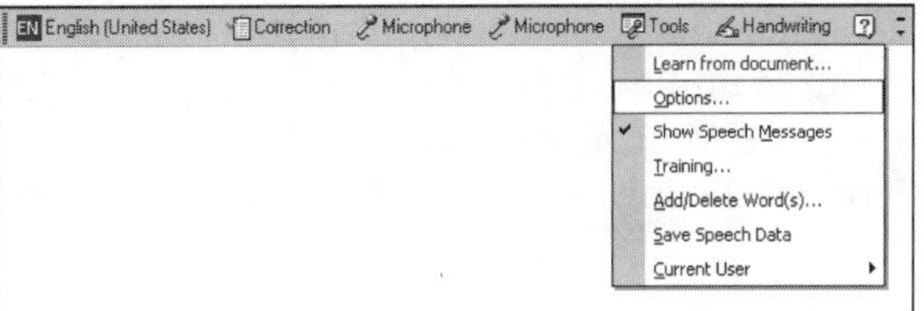

FIGURE 11.18

The Tools submenu can be opened by clicking the drop-down arrow at the end of the Language bar and choosing Speech Tools.

CREATING A PROFILE

If you share a computer with another person and plan to use Speech Recognition as a tool, you'll want to create an individual Speech Recognition profile. All people have distinct voice patterns. These patterns need to be trained and processed by the speech recognition engine. To achieve optimal results in a multi-user environment, you'll want to create a profile that is unique and readily recognizable to the speech recognition engine.

CREATE YOUR OWN SPEECH RECOGNITION PROFILE

1. From the Tools menu, choose Speech to activate the Language bar.
2. On the Language bar, click Tools and then Options to open the Speech Properties dialog box, as shown in Figure 11.19.
3. Click New.

FIGURE 11.19

Create a speech recognition profile when working in a multi-user environment if you share a computer with other users.

4. Follow along with the Profile Wizard to complete your profile and voice training.

Click Pause at any time during the training if you need to take a break. Click Resume when you're ready to begin again.

If the wizard stops highlighting words as you speak, stop and begin reading from the point immediately following the last highlighted word.

5. From the Language bar, click Tools and select Current User. You should see your name listed and checked.

If more than one profile exists on your computer, make sure that your profile is activated each time you use Speech Recognition.

ADDITIONAL TRAINING

The initial training wizard is useful for getting started with Speech Recognition, but in all likelihood, you'll need to spend more time training with the speech recognition engine for it to more accurately become familiar with the patterns of your voice in order to increase accuracy and reduce the number of incorrect entries. The more you practice, the more accurate the speech recognition will become. If you work alone, you can train as the current user, but if you share a computer, it's better to practice training as an individual profile.

RETRAINING AS CURRENT USER

1. From the Tools menu, choose Speech to activate the Language bar, or alternate-click the Language icon (EN) on the lower-right side of the Taskbar and choose Show The Language Bar.
2. From the Language bar, click Tools and select Training from the drop-down list.
3. Follow the training wizard and select an appropriate excerpt for the practice exercise.
4. If possible, choose an excerpt that you have not previously used.

5. As you read this time, say the punctuation marks—that is, "comma," "period," "question mark," "paragraph," and so on.
6. Continue as often as necessary to improve overall accuracy.

RETRAINING WITH A PROFILE

NOTE

This exercise assumes you have created an individual profile.

1. From the Tools menu, choose Speech to activate the Language bar, or alternate-click the Language icon (EN) on the Taskbar and choose Show The Language Bar.
2. From the Language bar, click Tools and select Options.
3. Select (check) your profile and click Train Profile, as shown in Figure 11.20.
4. Fill in any necessary information, if applicable, and follow the training wizard.
5. Select an appropriate excerpt from the list of choices and follow the training instructions.
6. Continue as often as necessary to improve overall accuracy.

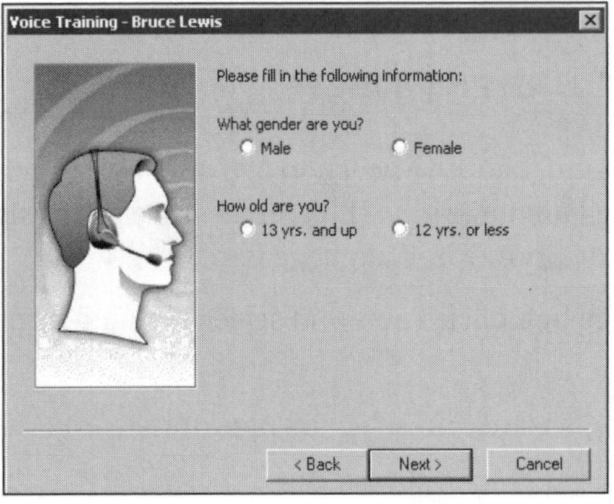

FIGURE 11.20

Training your profile will increase speech recognition accuracy.

USING DICTATION

The two main components of Speech Recognition are Dictation and Voice Commands. Dictation allows you to enter text into a document by speaking into a microphone. Voice commands allow you to execute application-specific commands by speaking them. When the Language bar is activated, you can turn on Dictation mode in one of two ways: By saying "Dictation" into the microphone (assuming it's turned on) or by clicking the Dictation button on the Language bar. As mentioned earlier, it's very important that you practice training the speech recognition engine to identify the patterns of your voice before attempting to use this feature.

USING DICTATION

1. Create a new document.
2. From the Tools menu, choose Speech, or alternate-click the Speech icon (EN) and choose Show The Language Bar.
3. From the Language bar, click Microphone to turn on the microphone.
4. Say "Dictation" to activate Dictation mode, or click the drop-down arrow at the end of the Language bar and choose Dictation.
5. Dictate the following paragraph, remembering to speak clearly and evenly: **A Person charged in any state with treason, felony, or other crime, who shall flee from justice, and be found in another state, shall on demand of the executive authority of the state from which he fled, be delivered up, to be removed to the state having jurisdiction of the crime.**

TIP

Say "comma" after each word, wherever appropriate, and "period" at the end of the sentence.

6. When you finish, click the Microphone button on the Language bar to turn the microphone off, or say "microphone off." Check the document for errors. How accurate was the dictation? If the number of errors is relatively high, then practice training the speech recognition engine more.

As noted in the Tip accompanying the preceding exercise, you can insert specific characters, such as commas, colons, exclamation points, and more, by saying them as you dictate. Table 11.4 provides a list of dictation

TABLE 11.4 DICTATING NUMBERS, PUNCTUATIONS, AND SYMBOLS

WHAT TO SAY	WHAT GETS INSERTED
Period/Dot	.
Comma	,
Semi colon	;
Question mark	?
Exclamation point	!
Ampersand	&
Asterisk	*
At sign/At	@
Backslash	\
Slash	/
Vertical bar	|
Hyphen	-
Dash	-
Double dash	--
Equals	=
Plus	+
Plus sign	+
Pound sign	#
Percent	%
Percent sign	%
Dollar sign	$

commands, along with the resulting insertion Word makes when you're using Dictation mode.

The accuracy attained using Dictation mode increases proportionately with the amount of time you spend training the voice recognition engine.

TABLE 11.4 DICTATING NUMBERS, PUNCTUATIONS, AND SYMBOLS

WHAT TO SAY	WHAT GETS INSERTED
Underscore	_
Tilde	~
Ellipsis	...
Greater than	>
Less than	<
New line	Enter
New paragraph	Enter twice
Open parenthesis	(
Left paren	(
Close parenthesis	)
Right paren	)
Quote	“
Open quote	“
Close quote	”
Single quote	‘
Open single quote	‘
Close single quote	’
Numbers 1-20	Numbers are spelled out when inserted
Numbers >20	Numbers are inserted as digits
First/Second/Third, and so on	first/second/third
One-half	1/2

USING VOICE COMMANDS

In addition to the dictation capabilities Speech Recognition offers, you can also use voice commands to perform standard application-specific operations such as Open, Close, Save, and so forth. You can even use voice commands to format text, change font size, and update styles! To use any of the recognizable commands, either click the Voice Command button on the Language bar or say “Voice Command,” if the microphone is turned on.

USE VOICE COMMANDS TO WORK WITH DOCUMENTS

1. Start Word.
2. From the Tools menu, choose Speech, or alternate-click the Language icon.
3. From the Language bar, click Microphone to turn on the microphone.
4. Say "Voice Command," or click Voice Command on the Language bar.
5. Say "File"—the File menu should expand.
6. Say "New"—the New Document Task Pane should open.
7. Say "Blank Document."
8. Switch to Dictation mode by saying "Dictation."
9. Say "This is a new document (period)."
10. Switch back to Voice Command mode by saying "Voice Command."
11. Say "File," once the File menu expands, then say "Save."
12. Say "File Name."
13. Say "Practice File" to name the file.
14. Say "Save."
15. Say "File;" once the File menu expands, say "Exit."

Use voice commands to select the following items:

- **Toolbar buttons**. Say the name of the specific toolbar button.
- **Menu items**. Say the name of the menu to expand it. Once the menu expands, say the name of the corresponding command.

You can also use voice commands for many keyboard operations. Table 11.5 lists the options.

CORRECTING SPEECH RECOGNITION ERRORS

You may find that certain words or phrases come out wrong when you use Speech Recognition. To correct mistakes, select the incorrect word using the mouse or keyboard. Repeat the correct word into the microphone until the selected incorrect word is corrected. If the word in question is something like a

TABLE 11.5 ADDITIONAL VOICE COMMANDS

VOICE COMMAND	KEYBOARD EQUIVALENT
Enter	Press Enter
Return	Press Enter
Backspace	Press Backspace
Delete	Press Backspace
Back one word	Press Ctrl+left-arrow
Last word	Press Ctrl+left-arrow
Spacebar	Press the Spacebar
Space	Press the Spacebar
Escape	Press Esc
Cancel	Press Esc
Right-click	Right-click a menu
Context menu	Right-click a menu
Right-click menu	Right-click a menu
Tab	Press Tab
Shift Tab	Press Shift+Tab
End	Press End
Go End	Press End
Home	Press Home
Go Home	Press Home
Up	Press up-arrow
Go Up	Press up-arrow
Down	Press down-arrow
Go Down	Press down-arrow
Left	Press left-arrow
Go Left	Press left-arrow
Right	Press right-arrow
Go Right	Press right-arrow
Previous Page	Press Ctrl+Page Up
Next Page	Press Ctrl+Page+ down-arrow
Page Down	Press Page Down
Page Up	Press Page Up

company or client name, you may have to add it to the speech recognition dictionary. For information on this, see the next section.

TIP

If you continue to experience a consistently high number of errors, practice training the speech recognition engine using the excerpts from the training dialog box.

ADDING AND DELETING WORDS

Some words or phases—often the name of your firm or the name of a client—won't be recognizable to the speech recognition engine no matter how often you say them. The speech recognition engine attempts to match known words (those in the speech engine dictionary) with the words you speak into the microphone. When necessary, you can change the dictionary to add or remove words that the speech recognition engine doesn't recognize or that you no longer use.

ADDING WORDS TO THE SPEECH RECOGNITION DICTIONARY

1. Create a new document.
2. Activate the Language bar.
3. From the Language bar, click Speech Tools and select Add/Delete Words from the drop-down menu.
4. Under Word, type the word you wish to add to the dictionary.
5. Click Record Pronunciation and say the word. When the speech recognition engine recognizes the word, it will be added to the dictionary list of custom words.

HANDWRITING RECOGNITION

Handwriting recognition is new to Word 2002. By using a handwriting device such as a digital pen (or the mouse, for that matter), you can enter text by writing instead of typing. Handwritten text is automatically converted to typewritten characters at the point where the insertion point is located. If you're a notoriously poor typist yet need to draft a document, then this feature might be just what the doctor ordered.

You can also insert handwriting as a sort of digital ink to display text in a printed or cursive form. This can be useful for files that need to be sent electronically but require an actual signature. It can also be used to add a more personal touch to less formal documents.

REQUIREMENTS

To use handwriting recognition, your computer will need the following minimum requirements:

- **Writing Tool**: A handwriting tool connected to your computer (such as a pen stylus and tablet). You can also use your mouse with the primary mouse button held down (not as effective as an input tool).
- **PC**: Minimum processing speed 75MHz with 24MB of RAM with Windows 98 or higher, or 75MHz with 40MB of RAM with Windows NT or higher.
- **Software**: Windows 98 or higher, or Windows NT or higher.

INSTALLING HANDWRITING RECOGNITION

Installing handwriting recognition is a simple matter.

INSTALL HANDWRITING RECOGNITION

1. From the Start menu, choose Settings and choose Control Panel.
2. From within the Control Panel dialog box, double-click Add/Remove Programs.
3. Click Change Or Remove Programs.
4. Select Microsoft Office from the list of installed programs and click Change.
5. In the Microsoft Office Setup dialog box, select Add Or Remove Features and click Next.
6. Click the plus (+) sign next to Office Shared Features to expand the submenu.
7. Click the plus (+) sign next to Alternative User Input to expand the submenu.
8. Click the drop-down arrow next to Handwriting, choose Run From My Computer, and click Update.

You may have to restart your computer for the settings to take effect. Once you've installed Handwriting Recognition, the Language bar will contain additional commands to help you work with this feature.

If, after installing Handwriting Recognition, you don't see the handwriting commands on the Language bar, alternate-click the toolbar itself and choose Settings. From the Text Input dialog box, click Add. Under Input Language, choose an appropriate language and select the correct keyboard layout. In most cases, you will choose English (United States) as the language and United States-International as the keyboard layout. At the time of publication, handwriting recognition is available in English, Korean, Japanese, and Simplified and Traditional Chinese.

Microsoft recommends that you remove Handwriting Recognition if you're not using it. This feature uses memory and can slow down the performance of your computer.

USING HANDWRITING RECOGNITION

Once you've determined that your computer meets the minimum hardware and software requirements necessary for handwriting recognition and you've performed the necessary installation, you're ready to start writing. You can use the Handwriting Recognition tool to convert written text to typeset characters, or simply write text into a document.

The enlarged Language bar, as shown in Figure 11.21, contains a Handwriting button that opens a drop-down menu with options that can be used to control the method and format in which handwritten text is displayed in your document.

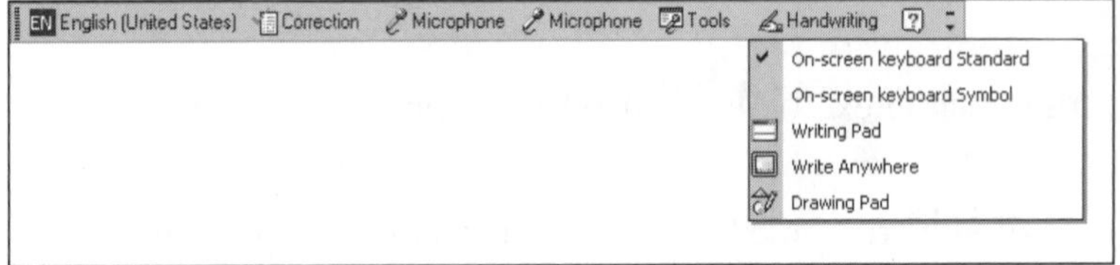

FIGURE 11.21

Use the Language bar to activate Handwriting Recognition if it's installed on your computer.

The menu includes the following options:

- **On-screen Keyboard Standard**. When selected, this option displays a fully functional on-screen keyboard similar to the one attached to your computer.
- **On-screen Keyboard Symbol**. This option displays an on-screen keyboard that replaces each of the regular keys with a selection of commonly used symbols.
- **Writing Pad**. Use the writing pad to enter text as either typeface or handwritten characters.
- **Write Anywhere**. Choose this option to write anywhere on the active screen. Your handwriting is identified and inserted at the insertion point.
- **Drawing Pad**. Use the drawing pad to draw and insert objects into your document.

PRACTICE USING HANDWRITING RECOGNITION

1. Create a new document. Turn on Show/Hide. Type **Sincerely,** and press Enter four times. Type your name, as though you were setting up a letter signature block.
2. Alternate-click the Language icon (EN) to activate the Language bar.
3. On the Language bar, click the Handwriting button and select Write Anywhere from the drop-down list to open the Write Anywhere box, as shown in Figure 11.22.

TIP

Click the drop-down arrow on the upper-left side of the Write Anywhere box to open a drop-down menu that allows you to switch between Write Anywhere, Writing Pad, and Drawing Pad. You can also choose to set specific options.

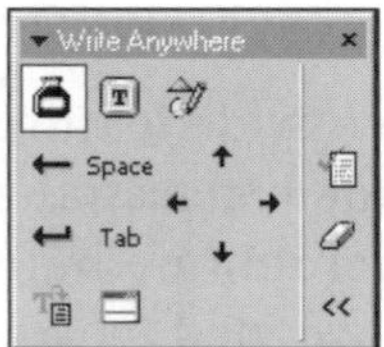

FIGURE 11.22

Hover your mouse pointer over any of the icons on the Write Anywhere box to display a helpful ScreenTip.

4. Place your insertion point at the third paragraph mark.

NOTE

Handwritten text is inserted where your insertion point is located, just as though you were using the keyboard.

5. Click and hold the mouse and spell out your name.

TIP

When using Write Anywhere, you can write anywhere on the active screen, and the text will still get placed at the insertion point.

6. After a brief pause, the written text will appear in the correct location. Hint: Click Recognize Now on the Write Anywhere box to quickly insert written text. Close Write Anywhere.

SUMMARY

Chapter 11 has covered those features in Word that help make it such a powerful, time-saving application. We started out talking about Find and Replace, searching for files, spelling and grammar checking, and custom dictionaries. We then moved on to Language, Thesaurus, Translation, and Word Count. The chapter concluded with a discussion of Word's exciting new speech and handwriting recognition tools.

TROUBLESHOOTING TOOLS

I closed the Language bar and it's gone. How do I get it back?

From the Start menu, choose Settings and then Control Panel. Double-click Text Services and then click Language Bar. Check the option to Show The Language Bar On The Desktop.

Strange things are happening when I move between Office applications—it's like the computer is taking over! What's going on??

Remember that Speech Recognition is an Office-wide feature, and Speech Recognition is most likely still turned on. To remedy the strange behavior of your computer, remember to turn off the microphone before switching between applications. Speech Recognition is designed to work with all the Office programs. Click the Microphone button on the Language bar to turn off Speech Recognition.

I can't remember where I saved an important document, and the client needs it now—what should I do?

Use the new Search feature to locate documents locally or on the network. From the File menu, choose Search to open the Search Task Pane. Switch between Basic and Advanced search by clicking the hyperlink at the bottom of the pane. Enter the appropriate search criteria, such as document title, keywords, or author, and then choose the search locations. Place a check next to the folders or network drives where you think the document may be located. Expand menus by clicking the plus (+) signs. Last, choose a selected file type. For example, if you're looking for a Word document, unselect all other file types to speed up the search. When everything is set, click Search.

My handwriting doesn't seem to be recognized when I use the Text feature—is there any way to train the computer to recognize my handwriting?

If your handwriting doesn't properly translate to typeface characters, then you might try the following: Switch from cursive to printing, write clearly, leave more spaces between words, and write entire words at a time.

The performance of my computer has noticeably slowed down since I installed speech and handwriting recognition. Is there any way to use these features without affecting my ability to work quickly and efficiently?

To use Speech Recognition, your computer needs a processor of at least 400MHz and 128MB of RAM. Handwriting Recognition requires at least 75MHz with 24MB of RAM. These are just the minimum requirements—to boost performance, you may have to add more memory or upgrade to a faster computer. Remember, if you're not using Handwriting or Speech Recognition, don't install it—it takes up a lot of processing speed and memory even when you're not using it.

The Spelling Checker keeps incorrectly marking words that are spelled correctly—is there any way to fix this without turning the Automatic Spelling Checker off?

Word uses a standard dictionary as the basis for checking spelling. Words that the Spelling Checker doesn't find in the standard dictionary get marked as being spelled incorrectly—whether they are or not. When a word that you know to be correct (such as the name of a client) gets flagged, alternate-click it and choose Add from the drop-down menu. This adds the word to the custom dictionary. The next time you type the word in a document, it won't get flagged.

I know that there are spelling mistakes in the document. I've checked, and the option to check spelling and grammar automatically is turned on—why is Word skipping these words when I run the Spelling Checker?

Someone has probably chosen to Ignore the words or phrases during a previous spelling check. When a word is flagged as "ignore," this is saved with the document. To reset these incorrectly flagged words, choose Options from the Tools menu. Click Recheck Document in the Spelling & Grammar tab.

If this does not correct the problem, to determine the cause of this problem, select the text that you know is spelled incorrectly. From the Tools menu, choose Language, Set Language. In the Language dialog box, check whether the option Do Not Check Spelling Or Grammar is selected. If the option is enabled, you might also want to select the entire document and verify that there are no other areas where Word is instructed not to check spelling or grammar. Converted documents often have this option enabled by default.

At the end of every sentence, a grammar error appears under the period and space after it. What is causing this?

There is an option in Word to check the number of spaces after the end of a sentence. To check or change this option, from the Tools menu, choose Options. Select the Spelling & Grammar tab and click Settings. Change Spaces Required Between Sentences to One, Two, or Don't Check, depending on your preference.

Chapter 12

Using Tables in Legal Documents

In This Chapter

- Parts of a table
- Creating a table
- Table navigation
- Modifying the table structure
- Setting table properties
- Creating nested tables
- Setting default dimensions
- Table math

Tables are not only essential to office and legal documents, they are also one of the easiest Word tools to use. One prominent law firm estimates that approximately 60 percent of its documents contain some form of table. Tables can serve as fax cover sheets to store recipient information, as captions in pleadings, as charts tracking medical chronology, as pleading indices, and as signature blocks, to name just a few of their many uses. Even if you don't use Word to create these types of documents, you'll still find the Table feature extremely useful for storing, aligning, and presenting information.

TABLES 101

A table is made up of rows and columns that intersect to form cells. The maximum number of columns in a Word table is 63. The maximum number of rows is 32,767. Each cell can contain text, numbers, graphics, or tables nested inside of other tables. Working with tables is made easier by the table components shown in Figure 12.1 and described in detail in the following bullet points.

- **Cell**. A cell is formed at the intersection of a row and column. Text, graphics, or other tables can be inserted into a table cell.
- **Row**. A row is a horizontal collection of cells within a table or spreadsheet.
- **Column**. A column is a vertical collection of cells within a table or spreadsheet.
- **Table Move Handle**. The move handle allows you to drag the table to a new location on the page. It appears when you are working in Web Layout or Print Layout view, and are within a table.
- **End-of-Cell Marker**. The end-of-cell markers store cell formatting and appear within every cell. These symbols only appear onscreen; they do not print.
- **End-of-Row Marker**. At the end of each row is an end-of-row marker. This marker's function is similar to the paragraph mark and contains formatting information.

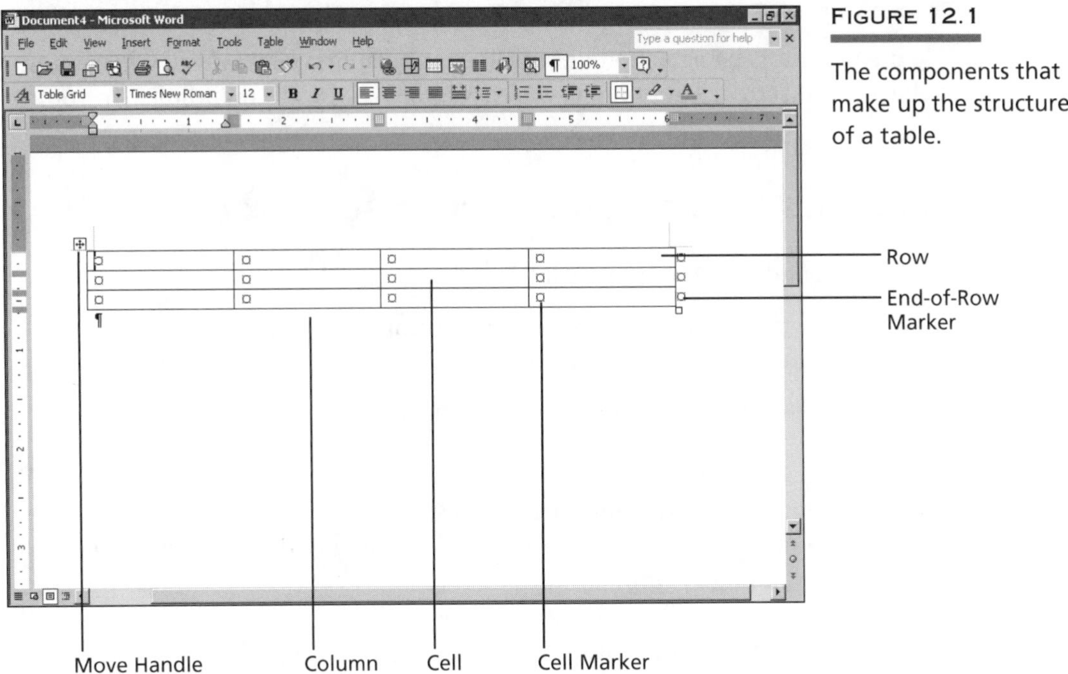

FIGURE 12.1

The components that make up the structure of a table.

NOTE

To see the end-of-row and end-of-cell markers, you need to turn on the display of nonprinting characters onscreen. Do this by clicking the Show/Hide button on the Standard toolbar. The keyboard combination for toggling the Show/Hide feature is Ctrl+Shift+8 (use the number on the main keyboard, not the numeric keypad).

- **Table Resize Handle**. The table resize handle—unsurprisingly—lets you change the size of a table. It appears in the lower-right corner of the table when the table is active. Click and drag when the pointer becomes a double arrow to change the size of a table.

CREATING A TABLE

As with most features in Word, you have more than one way to create a table. You can use a menu command or a toolbar button, or you can draw the table yourself. Whatever you choose, the result is the same—you get a new table.

CREATE A TABLE USING A TOOLBAR BUTTON

To create a table using a toolbar button, you must first click where you want the table to be inserted. After that, it's as easy as clicking and expanding a button.

CREATE A TABLE USING A TOOLBAR BUTTON

1. Click and hold the Insert Table button on the Standard toolbar.
2. Drag with the mouse to expand the button to show as many rows and columns as you want to insert.
3. Release the mouse button to create the table.

Creating a table using this method is easy, but it does have at least one drawback. It would be difficult if not impossible to create an extremely large table just from expanding the toolbar button.

CREATE A TABLE USING A MENU COMMAND

Tables are so important to Word that they have their own dedicated menu, with commands that help you create, manipulate, and format elements of a table. To create a table using a menu command, from the Table menu, choose Insert, Table. In the Insert Table dialog box, specify the quantity of rows and columns for the table as well as any special formatting and table properties.

The Insert Table dialog box, which is shown in Figure 12.2, is a great way to create a table when you need a large table or want to specify exact formatting.

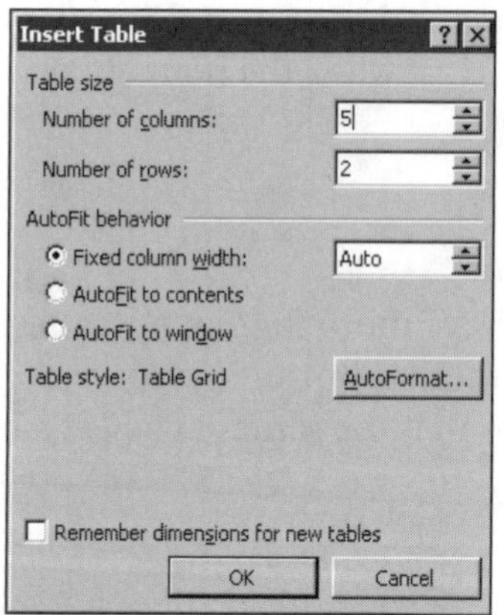

FIGURE 12.2

The Insert Table dialog box allows for greater control of the size, format, and AutoFit behavior of the table.

CREATE A TABLE USING THE TABLE MENU

1. From the Table menu, choose Insert, Table.
2. In the Number Of Columns field, type **4**. The maximum is 63.
3. Type **200** as the Number Of Rows. The maximum is 32,767.
4. Click OK to insert the table. (Ignore the other options in the dialog box, which are covered later in the chapter.)
5. Press Ctrl+A to select everything in the document, and then press Delete. That lets you start fresh creating other tables in later exercises.

CREATE A TABLE FROM TEXT

Sometimes information already exists and just needs to be converted from text into a table. Word includes the ability to quickly convert text to a table, or a table to text.

CONVERT TEXT TO A TABLE

1. Type **Ruth Bader Ginsburg** and press Enter. Type **David Hackett Souter** and press Enter. Type **John Paul Stevens** and press Enter.
2. Select the list of names.
3. From the Table menu, choose Convert, Text To Table. The Convert Text To Table dialog box opens, as shown in Figure 12.3.

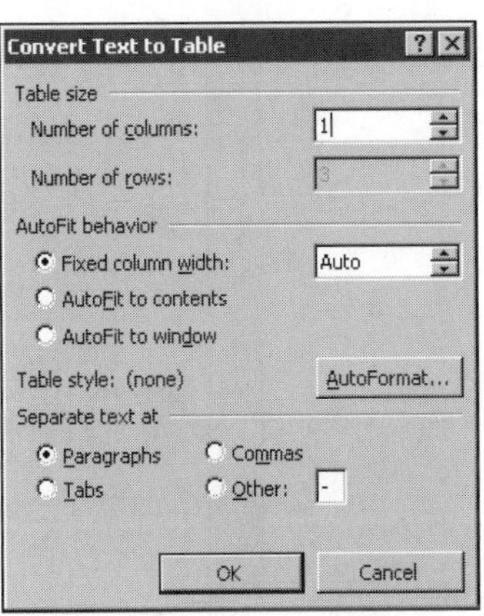

FIGURE 12.3

Converting text to a table quickly transforms existing text into tabular format.

4. Click the Other option button (in the Separate Text options at the bottom of the dialog box). Delete any character that appears in the box to the right of Other.
5. In the Other box, press the Spacebar. This tells Word that you want to use spaces to designate when to create a new column in the table.
6. Click OK to convert the text to a table with three columns. Figure 12.4 shows the finished result.

CREATE A TABLE FROM EXCEL DATA

Why reinvent the wheel when you don't have to? If information exists in another application, before retyping it, you should attempt to copy and paste it into Word. In this exercise, you will use information stored in Microsoft Excel and bring it into Word.

CREATE A WORD TABLE FROM EXCEL DATA

1. Open Microsoft Excel and Word. If you don't have an existing Excel spreadsheet, just type some information in several of the cells.
2. Select the text and copy it.

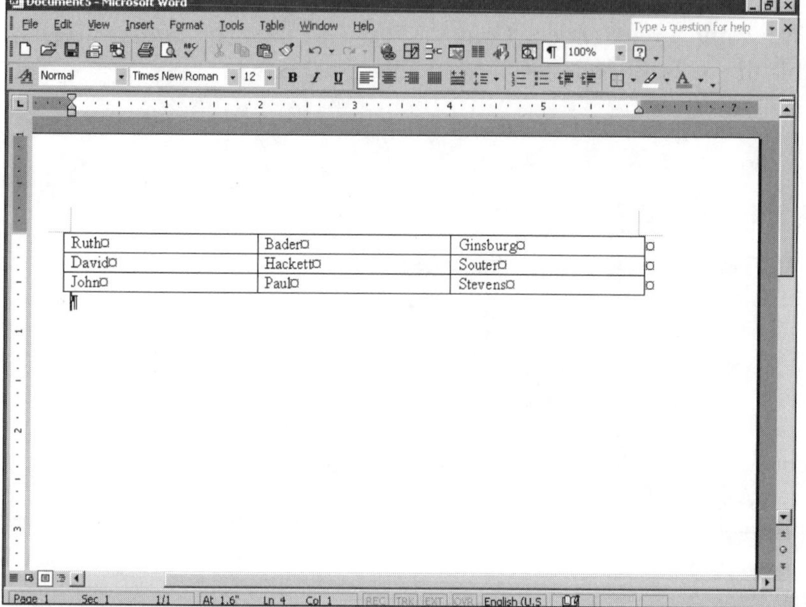

FIGURE 12.4

The text has been converted into a table with three columns.

NEW FEATURE!

When you copy and paste in the table exercise, you will see a picture of a Clipboard with a downward-pointing arrow in the lower-right corner of the table. This represents a new feature in Word 2002, the Paste Options button.

When information is copied and pasted from Excel to Word, the options are to Keep Source Formatting, Match Destination Table Style, Keep Text Only, Keep Source Formatting And Link To Excel, Match Destination Table Style And Link To Excel, and Apply Style Or Formatting.

Paste Options are covered in depth in other chapters of this book but, since they appear when copying and pasting information to create tables, they are worth mentioning here.

3. Switch to Word and, from the Edit menu, choose Paste. The information is pasted into the Word document as a table.
4. Press Enter a few times to give yourself a little room.
5. From the Edit menu in Word, choose Paste Special. The Paste Special dialog box opens, as shown in Figure 12.5.
6. Select Microsoft Excel Worksheet Object and click OK. This inserts the same information but preserves the object in Microsoft Excel format. To edit the Excel object, double-click the object.

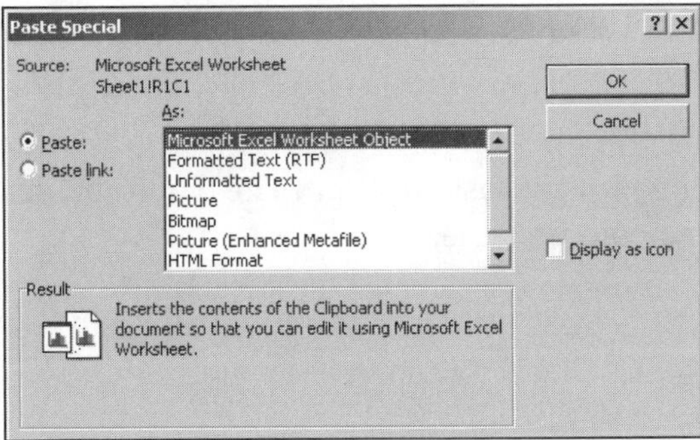

FIGURE 12.5

Control how information from other sources appears by using the Paste Special dialog box.

NOTE

The Paste Special dialog box includes an option to paste a link to the original source document. This is a great way to keep information up to date. If the source document is available, click the embedded Excel object and press F9. This forces a recalculation and will update the data to reflect any changes made to the source file. Creating a link to the Excel spreadsheet is also an option in the Paste Options menu.

7. Click in the Word document (that is, outside the Excel object) and press Enter again to give yourself some room.
8. From the Edit menu, choose Paste Special. Select Unformatted Text and click OK. This inserts the text only without formatting. Column separators are changed to Tab characters. Each row is separated by a paragraph mark.

TIP

The Paste Options button also allows you to paste as text only. The result is a comma-delimited table.

CREATE A TABLE USING AUTOCORRECT

You can also create a table by typing a few characters on the keyboard. Word has a built-in AutoFormat As You Type feature that recognizes combinations of plus signs (+) and hyphens (-) to quickly create a one-row table with one or more columns. On a blank line, type plus signs where the columns should begin and end, and hyphens for the number of spaces in the cells.

To get this feature to work, enable the AutoCorrect Options, AutoFormat As You Type feature. From the Tools menu, choose AutoCorrect Options. The AutoCorrect dialog box opens, as shown in Figure 12.6. Select the AutoFormat As You Type tab and check the Tables check box. Click OK to close the dialog box.

CREATE A TABLE USING AUTOFORMAT AS YOU TYPE

1. On a blank line, type +----------+---+----------+.
2. Press Enter after typing the last plus sign. The typed characters should convert to a three-column table.

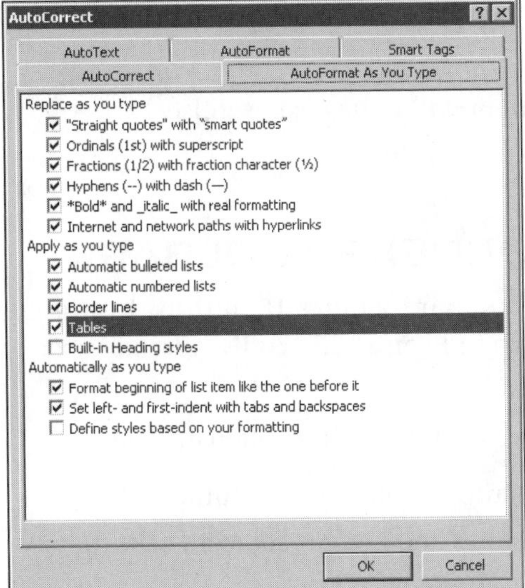

FIGURE 12.6

Control what Word "corrects" automatically in the AutoCorrect dialog box.

CREATE A TABLE USING DRAWING TOOLS

The Standard toolbar contains a Tables And Borders button that, when clicked, displays an entire toolbar. This toolbar includes buttons that let you draw, erase, and format text and lines, merge and split cells, and perform mathematical operations. When the Tables And Borders toolbar appears, the first button, Draw Table, is activated automatically.

TIP

You can also activate the Tables And Borders toolbar from the Table menu by choosing Draw Table.

DRAW A SIMPLE TABLE

1. Click the Tables And Borders button on the Standard toolbar or choose Draw Table from the Table menu.
2. Draw a rectangle approximately four inches long by two inches deep.
3. Draw a vertical line down the center to divide the table in two.
4. Draw more lines to separate the table even further, creating rows and columns.

5. Click the Draw Table button on the Tables And Borders toolbar to toggle off Drawing mode.
6. Leave this document open for the next exercise.

TABLE AND BORDERS TOOLBAR

The Tables And Borders toolbar includes 18 buttons for frequently accessed table commands, as shown in Figure 12.7. You've already used the Draw Table button.

The toolbar buttons behave as shown in the following list:

- **Draw Table**. Lets you draw a table in the document.
- **Eraser**. Erases the cell lines and merges adjacent cells that were separated by the lines.
- **Line Style**. Adds a border style to the lines of the table.
- **Line Weight**. Changes the thickness of the line.
- **Border Color**. Adds color to the border of the table.
- **Border**. Gives you several border alternatives for the table in a drop-down list.

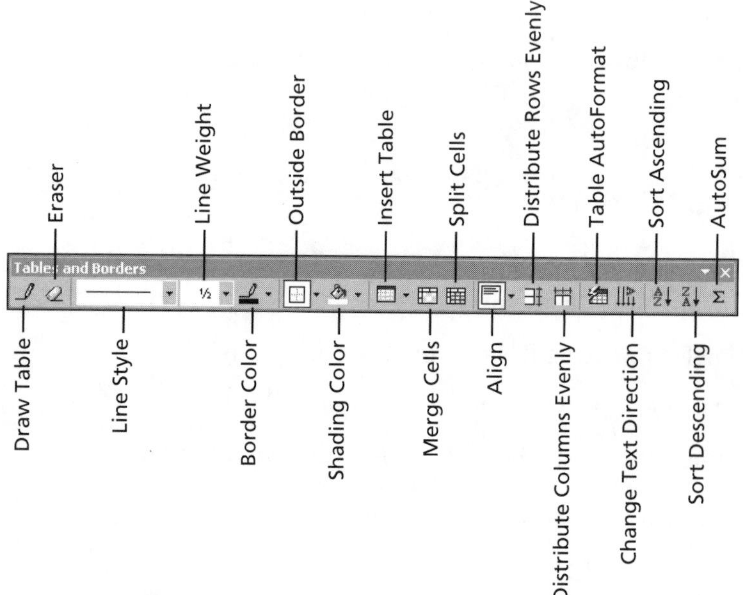

FIGURE 12.7

Create a table and format, sort, and apply other attributes to your table directly from the Tables And Borders toolbar.

- **Shading Color**. Fills active cells with the color selected from the palette.
- **Insert Table**. Gives you a menu of choices for inserting and working with a table, individual rows, columns, or cells.
- **Merge Cells**. Merges selected cells into one cell.
- **Split Cells**. Splits a cell into multiple columns or rows.
- **Align**. Lets you choose from nine different alignments, both vertically and horizontally, for the text within the table.
- **Distribute Rows Evenly**. Changes the selected rows to equivalent row heights.
- **Distribute Columns Evenly**. Changes the selected columns to equivalent column widths.
- **Table AutoFormat**. Opens the AutoFormat dialog box, with options for applying built-in formatting styles to the active table.
- **Change Text Direction**. Changes the direction of the text in the active cells from horizontal to vertical or vice versa.
- **Sort Ascending**. Sorts the table in ascending order.
- **Sort Descending**. Sorts the table in descending order.
- **AutoSum**. Inserts an =(Formula) field that calculates and displays the sum of the values in the table cells above or to the left of the cell containing the insertion point.

The Borders, Shading Color, and Text Alignment buttons can float. To do this, expand the button and then place your mouse pointer over the Drag To Make This Menu Float lines located at the top of the button. Drag the button off the toolbar.

USE THE TABLES AND BORDERS TOOLBAR

1. Click the Draw Table button to activate the feature.
2. Click the Line Style button, select the double line border, and then trace over an existing line in the table. This changes the line style of that border.
3. Draw a new line through the table and note how the line style is now the same style as the one selected in Step 2.
4. Click the Line Weight button, select the 1½-point weight, and then draw over an existing line or create a new one.

5. Click the Border Color button (not the down-arrow beside it). The Borders And Shading dialog box opens. Close the dialog box.
6. Click the down-arrow next to Border Color, select a color from the palette, and then apply it to an existing line.
7. Click the Eraser button and trace over or click on an existing line to erase it.
8. Click within one cell and then change the Borders button to apply a different type of border.
9. Experiment with the Shading Color and the Distribute Rows Evenly and Distribute Columns Evenly buttons.
10. Select two or more cells and click the Merge Cells button.
11. Click the Split Cells button and split a cell into two columns and one row.
12. Type text in a cell and change the Alignment and Text Direction.
13. Click the down-arrow next to the Insert Table button and see all the options for inserting cells, rows, and columns, as shown in Figure 12.8.
14. Close the Tables And Borders toolbar.
15. Close the document without saving.

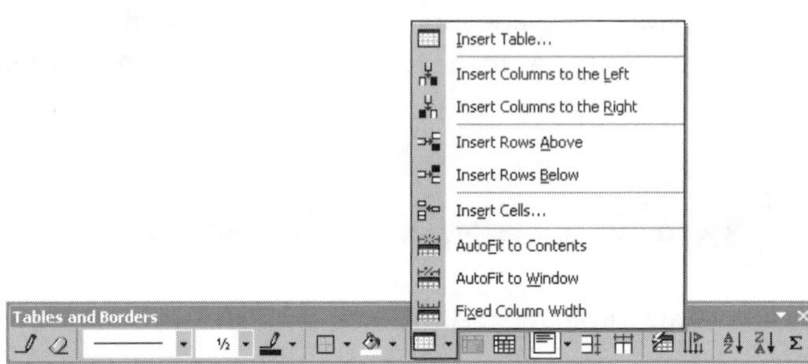

FIGURE 12.8

The Insert Table button on the Tables And Borders toolbar offers many of the same commands that are on the Table menu.

TABLE NAVIGATION

Moving around in a table is easy. Move forward one cell at a time by pressing the Tab key. To move back one cell, press Shift+Tab. These and other useful navigation shortcuts are shown in Table 12.1.

TABLE 12.1 TABLE NAVIGATION KEYBOARD SHORTCUTS

PRESS THIS	TO DO THIS
Tab	Move to the next cell.
Shift+Tab	Move to the preceding cell.
Alt+Home	Move to the first cell in a row.
Alt+End	Move to the last cell in a row.
Alt+Page Up	Move to the first cell in a column.
Alt+Page Down	Move to the last cell in a column.
Shift+left-arrow or right-arrow	Select character by character in the current cell, and then select the entire adjacent cell.
Shift+up-arrow or down-arrow	Select text row by row in the current cell, and then select the entire adjacent cell.
F8+up-arrow or down-arrow	Select the current cell and the cell above or below. (Press the Esc key to end the selection.)
F8+left-arrow or right-arrow	Select the characters in the current cell and then all adjacent cells. (Press the Esc key to end the selection.)
Alt+5 (numeric keypad)	Select the entire table. (The Num Lock key must be turned off.)

ENTER INFORMATION IN TABLES

Once a table is created, you can type text, insert graphics, or insert another table within the table cells. By default, Word resizes table cells to accommodate information size. If you do not want the column width to change automatically, adjust the Table Properties in the Table menu.

TOGGLE THE AUTOMATICALLY RESIZE TO FIT CONTENTS OPTION

1. Create a new document. Insert a two-column, two-row table.
2. Type your first name in the first table cell, and then press Tab to move to the next cell in the table.
3. Press the A key continuously until the table cell expands to fit the contents.
4. From the Table menu, choose Table Properties.
5. Select the Table tab as shown in Figure 12.9 and click Options. Uncheck the Automatically Resize To Fit Contents option.

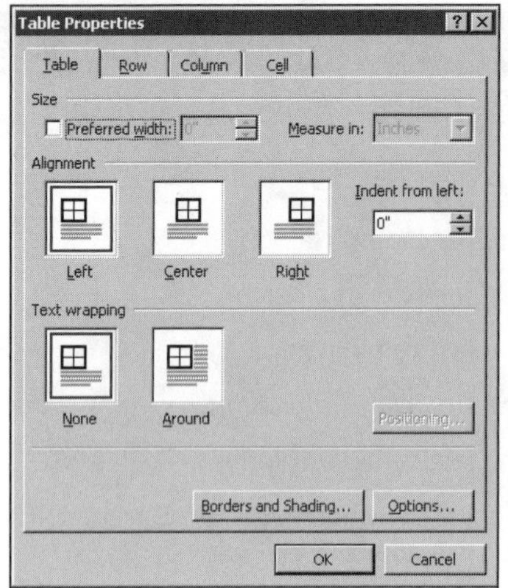

FIGURE 12.9

Set table size, alignment, and text wrapping options from the Table tab.

6. Click OK and try the exercise again. You can control the automatic resizing of table cells by following these steps.
7. Close the document without saving.

AUTOFIT CONTENTS

Word allows you to fine-tune how the content of a cell is formatted. You can use AutoFit To Contents and have the cell automatically expand as you type text. You can use AutoFit To A Window to make the table expand to fill the window or AutoFit To A Fixed Column Width to set a specific size. All AutoFit options are found under the Table menu, as shown in Figure 12.10.

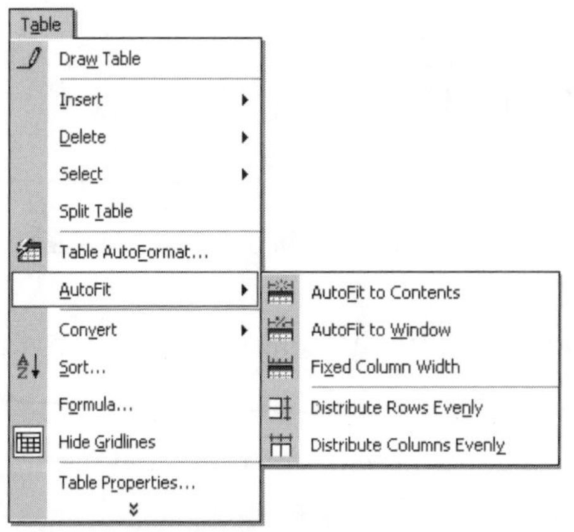

FIGURE 12.10

A variety of AutoFit options are available from the Table menu.

CREATE A PLEADING INDEX

So far, you've learned to create a table and how to use some of the special toolbar buttons on the Tables And Borders toolbar to apply formatting. In the following exercise, you will use the material covered so far to create a pleading index.

CREATE A PLEADING INDEX

1. Create a new document.
2. Type **PLEADING INDEX** and then apply bold, centered formatting. This is the title of your document.
3. Press Enter and type **File Name**.
4. Press Enter and type **File Number**.
5. Press Enter one or more times to add more space below the headings.
6. Insert a table that has three columns and two rows. Don't worry about the size of the columns now. You'll set these in a moment.
7. Click in the first column and, from the Table menu, choose Select and then choose Column.
8. From the Table menu, choose Table Properties and select the Column tab. The Column tab is shown in Figure 12.11.

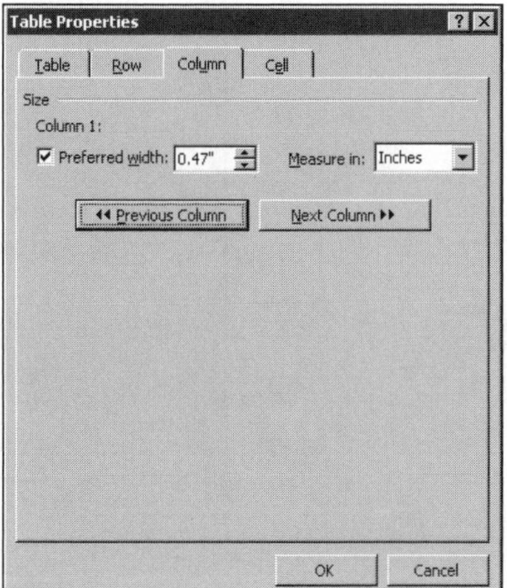

FIGURE 12.11

Use the Column tab to set the exact width.

9. Change column 1 to **0.39"**, column 2 to **4.5"**, and column 3 to **1.26"** and then click OK to save the changes and close the dialog box.

TIP

You can click the Next Column and Previous Column buttons to move easily from one column to the next without having to close the Table Properties dialog box.

10. Click in the first row, second column and type **Pleading Title**.
11. Type **Date** in the first row, third column.
12. From the Table menu, choose Select, Row. Alternate-click on the selected row and choose Cell Alignment.
13. Choose the option to align cell text in the center of the cell. Text will now be center-aligned in each of the cells.
14. You've just created a Pleading Index. Press Tab at the end of the table to automatically add a new row. The finished Pleading Index is shown in Figure 12.12.

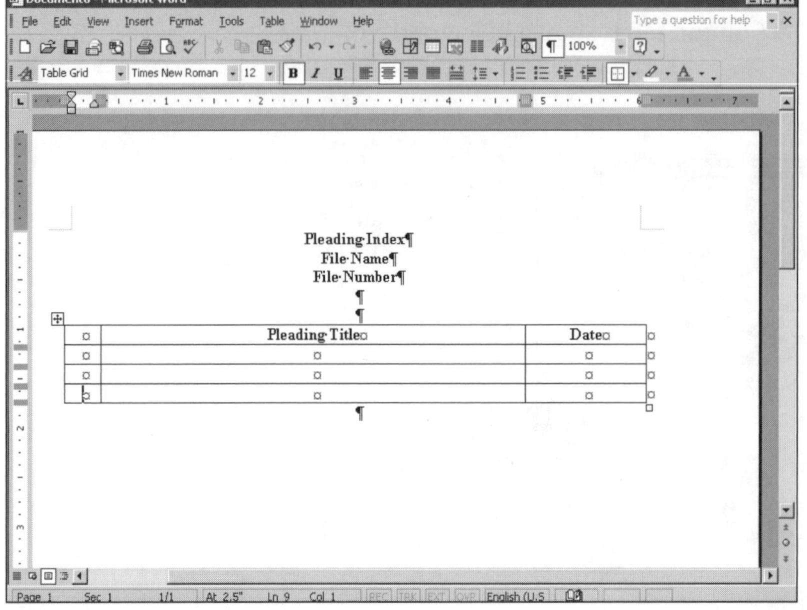

FIGURE 12.12

You can save this Pleading Index as a template and distribute it throughout your firm.

CHANGING TABLE STRUCTURE

It's not very practical to create a new table each time you need to add a new column or row. Word provides several ways to add these elements quickly. This section addresses how to work with cells, rows, columns, and tables.

WORKING WITH CELLS

A cell is a holding place for text or graphics. You can insert or delete cells, but you'll need to tell Word how to rearrange the table to accommodate the change.

ADD AND DELETE CELLS

1. Create a table that has a few rows and columns.
2. From the Table menu, choose Insert, Cells. The Insert Cells dialog box shown in Figure 12.13 opens.
3. Select Shift Cells Right and click OK. This inserts a cell to the right of the active cell, but notice how it only changes the active row if the table contains more than one row.
4. From the Table menu, choose Delete and then Cells.
5. Select Shift Cells Left and click OK.

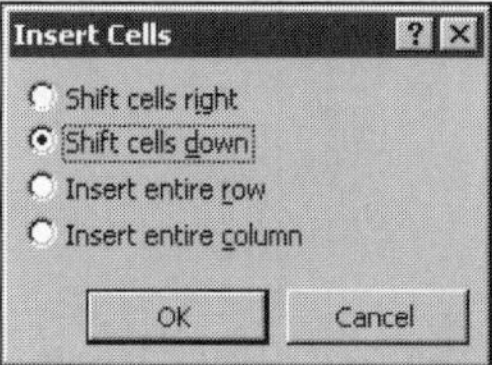

FIGURE 12.13

When you work with cells, as opposed to rows or columns, you must specify what you want Word to do with the rest of the table.

CHANGING THE SPACING BETWEEN CELLS

By default, table cells are directly adjacent to one another. If you need extra space (sometimes called *padding*) between cells, you can adjust the cell spacing as shown in the following exercise.

ADD SPACE BETWEEN CELLS

1. Click in any cell within a table.
2. From the Table menu, choose Table Properties and then select the Table tab.
3. Click Options.
4. Select Allow Spacing Between Cells and type **0.1"**.
5. Click OK to save the changes and then OK again to close the Table Properties dialog box. A table with spacing around each cell is shown in Figure 12.14.

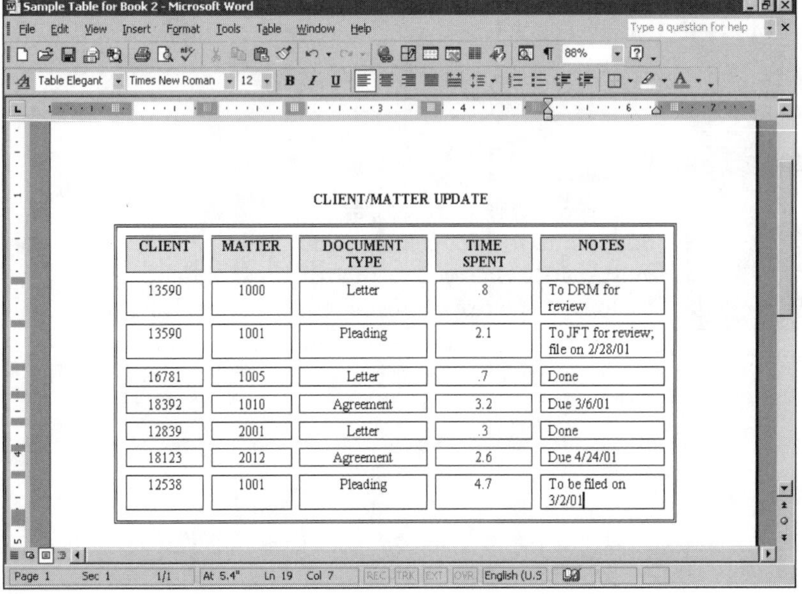

Sample Table for Book 2 - Microsoft Word
CLIENT/MATTER UPDATE
CLIENT | MATTER | DOCUMENT TYPE | TIME SPENT | NOTES
13590 | 1000 | Letter | .8 | To DRM for review
13590 | 1001 | Pleading | 2.1 | To JFT for review; file on 2/28/01
16781 | 1005 | Letter | .7 | Done
18392 | 1010 | Agreement | 3.2 | Due 3/6/01
12839 | 2001 | Letter | .3 | Done
18123 | 2012 | Agreement | 2.6 | Due 4/24/01
12538 | 1001 | Pleading | 4.7 | To be filed on 3/2/01
Page 1 Sec 1 1/1 At 5.4" Ln 19 Col 7 English (U.S

FIGURE 12.14

Cell spacing helps to set apart information within the same table.

WORKING WITH ROWS

One of the easiest ways to add a new row is to place your insertion point in the last cell of the table and press Tab. You can also alternate-click on a row or select a command from the Table menu to accomplish this task. You can also define whether the row should be inserted above or below the current row from the Table menu.

ADD AND DELETE ROWS

1. Create a table that has four columns and one row.
2. Click in the last cell of the table and press Tab. A new row is added to the table automatically.
3. Click within the table and, from the Table menu, choose Insert, Rows Above to insert a row above the active row.
4. From the Table menu, choose Insert, Rows Below to insert a row below the active row.
5. From the Table menu, choose Select, Row to select the active row.
6. With the row selected, alternate-click on the row and choose Insert Rows to insert a row above the active row.
7. Select multiple rows by clicking and dragging with the mouse as you would select text.

TIP

Be sure to select the entire row, including the end-of-row marker. If the entire row is not selected, the Insert Row and Delete Row commands will not be available in the shortcut menu.

8. Alternate-click on the selected rows and choose Insert Rows again. The number of rows inserted is equal to the number of rows selected.
9. Click within any row in the Table.
10. From the Table menu, choose Delete, Row. The active row is deleted.
11. Select any row within the table.
12. Alternate-click the selected row and choose Delete Rows. The active row is deleted.

RESIZING ROWS

There are several ways to resize rows. You can define an exact row size, as you did when creating the Pleading Index, or you can use the ruler to change the row size by dragging.

RESIZE ROWS

1. Click within the table. From the Table menu, choose Table Properties.
2. Select the Row tab, shown in Figure 12.15.
3. Click the Specify Height option, set the height of the row to 1", and click OK.
4. From the Table menu, choose Table Properties again, this time selecting the Column tab.
5. Change the Column Preferred Width to something different and click OK. Now look for gray lines on the ruler where your row and columns are located.
6. Click and drag the gray lines to a new position on the ruler. This method also resizes both columns and rows.

TIP

If you don't see both the horizontal and vertical rulers, change to Print Layout View and, from the View menu, choose Ruler.

7. Hold the Alt key as you click and drag the column or row to see the exact measurements. The result is shown in Figure 12.16.

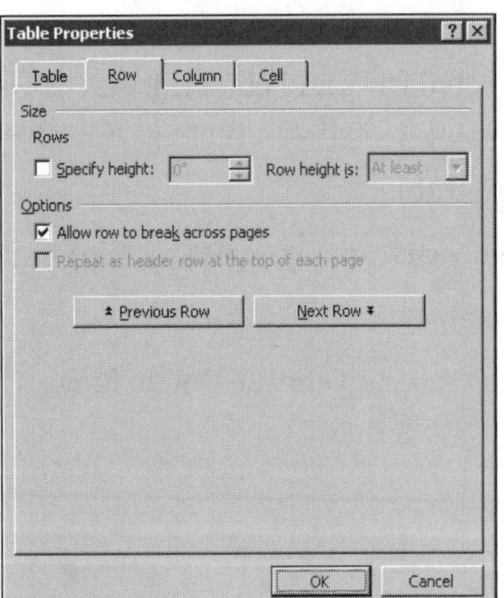

FIGURE 12.15

The Row tab allows you to specify the row height, whether to allow a row to break across pages, and whether or not to repeat the heading.

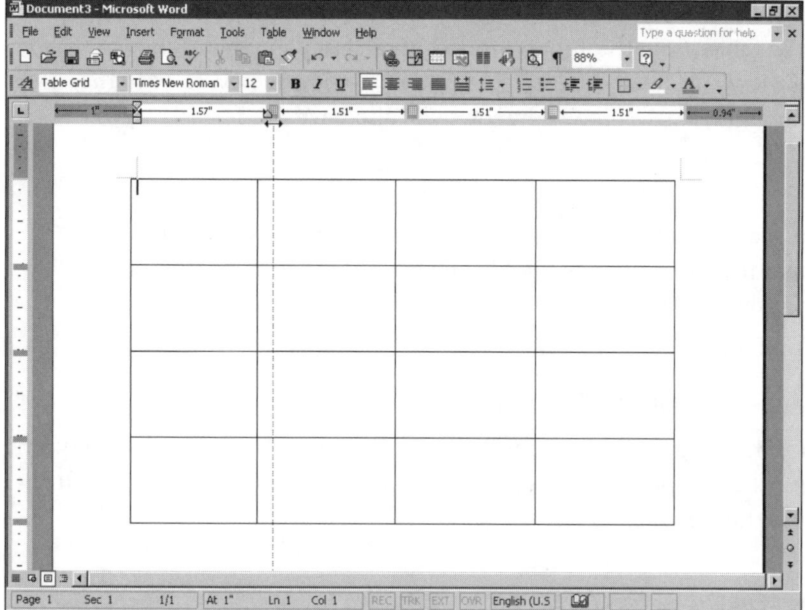

FIGURE 12.16

View exact measurements while holding down the Alt key and dragging the table column with the mouse.

KEEPING ROW INFORMATION TOGETHER

If you have a large amount of information in one cell, the cell may split across two pages. The default for Word tables is to allow rows to break across pages, but you can turn this setting off as illustrated in the next exercise.

PREVENTING ROWS FROM BREAKING ACROSS PAGES

1. In a new document, create a table that contains four columns and 50 rows.
2. Click in the first column cell in the last row at the bottom of the first page.
3. Type enough text into the cell until it wraps to the next page.
4. Click within the table. From the Table menu, choose Table Properties.
5. Select the Row tab and turn off the option Allow Row To Break Across Pages.
6. Click OK to close the Table Properties dialog box. Notice how the entire row has moved to page 2.

TIP

To prevent page breaks from being inserted within any of the rows in a table, select the entire table (from the Table menu, choose Select and then Table). Clear the Allow Rows To Break Across Pages option. If you add new rows to the table after clearing this option, the new rows will also have this formatting applied.

NOTE

The option to allow rows to break across pages is a formatting setting. If you clear this format for the last row of a table and then insert additional rows at the end of the table, the new rows will also have this option cleared.

REPEATING HEADING ROWS

When you are working with large, multipage tables, rows spill onto subsequent pages. When this happens, it's a good idea to have Word repeat the column headers across the top of each new page.

REPEAT HEADING ROWS

1. Create a new document.
2. From the Table menu, choose Insert, Table.
3. Set the Number Of Columns to 3 and the Number Of Rows to 500.
4. Click OK to create the table.
5. Click in the first cell of the table, type **City**, and press Tab.
6. Type **State** in the next cell in the first row and **Postal Code** in the final cell in the first row. Your table should resemble the one shown in Figure 12.17.
7. Scroll to the second page and note that the heading does not automatically repeat.
8. Return to the first page and select the first row of the table, where you typed the column headings.
9. From the Table menu, choose Heading Rows Repeat.
10. Scroll to the next page to see that the heading rows now show up on subsequent pages.

NOTE

You can select more than one row as a heading, but you must include the first row of the table in the heading selection.

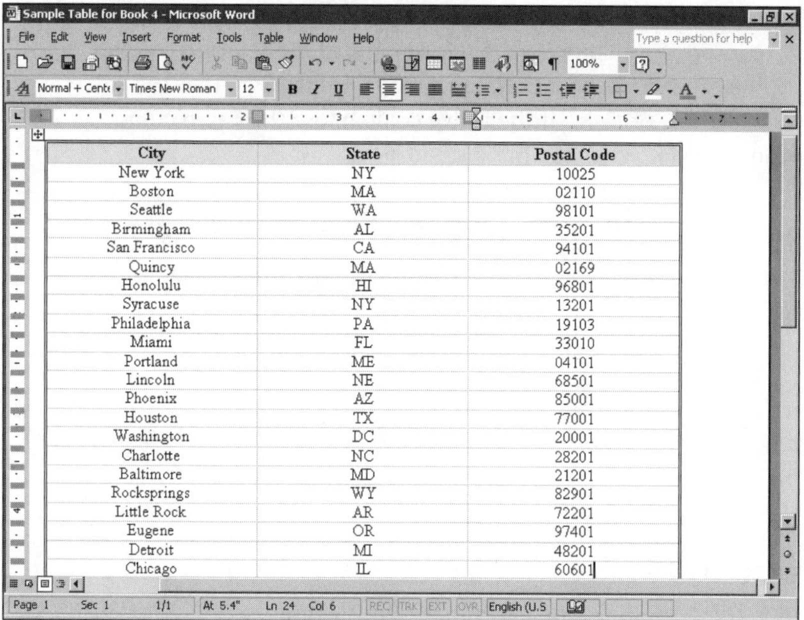

City	State	Postal Code
New York	NY	10025
Boston	MA	02110
Seattle	WA	98101
Birmingham	AL	35201
San Francisco	CA	94101
Quincy	MA	02169
Honolulu	HI	96801
Syracuse	NY	13201
Philadelphia	PA	19103
Miami	FL	33010
Portland	ME	04101
Lincoln	NE	68501
Phoenix	AZ	85001
Houston	TX	77001
Washington	DC	20001
Charlotte	NC	28201
Baltimore	MD	21201
Rocksprings	WY	82901
Little Rock	AR	72201
Eugene	OR	97401
Detroit	MI	48201
Chicago	IL	60601

FIGURE 12.17

The heading row can be repeated on subsequent pages if the table spills over one page.

If you insert a manual page break (Ctrl+Enter) in a table, Word does not repeat the heading.

WORKING WITH COLUMNS

Columns are added, deleted, and resized exactly the same as rows. You can use a menu command, alternate-click on a selected column, or use the Draw Table tool to draw one of your own.

INSERT AND DELETE COLUMNS

1. Click within a table. From the Table menu, choose Insert, Columns To The Left.
2. From the Table menu, choose Insert, Columns To The Right.
3. From the Table menu, choose Select, Column.
4. Alternate-click on the selected column and choose Insert Columns.

If you alternate-click a column to insert another column, Word does not give you the option to insert the column to the left or right of the selected column. It always inserts the column to the left. If you need to control whether the column is inserted to the left or right of the active column, use the Table menu option or the Tables And Borders toolbar instead.

5. Alternate-click on a selected column and choose Delete Columns.
6. Click within a column and, from the Table menu, choose Delete, Columns.

If a table only has one column, you cannot use the alternate-click method to delete the column.

RESIZING COLUMNS

There are four ways to change the column width of a table:

- Drag the border of the table.
- Drag the column marker on the ruler.
- From the Table menu, choose Table Properties and then select the Column tab.
- Double-click the column boundary on the right side to expand the column to AutoFit the longest string of text in the cell.

A common problem for people new to Word is accidentally selecting a single cell and then adjusting the column. The settings applied affect only the selected cell, which probably does not yield the desired result. When this happens, press Ctrl+Z to undo the column resize and then deselect the cell before making the adjustment.

PLEADING CAPTIONS

A pleading caption is a prime candidate for a table. Information must be aligned with other information and separated into columns. The following exercise walks you through creating a basic pleading caption.

Your firm may use a macro package for pleading captions or may use a different format from the one used in the exercise.

CREATE A PLEADING CAPTION

1. Create a new document.
2. Insert a table with three columns and one row.
3. Select the middle column, and then from the Table menu, choose Table Properties.
4. From the Table Properties dialog box, select the Column tab. Set the Preferred Width of Column 2 to 0.09".
5. Click Previous Column to select the first column of the table. Set the Preferred Width of Column 1 to 3.31".
6. Click Next Column twice to select the third column of the table. Set the Preferred Width of Column 3 to 3".
7. Click OK to close the dialog box.
8. Click in Column 2 and type **:** (the colon) followed by the Enter key 10 times.
9. From the Format menu, remove the borders of the table by choosing Borders And Shading. Select the Borders tab and, in the Setting section, select None and click OK to close the dialog box. Keyboard shortcut users can press Alt+Ctrl+U from within the table.

Figure 12.18 shows an example of a finished pleading caption.

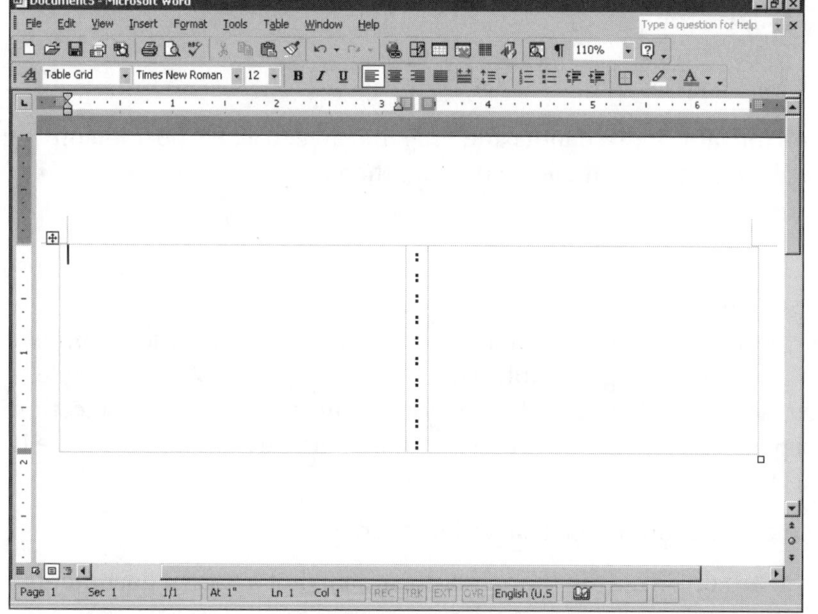

FIGURE 12.18

The pleading caption has three columns of varying sizes.

WORKING WITH THE ENTIRE TABLE

Tables sit on top of the document layer and can be moved and manipulated much like graphic objects. A table move handle appears when you work in Print Layout or Web view and click within the table. This handle allows you to drag the table to a new location in the document. The move handle (shown in Figure 12.19) is located at the top-left corner of the table.

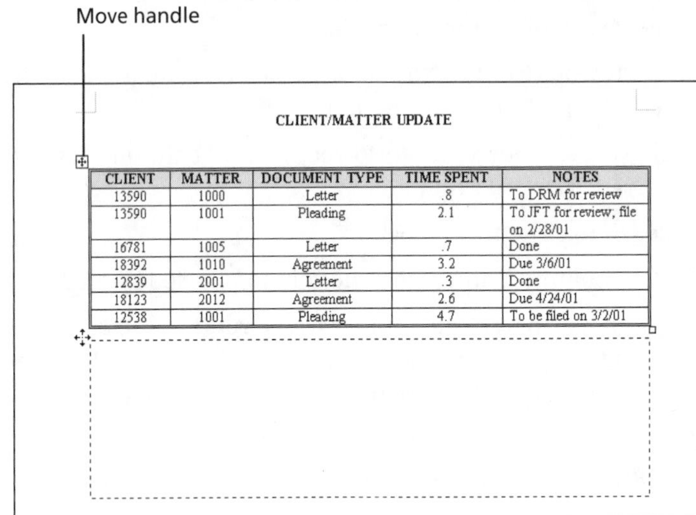

CLIENT/MATTER UPDATE

CLIENT	MATTER	DOCUMENT TYPE	TIME SPENT	NOTES
13590	1000	Letter	.8	To DRM for review
13590	1001	Pleading	2.1	To JFT for review; file on 2/28/01
16781	1005	Letter	.7	Done
18392	1010	Agreement	3.2	Due 3/6/01
12839	2001	Letter	.3	Done
18123	2012	Agreement	2.6	Due 4/24/01
12538	1001	Pleading	4.7	To be filed on 3/2/01

FIGURE 12.19

The move handle makes repositioning a table easy.

MOVE A TABLE

1. Click within a table.
2. Click on the table move handle and drag the table to a new position on the page (or anywhere in the document), then release the mouse.

COPY A TABLE

In Word 2002, you can now copy a table to a new location within the document by holding Ctrl and dragging the table with the move handle. When the table is being copied (as opposed to moved), the mouse pointer changes to a selection arrow with a plus sign. Release the mouse and then the Ctrl key, and the table is copied to the new location.

There are some limitations to the feature however:

- Tables can be copied only in the active document, not between documents.

- Tables cannot be copied into the header and footer or the Reviewing Pane.
- The move handle that is used to select the table to be copied is only available in Print Layout and Web Layout view.

COPY A TABLE

1. Create a new blank document and insert a table.
2. Click within the table. Make sure you are in Print Layout or Web Layout view.
3. Rest your mouse pointer over the table until you see the table move handle on the upper-left corner of the table.
4. Hold the Ctrl key and click and drag to copy the table to a new location within the document.
5. Release the mouse and the Ctrl key.
6. Close the file without saving.

TIP

Tables can be copied into the Footnote pane using this method.

RESIZE A TABLE

A table can be resized by dragging the table resize handle located in the bottom-right corner of the table. When you do this, the point size of the text remains the same, just the table structure is resized. The resize handle is shown in Figure 12.20.

CLIENT/MATTER UPDATE

CLIENT	MATTER	DOCUMENT TYPE	TIME SPENT	NOTES
13590	1000	Letter	.8	To DRM for review
13590	1001	Pleading	2.1	To JFT for review; file on 2/28/01
16781	1005	Letter	.7	Done
18392	1010	Agreement	3.2	Due 3/6/01
12839	2001	Letter	.3	Done
18123	2012	Agreement	2.6	Due 4/24/01
12538	1001	Pleading	4.7	To be filed on 3/2/01

Resize handle

FIGURE 12.20

Click and drag the resize handle to the desired table boundary size.

RESIZE A TABLE

1. Click within a table. Rest your mouse pointer over the table until you see the table resize handle on the lower-right corner of the table.
2. Click and drag to resize the table.
3. Close the file without saving.

SPLIT A TABLE

If a table is located at the very beginning of a document, before any text, you can add space before the table by clicking in the first cell and pressing Enter. This is extremely useful if you need to add a title or table caption before the table but didn't leave the extra room. Sometimes you might want to split a table into two separate tables so you can format each table differently or type paragraph text between the tables. A table can be split into two separate tables by choosing Split Table from the Table menu.

SPLIT A TABLE

1. Create a new document.
2. Create a table with four columns and five rows.
3. Click in the cell in the first column, third row.

NOTE

Place your cursor in the row that will be the first row of the new table. The split command will break the table horizontally above the cursor position.

4. From the Table menu, choose Split Table, as shown in Figure 12.21. The table is split into two separate tables, one above the other.

TIP

Keyboard users can press Ctrl+Shift+Enter to split the table.

WRAP TEXT AROUND A TABLE

You can make a page with tables more visually appealing by placing a table alongside text rather than one table below the other. This is also a great way to

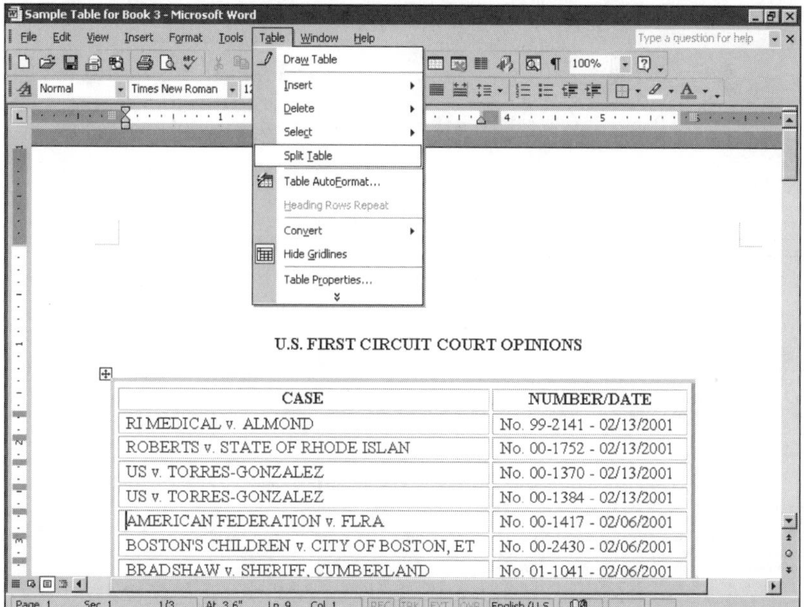

FIGURE 12.21

You can use Split Table to make two separate tables.

make more information fit on one page. As you look at Figures 12.22 and 12.23, you can see how wrapping text around a table can lend a more professional appearance to the page.

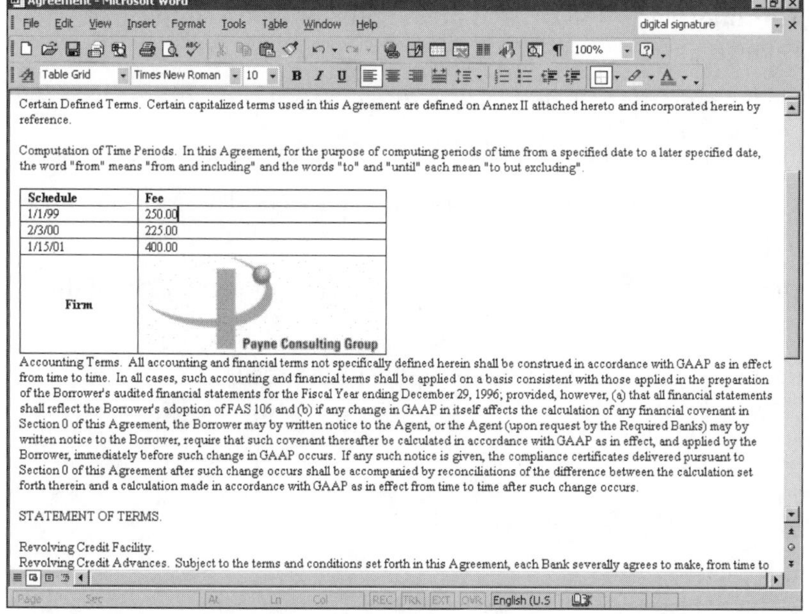

FIGURE 12.22

A table can be inserted between paragraphs of text.

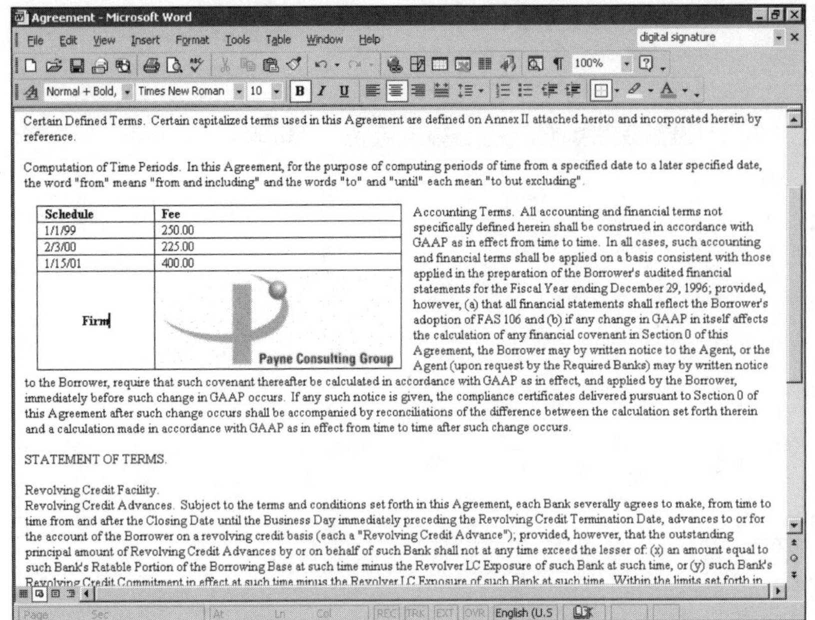

FIGURE 12.23

Text can be positioned to wrap around a table.

WRAP TEXT AROUND A TABLE

1. Create a new document.
2. On a blank line, type =**RAND()** and press Enter, or type a couple paragraphs of text.
3. Insert a table after the text, and click within the table.
4. From the Table menu, choose Table Properties and select the Table tab.
5. Select the Text Wrapping Around option and click OK. The Table tab and Text Wrapping Options are shown in Figure 12.24.
6. Select the table and drag it to the center, to the left, or to the right of the text.
7. Move the table to different locations on the page to see the effect.

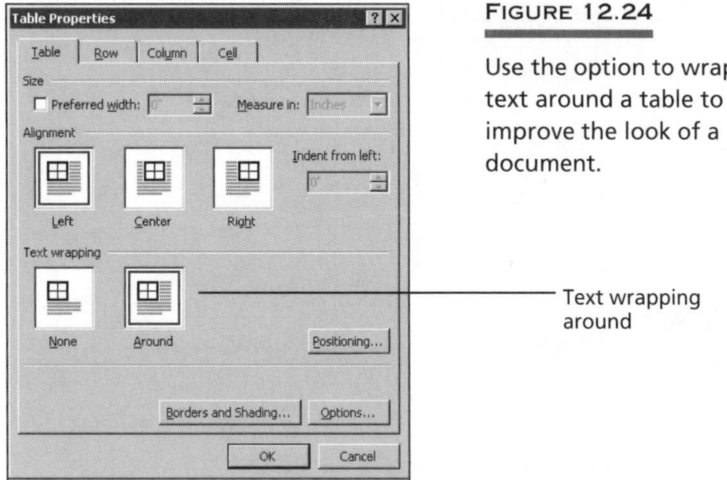

FIGURE 12.24

Use the option to wrap text around a table to improve the look of a document.

SPECIFY THE DISTANCE OF THE TABLE FROM TEXT

If text is set to wrap around a table, you can specify exactly how far the text should be offset from the table. To do this, follow the steps in the next exercise.

SET DISTANCE OF TABLE FROM TEXT

1. Click within a table that has Text Wrapping enabled.
2. From the Table menu, choose Table Properties.
3. Select the Table tab and click Positioning. The Table Positioning dialog box opens, allowing you to set the distance and positioning of the table and text, shown in Figure 12.25.
4. Change the Top, Bottom, Left, and Right distance in the Distance From Surrounding Text area.
5. Click OK twice to close the dialog boxes and return to the document.

CHANGE THE TABLE PAGE SETUP

If you are printing a page with Landscape Page Setup instead of Portrait, you may want to specify the table width.

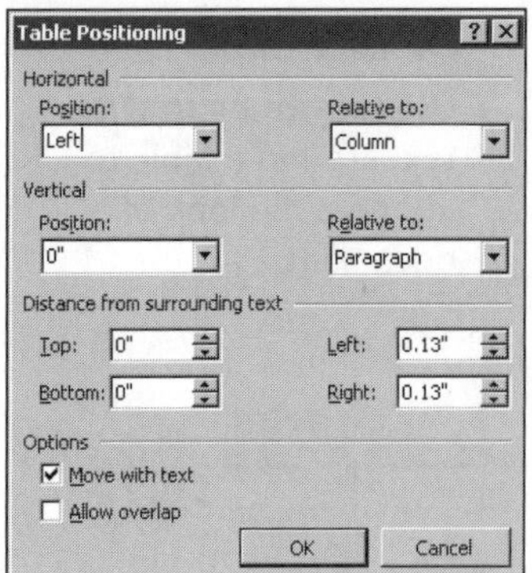

FIGURE 12.25

You can change the distance of the table from the text.

SPECIFY THE WIDTH OF A TABLE

1. Create a table with four columns and five rows.
2. From the File menu, choose Page Setup.
3. Select the Margins tab. The Margins tab is shown in Figure 12.26.
4. Change the Orientation to Landscape. Click OK to close the Page Setup dialog box.

NOTE

In Word 2000, the Landscape command was controlled from the Paper Size tab. This command is now located on the Margins tab.

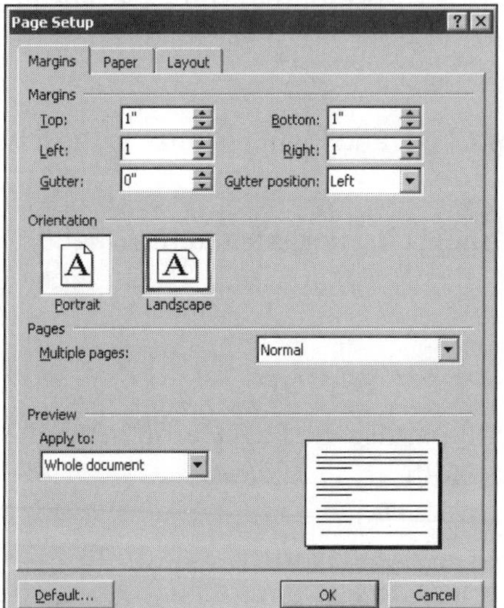

FIGURE 12.26

Set margins, change the orientation, and select multiple page settings from the Margins tab.

5. Click within the table and choose Table, Table Properties.
6. Select the Table tab and change Preferred Width to 9".
7. Click OK to apply the formatting. Keep this table open for use in the next exercise.

AUTOFORMAT TABLES

Have you ever wanted to add a bit of pizzazz to your table but don't have the artistic touch? Don't worry, Word can take care of the formatting for you. Table AutoFormat includes 45 default formats that can be applied—and you can also create and name your own formatting schemes that can be applied later.

MUCH IMPROVED TABLE AUTOFORMAT

If you've used Word AutoFormat before, you may be surprised by the changes in the Table AutoFormat dialog box, which is shown in Figure 12.27. The dialog box now has a better look and feel, and the preview area is much larger than previous versions.

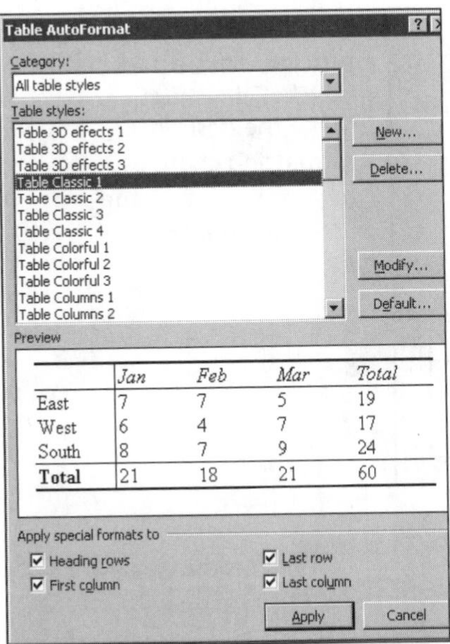

FIGURE 12.27

Select and apply a Table Style from the list—or create a new one.

APPLY TABLE AUTOFORMAT

1. Click within a table. From the Table menu, choose Table AutoFormat.
2. Select a Table Style and look at the preview.
3. Select a different Table Style.
4. Click Modify to see how you can change the selected Table Style. Click Cancel.
5. Click New. Name the Style **Financial Tables**. The New Style dialog box opens, as shown in Figure 12.28.
6. Change the Style Based On setting to something from the drop-down list.
7. Specify whether to apply the formatting to the entire table or just to the headers, specific rows, or specific columns.
8. Change the font style, font size, line color, border, or any other formatting option.
9. Click the Format button to see that you can change the Table AutoFormat to include Table Properties, Borders And Shading, Stripes, Font, Paragraph, and Tabs.
10. Click OK, and then click either Apply or Cancel.

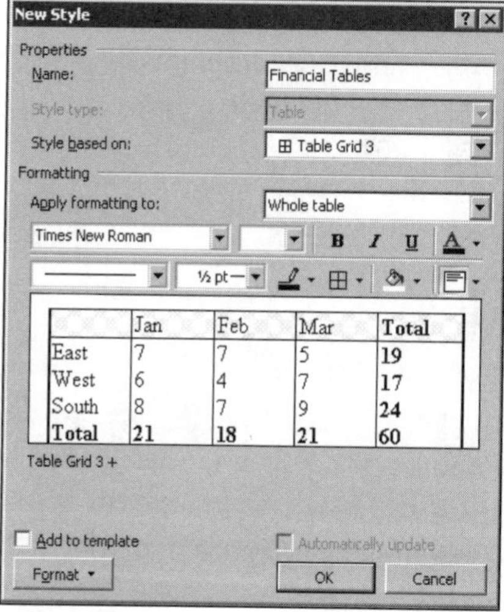

FIGURE 12.28

Make the desired formatting changes to your new style and use it again later.

People who work extensively with numbers in tables asked Microsoft for the ability to automatically format table cells with alternating shading patterns much like paper that can be purchased in supply stores used for bookkeeping. By formatting a table in this manner, the information is easy to read when you are looking down columns of data.

Microsoft has added a new Stripes format that achieves this result. Click the Format button and select Stripes. Specify the number of rows and columns in a band of stripes and click OK. Going through columns and rows is made easier with the alternating formatting.

SETTING UP A DEFAULT TABLE

If you find yourself creating the same types of tables repeatedly, you will like this new option—it allows you to set the default dimensions for all new tables you insert using the Insert command from the Table menu.

APPLY TABLE DIMENSIONS

1. From the Table menu, choose Insert and then choose Table.
2. Specify the number of rows and columns.
3. Check the Remember Dimensions For New Tables option. Click OK.
4. From the Tables menu, choose Insert, and then choose Table. Note that Word remembers what you set previously as the preferred table dimensions.

Click Default in the Table AutoFormat dialog box to set the preferred format for all newly created tables.

NESTED TABLES

Tables can be nested within other tables. This feature would be useful when the entire document is a table, as in a letter where one table exists in the header and footer layer and you choose to insert a table into the body of the document. It also comes in handy when one cell of a larger table requires more complex information than a single area can comfortably present.

If you share documents with clients who use Word 97 or earlier versions of the software, remember that nested tables don't work in versions prior to Word 2000. Word 2002 has a setting that allows you to choose to disable features not available in specific previous versions of Word. From the Tools menu, choose Options. Select the Save tab, select the option Disable Features Introduced After, and specify Word 97 or Word 6.0/95.

The Save tab is shown in Figure 12.29.

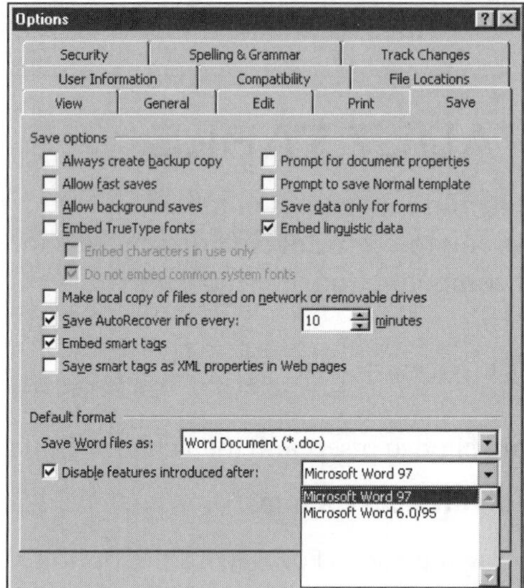

FIGURE 12.29

Word 2000 had a setting to disable features not available in Word 97. Word 2002 allows you to specify the next earlier version as well.

CREATE A NESTED TABLE

1. From the Table menu, choose Insert and then Table. Click in a table cell.
2. From the Table menu, choose Insert, Table, and then click OK. This inserts a new table within the original table. A nested table is shown in Figure 12.30.
3. Close the document without saving.

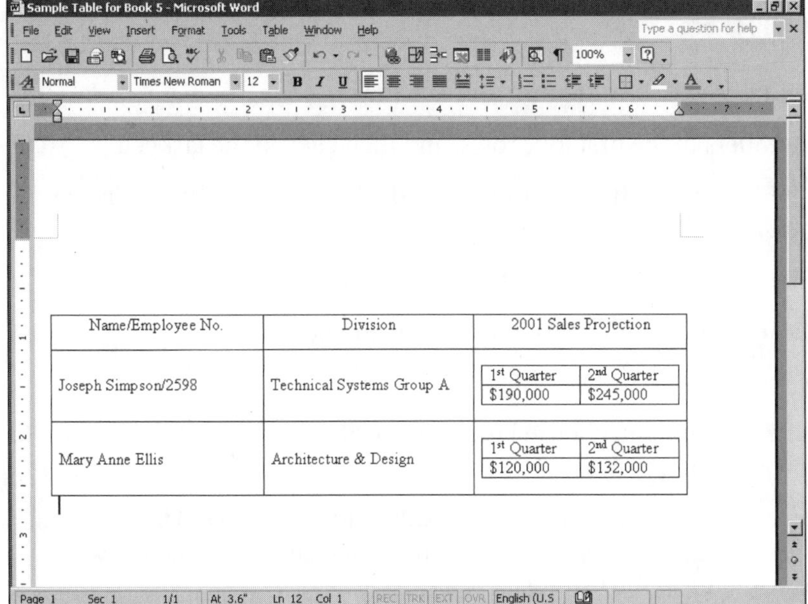

FIGURE 12.30

One or more tables can be nested within other tables.

TABLE MATH

You can perform simple math in tables, which comes in handy most often for summing rows or columns of numbers. The fastest way to get a sum is to click in a cell adjacent to the numbers you want to add, and then move the mouse pointer to the Tables And Borders toolbar and click the AutoSum button. More advanced functions, such as average, count, and number formatting, require use of the Formula command on the Table menu.

If you are performing a lot of calculations, you should consider using Microsoft Excel instead of Word. Excel formulas update automatically, whereas Word formulas do not. More important, Excel is a spreadsheet program designed specifically for number crunching. See Chapter 18, "Microsoft Office Integration: Tying It All Together," for more on the power of combining Word with Excel.

SIMPLE ADDITION FORMULA

Adding numbers is a breeze in Word tables. First type the numbers to be summed and then either click the AutoSum button on the Tables And Borders toolbar or choose Formula from the Table menu.

BASIC MATH

1. Create a table with one column and five rows.
2. Type numbers in the first four rows, and then click in the last cell.
3. Click the Tables And Borders button on the Standard toolbar to display the Tables And Borders toolbar.
4. Click the Draw Table button to turn off Drawing mode.
5. Click AutoSum on the Tables And Borders toolbar.
6. Delete the result in the last cell.
7. From the Table menu, choose Formula. Word will try to guess the formula that you are trying to use.
8. The dialog box shown in Figure 12.31 shows the formula =SUM(ABOVE). If you are attempting to add numbers from the left, substitute the word *LEFT* for *ABOVE* in the formula.
9. Select the third option (currency) in the Number Format drop-down list. Click OK.

NOTE

Numbers typed as text in the table cannot be formatted with percentages, decimals, or currency through a Word command. Of course, you can type dollar signs, percent signs, or decimal points when you input the numbers. Consider inserting an Excel worksheet into a document if number formatting is important or if the table needs to contain a large number of complex calculations.

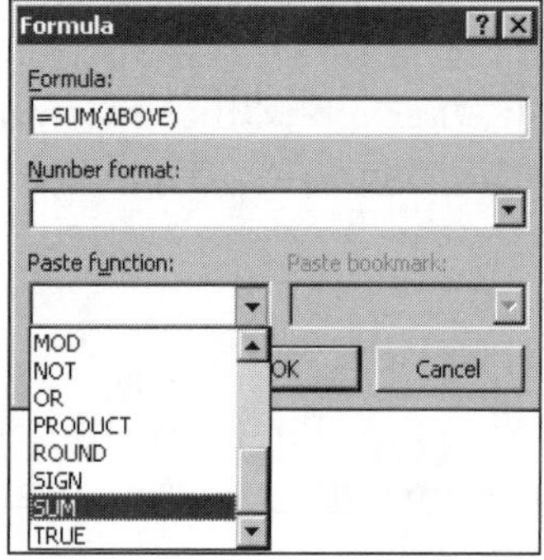

FIGURE 12.31

You can type in a formula, or you can use the drop-down fields to create a formula.

Word adds the cells above or to the left of the formula until it reaches the end of the table or a blank cell. That makes blank cells a great way to use subtotals in a table. However, if you want to add all the cells in a row or column whether they have values in them or not, type a zero in each blank cell.

UPDATING A FORMULA

As numbers in the table change, you might expect the calculation to update as well. Unfortunately, this is not the case in Word. Table results go into fields, and to update a field, you must first select it and then press F9.

If you are responsible for training in your firm, you will want to make sure to stress that table formulas do not update automatically. Often, individuals will change the numbers and not check the resulting total to make sure that it has been updated. They may then send the document to a client with incorrect information. One solution is to create a simple macro and assign it to a toolbar button that will Select All within the document and update fields (by pressing F9).

USE DECIMALS IN TABLES

You can use tabs in tables, but you will need to press Ctrl+Tab to move to the tab stop since the default behavior in a table is to move to the next cell when you press Tab. When working with figures that have decimals in your cells, you must first set a decimal tab stop and then use the Ctrl+Tab combination to move to the tab position. Make certain that you choose to align numbers only with decimal tabs, as opposed to text.

SET AND USE TABS IN A TABLE

1. Click within any table cell. Click once on the ruler to insert a Left tab.
2. From the Format menu, choose Tabs.
3. Specify a Decimal tab at a different Tab Stop Position and click Set.

NOTE

Do not select columns containing text when setting a decimal tab. Because text has no decimals, Word will assume that the decimal is at the end of the text. This will cause the text to be out of alignment with the numbers in the cells. To align text, use paragraph alignment or another type of tab.

4. Click OK.
5. Press Ctrl+Tab to move to the first tab stop. Press Ctrl+Tab to move to the next tab stop.

CAUTION

Do not set a decimal tab in a column that has been centered or right-aligned. If you do so, the numbers may not align correctly on the decimal. Select the numbers and press Ctrl+L to left-align the cells before setting the decimal tab.

6. Close the document without saving.

MORE COMPLEX MATHEMATICS

Occasionally, you may need to add values from several different tables. You can do this by creating a bookmark and referencing the bookmark in your grand total formula calculation.

USE BOOKMARKS TO TOTAL MULTIPLE TABLES

1. Create a new document and insert a table with three rows and one column.
2. Place numbers in the first two cells.
3. Click in the last cell where the formula will go.
4. From the Table menu, choose Formula and click OK.
5. Create another table with three rows and one column. Repeat Steps 2 through 4.
6. Create a third table with just one cell. The three tables are shown in Figure 12.32.
7. Select the first table's formula. From the Insert menu, choose Bookmark and name the bookmark **MyTotal1** (no space).

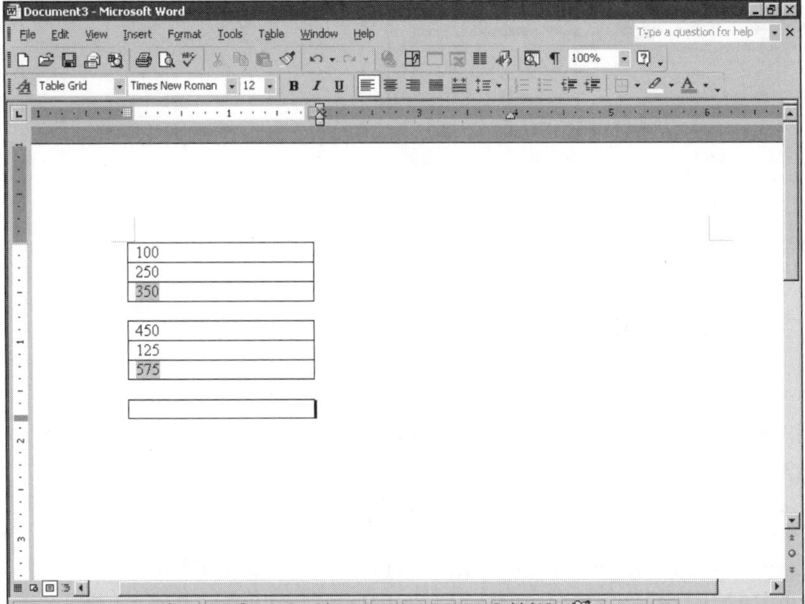

FIGURE 12.32

You can use bookmarks to add multiple table cell results together.

8. Click Add to add the bookmark.
9. Select the second table formula. From the Insert menu, choose Bookmark, name the bookmark **MyTotal2**, and click Add. The two bookmarks are shown in Figure 12.33.
10. Click in the cell in the third table. From the Table menu, choose Formula.

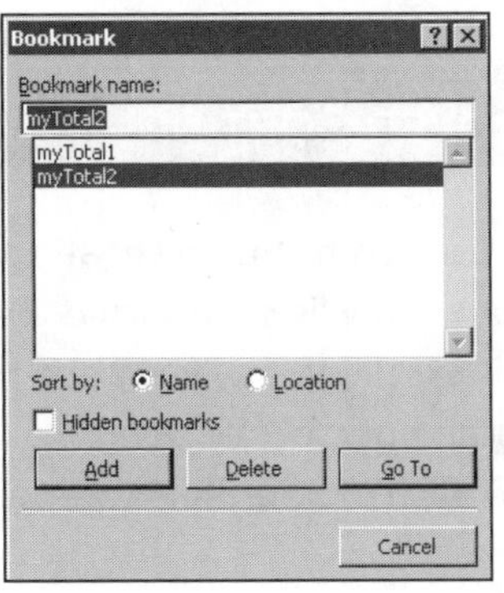

FIGURE 12.33

Bookmark names cannot contain any spaces.

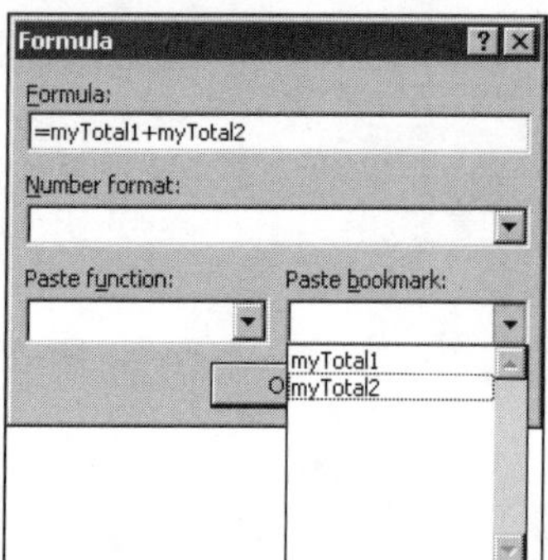

FIGURE 12.34

Pasting bookmarks to create a formula is simple to do.

11. Click after the = (equal sign) and then click the drop-down arrow next to Paste Bookmark.
12. Select the first bookmark in the list, MyTotal1, and type + (a plus sign).
13. Select the second bookmark, MyTotal2. The formula should be =MyTotal1+MyTotal2. The complete formula is shown in Figure 12.34.
14. Click OK to add the two table values together.

SORTING IN A TABLE

Word allows you to sort data easily. In tables, you can sort by column, text, number, or date. There are more options than ever to perform just the right sort.

NEW AND IMPROVED SORTING!

One of the requests that Microsoft received from the Legal Advisory Council was to allow more control over how lists are sorted. Because of this, the Sort feature in Word 2002 is excellent! Say you have the words *Miller, Dennis* in the same cell. You can now sort by *Dennis,* or by *Miller.* Furthermore, you can tell Word how each of your fields are separated (in this example, by a comma).

SORT TABLE INFORMATION

1. Create a new document.
2. Insert a one-column, five-row table and type the following items, one in each cell:

   George Washington

   John Adams

   Thomas Jefferson

   James Madison

   James Monroe
3. From the Table menu, choose Sort. The Sort dialog box is shown in Figure 12.35.
4. Click Options, choose to separate fields by Other, and press Spacebar in the Other box. Click OK.
5. Select Word 2 from the Using drop-down list. This instructs Word to sort by the second word in the cell. The Sort dialog box is shown in Figure 12.36.
6. Click OK. Word sorts the list by the last name field, which is the second word in the cell.

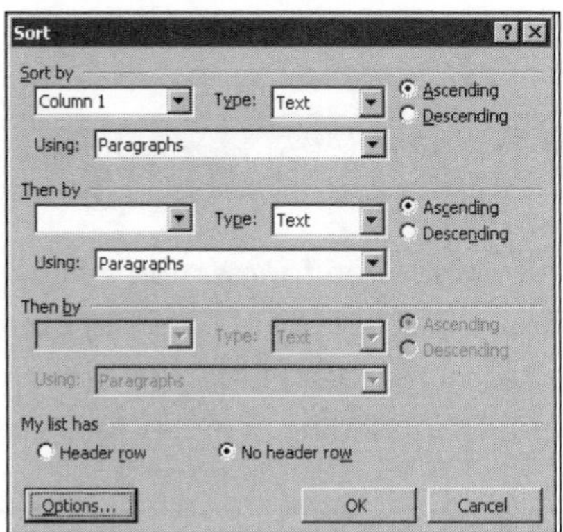

FIGURE 12.35

You can sort by last name or first name.

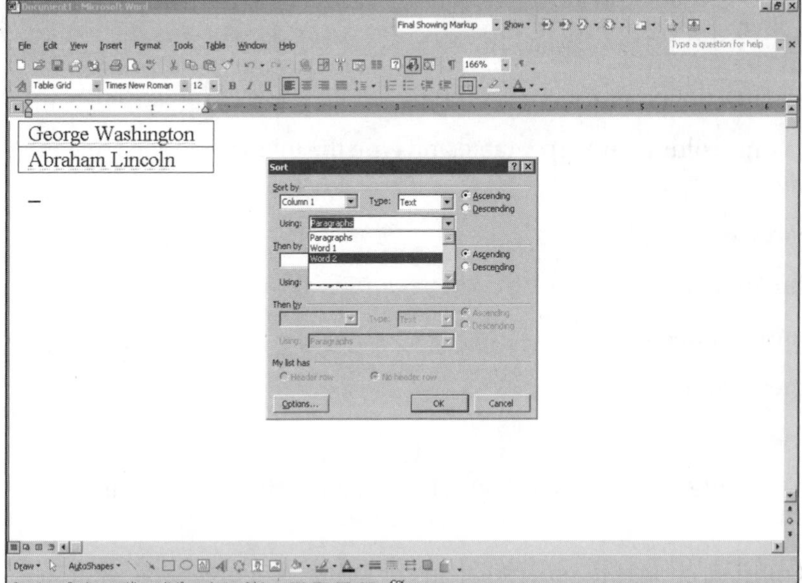

FIGURE 12.36

The Sort dialog box includes options to sort by words or fields.

CREATING FINANCIAL TABLES

Firms specializing in mergers and acquisitions face the challenge of constructing financial tables on a regular basis. These tables are so complex that it often takes 45 minutes to an hour to create each one.

The good news is that once you create the table the first time, you can make each type of financial table into an AutoText entry, which will save a tremendous amount of time. A financial table is shown in Figure 12.37.

> **ON THE CD-ROM**
>
> Since there are many instructions required for creating a financial table, and a limited amount of pages available for this book, an exercise is included on the CD-ROM that accompanies this book that walks you through all of the steps required for building complex financial tables.

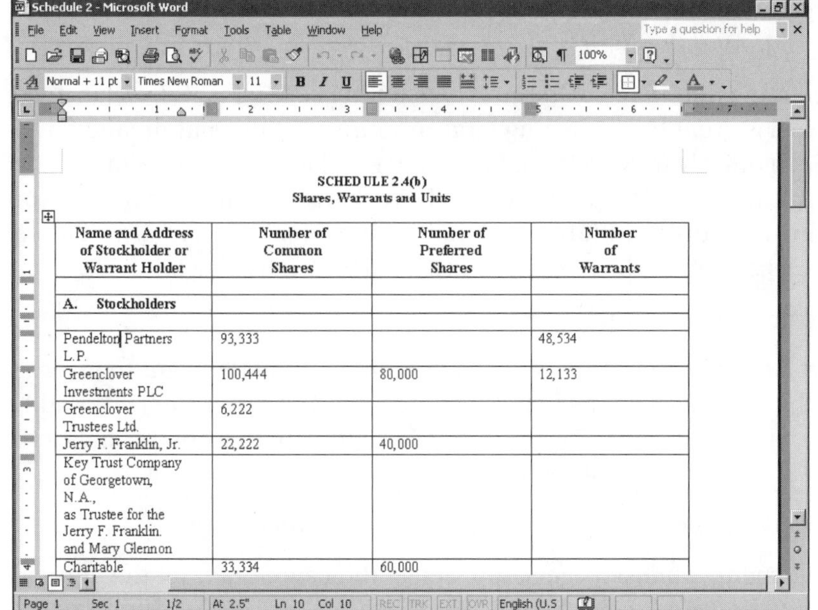

FIGURE 12.37

If you create a financial table in Word and want to reuse it, create a new AutoText entry.

SUMMARY

While some features such as marking citations, numbering, and styles require much thought, creating functional and impressive tables takes very little effort. Tables can contain formulas, text, even graphics, and they can be manipulated, much like any information in documents. Once you have mastered creating and formatting tables, you will look for and find more ways to use them in your documents than you ever believed possible.

TROUBLESHOOTING TABLES

In one of my rows, the text is cut off and only shows the top half of the characters. What could be causing this?

The cut-off characters are most likely caused by having the table row height property set to an exact number instead of a minimum value. To fix this problem, click within the row. From the Table menu, choose Table Properties and select the Row tab. Change the Row Height Setting to At Least.

I need to create a table with 64 columns but the maximum in Word is 63. What can I do to get around this limit?

If you are creating that many columns, you should use Microsoft Excel instead of Word. Excel is great for managing large amounts of information and, even better, you can quickly move to specific cells in Excel in just a few seconds. You cannot do this in Word. If you find yourself working with more than three or four columns in your Word table, consider using Excel as an alternative. In Excel, you can have up to 256 columns and 65,536 rows in each worksheet.

How do I get text above my table?

If you insert a table at the beginning of a document and later want to insert a line before the table, click in the first cell of the table and press Enter. This adds a line before the table begins. You can also click in the first row of the table and select Split Table from the Table menu.

How do I get my one-page table to be centered vertically on the page?

From the File menu, choose Page Setup. Select the Layout tab, set the Vertical Alignment to Center, and then click OK.

Why is my table getting cut off at the bottom of the page?

Text wrapping is the main reason for a table not spanning more than one page. Text wrapping is a great feature that allows you to put text right beside your table without using a text box. If your table runs longer than one page, however, text wrapping no longer works properly and you must remove it. To do this, click in the table. From the Table menu, choose Table Properties. In the Table tab, under Text Wrapping, click None.

If I use table styles and then send the document to a client who uses Word 2000, what will happen?

Table styles did not exist in previous versions of Word; however this feature translates very well to previous versions. When a document that contains table styles is opened in Word 97 or 2000, the formatting is in place and the applied table styles are treated as direct formatting. If the document that contains table styles is saved to HTML, the table styles are preserved.

Chapter 13

Legal Forms and Fields

IN THIS CHAPTER

- Designing legal forms
- When to create a template and when to use a form
- Using form fields
- Protecting your work
- Inserting fields into a document
- Controlling field properties

Many law firms are looking to reduce the amount of paper they generate—working toward becoming a paperless office. One of the ways of pursuing this goal is to create forms that users fill out in either Word or e-mail electronically. Examples of forms that can be used online are check request and office supply request forms, real estate forms, and patent or trademark forms.

In 20 minutes or less, anyone can learn to create forms that use Microsoft Word. This chapter first covers how to construct legal forms in Word, and then provides an introduction to working with fields.

INTRODUCTION TO FORMS

A form is a document that is used to extract specific information from others and that contains boilerplate text that does not change—regardless of who is using the form. The responses from users may differ, but the initial text and options are preset.

In Word, forms are created using the Forms toolbar, which allows the designer to insert various fields and specify the type of content expected for them. Before being distributed to others for completion, a form must be *protected*—that is, the document, along with the fields and their labels, are locked so they can't be changed, and the areas (fields) where the user will enter data are activated.

STEPS TO CREATING A FORM

Forms are easy to create, especially if you follow these steps:

1. Start by creating a new document and saving it as a template. This makes the form read-only when someone uses it to fill out the form.
2. Design the form. Most people make the mistake of hurriedly creating forms without much planning. Take a few moments to design your form. Consider placing information in table cells. This makes the layout and formatting of the form much easier.
3. Display the Forms toolbar and add form fields, defining them as Text, Check Box, or Drop-Down, as needed. If required, set options for each for formatting, default text, or macro execution.

4. Protect the form. Add a password if you want to prevent others from altering your work.
5. Hide the Forms toolbar, save the file once more, and close it. Now it's ready to be sent to others for their use.

TEMPLATES VERSUS FORMS

People often confuse templates and forms. To make matters even more confusing, all forms are templates but not all templates are forms.

The reason you create a template is to set up the basic formatting needs of a document. For example, when you create a letter template, it might include the firm's logo and electronic stationery, styles for constants such as address, signature block, and date, and formatting specific to a letter. You don't want to limit what the user can add and modify, however, since each letter may be different.

A form is a document where you need specific information placed in specific locations, and where the format should not change. A form allows you to limit what information is entered, as well as how and where it appears on the page. A form is saved as a template so that others can create new documents based on the format of the form.

Forms contain specific data entry areas called *form fields,* which are inserted from the Forms toolbar. The form is later protected and then deployed to others, if others will use the form. Templates do not usually contain form fields or require protection.

CREATE A BASIC TEMPLATE FOR THE FORM

1. Create a new document.
2. From the File menu, choose Save As.
3. Click the Save As Type drop-down arrow and select Document Template (*.dot) from the list of choices.
4. Name the template **Check Request Form** and click Save.
5. From the View menu, choose Toolbars, and then click Forms to activate the Forms toolbar. In the remaining exercises for forms, you will use this toolbar to insert form fields, set options, and protect as well as unprotect the form.

FORM DESIGN

Professional developers use tables to organize their forms. This is highly recommended since it offers many advantages over placing text randomly within a document. When you insert the table and then add text and form fields into table cells, the information appears organized, borders and shading can be applied easily, gridlines can be turned off to make the form look more like a printed document, and each table cell is assigned a cell address that can be used when you need to specify a location.

DESIGN A FORM

1. Type **CHECK REQUEST FORM** as the title of the form. Format this text as centered, bold, and 14 points. Press Enter twice, and then format the text as left aligned, non-bold, and 12 points.
2. Insert a table containing four columns and five rows.
3. Click in row four of the table. In this same row, select column cells two through four. From the Table menu, choose Merge Cells to merge the selected cells into one.
4. Type text as shown in Figure 13.1 to create the boilerplate for the Check Request form.

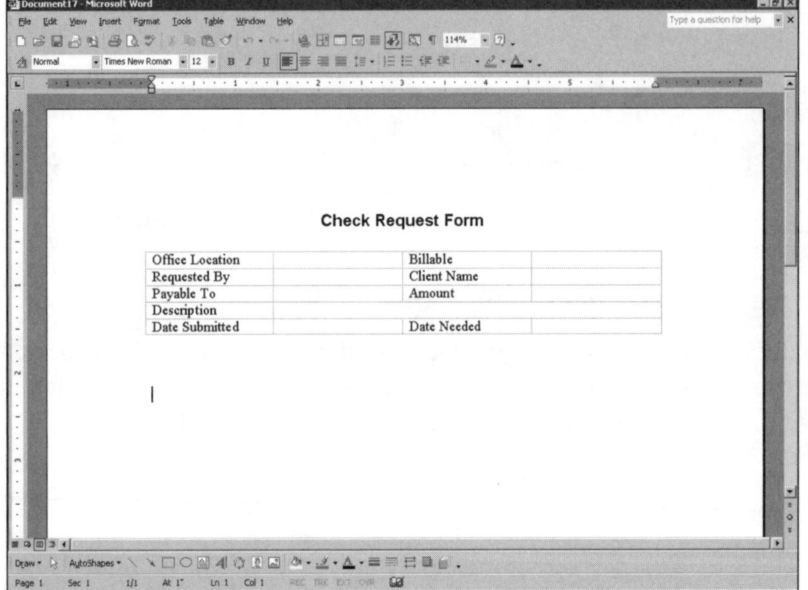

FIGURE 13.1

It is useful to have table gridlines showing when designing a form; however, most people turn them off before deploying the form to others or after applying borders.

5. After you have typed the text, from the Format menu, choose Borders And Shading and add the borders, as shown in Figure 13.1.
6. Click the Save button on the Standard toolbar and leave the file open for the next exercise.

THE FORMS TOOLBAR

Once the basic design of the form is complete, it's time to use the Forms toolbar to add form fields that make using the form easier. If the Forms toolbar is not visible, from the View menu, choose Toolbars and then select Forms. The Forms toolbar opens, as shown in Figure 13.2.

The following list provides a description for each button on the Forms toolbar.

- **Text Form Field.** Inserts a Text form field.
- **Check Box Form Field.** Inserts a Check Box form field.
- **Drop-Down Form Field.** Inserts a Drop-Down form field.
- **Form Field Options.** Allows you to change options, such as default text.
- **Draw Table.** Turns the mouse pointer into a table-drawing tool to insert an irregular-sized table.
- **Insert Table.** Inserts an evenly spaced table.
- **Insert Frame.** Adds a frame around selected text.
- **Form Field Shading.** Toggles the gray shaded background on form fields on and off.

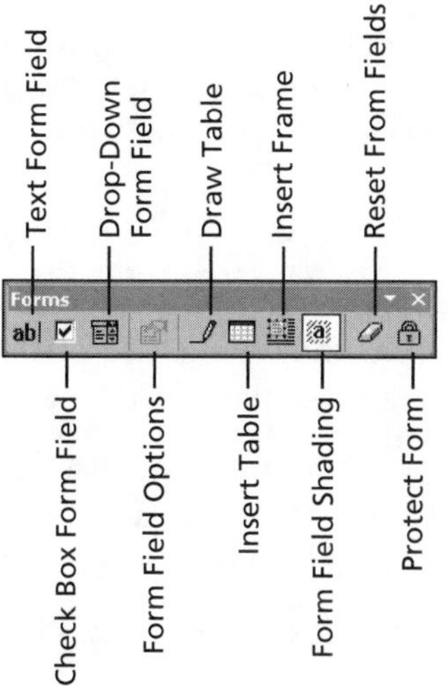

FIGURE 13.2

The Forms toolbar includes all the tools that you need to create, format, and protect a custom form.

NEW FEATURE!

In previous versions of Word, when a form was unprotected, all values previously entered into the form fields were reset and, therefore, lost. This was a big area of frustration for law firms. In Word 2002, the data in form fields is not automatically reset when the form is protected and unprotected by clicking the Protect Form button on the Forms toolbar. A Reset Form Fields button has been added to the Forms toolbar for this purpose. This button is useful during the testing process before deployment.

- **Reset Form Fields**. Resets the data in the form fields.
- **Protect Form**. Toggles protection of the form on or off, preventing or allowing changes to field definitions and boilerplate text.

Although form fields are not automatically reset when a form is reprotected by using the Protect button on the Forms toolbar, form fields *are* automatically reset when you choose Protect Document from the Tools menu.

TYPES OF FORM FIELDS

There are three types of form fields available on the Forms toolbar: Text, Check Box, and Drop-Down. For text—not just words but currency, dates, numbers, and even calculations—use a Text form field. For yes/no or true/false information, a Check Box form field is preferable. When you wish to limit the choices to a list that you provide in advance, use a Drop-Down form field.

TEXT FORM FIELD

A Text form field allows the user to enter regular or formatted text as well as numbers and dates by clicking on the field and typing. Calculations can also be performed, with the result appearing in the Text form field.

To insert a Text form field into the document, move the insertion point to the appropriate location in the document and click the Text Form Field button on the Forms toolbar. An example of a Text form field is shown in Figure 13.3.

If the form field does not appear shaded, click the Form Field Shading button on the Forms toolbar.

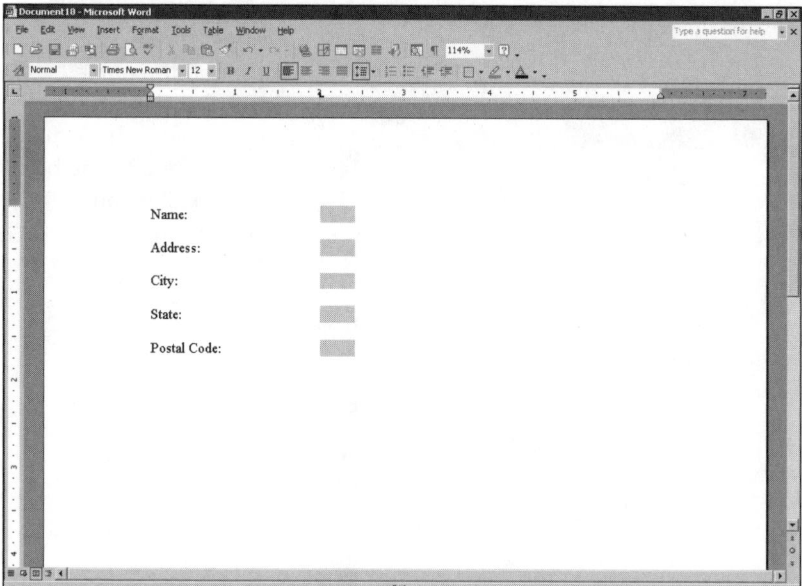

FIGURE 13.3

Form fields can be either shaded or nonshaded. Shading makes fields easier to recognize; omitting the shading makes the document look more polished—but nonshaded fields are somewhat more difficult to use.

CHECK BOX FORM FIELD

A Check Box form field allows the user to make a yes/no or true/false type of response. To insert a Check Box form field, move the insertion point to the appropriate location and click the Check Box Form Field button on the Forms toolbar. Once the form is protected, an X will appear within the box when it is clicked. The check box can also be checked or unchecked by pressing the Spacebar when the field is active. Figure 13.4 shows an example of a Check Box form field enabled.

DROP-DOWN FORM FIELD

A Drop-Down form field includes a list of up to 25 items that appear when the form is protected and the user clicks on the field, or on the drop-down arrow next to the field.

This type of form field is especially useful for restricting data entry. There is no chance for the user to type an incorrect response, use improper capitalization, or format the text incorrectly.

To insert a Drop-Down form field, move the insertion point to the appropriate location within the document. Click the Drop-Down Form Field button on the Forms toolbar. Later in this chapter, you will add items to the list of choices. Until items are added to the list, the Drop-Down form field will appear to be an empty box.

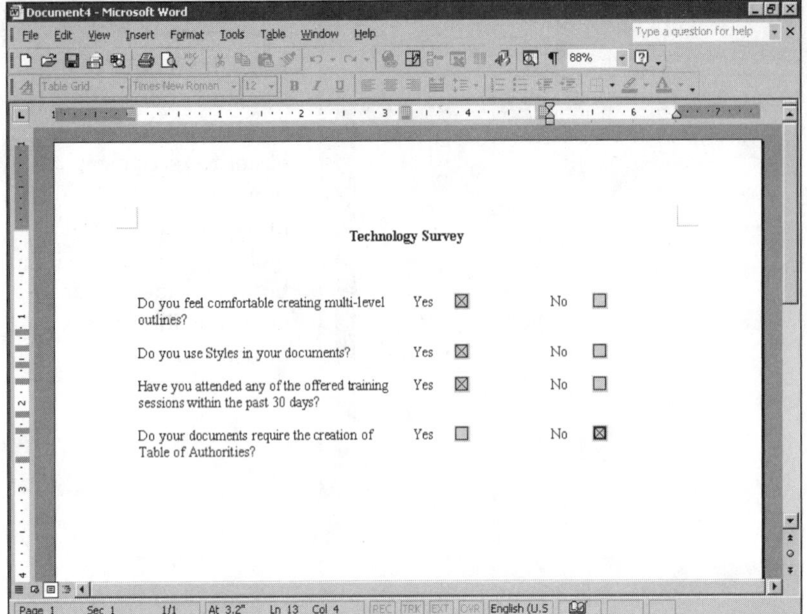

FIGURE 13.4

Although the name Check Box Form Field implies that a check mark will be added to the box when enabled, an X mark is used instead.

ADDING FORM FIELDS

Adding form fields is easy since all three types are inserted by clicking the appropriate button on the Forms toolbar.

ADD FORM FIELDS

1. Using the Check Request Form, insert Text form fields in the cells to the right of Date Submitted, Date Needed, Requested By, Client Name, Payable To, Amount, and Description.
2. Insert a Drop-Down form field in the cell to the right of Office Location.
3. Insert a Check Box form field in the cell to the right of Billable.

FORM FIELD OPTIONS

Once form fields are added, you can set options for formatting and content. Word provides three ways to set options for form fields:

- Click the Form Field Options button on the Forms toolbar.
- Alternate-click a form field in the document and choose Properties from the shortcut menu.

- Double-click the form field.

Some options are common to all form fields. You can set up any form field to run a macro when the insertion point enters or exits the field. Word assigns a generic bookmark name to each form field, but you can always change the bookmark name, if desired. Help text can be added to a form field by clicking the Add Help Text button. This feature is designed to provide assistance to people using the forms that you create.

NOTE

For Text form fields, if you want the user to type regular text with no special formatting, it is not necessary to set any form field options. It is also unnecessary to set any options for Check Box form fields that you want to be unchecked when the user initially opens the form.

SET TEXT FORM FIELD OPTIONS

1. Move your insertion point to the Date Submitted Text form field and click the Form Field Options button on the Forms toolbar. The Text Form Field Options dialog box opens, as shown in Figure 13.5.
2. To explore the options available for numbers, choose Number from the Type drop-down list. Notice the various options available in the Number Format drop-down list, which includes Decimals, Comma Styles, Currency, and Percentage.
3. From the Type drop-down list, choose Current Date. A Date Format drop-down list becomes available.
4. From the Date Format drop-down list, choose the third format: MMMM d, yyyy.

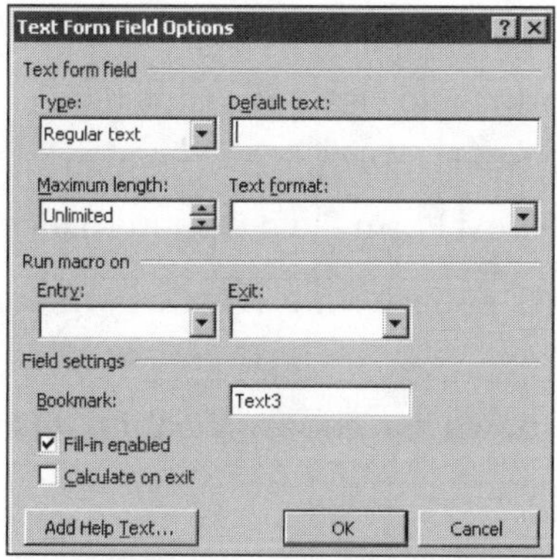

FIGURE 13.5

Some options for form fields are set automatically. For example, when a form field is inserted, a bookmark name is assigned.

ELEMENTS OF THE TEXT FORM FIELD OPTIONS DIALOG BOX

Type is a drop-down list of text choices. The choices for Type are Regular Text, Number, Date, Current Date, Current Time, and Calculation. For each type, there are corresponding formatting options. The length of the text entered into the Text Box Form Field can be limited by typing a number into the Maximum Length box or using the spinner to change the value from Unlimited, which is the default.

A default value can be entered for regular text, number, and date types.

The field has two additional options: Fill-In Enabled and Calculate On Exit. Uncheck the Fill-In Enabled box to prevent users from entering or changing data within the field. When the Current Date or Current Time type is selected, the Fill-In Enabled box will not be available. If the field is part of a calculation, check the Calculate On Exit box to update the calculation when the field is exited.

When Regular text is selected in the Type drop-down list, the Text Format drop-down list choices available are Uppercase, Lowercase, First Capital, and Title Case. When you choose one of these options, when the form field is exited, the formatting options you selected will be applied to the text, regardless of what format the user types.

NOTE

Notice that the Fill-In Enabled check box is no longer available. The text box will automatically display the date the form is filled out, without allowing the user to choose or type an alternate date.

5. Click OK to close the Text Form Field Options dialog box.
6. Move your insertion point to the Date Needed form field and double-click on the form field to open the Text Form Field Options dialog box.
7. From the Type drop-down list, choose Date. A Date Format drop-down list becomes available.
8. From the Date Format drop-down list, choose the third format: MMMM d, yyyy.

9. Click OK. The remainder of the Text Box form fields can be left in their generic state, but if you'd like some practice, try setting the options for the Client Name to be entered in Uppercase format and Amount as currency.

If the form field is going to be part of a calculation, you may consider changing the Bookmark name to something more descriptive of the field instead of Text1, Text 2, and so on. For example, in an expense form, you may designate the Bookmark of a field to be Hotel, Airfare, or Misc. You can then use these descriptive fields to generate the total calculation in the form as "= sum(hotel, airfare, misc)". This is very handy in complex forms.

POPULATING A DROP-DOWN FORM FIELD

Using Drop-Down form fields, you can limit choices to a predefined list. A Drop-Down form field can contain up to 25 items. Each item name can be up to 60 characters in length.

ADD ITEMS TO A DROP-DOWN FORM FIELD

1. Move your insertion point to the Office Location Drop-Down form field and click Form Field Options on the Forms toolbar. The Drop-Down Form Field Options dialog box opens, as shown in Figure 13.6.

2. In the Drop-Down Item box, type **New York** and then click Add. New York is added to the Items In Drop-Down List box.

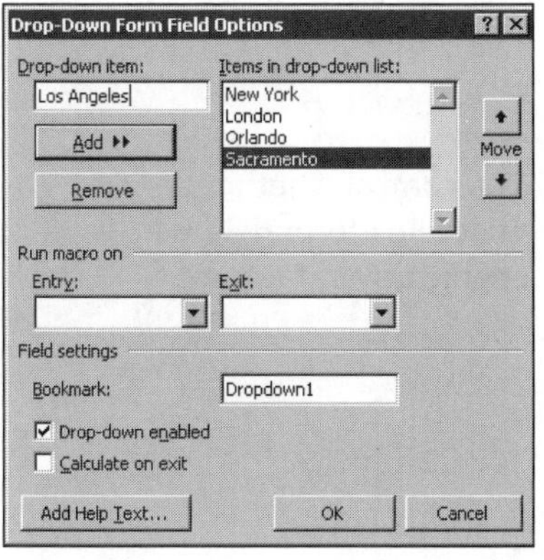

FIGURE 13.6

Select an item and click the Move Up or Move Down arrows to reposition the item within the list.

3. Type the following items into the Drop-Down Item box, clicking Add after each item: **London**, **Orlando**, **Sacramento**, **Los Angeles**.

To remove an item from the list, select the item in the Items In Drop-Down List box and click Remove.

The list is not organized in alphabetical order. To reorder the list manually, select one of the items and then click the Move Up or Move Down arrows to reposition the items in the list until they appear in the order you prefer.

4. Create one last entry for the list. This is a special entry that goes at the top of the list to prevent any of the cities appearing as a default value for the Drop-Down form field. Press the Spacebar 15 times or equal to the longest entry within your list. Click Add and move this item to the top of the list.
5. Click OK and save the file. Leave the Check Request Form open for the next exercise.

CHECK BOX FORM FIELD OPTIONS

In some instances, you may want to have a Check Box form field appear already checked when a user creates a new document based on your form. In certain forms that require a lot of data, such as a Civil Cover Sheet, you may need to adjust the size of the check box. You can change the initial value of a Check Box form field in the Check Box Form Field Options dialog box, as shown in Figure 13.7.

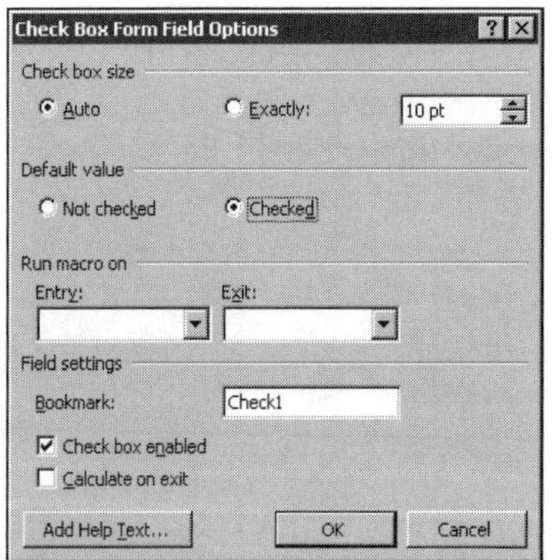

FIGURE 13.7

You control whether a Check Box form field is enabled by default.

CHANGE THE INITIAL VALUE OF A CHECK BOX

1. Double-click the Check Box form field for Billable to display the Check Box Form Field Options dialog box.
2. Under Default Value, click the Checked option and then click OK. The check box will now appear to be checked when a new document is created based on the Check Request Form template.

ADDING HELP TO FORM FIELDS

Two different types of help can be added to each form field: Status Bar text and Help Key text. Status Bar help is displayed on the status bar of the window when the insertion point is within the field. Help Key text appears in a message box if the user presses F1 when the insertion point is in the field. Adding help text is not required, but it may help to clarify the type of entry required for the form field.

To add help text to a form field, move your insertion point to a form field and then click the Form Field Options button on the Forms toolbar. In the Form Field dialog box, click the Add Help Text button. The Form Field Help Text dialog box opens, as shown in Figure 13.8, with two tabs: Status Bar and Help Key (F1).

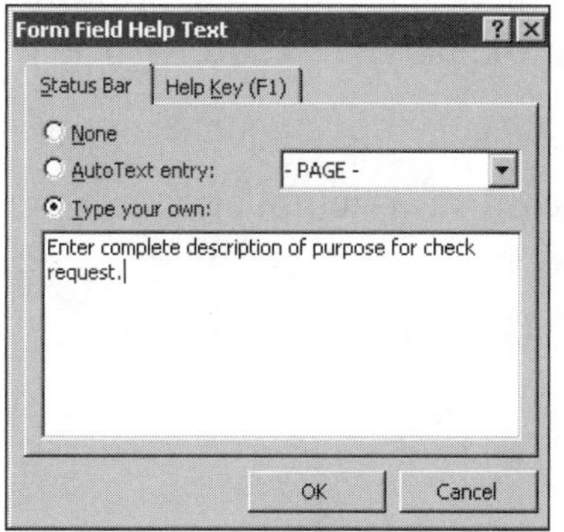

FIGURE 13.8

Text can be typed or existing AutoText can be used to display help instructions.

ADD HELP TEXT TO A TEXT BOX FORM FIELD

1. Move your insertion point to the Description Text form field and click the Form Field Options button. The Text Box Form Field Options dialog box opens.
2. Click Add Help Text.
3. Select the Status Bar tab, if it is not already active.
4. Select the Type Your Own option and type the following text: **Enter complete description of purpose for check request.**
5. Select the Help Key tab and select the Type Your Own option again. Type the same text as in Step 4.
6. Click OK, and then OK again.

Once the form is protected, whenever the user clicks the field that includes help (Description, in this example), Word's status bar will show the text typed for help. If F1 is pressed while the field is active, a message box, as shown in Figure 13.9, will appear containing the specified help message.

PROTECTING THE FORM

The form cannot be used until it is protected. This is perhaps the easiest of all steps because no matter what type of form field is used, the form is protected by clicking Protect Form on the Forms toolbar or by choosing a menu command.

A protected form is different from a regular document in several ways:

- Text and formatting of a protected form cannot be edited.
- The entire document cannot be selected.
- Most formatting commands, such as bold, italic, and underline, cannot be used within the fields.

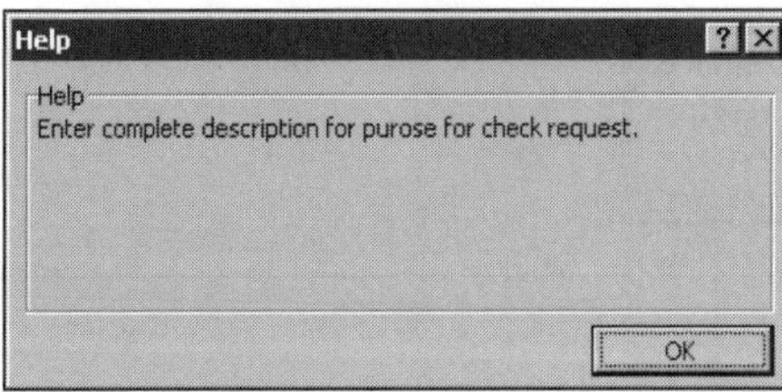

FIGURE 13.9

Adding help to forms that you create not only makes the form easier to use, it also reduces support calls for instruction on how to use the form correctly.

- Many menu commands and toolbar buttons will not be available when working in forms.
- The Spelling Checker will ignore protected sections of the document, although you can now check the spelling for unprotected sections of the form.
- Undo doesn't work for changes made to a form before it was protected.

There are two ways to protect a form: From the Tools menu, choose Protect Document and then click OK, or click Protect Form on the Forms toolbar. The Tools menu method gives you more options for protecting a document, allowing you to add a password and to choose to protect only specified sections of the document.

The Protect Form button toggles between Protect and Unprotect. To unprotect a form, from the Tools menu, choose Unprotect Document, or click the Unprotect/Protect Form button on the Forms toolbar. The Protect button will be surrounded by a blue box when the form is protected.

Reprotecting a form using the Tools menu method will reset the form fields to their original state—whether blank or containing a default value. Data entered into form fields will be retained when using the toolbar button method to reprotect a form.

PROTECTING A FORM WITH A PASSWORD

To ensure that the form cannot be unprotected by others, you can set Word to require a specified password before permitting modification of the form. Be careful, however—passwords are not easily recovered if forgotten. (In many cases, you wind up having to consult a password-hacking company.) Also, remember that passwords are case-sensitive.

PROTECT A FORM WITH A PASSWORD

1. From the Tools menu, choose Protect document. The Protect Document dialog box opens.
2. Make sure that the Forms option is selected. Type a password in the Password box. For security, the password looks like a string of asterisks regardless of what you type.
3. Click OK.

4. Reconfirm the password by typing it again. Click OK. If the password matches the first attempt, the dialog box closes and the password is assigned. If, for some reason, the password does not match the first attempt, a message box appears asking you to reenter the password.

If you attempt to unprotect a document that has been protected with a password, you will be prompted to enter the password before the document can be unprotected. You will be prompted for the password whether you use the Tools, Unprotect Document method or click the Unprotect Form button on the Forms toolbar. If you want to reprotect the form, you will need to reassign the password.

NOTE

It's possible to protect a form without a password—but, if you don't assign a password, anyone can unprotect the form and alter your work. They may also reset information by accident.

Therefore, even if you use a generic firm password such as "password" or your firm's initials, it's better than having no password at all. This keeps inexperienced users from undoing all of your hard work.

PROTECTING SECTIONS OF A FORM

Because of the limitations placed on protected documents, it may be necessary to protect only certain portions of the form. To accomplish this, you must divide your form into sections. Insert section breaks to separate the sections of your document that need protection from the sections that do not. You only need to protect the sections that contain form fields.

To apply protection to one or more sections in a form, from the Tools menu, choose Protect Document. The Protect Document dialog box opens. Under Protect Document For, choose Forms and then click Sections.

The Section Protection dialog box opens, as shown in Figure 13.10. Uncheck the sections of the document that you do not wish to protect and click OK.

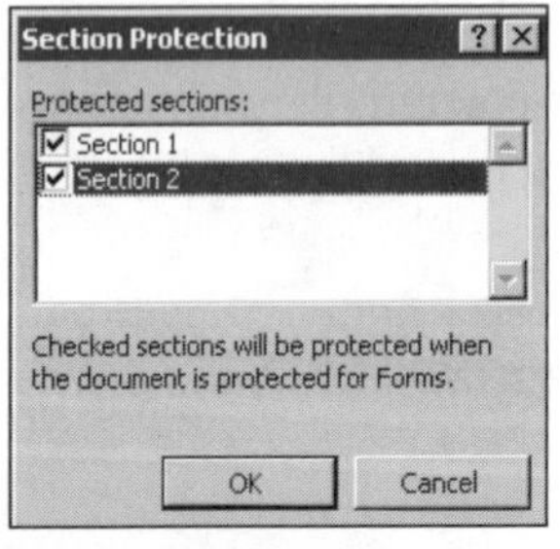

FIGURE 13.10

The first section of your document may contain form fields for a specific data form while the second contains an area where users can type general comments. If you insert a section break and protect the first part of the form, Section 1 only, the form is enabled in Section 1, and the users can type and format freely in Section 2.

INSERTING SECTION BREAKS FOR FORMS

To insert a section break, from the Insert menu, choose Break. Under Section Break Types, choose either Next Page to start a new page or Continuous Section Break to keep the text on the same page.

WORD FIELDS IN LEGAL DOCUMENTS

Up until this point, all fields discussed in this chapter have been related to forms. Using just form fields can be very limiting due to the restrictions in place when working with form documents. That's why Microsoft Word offers many more fields than just those used in forms.

These other fields are not inserted from the Forms toolbar, and the document does not need to be protected for the fields to work.

Word fields are special codes to instruct Word to insert information anywhere in a document. This information can be updated manually or automatically, depending on the type of field. Fields can be used to insert text, graphics, page numbers, and other information into documents.

TYPES OF FIELDS

Word 2002 includes more than 70 different fields that can be added to documents. These fields can be divided into three types: result, marker, and action fields.

RESULT FIELDS

The most frequently used fields in Word are result fields. Result fields retrieve information and place it within the document. One example of a result field is FILENAME, which automatically retrieves the name of the document and places that information in the field.

MARKER FIELDS

Marker fields differ from result fields in that they do not return a result. Instead, the field supplies information to Word. An example of a marker field is an Index Entry field (XE). An XE field is used to mark entries for an index. Marker fields cannot be updated automatically. Instead, the text within the field code needs to be changed manually to change the information supplied to Word. Word then uses the XE fields to extract information when generating an index.

ACTION FIELDS

Action fields are special fields that tell Word to perform a specific action. For example, an ASK field instructs Word to prompt for information to be entered and assigns a bookmark to represent the user's response.

INSERTING FIELDS

You can insert most fields by choosing Field from the Insert menu to open the Field dialog box. From the Field dialog box (shown in Figure 13.11), choose the category and field name you want to insert, select any properties and options, and then click OK.

If you are familiar with the field codes and syntax, you can insert a field manually by pressing Ctrl+F9. Some fields can be inserted using keystrokes. Some fields are inserted automatically. For example, inserting a table of contents by choosing Insert, Reference, Index And Tables, Table Of Contents, and then clicking OK will automatically insert a TOC field into the document. A hyperlink field is automatically inserted when choosing Insert, Hyperlink, selecting hyperlink options, and then clicking OK.

Manually entering a field code is not recommended for users new to fields. The syntax of a field code is very rigid, and a space or quotation out of place can cause an error in the field. The Field dialog box provides easy-to-understand instructions and adds the proper syntax, as needed.

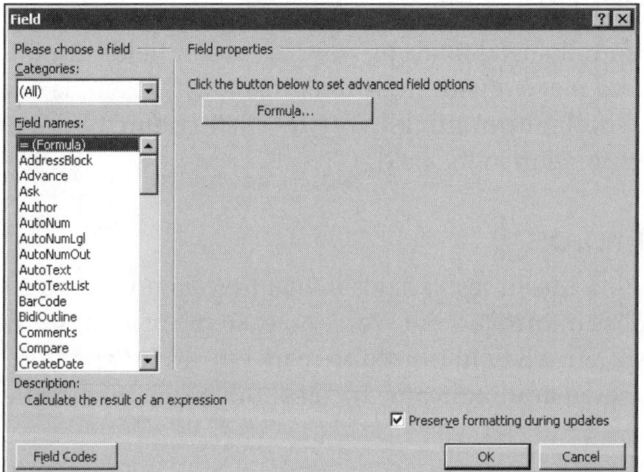

FIGURE 13.11

The Field dialog box in Word has become far more user-friendly than in previous versions.

THREE METHODS FOR INSERTING DATE FIELDS

- Press Alt+Shift+D to insert a Date field with the default date settings.
- From the Insert menu, choose Date And Time. The Date And Time dialog box opens, allowing you to choose one of the available formats. If desired, click Update Automatically. Figure 13.12 shows the Date And Time dialog box.

The option to Update Automatically is a cause for concern in most law firms. When selected, the date code will change to the current date each time the document is opened or printed. Although this may seem practical when drafting a document, it might cause problems if not changed in the final copy.

- From the Insert menu, choose Field. From the Categories drop-down list, choose Date And Time. The Field dialog box changes, as shown in Figure 13.13. From the Field Names list, choose Date. In the Field Properties

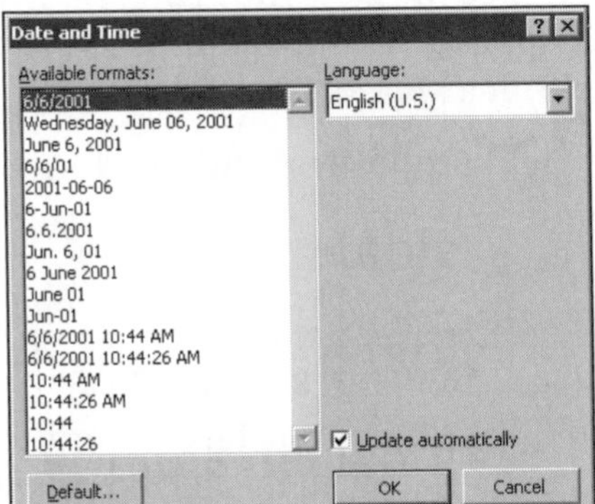

FIGURE 13.12

The Default button set your current choice as the default date and time format.

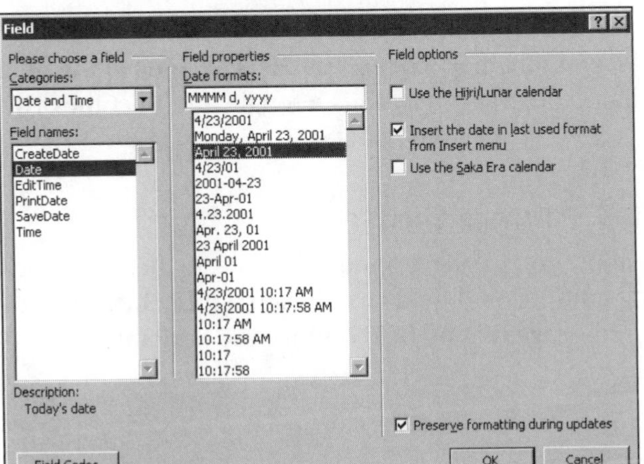

FIGURE 13.13

When different categories and fields are selected, the options for the dialog box change.

section, make a selection from Date Formats, or select the option Insert The Date In Last Used Format From Insert Menu. Click OK.

INSIDE THE FIELD DIALOG BOX

When you open the Field dialog box, you will find no shortage of types of fields and information that can be added to a document. There are fields for AddressBlock, Advance, Ask, Author, AutoNum (inserts an automatic number), AutoNumLgl (inserts an automatic number in legal format), AutoNumOut, AutoText, and AutoTextList. And these are just the fields that begin with the letter "A"—there are many more to choose from.

FIELD CATEGORIES

The Field dialog box is divided into three sections. In the first section, you choose a field. A drop-down list contains categories and displays a list of field names. If (All) is selected in the Categories list, all available fields are shown in Field Names. Categories narrow the Field Names list to the ones in the selected category. For example, if you choose the Date And Time category, only fields relating to dates and times will appear. Selecting Mail Merge in the categories list displays only fields applicable for a Mail Merge operation.

The second section contains Field Properties, and the third contains Field Options.

THE FIELD PROPERTIES SECTION

Field properties allow you to choose properties for the field in user-friendly format instead of codes. For example, in previous versions of Word, you would have to choose or type MMMM to insert the date with the full month spelled out. This involved remembering often tricky or obscure coding. Now you can choose the spelled-out month name from the list, and Word does the work for you.

If you prefer viewing the field codes, click Field Codes in the bottom-left corner of the Field dialog box. This button is a toggle and becomes Hide Codes when enabled.

THE FIELD OPTIONS SECTION

Field options allow you to select options by clicking desired check boxes instead of memorizing complicated field switches. If applicable, the Field Options section displays a message that no field options are available.

Most fields have the option to preserve formatting during updates. Checking this box adds the code * MERGEFORMAT to the field. This means that the formatting of the field will be retained when the field is updated. Imagine a Will or Trust document where the name of the testator is repeated throughout the document. This can be set up with an ASK field that originally asks for the testator's name and then uses REF field codes to repeat the name as needed throughout the document. In this type of document, different instances of the testator name require different formats—Title Case, Upper Case, Bold, Underlined, and more. If the option Preserve Formatting Changes During Updates is applied to each REF code, each instance of the name can be formatted independently of the original entry.

PRESERVE FORMATTING OF A FIELD

1. Open the file Trust.dot from the CD-ROM and position your cursor at the top of the document.
2. From the Insert menu, choose Field. The Field dialog box opens.
3. Select (All) from Categories and click on Ask under Field Names.
4. In Prompt:, type **Enter Testator's Full Name.**
5. In Bookmark Name, type **TestatorName** (with no spaces).
6. Select Prompt Before Merging Bookmark Text and click OK.
7. The ASK field triggers a dialog box as shown in Figure 13.14. Type **Testator Name** and click OK. This will store a default value of Testator Name in the bookmark.

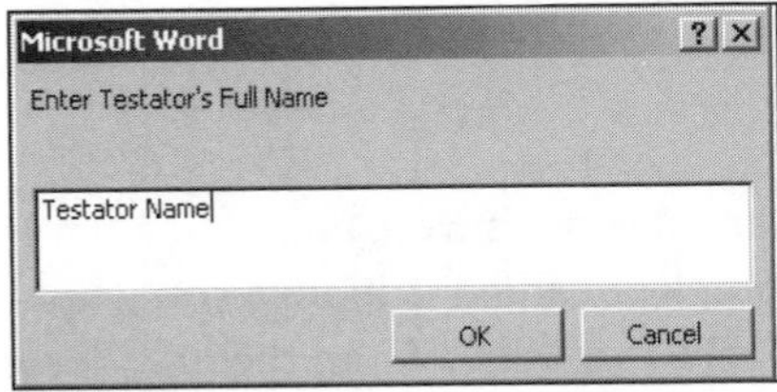

FIGURE 13.14

Use an ASK field to prompt the user to enter specific information that is stored in a bookmark to be referenced as needed in the document.

8. Position your cursor between the words "THE" and "TRUST" at the top of the document.
9. From the Insert menu, choose Field. The Field dialog box opens.
10. Select Links and References from Categories and click on REF under Field Names.
11. Select TestatorName from Bookmark Name.
12. Select Preserve Formatting Changes During Updates and click OK.
13. Format the newly inserted field as Bold and All Caps.
14. Select the Testatorname found in line 4 in the paragraph below the heading and press Delete.
15. From the Insert menu, choose Field. The Field dialog box opens.
16. Select Links and References from Categories and, under Field Names, click REF.
17. Select Testator from Bookmark Name and Title Case from Format.
18. Select Preserve Formatting Changes During Updates and click OK.
19. Select and delete TestatorName in the last line.
20. Repeat steps 9–12 to insert another reference.
21. Select the last reference inserted and format as Underlined.
22. Click Save to retain your changes.
23. To test the fields, press Ctrl+A, F9 to access the Testator Name dialog box.
24. Enter a name in the dialog box that appears and click OK. Notice how all the fields change but the formatting remains intact.
25. Close the document without saving.

NOTE

In the previous example, the ASK and REF fields were added to a template document. When the template was completed and distributed, you would access the template from the New Document Task Pane. When the new document opened, the prompt to enter the testator's name appeared, and all the references would update once you clicked OK.

FIELD SHADING

When you want to see where fields are located in your document, you can choose to display fields with a shaded background, either when selected or always.

TURN ON FIELD SHADING

1. From the Tools menu, choose Options. Select the View tab.
2. Under Field Shading:, choose Always to always show fields with a shaded background. The other choices available are When Selected to show fields with a shaded background only when selected, and Never for no field shading.

It's a good idea to show fields with shading so you can quickly identify field locations. The shading does not print.

VIEWING FIELDS

Most times, when fields are inserted, the desired effect is to view the result and not the field code. For example, if the AUTHOR field code is in a document, you probably don't want to see { AUTHOR * MERGEFORMAT }, which is the actual field code inserted behind the scenes; you want the name of the author. But when a field is not producing the result that you are looking for, it's helpful to display the field code instead of the field result to help troubleshoot the problem.

If a document contains multiple fields, you can toggle all of them at once to display the code instead of the result. To do so, press Alt+F9. Repeat this keystroke to toggle the field code display back to field results.

To see the field code for an individual field, alternate-click the field and choose Toggle Field Codes from the shortcut menu. The keyboard shortcut for toggling the individual field is Shift+F9 when the insertion point is within the field.

UPDATING FIELDS

Updating a field prompts Word to display the most current information as the field result. For example, updating a DATE field would display the current date. Some fields update automatically. For example, a PAGE field updates when additional pages of text are added to the document.

There are several ways to update fields that do not update automatically. Fields can be updated individually or all at once. There is even an option to update all fields when a document is printed.

To update an individual field:

- Place the insertion point within the field and press F9.
- Alternate-click the field and choose Update Field from the shortcut menu.

To update all fields in the document:

- Press Ctrl+A to select the entire document and press F9.
- From the Tools menu, choose Options, then select the Print tab. Under Printing options, check Update Fields. All fields will be updated when the document is printed.

PREVENTING FIELDS FROM UPDATING

On occasion, it's advantageous to prevent fields from being updated. There are two methods to accomplish this: The fields can be locked and later unlocked, or they can be unlinked. When you unlink a field, the field changes permanently to text.

LOCKING AND UNLOCKING FIELDS

To lock a field, click within the field and press Ctrl+F11. This prevents the field from being updated until it is unlocked.

To unlock a field, click within the field and press Ctrl+Shift+F11. The field can then be updated by pressing F9.

NOTE

A locked field looks the same as an unlocked field. The only way to determine if a field is locked is by alternate-clicking on the field. A grayed-out Update Field command is an indication that the field is locked.

UNLINKING FIELDS

Unlinking a field permanently converts the field to text. To unlink a field, press Ctrl+Shift+F9 or Ctrl+6 (use the 6 on the keyboard, not the numeric keypad). If you need to unlink all the fields in a document at once, you can press Ctrl+A and then Ctrl+Shift+F9—but make sure there are no fields you'd rather keep as fields before you use this shortcut.

FIELD SHORTCUT KEYS

There are several keyboard shortcut combinations that speed up inserting and working with fields. Table 13.1 includes the shortcuts for working with fields in Word.

TABLE 13.1 KEYBOARD SHORTCUTS FOR FIELDS

SHORTCUT KEY	RESULT
F9	Updates selected fields.
Shift+F9	Toggles selected fields to show the field code or field result.
Alt+F9	Updates all fields in the document.
Ctrl+F9	Manually inserts a field.
Ctrl+Shift+F9	Unlinks a field and converts it to text.
Ctrl+6	Unlinks a field and converts it to text.
Ctrl+F11	Locks a field to prevent updating.
Ctrl+Shift+F11	Unlocks a field.

SOME FIELDS USEFUL FOR LEGAL WORK

Several fields are so useful that you will want to master them and have them as part of your repertoire. The more you work with fields, the more uses you will find for them. Here's a good list to start with:

- **CreateDate**. Returns the date that the document was created. The date format includes the Hijri/Lunar calendar or the Saka Era calendar.
- **Date**. Inserts the current date specified by your computer. The field code is { DATE * MERGEFORMAT }.
- **PrintDate**. Inserts the date that the document was last printed. The field code is { PRINTDATE * MERGEFORMAT }.
- **SaveDate**. Inserts the date that the document was last saved. The field code is { SAVEDATE * MERGEFORMAT }.
- **Author**. Inserts the name of the document's author from Tools, Options, User Information. The field code is { AUTHOR * Upper} for uppercase author name.

- **Filename**. Returns the file name as the result. The field code is { FILENAME * MERGEFORMAT }.
- **Filename \p**. Returns the full path of the file name and location. Most firms make a lot of use of this field, especially in document footers. The field code for the full path is { FILENAME \p *MERGEFORMAT }.
- **NumPages**. Inserts the number of pages in the document. The field code is { NUMPAGES * Arabic *MERGEFORMAT }.
- =**(Formula)**. Calculates the result of whatever expression is typed into the field. For example, press Ctrl+F9 to insert an empty field. Type **=55*79** and press F9 to update the field. The field is calculated for you.
- **TA**. Marks a table of authorities entry.
- **TC**. Marks a table of contents entry.
- **TOA**. Creates a table of authorities.
- **TOC**. Creates a table of contents.
- **XE**. Marks an index entry.
- **ListNum**. Inserts an element in a list.
- **AutoNumLgl**. Inserts an automatic number in legal format and includes options to display the number without the trailing period. Also available is the option to specify a separator character that is inserted between the number and the text.
- **MacroButton**. Runs a macro. This field is used extensively in template development to create "click and type" fields. Press Ctrl+F9 to insert a field. Type **macrobutton nomacro Click here and Type**. Press F9 to update the field.

If you want to dig in and learn more about fields, consider taking a Master Series or Intro to VBA class from Payne Consulting Group. For more information on these classes, or on a class specific to advanced fields, visit our Web site at www.payneconsulting.com.

SUMMARY

Creating Word forms is fast, easy to learn, and does not require a large investment of time or frustration. When creating a form, the Forms toolbar provides all the tools necessary for creating a robust solution to your firm's form needs.

Word provides more than 70 types of non-form fields that can produce results, mark information to be used later (for example, in a table of authorities), or prompt for information to be entered (as is the case with ASK fields).

Many fields are useful for law firms. The more you use forms and fields, the more applicability you will find.

TROUBLESHOOTING FORMS AND FIELDS

My document contains field codes instead of the result. I've tried the keyboard shortcut to toggle to display results, but the codes are not changing.

From the Tools menu, choose Options and select the View tab. Uncheck Field Codes and click OK.

I protected my form, but the password doesn't work.

Passwords are case-sensitive, so try toggling the Caps Lock key—it may have been activated when you set the password, or it may be activated incorrectly now. It's a good idea to keep a list of passwords that have been applied to your documents in a safe location as well.

The table of contents in my document is not updating.

There are several possible scenarios: The field could be locked, or it may have been unlinked and converted to text. To troubleshoot, turn on Field Shading. Click on the table of contents to see if the table of contents is a field. If it is, the field is probably locked. Press Ctrl+Shift+F11 to unlock the field. If the table is not a field, it may have been typed manually or converted to text. If you used styles or applied Outline Level using the Outlining toolbar, the table of contents can be regenerated in seconds. From the Insert menu, choose Reference, and then Index And Tables. Select the Table Of Contents tab and click OK.

Every time something is typed in a form field, it is formatted in lowercase, even when mixed and uppercase formatting is used.

Unprotect the form, double-click the field to open the Form Field Options dialog box, and change or remove the Text Format option.

CHAPTER 14

AGREEMENTS, BRIEFS, AND OTHER LONG DOCUMENTS

IN THIS CHAPTER

- Document comments
- Footnotes and endnotes
- Hyperlinks
- Bookmarks
- Cross references
- Captions and tables of figures
- Tables of contents
- Tables of authorities
- Indexes
- Constructing complex documents from scratch

Long, complex legal documents have traditionally been both the boon and bane of a law firm's existence. These documents can range anywhere from loan closing documents to lengthy briefs filed with the courts. What makes these documents so different from documents created in other industries? Among other things, they can push the limits of any word processing software. Any one of these legal documents can require a table of contents, a table of authorities, long lists of footnotes or endnotes (or both), internal cross references, an index, and other complex features not usually found together in one document. For example, patent law documents can require inclusion of scientific equations as well as unusual line numbering.

What do all these documents have in common? Whether you are meeting a court-mandated deadline or closing a difficult negotiation, these documents must be produced as quickly and seamlessly as possible. In an effort to take pressure off the people producing these documents, Microsoft has worked hard to address their needs.

You may ask, "How did Microsoft do this?" The answer is that Microsoft has simplified the use of all the features listed in the first paragraph, as well as improving the functionality of each. In this chapter, you'll have an opportunity to experience some of these dramatic improvements and how they affect the creation and manipulation of long, complex documents. This chapter and the next (Chapter 15, "Document Collaboration") will show you how much easier it now is to work on documents created and edited by multitudes of people. You'll see how the collaboration tools have been significantly enhanced to assist lawyers when sharing documents not only within their office but also with others in the global legal arena.

DOCUMENT COMMENTS

Document comments are notes placed in a document to communicate information that isn't part of the document itself. Comments don't normally appear in the printed document, and although there is an option to print document comments, this tool is usually used to provide online information about the construction of the document as well as communicate information about the document's content. In the latter situation, there are times when attorneys need to make notes to themselves and others but not include the note in the actual text of the working document. Among other things, document comments can be used to share background information, address strategy issues, identify key points, and add suggestions for areas of improvement and further research. Like tracked changes, document comments now appear in balloons located in the margin of the document with a dashed line drawn to the insertion point of the comment in the text. Comments are much easier to read in this new format. Figure 14.1 shows an example of comments in Word 2002.

INSERTING COMMENTS

There are several ways to insert document comments. From the Insert menu, choose Comment. You can use the keyboard shortcut Ctrl+Alt+M to insert the comment, or you can click New Comment on the Reviewing toolbar.

If your computer has a sound card and a microphone, you can also insert voice comments in the document. The voice comment is recorded as a sound object. To record a voice comment, click the drop-down arrow on the New Comment button on the Reviewing toolbar. Select Voice Comment from the list and record your comment.

Voice comments can be useful for conveying nuances of meaning, but bear in mind that sound objects can dramatically increase the file size of your document—and can be heard only by reviewers who have sound cards on their computers. Also, there is no option to print voice comments, so they cannot become part of the paper record.

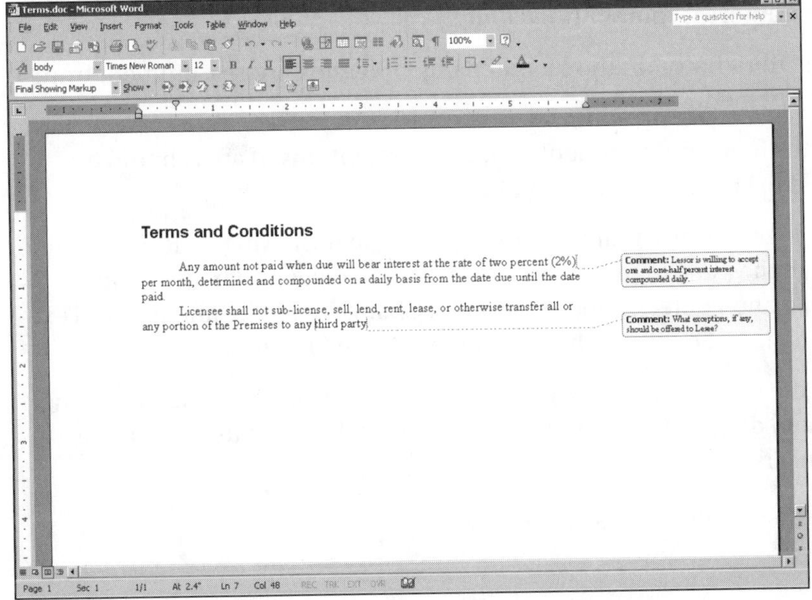

FIGURE 14.1

Document comments can include formatted text, as well as graphics, in the Comments balloon.

INSERTING COMMENTS

1. Create a new blank document.
2. Switch to Normal view by choosing Normal from the View menu, or pressing Ctrl+Alt+N.
3. Type **Any amount not paid when due will bear interest at the rate of two percent (2%) per month, determined and compounded on a daily basis from the date due until the date paid.** and press Enter twice.
4. Type **Licensee shall not sub-license, sell, lend, rent, lease, or otherwise transfer all or any portion of the Premises to any third party.** Press Enter twice.
5. Select "two percent (2%)" in the first paragraph.
6. From the Insert menu, choose Comment. The Reviewing Pane appears at the bottom of the screen.

When a comment is inserted into a document, the Reviewing toolbar automatically appears.

To activate the Reviewing toolbar at any time, alternate-click on any toolbar and select Reviewing from the list of available toolbars.

7. Type the comment text **Lessor is willing to accept one and one-half percent interest compounded daily.**
8. Select "third party" in the second paragraph and choose Comment from the Insert menu.
9. Type the following comment text: **What exceptions, if any, should be offered to Lessee?** (See Figure 14.2.)
10. Using the vertical scrollbar on the right of the Reviewing Pane, scroll through the pane to reveal other information displayed in the pane (Header and Footer Changes, Text Box Changes, Header and Footer Text Box Changes, Footnote Changes, and Endnote Changes).
11. Close the Reviewing Pane by clicking on the top border of the Reviewing Pane and dragging it down to the bottom of the screen until the pane disappears.
12. Leave the document open for the next exercise.

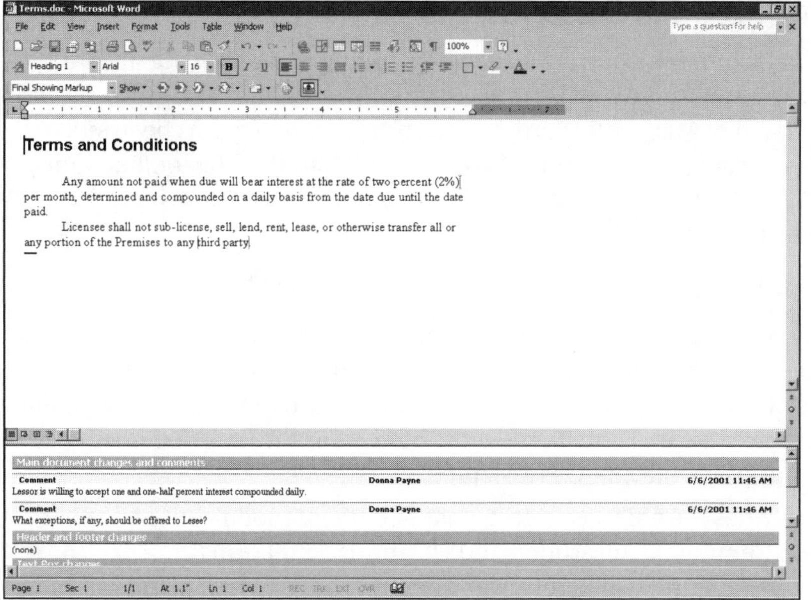

Figure 14.2

The Reviewing Pane displays the type of collaborative modification made in the document, noting who made the comment as well as the date and time it was made.

You can also close the Reviewing Pane by either double-clicking on the top of the Reviewing Pane or clicking the Reviewing Pane button located on the Reviewing toolbar.

The comment indicators appear in the text as nonprinting colored brackets surrounding the commented text. Hover your mouse pointer, without clicking, over the commented text in the document, and the comment appears in a shaded box. The color of the brackets and shaded box varies by author.

If the shaded comment box does not appear on the screen, the ScreenTips option is probably not activated. To activate the option, from the Tools menu, choose Options and select the View tab, then the ScreenTips option.

The comments will appear as ScreenTips only if there is an open and closed comment indicator. If text was not selected when the comment was inserted, the "I" bar indicator is displayed but you cannot view the comment with screen tips in this case.

REVIEWING TOOLBAR

The Reviewing toolbar is a powerful aid when editing and reviewing documents. This toolbar is where you will find many of the collaboration tools that make this version of Microsoft Word so powerful. The toolbar has been substantially improved from prior versions of Word. You'll find that the toolbar appears automatically when you activate any of the collaboration tools. Figure 14.3 shows the Reviewing toolbar.

Here is a brief description of the buttons on the Reviewing toolbar:

- **Display For Review**. Provides a variety of display options to view reviewer's marks or changes, which include document comments as well as tracked changes. Reviewers can view the original document, the original document with changes, the final document with changes, or the final document as it would appear with all changes accepted.
- **Show**. Provides the ability to select what document modifications appear onscreen: Comments, Insertions And Deletions, and Formatting. It also allows you to control which reviewer's changes are on view, display or hide the Reviewing Pane at the bottom of the screen, and display the Track Changes option settings.
- **Previous**. Displays the previous modification or comment (depending on the Show option settings).
- **Next**. Displays the next modification or comment (depending on the Show option settings).
- **Accept Change**. Accepts Track Change modifications; options include accepting the selected change, the changes shown, or all changes in the document.

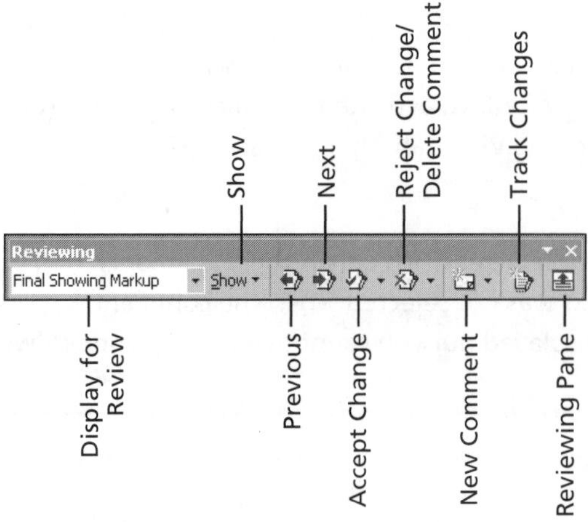

FIGURE 14.3

The Reviewing toolbar provides easy access to common collaboration tools, such as New Comment and Track Changes.

- **Reject Change/Delete Comment.** Rejects Track Change modifications or deletes document comments; options include ability to reject the selected change or delete the selected comment, reject all changes shown, reject all changes in the document, delete all comments shown, or delete all comments in the document.
- **New Comment.** Inserts a comment into the document; includes the ability to edit an existing comment, delete the selected comment, or insert a voice comment.
- **Track Changes.** Toggles the Track Changes feature on or off.
- **Reviewing Pane.** Toggles the Reviewing Pane on or off the bottom of the screen.

If you are reviewing a document that was sent to you using the Send To, Mail Recipient (For Review) command, you may also see a Reply With Changes button. This button is a quick way to send back to the sender a document that you have reviewed.

REVIEWER SCREENTIPS

As mentioned earlier, you can hover your mouse pointer over a document comment to display the ScreenTip. The ScreenTip includes the comment text, as well as the comment's author (whom Word calls a Reviewer), and the date and time the comment was inserted into the document. When you have several people working on the same document, it is important to make sure that all reviewers have the ScreenTip option selected. It is also important that each reviewer's name appear in the document comment. This information is obtained from the User Information tab of the Options dialog box found under Tools, Options.

Unless you've specifically selected the option to print comments, the brackets surrounding the commented text will not print; however, they will show on the screen regardless of whether the Show/Hide feature is activated.

VIEWING COMMENTS

There are several ways to view comments in a document. Two methods have already been discussed: the ScreenTip you get when you hover your mouse pointer over the comment in the text of the document and the Reviewing Pane located at the bottom of the screen. Print Layout and Web Layout views also provide another method for viewing comments. The comments appear in balloons in the margin of the document. The size and location of the balloon in the margin is specified under Tools, Options on the Track Changes tab. The next exercise gives you a look at the various viewing methods.

VIEWING COMMENTS

1. The document from the preceding exercise should still be open. Hover your mouse pointer over the text "two percent (2%)" and note the shaded box that appears containing the comment text.
2. On the Reviewing Toolbar, click the Reviewing Pane button (the far-right button on the toolbar) to view the comment in the Reviewing Pane at the bottom of the screen. Click the Reviewing Pane button again to close the pane.
3. Change the view of your document by choosing View, Web Layout. The comment appears in a balloon located in the right margin of the document.
4. Change the view of your document back to Normal by choosing View, Normal. The Comment balloon disappears.
5. Change the view of your document again by choosing View, Print Layout. The Comment balloon reappears.
6. Leave the document open for another exercise.

The Comment balloons appear with both the Web Layout and Print Layout views. If, at a minimum, the comment brackets aren't visible, you can choose Markup from the View menu to display them. However, keep in mind that you can quickly view all the comments in a document by activating the Reviewing Pane, which will place all the comments at the bottom of the screen, even in Web Layout and Print Layout views.

You can also choose to view all the comments in a document, or just the comments made by a selected individual or group of individuals. The different options for viewing comments by reviewer are found under the Show menu of the Reviewing toolbar, which is shown in Figure 14.4.

NOTE

Reviewers can respond directly to a document comment by clicking inside the comment and then choosing Insert, Comment, or clicking the New Comment button on the Reviewing toolbar.

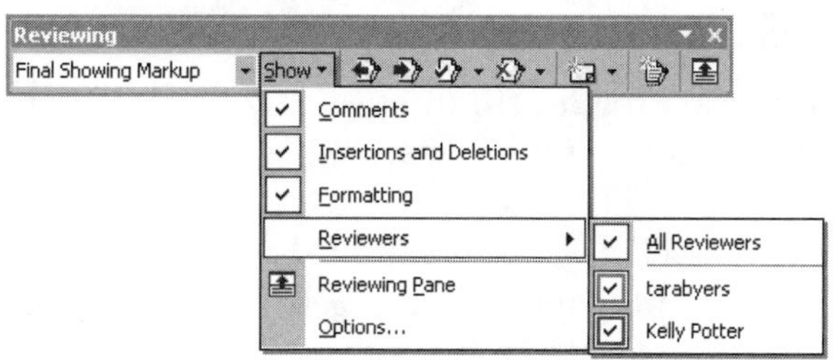

FIGURE 14.4

The Show, Reviewers option on the Reviewing toolbar allows you to review comments from an individual reviewer, a group of reviewers, or all comments in a document.

BROWSING BY COMMENTS

In addition to viewing all the comments at one time in the Reviewing Pane, there are other ways to view comments, such as browsing from comment to comment. The Browse Object on the vertical scrollbar offers the option to browse or move from one comment to the next. Click on the Browse Object and then select Browse By Comment, which is represented by a yellow sticky note graphic. This activates the Browse Object for comments so you can click on the blue double-arrows to scan through the document comment by comment. You can also use the Previous and Next buttons on the Reviewing toolbar to browse through the document by comment as well as by tracked changes.

BROWSING BY COMMENT

1. The document from the preceding exercise should still be open. Press Ctrl+Home to move to the top of the document and press Ctrl+Enter twice to insert two page breaks.
2. Press Ctrl+Home to move back to the top of the document.
3. Click the Browse Object button on the vertical scrollbar and select Browse By Comment to move to the first commented text in the document.

Keyboard users can press Ctrl+Alt+Home to activate the Browse Object menu.

4. Browse to the next comment by clicking Next Comment, or the downward-pointing double-headed arrow below the Browse Object.
5. Press Ctrl+Home to move back to the top of the document.
6. Click Next on the Reviewing toolbar to move to the first Comment balloon.
7. Click the Next button again to move to the second Comment balloon.

EDITING COMMENTS

Sometimes it is necessary to edit comment text, or even delete specific comments in a document. Comments can be easily edited through the Reviewing Pane, or by directly editing the comment text in the balloons in the margin while in Print Layout or Web Layout view. If the balloons are not visible, you can alternate-click on commented text (located between the colored brackets) in a document and choose Edit Comment from the shortcut menu.

To change the way comment text appears in balloons, click inside a balloon and then—from the Format menu—choose Styles And Formatting to activate the Styles And Formatting Task Pane. The Comment Text style appears in the Formatting Of Selected Text box. Click the drop-down arrow after the Comment Text style and select the option to modify the style.

DELETING COMMENTS

Now and then it becomes necessary to delete a comment or two. You will even find times when it is necessary to delete every single comment throughout the entire document. Prior to sending documents to anyone (co-workers, outside counsel, clients, or others), it's important to consciously evaluate who will be receiving the document and what information you want them to be able to see. Word documents include hidden information, sometimes referred to as *metadata,* which can include text deleted from the document, the names of the past 10 authors, and file locations, to mention a few of the types of information that may be available. For more information on metadata, please refer to Chapter 20, "Document Forensics." Comments can also be considered metadata. Word offers numerous ways to delete comments in a document, as shown in Figure 14.5.

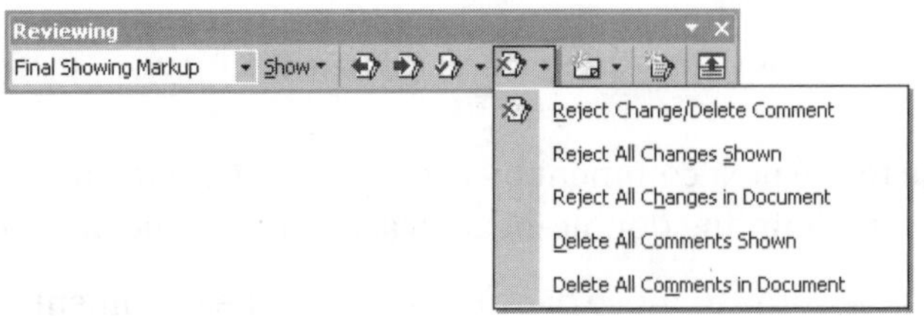

FIGURE 14.5

The Reject Change/Delete Comment menu offers a variety of choices regarding the deletion of changes and comments.

DELETING COMMENTS

1. The document from the preceding exercise should still be open. Switch to Normal view by choosing Normal from the View menu, or by using the keyboard shortcut Ctrl+Alt+N.
2. Alternate-click on the first text marked for comment ("two percent (2%)").

Commented text in the document is surrounded by brackets. If the comment brackets aren't visible, choose Markup from the View menu to display them.

3. From the shortcut menu, choose Delete Comment. Word removes the comment.
4. Press Ctrl+Z, or click the Undo button on the Standard toolbar to undelete the comment.
5. To remove the comment using a different method, click the Reject Change/Delete Comment button on the Reviewing toolbar.
6. Press Ctrl+Z, or click the Undo button on the Standard toolbar to undelete the comment.
7. Switch from Normal view to Print Layout view.
8. Alternate-click in the balloon of the first comment, and from the shortcut menu, choose Delete Comment.
9. Press Ctrl+Z, or click the Undo button on the Standard toolbar to undelete the comment.
10. To delete all the comments in the document at one time, click the drop-down arrow on the Reject Change/Delete Comment button and select Delete All Comments In Document.

PRINTING COMMENTS

By default, the option to print comments is not automatically selected when you install Word. This is a useful protection for a law firm—you wouldn't want comments about negotiation fallback positions, for example, to be presented to opponents who might otherwise agree to more favorable terms. You can activate the print option, when necessary, by choosing Print from the File menu.

NOTE

If you have the Warn Before Printing/Saving/Sending A File That Contains Track Changes Or Comments option activated under the Tools, Options, Security tab, you will need to click Yes to acknowledge that the document to be printed has comments.

From the Print What list, choose Document Showing Markup. This affects only the current document, not all documents.

NOTE

Comments are printed along with Track Changes. This is different from previous versions of Word where you could choose to print only comments from either the Print dialog box or Tools, Options.

FOOTNOTES AND ENDNOTES

Any type of document can hold a footnote or endnote, from common letters to legal briefs. Footnotes and endnotes are used to provide additional information and references related to information in the body of the document. Fortunately, inserting and modifying footnotes and endnotes is a piece of cake. Word automatically numbers them for you. If you add, move, or delete them, the numbers automatically change to fit the new situation.

NOTE

This chapter discusses footnotes for most of the examples regarding footnotes and endnotes. The two features function almost identically; however, where differences occur, we present specific instructions and options.

Footnotes and endnotes are made up of the components listed in Table 14.1.

TABLE 14.1 ELEMENTS OF A FOOTNOTE OR ENDNOTE

FEATURE	DESCRIPTION
Footnote or Endnote Reference Marks	These are usually numbers, but they can also be characters, or a combination of characters, that indicate that additional information is contained in a footnote or endnote.
Separator Line	Also referred to as the *Note Separator*, this is the short horizontal line that separates the body text of the document from footnotes and endnotes.
Footnote Text	The text of the footnote, which appears at the bottom of the page.
Endnote Text	The text of the endnote, which appears at the end of the document.

INSERTING FOOTNOTES AND ENDNOTES

Adding footnotes and endnotes could not be easier in Word. The footnotes and endnotes are automatically numbered as you insert them into the document. One exciting new feature is that you can use different number formats from one section to another. In this next exercise, you add footnotes to text created earlier in this chapter.

You can include both footnotes and endnotes so they appear in the same document, in the same section, or even on the same page.

INSERTING FOOTNOTES

1. The file from the preceding exercise should still be open. Switch to Normal view by pressing Ctrl+Alt+N, or from the View menu, choose Normal.
2. Place your insertion point after the word *daily* in the first sentence.
3. From the Insert menu, choose Reference, Footnote. The Footnote And Endnote dialog box opens, as shown in Figure 14.6, allowing you to insert a footnote. Alternatively, you can use the keyboard shortcut Ctrl+Alt+F.
4. Click Insert and add a footnote to the document via the Note Pane at the bottom of your screen.
5. Type **Lessor may be willing to consider option to compound on a weekly basis.**

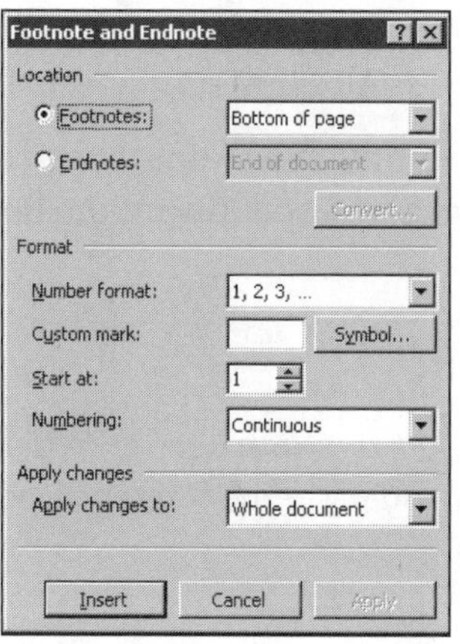

FIGURE 14.6

The Footnote And Endnote dialog box offers many options for controlling the location and look of your footnotes and endnotes.

6. Place your insertion point at the end of the first paragraph in the document text, immediately after the period.
7. Use the keyboard shortcut Ctrl+Alt+F to insert another footnote.

When you use shortcut keys to insert footnotes or endnotes, the dialog box does not open. This prevents you from being able to use a custom mark unless a custom mark has been used previously. If a custom mark has been used previously in the document, the shortcut key will activate the Footnote and Endnote dialog box so you can pick the custom mark.

8. Type **Based upon the prime rate.**
9. Place your insertion point after the word *Premises* in the second paragraph, and from the menu, choose Insert, Reference, Footnote to insert an endnote.

The keyboard shortcut to insert an endnote is Ctrl+Alt+D. Word 97 users may remember that pressing Ctrl+Alt+E inserted an endnote in that version of Word. However, in Word 2000 and 2002, Ctrl+Alt+E inserts the currency symbol for the Euro.

10. Under Location, select Endnote and click Insert to insert an endnote. The Note Pane appears.

When inserting both footnotes and endnotes into the same document, the Number Format automatically changes, so the reference marks will be different.

11. Type **Legal description of which is included in Exhibit A to this Agreement.**
12. Click Close on the Note Pane or press Alt+Shift+C to close the pane.
13. Switch to Print Layout view and examine the endnote appearing after the text of the document. View the footnote appearing at the bottom of its referenced page.

To move or copy a footnote or endnote, select the Note Reference Mark in the text of the document and then cut or copy and paste the reference mark in the new location.

CAUTION

If you use custom marks when formatting your number reference, keep in mind that they will not automatically update when you add, move, or delete the footnote or endnote.

VIEWING AND EDITING FOOTNOTES AND ENDNOTES

Footnotes appear differently depending on which view is active. In Print Layout view, the footnotes appear at the bottom of the page. You can even edit the text in Print Layout view. It is easier, however, to edit the footnote text through the Note Pane from Normal view.

MODIFYING A FOOTNOTE

1. The document from the preceding exercise should still be open. Switch to Normal view by pressing Ctrl+Alt+N, or from the View menu, choose Normal.
2. To edit a footnote or endnote, choose View, Footnotes.
3. When the document contains both footnotes and endnotes, the View Footnotes dialog box, as shown in Figure 14.7, appears. Select the View Footnote Area option, click OK, and the Note Pane will appear.
4. At the end of the footnote text, before the period, type **as determined from time to time**.
5. Click Close on the Note Pane.

TIP

Double-click the reference to switch back and forth between the Note Pane and the Note Reference in the document text.

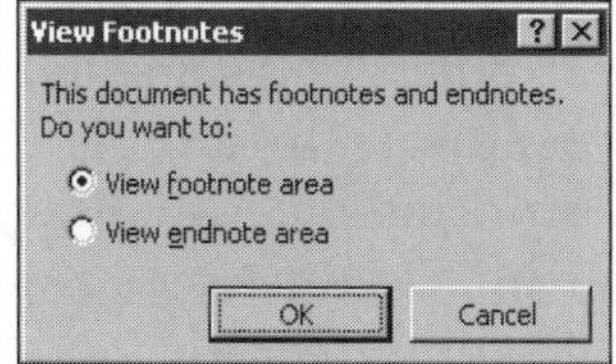

FIGURE 14.7

The View Footnotes dialog box appears only when you have both footnotes and endnotes in the same document.

MODIFYING THE NOTE SEPARATOR

There are two line separators, the Note Separator (which separates the document text from the footnotes at the bottom of the page) and the Note Continuation Separator (which appears when lengthy footnotes must be split between multiple pages). In the next exercise, you'll modify the line separators.

MODIFYING THE LINE SEPARATOR

1. The document from the preceding exercise should still be open. From the View menu, choose Normal.
2. From the View menu, choose Footnotes, and the Note Pane appears.

If the document contains both footnotes and endnotes, a message will appear asking whether you want to view the footnote area or the endnote area.

3. In the Footnotes box, select Footnote Separator from the drop-down list.
4. Delete the current separator and type *** **Footnote Begins Here** ***. Click Close to exit the Note Pane.

When you edit the Note Separator, you can use text or even clip art divider lines.

5. To view the Note Separator, switch back to Print Layout view.
6. Switch back to Normal view and choose View, Footnotes.
7. Select Footnote Separator from the drop-down list and click the Reset button to restore the default Note Separator.
8. Close the Note Pane.

BROWSING BY FOOTNOTES

Sometimes it is difficult to find the small Note Reference Mark in a page full of text. Or, when working collaboratively with others, it is sometimes necessary to jump quickly from one footnote or endnote to another. Word offers several ways to browse from one footnote or endnote to another. You can also view all footnotes or all endnotes at one time in the Notes Pane. In the next exercise, you use two of Word's Browse features to locate footnotes and endnotes in a document.

BROWSING BY FOOTNOTE OR ENDNOTE

1. The document from the preceding exercise should still be open. From the View menu, choose Normal.
2. From the View menu, choose Footnotes and click OK to view the footnotes.
3. In the Note Pane, choose All Footnotes from the Footnotes list. All the footnotes in the document appear so you can view or edit them.
4. Click Close on the Note Pane.
5. Press Ctrl+Home to move to the beginning of the document.
6. Click the Browse Object, or press Ctrl+Alt+Home to display the Browse Object icons.
7. Select either the Browse By Footnote icon or the Browse By Endnote icon to move through the document viewing each. Figure 14.8 shows the Browse Object icons.
8. Click the double-headed arrows above and below the Browse Object to move to the next or preceding footnote or endnote. Keyboard users can use Ctrl+Page Up or Ctrl+Page Down to move to the next or preceding footnote or endnote.

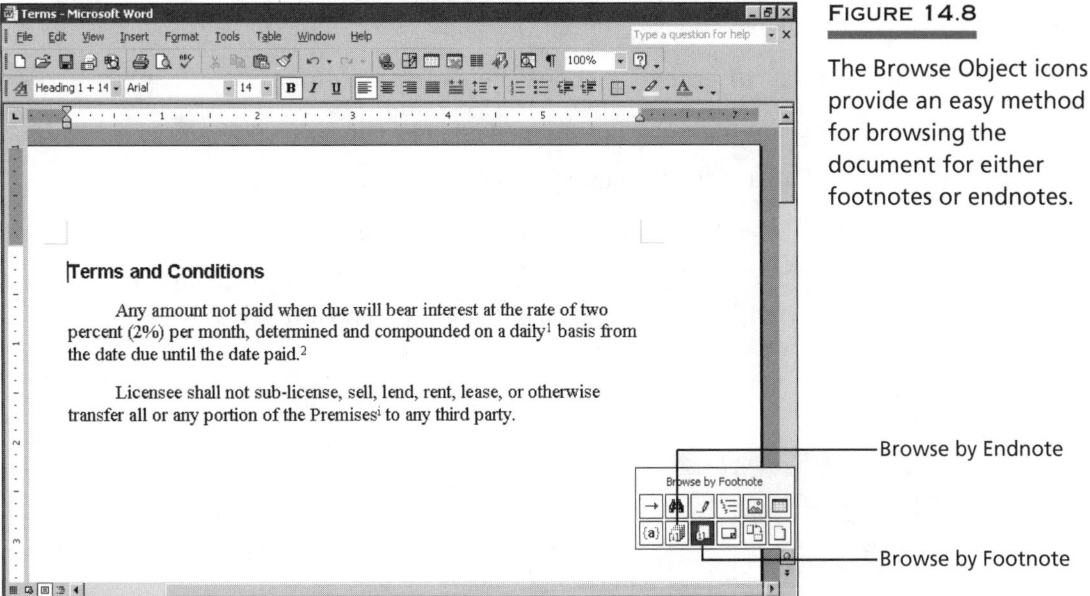

FIGURE 14.8

The Browse Object icons provide an easy method for browsing the document for either footnotes or endnotes.

When the double-headed arrows above and below the Browse Object are black, the Browse selection is set to Page. If any other Browse selection is activated, the arrows are blue.

DELETING FOOTNOTES AND ENDNOTES

If you need to delete a footnote or endnote, do not open the Note Pane and delete the text. The reference mark will remain in the document and the footnote at the bottom of the page will be empty. Instead, you must select and delete the reference mark in the text of the document; that will delete both the reference mark and the footnote or endnote text. When you delete a footnote or endnote reference mark, subsequent notes in the document automatically renumber.

CONVERTING FOOTNOTES AND ENDNOTES

Periodically, you may create a document with footnotes and have to convert them to endnotes, or vice versa. Word offers a conversion utility that will automatically convert selected footnotes or selected endnotes. You also have the option to switch the footnotes to endnotes while at the same time switching all endnotes to footnotes.

CONVERTING ALL NOTES

1. The document from the preceding exercise should still be open. From the View menu, choose Normal.
2. From the Insert menu, choose Reference, Footnote.
3. In the Footnote And Endnote dialog box, click Convert.
4. The Convert Notes dialog box shown in Figure 14.9 opens.
5. Select Swap Footnotes And Endnotes and click OK.
6. Click Close on the Footnote And Endnote dialog box; all the endnotes convert to footnotes, and all the footnotes convert to endnotes.

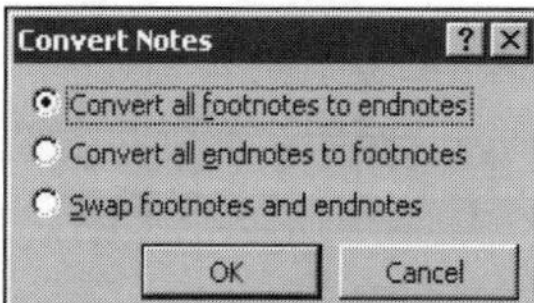

FIGURE 14.9

The Convert Notes dialog box offers several choices for converting notes in the active document.

7. From the Insert menu, choose Reference, Footnote. Click Convert.
8. Select Convert All Endnotes To Footnotes and click OK.
9. Click Close on the Footnote And Endnote dialog box, and all the endnotes convert to footnotes.
10. From the Insert menu, choose Reference, Footnote.
11. In the Footnote And Endnote dialog box, click Convert, and the Convert Notes dialog box opens.
12. Select Convert All Footnotes To Endnotes and click OK.
13. Click Close on the Footnote And Endnote dialog box, and all the footnotes convert to endnotes.

You don't have to convert all the notes in a document. You can also convert individual notes one at a time.

CONVERTING SELECTED NOTES

1. The document from the preceding exercise should still be open. From the View menu, choose Normal.
2. From the View menu, choose Footnotes. This option will also allow you to view endnotes.
3. From the Notes Pane, alternate-click on an endnote.
4. From the shortcut menu, select Convert To Footnote, and the selected endnote converts to a footnote.

HYPERLINKS

With the influx of Internet and intranet Web sites, many people are familiar with hyperlinks. Well, the actual term *hyperlink* may not be that well known, but the function of the hyperlink is. Mention the colored, underlined words that you click on to go to a different area of a Web site or a completely different site, and you will see heads nod with understanding.

A hyperlink is an object, text or otherwise, that directs you to a document, Internet Web site, or e-mail address. When used in a Word document, a hyperlink can direct the reader to a different document, another part of the same document, or a Web site, or it can start an e-mail message.

In order for links to the Internet to work, you must have access to the Internet through a Web browser, such as Internet Explorer or Netscape Navigator.

Imagine sending a firm profile to a client where clicking on a hyperlink brings the client directly to your firm's Web site. It is also a great way to direct a new or temporary employee to current files. Rather than spending a lot of time training the employee on the network and file structure, create a document with hyperlinks to the documents that will be edited.

INSERT A HYPERLINK

1. Create a new blank document.
2. From the Insert menu, choose Hyperlink, or press Ctrl+K. The Insert Hyperlink dialog box opens, as shown in Figure 14.10.
3. Select Existing File Or Web Page under Link To.
4. In the Text To Display field, type the text that you wish to display for the hyperlink.

Text To Display is a great feature—it allows you to give a name to the location rather than show the user the complete path name to the file.

5. Click ScreenTip, enter the text that should appear when the mouse pointer hovers over the hyperlink, and click OK.
6. Navigate to the location of the document for the hyperlink.
7. Select the document and click OK. The hyperlink is inserted into the document.

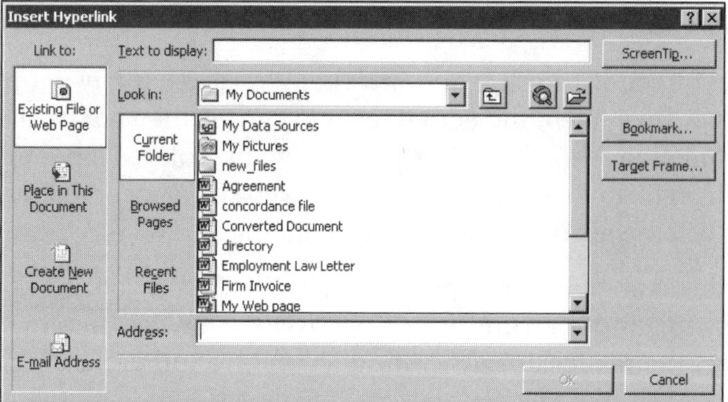

FIGURE 14.10

Select the type of hyperlink you wish to insert.

8. Click on the hyperlink to access the document.

NOTE

If clicking on the hyperlink does not open the document, try holding the Ctrl key down while you click. Word 2002 has an option called Use Ctrl+Click To Follow The Hyperlink. With this turned on, you cannot just click on a link—and you won't head off into cyberspace without warning if you accidentally click on one. This option is found in the Edit tab from Tools, Options.

9. Press Ctrl+F6 to go back to the document that contains the hyperlink.

NOTE

When the hyperlink has been viewed, the color of the hyperlink will change from blue to purple. This is controlled by the Hyperlink and Followed Hyperlink styles.

OTHER HYPERLINK CHOICES

In the preceding exercise, the hyperlink was linked to an existing file or Web page. These are the other options available in the Insert Hyperlink dialog box:

- **Place In This Document.** Select a location within the current document for the hyperlink. This can be bookmarked text or a heading.
- **Create New Document.** If you are planning to create something new for the hyperlink, this is the choice. Once the new document is created, you can edit it at any time.
- **E-Mail Address.** Insert an e-mail address hyperlink, which will activate a new message to the addressee when clicked.

BOOKMARKS

When you read a book and need to mark the place where you left off, you can insert a bookmark. Word includes the same functionality. Once a bookmark is added, you can use Go To (F5 or Ctrl+G) to navigate to the specific bookmark position. Note that although the Go To dialog box defaults to asking for a page number, you can simply type in a bookmark name instead of a page number and go straight to the bookmark; there's no need to change the Go To What list selection first.

From the Insert menu, choose Bookmark. Type a name for the bookmark that does not start with a numeric value or include any spaces and click Add. Bookmarks are extremely useful but often underutilized in legal documents.

CROSS REFERENCES

Cross references occur in a document when you want to refer the reader to another location in your document. For example, on the first page of a brief, the text might appear: "For more information, see Page 14." This is a cross reference. With all the editing legal documents go through, however, internal cross references become very difficult to maintain by hand because the referenced page numbers keep changing. Word simplifies the process by keeping track of the page numbers for you.

Cross references are easy to insert, and you can insert a cross reference to almost anything in Word. Some of the things that you can insert a cross reference to include a numbered item, heading, bookmark, footnote, endnote, equation, figure, or table.

INSERT A CROSS REFERENCE

1. Open a document that contains automatic paragraph numbering.
2. Position your insertion point where the cross reference should appear.
3. Type **For more information, see** and press the Spacebar.
4. From the Insert menu, choose Reference, Cross-Reference. The Cross Reference dialog box opens, as shown in Figure 14.11.
5. Choose Numbered Item from Reference Type.
6. Select the numbered item you wish to reference from the list that appears under For Which Numbered Item.
7. From the Insert Reference To drop-down list, choose Paragraph Number (Full Context).

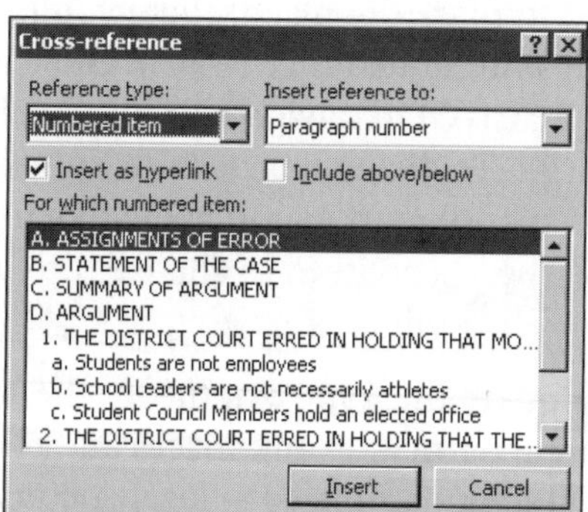

FIGURE 14.11

Choose the type of reference and how it should appear. Cross references can even be formatted as hyperlinks.

NOTE

There are three choices for paragraph numbering in the Insert Reference To box. Table 14.2 describes these three options.

8. Click Insert.
9. Click Close.

TIP

By default, the cross reference is inserted as a hyperlink. Click on the cross reference to be directed to the referenced location.

NOTE

Cross-reference fields do not update automatically when the document is edited. To update a cross reference, select it and press F9. Alternatively, you can update all fields in the document at one time by pressing Ctrl+A to select the entire document and then pressing F9 to update.

TABLE 14.2 PARAGRAPH NUMBER CROSS-REFERENCE OPTIONS

REFERENCE TYPE	DESCRIPTION
Paragraph Number	The cross reference is inserted relative to the position of the current paragraph. For example, if the reference being inserted is paragraph III.C.3 and it is being inserted into paragraph III.C, it will appear as paragraph 3. If the cross reference is being inserted into II.A.1, it will appear as III.C.3.
Paragraph Number (No Context)	The paragraph number will be inserted without consideration for the position. Using the same example, it would always be paragraph 3.
Paragraph Number (Full Context)	The paragraph number will be inserted without consideration for the position. Using the same example, it would always be paragraph III.C.3. This is the most commonly used option since there is never a question where the reference is located.

CAPTIONS

Have you worked with patent applications or other long documents full of pictures, diagrams, or tables? Word's Caption command inserts a caption above or below these types of objects. The captions contain a label indicating the type of object and also include caption numbers to easily track and cross-reference the object.

ATTACH A CAPTION TO A TABLE

1. Create a new document.
2. Insert a small table.
3. From the Insert menu, choose Reference, Caption. The Caption dialog box opens, as shown in Figure 14.12.
4. From Position, select Above The Selected Object (or Below The Selected Object, if you prefer) to indicate where the caption should appear.
5. Click Numbering, choose the type of numbering to be used in the caption, and then click OK.
6. Press the Spacebar and type **Product Comparison** after "Table 1" in the Caption field.
7. If desired, choose a different Label from the drop-down list, or click New Label to create a new one.
8. Click OK to insert the caption. It appears as shown in Figure 14.13.

AUTOCAPTION

If you are inserting a large number of captions in a document, as is the case with chapters in books, patent applications, or other documents, you may want to use the AutoCaption option to instruct Word to automatically add a caption to specified object types. When AutoCaption is selected, every time that type of object is inserted into the document, a caption is inserted as well.

From the Insert menu, choose Reference, Caption. Click AutoCaption. Select the type of object to add an AutoCaption to from the AutoCaption dialog box, as shown in Figure 14.14. If necessary, choose the New Label and Numbering options then click OK.

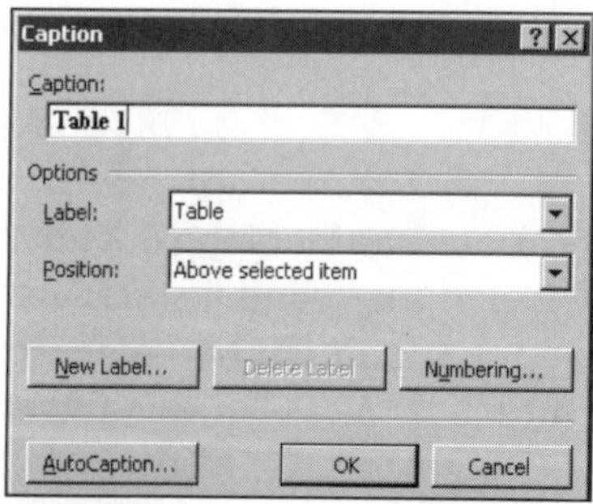

FIGURE 14.12

Captions provide general information to the reader as well as cross-referencing and tabling ability for the document author.

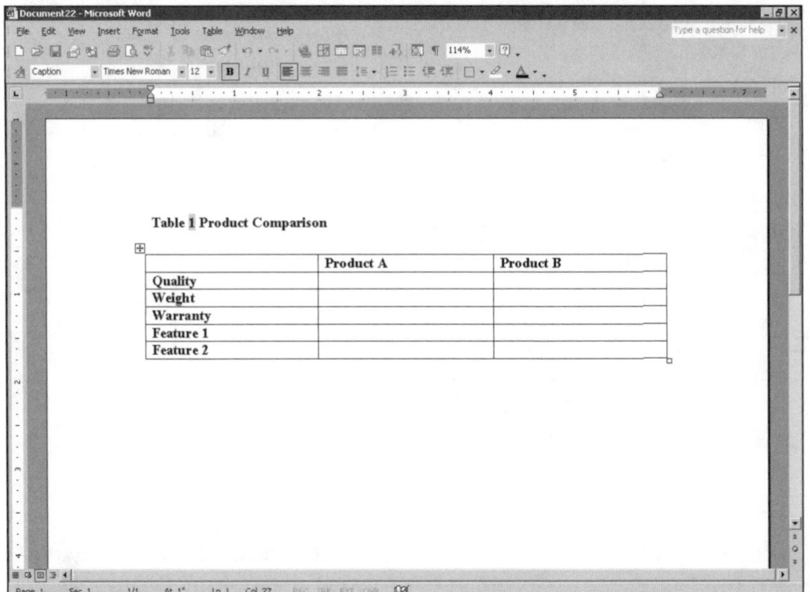

FIGURE 14.13

Captions can appear above or below an object.

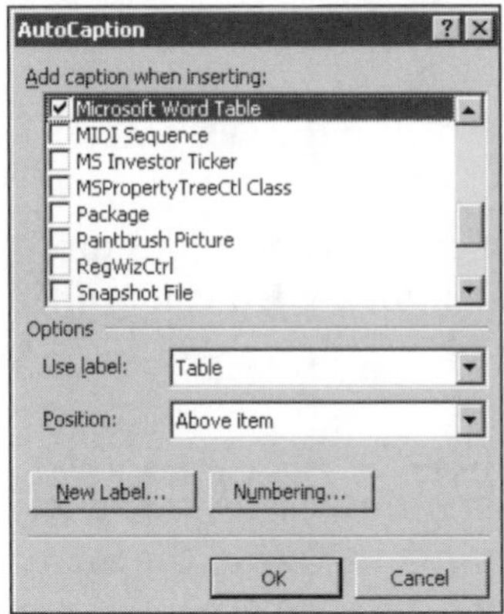

FIGURE 14.14

Check marks indicate which object types will automatically have a caption inserted.

To remove the AutoCaption, follow the same steps as outlined in the preceding example, but uncheck the object so AutoCaption no longer occurs.

TABLES OF FIGURES

The largest benefit to using captions is the ability to generate a list of the captioned items. This could be a Table of Tables, a Table of Figures, or any other label used in a caption.

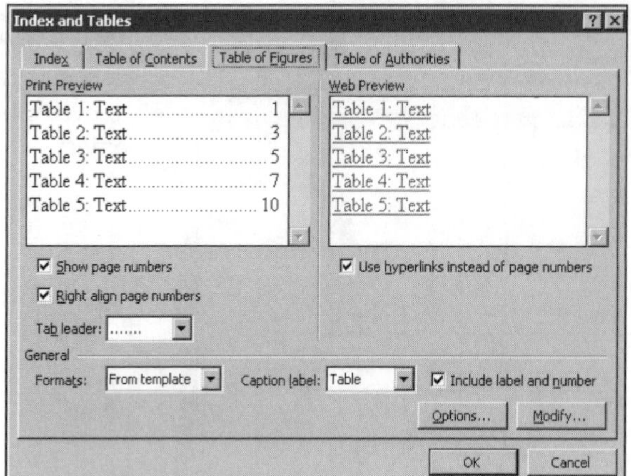

FIGURE 14.15

Generate a list of the figures, tables, or other objects within seconds.

To insert a Table of Figures, place your insertion point where you want the table to appear. From the Insert menu, choose Reference, Index And Tables. Select the Table of Figures tab, as shown in Figure 14.15. Select the desired options and click OK.

TABLES OF CONTENTS

As a document grows longer, the need for a table of contents becomes more apparent. Creating a table of contents in Word is straightforward, if you format the document with styles.

USING STYLES FOR A TABLE OF CONTENTS

Styles are the preferred method for formatting documents. One of the many benefits to using styles is the way they speed up creating the table of contents. If you use styles to format headings, the table of contents can be generated by anyone within seconds.

CREATE A TABLE OF CONTENTS USING STYLES

1. From the CD-ROM, open Brief.doc. Notice that the headings in the document have been formatted with styles.
2. Place the insertion point in the Table of Contents page, where the table should be inserted.
3. From the Insert menu, choose Reference, Index And Tables.

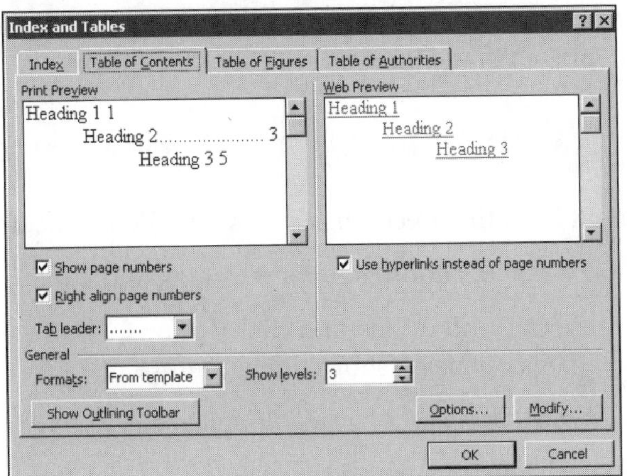

FIGURE 14.16

Select from a variety of formatting options when inserting the table of contents.

4. Select the Table Of Contents tab to display the available options, as shown in Figure 14.16.
5. From the Formats drop-down list, choose From Template.

NOTE

Each Format choice has a distinct look for the table of contents. The From Template option will format the table of contents using the TOC styles that exist in the template used to create the document.

6. Select 3 from Show Levels. This will insert all topics marked with Heading styles 1 through 3 only.
7. Click OK to insert the table of contents.
8. Save the document and keep it open for the next exercise.

Not everyone uses Word's Heading 1 through Heading 9 styles, exclusively, for their document headings. You can manually mark table of contents entries, then choose the Table Entry Fields option in the Index And Tables dialog box, or use the Outlining toolbar to assign a level to the text.

USE CUSTOM STYLES IN THE TABLE OF CONTENTS

Did you format your document using styles other than Word's built-in Heading styles? Creating a table of contents is still quick—just tell Word which styles to use to generate the table. This is accomplished through the Options button on the Table of Contents tab in the Index And Tables dialog box.

USE A CUSTOM STYLE IN THE TABLE OF CONTENTS

1. The document from the preceding exercise should still be open.
2. From the Insert menu, choose Reference, Index And Tables.
3. Select the Table Of Contents tab and click Options. The Table Of Contents Options dialog box opens, as shown in Figure 14.17.
4. Locate Heading from the list of available styles.
5. In the TOC Level field, type **1** and click OK.
6. Click OK to update the table of contents.
7. Click Yes when prompted to replace the selected table of contents.
8. The text formatted with Heading style should now appear in the table of contents.

Any changes made to options in the Table Of Contents Options dialog box will apply to the current table of contents. Each time you generate the table of contents through the Index And Tables dialog box, you will need to reselect the options even from within the same document because the old TOC is replaced with a new TOC. To prevent this, you can update the table of contents by alternate-clicking the table of contents, pressing F9, or clicking Update TOC on the Outlining toolbar.

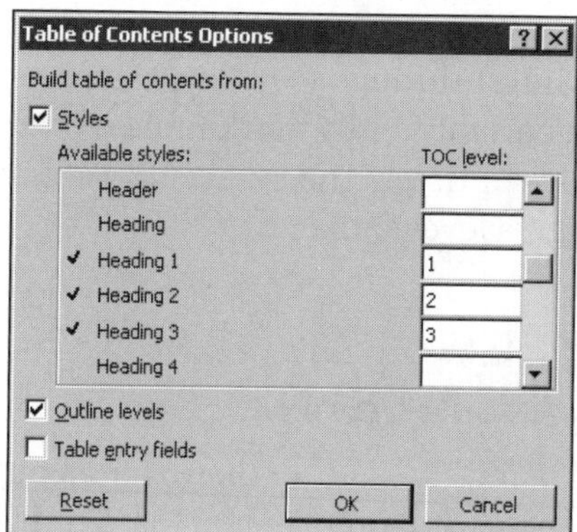

FIGURE 14.17

Styles used in the document appear in the dialog box. Type a heading level number in TOC Level next to the custom style and click OK. Text formatted with the custom style will appear in the table of contents.

USING THE OUTLINING TOOLBAR

There is a new feature in Word that allows you to display a toolbar, select text to appear in the table of contents, assign it a level, and have Word insert this text in the table of contents. By doing so, you can place specific paragraphs into the table of contents without having to apply a heading style or manually mark them.

To access the Outlining toolbar, alternate-click on any toolbar and select Outlining. The toolbar appears, as shown in Figure 14.18.

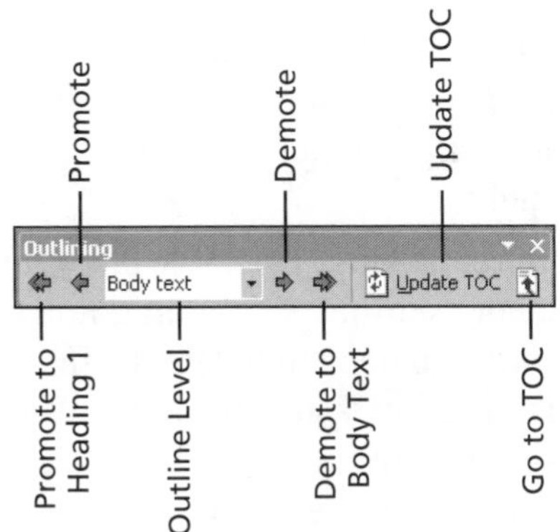

FIGURE 14.18

Set outline levels for paragraphs, update the table of contents, or go to the table of contents from the Outlining toolbar.

CREATE A TABLE OF CONTENTS FROM OUTLINE LEVELS

1. The document from the preceding exercise should still be open. Display the Outlining toolbar.
2. Select the italicized "Assignments of Error" paragraph.
3. From the Outline Level drop-down list, select Level 2.
4. Apply Level 2 to "Issues Pertaining to Assignments of Error."
5. Click Update TOC to add these new entries to the table of contents. The Update TOC dialog box opens, as shown in Figure 14.19.

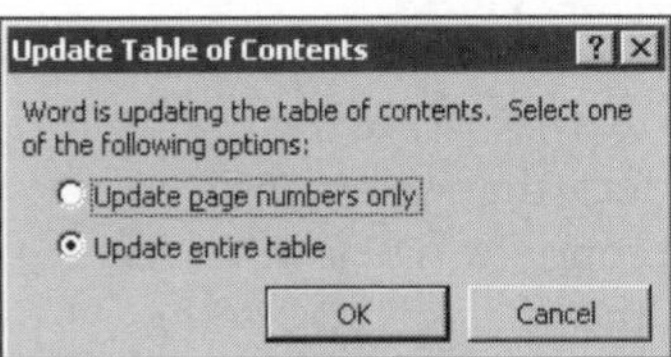

FIGURE 14.19

Choose Update Entire Table to ensure text and page numbers are both updated.

6. Click Update Entire Table and click OK.
7. Click Go To TOC. The entries that you just added should now appear in the table of contents.

MARKING TABLE ENTRY FIELDS MANUALLY

The least desirable method for generating a table of contents is to use table entry fields. There are two very good reasons to think twice about using the manually marked table entry field method:

- **Paragraph Numbering is not included**. Word's Mark Table of Contents Entry feature picks up text only, no formatting. If the paragraph you are marking contains an automatic paragraph number, you will need to manually type it into the table entry field.
- **Any changes to text will require remarking**. The table entry fields do not change when the text changes. For example, if the paragraph changes from "Introduction" to "Overview," you will need to delete the first table entry field and insert a new one. This can be catastrophic if the text has not changed but the number has—every numbered paragraph's table entry field after the change will need to be modified as well.

MANUALLY MARK TABLE OF CONTENTS ENTRIES

1. Create a new document.
2. Click the Numbering button on the Formatting toolbar.
3. Type **Introduction** and press Enter.
4. Press Tab, type **Definitions**, and press Enter.
5. Press Shift+Tab, type **Summary of Facts**, and press Enter.
6. Type **Conclusion**.
7. Select Introduction and press Alt+Shift+O to open the Mark Table Of Contents Entry dialog box shown in Figure 14.20.

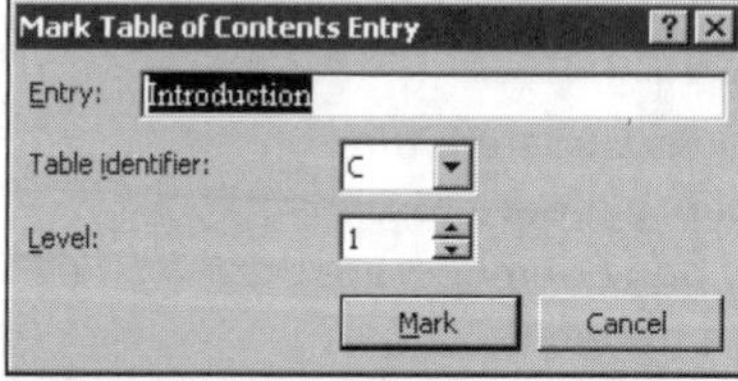

FIGURE 14.20

Verify that the text is correct, then select the appropriate TOC level for the selected TOC entry.

8. Click in front of "Introduction" in the Entry box and type **1.** followed by two spaces.
9. Choose 1 from the Level drop-down list.
10. Click Mark to mark the entry.
11. Select the Definitions paragraph and click in the Mark Table Of Contents Entry dialog box, or press Alt+Shift+O to open it.

TIP

You can leave the Mark Table Of Contents Entry dialog box open as you mark entries. Just click outside the dialog box, select the text, and click back in the dialog box to activate it again.

12. Click in front of "Definitions" in the Entry field. Type **a.** followed by two spaces.
13. Choose 2 under Level and click Mark.
14. Mark "Summary of Facts" and "Conclusion" as Level 1 entries. Be sure to include the paragraph number and correct level.
15. Click Close on the Table Of Contents Mark Entry dialog box.
16. Press Ctrl+End to go to the bottom of the document and insert a page break by pressing Ctrl+Enter.
17. From the Insert menu, choose Reference, Index And Tables, and select the Table Contents tab.
18. Click Options.
19. Select Table Entry Fields to instruct Word to use the entries in your document for the table of contents.
20. Click OK twice to insert the table.

UPDATING THE TABLE OF CONTENTS

As edits are made to the document, the table of contents will not reflect the changes until the table has been updated.

There are four ways to update a table of contents:

- Alternate-click on the table of contents and choose Update Field from the shortcut menu.

- Place your insertion point in the table of contents and press F9.
- Click Update TOC on the Outlining toolbar.
- From the Tools menu, choose Options and select the Print tab. Check Update Fields.

FORMATTING THE TABLE OF CONTENTS

The first thing to remember is that the table of contents is a field. If you edit the results, the manually entered information does not stick. For this reason, typing anything in a field—even pressing Enter while the insertion point is in the field—is not a good idea.

The second thing to remember when working with a table of contents is that when the table is generated, each level is formatted with the corresponding TOC style. For example, Level 1 entries are formatted with TOC 1, Level 2 with TOC 2, and so on. The TOC styles are the only styles in Word that have Automatically Update Style turned on by default.

Therefore, if you want to change the look of your table of contents, you should update the TOC styles. This will ensure that any changes you make will remain after updating and printing.

CHANGE THE FORMAT OF THE TABLE OF CONTENTS

1. The document from the preceding exercise should still be open.
2. Go to the table of contents.
3. Click in the "Statement of Cases" paragraph.

NOTE

By default, Word inserts the table of contents with a hyperlink to the specified pages. When this is in effect, it is difficult to click within the Table of Contents field. To change this behavior so Word still treats the field as a hyperlink but allows you to click within the field, from the Tools menu, choose Options and select the Edit tab. Check the Use Ctrl+Click To Follow Hyperlink option and then click OK.

4. From the Format menu, choose Paragraph.
5. Type **12** in the After box and click OK.
6. Notice all TOC 1 paragraphs are formatted with 12 points of space after.

INNER PARAGRAPH STYLES

For years, law firms have requested the ability to type text to be included in the table of contents and have it appear on the same line as text not to be included in the table of contents. For example:

> **1. Heading for Table of Contents**. This is non-heading text and should not appear in the table of contents. This is non-heading text and should not appear in the table of contents.

It seems like such a simple thing to do—but until this version, firms had to resort to various and sometimes strange methods to accomplish it.

HIDDEN PARAGRAPH MARK

By far the most common workaround to having text appear on the same line as information to be included in the table of contents has been the old hidden paragraph trick. Here, text would be entered and formatted with a heading style on one line. Next, the user would press Enter to create a new and distinct paragraph formatted with a nonheading style, and then select the paragraph mark separating the two paragraphs and format it as hidden text. That way, when Show/Hide was turned off, the text appeared on the same line. This was kludgey, but it worked.

Since most law firms needed to have text formatted in this manner, many sought to make the process easier by writing a macro to automate this step. Additionally, to differentiate hidden paragraphs from normal paragraphs, many firms also chose to format the hidden paragraph mark as red.

Some third-party vendors have products that help to generate tables of contents. This can cause problems when the utilities do not use native Word and attempt to introduce other elements for controlling the table of contents. The biggest problem is that clients, who do not have the same macro package will have difficulty when it is necessary to update or generate a table of contents from a revised document.

STYLE SEPARATOR

Want proof that Microsoft listened to law firms? The new Style Separator feature in Word provides an answer to the table of contents problem. Using this feature, text for the table of contents can exist on the same line as non-TOC text, without your having to manually hide paragraph marks. The addition of this feature is a direct result of Microsoft's working closely with the Legal Advisory Council.

The Style Separator does not appear by default on any toolbar or menu command. However, it can be added quickly. From the View menu, choose Toolbars, Customize. Select the Commands tab. Under Categories, select All Commands; under Commands, select InsertStyleSeparator and drag it to a toolbar or menu.

The keyboard shortcut for the Style Separator is Ctrl+Alt+Enter.

The Style Separator exercise assumes that you've installed the appropriate button on a toolbar or menu.

USE STYLE SEPARATOR

1. Create a new document.
2. Type **Agreement.** and apply Heading 1 style to the text.
3. With the insertion point still within the text, click the Style Separator button. Word automatically inserts something that looks just like a hidden paragraph mark, but—unlike a manually marked hidden paragraph—the following text always appears on the same line even when Show/Hide is enabled.
4. Type **This text will not appear in the table of contents.** and press Enter.
5. Type **Definitions.** and apply the Heading 2 style by pressing Ctrl+Alt+2.
6. Click Style Separator and then type **My text will appear here but not in the table of contents.**
7. Press Enter.
8. From the Insert menu, choose Reference, Index And Tables.
9. Select the Table Of Contents tab and click OK. Text formatted with heading styles are inserted into the Table of Contents field. Text that appears after the Style Separator is not included. The result is shown in Figure 14.21.

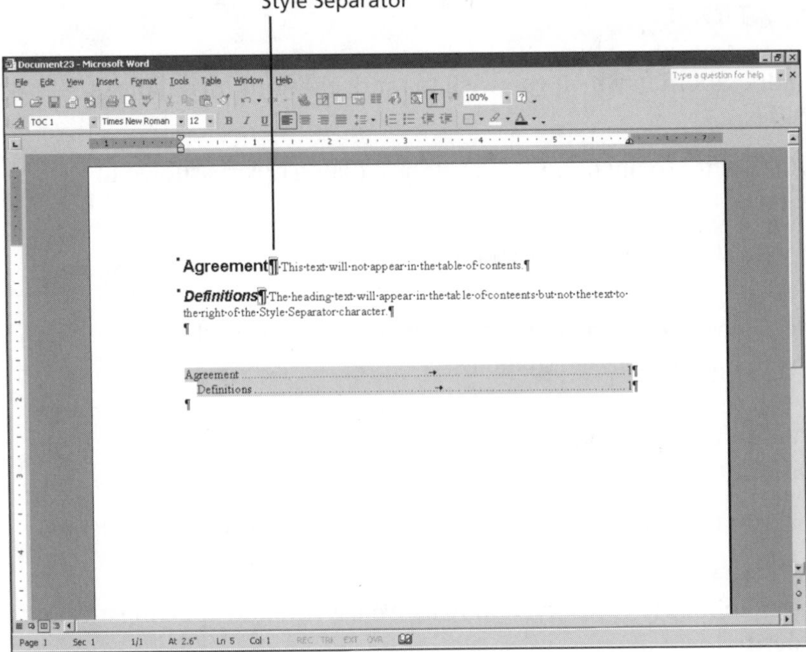

FIGURE 14.21

The Style Separator is Microsoft's reply to one of the most common requests from people constructing legal documents.

TABLES OF AUTHORITIES

Word's Table of Authorities command will help mark and generate a list of cases, statutes, and rules of legal documents. Citations are marked and then compiled into the table of authorities.

MARKING CITATIONS

Rather than spending a lot of time searching for citations in the document, you can use Word's Mark Citation dialog box to move directly from one citation to the next.

There are certain terms that Word looks for when searching for a citation: *in re, v., Id., Supra, bid, Infra, Cong.* (for Congress), *Sess.* (for Session), *(19xx)* (to find dates in parentheses; x is any number) and ¶. Word also stops at short forms of citations that are not marked.

When marking the citations, you can mark both long and short citations at the same time. The long citations form will appear in the table of authorities, along with the page numbers of their corresponding short form citations.

MARK CITATIONS

1. Open a document in which you wish to mark citations for a table of authorities.
2. Press Alt+Shift+I to open the Mark Citation dialog box, as shown in Figure 14.22.
3. Click Next Citation to search for citations.

Word may select noncitation text during its search. If this happens, click Next Citation again until you find a valid citation.

4. When Word finds a citation, click in the document and select the text of the citation.
5. Click back in the dialog box. The selected text will appear in the Selected Text box.
6. Edit the citation, as necessary, removing excess text and applying formats where desired.

Use shortcut keys to apply formats within the dialog box. For example, select the case name and press Ctrl+U to underline it.

7. Edit the Short Citation text to match the short form cites in your document.

Various forms of the short citations can appear in the document. It is important to review the document so you can include the correct short form cite(s) for each citation. This will make using Mark All to find short citations easier and more reliable.

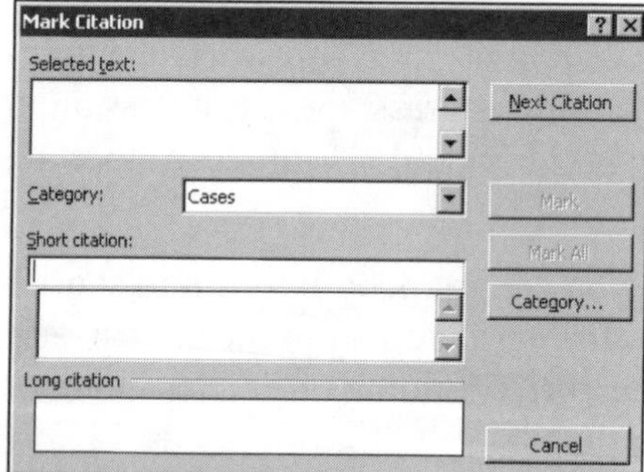

FIGURE 14.22

Click Next Citation to have Word search for citation-type terms.

8. Select the Category and select the type of citation or reference.
9. Click Mark All to mark the long citation and all the corresponding short form citations within the document.
10. Repeat steps 3 through 9 to mark the rest of the citations.
11. Leave this document open for the next exercise.

GENERATING THE TABLE OF AUTHORITIES

The Index And Tables dialog box offers format options for inserting a table of authorities from the marked entries. Now that you have marked the table of authorities entries, you can generate the table of authorities.

INSERT THE TABLE OF AUTHORITIES

1. The document from the previous exercise should still be open.
2. Place your insertion point where you want the table of authorities to be inserted (usually immediately after the table of contents).
3. Turn off Show/Hide.

Hidden text must be turned off so the document paginates properly—otherwise, the page numbers may not be accurate in the table of authorities.

4. From the Insert menu, choose Reference, Index And Tables and select the Table Of Authorities tab, as shown in Figure 14.23.

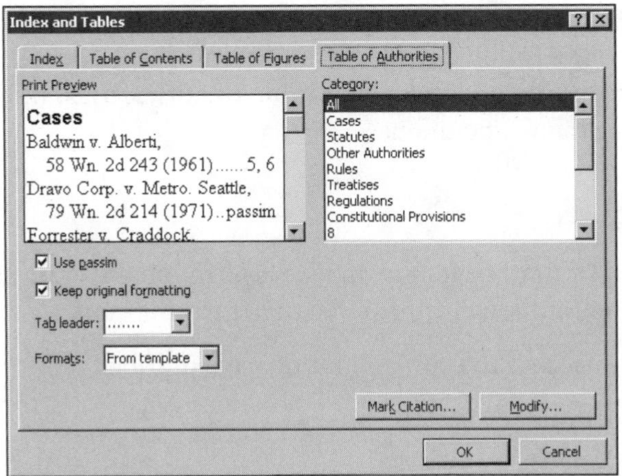

FIGURE 14.23

Select which categories to include in the Table of Authorities.

5. Uncheck Use Passim.

When Passim is selected, if a citation is referenced on more than five pages, the page numbers won't be listed in the table of authorities. Instead, the word *Passim* will appear.

6. Click All from Category. This will include all categories in the table of authorities. Select Individual.
7. Select other options, as needed.
8. Click OK to insert the table of authorities.

UPDATING THE TABLE OF AUTHORITIES

You can update a table of authorities with similar methods used for updating tables of contents: Select the table, alternate-click, and press F9, or turn on Update Fields from the Tools, Options, Print tab.

As you continue to edit the document, more citations may be inserted and others deleted. To add new citations, mark the citation as shown in the preceding exercise. If new short citations are added, select the existing long citation, press Alt+Shift+I, and click Mark All.

To delete an entry from the table of authorities, find the TA field in the document and delete it. The changes will be reflected when you update the table of authorities.

INDEX

An index is a set of words, phrases, topics, and references contained within the document. Once the index entries have been marked, you can maintain the index much like a table of contents or table of authorities, updating it when changes are made to the document.

MARKING

Index entries can be marked in one of two ways: manually or by using a concordance file. An index entry will appear in one of three formats:

- A word or phrase and the corresponding page number

- A subject matter and the corresponding page range in which it appears
- A word or phrase referencing another index entry

INDEX ENTRIES

To mark an index entry, select the text that you wish to mark and press Alt+Shift+X to open the Mark Index Entry dialog box.

MARK INDEX ENTRIES

1. The document from the preceding exercise should still be open.
2. Select the word *Error* at the beginning of the brief.
3. Press Alt+Shift+X. The selected text appears in the Mark Index Entry dialog box, as shown in Figure 14.24.
4. From Options, choose Current Page.
5. If desired, choose the Page Number format to be Bold or Italic.
6. Click Mark All to mark all the entries in the document.

If the entry appears throughout the document, click Mark All to mark all entries at once. Mark will affect only the current entry.

7. Select "Assignments of Error."

You can leave the Mark Index Entry dialog box open as you mark entries. Just click outside the dialog box, select the text, and click back in the dialog box to activate it again.

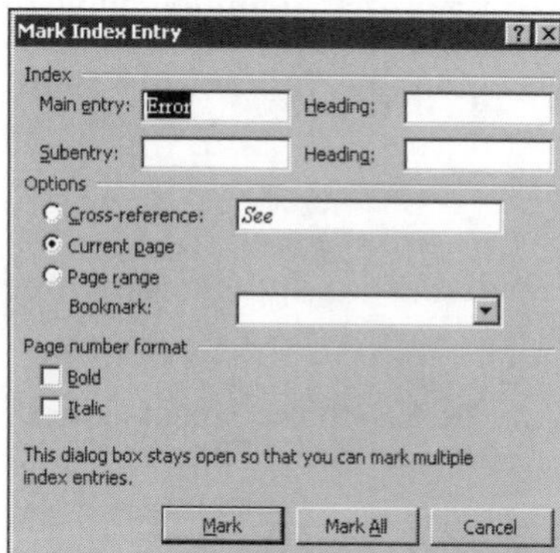

FIGURE 14.24

The index entry can reference a page number, another index entry, or a range of pages.

8. Click on the Mark Index Entry dialog box, or press Alt+Shift+X.
9. From Options, choose Cross-Reference.
10. After "See," type **Errors.**
11. Click Mark All.

NOTE

Index entries appear as fields in the document that look like this: {XE "entry"}. The text within the quotation marks is what will appear in the index. If you do not see the fields, click Show/Hide to view hidden text.

12. Mark a few more entries.
13. Leave this document open for the next exercise.

CONCORDANCE FILES

A concordance file is a list of words that need to be marked within the document. A concordance file is ideal when more than one person is working on a document. One person can create a concordance file while the other person is editing the document. When completed, the concordance file is used to mark the index entries.

To create a concordance file, insert a two-column table into a new document. The first column will contain the words and phrases that Word should search for. The second column will contain the corresponding index entry.

Once the concordance file is created, use Word's AutoMark command to mark the index entries in the document.

USE A CONCORDANCE FILE TO MARK INDEX ENTRIES

1. The document from the preceding exercise should still be open.
2. From the Insert menu, choose Reference, Index And Tables. Select the Index tab.
3. Click AutoMark.
4. The Open Index AutoMark File dialog box appears, as shown in Figure 14.25.
5. Navigate to the exercise files on the CD-ROM. Select Concordance File and click Open.

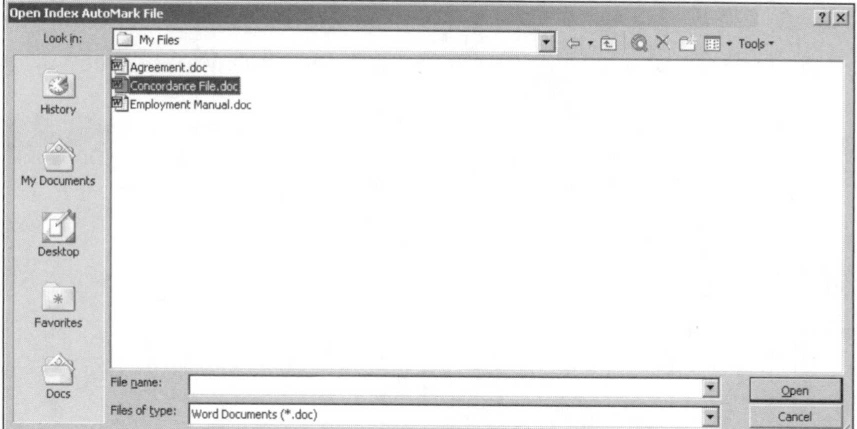

FIGURE 14.25

The concordance file contains a table of words and phrases to be included in the index.

6. The Status bar indicates the number of entries that were marked.
7. Leave this document open for the next exercise.

GENERATING THE INDEX

Once all index entries are marked, generating the index is easy. Place your insertion point where you wish to insert the index, and from the Insert menu, choose Reference, Index And Tables.

INSERTING THE INDEX INTO YOUR DOCUMENT

1. The document from the preceding exercise should be open.
2. Turn off Show/Hide.
3. Press Ctrl+End to move to the end of the document.
4. From the Insert menu, choose Break. Select Next Page and click OK.
5. Type **Index** and press Enter twice.
6. From the Insert menu, choose Reference, Index And Tables, and select the Index tab, as shown in Figure 14.26.
7. Choose a desired format from the Formats drop-down list.

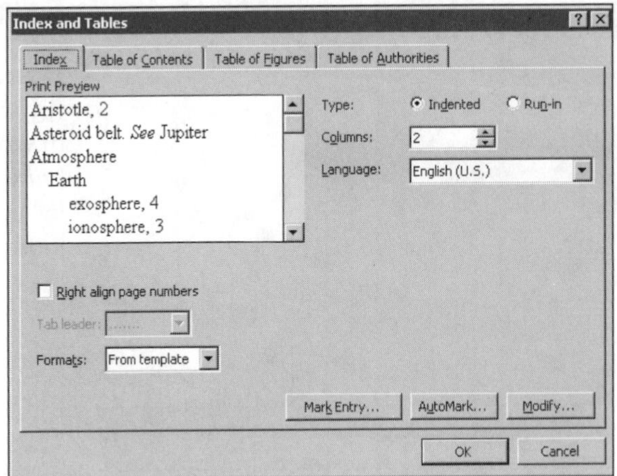

FIGURE 14.26

The Preview area of the Index And Tables dialog box shows how the index will look with the selected options.

8. Select the preferred page number alignment, number of columns, and format for subentries.
9. Click OK. Word inserts the index into the document.
10. Leave this document open for the next exercise.

Alternate-click within the index and choose Update Fields to update the index.

CONSTRUCTING COMPLEX DOCUMENTS FROM SCRATCH

The ideal situation when starting a new document would be to base it on a template, as shown in Chapter 10, "Templates." But, with the large mixture of legal documents that are created, you may not have immediate access to a template that meets your needs.

When this happens and you sit down to create a long, complex document, the task may seem daunting. But, with a little planning, the process can be fairly straightforward. It is best to start with the necessary document layout items before adding text.

This section walks you through the steps for creating a long or complex document.

PAGE SETUP

The margins, orientation, and paper size are usually specific to the document type, so this would be a good place to start. Create a new blank document. From the File menu, choose Page Setup and set the margins, paper size, and orientation of the document.

DOCUMENT BASICS

Along with the basic page formatting options, each document type has a basic blueprint—specific pages for particular parts of the document. For example, in an agreement, you may have a title page, a table of contents page, any number of pages in the body of the agreement, and a set of appendix pages. So, the next logical step is to insert the section and page breaks required to designate these different sections in the document.

CREATE A FLOOR PLAN FOR AN AGREEMENT

1. Create a new blank document.
2. From the File menu, choose Page Setup.
3. Set the margins, orientation, and paper size then click OK.
4. Type **AGREEMENT** and press Enter.
5. From the Insert menu, choose Break.
6. Select Next Page Section Break and click OK.
7. Type **TABLE OF CONTENTS** and press Enter.
8. Follow steps 5 and 6 to insert a Next Page Section Break.
9. Type **DEFINITIONS** and press Enter.
10. Follow steps 5 and 6 to insert a Next Page Section Break.
11. Type **APPENDIX** and press Enter.
12. Press Ctrl+Home to move to the top of the document.
13. From the File menu, choose Page Setup.
14. On the Layout tab, set Vertical Alignment to Center.
15. Under Apply To, choose This Section.
16. Click OK.
17. Save the document and leave it open for the next exercise.

HEADERS AND FOOTERS

Now that the blueprint of the document is prepared, it's time to focus attention on the details of the document itself. With the sections set up, adding headers and footers is the next logical step.

ADD PAGE NUMBERS TO THE FOOTER OF THE DOCUMENT

1. The document from the preceding exercise should still be open.
2. Press Ctrl+Home to move to the top of the document.
3. From the View menu, choose Header And Footer.
4. Press Tab twice to move to the right side of the header.
5. Type **Confidential**.
6. Click Show Next to move to the Table of Contents page.
7. Click Switch Between Header And Footer to move to the footer.
8. Click Same As Previous to unlink this footer from the previous footer.
9. Press Tab to move to the middle of the footer and click Insert Page Number.
10. Click Format Page Number, select the lowercase roman numeral format.
11. Set the Start At value to be i and click OK.
12. Click Show Next to move to the Definitions page.
13. Click Same As Previous to unlink this footer from the previous footer.
14. Click Format Page Number, select Arabic, and then set Start At to 1.
15. Click Show Next to move to the Appendix page.
16. Repeat steps 13 and 14 to set the Appendix page number format to uppercase alphabetic, starting at A.
17. Save the document and leave it open for the next exercise.

For more information on headers and footers, see Chapter 7, "Formatting a Document."

STYLES

It is almost time to enter the text. To make formatting consistent and effortless, basic styles should be set up next. This includes a style for the body text format for the main text of the document, as well as heading styles with numbering, if applicable.

SET UP BODY TEXT STYLE

1. The document from the preceding exercise should still be open.
2. Open the Styles And Formatting Task Pane.
3. Select All Styles from the Show drop-down list at the bottom of the pane.
4. Select Modify from the drop-down list beside Body Text. The Modify Style dialog box opens, as shown in Figure 14.27.
5. Click Format and choose Paragraph.
6. Under Special, set the First Line Indent to 0.5.
7. Choose Double from Line Spacing.
8. Reset all other options to 0 and click OK twice.
9. Save the document and leave it open for the next exercise.

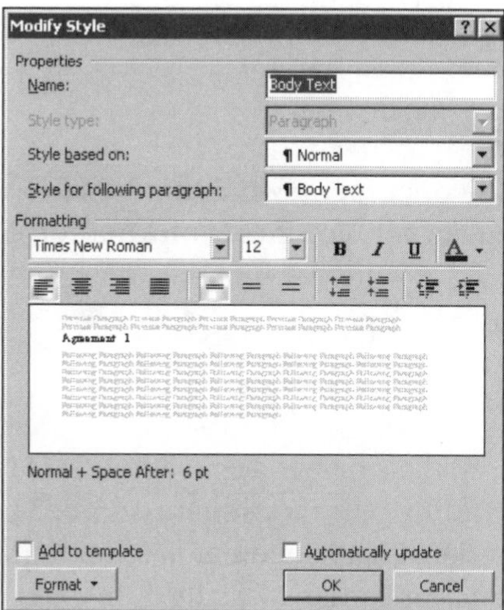

FIGURE 14.27

Choose from a variety of formats to modify the style.

NUMBERING

Paragraph numbering works best when attached to heading styles, as shown in Chapter 8, "Bullets and Numbering."

CUSTOMIZE HEADING STYLES TO INCLUDE NUMBERING

1. The document from the preceding exercise should still be open.
2. In the Styles And Formatting Task Pane, choose Modify Heading 1 style.
3. Click Format and choose Numbering.
4. Select the Outline Numbered tab.
5. Select the first gallery position from the bottom row and click OK.
6. Click OK in the Modify Style dialog box.

For more information on customizing heading styles, see Chapter 9, "Styles," and Chapter 8, "Bullets and Numbering."

TYPE TEXT

There is no way to predict and create styles for all formatting needs before you start typing. The needs of a document change as the document is constructed, and even later, as it is edited. In the preceding exercise, the Body Text and Heading styles were set up. Use these styles to insert and format text. Create and format other styles as the need arises.

TABLE OF CONTENTS

After the text is inserted into the document, generate the table of contents on the page that was created for it earlier. For more information on creating the table of contents, see the "Tables of Contents" section earlier in this chapter.

SUMMARY

Long and complex documents, such as patent applications and briefs, are good examples of why the legal community puts more strain on word processing software than any other vertical market. Legal documents often require special formatting, unique tables, equations, and other specialty items.

To make working in these complex documents easier, Microsoft has brought many of the tools in Word to the forefront. Additionally, Word has now added security to warn when a document is about to be printed or sent to others that contains comments and tracked changes.

TROUBLESHOOTING LONG DOCUMENTS

When I try to see who made a change or added a comment, why does it show up as an unidentified reviewer?

The reviewer has not customized the User Information tab under Tools, Options, so Word does not know what name to display.

Why does the name associated with changes or comments change to "Author" when I save my document?

The Remove Personal Information From This File On Save option on the Security tab, under Tools, Options, has been selected.

I deleted the footnote text, but the footnote reference wasn't deleted. How do I get rid of the entire footnote?

To delete the entire footnote, you must delete the footnote Reference Mark in the text of the document. You cannot remove a footnote or endnote just by deleting the note text. The note reference is maintained in the last paragraph mark of the Note Pane, and that mark cannot be deleted when you delete the note text.

"I deleted a footnote reference, but the other footnotes didn't renumber.

Track Changes is still turned on for the file, so the footnote continues to exist as deleted text. When all the revisions are accepted, Word will renumber the footnotes. If you want to adjust the numbering immediately, select the deleted footnote reference mark and accept that tracked change.

I would like to modify my Note Separator but can't get the Note Pane to open. What do I need to do?

To view the Note Pane, you must be in Normal view. Switch to this view by choosing View, Normal from the menu bar. Once you are in Normal view, choose View, Footnotes from the menu bar to view the Note Pane. You can also double-click the note reference in the body of the document.

The page numbers in the table of authorities do not match my document.

When you generate a table of authorities, you must turn off Show/Hide to get accurate page numbering. Click Show/Hide to turn off the paragraph marks in the document then alternate-click on the table of authorities and choose Update Field. The page numbers should now be correct.

I am working with a document that was manually marked for the table of contents. One of the marked entries is showing up in the wrong level in the table of contents.

Manually marked table of contents entries appear in the document as a field similar to this: {TC "Introduction" \f c \l "3"}. Select the marked entry, alternate-click, and choose Toggle Field Codes from the shortcut menu. The number at the end of the field (after the \l) indicates the level it will have in the table of contents. Change the field to reflect the correct level and update the table of contents.

Chapter 15

Document Collaboration

IN THIS CHAPTER

- Track Changes and using the Reviewing toolbar
- Comments
- Compare and Merge and using Word Versions
- Third-party comparison applications
- Sending documents for review
- Routing documents
- Sharing documents externally
- Metadata and tracked changes
- Online sharing and collaboration
- Master Documents

Contracts, agreements, and other types of legal documents often pass through many hands and many versions before the final document is created. Therefore, if Word is to be used successfully in a law firm, the product must be robust enough to handle multiple edits by multiple authors, have the ability to merge all changes into one document, and provide flexibility in formatting revisions.

Truth be told, previous versions of Word did not cut it for many long and complex legal documents, and many training companies recommended that their law firm clients purchase third-party solutions for keeping track of changes, versions, and comparisons. With Word 2002, Microsoft has totally rewritten how Track Changes and Compare and Merge documents work. Its programmers worked with law firms and the Legal Advisory Council, and the result is a more robust, reliable comparison utility built into Word.

TRACK CHANGES: AN OVERVIEW

Whether it's an amended contract, a marked-up agreement, or a revised IP form, Track Changes can help to identify text that has been added or removed from documents. With Track Changes, you control not only the appearance of inserted and deleted text but also the manner in which modified text is displayed onscreen. Using the Reviewing toolbar, you can choose to accept or reject proposed changes one at a time or all at once. You can even review and merge changes made by multiple reviewers. Track Changes is enabled in several ways—directly from the status bar by double-clicking TRK (see Figure 15.1), from the Tools menu by choosing Track Changes, from the keyboard by pressing Ctrl+Shift+E, or from the Reviewing toolbar.

CONTROLLING TRACK CHANGES

Law firms typically prefer to mark changes according to their individual firm preference. For example, should changes be marked in color? Will you create a legal blackline document to show changes? How should inserted text and format changes appear onscreen and in the resulting document? All of these settings and more are available through the Track Changes tab in the Options dialog box.

IS TRACK CHANGES SAFE?

In previous versions of Word, Track Changes was perceived as not being safe or accurate, hence the popularity of third-party comparison products such as CompareRite and DeltaView. Often, deletions that had been accepted using Track Changes would reappear when or if a document became corrupt. As a result of this and other annoyances, Track Changes received a bad name. In the latest version of Word, Microsoft spent a great deal of time overhauling the Track Changes feature so it would better meet the needs of law firms. You will find it produces a more accurate and stable result. As for whether or not the feature is safe—we used the feature throughout the creation of this book and did not experience the problems that previously existed. However, as with any product that includes a feature that is either new or redesigned—proceed with caution.

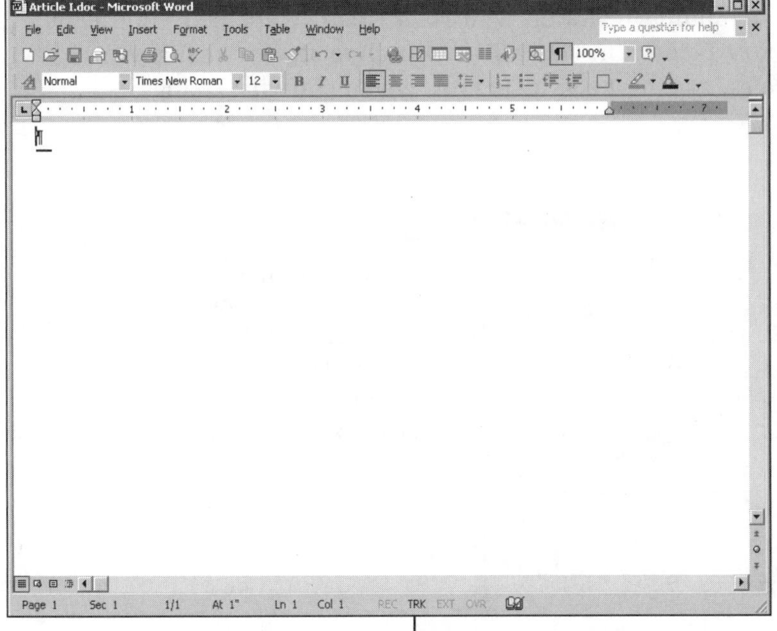

FIGURE 15.1

The quickest way to enable the Track Changes feature is to double-click TRK on the status bar.

From the Tools menu, choose Options and select the Track Changes tab. If you find it distracting to see all the tabs in the dialog box, you can show only the Track Changes tab. To do this, display the Reviewing toolbar. Click Show and choose Options. The Track Changes dialog box opens, as shown in Figure 15.2.

The following section provides an explanation of each option in the Track Changes dialog box. If you've worked with previous versions of Word, you'll notice some major differences and new features—including Markup balloons, which appear in the margins when you're working in Print Layout or Web Layout view.

Markup and Comment balloons are new to Word 2002. They are visible from Print Layout and Web Layout views and can be edited directly. The technique is similar to the marks used when an editor reviews and marks up a document by hand. Most people find them easy to read and understand.

TRACK CHANGES OPTIONS

- **Insertions**. This option controls how new text inserted into a document with Track Changes enabled is formatted. Many law firms prefer the default Underline option, or Double-Underline, to mark inserted text.
- **Color**. Control the color used for marking inserted text. If you're sending a document to multiple reviewers with Track Changes enabled, choose the default option, By Author. This will mark each reviewer's changes in a different color, making it easy to identify who made what change.

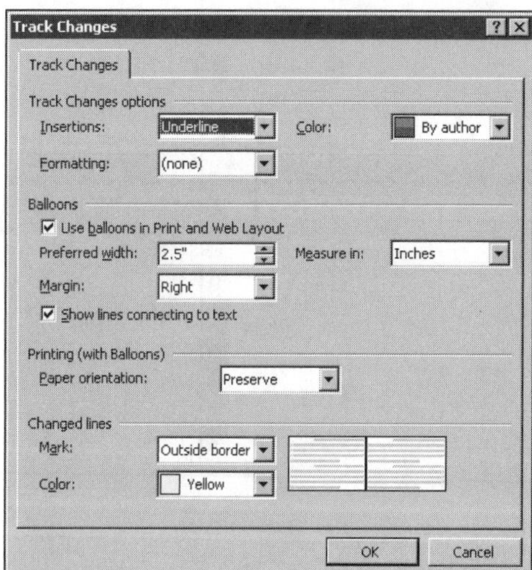

FIGURE 15.2

The Track Changes dialog box allows you to set specific options for controlling the appearance of edited text.

FORMAT OF DELETED TEXT

With the introduction of Markup balloons, Word 2002 no longer offers an option for how deleted text is displayed. In Print Layout or Web Layout views, deleted text appears in Markup balloons. In Normal or Outline views, it is shown with strikethrough formatting.

- **Formatting**. This setting controls how inserted text is formatted. For example, inserted text can be a designated color and can appear as bold, italic, underline, or double-underline.

BALLOONS

- **Use Balloons In Print And Web Layout**. Deleted text is displayed in Markup balloons in either the left or right margin. This is extremely useful because it places the deleted information off in the margin and provides more visible space for viewing the actual text of the document. Markup balloons are shown in Figure 15.3.

NOTE

Inserted text will also be displayed in Markup balloons when the Display for Review option is set to Original Showing Markup.

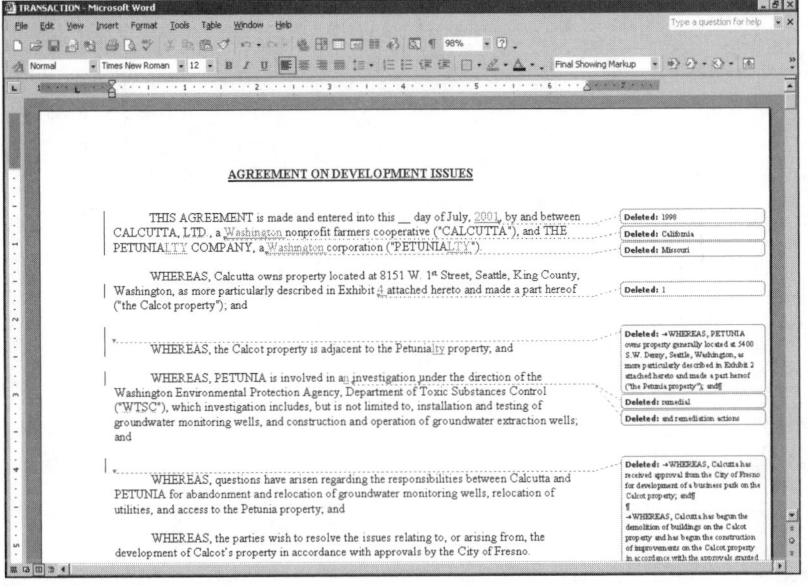

FIGURE 15.3

Markup balloons put deleted material off to one side, making it easier to read the current text.

- **Preferred Width**. Increase or decrease the size of Markup balloons by clicking the up or down spinners.
- **Measure In**. Choose Inches or Percentage to determine the size of Markup balloons.
- **Margin**. Position Markup balloons in either the right or left margin.
- **Show Lines Connecting Text**. When this option is checked, lines connect Markup balloons with the location of deleted text. This makes it easy to associate changes that appear in margins with corresponding text within the document.

PRINTING (WITH BALLOONS)

- **Paper Orientation**. Click the drop-down arrow and choose Preserve (keeps current page orientation), Auto (adjusts page orientation, if necessary, to make room for Markup balloons), Force Landscape (automatically changes page orientation to landscape to accommodate Markup balloons).

CHANGED LINES

- **Mark**. When this option is selected, the paragraph where text has been inserted, moved, changed, or deleted will be marked with a thin line on the left, right, or outside border. This is intended to draw attention to the page that contains changes that might otherwise be overlooked. Figure 15.4

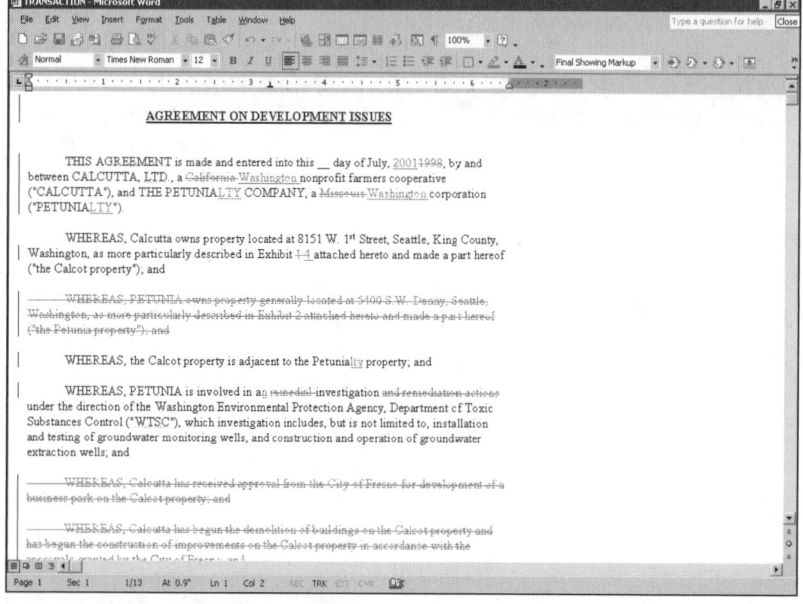

FIGURE 15.4

Marking changes in the margin helps you quickly identify those sections of the document where changes have been made.

shows a revised document with Mark enabled; it also illustrates the appearance of deleted text in Normal view where Markup balloons are not used.

- **Color**. Click the drop-down arrow and select a color for Mark lines, or stick with the default, Auto.

USING TRACK CHANGES

Remember the old days when you had to sit down with a red pencil and manually mark all the changes to a document and then apply them to the electronic document? Thankfully, those days are over for most of us, and we now have a better way to do what was previously a tedious and time-consuming task. Track Changes literally tracks all of the changes made to a document.

The options you set in the Track Changes dialog box will determine the exact appearance of modified text. These options are persistent for all Word documents on your computer and are not document-specific.

Each tracked change can be accepted or rejected one at a time or all at once using options on the Reviewing toolbar. This differs from previous versions where the Track Changes menu command expanded to reveal a submenu with these options.

TURN ON TRACK CHANGES AND USE THE REVIEWING TOOLBAR TO ACCEPT AND REJECT PROPOSED CHANGES

1. Create a new document. Switch to Normal view.
2. Type (c) **Whether Congress has the authority under Article I to abrogate a State's immunity in its own courts is, then, a question of first impression.**
3. Double-click TRK on the status bar to turn on Track Changes. The Reviewing toolbar automatically appears.

You may need to move or dock the toolbar to see the document text without interruption.

4. Place your insertion point at the end of the first sentence and type **History, practice, precedent, and the Constitution's structure show no compelling evidence that this derogation of the State's sovereignty is inherent in the constitutional compact.**
5. Select the entire first sentence and press Delete.
6. Your document should look similar to the one shown in Figure 15.5.

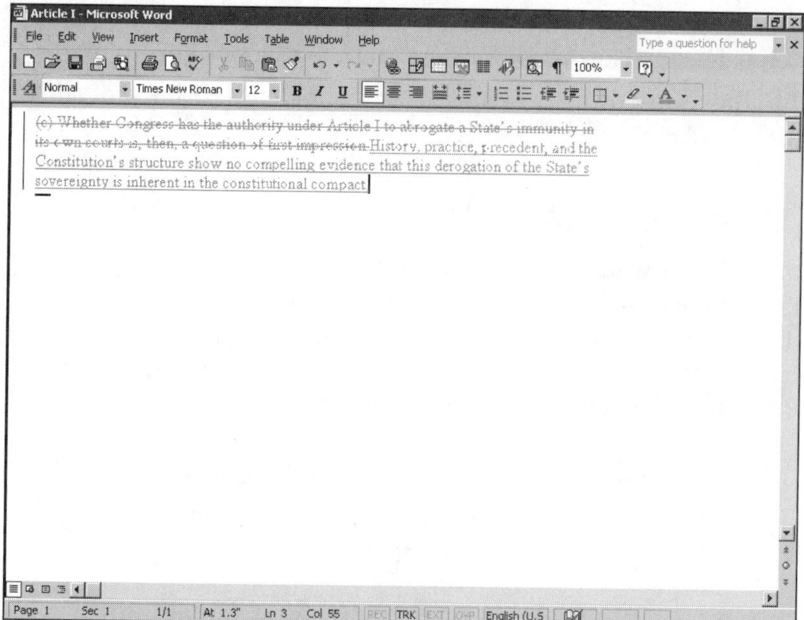

FIGURE 15.5

By default, inserted text is formatted as underlined and deleted text with strikethrough formatting.

7. Leave this document open for the next exercise.

REVIEWING TOOLBAR

By default, the Reviewing toolbar appears each time you turn on Track Changes. You can also activate it by alternate-clicking any visible toolbar and choosing Reviewing from the drop-down list.

The Reviewing toolbar, shown in Figure 15.6, contains a number of options and features that allow you to work with Track Changes and Comments. You can use it to turn on or off Track Changes, accept and reject changes, insert and delete comments, open and close the Reviewing Pane, and preview how a document with tracked changes will appear in various states (Original, Final, Original Showing Markup, and Final Showing Markup).

FIGURE 15.6

The Reviewing toolbar can be used to work with Track Changes, Comments, Routed Documents, and Documents Sent For Review.

New Feature!

In previous versions of Word, there were a couple of options available for reviewing and accepting or rejecting changes made with Track Changes. You could use the Reviewing toolbar to accept or reject changes, or you could choose from one of the three options found on the Tools, Track Changes menu: Highlight Changes, Accept or Reject Changes, or Compare Documents. In this version of Word, everything related to Track Changes is rolled into one streamlined component—the Reviewing toolbar. The only exception is Compare and Merge (formerly Compare Documents), which is now a separate command on the Tools menu.

Hold your mouse pointer over an option to see an identifying ScreenTip. Here is a description of each of the options found on the Reviewing toolbar:

- **Display For Review**. Choose one of four options to display a different view of the changes in the document. Final Showing Markup shows the final document with full markup, Final shows how the document will appear if all changes are accepted, Original Showing Markup shows the original document with full markup, and Original shows the document as if no changes were made or all changes are rejected.
- **Show**. Click the drop-down menu and choose from the following options: Comments (shows online comments), Insertions And Deletions (shows marked text), Formatting (shows formatting changes in a document), Reviewers (allows you to choose whether to show or exclude changes or comments from specific reviewers), Reviewing Pane (opens a display at the bottom of the document window), and Options (opens the Track Changes dialog box, where options are set for marking changes).

Note

The Reviewers command on the Show drop-down menu includes the names of reviewers for all opened documents. To see reviewer names for the active document only, close all open documents, restart Word, and then open the document and return to the Reviewers command.

- **Previous**. Move to the nearest tracked change before the insertion point.
- **Next**. Move to the next tracked change after the insertion point.
- **Accept Change**. Click and choose one of three options: Accept Change, Accept All Changes Shown, and Accept All Changes In Document.

- **Reject Change/Delete Comment**. Click and choose one of five options: Reject Change/Delete Comment, Reject All Changes Shown, Reject All Changes In Document, Delete All Comments Shown, and Delete All Comments.
- **New Comment**. Click and choose one of four options: Insert a New Comment, Edit an Existing Comment, Delete a Comment, or Create a Voice Comment.
- **Track Changes**. Click to turn Track Changes on or off. The button works as a toggle for the feature.

This button enables changes to be tracked or turns off tracking but does not hide the existing Track Changes already in the document.

- **Reviewing Pane**. Click to open or close the Reviewing Pane, where you can review and edit changes and comments. The Reviewing Pane is divided into sections that may include Main Document Changes And Comments, Header And Footer Changes, Text Box Changes, Header And Footer Text Box Changes, Footnote Changes, and Endnote Changes. The Reviewing Pane can be resized to display more information at once by placing the mouse pointer, without clicking, over the Resize line that divides the document window from the Reviewing Pane and then clicking and dragging the Resize line to a new position.

REVIEW CHANGES MADE TO A DOCUMENT

1. Return to the document from the preceding exercise.
2. Switch to Print Layout view. Notice the deleted text appears in a Markup balloon in the right margin, as shown in Figure 15.7.

Word changes the zoom in the background of the document to add the Markup balloons. Margins nor pagination are affected.

3. On the Reviewing toolbar, click the drop-down arrow next to the Display For Review button and click through and view each of the four display options and results. End with Final Showing Markup.

Notice that when you choose Original Showing Markup, the Markup balloon contains inserted text rather than deletions.

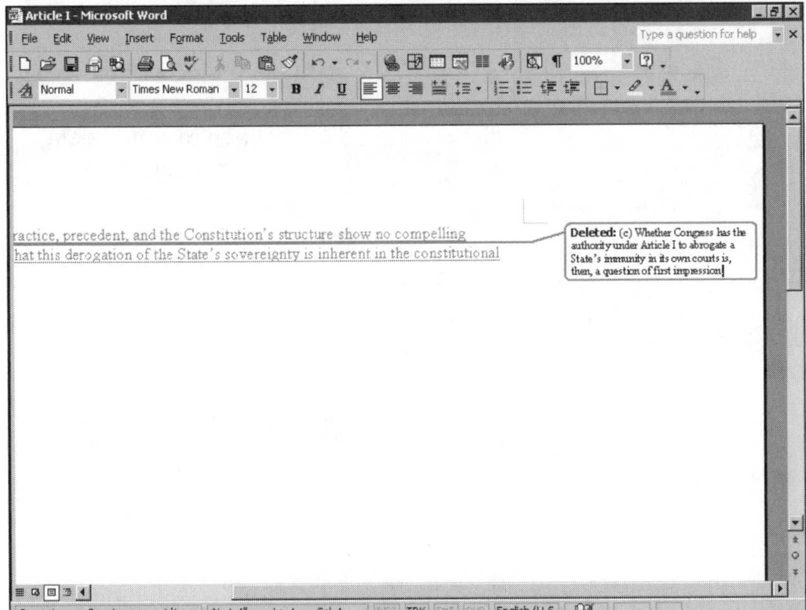

FIGURE 15.7

Markup balloons can show comments, as well as deleted or inserted text, depending on what is selected in the Display For Review button on the Reviewing toolbar.

4. Click the Next button to move from change to change. Click Yes, if prompted, to search through the document.
5. Click the drop-down arrow next to Accept Change and choose Accept All Changes In Document.
6. Click the Track Changes button to turn off Track Changes.
7. Leave this document open for the next exercise.

Occasionally, not all deleted text can fit in Markup balloons. When this occurs, ellipses display in the balloons, indicating that additional text is available but not displayed. Double-click the ellipsis (as shown in Figure 15.8) to open the Reviewing Pane.

If you've already worked through the Comments exercises in Chapter 14, you can skim the "Comments" section here—we've repeated some information for completeness because the feature is part of the Reviewing Toolbar and Pane, and some readers may turn to this chapter first.

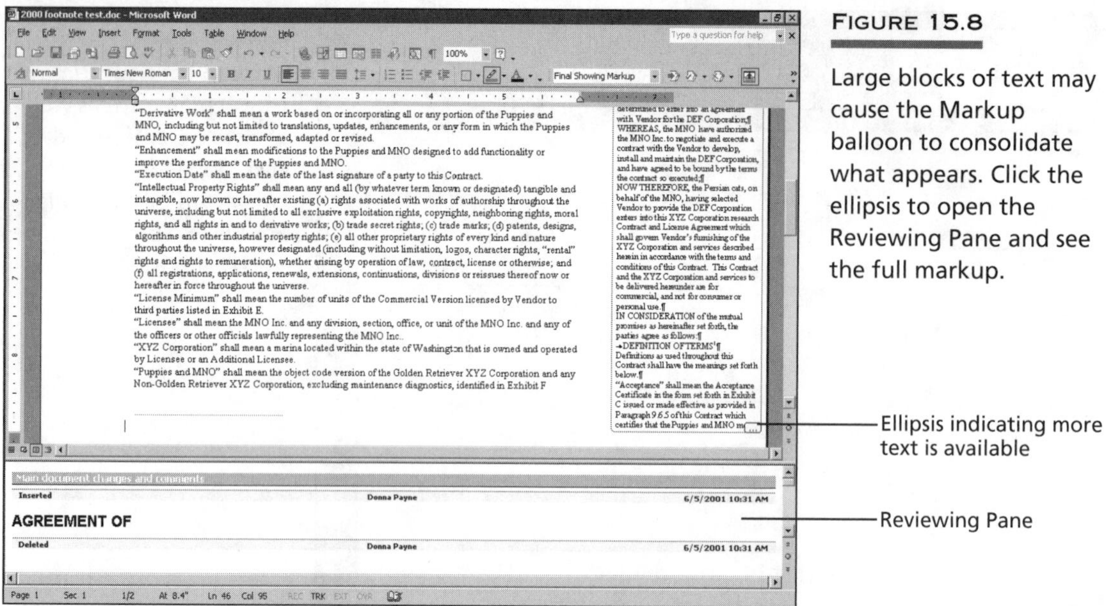

FIGURE 15.8

Large blocks of text may cause the Markup balloon to consolidate what appears. Click the ellipsis to open the Reviewing Pane and see the full markup.

COMMENTS

Sticky notes are useful for drawing attention to sections of a document that need further comment and for pointing out where a signature goes, but too often these types of notes fall off the document and land on the floor. Word provides an easier way for you to add comments during the review process. Online comments can be quickly inserted, edited, and deleted—and even printed with the document, if necessary. The easiest way to affix comments is by selecting the appropriate text for the comment and choosing Insert, Comment. You can also click Insert Comment on the Reviewing toolbar. When you insert comments while working in Normal view, the Reviewing Pane opens at the bottom of the document window, providing a place for you to add comment text. The information displayed in the Reviewing Pane includes the Comment Number (comments are numbered sequentially), Comment Text, Author, and Date. If you happen to be working in Print Layout or Web Layout view, Word displays editable Comment balloons in the left or right margins.

DIFFERENCES BETWEEN COMMENTS IN WORD 2002 AND PREVIOUS VERSIONS

Comments are displayed differently in Word 2002 than in previous versions. In Normal view, Comments are no longer identifiable as yellow marked text. Instead, they appear as either a colored nonprinting I-beam at the point of insertion or brackets surrounding the text. In Print Layout view, the comments appear in colored Comment balloons to the left or right of the text. In Normal view, hover your mouse pointer, without clicking, over the commented text in the document and the comment appears in a shaded box. The color of the brackets and shaded box varies by author. You can also open the Reviewing Pane, which appears at the bottom of the document window.

NOTE

If your computer is configured with a sound card and microphone, you can add voice comments to documents. To do so, click Voice Comment on the Reviewing toolbar, record the comment, and then close the Recording dialog box. For others to access your voice comments, however, they will also need the appropriate hardware. Be careful with this feature—voice comments dramatically increase file size and should not be used in place of dictation devices. Also, there is no option to print voice comments, so they cannot become part of the paper record.

ADD COMMENTS TO YOUR DOCUMENT

1. The document from the preceding exercise should still be open. If it's not, type any text and continue with Step 2.
2. Switch to Print Layout view and display the Reviewing toolbar.
3. Place your insertion point at the end of the paragraph.
4. From the Reviewing toolbar, click New Comment. Notice the Comment balloon in the right margin.
5. In the Comment balloon, type **Expand on this topic.**
6. Switch to Normal view and click Reviewing Pane on the Reviewing toolbar.
7. At the bottom of the document window, place your insertion point in the comment and, after the word *topic,* type **and report back when complete.**

8. Click the Reviewing Pane again to close the pane. Switch to Print Layout view.

You can also quickly close the Reviewing Pane by double-clicking the split bar between the document text and the Reviewing Pane.

9. Click the drop-down arrow next to New Comment and click Delete Comment.

If Delete Comment is not activated, click inside the Comment balloon and then try again. You can delete all comments in a document by clicking the drop-down arrow next to Reject Change/Delete Comment on the Reviewing toolbar and clicking Delete All Comments In Document.

Comments made by different users appear in different colors. You can move from one comment to the next by clicking the Previous and Next buttons on the Reviewing toolbar. The Browse Object, on the vertical scroll bar, also allows you to move from one comment to the next quickly.

PRINTING COMMENTS WITH A DOCUMENT

Comments that you place in documents can be printed along with the document. From the File menu, choose Print to open the Print dialog box. Click the drop-down arrow next to Print What and select Document Showing Markup, as shown in Figure 15.9. The comments will appear in Comment balloons on the

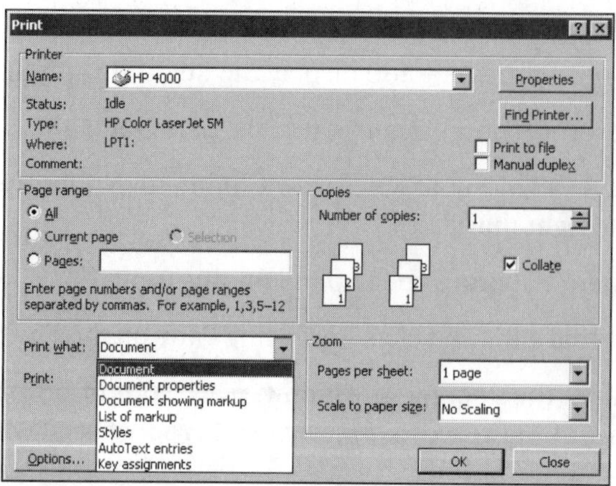

FIGURE 15.9

You can print the document as it will appear in final format, showing markups, comments, and more.

NEW FEATURE!

If a document that contains Markup balloons is saved to previous versions of Word (Word 2000, 97, 95, or 6.0), changes are not deleted from the document. Instead, they appear the way they would in that version of Word. If the document is then reopened in Word 2002, the Markup balloons again display. It is possible for some information to not display after switching between these versions (author name, date, and time); however, the changes will appear intact.

left or right margin depending on the option you set on the Track Changes tab. The default is to print these comments in the right margin.

NOTE

Comments are printed along with Track Changes. This is different from previous versions of Word where you could choose to print only comments from either the Print dialog box or Tools, Options.

AVAILABLE PRINT OPTIONS FOR TRACK CHANGES AND COMMENTS

If you wish to see all the changes that have been made to your document in list format, open the Print dialog box and then select List Of Markup from the Print What drop-down list. When you choose this option, Word prints a separate sheet with a list of the following items:

- **Main Document Changes And Comments**. Lists insertions, deletions, and comments by page, author, and date.
- **Header And Footer Changes**. Lists insertions and deletions made to headers and footers by page, section, author, and date.
- **Text Box Changes**. Lists inserted and deleted text boxes by page, author, and date.
- **Header And Footer Text Box Changes**. Lists inserted and deleted text boxes in headers and footers by page, author, and date.
- **Footnote Changes**. Lists inserted and deleted footnotes by page, author, and date.
- **Endnote Changes**. Lists inserted and deleted endnotes by page, author, and date.

COMPARE AND MERGE

Legal users often need to identify the differences between two documents or two versions of the same document. The Compare and Merge feature was developed to accomplish just this task. Compare and Merge analyzes two documents and produces an output file, using Track Changes to show where the versions differ. For example, you might want to see what modifications have been made to an agreement that was sent to a client and returned with changes. With Compare and Merge, you open the latest version and compare it to the original. Inserted text appears with single or double underlining, and deleted text is formatted as strikethrough. You can even use the Reviewing toolbar to accept or reject each change and save the output file as the final version—or print the redlined copy to make a note of the changes.

MERGE DOCUMENTS COMMANDS

If you have changes in multiple documents that need to be merged into one document, use the Merge command in the Compare And Merge Documents dialog box. The Merge button (Figure 15.10) includes a drop-down list with the following items:

- **Merge**. Track changes are displayed to reflect additions when the documents are merged. All changes will be reflected in the document you open last (e.g., Agreement 1.14.01).
- **Merge Into Current Document**. The active document displays the changes as additions (e.g., Agreement 1.15.01).
- **Merge Into New Document**. A new document is created and changes appear as additions.

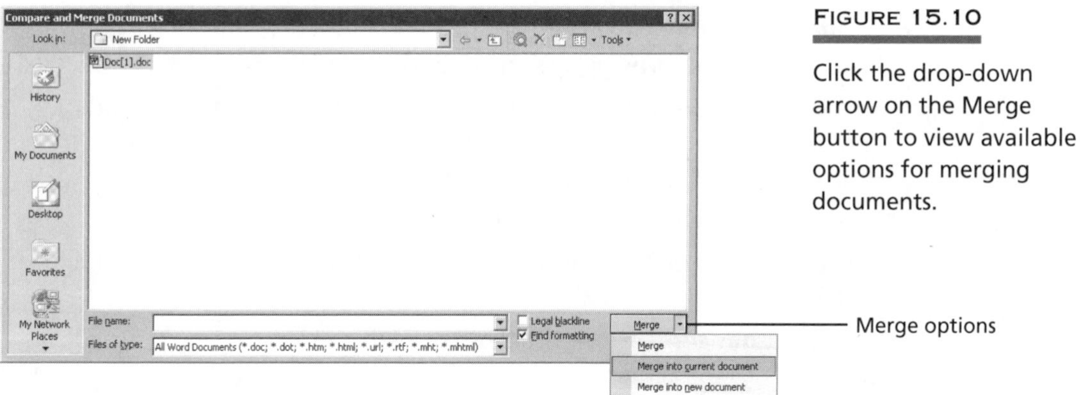

FIGURE 15.10

Click the drop-down arrow on the Merge button to view available options for merging documents.

The next exercise will merge two versions of a document. The merged changes display as additions with Word's Track Changes feature.

USE MERGE

1. Create a new document.
2. Type **Revolving Credit Borrowings. Each Revolving Credit Borrowing shall be: (i) if comprised of Alternate Base Rate Advances, in an amount at the option of the Borrower.**
3. Save the document as **Agreement 1.14.01**. Close the document.
4. Create a new document. Type **Non-Revolving Credit Borrowings. Each Non-Revolving Credit Borrowing shall be: (ii) if not comprised of Alternate Base Rate Advances, in an amount at the option of the Borrower. The Borrower shall be entitled to have more than one Non-Revolving Credit Borrowing outstanding at one time.**
5. Save the document as **Agreement 1.15.01**. Leave this document open.
6. From the Tools menu, choose Compare And Merge Documents. The Compare And Merge Documents dialog box opens, as shown in Figure 15.11.
7. Navigate to the saved document Agreement 1.14.01 and click Merge.

NOTE

If the Merge button does not appear in the Compare And Merge Documents dialog box, turn off the Legal Blackline option and the Compare button becomes the Merge button.

8. Switch to Print Layout view. On the Reviewing toolbar, change the view to Original Showing Markup.

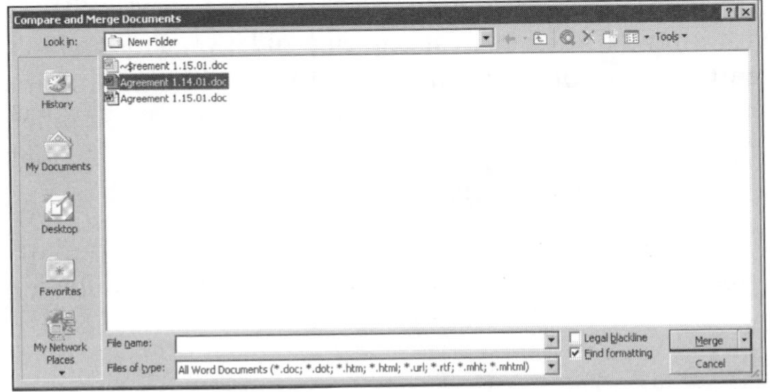

FIGURE 15.11

Open the latest version of the file and then choose Compare And Merge Documents from the Tools menu.

9. Click the drop-down arrow next to Accept Change and choose Accept All Changes In Document.
10. Save the document as **Revised Agreement 1.16.01**.

COMPARE DOCUMENTS COMMANDS

You may have noticed the Legal Blackline option on the Compare And Merge Documents dialog box. Legal Blackline opens a separate document showing the result of merging the two documents, with the additions as well as deletions. If Legal Blackline is chosen, the Merge button changes to Compare.

Law firms asked for this functionality. They felt that it was too easy to save over the original document by mistake.

WHY WORD VERSIONS MAY NOT BE WHAT YOU THINK THEY ARE

For those of you who have worked extensively with document management software, the concept of versions should be quite familiar. Products such as DOCS Open, iManage, and WORLDOX allow you to create multiple versions of a document and compare them later. Agreements, contracts, and other types of documents often go through numerous revisions and multiple versions of the same document can exist at any time. In the context of a document management system, each version actually exists as a separate file. Popular comparison tools, such as DeltaView, compare document versions and create output files that compile the results into a separate redlined document. The redlined document reflects the difference between two versions or two documents using conventional markup options. They can also be set up to provide statistics on the number of insertions, deletions, moves, and more.

Word has its own Versions feature listed under the File menu, but it works very differently from the way most legal users think of versions. Word saves each version of the document within the same file. You can view older versions and roll back, if necessary, but you cannot use Compare and Merge to differentiate between two versions, nor can you assign version numbers to the file. Another drawback is that Word Versions can bloat the file size. Versions should be used on limited occasions—or better yet, don't use it at all.

If your firm does not use a document management system, you can choose Save As from the File menu and assign a new document name to reflect the different versions.

Compare And Merge cannot be used to compare versions as defined by Word because each new version is actually an appended component of the original file. Compare And Merge works by comparing two uniquely named files. So, in order to use Compare And Merge, you'll need to use the Save As feature to create separate document files for each version.

So why would legal users want to use Word's Versions feature? The short answer is that they wouldn't. We strongly advise our clients not to use this feature. It's bad enough that you can't compare Word's versions, but the feature is actively dangerous—it dramatically increases file size, resulting in a greater likelihood of document corruption. We recently received a one-page document from a client who was having trouble opening it and reported that the file was also behaving erratically. Upon closer inspection, we found that the Automatically Save A Version On Close option was turned on and the size of the file was close to 32MB! Every time the client closed this one-page document, Word created a new version appended to the same file.

We recommend that you either remove the versions command from the File menu altogether or direct your users to avoid it. In addition, provide training to your users on the proper procedures for creating versions using document management software or the Save As feature in Word.

When Versions is enabled in a document, you also run a risk that hidden information, or metadata, will be exposed when the file is sent to others. The file can be opened and all previous changes (additions and deletions) can be revealed.

IDENTIFYING A DOCUMENT WITH VERSIONS AND TURNING AUTO VERSIONING OFF

1. From the CD-ROM, open exercise file **Article II**.
2. From the File menu, choose Versions to open the Versions dialog box, as shown in Figure 15.12.
3. Uncheck the Automatically Save A Version On Close option.

Do not use the Automatically Save A Version On Close feature. The file will quickly balloon in size and will be more likely to become corrupt.

4. Select each version and click Delete.

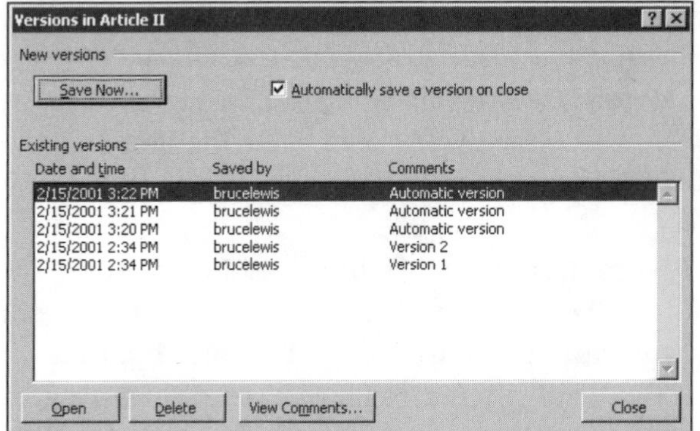

FIGURE 15.12

The Versions dialog box shows all existing versions of a document, the date and time each version was created, as well as who created the version and any comments that have been added.

To quickly select the entire list of versions, select the version at the top of the list, hold down the Shift key and select the last version in the list, and press the Delete key on your keyboard.

5. Click Close.

COMPARING VERSIONS OF A DOCUMENT

Remember, it isn't possible to use the Compare and Merge feature to compare two Word Versions of the same document. To run any type of comparison, you'll need to create two separate files using the Save As feature.

CREATE TWO VERSIONS OF A DOCUMENT USING SAVE AS AND RUN COMPARE AND MERGE

1. Create a new document.
2. Type **This section of the Federal Register contains notices to the public of the proposed issuance of rules and regulations.**
3. Save this document to C:\My Documents (or your default local document directory) as **Proposed Rules**. This is the original document (that is, version 1).
4. From the File menu, choose Save As.
5. Name the file **Proposed Rules v2** and click Save. Notice that the new document title appears in the title bar.

6. Delete the word *section* and replace it with **article.**
7. Place your insertion point at the end of the sentence and add the following text: **The purpose of these notices is to give interested persons an opportunity to participate in the rule making process prior to the adoption of the final rules.**
8. Click the Save button on the Standard toolbar to save the changes.
9. From the Tools menu, choose Compare And Merge Documents.
10. Navigate to C:\My Documents (or wherever you saved version 1), select Proposed Rules, and click Compare. (Make sure the Legal Blackline option is checked.)
11. Press Ctrl+S to activate the Save dialog box.
12. Name the document **Proposed Rules Redline Copy** and click Save.
13. Switch to Print Layout view. From the Reviewing toolbar, click the drop-down arrow next to the Display For Review button and select Final Showing Markup.
14. Click the drop-down arrow next to Accept Change and choose Accept All Changes In Document.

COMPARISON SOFTWARE: WORD VERSUS THIRD-PARTY APPLICATIONS

Okay, now that you've had a chance to look at Word's versioning and comparison features, it's time to see how the leading third-party comparison utilities stack up.

COMPARERITE

CompareRite was a product available from Lexis-Nexis that for years was the preferred (and only) third-party comparison utility for law firms. Lexis-Nexis has announced that they will retire the product. They are no longer selling CompareRite. Maintenance contracts and general support will be terminated effective February 1, 2002. For more information, visit the Lexis-Nexis Web site at www.lexis-nexis.com.

DELTAVIEW

A relative newcomer to the legal market, DeltaView has been winning accolades for its performance as a document-comparison utility. DeltaView provides a full-featured set of options for users who require detailed document comparison. Developed by Workshare Technology, DeltaView allows users to create "rendering sets" with unique characters, colors, numbers, and other types of information to highlight inserted, deleted, and moved text and tables. When a comparison is run, the resulting output file is generated directly in the DeltaView Desktop window. Inserted, deleted, and moved text can be easily identified using traditional markup options or with colors. Changes can also be numbered to allow users to search for specific changes or move through the numbered changes one by one.

One of the real advantages DeltaView offers is the ability to e-mail the redlined document (output file) directly from the DeltaView Desktop. An example of the DeltaView comparison result is shown in Figure 15.13. Users even have the option of e-mailing the documents used in the comparison process along with the output file.

DeltaView integrates with document management systems such as DOCS Open, iManage, and WorldDox. It also works locally with Windows Explorer. To learn more about DeltaView, visit the company Web site at www.workshare.net.

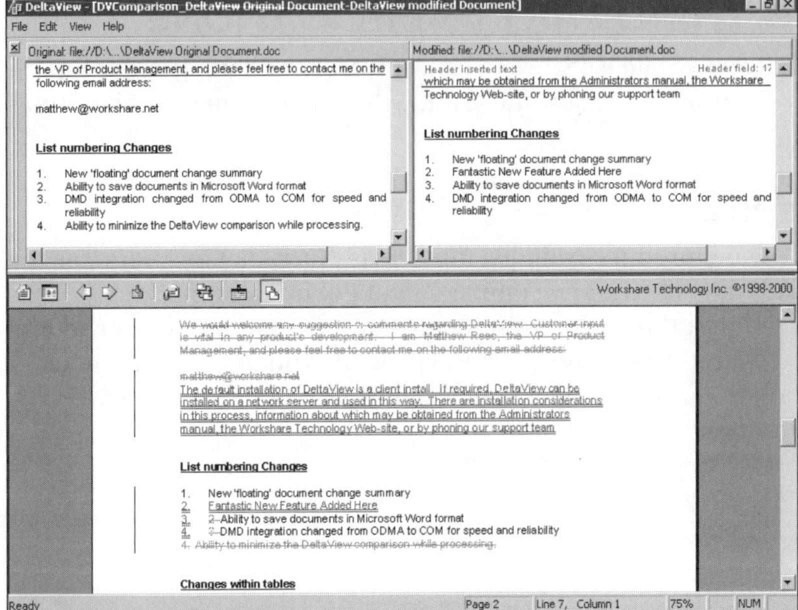

FIGURE 15.13

DeltaView has a few more features than Word's comparison functionality, including change numbers, the ability to create and save rendering sets, and greater control over how insertions and deletions are marked.

SENDING FILES FOR REVIEW

There may be times when the document you're working on needs a second pair of eyes before going out the door to a client. The Send To Mail Recipient For Review feature allows you to send a document to one or more colleagues who review the document, make any appropriate changes, and send the document back to you. Each reviewer receives the document as an attachment in an e-mail message which, when opened, has Track Changes automatically turned on. Once the reviewed document is returned, a message box appears asking if you want to merge the changes with the original document. Click Yes, and the changes are marked in the original for all reviewers, and you can accept or reject the proposed changes using the Reviewing toolbar.

Since the reviewing process requires the participation of other users, you'll need to solicit help from two members of your firm to complete the following exercise.

SENDING A DOCUMENT FOR REVIEW AND ANALYZING PROPOSED CHANGES

1. Create a new document. Type **The Congress shall have power to lay and collect taxes on incomes, from whatever source derived, without apportionment among the several States, and without regard to any census or enumeration.**
2. Save the document to C:\My Documents (or your default documents directory) and name it **Sixteenth Amendment**.
3. From the File menu, choose Send To and select Mail Recipient (For Review).

NOTE

You will need Outlook 2000 or higher to complete this exercise.

4. Outlook will generate an e-mail message with the file attached. The Subject line will read: "Please review 'Sixteenth Amendment'"—you don't have to compose anything. (See Figure 15.14.)
5. Address the message to two members of your firm and click Send.

NOTE

You can send a document to multiple reviewers.

6. The reviewers will receive a message containing the attached file. Advise them that they will need to double-click the attachment to open it.

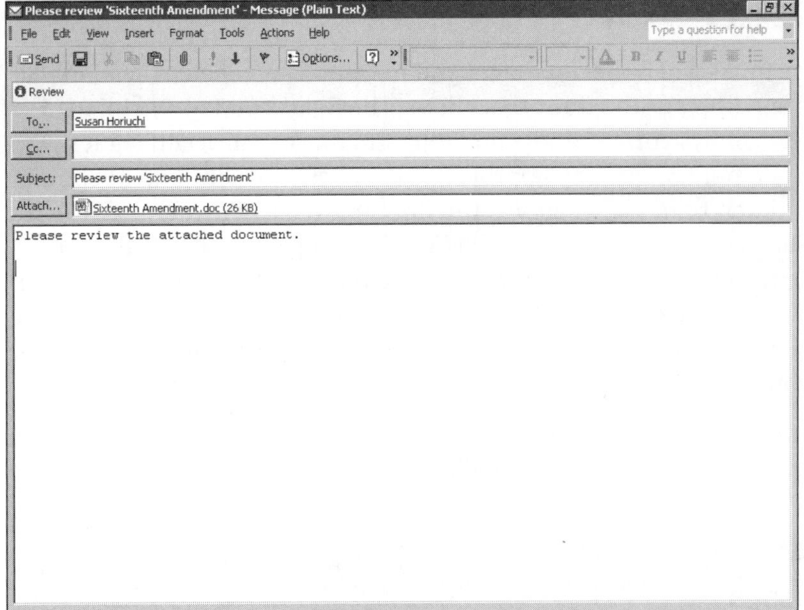

FIGURE 15.14

Sending files for review allows you to solicit feedback from others and then merge the changes back into the original file.

7. Once the attached file opens, the Reviewing toolbar automatically appears. Have the reviewers make a few changes and then click the Reply With Changes button. This generates a return e-mail message with the modified document attached. The reviewers can add any comments in the body of the message and click Send.

8. When you receive and open the return message, double-click the modified attachment. Figure 15.15 shows the message that appears: " 'Sixteenth Amendment' [or whatever you named the document] was sent for review. Do you want to merge changes in 'Sixteenth Amendment' back into 'C:\My Documents\Sixteenth Amendment' [the full document path]?"

9. Click Yes—this will merge all the changes into the original file and allow you to use the Reviewing toolbar to accept or reject each change, as necessary.

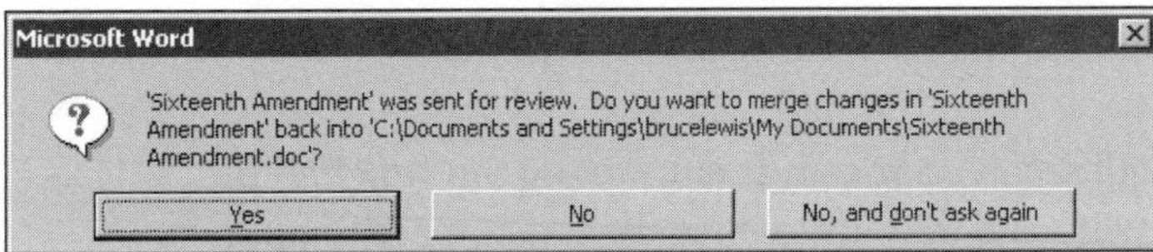

FIGURE 15.15

If you send the file to reviewers, when the file is returned, you can merge all changes into the original file—without having to use the Compare and Merge feature.

NOTE

If you've sent the document to multiple reviewers, click Show, All Reviewers from the Reviewing toolbar to see all the proposed changes from all reviewers. Alternatively, you can selectively view the changes from specific reviewers by checking or unchecking each reviewer's name.

10. Use the Reviewing toolbar to accept or reject the changes.

NOTE

If you've sent the document out to multiple reviewers but want to end the Review process, click End Review on the Reviewing toolbar.

11. From the File menu, choose Save or press Ctrl+S to save changes.
12. Close the document.

ROUTING FILES

Similar to Send Files for Review, Word's Routing feature allows you to route a document to one or more recipients for editing and review. Send Files For Review sends the original document to each reviewer simultaneously, whereas a routed document can be sent to one person at a time or all at once—ultimately ending up back at its source. When a document is routed, it is by default protected for Tracked Changes so the author will be able to view the proposed changes from each of the routing recipients. Recipients who receive the file in this manner cannot turn off Track Changes if Protect For Tracked Changes is selected when creating the Routing Slip.

NOTE

The following exercise requires the participation of two additional members of your firm. It also assumes that your firm is using Outlook 2000 or 2002.

ROUTE A DOCUMENT FOR REVIEW

1. Create a new document. Type **Excessive bail shall not be required, nor excessive fines imposed, nor cruel and unusual punishments inflicted.**
2. Save the document to C:\My Documents (or your default local documents directory) as **Amendment VIII**.
3. From the File menu, choose Send To and select Routing Recipient.

New Feature!

Microsoft built additional security measures into Outlook 2002 to help control and, hopefully, eliminate the spread of malicious e-mail viruses. Each time you attempt to route a document, a warning dialog will appear, as shown in Figure 15.16, stating that Outlook has detected another program attempting to access your e-mail addresses. In this case, that program happens to be your copy of Word and since you are doing this on purpose, click Yes to allow access. If you are ever unsure when you see this prompt, always click No and contact your system administrator.

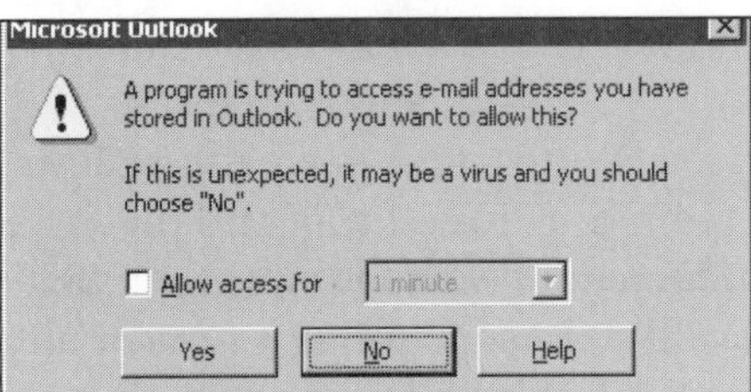

FIGURE 15.16

Make sure you know which program is trying to access your e-mail address list. Most viruses are spread through e-mail and Outlook has been the preferred target of many virus writers.

4. Click Yes on the warning dialog box to open the Routing Slip dialog box, as shown in Figure 15.17.
5. Add two routing recipients by clicking the Address button and selecting two people from your firm to whom you want to send the document.
6. In the Subject line, type **Amendment VIII**.
7. In the Message text box, type: **Please review this document and make any necessary changes.**
8. In the Route To Recipients section, select One After Another.
9. Check the Track Status option to be notified via e-mail as your document is routed to each of the designated recipients.
10. Check Return When Done to have the document automatically returned to you after the last person on the routing list closes the file.
11. Click the drop-down arrow next to Protect For and choose Tracked Changes, Comments, Forms (if your document has form fields), or None. The default is Tracked Changes.

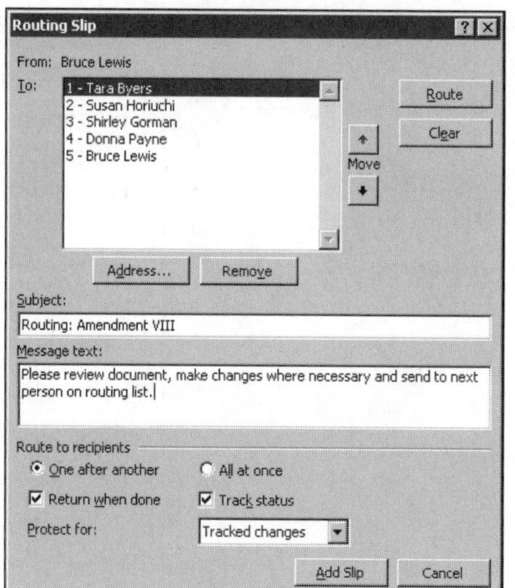

FIGURE 15.17

The order of the names will determine the routing order of the document.

NOTE

The Protect For list option prevents users from turning off Track Changes without first choosing Unprotect Document from the Tools menu. Reviewers can insert comments into the document without changing the document itself. The option also protects form fields when documents contain fields.

12. Click Route.
13. The first recipient will receive an e-mail with the routed document attached to a message similar to the one in Figure 15.18.

NOTE

It is important that each routing recipient follow the instructions in the e-mail message by routing the document to the next person on the routing list. Otherwise, the file will stall with one person and not be routed to the next person on the list. This is where the Track Status option comes in handy—if you have a document that's being routed from person to person, it's useful to be able to keep an eye on where it is and follow up if it seems to be spending too much time in one place.

14. Once the last recipient has routed the document back to you, open the e-mail message containing the attachment then open the file by double-clicking.
15. From the Tools menu, choose Unprotect Document and turn off protection for Track Changes.
16. Display the Reviewing toolbar and accept or reject the proposed changes.

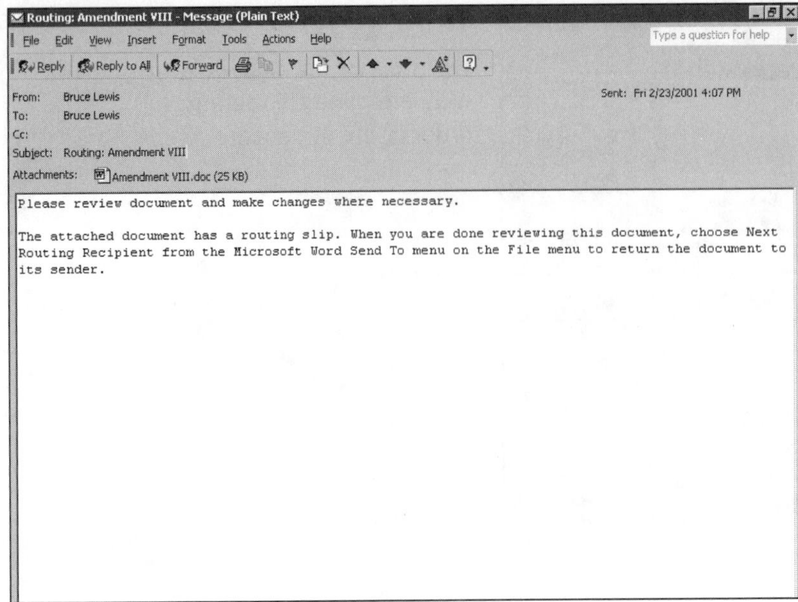

FIGURE 15.18

Remember to route the document to the next recipient after making changes.

17. From the File menu, choose Save As, navigate to C:\My Documents (or to the directory where you stored the original file), and click Save.

NOTE

If you click Save instead of Save As, Word actually saves the changes to the temp folder on your computer where the attached file to the e-mail is stored. You must use the Save As feature to overwrite the original file with the changes from the attached file.

18. Click Yes when prompted, to overwrite the existing file **Amendment VIII**.
19. The file **Amendment VIII** now contains all the accepted changes from the routing recipients.

SHARING DOCUMENTS EXTERNALLY

Documents are often passed back and forth between client and attorney or between their respective secretaries. The ubiquitous nature of e-mail has made this process more efficient while at the same time potentially more damaging. Leading document management systems integrate with most of the e-mail systems on the market and allow users to e-mail documents directly from the Document Management Desktop. This can be very useful when sending multiple documents at the same time.

You can also e-mail documents directly from within Word, as either an attached file(s) or as the body of the e-mail message itself. Most legal users will choose to send the file as an attachment because embedding the document into the body of the message limits the ability to edit on the receiving end.

Before sending a document as the *body* of an e-mail message (File, Send To, Mail Recipient), make sure the recipient's mail system is configured to handle mail in HTML format—this is how Word sends the file. Use this option for viewing purposes only, not when the recipient will need to edit the file.

SEND A DOCUMENT AS AN ATTACHMENT

1. Create a new document.
2. Type **The powers not delegated to the United States by the Constitution, nor prohibited by it to the States, are reserved to the States respectively, or to the people.**
3. Save the document to C:\My Documents (or a local document directory) and name it **Amendment X.**
4. From the File menu, choose Send To and select Mail Recipient (as Attachment). Figure 15.19 shows the e-mail message containing the attached document.

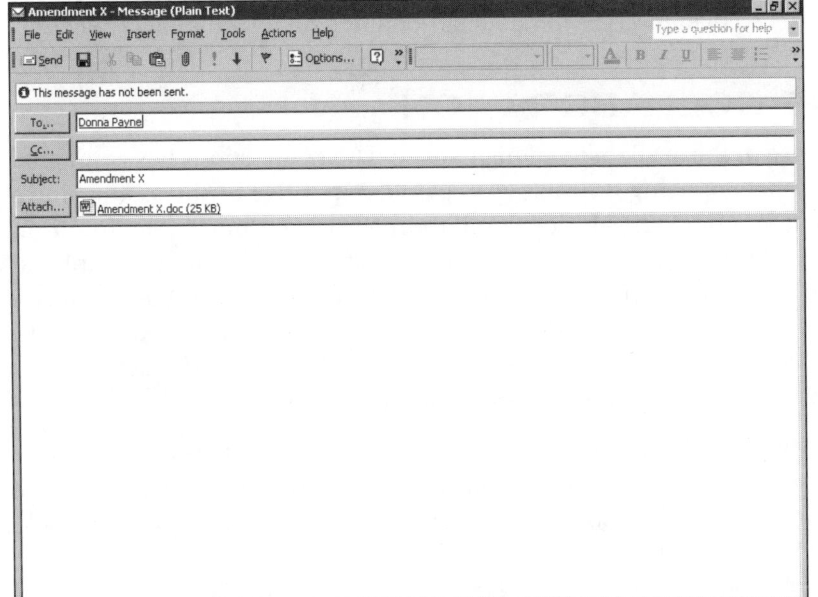

FIGURE 15.19

If you're using Outlook 2002 and wish to attach multiple documents, click Attach and navigate to the appropriate directory. Select the appropriate document and click Insert. Repeat this process until all documents are added. You will see a list of file attachments in the Attach line of your pending e-mail message.

5. Address the e-mail message to the appropriate recipients, amend the Subject line as needed, then type a message and click Send.

NOTE

This exercise assumes you're using Word 2002 and Outlook 2002. If your e-mail system doesn't look like the one in this exercise, contact your system administrator for details regarding your system.

METADATA AND TRACKED CHANGES

Metadata has become a topic of great interest to law firms recently as more information about it has been publicized and growing numbers of users have become aware of the threat it poses to both client and firm confidentiality. Metadata can be loosely defined as invisible information that resides within Word documents (and some Excel and PowerPoint files, for that matter).

Since comments and tracked changes can be displayed or hidden, many firms have found themselves in the embarrassing position of unknowingly sending files to clients or co-counsel that contained regrettable observations that had not been removed.

Microsoft has added additional security to warn before sending, saving, or printing a file that contains comments or tracked changes. From the Tools menu, choose Options. Select the Security tab and check Warn Before Printing, Sending Or Saving A File That Contains Tracked Changes Or Comments.

Metadata will be covered in greater detail in Chapter 20, "Document Forensics."

ONLINE COLLABORATION

The steady rise in the availability of high-speed data connections has combined with the prospect of using technology to gain competitive business advantage to create a demand for the ability to collaborate in real time via the Internet. Microsoft NetMeeting is a utility that lets users from different geographical regions work together online by connecting to a central server. Your firm can use NetMeeting to connect satellite offices or conduct virtual meetings with clients. NetMeeting can be used to share documents, give PowerPoint presentations, or review quarterly financial statements created in Excel.

To use NetMeeting, participants must have it installed on their PCs. The host will need NetMeeting 2.11 or above. With NetMeeting, one user hosts the online gathering and invites others to join by sending a meeting request from Outlook, as shown in Figure 15.20.

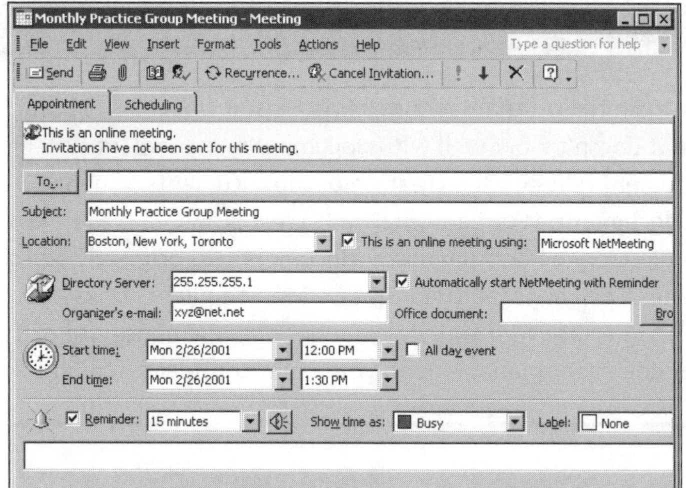

FIGURE 15.20

Some firms are using NetMeeting to reduce travel costs by conducting meetings online rather than attending in person.

Participants can launch NetMeeting by clicking Start, Programs, NetMeeting or by choosing Tools, Online Collaboration, Meet Now. They then enter the name or IP address of the central server to join in the online meeting. The meeting host can send specific files to each participant so each member can have the most current, relevant information for the meeting. Meeting participants can even chat with one another using a special chat window or make comments to a NetMeeting Whiteboard. Contact your system administrator to see if your firm is set up to use NetMeeting.

MASTER DOCUMENTS

Master Document is a feature in Word that most law firms rarely use. However, based on questions and feedback from some of our clients and readers, we've decided to include a discussion of it in this book.

The Master Document feature allows you to break one large document into several smaller subdocuments, all the while maintaining a link between the files. This can be useful for really big files (in the megabyte range), files that are graphics intensive (which tend to open and paginate slowly), or files that are made up of many articles, sections, or chapters. Each subdocument in a master document actually exists as a separate file and can be opened, edited, and saved as such. You can create a master document solely for your own use or for a workgroup or practice group.

MASTER DOCUMENT WOES

The main reason that law firms find Master Document impractical is that it doesn't work well with document management systems. Master Document relies on the creation of subdocuments. When you create subdocuments, Word automatically creates and links the files locally to the directory where the master document was originally saved. The Master Document feature is not ODMA compliant, which means it won't interface well with a document management system. If your firm uses document management, you might consider skipping this section.

To create a master document, create a new document and switch to Outline view. Use heading styles as you type text. Each heading will eventually become a separate subdocument. The Outlining toolbar, as shown in Figure 15.21, contains a number of options that can be used to create, delete, and insert subdocuments, as well as merge and lock them when appropriate.

NOTE

The Outlining toolbar automatically appears in an expanded mode when you switch to Outline view.

Once you've created an outline, the next step is to convert each heading into a subdocument.

NOTE

The following exercise assumes that Word is not integrated with a document management system. If your firm uses document management then skip this exercise and practice in a nonintegrated environment.

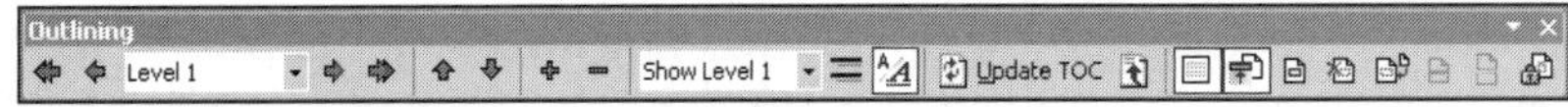

FIGURE 15.21

The Outlining toolbar has various options for working with a master document.

CREATE A MASTER DOCUMENT WITH SEVERAL SUBDOCUMENTS

1. Create a new document. Turn on Show/Hide.
2. From the View menu, choose Outline.
3. Type **Chapter One** and press Enter.
4. Repeat Step 3 (that is, type **Chapter Two** and so on) until you have four chapters. Your document should look like the one in Figure 15.22.
5. Place your insertion point anywhere in the first paragraph (Chapter One) and, from the Outlining toolbar, click Create Subdocument.
6. Do the same for Chapters Two, Three, and Four.
7. From the File menu, choose Save.

Heading 1 is applied to Level 1 paragraphs in Outline view.

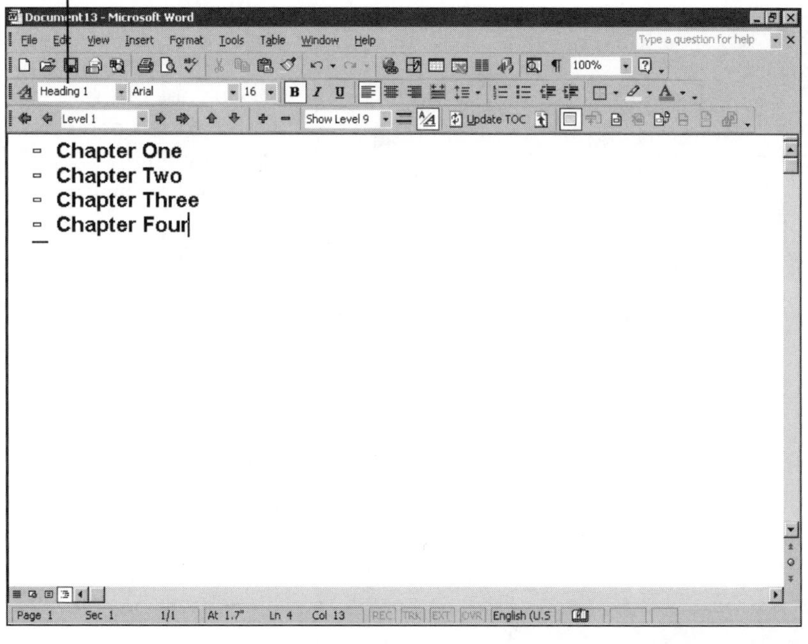

FIGURE 15.22

Notice that each chapter heading is linked to Heading 1 style.

8. Navigate to C:\My Documents (or your default document directory) and save the master document as **Firm Handbook**.
9. From the Outlining toolbar, click Collapse Subdocuments. Your document should look like the one in Figure 15.23. Notice that each of the subdocuments has been saved to the same directory.
10. Click the first hyperlink to open Chapter One.doc. Notice that Word opens up a separate document window for the file.
11. Press Enter after Chapter One and type **Introduction**. Press Ctrl+S to save the changes.
12. Close Chapter One.doc.
13. Return to Firm Handbook.doc and, from the Outlining toolbar, click Expand Subdocuments. Notice that the changes you added appear in this view.
14. From the View menu, choose Normal. This displays the Master Document in its entirety.

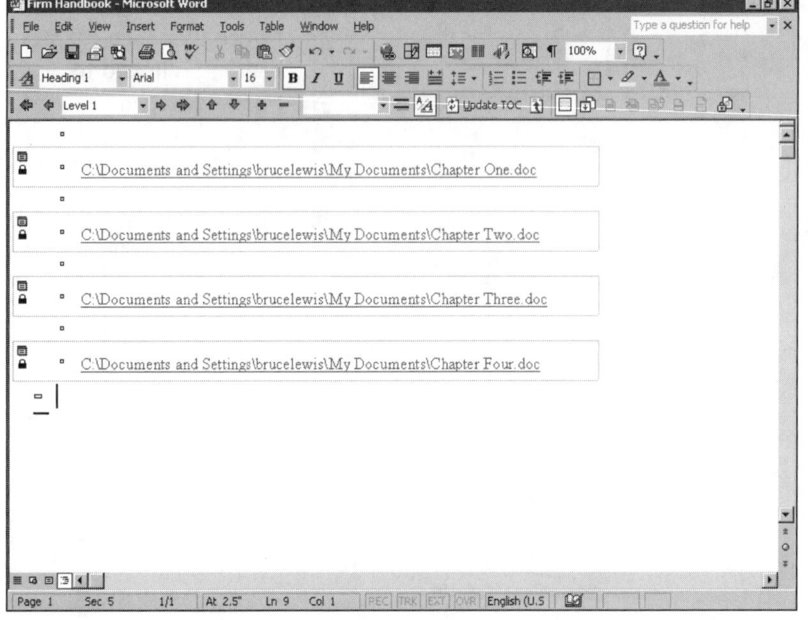

FIGURE 15.23

Click on any of the hyperlinks to open up a subdocument in a separate document window.

PRINTING MASTER DOCUMENTS

The easiest way to print a master document is to use the following steps:

1. Open the master document.
2. Switch to Outline view and expand the subdocuments.
3. Switch to Normal view and, from the File menu, choose Print.

WORKING WITH SUBDOCUMENTS

Once you've created a master document with subdocuments, you can open and work with each subdocument individually. To do so, open the master document, switch to Outline view, and collapse the subdocuments by clicking Collapse Subdocuments on the Outlining toolbar. Once you have collapsed the subdocuments, click the appropriate hyperlink to open a specific subdocument. Since subdocuments are actually separate files, Word opens up a new document window. Make the necessary edits and save the changes. When you finish, close the document.

VIEWING ENTIRE CONTENTS OF A MASTER DOCUMENT

There may be times when you want to view everything in a master document rather than working with individual subdocuments. You can do so easily. First, open the master document and switch to Outline view. Expand all the subdocuments and then switch to Normal or Print Layout view.

PRINTING SUBDOCUMENTS

To print a subdocument, open the master document, switch to Outline view, collapse the subdocuments, click the appropriate hyperlink and, from the File menu, choose Print.

INSERTING ADDITIONAL SUBDOCUMENTS

You can insert existing documents as subdocuments into a master document. To do so, open the master document, switch to Outline view, place your insertion point where you want the subdocument to appear, and click Insert Subdocument on the Outlining toolbar. From the Open dialog box, navigate to the directory where the document you wish to insert resides, select it, and click Open.

SHARING AND PROTECTING SUBDOCUMENTS

One of the real strengths of Word's Master Document feature is the ability that it provides for multiple users to collaborate on one document simultaneously. A master document that is stored on a shared network drive can be accessed and edited by various members of a practice group, review panel, or project team. Each member can open the document and work on specific subdocuments. Word also has built-in protection to ensure that only one person at a time can work on a subdocument. Whenever a subdocument is open, it becomes locked. If other users attempt to access the subdocument they will get a read-only copy. Users can even choose to receive notification once the locked subdocument becomes available, as shown in Figure 15.24.

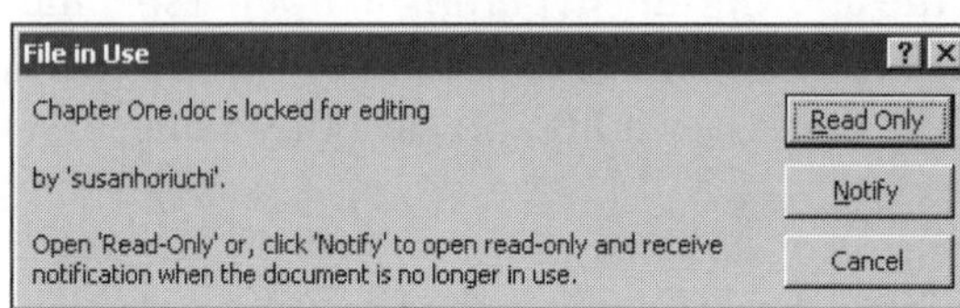

FIGURE 15.24

Subdocuments become locked once someone opens them.

SUMMARY

Chapter 15 focuses on the features in Word that assist with document collaboration. The chapter opens with an examination of Track Changes, Comments, Compare And Merge, and Versions. The second half focuses on third-party comparison software, reviewing and routing files, and a brief overview of metadata with respect to tracked changes and comments. The chapter concludes with a look at collaborating online using NetMeeting and working with master documents.

TROUBLESHOOTING DOCUMENT COLLABORATION

I've inserted a number of comments in my document but I can't see them—where have they gone?

In Word 2002, the appearance of online comments has changed a bit. If you're in Normal view, the only indication of a comment is a either a colored I-beam or brackets positioned at the point where you inserted the comment—easy to miss. To readily and easily view comments, switch to Print Layout view and make sure the Use Balloons In Print And Web Layout option is checked in the Track Changes tab of the Tools, Options dialog box.

Whenever I use Compare And Merge, Word rolls all the changes between the two documents I'm comparing into the open document. I then have to use Save As to create a separate redlined document so as not to change the original. Is there any way to avoid this?

When you use Compare And Merge, make sure to check the Legal Blackline option before comparing. This will create a separate output document, which will open in its own document window. You can save it, print it, or simply use it as a temporary visual aid.

I used Word's Versions feature and then tried to compare two versions of a document using Compare And Merge but I couldn't find the second version—why not?

Word's Versions feature is very different from versions in the context of a document management system. Word creates each new version as a component appended to the original file with the same file name. So it's actually impossible to create multiple versions for the purpose of comparing. And Word's Versions feature can make small files bloat quickly—be careful with this feature!

I'm really worried about accidentally sending documents out that may have comments—is there any way to quickly remove online comments?

Yes—to remove comments manually, activate the Reviewing toolbar, click the drop-down arrow next to the Delete Comment button, and choose Delete All Comments In Document. If you want a more foolproof automated system that integrates with Outlook, go to www.payneconsulting.com and find out about the Enterprise edition of the Metadata Assistant.

I just sent a document out to another member of my firm and received it back with changes. I want to save it back to our document management system without having to create a new profile. Is this possible?

No. When you send a document as an attachment you're actually sending out a copy—not the original. When you receive the copy back as a marked-up attachment and attempt to save it, your document management system doesn't recognize it so it prompts you to profile it as an original document. Most document management systems have an option that lets you send *internal* documents as links. This maintains the profile and original document number. If you send any documents within your firm as links, all changes will be made to the original, not a copy.

CHAPTER 16

MAIL MERGE

IN THIS CHAPTER

- Mail Merge tools
- Sending letters with Mail Merge
- Printing a directory of address data
- Producing labels and e-mail messages
- Managing and selecting data for Mail Merge

Microsoft has completely redesigned how Mail Merge works in Word 2002. You'll find a leaner, meaner, and cleaner version of this utility, much simpler to use than any of its predecessors—but still compatible with most old merge main document files. Using the Mail Merge feature, you can create personalized letters, envelopes, labels, faxes, e-mail messages, directories, and more. The Mail Merge Wizard, along with the new Mail Merge Task Pane, can help a novice get through even the first Mail Merge like a pro.

You'll find that using Mail Merge is the simplest way to set up mass mailings, whether you're sending corporate annual meeting notices or creating labels for preprinted firm announcements. Best of all, for anyone who uses a document management system, this version of Word works *with* your document management system—not against it.

MAIL MERGE OVERVIEW

Performing a Mail Merge using the Mail Merge Wizard involves a four-step process:

1. Create or open the main document.
2. Create or open the source document.
3. Insert merge fields into the main document.
4. Perform the merge process.

TIP

For anyone who has used WordPerfect's merge feature, the Word main document is the same as WordPerfect's primary document and the Word source document is the same as WordPerfect's secondary document.

Initially setting up the Mail Merge will take some time, but the Mail Merge itself can be completed in a matter of seconds once it's set up. The following sections describe and demonstrate the steps involved in a Mail Merge to create a main document that contains the standard text, create a data source containing name and address information, insert merge fields into the main document, and finally merge the main document and data source together to create the final product. Keep in mind, if your firm's client information is already stored in a database, your work is halfway complete.

NOTE

You can use Mail Merge to create any type of document that maps fields to data, not just mailings or directories. For example, you could create personalized stock certificates for each shareholder using the merge process.

MAIL MERGE TOOLS

Before starting a Mail Merge project, it will be helpful to identify some of the new Mail Merge tools available in this version of Word.

MAIL MERGE TOOLBAR

The Mail Merge toolbar includes 22 buttons for performing and working with Mail Merge documents. If you have used Mail Merge in previous versions of Word, you will notice that there are several new buttons, including Insert Word Field, View Merged Data, and Check For Errors. When the main document of your Mail Merge is onscreen, the toolbar automatically appears. You can also alternate-click any toolbar button and choose Mail Merge to display the toolbar at any time. Figure 16.1 shows the new and improved Mail Merge toolbar.

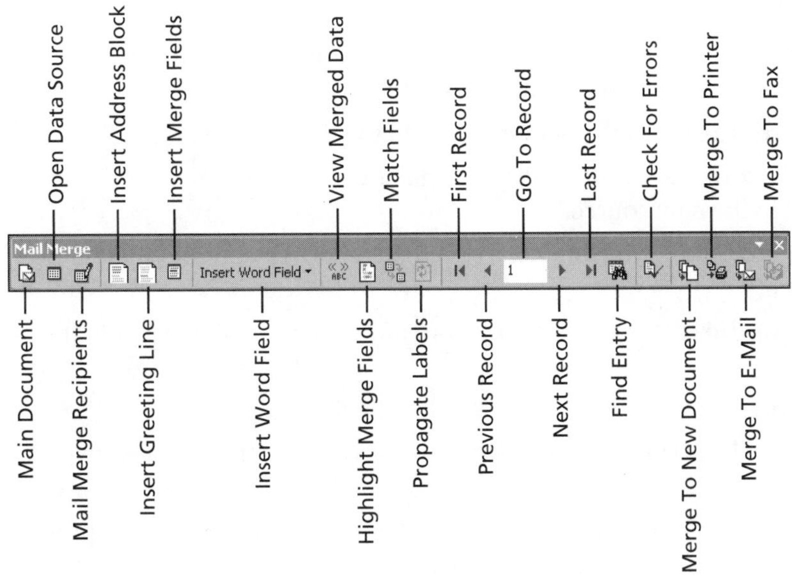

FIGURE 16.1

The Mail Merge toolbar includes buttons for each of the steps needed to create a Mail Merge.

Here is a list of the Mail Merge toolbar buttons, along with a brief description of each.

- **Main Document Setup**. Opens a dialog box that helps you select and create the main document (your letter, e-mail message, envelope, or whatever).
- **Open Data Source**. Allows you to select the data source or variable information that will be merged with the main document to create a personalized document for each recipient.
- **Mail Merge Recipients**. Displays a table listing all the recipients in the data source; this list can be edited and manipulated.
- **Insert Address Block**. Allows you to designate what information is included in the Address Block of the main document.
- **Insert Greeting Line**. Allows you to designate what greeting information is included in the main document.
- **Insert Merge Fields**. Allows you to select any of the fields available—either Address fields or Data fields—and insert them into the main document.
- **Insert Word Field**. Allows you to insert Word fields such as Ask, Fill-In, Next Record, Set Bookmark, and more.
- **View Merged Data**. Shows you an example of how the data merges with the main document.
- **Highlight Merge Fields**. Highlights the merge fields in the main document so they are easy to identify.
- **Match Fields**. Allows you to match fields in your database with the Address Block fields.
- **Propagate Labels**. Allows you to generate labels once the main label document has been set up and the data source has been defined.
- **First Record**. Takes you to the first record in the data source.
- **Previous Record**. Takes you to the record above the location of your insertion point in the data source.
- **Go To Record**. Allows you to go to a specified record (by number) in the data source.
- **Next Record**. Takes you to the next record after your insertion point in the data source.
- **Last Record**. Takes you to the last record in the data source.
- **Find Entry**. Allows you to search all fields or a specified field for any text string.
- **Check For Errors**. Allows you to check the Mail Merge for errors; also provides multiple options for viewing errors.

- **Merge To New Document**. Creates a new document containing the personalized Mail Merge product when the main document and data source information are merged together.
- **Merge To Printer**. Prints the completed Mail Merge product automatically when the main document and data source information are merged together.
- **Merge To E-Mail**. Creates new e-mail messages for each recipient when the main document and data source information are merged together.
- **Merge To Fax**. Creates fax coversheets for each recipient when the main document and data source information are merged together.

USING THE MAIL MERGE WIZARD

When the Mail Merge Wizard is activated, the Mail Merge Task Pane appears. The wizard walks you through the steps required to create customized letters, e-mail messages, envelopes, labels, or a directory. Figure 16.2 shows Step 1 of the new Mail Merge Wizard.

NOTE

Experienced Mail Merge users can bypass the Mail Merge Task Pane entirely and just use the Mail Merge toolbar to complete each step of the merge process.

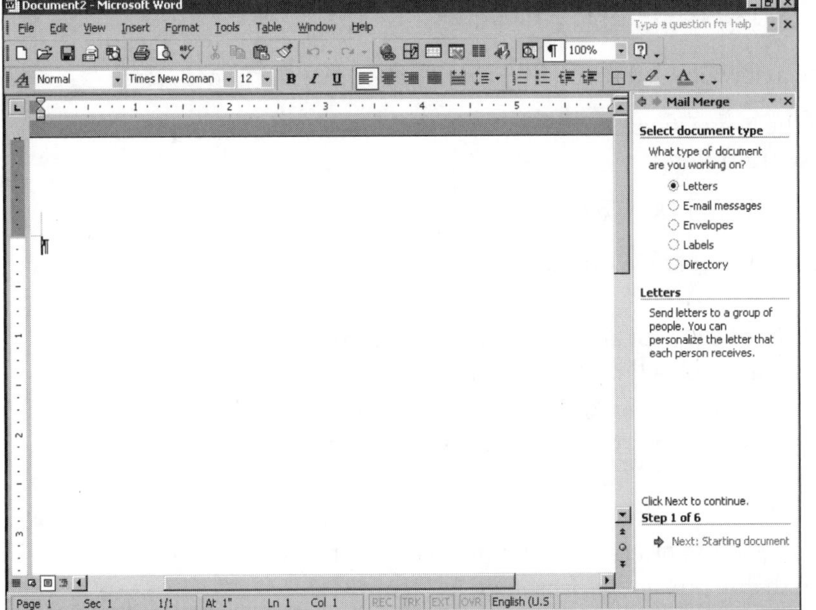

FIGURE 16.2

The Mail Merge Task Pane offers step-by-step instructions for the Mail Merge process.

USING THE MAIL MERGE WIZARD

1. To start the Mail Merge Wizard, from the Tools menu, choose Letters And Mailings, Mail Merge Wizard. The task pane appears on the right.
2. Under Select Document Type, select the various options (letters, e-mail messages, and so on) and review the description provided for each.
3. At the bottom of the task pane, click Next: Starting Document.
4. Under Select Starting Document, select the various options available.
5. Click Previous to return to Step 1.
6. Close the document without saving.

The Mail Merge Wizard and task pane not only clearly describe each of the steps of the Mail Merge process, they walk you through the entire process while your document is onscreen.

LETTER WIZARD

Another wizard helpful to new users of Word is the Letter Wizard. This wizard will walk you through the process of creating your own letter that can also be used with the Mail Merge Wizard.

USING THE LETTER WIZARD

1. Create a new blank document. From the File menu, choose New.
2. From the New Document Task Pane, under New From Template, click General Templates.
3. Select the Letters & Faxes tab.
4. Double-click Letter Wizard.

NOTE

If the Letter Wizard does not appear in the Letters & Faxes tab, you might need to install the wizard. Some firms choose not to install some of the default Microsoft templates and wizards, so the Letter Wizard may not be available. In that case, either skip this exercise or see your system administrator about obtaining a copy.

5. Select the Send Letters To A Mailing List option and the Mail Merge Helper dialog box opens, as shown in Figure 16.3.

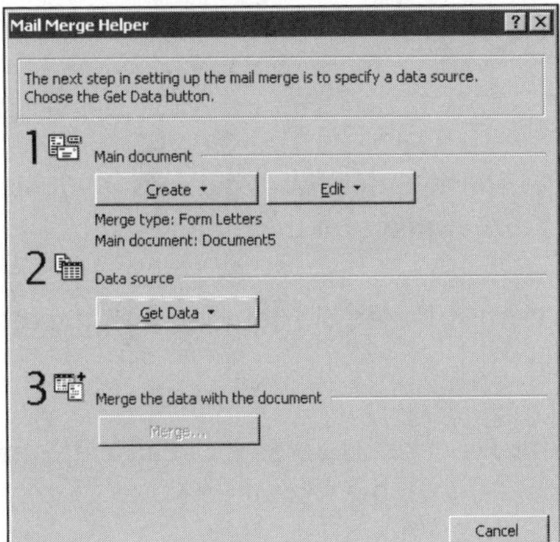

FIGURE 16.3

The Mail Merge Helper dialog box walks you through the process of creating the main document, the data source, and merging the document with the data source.

NOTE

The Mail Merge Helper dialog box was also used in previous versions of Word.

6. Click Cancel to close the Mail Merge Helper dialog box.
7. Close the document without saving.

MERGE LETTERS

It's easy to create merge letters using the Mail Merge Wizard. The process involves two primary steps: create the document, and then select the recipients and other options. Two more steps are required to finish the mailing: add fields to the main document, then combine the main and source documents.

STEP 1: CREATE THE MAIN DOCUMENT

The first step in the merge process is to create the main document. The main document contains the standard text and graphics that appear unchanged in every one of the merged documents. In this exercise, you create a Mail Merge form letter. The standard text will include the body and the signature block of the letter.

TIP

If you are already familiar with the Mail Merge process or prefer not to use the Mail Merge Wizard, you can use the Mail Merge toolbar.

CREATING A FORM LETTER

1. Create a new document.
2. From the Tools menu, choose Letters And Mailings, Mail Merge Wizard. The Mail Merge Task Pane appears on the right.

NOTE

If the insertion point is in the header, footer, or Footnote Pane, the Letters And Mailings submenu is disabled.

3. Under Select Document Type, select Letters. Click Next: Starting Document to move to the next step in the wizard.
4. Under Select Starting Document, select Start From A Template.
5. Under Start From A Template, click Select Template.
6. Choose one of your firm's standard letter templates, if available; otherwise, select one of Word's default templates but delete the instructional text in the document.
7. Insert a date at the top of the letter, if one does not already exist.
8. Where the body text of the letter should appear, type the following text: **Our annual Employment Law seminar has been scheduled for Friday, May 16th. It will be held at the Seattle Sheraton & Towers, Grand Ballroom, between the hours of 9:00 a.m. and 4:00 p.m. Please RSVP by returning the enclosed self-addressed, stamped postcard. We hope to see you there.**

   Sincerely,
9. Press Enter three times and type the name of your law firm or company.
10. Leave this document open for the next exercise.

The main document has been created and the standard text has been added. The next step of the merge process involves the data source.

STEP 2: SELECT RECIPIENTS

The second step in the merge process is to create or open an existing data source. A data source contains the data or variable information that changes from letter to letter. In this example, the inside address and salutation information are contained in the data source.

A data source can be a Word document, an Excel spreadsheet, a set of Outlook Contacts, an Access or SQL database—in fact, any MAPI-compliant database will do.

TIP

If you are selecting a Microsoft Excel spreadsheet as your data source and the spreadsheet has information on multiple tabs, you must select the tab containing the information needed before clicking OK.

Data sources contain two types of information. All the information about one specific recipient (for example, name, street address, city, state, ZIP code, and salutation name) is called a *data record.* Each of those individual pieces of information (name, street address, and so on) is called a *data field.*

When you click Select Recipients on the Mail Merge Task Pane, you can choose from the three options listed in Table 16.1.

TABLE 16.1 OPTIONS FOR SELECTING RECIPIENTS

OPTION	RESULT
Use An Existing List:	This option will offer you the last data source used; you have three choices: (1) select a different list, (2) edit the recipient list displayed, or (3) click Next: Write Your Letter to accept the default Word data source without editing.
Select From Outlook Contacts:	This option will offer you the last Outlook Contacts list used; you have three choices: (1) click Contacts Folder so you can select a different Contacts folder in Outlook, (2) edit the recipient list displayed, or (3) click Next: Write Your Letter to accept the default Outlook Contacts data source without editing.
Type A New List	Create a new Word data source.

CREATING A DATA SOURCE IN WORD

When you create a data source in Word, the information is stored in a Microsoft Office Address Lists (*.mdb) database. However, it is easier to think of the data source as a table with columns and rows of information. Each column corresponds to a category of information, the data field. Each row of information corresponds to information in a unique data record, such as the name and address of a single recipient. When you complete the merge process, individual recipient information is mapped to fields in the main document. In previous versions of Word, the data source created by the Mail Merge Wizard was a Word table. Each table column was a data field and the maximum number of columns allowed in a Word table is 63. Using the Office Address Lists database for the data source removes this limitation.

If you've used Microsoft Access, you may recognize the .mdb file type as the same file type used in Microsoft Access databases. While the Office Address Lists database uses the same file extension, you do not need to have Access installed to be able to use the feature.

The next exercise creates a simple recipient list in Word to use as your data source.

CREATING A DATA SOURCE

1. At the bottom of the Mail Merge Task Pane, click Next: Select Recipients.
2. Under Select Recipients, click Type A New List.
3. Under Type A New List, click Create and the New Address List dialog box opens, as shown in Figure 16.4.
4. Leave the dialog box open for the next exercise.

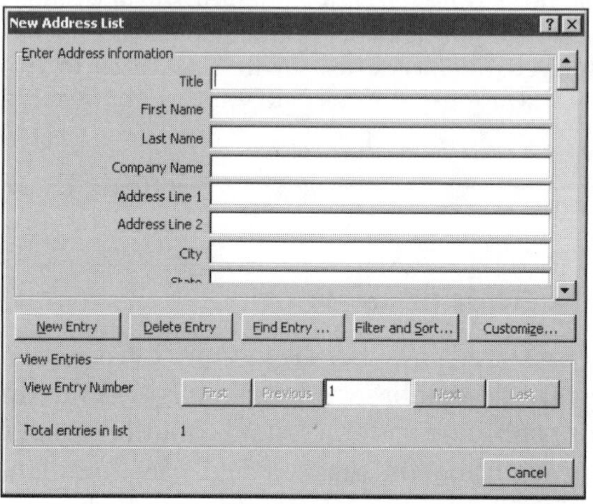

FIGURE 16.4

The New Address List dialog box simplifies the process of inputting name and address information into a data source.

MODIFYING THE DATA SOURCE

The New Address List dialog box contains standard data fields for the data record. You may want to add fields to this list or even remove extraneous fields that will not be used. Keep in mind, however, that it is perfectly OK to leave unused fields in a data source even though you will not use the data contained in them. Your main document will retrieve information only from the fields that you designate.

Before you begin, you should carefully plan what types of information will need to be maintained in the data source and identify all the data fields to be included in the data record. It is also a good idea to break down into small pieces the information contained in each data record. For example, rather than having one field contain the entire recipient name, it would be better to break it down into fields such as Title, First Name, and Last Name. This gives you the option to use either the First Name or the Title plus Last Name in the salutation.

MODIFYING THE DATA FIELDS IN THE NEW ADDRESS LIST

It is easy to add more data fields to your data source from the New Address List dialog box. These fields will then be available to your main document. In the next exercise, you add and remove several data fields.

MODIFYING THE DATA SOURCE

1. From the New Address List dialog box, click Customize. The Customize Address List dialog box opens, as shown in Figure 16.5.

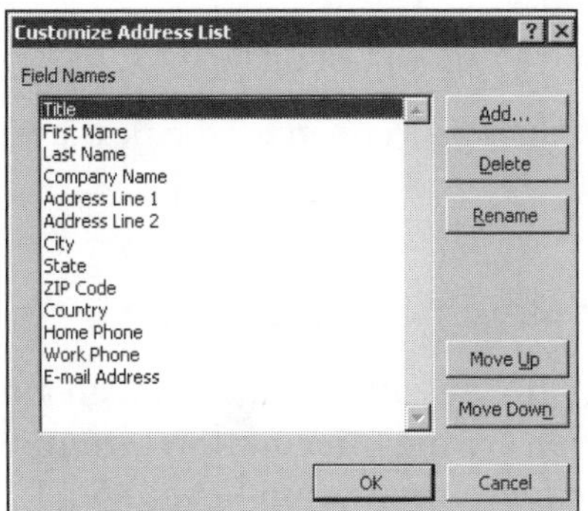

FIGURE 16.5

You can add or remove data fields from the Customize Address List dialog box.

2. From the Field Names list, select Country and click Delete. At the prompt, click Yes to confirm the deletion. The Country data field is removed from the list.
3. From the Field Names list, select and delete the Home Phone and Work Phone fields.
4. Click Add on the Customize Address List dialog box. The Add Field dialog box opens, as shown in Figure 16.6.

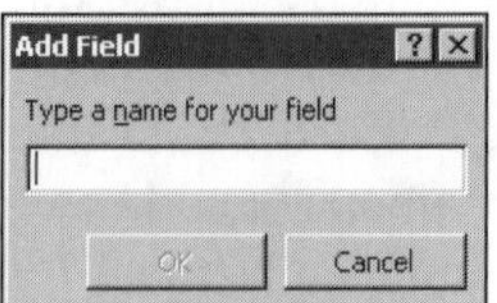

FIGURE 16.6

You can easily add more data fields to your data source.

5. Type **Attorney** for the name of the new data field and click OK. "Attorney" now appears in the list of data fields, where it can be used to develop a signature block for the letter.

TIP

Data field names must be unique.

6. If the Attorney data field does not appear at the bottom of the list, click the Move Up or Move Down buttons to reorder the fields.
7. Repeat steps 4 and 5 to add a field for client-matter number, typing **Client-Matter** for the field name. The client-matter field will be used in a later exercise, not in the current letter. (This demonstrates that data sources can contain fields not used in the main document.)
8. Click OK to return to the New Address List dialog box.
9. Leave the New Address List dialog box open for the next exercise.

ADDING RECORDS TO THE NEW ADDRESS LIST

The New Address List data form provides an easy mechanism for adding information to your data source. When typing information into the New Address List, you can use either Tab or Enter to move from field to field. Use Shift+Tab to return to a previous field.

Adding Data Records

1. Input the following data:

   Title: **Ms.**
   First Name: **Alma**
   Last Name: **Bell**
   Company Name: **Bell & Perez LLP**
   Address Line 1: **123 Edmonds Street**
   Address Line 2: **Suite 230**
   City: **New Orleans**
   State: **LA**
   ZIP Code: **70132**
   E-mail Address: **ab@BellPerez.com**
   Attorney: **Doug Wigington, Esq.**
   Client-Matter: **1001-4**

2. Click the New Entry button to save the data record and then add the following two records:

   Title: **Mr.**
   First Name: **George**
   Last Name: **Douglas**
   Company Name: **Netherton, Penland & Madison**
   Address Line 1: **55 Park Avenue**
   Address Line 2: **Suite 1400**
   City: **Chicago**
   State: **IL**
   ZIP Code: **60606**
   E-mail Address: **GDouglas@NPMLaw.com**
   Attorney: **Jeff Peterson, Esq.**
   Client-Matter: **1022-3**

   Title: **Mrs.**
   First Name: **Diana**
   Last Name: **Snead**
   Company Name: **Gullikson Consulting, Inc.**
   Address Line 1: **1616 First Avenue**
   Address Line 2: **Suite 2200**
   City: **Seattle**
   State: **WA**
   ZIP Code: **98101**
   E-mail Address: **DianaSnead@Gullikson.com**
   Attorney: **Chris Taylor, Esq.**
   Client-Matter: **1302-1**

3. Click Close when you finish.
4. At the Save Address List dialog box (which appears automatically when you click Close), type the name **Employment Law Data Source** in the File Name box and click Save. Click OK on the Mail Merge Recipients dialog box.

NOTE

The maximum number of fields in the Mail Merge Recipients dialog box is 255.

5. Leave the document open for the next exercise.

MODIFYING THE DATA SOURCE

The data source can be modified at any time during the Mail Merge creation process. When information in the data source needs to be corrected, it's important to edit the data source, never the completed merge document. If you change the merge document but not the source, the same corrections would need to be made once again the next time the data source is used. In the next exercise, you will edit the data source by adding another recipient to the database.

EDIT THE DATA SOURCE

1. On the Select Recipients Mail Merge Task Pane, select Use An Existing List.
2. Under Use An Existing List, click Edit Recipient List and the Mail Merge Recipients data form appears.
3. Click Edit and the Edit Address List data form shown in Figure 16.7 appears.

FIGURE 16.7

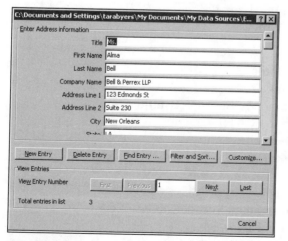

From the Edit Address List data form, you can edit existing records, add or remove recipients, customize the data form, and perform many other functions.

NOTE

The Edit button is enabled only for specific data source file types such as .doc, .rtf, and .txt, as well as data sources created with the Office Address Lists database .mdb. Excel and Access data sources must be edited directly in their application rather than through the Mail Merge Recipients dialog box.

4. Click New Entry and input the following recipient information:

   Title: **Ms.**
   First Name: **Tammy**
   Last Name: **Crisp**
   Company Name: **Crisp & Associates**
   Address Line 1: **2465 18th N.E.**
   Address Line 2: **Suite 10**
   City: **Seattle**
   State: **WA**
   ZIP Code: **98101**
   E-mail Address: **TCrisp@Crisp.com**
   Attorney: **Harvey Jones, Esq.**
   Client-Matter: **2101-1**

5. Click Close when you finish.
6. Click Find in the Mail Merge Recipients dialog box and the Find Entry dialog box opens. (If the data source is small, it is easy to find a record by hand—but it's much easier to use the Find option once the source is larger than a handful of records.)
7. Type **George** in the Find box.
8. Change the Look In box to This Field and select First Name from the list.
9. Click Find Next and the record is selected in the Mail Merge Recipients dialog box. If there were more than one occurrence of George as a First Name, you would click Find Next until the correct record appeared.
10. Click Cancel to close the Find Entry dialog box. Click OK to return to the document.
11. Leave the document open for the next exercise.

NOTE

You may have noticed the Validate button on the Mail Merge Recipients dialog box. If you have validation software installed on your computer, you can click this button to validate for complete address fields for city, state, and postal code. If no validation software is installed, click Yes to go to the Microsoft Office Update Web page for information on how to obtain the software.

Address validation is currently available for addresses in the United States and Canada only.

STEP 3: ADDING FIELDS TO THE MAIN DOCUMENT

The next step in the Mail Merge process is to complete the main document by inserting the merge fields where the data should appear in the letter. Data fields are placed everywhere information from the data source should appear in the document. The Mail Merge Wizard includes two of the most common merge fields—AddressBlock and GreetingLine. The AddressBlock field is the placeholder for the name and address of the recipient. The GreetingLine field is the placeholder for the salutation. The wizard allows you to customize these fields while automatically including the ability to adapt to missing information in the address or salutation so you don't end up with blank lines. The next exercise gives you a look at the options available with each of these fields.

NOTE

Be sure to include the correct spacing; both between words and, when inserting the address block, paragraph spacing before and after when adding merge fields in the document. Otherwise, when the merge is complete, the merged text may be combined with the standard text or have too much spacing between the lines.

COMPLETING THE LETTER

1. At the bottom of the Mail Merge Task Pane, click Next: Write Your Letter.
2. Click in the letter where you want the letter's inside address (name, address, city, and so on) to appear. This places your insertion point where the merge field will be inserted.
3. From the Mail Merge Task Pane, click Address Block to open the Insert Address Block dialog box, as shown in Figure 16.8.
4. Accept the default options and click OK. Press Enter twice.
5. From the Mail Merge Task Pane, click Greeting Line. The Greeting Line dialog box opens, as shown in Figure 16.9.

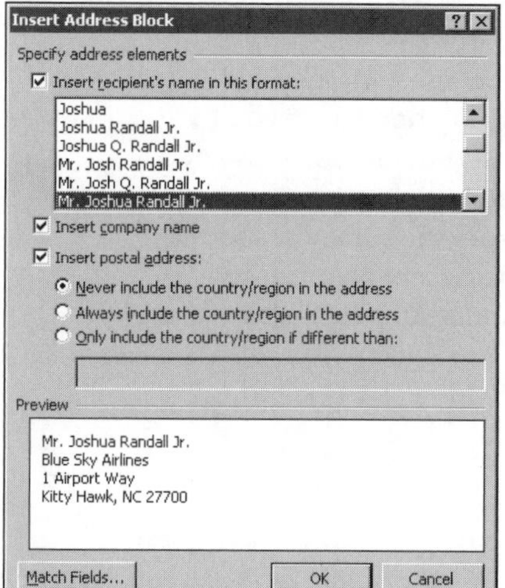

FIGURE 16.8

The Insert Address Block dialog box allows you to easily format the address block information in the main document.

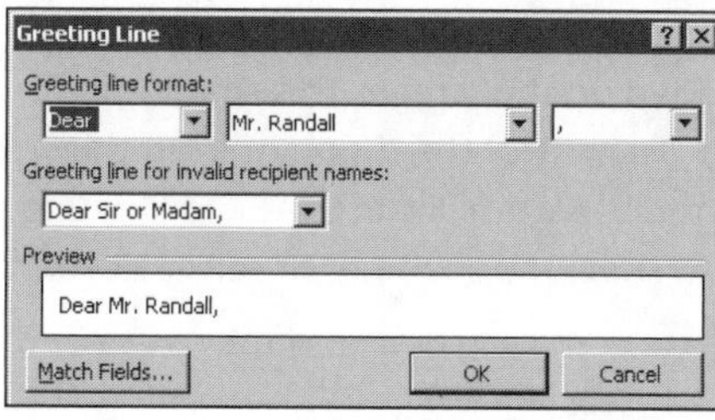

FIGURE 16.9

The Greeting Line dialog box allows you to easily format the salutation information in the main document.

6. From the Greeting Line dialog box, change the punctuation following the salutation from a comma to a colon, then click OK.

Even though field codes show up on the screen with double chevrons—double arrows called guillemets—surrounding them, you cannot insert a merge field by manually typing the chevron symbols and field name into a document.

7. Press Ctrl+End to move to the end of the document or click and place your insertion point where the signature block should appear.
8. Click More Items. The Insert Merge Field dialog box opens, as shown in Figure 16.10.
9. From the Insert Merge Field dialog box, select Attorney from the Database fields in the list and click Insert and then close the dialog box.

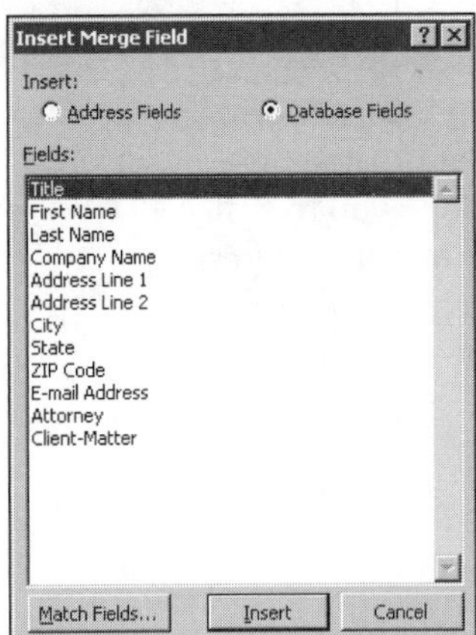

FIGURE 16.10

The Insert Merge Field dialog box allows you to insert database fields from your data source, or from the common address field components listed under Address Fields.

All merge fields have now been placed in the document.

The merge fields may appear shaded on the screen. This shading is for display purposes only and does not print. To control the shading, from the Tools menu, choose Options, and then select the View tab. From the Field Shading field, select Always or When Selected to show the shading, or select Never to remove the shading from the screen.

EDITING MERGE FIELDS

Once fields have been added to the main document, they can be edited, if necessary. One example of when editing a field is useful is when the information should be formatted a certain way, such as with all capital letters. Individual fields such as *first name, last name,* etc., can be edited. Consolidated fields such as *Address Block* and *Greeting* cannot be edited.

To edit a field, insert it into the document, alternate-click on the field code, and choose Edit Field from the shortcut menu. Depending on what type of field is being edited, a dialog box similar to Figure 16.11 opens.

PREVIEWING THE MERGE

Before sending your document to the printer, you'll want to preview the merged document to check for any mistakes. This not only gives you an opportunity to fine-tune the document, it could also potentially save you lots of paper depending on the number of records to be merged. Figure 16.12 shows an example of previewing the document.

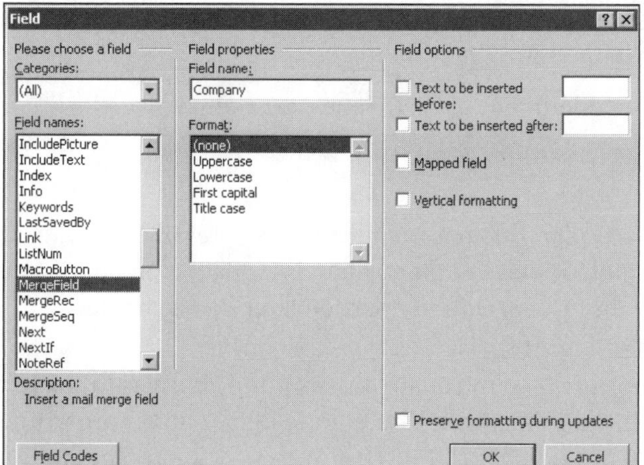

FIGURE 16.11

Fields can be edited after they are added to the main document.

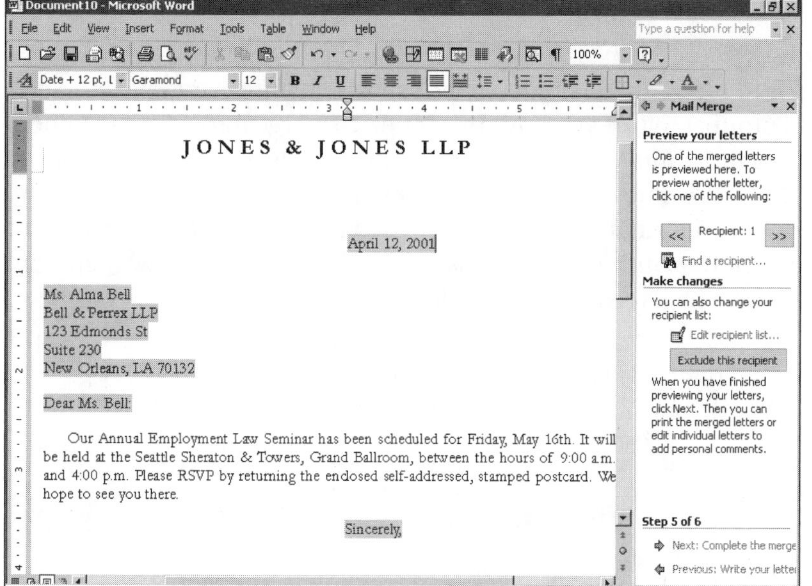

FIGURE 16.12

Previewing your document before sending it to print will give you an opportunity to view the document for layout and formatting mistakes.

PREVIEWING THE LETTER

1. In the Mail Merge Task Pane, click Next: Preview Your Letter.
2. To preview the letters in order, click the Next/Preview button (these buttons have pairs of arrowheads (or guillemets) pointing either left or right).

3. To preview a specific letter, click Find A Recipient, then enter the search criteria in the Find Entry dialog box.
4. Leave the document open for the next exercise.

NOTE

To exclude a particular recipient from the merge, preview the recipient's letter and then click Exclude This Recipient. More information on filtering records will be provided in the "Query Options" section later in this chapter.

Take this opportunity to make any last-minute changes to the letter or recipient list before printing. This would be your last chance before printing to filter out recipients you did not want in the list or to sort the recipient list by ZIP code to obtain a bulk-mailing discount. These activities will be discussed later in this chapter in the "Query Options" section.

STEP 4: COMPLETING THE MERGE

The last step is to merge the main document and recipient list together and create a finished product. While you have the option to merge the completed document directly to the printer, we recommend that you select the option to merge the information into a new document. This will give you an opportunity to check the layout and formatting of the completed project in detail before sending the document to print. In this exercise, you will merge to a new document so you can view the final result of the merge process.

NOTE

The Merge To Print option will send the merge document to the printer without creating a new document.

COMPLETING THE MERGE

1. In the Mail Merge Task Pane, click Next: Complete The Merge.
2. Click Edit Individual Letters.
3. The Merge To New Document dialog box opens, as shown in Figure 16.13. Select All and click OK. You can preview the letters one last time before printing.
4. Print the merge document by choosing File, Print and clicking OK.

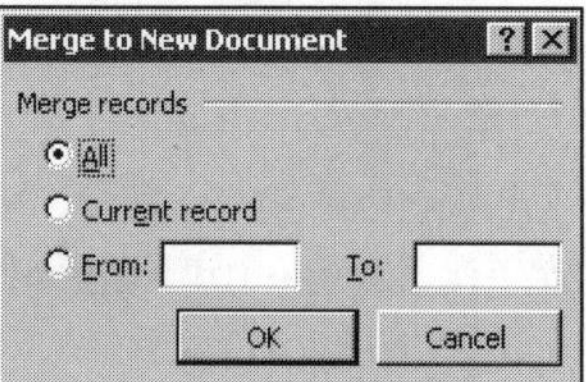

FIGURE 16.13

The Merge to New Document dialog box gives you the option to select the records you want to merge.

Congratulations! You have now completed a Mail Merge. All the merged information has been combined into one document named Letters1. Each individual letter is separated from the next by a section break. Since the main document is only one page long, each letter is a separate page in the completed merge document. Prior to printing the document, you could add personalized messages to selected letters.

Because Word places each letter in a separate section, you need to be careful when printing just selected letters that may be more than one page long. The Merge To Printer dialog box will provide options to print all the records, just the current record, or a range of records. When printing selected records in the merged document, make sure you indicate the sections rather than the pages to be printed. (For example, to print the third, fourth, sixth, and twelfth letters, type **s3-s4,s6,s12**.)

You can save the completed merge document for future use, if necessary. However, if you did not make any customizations to selected letters in the completed merge, there is no need to save the document; just save the main document and recipient list for future merges.

SAVE THE MERGE LETTER AND DATA SOURCE

1. Close the document with the completed merge product (named Letters1) and click No to close it without saving.
2. Close the main merge document and click Yes at the prompt to save the document.
3. Name the document **Employment Law Letter** and click Save.

CREATING ENVELOPES FROM YOUR MAIL MERGE

You can use the same data source to create envelopes for these letters using the Mail Merge Wizard. Keep in mind, if there are a large number of recipients and you do not have an automatic envelope feeder on your printer, it may be easier to create labels rather than envelopes. But printed envelopes look more formal and impressive than labels, so it's useful to know how to create envelopes when they're worth the extra work—or when you're sending so few letters at a time that the effort doesn't amount to anything.

Creating an Envelope Merge

1. Create a new blank document.
2. Start the Mail Merge Wizard. From the Tools menu, choose Letters And Mailings, Mail Merge Wizard. The Mail Merge Task Pane appears.
3. Under Select Document Type, select Envelopes.
4. At the bottom of the task pane, click Next: Starting Document.
5. Under Select Starting Document, select Change Document Layout and then click Envelope Options to review and change the envelope settings.
6. The Envelope Options dialog box opens, as shown in Figure 16.14. Select Size 11 from the Envelope Size drop-down list and click OK.

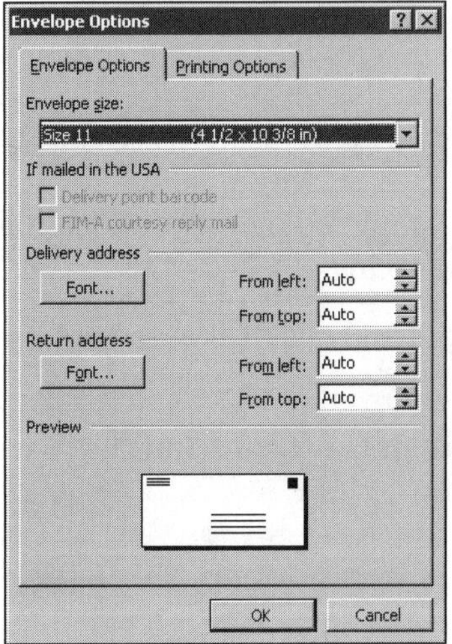

Figure 16.14

The Envelope Options dialog box allows you to change the envelope type, address fonts, and printer feed options for the envelope.

The Font buttons in the Envelope Options dialog box affect only the current job. To change the font of the delivery address and return address permanently, open the Normal template and modify the Envelope Address and Envelope Return styles.

You can automatically include a return address on your envelope in the upper-left corner. This information can be input and modified by choosing Tools, Options from the menu bar, selecting the User Information tab, and then typing the information into the Mailing Address box.

7. At the bottom of the task pane, click Next: Select Recipients.

In the preceding exercise, a data source that contains the name and address information was created. If you have name and address information located in Outlook Contacts, choose the Select From Outlook Contacts option. If the address information is located in any other MAPI-compliant database, select the Use An Existing List option, browse to the database location, and select the file.

8. From the Mail Merge Task Pane, under Select Recipients, choose the Use An Existing List option.
9. Click Browse.

The default folder browsed is My Data Sources in the My Documents folder.

10. From the Select Data Source dialog box, select Employment Law Data Source and click Open. This is the address list created in the earlier exercise.
11. From the Mail Merge Recipients dialog box, click OK to select the entire database.
12. At the bottom of the task pane, click Next: Arrange Your Envelope.

If you are not already working in Print Layout view, switch to it. From the View menu, choose Print Layout.

13. Turn on Show/Hide to view the text box on the envelope where the recipient address should appear. Place your insertion point where the address should appear.

The Address Block area of the envelope is placed in a text box. When you click within the text box, its borders appear. To move the text box, click and drag it to a new location. The text box can also be resized by clicking on the border to access the sizing handles. Click and drag the border to resize. Figure 16.15 shows the Address text box automatically placed on an envelope during the merge process.

14. Under Arrange Your Envelope in the task pane, click Address Block.
15. The Insert Address Block dialog box opens. Click OK and the Address-Block field, shown in Figure 16.16, appears.
16. Press Enter to move your insertion point under the Address field and click Postal Bar Code in the task pane to insert a barcode. The Insert Postal Bar Code dialog box opens, as shown in Figure 16.17.

Placing a barcode on an envelope or label can speed up delivery of your letter. Barcodes are valid only for addresses within the United States, so this option appears only if you are using the U.S. English version of Word. To use this option, you must select a label or envelope type that supports the POSTNET bar code.

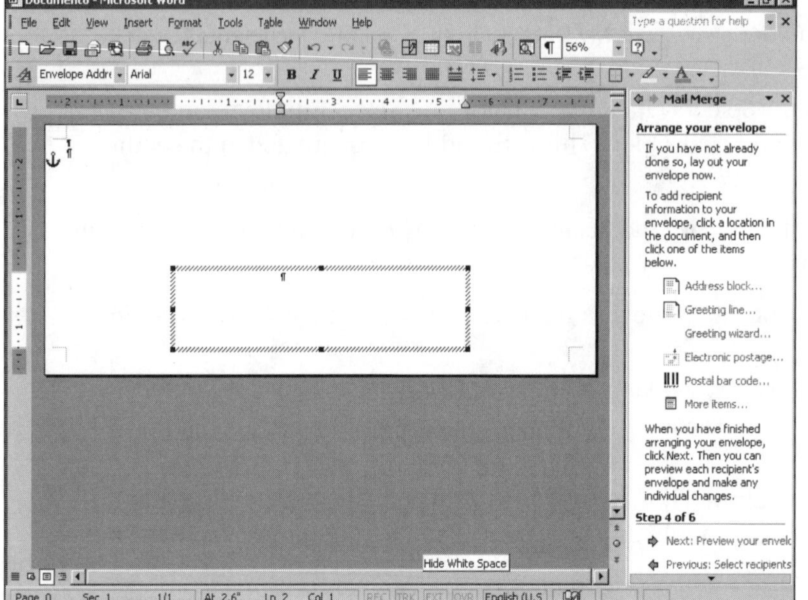

FIGURE 16.15

The Address text box area of an envelope can be moved and resized.

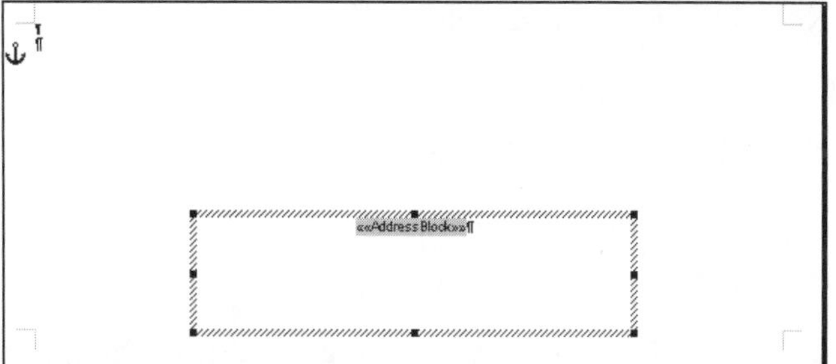

FIGURE 16.16

At the conclusion of the merge, the AddressBlock field is replaced with the merged names and addresses from your list.

FIGURE 16.17

To generate an accurate barcode, Word needs to know the data fields in the data source that contain the street address and ZIP code.

17. Select ZIP Code in the Merge Field With Zip Code box.
18. Select Address_Line_1 in the Merge Field With Street Address pull-down menu and click OK. A barcode now appears under the Address Block.

ELECTRONIC POSTAGE

Electronic postage is part of a new e-Service offered by Microsoft off the Web. You can purchase postage online and then print the stamps directly on your envelopes and labels. Different companies offer different electronic postage solutions, but all are held to the same U.S. Postal Service requirements, ensuring security and an appropriate interface with post office operations.

To add electronic postage, you must first install an electronic postage program. If you select this option, Microsoft Word prompts you to install one and offers to connect to the Microsoft Office Web site where you can get more information. This site also includes links to other sites that offer electronic postage.

19. Click Next: Preview Your Envelopes.
20. Preview your envelopes, using the arrow buttons.
21. Click Next: Complete The Merge.
22. Select Edit Individual Envelopes.
23. In the Merge To New Document dialog box, select All and click OK.
24. Print the merge document by choosing Print from the File menu, and then clicking OK.
25. Close the document with the completed merge product (named Envelopes1). Click No to close it without saving.
26. Close the main merge document and click Yes at the prompt to save the document.
27. Name the document **Employment Law Envelope** and click Save.

CREATING A DIRECTORY

Although databases such as Outlook Contacts are great for maintaining names and addresses for automated use, sometimes it is necessary to generate a printout of this information. You'll find that the more familiar you become with Mail Merge, the more uses you will find for this feature. You can use the Mail Merge feature to create client lists, membership directories, catalogs, supply lists, and more. The next exercise lets you create a document that lists all the client information typed in the earlier exercise.

NOTE

The Directory document type was called Catalog in earlier versions of Word.

CREATING A DIRECTORY

1. Create a new blank document.
2. Start the Mail Merge Wizard. From the Tools menu, choose Letters And Mailings, Mail Merge Wizard. The Mail Merge Task Pane appears on the right.
3. Under Select Document Type, select Directory.
4. Click Next: Starting Document.

5. Under Select Starting Document, select Use Current Document.
6. Type **NAME/ADDRESS**, press Tab, then type **CLIENT-MATTER #**.
7. Using the ruler, insert a left tab at 4" and press Enter three times.
8. Select the heading text, not the last two paragraph marks, and press Ctrl+B to bold the text (or use the Bold button on the Formatting toolbar).
9. Click Next: Select Recipients.
10. From the Mail Merge Task Pane, under Select Recipients, choose the Use An Existing List option.
11. Click Browse.
12. From the Select Data Source dialog box, select Employment Law Data Source and click Open. This is the address list you created in an earlier exercise.
13. From the Mail Merge Recipients dialog box, click OK to select the entire database.
14. At the bottom of the task pane, click Next: Arrange Your Directory.
15. Press Ctrl+End to place the insertion point at the end of the document.
16. Under Arrange Your Directory, click Address Block. Click OK to accept the default options on the Insert Address Block dialog box. The AddressBlock field appears under the NAME/ADDRESS heading.
17. Press Tab.
18. Under Arrange Your Directory, click More Items.
19. Select Client-Matter from the Database Fields, click Insert to place the Client-Matter field in the document, and then click Close.
20. Press Enter three times after the Client-Matter field to add space between records after they are merged.
21. Click Next: Preview Your Directory.
22. Preview the first entry of your directory. Use the arrow buttons to preview all the entries.
23. Click Next: Complete The Merge.
24. Select Merge To New Document.
25. In the Merge To New Document dialog box, select All and click OK. (See Figure 16.18.)
26. Print the merge document.

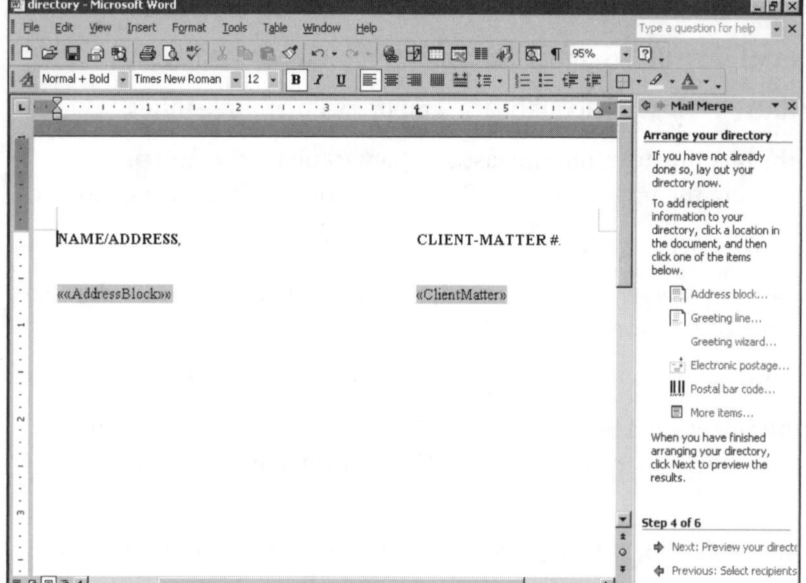

FIGURE 16.18

A Directory document with merge fields.

27. Close the document with the completed merge product (named Directory1), clicking No to leave it without saving.
28. Close the main merge document and click Yes at the prompt to save the document.
29. Name the document **Employment Law Client Roster** and click Save.

If you want the standard text (e.g., Name/Address) to appear at the top of each page, not before each record, place that information in the header of the document.

LABELS

Most of the time, it is quicker and easier to create labels rather than envelopes for your merge documents. You can create any type of label, not just mailing labels. Anything that needs to be completed in bulk can be done quickly with Mail Merge. Say you need to create file labels for your files—you can use a merge similar to the one in the directory exercise to get client info labels for your folders. But mailing labels will come in handy most often, so the next exercise uses the Mail Merge Wizard to create labels for the recipients of the letters.

CREATING A LABEL MERGE

1. Create a new blank document.
2. Start the Mail Merge Wizard. From the Tools menu, choose Letters And Mailings, Mail Merge Wizard and the task pane appears on the right.
3. Under Select Document Type, select Labels.
4. Click Next: Starting Document.
5. Under Select Starting Document, select Change Document Layout, and then click Label Options to review and change the label settings. The Label Options dialog box opens, as shown in Figure 16.19.
6. In the Label Options dialog box, select Label Products: Avery Standard. Select 5164-Shipping listed under the Product Number and click OK.
7. Click Next: Select Recipients.
8. From the Mail Merge Task Pane, under Select Recipients, choose the Use An Existing List option.
9. Click Browse.
10. From the Select Data Source dialog box, select Employment Law Data Source and click Open. This is the address list created in an earlier exercise.
11. From the Mail Merge Recipients dialog box, click OK to select the entire database.
12. At the bottom of the task pane, click Next: Arrange Your Labels.
13. Under Arrange Your Labels, click Address Block. Click OK to accept the default options on the Insert Address Block dialog box. The AddressBlock field appears in the top, left label.

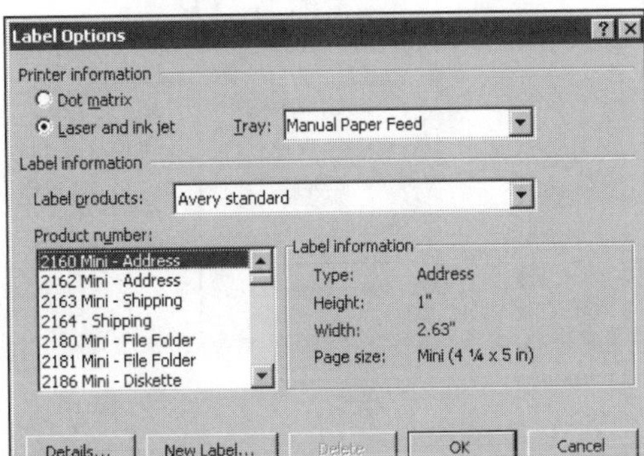

FIGURE 16.19

The Label Options dialog box allows you to change the type of labels and set the printer type.

14. Press Enter to move your insertion point under the Address field and click Postal Bar Code in the task pane to insert a barcode.
15. Select ZIP Code in the Merge Field With Zip Code box.
16. Select Address_Line_1 in the Merge Field With Street Address and click OK. A barcode now appears under the Address Block. (See Figure 16.20.)
17. Under Replicate Labels in the task pane, click Update All Labels. Word copies the layout with the field codes from the first label to all the other labels on that page.
18. Click Next: Preview Your Labels.
19. Preview the sheet of labels.
20. Click Next: Complete The Merge.
21. Select Edit Individual Labels.
22. In the Merge To New Document dialog box, select All and click OK.
23. Print the merge document.

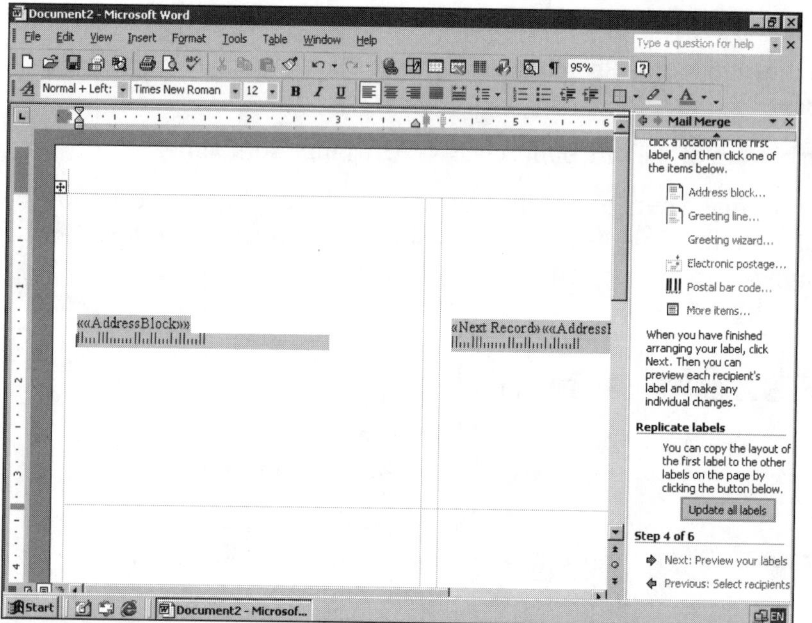

FIGURE 16.20

Once you have inserted the merge fields in the first label, the Replicate Labels option copies the information to all the labels.

24. Close the document with the completed merge product (named Labels1) and click No to leave it without saving.
25. Close the main merge document and click Yes at the prompt to save the document.
26. Name the document **Employment Law Labels** and click Save.

CREATING MERGE E-MAIL MESSAGES

You can use the Mail Merge Wizard to create a group e-mail distribution. This is a great way to send individualized e-mail messages to large groups of people. To use this feature, your e-mail system must be MAPI-compliant, like Microsoft Outlook.

NOTE

You should open your e-mail program and minimize it in the background while you complete the following exercise.

CREATING AN E-MAIL MERGE

1. Create a new blank document.
2. Start the Mail Merge Wizard. From the Tools menu, choose Letters And Mailings, Mail Merge Wizard and the task pane appears on the right.
3. Under Select Document Type, select E-Mail Messages.
4. Click Next: Starting Document.
5. Under Select Starting Document, select Use The Current Document.
6. Click Next: Select Recipients.
7. From the Mail Merge Task Pane, under Select Recipients, choose the Use An Existing List option.
8. Click Browse.
9. From the Select Data Source dialog box, select Employment Law Data Source and click Open.
10. From the Mail Merge Recipients dialog box, click OK to select the entire database.

11. Click Next: Write Your E-mail.
12. Type the following text in the document: **You will be receiving in the mail an invitation to Our Annual Employment Law Seminar scheduled for Friday, May 16th. I hope you will mark this date on your calendar now to join us at this popular event. We hope to see you there.**
13. Click Next: Preview Your E-mail Messages.
14. Click Next: Complete The Merge.
15. Under Merge, select Electronic Mail.
16. In the Merge To E-mail dialog box, select To E-mail Address and type **Employment Law Seminar Invitation** in the Subject Line field. Leave the Mail Format at HTML and Send Records set to All, then click OK.
17. Close the main merge document and click Yes at the prompt to save the document.
18. Name the document **Employment Law E-Mail** and click Save.

Open your e-mail program and check your Sent Items folder for the messages you just sent. Recall and delete them from your Sent Items folder.

QUERY OPTIONS

Mail Merge offers two choices when selecting recipient information during a Mail Merge. First, you can sort the records in ascending or descending order by any data field. It is very common with bulk mailings to sort the letters by ZIP code to get a reduced rate at the post office. Second, you can filter records from the list. Say you have a large database containing records for all your clients and you only want to send letters to the clients in Australia. You can easily filter the list to exclude everyone except those clients from Australia. The sort and filter options make it easy to manipulate information in your data source.

SORTING THE DATA

Sorting is a useful feature when dealing with large lists of information. Sometimes it's helpful to have a list sort one way for one situation and then have it sorted another way in another situation. For example, you might want to sort the list in alphabetical order by Last Name then First Name when creating a Client Address Book. Next, you might want to sort it by Attorney so each attorney's letters will be generated and grouped together to make it easier to divide and distribute the mass mailing for attorney signatures. The next exercise shows you how to sort records in a data source by ZIP code.

SORTING A DATA SOURCE

1. Open the Employment Law Letter created earlier in the chapter.
2. Start the Mail Merge Wizard.
3. Under Select Recipients, choose Use An Existing List.
4. Under Use An Existing List, choose Edit Recipient List.
5. From the Merge Mail Recipients dialog box, scroll to the right until you can see the ZIP Code column.
6. Click on the column heading titled ZIP Code and the recipient list reorders in ascending order.
7. Click on the ZIP Code column header again and the list is sorted in descending order.
8. You can also sort using up to three keys. Click Edit from the Mail Merge Recipients dialog box.
9. From the Edit Recipients dialog box, click Filter And Sort, and then click on the Sort tab.
10. In the Sort By field, click the drop-down list arrow and select ZIP Code from the list, then select Descending.
11. In the first Then By field, click the drop-down list arrow and select Last Name from the list, then select Ascending.
12. In the other Then By field, select First Name from the list, and then select Ascending.
13. Click OK and then Close to return to the Mail Merge Recipients dialog box. The list has been resorted according to the three sort criteria you provided.
14. Click OK to close the Mail Merge Recipients dialog box and return to the document.

FILTERING THE DATA

As mentioned earlier in this chapter, there may be times when you only need to use some of the records in a data source. Filtering the list could be as simple as excluding a person on the recipient list. In fact, while you are previewing your letter, under Make Changes in the task pane, you can select the option to Exclude This Recipient as you preview. Also, within the Mail Merge Recipients dialog box, you can exclude recipients without deleting their information. Those approaches all require identifying individual recipients to exclude, which is difficult if you want to send your letter to just a small proportion of the database. The next exercise shows you both how to eliminate a specific recipient and how to restrict your notices to clients living in a specific city.

FILTERING A DATA SOURCE

1. The Employment Law Letter should still be open from the preceding exercise. If it isn't, open it.
2. Under Select Recipients, choose Use An Existing List.
3. Under Use An Existing List, choose Edit Recipient List.
4. From the Merge Mail Recipient dialog box, note the check boxes next to each recipient. Click in the check box to deselect George Douglas. This record will not be included in the merge process.

If you have a large list and want to include most of the list in the merge, click Select All first, and then clear the specific records that should not be included in the merge. Likewise, if you want to exclude most of the list in the merge, click Clear All to deselect all records first then select the records you want to include in the merge.

5. Scroll to the right to see the column heading entitled City. Click the blue arrow next to the City column heading.
6. From the list, select Seattle. Just the Seattle recipients are displayed. Notice that the arrow turns blue when a column is filtered.
7. Click the arrow next to the column heading and select All from the list. Notice that the arrow turns black again.

If the list does not update to reflect the changes you made, click Refresh to update the screen.

The Blanks option on the Column drop-down list will display all the records in which the corresponding field is blank. Likewise, the Nonblanks option will display all records in which the field is not blank.

8. For more filtering and sorting options, select Advanced from the column drop-down list or click Edit from the Mail Merge Recipients dialog box.
9. From the Edit Recipients dialog box, click Filter And Sort then click on the Filter tab.
10. Click the arrow in the Field box and select City from the list.
11. Click the arrow in the Comparison box and select Equal To from the list.
12. Type **Seattle** in the Compare To box then click OK and Close to return to the Mail Merge Recipients list. Word now includes only Seattle recipients in the Mail Merge process.

The value typed into the Compare To box must match the data source exactly. If you make a mistake, you will get an error that says no data records exist for your query.

Once you filter the list, you can also use the check boxes to include or exclude specific records that did not match the original filter criteria.

13. Click OK to close the dialog box and return to the document.

MORE THINGS TO KNOW ABOUT MAIL MERGE

Since Mail Merge was completely redesigned, there are a lot of things that need to be covered, but not a lot of space to thoroughly discuss each feature. Some that deserve mentioning, however, are listed in this section.

USING OTHER CONTACT LISTS DURING A MAIL MERGE

In law firms, attorneys often share their contacts with their secretary or assistant. Word 2002 allows you to choose which Contact folder to use during the mail merge process—even if the information is stored in a public folder on your firm's network.

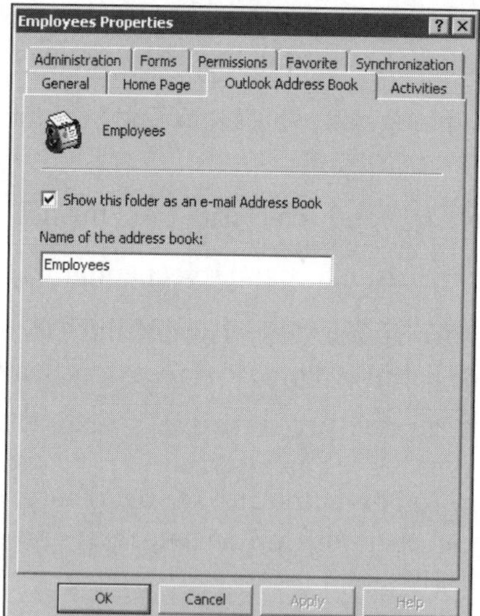

FIGURE 16.21

Secretaries and attorneys can share contact lists and use them for mail merge data sources.

To make this feature work, you need to: (1) Grant the person access to the contact folder and (2) install all converters and filters that make this possible. Once these steps are complete, alternate-click the folder in Outlook and choose Properties. Select the Outlook Address Book tab and check the option Show This Folder As An E-Mail Address Book (Figure 16.21). Click OK.

When you choose to use an Outlook folder as a data source for the mail merge, the added folder will be a selectable option, as shown in Figure 16.22.

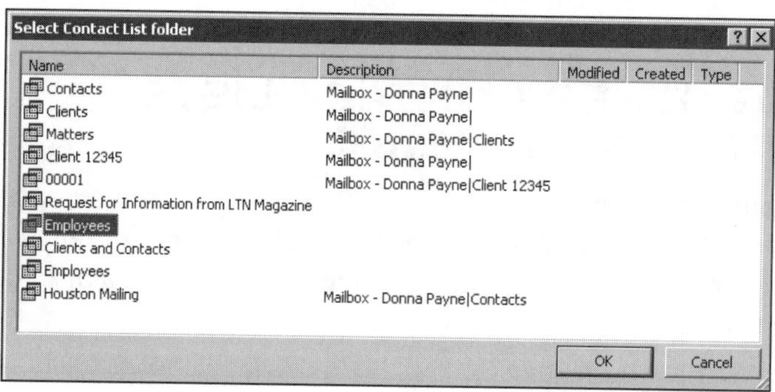

FIGURE 16.22

When more than one contact folder exists, Word prompts for you to choose which one to use for the mail merge.

USING OUTLOOK FIELDS DURING A MERGE

In Office XP, Word, and Outlook integrate more closely for performing the mail merge process. There are 44 Contact fields available for the merge, with only three not exposed in the mail merge. The three fields not available are: Categories, Home Phone, and Spouse.

OPENING EXISTING MERGE MAIN DOCUMENTS

If you create a Mail Merge main document then save and close it, you can reopen the document and pick up where you left off with the merge process. From the View menu, choose Task Pane and select Mail Merge, or from the Tools menu, choose Letters And Mailings, Mail Merge Wizard and all information saved (such as data source) is retained.

MAIL MERGE BACKWARD COMPATIBILITY

Not all features in Word 2002 are backwardly compatible. When a document created in Word 2002 is opened in previous versions of Word, merge fields such as Address Block and Greeting Line appear blank. All other Mail Merge features should work as intended in previous versions.

MAIL MERGE AND ODMA

Not all Mail Merge dialog boxes in previous versions of Word were ODMA-compliant. This meant that when a person chose to Open Data Source, Open Header Source, or Save As, he or she was presented with the Word native dialog boxes rather than the document management system. Word has integrated these dialog boxes with ODMA support in this version.

RESTORING MAIL MERGE HELPER AS IN PREVIOUS VERSIONS

If you prefer the way the Mail Merge Helper worked in previous versions, you can add a command to the menu to make this feature available. From the Tools menu, choose Customize. Select the Commands tab and select All Commands from the Categories list. Locate and drag MailMergeHelper to the Tools, Letters And Mailings submenu (or to a toolbar). This button displays the Mail Merge Helper dialog box.

SUMMARY

This chapter explores many of the options that Mail Merge has to offer. While the primary focus was on the Mail Merge Wizard, remember that you can complete a mail merge by just using the Mail Merge toolbar. The more you become familiar with this feature, the more ways you'll find to use it with all types of output, from letters, pleadings, and similar legal documents to mass mailings with faxes and e-mail messages.

TROUBLESHOOTING MAIL MERGE

Can I use main documents in Word 2002 that I created in earlier versions of Word?

You can use main documents that you created in the following versions of Word: Microsoft Word 2000, 97, 7.x, 6.x, or 2.x for Windows, if the main document is attached to a data source; Word 98 for Macintosh, if the main document is attached to the data source; Word 1.x for Windows, if the main document contains a data field that identifies the data source; Word for Macintosh or Word for MS-DOS, if the main document contains a data instruction that identifies the data source.

I want to create a catalog but I can't find an option to do this. Where should I look?

The Catalog feature is now called Directory.

How do I restore a Mail Merge main document back to a regular document?

You can restore a main document back to a regular document by opening the main document and activating the Mail Merge toolbar. Click the Main Document Setup button (first button on the left), select Normal Word Document, and then click OK on the Main Document Type dialog box.

When I print my document, merge fields print instead of my data. What can I do?

You have activated the Display Field Codes option. To turn this off, select Tools, Options from the menu bar, then click the Print tab and clear the Field Codes check box.

I want to use Microsoft Query to retrieve data but can't find it. Is it still available?

You can find Microsoft Query on the Select Data Source dialog box, which is a button on the Mail Merge toolbar. Click Tools on the Select Data Source menu and choose MS Query.

When I try to merge to e-mail, I get a message asking if I want to allow access to my Outlook addresses. What should I do?

When merging to e-mail with Microsoft Outlook, you may get an Outlook message telling you that a program is trying to access e-mail addresses and send e-mail. This is a security measure designed to protect you against computer viruses that replicate through e-mail. To continue with the merge process, select the Allow Access For check box and select the amount of time you need to complete the merge. Click Yes and then, if prompted again, continue clicking Yes until the merge is complete. These prompts do not appear if you send the message in HTML format, which is an option on the Merge To E-mail dialog box.

Is there a way to have the address block information automatically switch to all caps in a mail merge?

If you are going to use a barcode on your envelope or label, the address block should also appear in all caps. There are numerous field code switches available, including an option for All Caps. However, the easiest way to modify the font for both envelopes and labels is to bring up the Envelope Or Labels Options dialog box and click on Font. Select the All Caps option for the Delivery Address, then click OK twice to return to the document.

Is there a way to have the country appear in my address block only when the delivery address is located outside the United States?

As with other field codes, you can insert switches that activate certain options on fields. In this case, you need to use two switches. The first switch (\e) specifies the country to exclude (that is, the United States). The second switch specifies the country format (\c), but only when different from the value for \e. Alternate-click on the AddressBlock field code and add the switches.

Example: { ADDRESSBLOCK \f "<<_TITLE0_ >><<_FIRST0_>><< _LAST0_>><< _SUFFIX0_>>

<<_COMPANY_

>><<_STREET1_

>><<_STREET2_

>><<_CITY_>><<, _STATE_>><< _POSTAL_>><<

COUNTRY>>" \l 1033 \c 2 \e "U.S.A." }

However, the easiest way to include these switches is to open the Insert Address Block dialog box, select the Insert Postal Address, Only Include The Country/Region If Different Than option, and type in **U.S.A.**

Chapter 17

Graphically Speaking

IN THIS CHAPTER

- Graphics toolbars
- Inserting media and pictures
- Working with text boxes, Word Art, and drawing objects
- Organization charts
- Diagrams
- Equation Editor
- Applying borders and shading
- Using Document Grid
- Adding and removing watermarks

When you hear the term *graphics,* what is the first thing that comes to mind? Pictures, maybe? If so, you are probably asking yourself, "How do pictures come into play with legal documents?"

It is true that most legal documents primarily contain text; however, just as word processing has evolved, so has the legal document. Graphics are more than just pictures. Think of organization charts, graphs, photos, diagrams, and more. Even borders on the cover page of an agreement are graphical in nature.

GRAPHICS TOOLBARS

Toolbars in Word offer shortcuts to commands specific to the toolbar's subject. There are many types of graphics available in Word, each with a corresponding toolbar to assist you.

DRAWING TOOLBAR

The Drawing toolbar is the primary toolbar used when working with graphics. You can change properties, align, ungroup, rotate, flip, or insert objects with this toolbar.

When you turn the Drawing toolbar on, it automatically docks at the bottom of your screen, just above the status bar, but you can undock it and put it wherever is most convenient for you. A floating Drawing toolbar is shown in Figure 17.1.

The following formatting commands are available on the Drawing toolbar:

- **Draw**. This drop-down list contains commands available for organizing and manipulating objects. Menu commands include: Group, Ungroup, Regroup, Order, Grid, Nudge, Align or Distribute, Rotate or Flip, Text Wrapping, Reroute Connectors, Edit Points, Change AutoShape, and Set AutoShape Defaults.
- **Select Objects**. You can click this button and draw an invisible square around multiple objects. All objects within the boundary are selected.
- **AutoShapes**. This drop-down list includes commands for working with Lines, Connectors, Basic Shapes, Block Arrows, Flowchart, Stars and Banners, Callouts, and More AutoShapes.

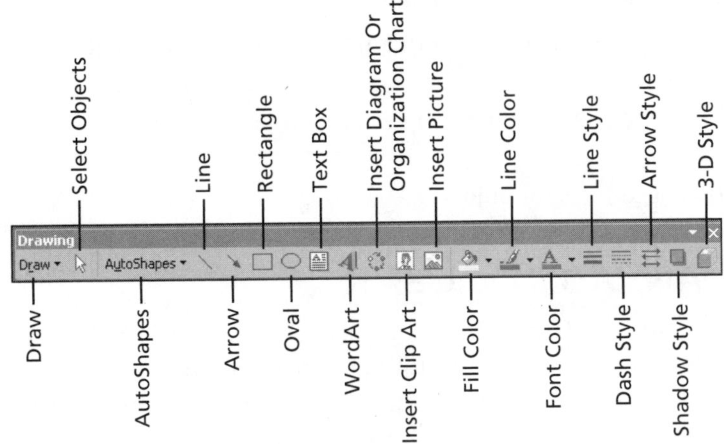

FIGURE 17.1

Insert shapes, diagrams, Clip Art, pictures, text boxes, and more from the Drawing toolbar.

- **Line**. This button, when clicked, allows you to draw a straight line.
- **Arrow**. This button allows you to draw a line with an arrowhead.
- **Rectangle**. You can draw a rectangle when this button is clicked. Hold the Shift key and drag with the mouse to create a square shape.
- **Oval**. This button draws an oval shape into the document or drawing canvas. Hold the Shift key and drag to draw a circle instead.
- **Text Box**. This button allows you to insert a rectangular-shaped object that may include text. Hold the Shift key and drag to draw a square text box.
- **Insert WordArt**. This button displays the WordArt Gallery. Preset colorful and artistic formats are available.
- **Insert Diagram Or Organization Chart**. Insert one of six types of charts into the document. Chart types include: Organization, Cycle, Radial, Pyramid, Venn, and Target.
- **Insert Clip Art**. This button displays the Insert Clip Art Task Pane where you can browse for and select clip art to be inserted into the document.
- **Insert Picture**. Opens the Insert Picture dialog box where you can browse for and select existing pictures.
- **Fill Color**. Selected objects are filled with the selected color. Click the drop-down arrow next to the button to select a different color or special fill effects.
- **Line Color**. This button changes the color of the line or border to the selected color.
- **Text Color**. Specify a font color.
- **Line Style**. Select the weight and style of lines for your objects.

- **Dash Style**. You can select different dash line styles.
- **Arrow Style**. This button includes different types of arrows that can be applied to selected lines.
- **Shadow Style**. Creates a shadow effect for selected objects or remove shadows.
- **3-D Style**. Creates 3-D effects for objects.

DRAWING CANVAS TOOLBAR

The Drawing Canvas toolbar (shown in Figure 17.2) is new to Word. This is where drawing objects and media clips are stored in the document. The canvas offers the ability to manipulate multiple graphics at one time. It's similar to an artist's canvas where paintings are created. One of the most important aspects of this new feature is that it offers the ability to expand the canvas, as needed, or make it fit the contents of your graphic objects.

The following commands are available on the Drawing Canvas toolbar:

- **Fit Drawing To Contents.** This button crops the canvas to make boundaries of the canvas fit the object better.
- **Expand Drawing**. Increase the size of the drawing canvas each time you click the button.
- **Scale Drawing**. Removes the crop handles from the drawing canvas so the image can be cropped or manipulated.
- **Text Wrapping**. Displays text-wrapping options. These options include: In Line With Text, Square, Tight, Behind Text, In Front of Text, Top and Bottom, Through, and Edit Wrap Points.

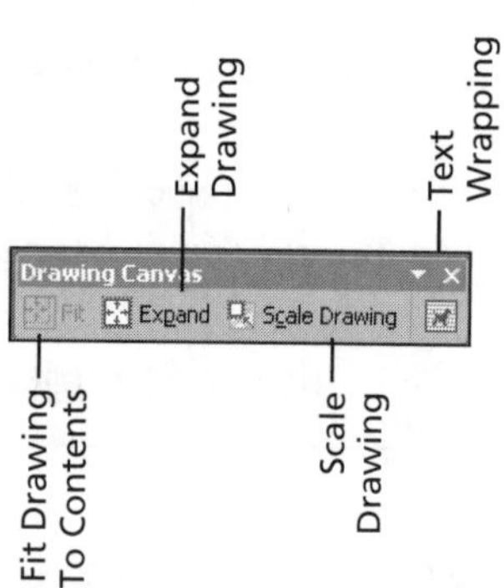

FIGURE 17.2

Manipulate drawing objects using the Drawing Canvas toolbar.

NOTE

If you do not see the Drawing Canvas when working with objects, you may need to turn it on. From the Tools menu, choose Options. In the General tab, select Automatically Create Drawing Canvas When Inserting AutoShapes.

OTHER TOOLBARS

Some toolbars appear automatically when you are working with specific items. For example, if you insert a WordArt object and select the object, the WordArt toolbar appears. The toolbars that control graphics include the following:

- Picture toolbar
- Diagram toolbar
- WordArt toolbar
- Organization Chart toolbar
- 3-D Settings toolbar
- Shadow Settings toolbar

These toolbars will be covered in more detail in their corresponding sections later in this chapter.

SIZING HANDLES

Once you add a drawing object to the document, you may find that the size needs to be adjusted. You must select a drawing object first to activate the sizing handles. Click and drag these handles to resize the object. Hold the Shift key and use the handles in the corners to resize an object while preserving its proportions; the ones in the centers of the sides change the width or height while leaving the other dimension alone. Hold the Ctrl key and use the handles to resize the object while retaining the center of the object in the same location.

> *Sizing handles* surround a drawing object when it is selected. When the mouse pointer is placed over a sizing handle, the pointer shape changes to double-arrows that indicate the directions you can move it.

INSERTING MEDIA

Microsoft defines *media* to include all pictures, clip art, sound clips, and movies. Inserting media into a document is quick and easy, regardless of whether you choose Clip Art from the Media Gallery or a picture obtained from a scanner, digital camera, or the Internet.

MEDIA GALLERY

The Media Gallery is the library that holds all the media clips found on your computer. The Media Gallery organizes the media clips into collections that include keywords for each individual clip. This makes searching for the right clip a breeze.

COLLECTIONS

Think of a collection as a folder of media clips. By default, you will start with the following collections:

- My Collections
- Office Collections
- Web Collections

Each collection has subfolders. Once you open these subfolders, you can view the contents and insert those clips into your document. You can also add, modify, and delete any of the collections or subcollections. The Clip Organizer is shown in Figure 17.3.

SEARCHING

Since you can have hundreds or even thousands of media clips, Word provides a way to search through the collections. You can perform a search using

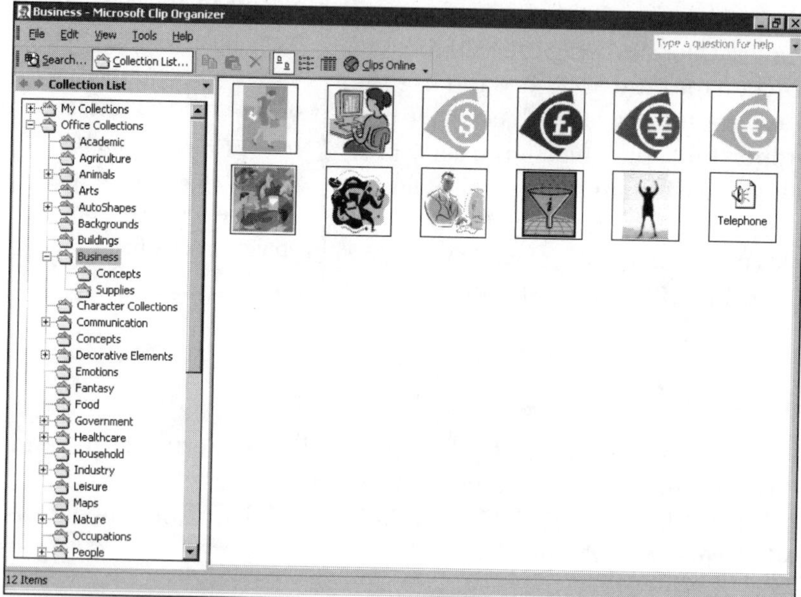

FIGURE 17.3

Organize media in your Collection List and search for media with the Clip Organizer.

keywords, type of media, or a specific collection. The search feature from within the Search Task Pane automatically activates when you choose Picture, Clip Art from the Insert menu.

SEARCH THE MEDIA GALLERY

1. Create a new document.
2. From the Insert menu, choose Picture, then Clip Art.

The first time you insert clip art, an Add Clips To Gallery dialog box will open, giving you the option to catalog your Media Gallery files now or later. You can specify which folders you want to organize them in by clicking the Options button. You can check off the box next to Don't Show This Message Again if you want to bypass this message in the future. Click the Later button to continue.

3. The Clip Art Task Pane opens on the right side of the document window, as shown in Figure 17.4.
4. Type **law** in the Search text box.
5. Click Search. The Search Task Pane displays the search results.

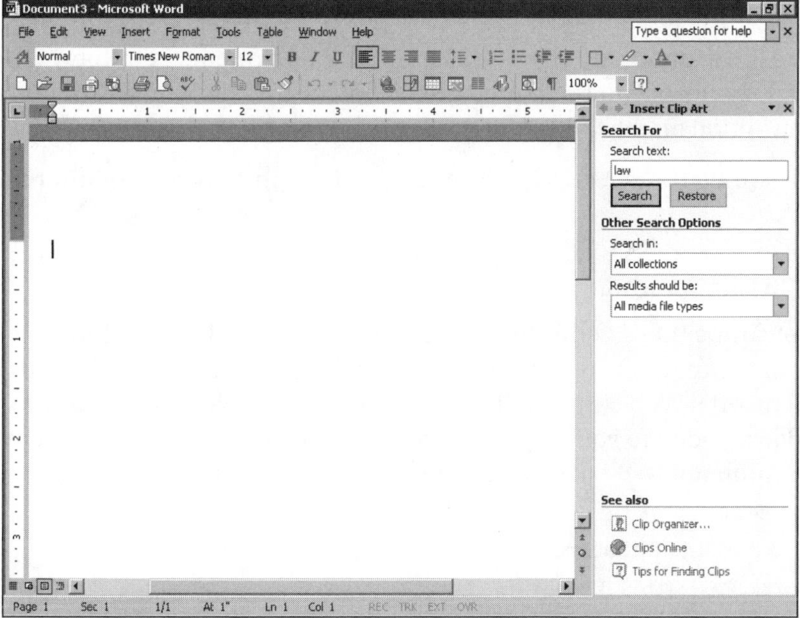

FIGURE 17.4

Search for media in the Clip Art Task Pane.

6. Leave this open for the next exercise.

CLIP ART

After you have located the desired clip art, you can choose to insert it, change keywords, view properties, or delete it from a collection.

INSERT CLIP ART

1. Using the document from the preceding exercise, hover your mouse pointer over the picture you want and click the drop-down arrow next to it.
2. Click Preview/Properties. An enlarged view of the clip art appears along with properties and keywords.
3. Click Close.
4. Double-click the clip art in the task pane to insert the clip art into the document.
5. Click the (X) Close button in the upper-right corner of the task pane to close the Clip Art Task Pane.

SETTING DEFAULTS FOR PASTING AND INSERTIONS

The default text wrapping for objects inserted into documents is Inline With Text. Word 2002 allows you to change this behavior by selecting a different text-wrapping option on the Edit tab of the Options dialog box (Figure 17.5).

The Insert/Paste Pictures As option applies to all graphics inserted into the document.

DESIGN GALLERY ONLINE

If you cannot find a media clip that serves your purposes by searching the gallery on your computer, you can access an even larger gallery located on the Internet. Microsoft's Web site contains an extensive collection of media clips that can be downloaded to your computer, and Word is set up to take you there from a menu command—no need to think about the Web address.

NOTE

Clips Online requires Internet access.

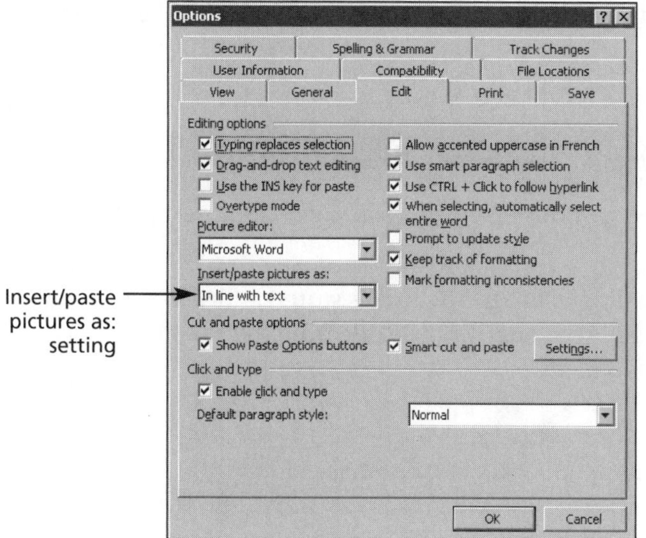

FIGURE 17.5

This setting affects inserting objects from the Insert, Picture menu command, through the Picture toolbar, Insert Object, WordArt toolbar, and Insert Clip Art.

DOWNLOAD A CLIP ONLINE

1. Create a new document.
2. From the Insert menu, choose Picture, Clip Art. The Clip Art Task Pane appears.
3. At the bottom of the task pane, click Clips Online. Your Internet browser will open and navigate to the Microsoft Media Gallery Web site.
4. Type a keyword or select a category and click Go.
5. Select a clip from the search results and choose Download. Follow the prompts to download.
6. Once the clip is downloaded into your Media Gallery, insert it in your document. You can then keep or delete the copy in the Media Gallery, and change its keywords.

INSERTING PICTURES

With the influx of scanners and digital cameras into homes and businesses, there are endless possibilities to choose from when it comes to pictures. You do not have to use one of Microsoft's pictures. Instead, insert one that is specific to the subject matter, and maybe even take a digital picture yourself and add it to your document.

Word makes it easy to browse all drives of a computer for picture file formats.

INSERT A PICTURE FROM FILE

1. Create a new document.
2. From the Insert menu, choose Picture, From File. The Insert Picture dialog box opens.
3. Navigate to the location where the picture is stored and select it. If you don't have a picture file of your own, use one from the CD-ROM that accompanies this book.
4. Click Insert.
5. Leave this document open for the next exercise.

MANIPULATING PICTURES

You have probably seen documents with pictures that are a little too dark or contain unnecessary space. These and other problems are fixable using the Picture toolbar, which is shown in Figure 17.6.

The buttons on the Picture toolbar work like this:

- **Insert Picture**. Opens the Insert Picture dialog box, which lets you navigate to pictures stored anywhere on your computer.

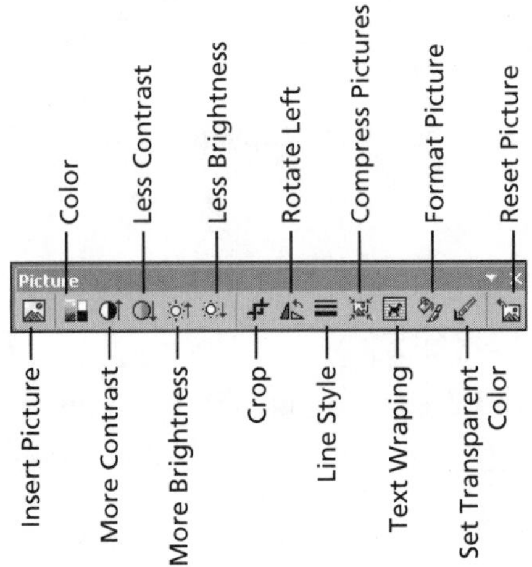

FIGURE 17.6

Use the Picture toolbar to adjust the quality of the inserted picture.

- **Color**. Lets you change the look of your picture by selecting one of the color options: Automatic, Grayscale, Black And White, or Washout.
- **More Contrast**. Increases the contrast level each time you click the button.
- **Less Contrast**. Decreases the contrast level each time you click the button.
- **More Brightness**. Increases the brightness of the picture.
- **Less Brightness**. Decreases the brightness of the picture.
- **Crop**. Lets you cut the unneeded parts of a picture.
- **Rotate Left**. Rotates the entire picture to the left 90 degrees. Click repeatedly until the picture reaches the angle you want.
- **Line Style**. Lets you select a line style for the border of the picture.
- **Compress Pictures**. Lets you decrease the file size of the picture by removing the cropped areas or decreasing pixels.
- **Text Wrapping**. Lets you select how the text should wrap around the picture. You can pull Text Wrapping out and make it a floating toolbar on its own.
- **Format Picture**. Activates a dialog box that contains all the picture options on various tabs.
- **Set Transparent Color**. Lets you convert any solid-colored area of the picture to a transparent color. When you click such an area with this tool, all pixels with similar colors to the one chosen will also become transparent.
- **Reset Picture**. Resets the picture back to the default.

To *crop* a picture means to cut unneeded portions from it.

The next exercise lets you try some of these tools on the picture inserted in the preceding exercise.

NEW FEATURES!

In Word 2002, you have the ability to change pictures from floating to inline from the Picture toolbar. Graphics and any drawing object can be rotated using the Rotation button on the Drawing toolbar.

MODIFY A PICTURE

1. The document from the preceding exercise should still be open.
2. Select the picture in the document. If the Picture toolbar is not displayed, alternate-click on any toolbar and choose Picture.
3. Pick Grayscale from the Color button.
4. Click Reset Picture to return the picture to its original color.
5. Click More Brightness a few times. Notice how the lighting for the picture changes.
6. Click the Less Brightness and Contrast buttons a few times to see how the picture changes with each click.
7. Select a Line Style to add a border to the picture.
8. Click Format Picture, which is shown in Figure 17.7. On the Size tab, change the Height and Width and click OK.

TIP

Double-clicking a picture will open the Format Picture dialog box and will select the Picture tab automatically.

9. Save this document as Picture.doc and leave it open.

TEXT WRAPPING

When text and graphics share the same page, the page often appears more professional if unnecessary surrounding white space is eliminated and the pictures

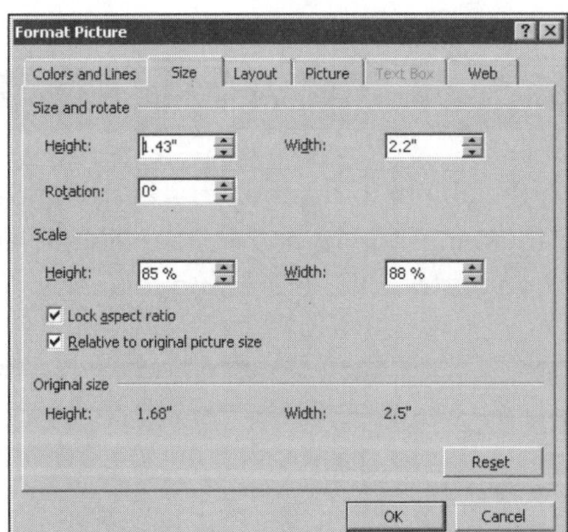

FIGURE 17.7

Adjust the picture, as needed, using the Format Picture dialog box.

are aligned more closely with text. Text Wrapping controls how the graphic appears in conjunction with text on the page. The graphic can move with text, and can float over, under, or closer to the text.

EXPERIMENT WITH TEXT WRAPPING

1. Open the file Logo.doc from the CD-ROM, or insert a graphic of your choice.
2. Click beside the logo and type the following text block:

   Jones and Jones, LLP
   2500 First Avenue
   Seattle, WA 98101
3. Notice how the text aligns in relation to the picture.
4. Select the logo, click the Text Wrapping button on the Picture toolbar, and choose Square. The text is now aligned top-right.
5. Select Behind Text from the Text Wrapping button.
6. Close the document without saving.

NOTE

Text Wrapping determines the type of sizing handles on an object. Black square handles indicate that the wrapping is set to Inline with Text. White circular handles cover all the other wrapping choices.

CROPPING

Cropping removes parts of a picture that are no longer desired. You can crop from the top, bottom, left, or right sides of the picture.

CROP PICTURE

1. The Picture.doc document created in the "Modify a Picture" exercise should still be open.
2. Select the picture and click Crop.
3. Click and drag the middle right handle to reduce the area on the right side of the picture.
4. Crop the bottom of the picture.
5. Crop the remaining sides to make it even.

NEW FEATURE!

In Word 2002, you have the option to permanently delete the cropped areas, thereby reducing the file size. Click Compress Picture from the toolbar and check Delete Cropped Areas Of Pictures. Click Apply to apply picture optimization and check the box Don't Show Me This Warning Again if you want to bypass this message in the future.

OBJECTS

Object is a very generic term, isn't it? Word considers an object any drawing item created within Word or with an applet program compatible with Word.

An *applet* is a mini application that inserts different objects into Word with various formatting choices available. Applets commonly used in law firms include Organization Chart and Equation Editor.

DRAWING OBJECTS

Most of the items found on the Drawing toolbar are drawing objects. Objects you can select include a basic line, square, or circle, a flowchart, other shapes, and more. Even a text box is considered a drawing object. To insert an object into a document, select an object from the Drawing toolbar and then click and drag the mouse to insert it into the document. Once the mouse button is released, the drawing object appears.

TEXT BOX

Text boxes are terrific! They allow you to place text anywhere in the document without the requirement of complex formatting. Does your pleading require numbered lines on the left side of the page? Do you need to put the word *Draft* in the top-right corner of an agreement? A text box is one way to satisfy both of these requirements.

Whether you start with an empty text box and type text, or select text in a document and add it to the text box, this feature offers the flexibility of having text "float" anywhere you need it to appear.

TEXT BOX IMPROVEMENTS

Word 2002 offers two new options for working with text boxes. When a text box is selected, from the Format menu, choose Text Box and select the Text Box tab shown in Figure 17.8.

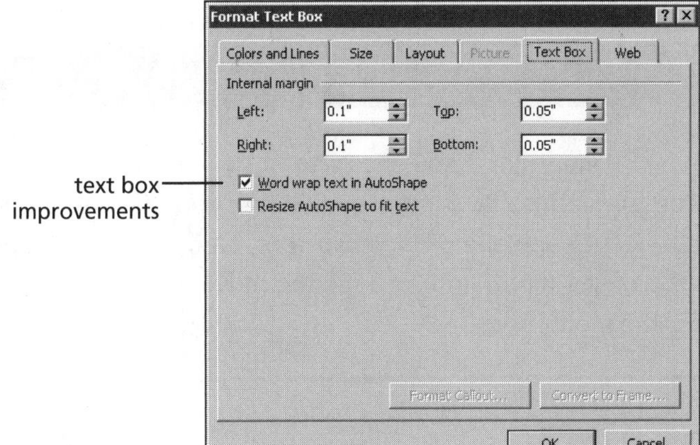

FIGURE 17.8

When a text box is linked, the new options are automatically turned off.

New options include Word Wrap Text In AutoShape, which wraps the text within the text box to the size of the text box. Resize AutoShape To Fit Text adjusts the size of the text box to fit the text.

INSERT TEXT BOXES

1. Create a new document. If the Drawing toolbar is not visible, alternate-click on any toolbar button and select Drawing.
2. From the Drawing toolbar, click Text Box. Notice the mouse pointer changes to crosshairs.
3. Click and drag diagonally in the Create Your Drawing Here section.
4. Type text into the text box.
5. Click the drop-down arrow next to the Line Color button on the Drawing toolbar and select a color for the border.

TIP

Select No Line to remove the border completely.

6. Position the mouse pointer on the border of the text box until the move handle appears. Click and drag the text box to the top-right corner of the document. This repositions the object.

NEW FEATURE!

Fill Color, Line Color, and Font Color buttons on the Drawing toolbar can be turned into floating menus. When you click the drop-down arrow next to any one of these buttons, place your mouse pointer at the top of the menu until you see the move handle. Click and drag to make the menu float.

WORDART

WordArt is fancy text that already has all of the formatting applied. The text can appear with shadows, vibrant color, and diagonal alignment. The feature is not used very often in legal documents but it's useful for newsletters and other types of entertaining documents.

To insert WordArt, click the Insert WordArt button on the Drawing toolbar, and then select a format and type some text. Of course, as with all graphics, you have an abundance of formatting options to choose from.

WORK WITH WORDART

1. Create a new document.
2. Click WordArt on the Drawing toolbar. The WordArt Gallery appears, as shown in Figure 17.9.
3. Select a WordArt style and click OK.
4. Type the text to insert and click OK. The WordArt appears in the document.
5. Select the WordArt to activate the WordArt toolbar, which is shown in Figure 17.10.
6. Experiment with the different formatting options on the WordArt toolbar.

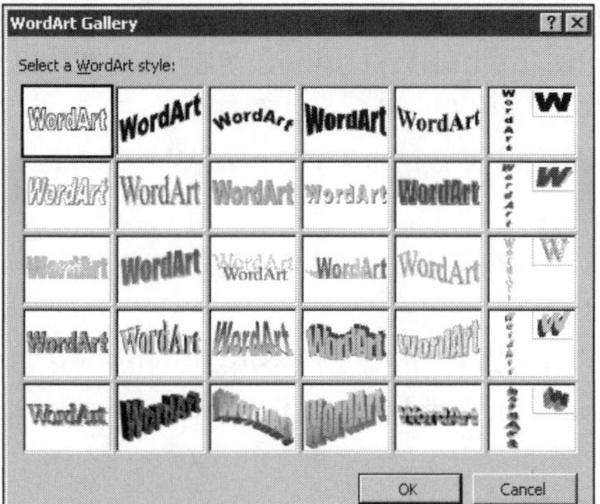

FIGURE 17.9

Select from the 30 styles in the WordArt Gallery.

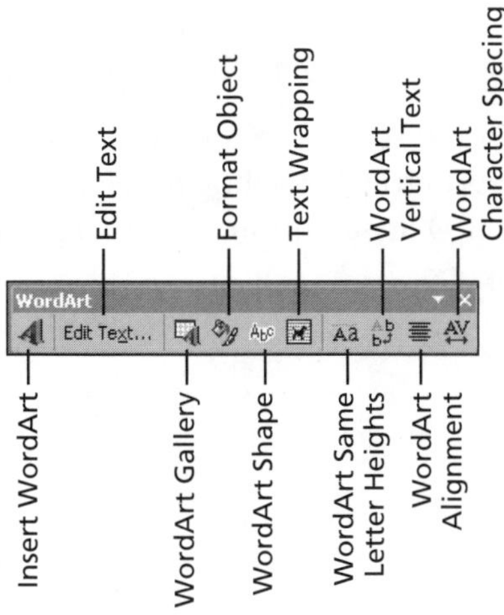

FIGURE 17.10

Use the WordArt toolbar to add fancy formatting, edit text, and more.

The buttons on the WordArt toolbar work like this:

- **Insert WordArt**. Opens the WordArt Gallery dialog box, which lets you select one of 30 different formats for the text.
- **Edit Text**. Allows you to change the text for the WordArt object when the object is selected or active. The Edit WordArt Text dialog box displays.
- **WordArt Gallery**. Opens the WordArt Gallery dialog box where you can change the preset format for the object.
- **Format Object**. Opens the Format WordArt dialog box. Tabs in this dialog box include Colors And Lines, Size, Layout, Picture, Text Box, and Web.
- **WordArt Shape**. Displays 40 shapes to choose from. The WordArt object changes to reflect the selected shape.

- **Text Wrapping**. Displays a list of text wrapping options including: Inline With Text, Square, Tight, Behind Text, In Front Of Text, Top And Bottom, Through, and Edit Wrap Points.
- **WordArt Same Letter Heights**. Toggles letters of WordArt to be the same height.
- **WordArt Vertical Text**. Toggles the WordArt between vertical and horizontal.
- **WordArt Alignment**. Displays a menu of six alignment options.
- **WordArt Character Spacing**. Displays a list of seven options for adjusting character spacing.

CUSTOMIZING DRAWING OBJECTS

The Drawing toolbar holds all the secrets for modifying drawing objects. Be creative—select an object and try out the features. Add some pizzazz with Shadow and 3-D settings. There is a separate toolbar for each of these commands.

To view the Shadow Settings toolbar, click the Shadow Style button on the Drawing toolbar and select Shadow Settings, as shown in Figure 17.11. To view the 3-D Settings toolbar, click the 3-D Style button on the Drawing toolbar and select 3-D Settings, as shown in Figure 17.12.

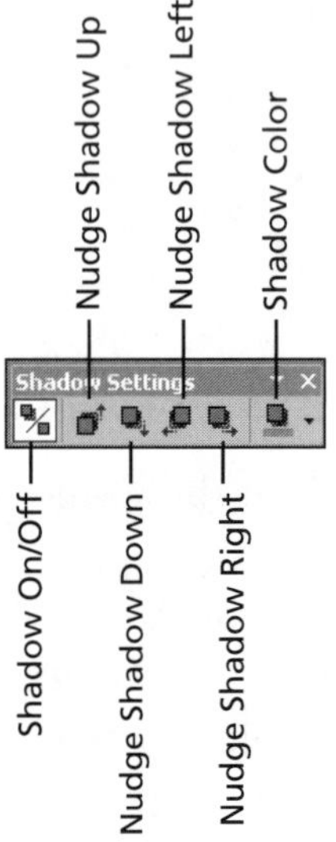

FIGURE 17.11

Make detailed changes to your shadowed objects using the Shadow Settings toolbar.

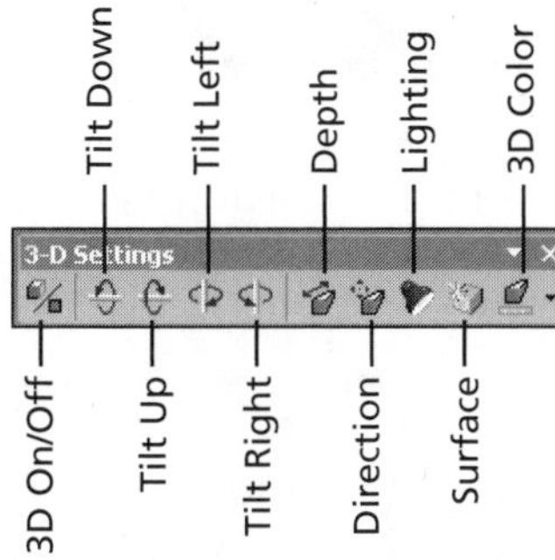

FIGURE 17.12

Make detailed changes to your 3-D objects using the 3-D Settings toolbar.

The buttons on the Shadow Settings toolbar work like this:

- **Shadow On/Off**. Toggles the selected object's shadow on and off.
- **Nudge Shadow Up**. Adjusts the selected object's shadow up.
- **Nudge Shadow Down**. Moves the shadow down.
- **Nudge Shadow Left.** Adjusts the selected object's shadow left.
- **Nudge Shadow Right.** Moves the shadow right.
- **Shadow Color.** Click the drop-down arrow next to the button to select a different shadow color.

TIP

Each time you click one of the four Nudge buttons, the shadow is moved by one point. Hold the Shift key while clicking the buttons to move the shadow by six points.

The buttons on the 3-D Settings toolbar work like this:

- **3D On/Off**. Toggles the selected object's 3-D effect on and off.
- **Tilt Down**. Tilts the selected 3-D object down.
- **Tilt Up**. Tilts the object up.
- **Tilt Left.** Tilts the selected 3-D object to the left.
- **Tilt Right.** Tilts the object right.
- **Depth.** Adjusts the depth of the 3-D effect from 0 points to Infinity. Click the button and choose a preset measurement or enter a custom one.
- **Direction.** Change the direction of the 3-D effect from one of the 11 preset choices.
- **Lighting.** Choose from Bright, Normal, or Dim lighting on the selected object as well as the direction the light is shining from. This button changes the brightness of the object.
- **Surface.** Pick a Metal, Plastic, Matte, or Wire Frame surface for the selected 3-D object.

TIP

When Wire Frame is selected, the color is removed from the object.

- **3-D Color.** Click the drop-down arrow next to the button to select a color for the 3-D effect.

APPLETS

Applets are separate programs that work within the Word document. Once accessed, the applet opens another window with menus and toolbars specific to the type of object with which you are working. When you finish working with the applet object, click back in the Word document to return to Word's features, menus, and toolbars.

ORGANIZATION CHART

The Organization Chart object has been significantly improved in Word 2002. There are enhancements for adding and removing parts of the chart as well as AutoFormat options to quickly apply formatting. The first noticeable difference is the ability to insert an organization chart directly from the Drawing toolbar.

CREATE AN ORGANIZATION CHART

1. Create a new document.
2. Click the Insert Diagram or Organization Chart button on the Drawing toolbar. The Diagram Gallery opens, as shown in Figure 17.13.

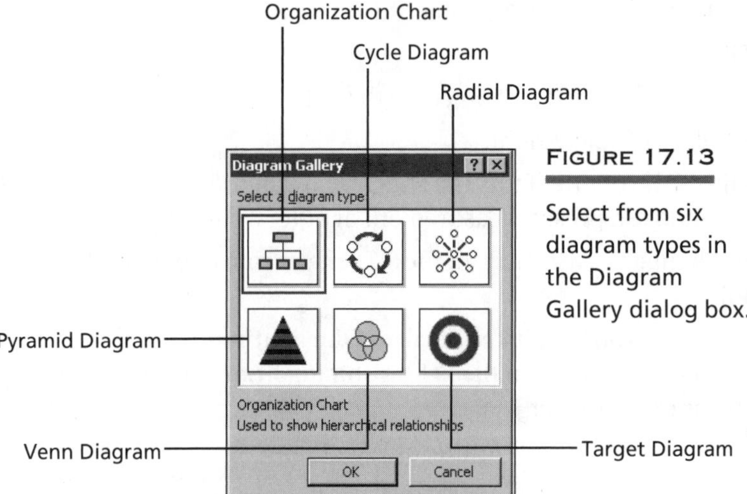

FIGURE 17.13

Select from six diagram types in the Diagram Gallery dialog box.

You can also open the Diagram Gallery dialog box by choosing Diagram from the Insert menu.

3. Select Organization Chart and click OK. Notice the Organization Chart toolbar appears automatically, as shown in Figure 17.14.
4. In the first box at the top of the chart, click and type **Jane Smith** and press Enter. Type **CEO**.
5. In the first box in the next layer of the chart, click and type **Frank Johnson** and press Enter. Type **Sales VP**.
6. In the second box, click and type **Open** and press Enter. Type **Marketing VP**.

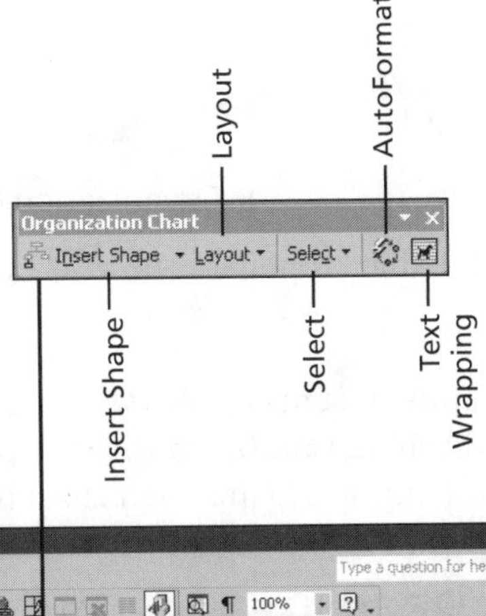

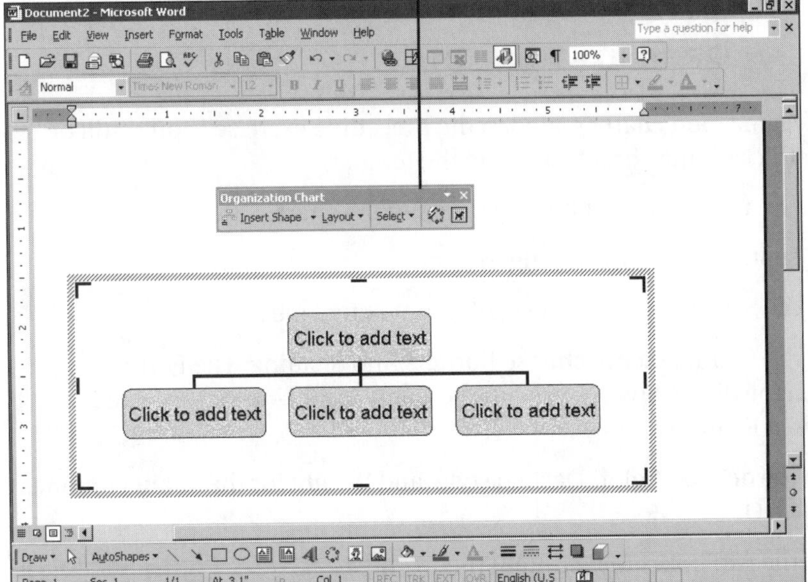

FIGURE 17.14

Since Word includes the Organization Chart applet, you no longer need fancy and expensive software to create professional organization charts.

7. Click the border of the third box and press Delete to remove it from the chart.

8. Click Insert Shape to add another level under Marketing VP.

TIP

The Insert Shape button on the Organization Chart toolbar can be turned into a floating menu. When you click the drop-down arrow next to the Insert Shape button, place your mouse pointer at the top of the menu until you see the move handle. Click and drag to make the menu float.

9. Select the newly added box.
10. Click the drop-down arrow beside Insert Shape and select Coworker.
11. Insert the following text into the new boxes:

    Sharon Timmond
    Media
    Open
    Internal

12. Press Esc twice to close the Organization Chart toolbar and return to Word.
13. Leave the document open for the next exercise.

The Select command presents a great way to choose individual levels, connecting lines, or the full chart. Combined with the power of borders and shading format options, modifying an organization chart is almost effortless.

FORMAT AN ORGANIZATION CHART

1. The organization chart created in the preceding exercise should still be open. Click on the chart to activate the toolbar.
2. Select the text in the first box at the top of the chart.
3. Click Center on the Formatting toolbar.
4. From the Select button, choose All Connecting Lines.
5. From the Format menu, choose Borders And Shading. The Format AutoShape dialog box opens with the Colors And Lines tab selected, as shown in Figure 17.15.
6. Select the desired Color, Dashed style, and Weight for the connector lines and click OK.
7. Select the two boxes that contain the word *Open*.

FIGURE 17.15

Change the look of the connecting lines of your organization chart from the Format AutoShape dialog box.

Use the Shift key to select noncontiguous boxes. Select the first box and then hold down the Shift key while selecting the next one. Continue holding Shift until all desired boxes or shapes are selected.

8. From the Format menu, choose Borders And Shading.
9. Select Yellow for the Fill Color and click OK.
10. Leave this chart open for the next exercise.

The AutoFormat command offers preset formats that apply to the entire chart. This is covered in the next section on working with diagrams.

DIAGRAM

Another new feature in Word is Diagram, which provides the ability to illustrate important points of a document. For example, the Diagram feature can help you prepare a merger contract that contains a Venn diagram to show the areas of overlap between two companies, or a patent application displaying a Cycle diagram of the process used by a new invention.

The five types of diagrams and the common use for each include:

- **Cycle**. Steps in a continuous process.
- **Radial**. The main element and its relationships.
- **Pyramid**. Foundation-based associations.
- **Venn**. Areas of overlap displayed with circle shapes.
- **Target**. This bulls-eye format plots the steps toward a goal.

As with all objects, try not to limit the usage to the descriptions. Pick the shape from the diagram that best demonstrates the point of your document. You can always modify the diagram type at any time.

Word comes with default formatting options that you can use if you are not feeling creative or willing to take the time to set up the options yourself. These AutoFormats save a lot of time and offer the graphically challenged a way to include style without having to outsource these projects.

CREATE A TARGET DIAGRAM

1. Create a new document.
2. Click the Insert Diagram Or Organization Chart button on the Drawing toolbar. The Diagram Gallery opens.
3. Choose Target and click OK.
4. In the upper-right corner text box, click and type **Finished!**
5. Type **Train** in one of the remaining text boxes, and type **Install** in the other.
6. Click Insert Shape to add another ring.
7. Type **Design**.
8. Add another ring and type **Support**.
9. Change the font size for all of the text to 9 points.
10. Select the last ring inserted.
11. Click Move Shape Forward twice to position this ring directly after the "Finished!" ring.
12. Click AutoFormat to access the Diagram Style Gallery, as shown in Figure 17.16.
13. Select a style and click Apply.

You can also select each ring individually and choose Borders And Shading from the Format menu to apply formatting.

14. Press Esc to return to the Word document.

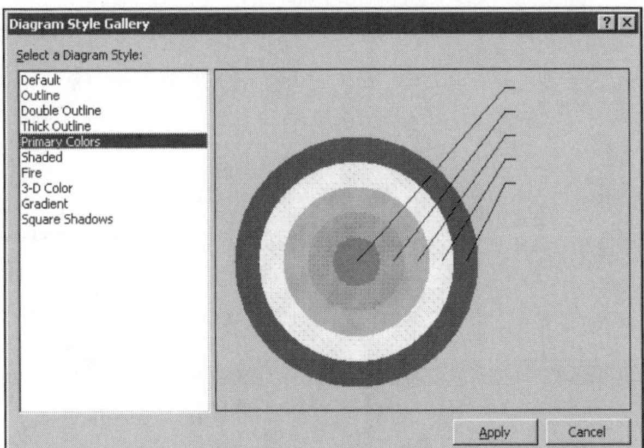

FIGURE 17.16

Select from a variety of diagram styles.

EXCEL SPREADSHEET

The Excel applet allows you to create an Excel spreadsheet or graph within Word. Excel is the best solution for crunching numbers, analyzing data, or creating data-driven charts. There is an entire section on integrating Word and Excel in Chapter 18, "Microsoft Office Integration: Tying It All Together."

EQUATION EDITOR

The Equation Editor is not widely used, yet it is extremely powerful and necessary in many types of legal documents. The Equation Editor is designed to create complex equations for patent applications or other scientific and technical documents. The best part about the Equation Editor is that you do not need to be a math or science genius to use it.

Accessed through the Insert, Object menu, the Equation Editor comes with its own toolbar and menu, as shown in Figure 17.17. Once the toolbar is visible, click the symbol or character you wish to insert.

THE EQUATION TOOLBAR

The toolbar looks a little daunting at first, but it's easier to follow once it's broken down into components.

- **Top Row**. The top row of the toolbar consists of the symbols used in the creation of equations. Related symbols are grouped together onto palettes for easy access.
- **Bottom Row**. The bottom row is made up of templates and fences. A *template* is a set of formatted empty slots in which the symbols from the top row are inserted. A *fence* is an item that is used to enclose parts of equations. A fence can be a bracket, parenthesis, vertical bar, or other specialized symbol.

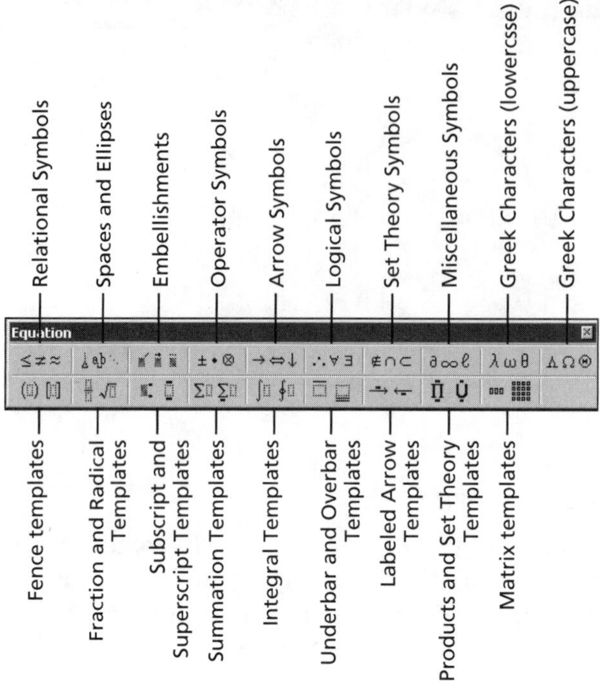

FIGURE 17.17

Create mathematical equations by inserting the proper symbols from the Equation toolbar.

Don't forget that you can use ScreenTips to view the name of each palette for more information on the function of each button.

USE THE EQUATION EDITOR

1. Create a new document.
2. From the Insert menu, choose Object.
3. Select Microsoft Equation 3.0 from the list and click OK. Notice the menu changes and the Equation toolbar appears.
4. Type **x** =.
5. From the Fraction And Radical Templates palette, select Full-Size Vertical Fraction Template, the first symbol on the top row.

Check the status bar for a description of the various buttons on the palette. As you place your mouse pointer over the various buttons, watch the status bar change.

6. Type **-b**.
7. From Operator Symbols, select ±.
8. From the Fraction And Radical Templates palette, select the Square Root Template (the first one on the fourth row).
9. Type **b**.
10. From the Subscript And Superscript Template, choose the Superscript option (the first one on the top row).
11. Type **2** and press Tab.
12. Type **-4ac** and press Tab twice. Your insertion point should move to the bottom of the fraction.
13. Type **2a+5y**.
14. Leave this equation open for the next exercise.

SHORTCUT KEYS

Table 17.1 lists some helpful shortcuts for working with the Equation Editor.

TABLE 17.1 EQUATION SHORTCUT KEYS

KEYBOARD	RESULT
Tab	Move forward in the equation
Shift+Tab	Move backward in the equation
Ctrl+D	Redraw
Ctrl+F	Fraction template
Ctrl+H	Superscript
Ctrl+L	Subscript
Ctrl+R	Square root
Ctrl+Shift+E	Text format
Ctrl+Shift+=	Math format
Ctrl+G, followed by a letter	Insert Greek symbol
Ctrl+Spacebar	Insert a space

FORMATTING EQUATIONS

A common misconception about equations is that they are inflexible because the symbols are chosen from a predetermined set on the toolbar. This is not the case. It is easy to change the font or add borders around previously entered pieces of the equation. The concept of formatting equations is similar to formatting text in Word; select the item you wish to change and apply the formatting. There are even styles in the Equation Editor.

FORMAT THE EQUATION

1. Your equation from the preceding exercise should still be open. If you do not see the Equation toolbar, double-click the equation.
2. Press Home to position the insertion point in front of the equation.
3. Type **Equation** and press Ctrl+Spacebar to insert a space.

The Equation Editor inserts the necessary spacing for the equation and suppresses the keyboard Spacebar to save you from inadvertently entering unneeded spaces. If you do need to insert extra space, use Ctrl+Spacebar.

4. Type **#1:** and press Ctrl+Spacebar twice.
5. Select the "Equation #1" text.
6. From the Style menu, choose Text. Notice the format of the text is no longer italic. The Text style differentiates text from vectors and variables.

Choose Other from the Style menu to change the font type or to include italic or bold formatting.

7. Select 2a+5y.
8. From the Fence Templates button (the first button on the second row), select the Parentheses (the first symbol on the top row).
9. Click outside of the equation to return to Word.

While editing large, complex equations, you may notice strange marks around the equation. If this occurs, use the Redraw command from the View menu to refresh the screen. Ctrl+D also produces the same result.

MANIPULATING OBJECTS

Both the Drawing toolbar and the Format menu offer an extensive selection of tools to modify drawing objects. The tools that become available depend on which object is selected. As you work with graphics, take a few minutes to observe and experiment with the tools as they appear.

BORDERS AND SHADING

The most common graphic element in legal documents would have to be borders. Borders are commonly applied to format title pages of agreements or contracts. Shading applied to text makes the text stand out a little more in the document. Borders can be added to characters, paragraphs, or entire pages.

Although shading is called for a little less often than borders, it can also be applied to characters and paragraphs.

APPLY BORDERS AND SHADING

The Outside Border button on the Formatting toolbar offers a quick way to add borders to selected characters and paragraphs. For more options, including page borders, use the Borders And Shading dialog box found on the Format menu.

APPLY BORDERS AND SHADING

1. From the CD-ROM, open Page Border.doc. This is a simple multipage agreement.
2. Select the paragraph that reads, "This Page was intentionally left blank."
3. Click the drop-down arrow beside of the Outside Border button.
4. Select Bottom Border. Notice the border now appears below the selected paragraph.
5. Select the title on the first page.
6. From the Format menu, choose Borders And Shading. The Borders and Shading dialog box opens, as shown in Figure 17.18.
7. From the Borders tab, select a double border from Style.
8. Choose a Color and Width for the border. Look at the Preview to see how the border will appear in the document.
9. Click the Left border button (under Preview) to turn off the left border.
10. Click the Right border button to turn off the right border.

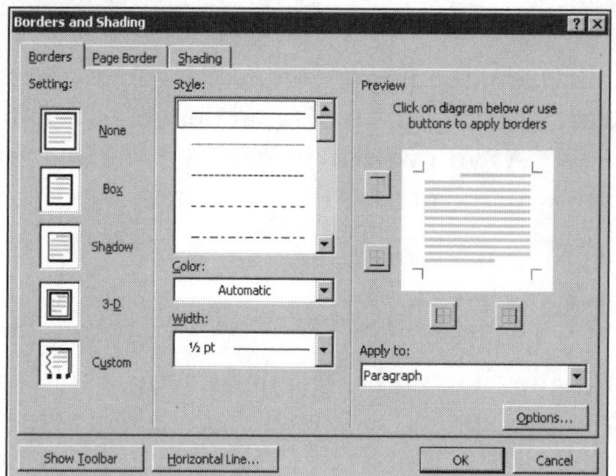

FIGURE 17.18

From the Borders tab, choose a border style, add color and change the width, then apply it to the paragraph or text.

11. Select the Shading tab and choose a light gray fill.
12. Click OK.

PAGE BORDERS

You may have noticed a separate tab in the Borders And Shading dialog box specifically for page borders. Even though paragraph and page borders are similar, page borders affect an entire document or selected sections.

Applying page borders to specific parts of the document requires a healthy understanding of section breaks. For more information, please see Chapter 7, "Formatting a Document."

ADD A PAGE BORDER

1. Open Page Border.doc, if it is not already open from the preceding exercise. This file is on the accompanying CD-ROM.
2. Place the insertion point on the first page.
3. From the Format menu, choose Borders And Shading. Select the Page Border tab, as shown in Figure 17.19.
4. Select the style, color, and width for the page border. Preview the selections in the Preview area of the dialog box.
5. Under Apply To, select This Section.
6. Click OK.

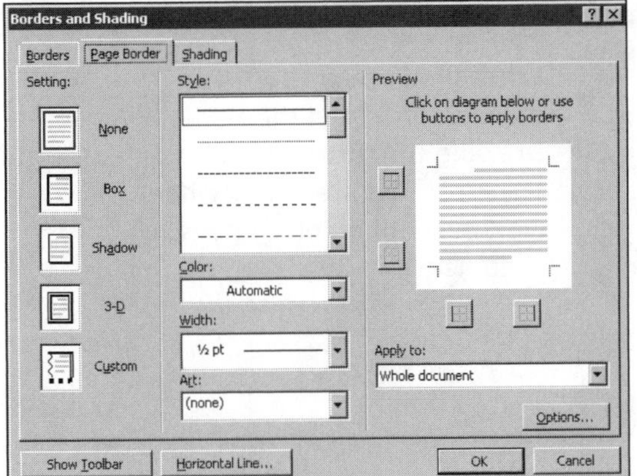

FIGURE 17.19

When you add a page border, you frame the document.

This document already contained different sections and section breaks. Therefore, the border is applied only to the first page of the document. Select Whole Document (under Apply To) if you wish the border to appear throughout the document.

WHAT ELSE DO I NEED TO KNOW ABOUT GRAPHICS?

In our earlier Word books, *Word 2000 for Law Firms* and *Word 97 for Law Firms,* graphics didn't command a chapter of its own. So, by now, you must be asking yourself, what else can there be to talk about? The Document Grid feature helps to align different types of graphics within a single document, and the Watermark feature makes it easy to apply watermarks to documents. Columns fit into this discussion, as well, since they arrange type in a fashion similar to graphics.

DOCUMENT GRID

The document grid has been around for the last few versions of Word but has become more obvious in Word 2002. The grid's function is to help line up drawing objects and pictures. In this version, it also assists with lining up text.

There is a grid in every Word document, although most people never see it. To view the grid or change how text and graphics relate to the grid, select Grid from the Draw button on the Drawing toolbar. The Drawing Grid dialog box will display as shown in Figure 17.20.

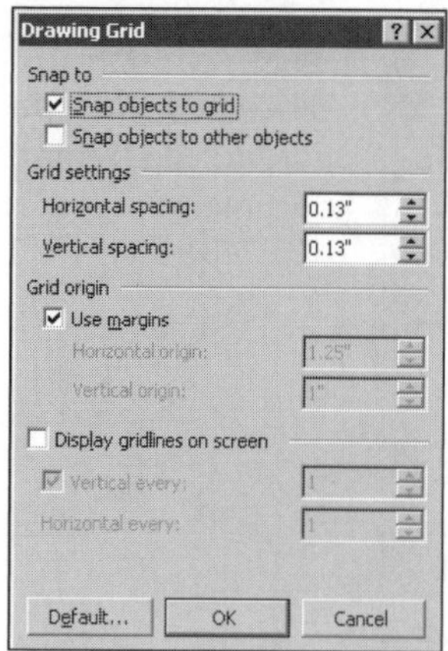

FIGURE 17.20

Set desired options for the drawing grid from the Drawing Grid dialog box. These settings are handy when working with graphic-intensive documents.

ADDING A WATERMARK

Have you ever tried to add a watermark in Word? In all earlier versions, there was no clear method to do it. In this version of Word, there is an actual command to help you insert watermarks.

A familiar watermark in legal documents is the word *DRAFT* appearing in a large, light-colored font that is inserted behind the text of the document, as shown in Figure 17.21. Other commonly used watermark text includes

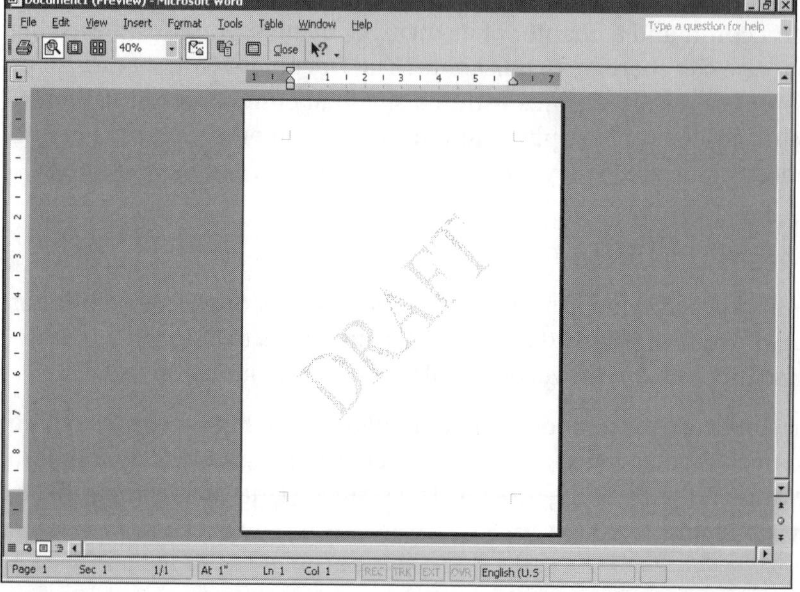

FIGURE 17.21

Add a watermark to your draft documents.

NEW FEATURE!

Word now offers a snappy new way to add watermarks to documents. From the Format menu, choose Background, then Printed Watermark.

CONFIDENTIAL, ORIGINAL, or *COPY.* These words, as well as others, have been set up in the new Watermark feature. If you prefer your firm's logo or a picture, these can also be used as watermarks.

ADD A WATERMARK

1. Create a new document.
2. From the Format menu, choose Background, then Printed Watermark. The Printed Watermark dialog box opens, as shown in Figure 17.22.

NOTE

It may be a bit confusing to choose Background since other backgrounds appear onscreen but do not print. In fact, the watermark is actually on the Header layer, but the commands are on the Background menu. Microsoft attempted to clear up any confusion by naming the command Printed Watermark. When a watermark is added to a document, it will print—provided the Drawing Objects option is selected to print in the Print Options dialog box.

3. Select Text Watermark.
4. From Text, select DRAFT.

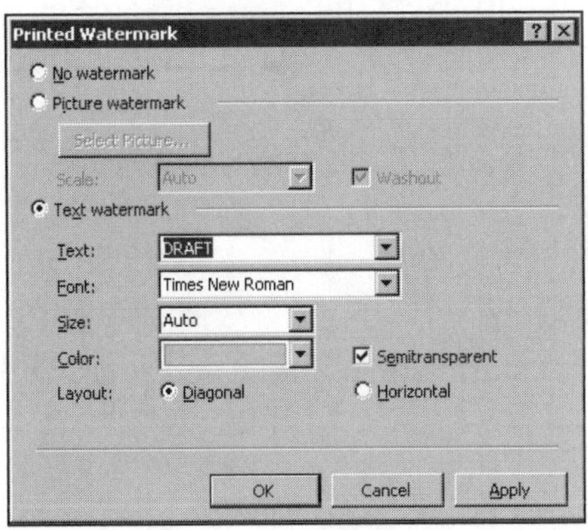

FIGURE 17.22

Select watermark attributes from the Printed Watermark dialog box.

If you do not see the word or phrase you are looking for, just type the text you want into the Text box.

5. Choose a Font style and Color.
6. Leave Semitransparent checked to mute the color.
7. Under Layout, select Diagonal.
8. Click OK to insert the watermark.

Try modifying the text watermark or inserting a picture watermark.

To remove the watermark, go back into the Printed Watermark dialog box, choose No Watermark, and click OK.

Since the Watermark feature was not available in previous versions, it is not backwardly compatible. If you need to add a watermark to a document that must be shared electronically with someone not using Word 2002, do not use this feature. Instead, view the header and footer, then insert and format a WordArt object.

FORMATTING WITH COLUMNS

A Word document can be divided into columns so text appears alongside other text, just as you might see in a newspaper. Creating columns in Word is a two-step process. Select the text first, then click the Columns button on the Standard toolbar and select the number of columns. That's all there is to it.

Newspaper-style columns format text to snake down the left side of the page and then continue on the right side of the page from top to bottom.

FORMAT A DOCUMENT INTO COLUMNS

1. Open Agenda.doc from the CD-ROM. If you prefer, type several paragraphs of text in a new document.
2. Select the paragraphs that start with a time (if you're using the Agenda.doc file).

3. Click Columns on the Standard toolbar. A column grid appears.
4. Drag the mouse across the grid to select the number of columns.
5. Release the mouse button and watch the text move into columns.

For advanced column formats, from the Format menu, choose Columns. Using this method, you can specify column size, add a line separator between columns, and more.

SUMMARY

There are many times when legal documents require graphics. The Equation Editor, Organization Chart, and other applets can be used to extend the power of Word by inserting pictures, drawing objects, and shapes into documents. All these items can be further customized by the extensive formatting options. Borders, shading, text boxes, and watermarks are also considered graphics and each one is commonly used in legal documents.

TROUBLESHOOTING GRAPHICS

I have a picture in the middle of my page that is behind the text. I cannot seem to click on it to change the text wrapping.

The picture may be a watermark, which is stored in the Header layer of the document. To remove it, do the following: From the Format menu, choose Background, Printed Watermark. Choose No Watermark to turn it off. To reposition the watermark, from the View menu, choose Header And Footer. Click and drag the watermark to the desired location.

When creating documents for our firm intranet, I'm unable to add a watermark from the Format, Background menu.

The Printed Watermark command is not available when working in a Web page document and is not visible when working in Web Layout view.

When I print my document, the organization chart does not show up.

Organization charts are considered Drawing Objects, and there is an option to choose whether or not to print them. From the Tools menu, choose Options. From the Print tab, verify that Drawing Objects is selected.

I am not able to drag my inserted photo to a new location.

The Text Wrapping command has been set to Inline With Text, which configures the picture to move with the paragraph text. Click the Text Wrapping button on the Picture toolbar and select Square. You should be able to drag the picture now.

Microsoft Equation 3.0 is not listed in the Insert, Object dialog box.

The Equation Editor is not part of the standard installation of Microsoft Office. If you don't see it, you may need to install it or contact your help desk or system administrator.

I have quite a few objects in my document and I am trying to get them positioned just right by dragging. However, when I let go of the mouse, they seem to jump a little to the right or left.

All Word documents contain a grid that helps line up text and objects using the Snap Objects To Grid command. You can turn this feature off using the Drawing toolbar. Click Draw and choose Grid. Or, to control one item at a time, hold the Alt key down while dragging your object.

Microsoft Office Integration: Tying It All Together

IN THIS CHAPTER

- E-mailing documents with Word and Outlook
- Integrating Word and PowerPoint
- Embedding Excel spreadsheets
- Using Access Reporting Tools in Word
- Creating effective charts
- Publishing to a Web page and HTML

Microsoft Word is a great word processing application. It is capable of handling desktop publishing projects, simple spreadsheets, and data management. Word is not, however, built for heavy spreadsheet work, database development, or graphic presentations. Other applications are much better suited for this type of work—and they integrate seamlessly with Microsoft Word.

MICROSOFT OFFICE INTEGRATION

Microsoft Office includes a suite of applications that work very well together. The contents vary depending on the version of Office that your firm purchased, but the main components are Microsoft Word, Access, Excel, PowerPoint, and Outlook. So how do all of these pieces fit together for you? Well, suppose your firm decides to conduct a client satisfaction survey—here's how it might work:

- **Store data in Access**. Input the gathered data and store it in Microsoft Access—the database application of Microsoft Office.
- **Excel query of database**. Use Excel to retrieve information to be analyzed and generate a report using functions to find average, minimum, and maximum responses per survey question, and then report the data with PivotTables and PivotCharts for a visual reflection of the findings.
- **Create a report in Word**. Write your conclusion report and copy the reports from Excel into the Word document for supporting facts. Include charts, worksheets, PivotTables, and PivotCharts. Set up these reports as handouts for a meeting.
- **Create a presentation in PowerPoint**. Once the results are tabulated and you are ready to present the data to the firm, send the Word document to PowerPoint to create an effective slide presentation. Use NetMeeting from within PowerPoint to schedule and hold an online meeting, or hold the meeting in person.
- **E-mail the report using Outlook**. Send a soft copy of the report and presentation, if desired, as an attachment to an Outlook e-mail message.

Any one application would have difficulty accomplishing all of this—but, by combining all that Microsoft Office has to offer, these tasks can be accomplished easily.

E-MAILING DOCUMENTS WITH WORD AND OUTLOOK

Let's face it, people rarely create documents for their own enjoyment. Documents are made to be shared. In the past few years, most people have gotten used to sending documents through electronic mail, *e-mail* for short, and Word makes this process easy. Documents can be sent electronically by clicking the E-Mail button on the Standard toolbar, or by choosing File, Send To and selecting the appropriate menu command.

SEND E-MAIL BY CLICKING A TOOLBAR BUTTON

The fastest way to send a Word document through e-mail is to click the E-Mail button on the Standard toolbar. The button toggles on and off a message header at the top of the document with standard e-mail fields. The integrated e-mail message and Word document are shown in Figure 18.1. For this feature to work, your firm must use e-mail software compatible with Microsoft Word.

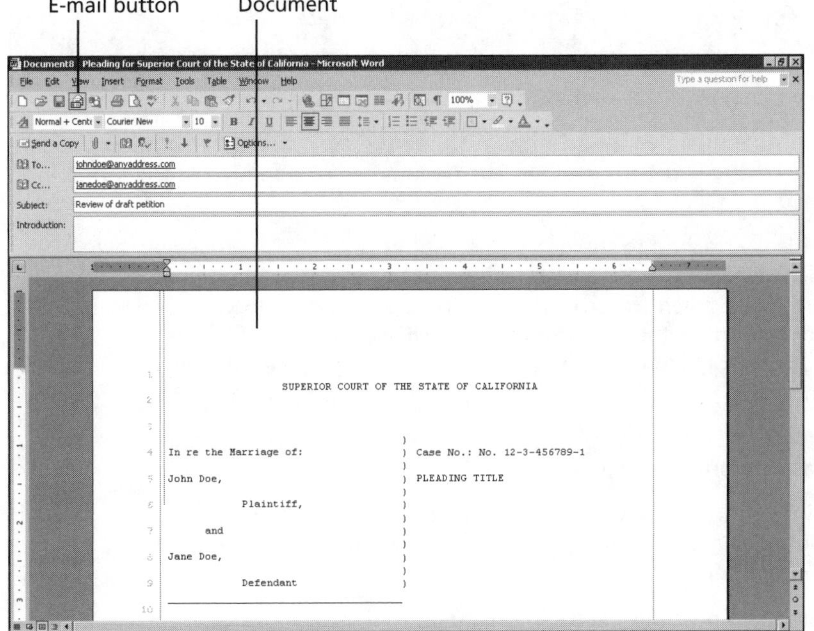

FIGURE 18.1

The e-mail header appears in the upper portion of the document.

E-MAIL A DOCUMENT USING THE E-MAIL BUTTON

1. Create a Word document and type some text.
2. Click the E-Mail button on the Standard toolbar.
3. Click the E-Mail button again to remove the e-mail header from the document.

Unless you know that the recipient is using the same e-mail application that you are, and the document being mailed will not need to be saved, you should not use the E-Mail button to send files. If you send a document using this method, the recipient receives the document as part of the body of the message—not as an attachment.

SEND A DOCUMENT VIA E-MAIL USING THE FILE MENU

The File menu offers more control over how files are sent. When you choose File, Send To, you are presented with e-mail choices for sending the document, as shown in Table 18.1.

TABLE 18.1 FILE, SEND TO COMMANDS

COMMAND	FUNCTION
Mail Recipient	Inserts an e-mail header onto the document. This is the same result as clicking E-Mail on the Standard toolbar. The document is embedded as the e-mail message text.
Mail Recipient (For Review)	The file is attached to the e-mail message. The text "Please Review the Attached Document" is added automatically to the outgoing message. When the recipient receives the file and opens it, a dialog box appears announcing that the file was sent for review. When the file is returned to the originator, Word asks if you want the file to be merged with the original to show any changes.
Mail Recipient (As Attachment)	Attaches the file to the e-mail message. The recipient opens and saves the file as with any e-mail attachment.
Routing Recipient	Allows you to define who receives the document and in what order. A routing slip also includes options for protecting and managing the document being routed.
Exchange Folder	Attempts to post the file to an Exchange folder on your network.

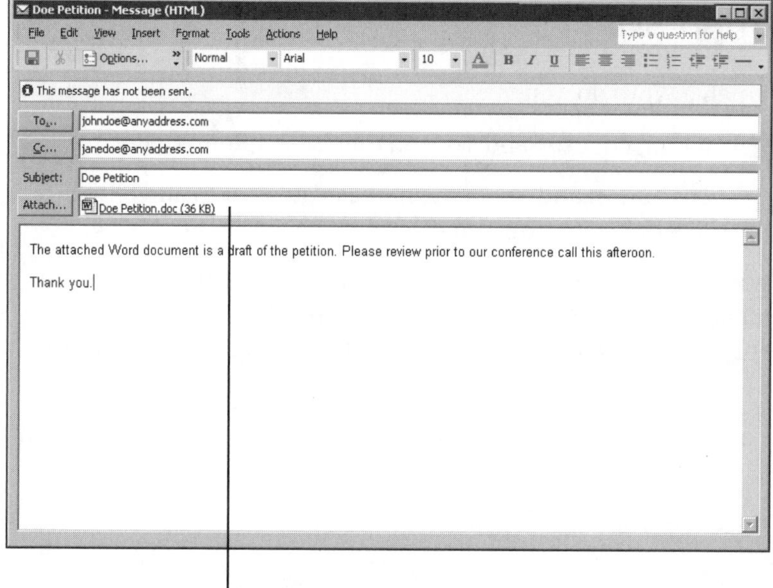

FIGURE 18.2

The Word file is automatically attached.

To send a document as an attachment, from the File menu, choose Send To, Mail Recipient (As Attachment). This will launch your e-mail application and automatically attach the Word document. Figure 18.2 shows the result of choosing the Mail Recipient (As Attachment) command.

SEND A DOCUMENT AS AN ATTACHMENT

1. Create or open a Word document.
2. From the File menu, choose Send To, Mail Recipient (As Attachment).
3. Type the recipient's e-mail address in the To box. Fill out any other fields.
4. Click Send.

If you do not have an option for Mail Recipient (As Attachment), you may need to enable it. From the Tools menu, choose Options. In the General tab, select Mail As Attachment and click OK.

Sometimes you need a bit more control over how a document is routed and to whom. When this is the case, you can add a routing slip.

ADD A ROUTING SLIP

1. Create or open a Word document.
2. From the File menu, choose Send To, and then select Routing Recipient.
3. Click the Address button and select the names you want to add to the routing slip. Click the To button and then click OK.
4. The order in which the recipients receive the routed document and routing slip can be controlled by selecting a name and clicking the Move arrows to promote or demote a name on the list. Under Route To Recipients, select the option One After Another.
5. Complete any other options. A completed sample routing slip is shown in Figure 18.3.
6. To route the document, click Route.

If a document is routed with the option One After Another selected, the first recipient receives an e-mail message with the document attached. The message will inform the recipient that the document is being routed, and will give instructions to route the document to the next recipient.

To add a routing slip but not yet send the document, click Add Slip. When you're ready to route the document, you can choose File, Send To, Next Routing Recipient.

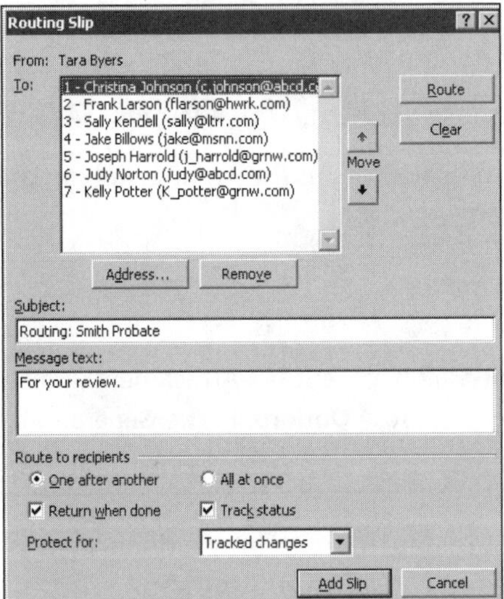

FIGURE 18.3

Create a routing slip for your document to be distributed to multiple recipients.

You can protect a routed document with any of the options shown in Table 18.2.

TABLE 18.2 ROUTING SLIP PROTECTION OPTIONS

SETTING	FUNCTION
None	Does not protect the routed document for changes or comments.
Track Changes	Track Changes is turned on and the recipients cannot turn off the feature.
Comments	Recipients can insert comments into the document but cannot change or delete comments from others.
Forms	Recipients can fill out a form document, but not make changes to the form itself.

USING WORD AS YOUR E-MAIL EDITOR IN OUTLOOK

In Outlook 2002, the default E-mail Editor is Word. This allows you to take advantage of many of Word's features when creating and reading e-mail messages, such as AutoCorrect, Automatic Bullets and Numbering, Styles, Tables, AutoFormat, Signatures, and Themes. This is evident from the toolbar and menu choices available when creating new messages in Outlook.

In addition, e-mail options such as signatures, stationary, and special fonts for different types of messages can be set in Word and will carry over to Outlook and vice versa.

In previous versions of Outlook, the default e-mail editor was the Outlook editor but there was an option to turn on Word as your e-mail editor.

Although many firms choose to turn this feature off in order to increase computer performance, there are some new options that allow you to access the Word E-Mail Editor in the following situations:

- **Create One E-Mail Message.** If you want to add special formatting such as Numbering to a single message, from the Actions menu in Outlook, choose New Mail Message Using, Microsoft Word (*message format*).

Message format will be HTML, Rich Text, or Plain Text.

- **View E-Mail Messages.** If you prefer to view Rich Text messages that you receive using Word, from the Tools menu, choose Options and select the Mail Format tab. Select Use Microsoft Word To Read Rich Text E-Mail Messages and click OK.

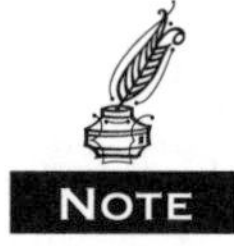

The option to use Word as your e-mail editor is controlled from within Outlook. From the Tools menu, choose Options and select the Mail Format tab. To turn off this feature, clear the Use Microsoft Word To Edit E-Mail Messages option and click OK.

INTEGRATING WORD AND POWERPOINT

PowerPoint is an easy-to-use graphics and presentation program. The good news is that Word and PowerPoint integrate so well that you can take any Word document that contains headings and send it to PowerPoint to create a presentation instantly—likewise, you can send a PowerPoint presentation to Word.

SENDING A DOCUMENT TO POWERPOINT

If you use heading styles in Word, you can send a document to PowerPoint to create a presentation.

Microsoft PowerPoint must be installed on your computer before you can complete the exercises in this section.

SEND A WORD DOCUMENT TO POWERPOINT

1. Create a new document at least two pages long and apply heading styles 1 through 3 in some of the paragraphs on both pages. Or, if you prefer, you can open the exercise titled "Word to PowerPoint" on the CD-ROM accompanying this book.
2. From the File menu, choose Send To, Microsoft PowerPoint. The result is shown in Figure 18.4.
3. Leave this document open for the next exercise.

Information formatted with Heading 1 style is made into a new slide, Heading 2 is a bullet point on the slide, and Heading 3 style text is a sub-bullet under Heading 2 style text. Text formatted with Normal style formatting is not exported to the presentation. For more information on using styles in Word, see Chapter 9.

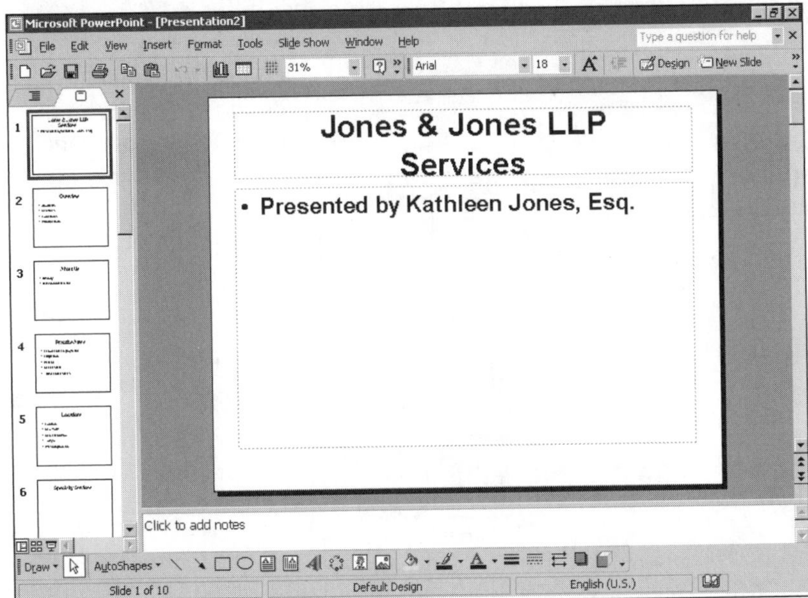

FIGURE 18.4

PowerPoint will automatically create slides when you export a document to it from Word.

FORMATTING THE EXPORTED DOCUMENT

Once the text from the Word document is in PowerPoint, you can do a great deal to enhance its impact. The best part about this is that applying formatting in PowerPoint is easy. Within five minutes, you can create a presentation that might easily have taken an hour or more to create from scratch.

FORMAT THE PRESENTATION IN POWERPOINT

1. The PowerPoint file from the preceding exercise should still be open.
2. From the PowerPoint Format menu, choose Slide Design. The Slide Design Task Pane shown in Figure 18.5 opens.
3. Place your mouse pointer, without clicking, over any design template.
4. Click the drop-down arrow next to your chosen design template and choose Apply To All Slides. The selected slide design is applied to all slides in the presentation.

NOTE

Design templates contain two formats—one for the title slide and one for the rest of the slide. The format is applied automatically depending on the layout of the slide.

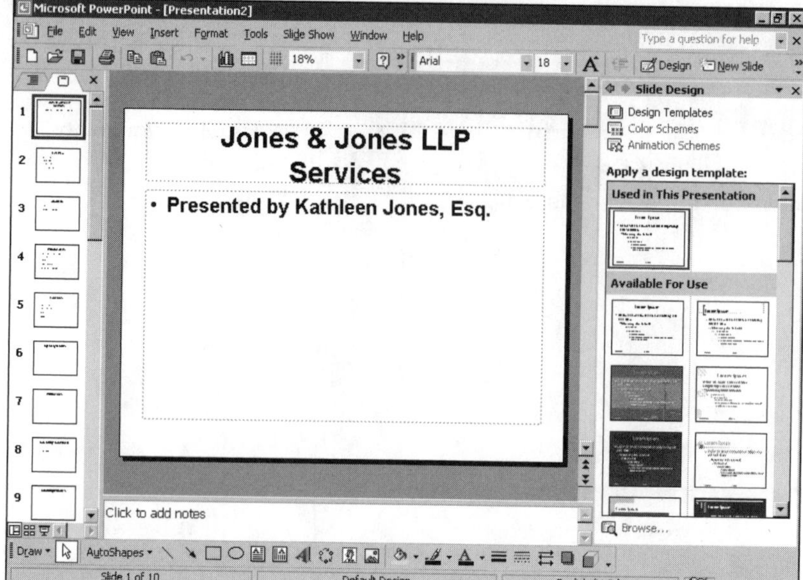

FIGURE 18.5

Choose from many design templates on the Slide Design Task Pane.

5. Select the first slide in your presentation. Most often this is a title slide that might require a unique format.
6. Locate a different slide design from the Slide Design Task Pane and click the drop-down arrow.
7. Select Apply To Selected Slides to change the design of individually selected slides.
8. Keep this file open for the next exercise.

SEND A POWERPOINT PRESENTATION TO WORD

Information can be sent from a PowerPoint presentation to create a Word document. By doing this, you can create handouts for your presentation, as well as an outline document to help you as you speak.

SEND A POWERPOINT PRESENTATION TO WORD

1. The PowerPoint file from the preceding exercise should still be open.

2. From PowerPoint, choose File, Send To and select Microsoft Word. The Send To Microsoft Word dialog box shown in Figure 18.6 opens.
3. Choose one of the page layout options and whether or not to create a link to the PowerPoint file so changes are reflected in the Word document.
4. Click OK. The resulting Word document is shown in Figure 18.7.

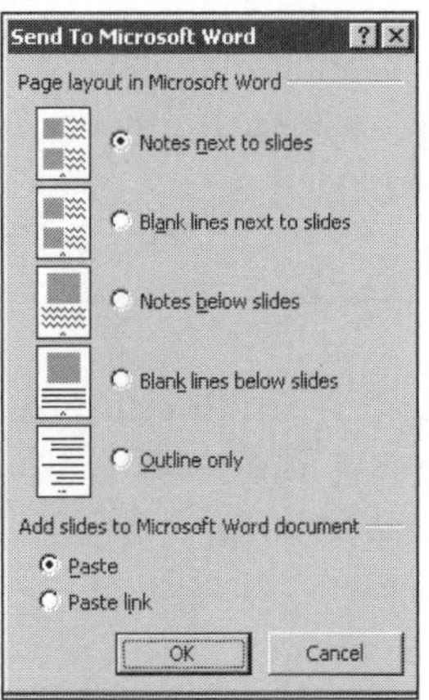

FIGURE 18.6

Select page layout options when sending a PowerPoint presentation to Word.

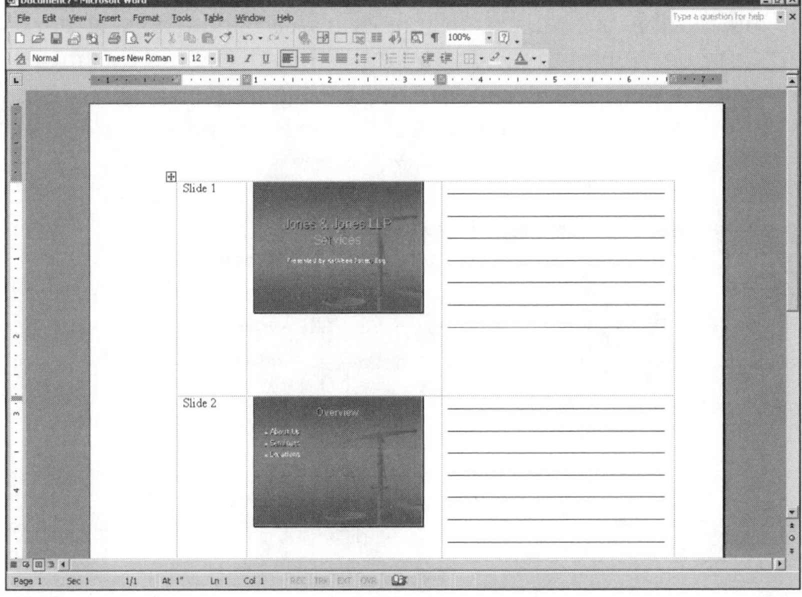

FIGURE 18.7

Word organizes PowerPoint slides into a table.

INTEGRATING WORD AND EXCEL

Excel has long been known as the most powerful spreadsheet program in the world. Excel is a number-crunching, data analysis, charting, PivotTable, report-generating giant.

Word allows you to create tables and use basic formulas, but when you need more, you need Excel. Excel includes more than 200 functions and an Insert Function Wizard that walks you through creating even the most complex formula. If it's more rows and columns that you need from Excel, the limit for rows is 65,536, and there can be up to 256 columns in each worksheet.

> Microsoft Excel uses the term *PivotTable* to describe a three-dimensional way to look at and analyze data. Fields can be dragged from one position on the table to another to change the way data is displayed. PivotTables contain Page, Column, Row, and Data fields. Calculations can be performed on the Data field of a PivotTable.

There are three ways to insert an Excel spreadsheet into a Word document: using a toolbar button, using a menu command, or copying and pasting the information from Excel into Word.

INSERT MICROSOFT EXCEL WORKSHEET TOOLBAR BUTTON

The Insert Microsoft Excel Worksheet button on the Standard toolbar functions much like the Insert Table button, except it inserts an embedded Excel worksheet into the Word document instead of a table. Click to expand the button and select how many rows and columns are required for the Excel worksheet. The expanded Insert Microsoft Excel Worksheet button is shown in Figure 18.8.

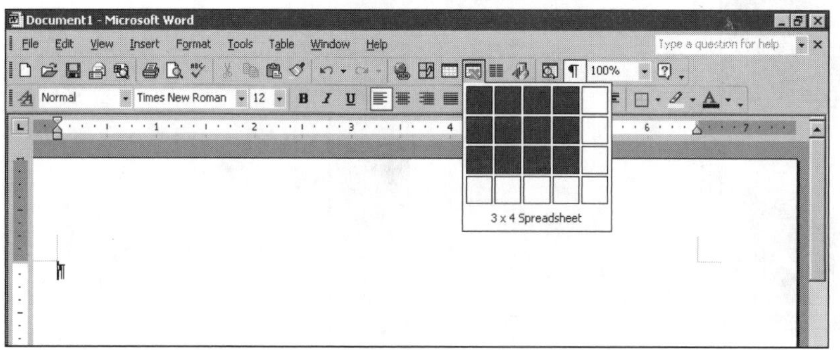

FIGURE 18.8

Insert an embedded Excel worksheet into your Word document.

NOTE

Microsoft Excel must be installed on your computer before you can complete the exercises in this section.

INSERT A WORKSHEET USING A TOOLBAR BUTTON

1. Create a new Word document.
2. Click the Insert Microsoft Excel Worksheet button on the Standard toolbar.
3. Drag your mouse to highlight the number of rows and columns that you want to insert into the Word document and release the mouse button to complete the process.

When the embedded Excel worksheet is active, Microsoft Excel menus and toolbars replace the ones from Word. Once you click out of the embedded worksheet, the Word menus and toolbars return.

An embedded Excel worksheet is shown in Figure 18.9.

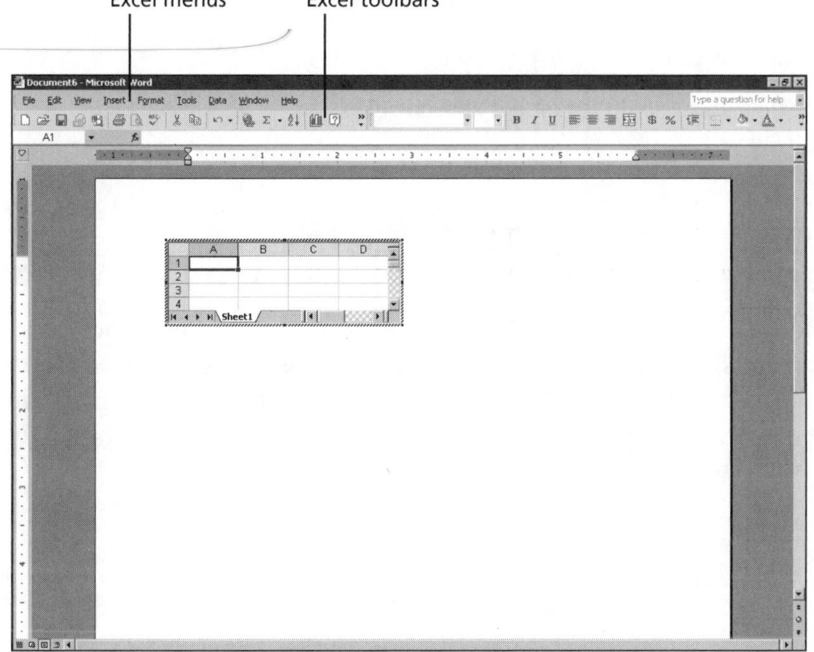

FIGURE 18.9

An embedded Excel worksheet allows you to access all the functionality of Excel without leaving Microsoft Word.

INSERT A WORKSHEET FROM A MENU COMMAND

The Insert Excel Worksheet button allows you to define, in advance, the number of columns and rows for the Excel worksheet. If you don't need to specify this in advance, you can insert the Excel worksheet by choosing Insert, Object, and selecting Microsoft Excel Worksheet. The Object dialog box is shown in Figure 18.10.

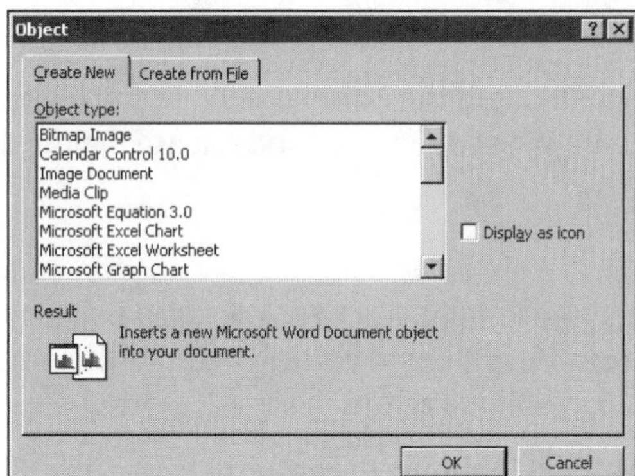

FIGURE 18.10

Choose from an array of object types to insert into your Word document.

INSERT A WORKSHEET FROM A MENU COMMAND

1. From the Insert menu, choose Object.
2. Select Microsoft Excel Worksheet and click OK.

USE COPY AND PASTE SPECIAL TO INSERT AN EXCEL WORKSHEET

The final method to insert an Excel worksheet is to use the Copy and Paste Special commands. By using Paste Special instead of Paste, you can have Word maintain a link rather than copy the data itself, and the information format can remain that of Microsoft Excel—and any updates to the Excel file can be set to show up in your Word document without further effort on your part.

COPY AND PASTE SPECIAL WITH AN EXCEL WORKSHEET

1. Open both Excel and Word, if necessary.
2. From the CD-ROM, open the exercise titled "Copy Excel Data." If you don't have access to a CD drive, type information into several cells.
3. Select the information you want to copy from the Microsoft Excel worksheet.
4. From the Edit menu, choose Copy.
5. Switch back to Microsoft Word.
6. From the Edit menu, choose Paste Special. The Paste Special dialog box opens, as shown in Figure 18.11.
7. Select Paste Link and Microsoft Excel Worksheet Object and click OK.

NOTE

If you do not need the Excel data to update from the original spreadsheet, do not click Paste Link.

8. Close both documents without saving.

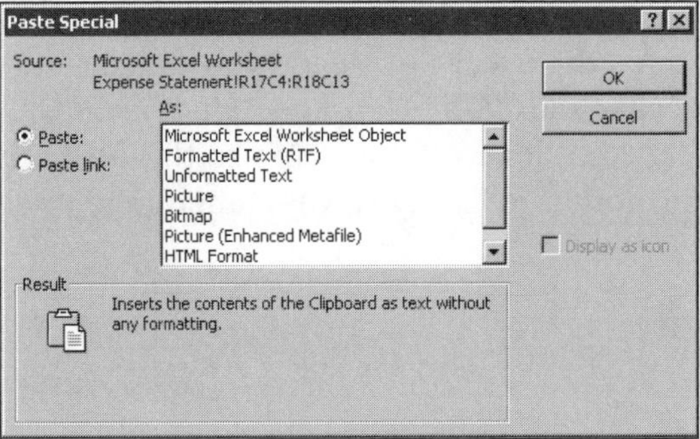

FIGURE 18.11

From the Paste Special dialog box, choose to either paste the Excel Worksheet Object or paste a link to the Excel Worksheet Object.

NEW FEATURE!

If you choose to Paste the copied Excel data instead of Paste Special, you can use the new Paste Options button that contains options to control formatting of the pasted text or to create a link to the original file.

WHEN TO USE EXCEL INSTEAD OF WORD

Excel is great for performing calculations and presenting data in an organized and flexible format. Because calculations update as changes to the numbers occur, it's a safer bet to keep important calculations that must remain current in Excel worksheets rather than Word tables.

Another time to use Excel instead of Word is when you need to perform more complex calculations than what Word offers. You can quickly calculate monthly payments using the Excel PMT function, calculate an Internal Rate of Return (IRR function) for a series of cash flows, or use Date functions to find the number of days between two dates, or other necessary information.

If you look at these examples and still do not know if Excel is applicable for your firm's usage, here are some practice groups that usually benefit from using Excel:

- **Real Estate**. Calculate square footage costs, monthly payments.
- **Trust and Estates**. Calculate percentage-based disbursements and perform other distribution-related calculations.
- **Mergers and Acquisitions**. Create and maintain financial tables that automatically update.
- **Corporate**. Calculate taxes, business plans, futures, and percentage-based bonus distributions.

AN INTRODUCTION TO USING EXCEL 2002

Once you have embedded the Excel worksheet, you can get started by creating formulas, reports, and charts. Excel's Insert Function Wizard walks you through creating even the most complex formulas. New to this edition of Excel is the ability to ask a question and have Excel list what function to use to achieve your goal.

USE THE EXCEL INSERT FUNCTION WIZARD

1. Create a Word document.
2. From the Insert menu, choose Object, and select Microsoft Excel Worksheet.
3. Click OK. The Excel worksheet is embedded in the Word document. The insertion point is still in the Excel worksheet, so Excel menus and toolbars are active while you work.
4. From the Insert menu, choose Function.
5. Type **Monthly Payments** in the Search For A Function box and click Go. Figure 18.12 shows the Insert Function dialog box.

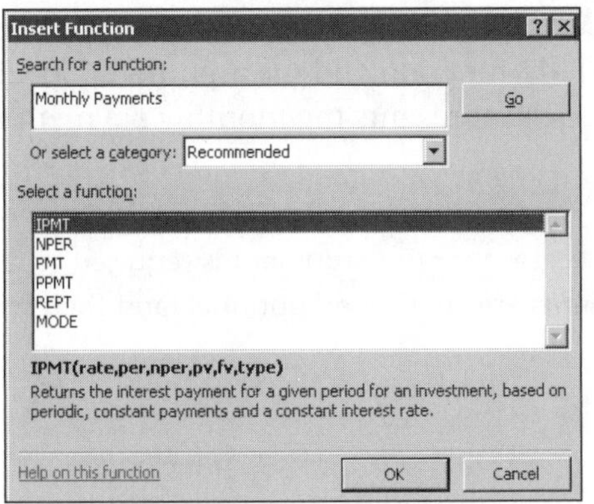

FIGURE 18.12

Use the Search For A Function box to locate an exact function in Excel.

6. Select PMT, the Payment function, and click OK. The Function Arguments dialog box opens, as shown in Figure 18.13, to help you construct the formula.
7. Type **.064/12** in the Rate box. In this calculation, .064 is the interest rate on the loan. This number is divided by 12 to calculate 12 monthly payments per year. Of course, you will want to substitute the current interest rate for this 6.4 percent when creating your own formula.
8. The Nper box represents the total number of payments for the duration of the loan. Type **60** in the Nper box for this exercise—that indicates the loan is for five years and you expect one payment per month. If you prefer, you can type **5*12** in the Nper box to let Excel do the calculation for you. If you were calculating a 30-year mortgage, the Nper would be 30*12 (30 years, 1 payment per month).

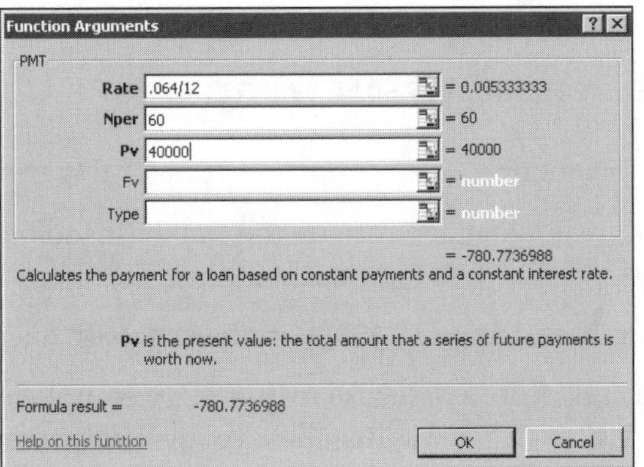

FIGURE 18.13

The Function Arguments dialog box will assist you with creating a formula.

9. Pv is the present value of the loan. For this exercise, type **40000** and click OK. The result of the PMT function and the arguments specified in this exercise is $780.77, which represents the monthly payment required on the $40,000 loan.

NOTE

Bold next to an argument indicates that the argument is required to create the formula. The nonbold arguments are considered optional, and therefore, not required.

INTEGRATING WORD AND ACCESS

The database application of Microsoft Office is called Access. Access is a relational database that can contain multiple tables of information that can be linked to other tables in the database. Access is a great application for this purpose because it can handle large amounts of data in an organized manner.

NOTE

Good as it is, Access isn't unlimited. If your performance and storage size requirements call for something more powerful, consider using SQL Server. Since SQL Server is not part of Microsoft Office, however, it is not covered in this chapter.

Access database information can be queried from within Microsoft Word. To do this, you'll need to display the Database toolbar.

NOTE

Microsoft Access must be installed on your computer before you can complete the exercises in this section.

QUERY ACCESS FROM WITHIN WORD

1. Create a new document.
2. Alternate-click any toolbar and turn on the Database toolbar. The Database toolbar is shown in Figure 18.14.
3. Click Insert Database. Figure 18.15 shows the Database dialog box.
4. Click Get Data and locate a database to query. If a complete installation was performed when Office was installed, you will have a sample database named Northwind. To see if this database is installed, search your hard drive for Northwind.mdb.

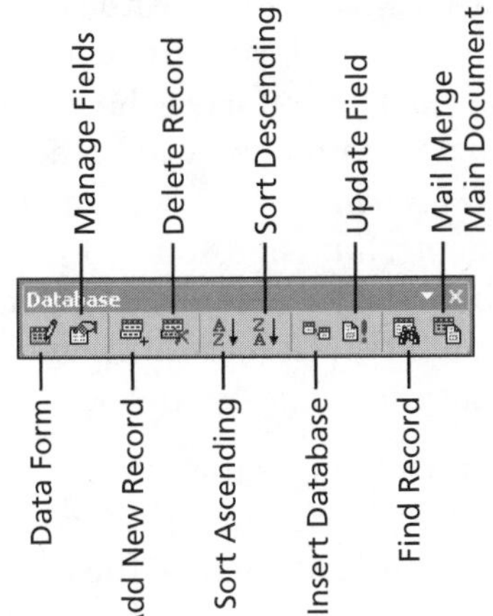

FIGURE 18.14

The Database toolbar will help you create and manage records used in a mail merge, for example.

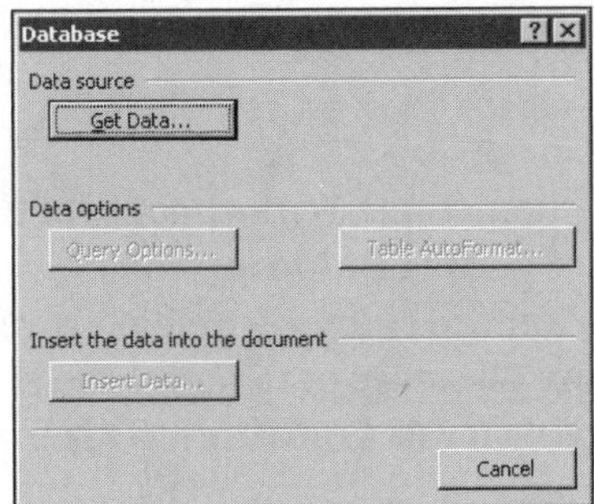

FIGURE 18.15

Use the Database dialog box to insert stored data into your Word document as a table.

5. Select a table to query. For this exercise, you can use Ten Most Expensive Products and click OK.
6. Click Insert Data, then OK. The information from the Access database appears in the Word document.

INTEGRATING WORD WITH THE WEB

Most software manufacturers have stated that they intend to change the way we all use software today. They say the goal is to take applications that currently reside on the desktop and have users access them from an Application Service Provider (ASP). Other manufacturers have changed the way they provide support by making the company Web site the first stop for consumers when they need additional drivers for printers, products, patches, and customer service.

The world is comfortable in a Web-based environment. And law firms are starting to realize the importance of having a strong Web presence to attract new clients and to provide information that can be accessed 24 hours a day. Firms are also realizing that the easiest way to share information within the firm itself, is to set up and maintain a firm intranet. This allows coworkers to share internal communications such as bulletins, documents, human resource forms, and present firm policies. The primary difference between the Internet and an intranet is that people must be within your firm or granted special access by your firm to access the intranet, and the Internet is generally accessible by anyone.

Microsoft Word integrates so well with Web pages that you can actually save a document as a Web page in just a matter of seconds. This section focuses on how to save Word documents as Web pages and some of the features available once files are saved in this format.

CREATE A WEB PAGE FROM A WORD DOCUMENT

1. Create a new document.
2. Type **Introduction** and press Enter. Type **We the people of the United States, in Order to form a more perfect Union, establish Justice, insure domestic Tranquility, provide for the common defense, promote the general Welfare, and secure the Blessings of Liberty to ourselves and our Prosperity, do ordain and establish this Constitution for the United States of America.**
3. From the File menu, choose Save As Web Page.
4. Save in C:\My Documents. Under File Name, type **My Web Page** and click Save.

Once you save your document as a Web page, you can view the document using any Web browser.

NOTE

When you save a document as a Web page it is saved in HTML format, which changes the file extension from .doc to .htm.

Word 2002 includes a new Web file format that strips out XML tags and Word HTML and style markup to produce clean HTML code. This format is called Web Page, Filtered and is available from the Save As Type drop-down list. If there is a possibility that you will need to edit your file again in Word, do not save to this format; instead, choose Save As Web Page to preserve formatting.

HTML is the standard markup language used for documents on the Web. *Tags* are used in HTML to tell the Web browser how to display text and graphics.

VIEW YOUR WEB PAGE IN A BROWSER

1. Open your Web browser.
2. From the File menu, choose Open.
3. Type **C:\My Documents\My Web Page.htm** and click OK.
4. Now you are looking at your document as a Web page. (See Figure 18.16.)
5. Keep this document open for the next exercise.

Looking at a document in a browser is similar to viewing the document in Web Layout view in Word. When you save a Word document as a Web page, HTML code is inserted into the document to let the browser know how to display the page.

There are a few features that you cannot use when creating a Web page in Word. They include page borders and multiple columns of text. The workaround for this is to create a table to get the same effect.

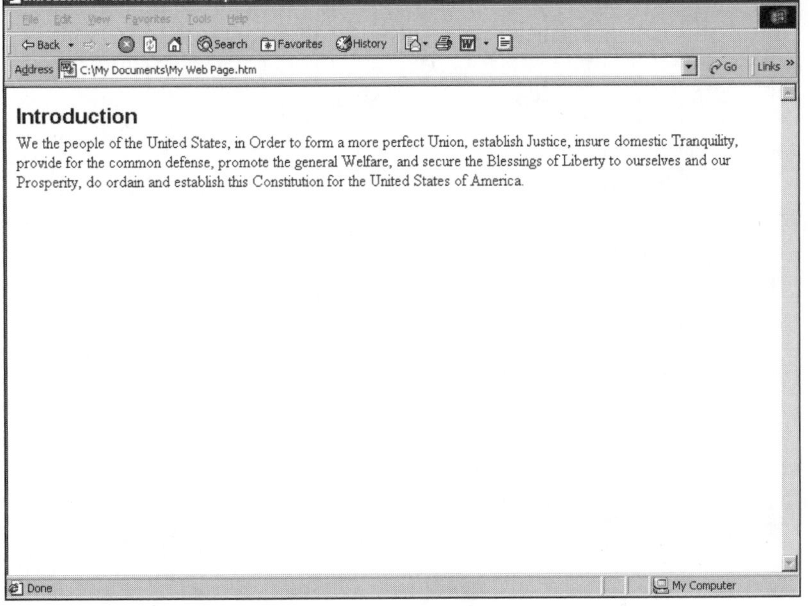

FIGURE 18.16

You can turn a Word document into a Web document with just a few mouse clicks.

VIEW HTML SOURCE OF YOUR WEB PAGE

1. My Web Page should still be open in Word from the preceding exercise.

HTML can only be viewed in a document that has been saved as a Web page. You can also view the HTML in any Web page.

2. From the View menu, choose HTML Source, as shown in Figure 18.17.
3. From the File menu, choose Exit to return to your document.

As you just saw from viewing the HTML source, there is a lot of code needed just to turn your document into a Web page. Aren't you glad you don't have to write all that code? The code you saw is HTML, and it was automatically written for you just by saving your Word document as a Web page. So, congratulations, you have just written an HTML Web page.

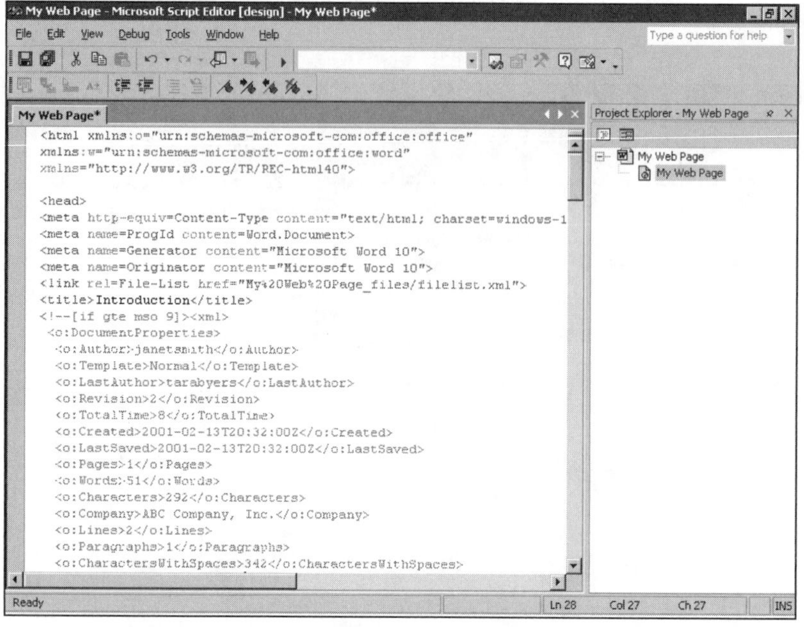

FIGURE 18.17

View the HTML source code behind your Web page.

ENHANCING THE WEB PAGE

You have seen how easy it is to turn a Word document into a Web page, although you may want to add some personality to the page to make it look like more than just a Word document saved as a Web page. You could start by adding a background to your page to give it a little color. Adding a background to the Web page is no different from adding it to a Word document.

ADDING A BACKGROUND TO YOUR DOCUMENT

1. My Web Page should be open from the preceding exercise.
2. From the Format menu, choose Background.
3. Select the desired background color.
4. Save the document and keep it open for the next exercise.

NOTE

To see what your Web page looks like now, you can repeat the "View Your Web Page in a Browser" exercise.

Adding a background to a Web page is pretty straightforward. However, if you wanted to change the font as well, and maybe add bullets to your document, you could change them all separately or use themes to change them all at once. Similar to styles in a Word document, themes were designed to help make a Web page look great. Themes allow you to apply bullets, add a background, and format the text.

ADDING A THEME TO YOUR WEB PAGE

1. The My Web page.htm file that you created earlier should still be open; open it, if necessary.
2. From the Format menu, choose Theme.
3. Select the desired theme and click OK.
4. Save the document and view it in your Web browser.

NOTE

To change an applied theme, repeat steps 1 through 3 of the preceding exercise. To remove a theme, choose No Theme from the Theme list.

BEYOND THEMES

Now that a background and theme have been applied, it's time to take this one step further. Most Web pages are divided into sections for easy navigation and readability. Figure 18.18 shows a document with different sections.

Sections are added by inserting frames into the document. Frames also allow you to organize the Web page. For example, you can include a header at the top of the screen, a navigation bar on the left, and the body of the document in the center. Each frame you create is, in fact, a different file, linked to the others using what is called a *frames page.*

ADD FRAMES TO YOUR WEB PAGE

1. Open the My Web page.htm file that you created earlier.
2. From the Format menu, choose Frames and then choose New Frames Page. The Frames toolbar opens.
3. Click New Frame Left on the Frames toolbar. A vertical gray bar called the *Frame border* appears in the center of the page.
4. Drag the Frame border so the new frame is taking up about a third of the page.

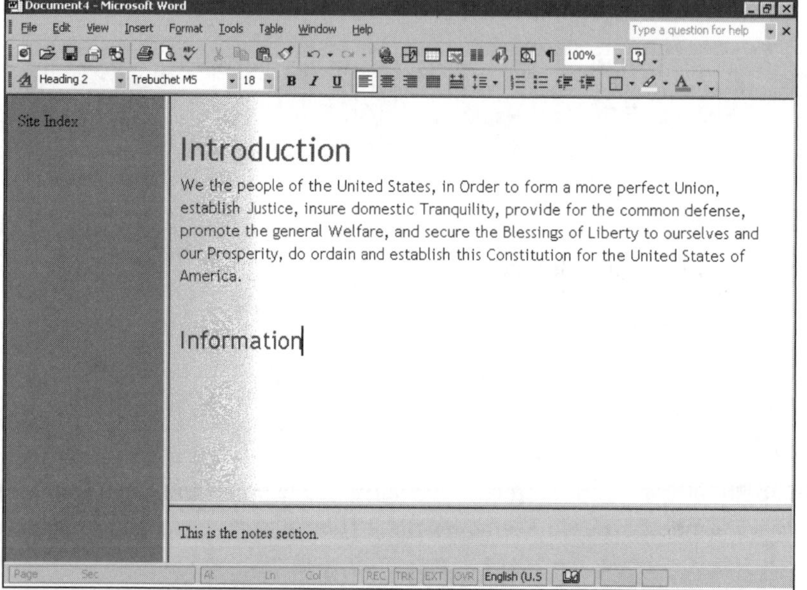

FIGURE 18.18

Organize your Web page by inserting frames.

5. Click in the new frame and add a background. Remember, backgrounds are found on the Format menu.
6. Save the document and view it in your Web browser.

Avoid having too many frames in one Web page; it can cause your Web page to load slowly in most browsers. If a page is too sluggish, many potential users will simply click away without waiting for it to appear.

Now that the new frame has been added, you can add anything to it—some text, an image, a different background—the sky's the limit.

WEB PAGE TABLE OF CONTENTS

A table of contents in a Word document is used to let people know what topics are included and where to find them. A Web page can contain a table of contents for the same reasons. Use heading styles in the document, and these headings are automatically added to the table of contents.

TABLE OF CONTENTS FRAME

1. Create a new Word document.
2. Type **This is heading 1**. Apply heading style 1 (Ctrl+Alt+1), and press Enter. Type **This is heading 2** and press Enter. Apply heading 2 style (Ctrl+Alt+2).
3. From the File menu, choose Save As Web Page, and name the file **Frames**.
4. From the Format menu, choose Frames and then Table Of Contents In Frame.
5. Save the Web page and view it in your Web browser.

SUMMARY

Microsoft Word is a great program but it's not practical to use it for everything. Microsoft Office applications such as Excel, PowerPoint, Access, and Outlook can be used in conjunction with Word to extend the capabilities available in Microsoft Word. Word documents can be saved as Web pages and posted to an Internet or intranet site. Once these files are saved in this format, themes and frames can be added to apply just the formatting you need.

TROUBLESHOOTING OFFICE INTEGRATION

I would like the inserted worksheet to appear as an icon. Can this be accomplished after the worksheet has already been added?

If the reviewers of a document are within your firm and have access to the network, you can embed the Excel worksheet as an icon. When the worksheet needs to be accessed, a simple double-click opens the file and produces the information. Even after this information is inserted as an icon or a worksheet object, it can be converted easily. Select the object and from the Edit menu, choose Worksheet Object, Convert. Check or uncheck Display As Icon.

Is there a way to export information from Access for a Word mail merge?

Yes, but you can also query information from within Word for a mail merge by using the Database toolbar. If you want to go through Access, open the table to be exported. From the File menu, choose Export. In the Export Table 'Table Name' To dialog box, change Save As Type to Microsoft Word Merge (*.txt). Name the file and click Export All. The file is saved as a text file that is separated by tabs and other formatting. From within Word, choose File, Open. Locate the file and open it. Select everything and, from the Table menu, choose Convert, Text To Table. You will probably need to change the formatting of the columns and rows but the data is now in Table format.

Is there a way to export Meeting Minder minutes and action items to Word?

Meeting Minder is a great tool if you're giving a presentation and want to jot down a few notes and assign tasks to individuals. This information can be exported from PowerPoint to Word and Outlook. From the PowerPoint Tools menu, choose Meeting Minder. Add meeting minutes and action items, if none yet exist. Click the Export button. Check Send Meeting Minutes And Action Items To Microsoft Word and click Export Now.

CHAPTER 19

DOCUMENT CONVERSION

IN THIS CHAPTER

- The types of files you can convert
- Options available for conversion
- Why converted documents often become corrupt
- How to clean a document correctly
- Third-party solutions

All law firms deal with file conversion on a daily basis—whether by sharing electronic documents with a client, co-counsel, other offices within the same firm, or even other practice groups that may use different versions of the software or an entirely different word processing application.

Other chapters in the book are important and instruct on how to use Word correctly in a law firm. But face facts—if numbering or styles are used incorrectly, the result is a poorly formatted document. If the conversion process is shabby, the result is an unstable, unusable, and corrupt document—something that no law firm can afford.

The goal of this chapter is to target areas of conversion that are confusing, offer advice for cleaning up documents that need to be converted, and provide help for avoiding common conversion pitfalls.

CONVERSION OVERVIEW

Since 1997, law firms have migrated in droves from WordPerfect to Word. Since then, firms have upgraded to newer versions of Word and the cycle will continue so long as we all use word processing software and new features and versions are introduced.

This never-ending cycle of upgrading requires everyone who works with legal documents to be up to speed on many issues that never needed consideration before—from what is converted and what is not to what causes corruption and how to recover files that have become corrupt. For these reasons, it's imperative to have a good understanding of the entire conversion process.

ROUND-TRIPPING IS A *BAD* IDEA!

The first rule for converting a document is to do it only once. *Round-tripping*—converting a document from one word processing system to another and back again—is poison. Sounds melodramatic—but if you've ever been stung by a document that got corrupted from round-tripping, you will appreciate the strong warning.

Round-tripping can occur easily. Say a client sends you a document created in Word but your firm still uses WordPerfect. You open the file originally created in Word, make edits, and then save the file as a Word or WordPerfect document. When the client reopens the document in Word, the file has been through a complete revolution of round-tripping. Both word processing applications seem to be able to read the document, but it has collected a heavy burden of hidden formatting codes from both systems. Eventually one or another of these orphan codes will trigger an unanticipated response, and the document will become corrupt and unusable.

Round-tripping is a big problem for firms that use multiple word processing applications. This is commonly referred to as being a *dual shop* or, according to Ross Kodner from MicroLaw, "being word processing ambidextrous." Firms that are dual shops should set policies designed to protect documents from corruption by stating that documents should remain in one application or the other and should not shuttle back and forth between the two.

Law firms must generate important, timely, and reliable document output; round-tripping is a bad idea.

WHAT YOU CAN AND CAN'T CONVERT

With the help of built-in text converters, Word 2002 is able to open and save to many different file types, including the more common formats such as WordPerfect, text, HTML, previous versions of Word, and Microsoft Works. The converters are broken down into two categories: import and export.

Import converters allow Word to open certain file types. *Export converters* allow Word to save to specific file types. This is important to remember because even if you are able to open a particular file type, this does not mean that you can save into that same format. For example, Word can open WordPerfect 6.x documents but, if you choose Save As and try to save it back to the original system, your closest option is to save to WordPerfect 5.x format.

> *Install On First Use* is an option that can be set during the installation process to load specific files or features when you first attempt to use them. When you specify many items as Install On First Use, the installation takes up less disk space and the application runs faster. There is a downside to Install On First Use, however. If you don't have the installation CD and don't have a connection to a server where it resides, you will not be able to load the converter until you can access the installation files—which can be a problem if you're on the road and need the converter on your laptop.

The most common converters are native to Word, which means they are a part of the basic Word installation with no exceptions. The standard installation includes a few other converters and even more are set to install the first time you use them. The Install On First Use feature allows access to file converters when you need them—without having to preload these files on your computer.

Table 19.1 shows a list of the available converters and whether they are native to Word, part of the standard installation, or set to install on first use.

TABLE 19.1 TEXT CONVERTERS

CONVERTER	NATIVE	STANDARD	INSTALL ON FIRST USE
HTML	X		
Lotus 1-2-3 Converter			X
Microsoft Excel Converter			X
MS-DOS Text	X		
MS-DOS Text with Layout	X		
Recover Text Converter		X	
Rich Text Format (RTF)	X		
Text Only	X		
Text with Layout	X		
Unicode Text	X		
Web Page	X		
Web Page, Filtered	X		
Web Archive	X		
Word 2.0 and 1.0 for Windows (import only)	X		
Word 4.x–5.1 for the Macintosh (import only)	X		
Word 6.0/95 Export Converter		X	
Word 6.0/95 for Windows, and Word 6.0 for the Macintosh	X		
Word 97 for Windows, and Word 98 Macintosh Edition		X	
Word 97–2002 and 6.0/95 RTF Converter		X	
Word for Macintosh 4.0–5.1 Converter			X
Word for Windows 2.0 Converter (export only)			X
WordPerfect 5.x Converter			X
WordPerfect 6.x Converter (import only)			X
Works 2000			X
Works for Windows 4.0			X
Word 6.0/95 for Windows, and Word 6.0 for the Macintosh (Asian versions)			X

TIP

If you choose to perform a complete installation of Word, all converters are installed.

VIEWING THE AVAILABLE CONVERTERS

In many firms, attorneys and staff do not install software on the computers. Instead, an IT department takes care of this for everyone. If you are unsure which converters have been loaded onto your computer and want to find out before you go on the road and get stuck without a converter, you can check both the import and export converters in seconds. To see which import converters have been installed, from the File menu, choose Open. Click the drop-down arrow next to Files Of Type and read the list of available converters. The export converters are visible by choosing Save As from the File menu and clicking the Save As Type drop-down arrow.

CAUTION

The converters listed as Install On First Use will show up on the Files Of Type and Save As Type drop-down lists whether they've been installed or not. If you select one of them, you will be prompted to install at that time. So, if you want to be absolutely sure you've got something available, try using it on a file before you leave home!

IDENTIFYING INSTALLED CONVERTERS

1. From the File menu, choose Open.
2. Click the drop-down arrow next to Files Of Type, as shown in Figure 19.1.

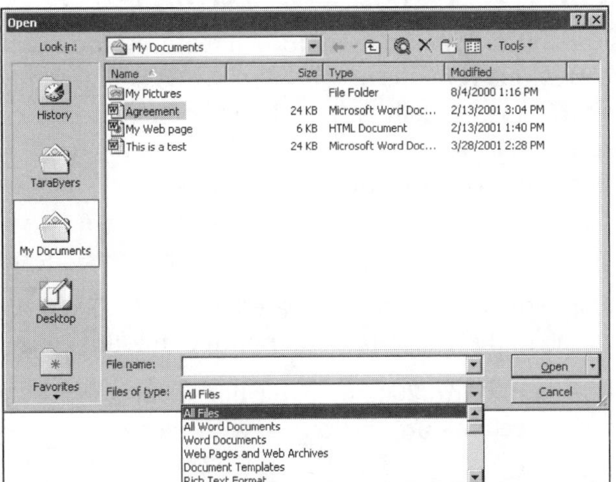

FIGURE 19.1

The available converters are not listed in alphabetical order. However, they are grouped by similar type. For example, all WordPerfect file types are grouped together.

The Save As dialog box lists available export converters.

OTHER CONVERTERS

If the converter that you need is not listed, you may be able to get it from the Office Converter Pack. This is accessed through the Office Resource Kit or on Microsoft's Web site. The following converters are in the Converter Pack:

- Borland dBase II, III, III+, and IV
- Lotus AmiPro 3.x for Windows
- Microsoft FoxPro 2.6
- Microsoft Windows Write 3.x
- Microsoft Word 3.x–6.0 for MS-DOS
- Microsoft Works 3.0 for Windows
- Revisable-Form-Text Document Content Architecture (RFT-DCA)
- WordPerfect 4.0 for MS-DOS
- WordStar 3.3–7.0 for MS-DOS and WordStar 1.0–2.0 for Windows

No converter is available for Lotus Word Pro. To get around this, use Lotus Word Pro to save the file to a different file format such as an earlier version of Word or WordPerfect and then open it in Word 2002. For more information on converting Word Pro documents, see Article Q139792 in Microsoft's Knowledge Base.

CONVERTING WORD DOCUMENTS

Each new version of Word includes additional features, tools, and functionality not available to previous versions of the software. Of course, converting a document from Word 97 to Word 2002 will not be as complicated as converting from WordPerfect to Word—but there are still some issues to be aware of when working with different versions of the same application.

DOCUMENTS CREATED IN AN EARLIER VERSION OF WORD

Word 2002 is able to open documents created in Word 2.0, 6.0/95, 97, and 2000. The formatting used in these versions is supported in Word 2002.

Going backwards from Word 2002 to an earlier version is not quite as simple. Many new and improved features are added with each new release of Word that were not available in previous versions and do not convert to older versions. Further, the file format for Word 95 is different from other versions, which can cause difficulty.

WORD 97 AND 2000

Word 97 and 2000 share the same file format as Word 2002 so both programs should open the Word 2002 file with relative ease. Keep in mind, however, that even with the same file format, new features introduced may not be supported in the previous version. For example, Nesting Tables is not available in Word 97 or earlier versions.

To disable features not supported in a previous version of Word, from the Tools menu, choose Options and select the Save tab. Check the Disable Features Introduced After option, and select the appropriate version from the drop-down list. When this option is selected, the formatting not supported in previous versions will be unavailable.

SAVE A DOCUMENT AS A PREVIOUS VERSION

1. Create a new blank document.
2. Type **This is a test of underline color**.
3. Select the text "underline color."
4. From the Format menu, choose Font.
5. Choose Double Underline from Underline Style and Red from Underline Color.
6. Click OK.
7. Save the document.
8. From the Tools menu, choose Options, and select the Save tab.
9. Select Disable Features Introduced After and Word 97, as shown in Figure 19.2.
10. Click OK. A message box opens, warning about features in the document that are not supported. This warning is shown in Figure 19.3.
11. Click Continue.
12. Save the document.

FEATURE CHANGE!

Word 2000 allowed you to disable features not supported in Word 97. Due to popular demand, Microsoft added Word 6.0/95 as a choice in Word 2002, which makes this feature even more powerful as it is more specific to individual versions of Word.

Word 2000 is not listed as an option because most new features in Word 2002 are backwards compatible to Word 2000. There are some features such as Watermark and the consolidated fields Addressblock and Greeting in Mail Merge that are not backwardly compatible, however.

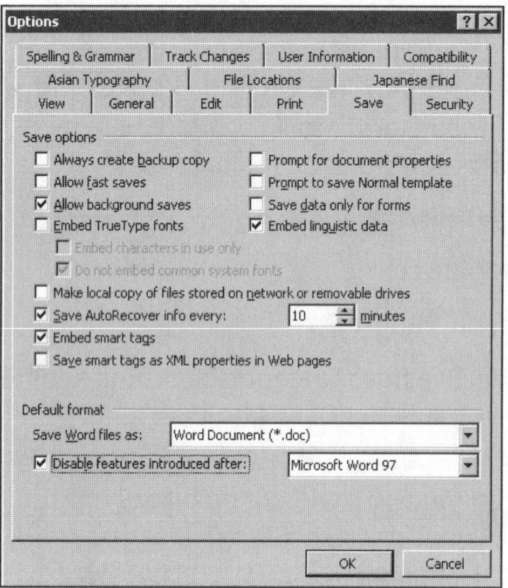

FIGURE 19.2

If you share documents with others who use older versions of Word, select Disable Features Not Supported After and select the appropriate version.

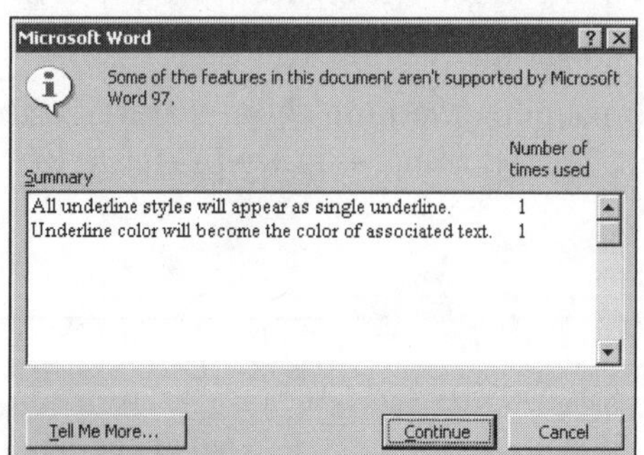

FIGURE 19.3

Each nonsupported feature is listed in the box, as well as how many times the feature has been used throughout the document.

WORD 6.0/95 AND EARLIER

Much to the delight of many WordPerfect users, Microsoft made what can be considered a mistake by changing the file format for Word 97. This was quickly remedied and Word documents now use the same file format between versions. However, to open a Word 2002 file in Word 95 or earlier, you must first install the Word 97–2002 import converter, which can be found on the Microsoft Web site.

NOTE

For Macintosh files, you must use the Word 97–98–2000 Import Converter, which is also available on the Microsoft Web site.

Should you need to save a Word 2002 document down to a previous version, the export converters will allow this to occur. Select the desired file type from Save As Type in the Save As dialog box.

NOTE

When saving a document in a version of Word earlier than Word 97 or as RTF (which stands for Rich Text Format), you may notice that the file size increases. This is due to image compression, which has been improved in Word 97, 2000, and 2002.

CONVERTING WORDPERFECT DOCUMENTS

At first glance, Word and WordPerfect may seem to be doing the same things. But these programs have fundamental differences in how they are designed to process information. WordPerfect works line by line, using pairs of codes to turn formats on and off, whereas Word looks at the entire paragraph, page, or document and stores the information about formatting for each separately from the text stream. To take codes from one program and try to convert them to the other program is a daunting task—and one that has yet to be perfected.

WORDPERFECT 5.X

Word 2002 offers an import and export converter for WordPerfect 5.x. With the differences in programs, certain features are not supported. Table 19.2 lists which features are supported on import and export.

WORDPERFECT 6.X

Word 2002 includes an import converter to handle WordPerfect 6.x files. By default, WordPerfect 7, 8, and 9 share the same file format as WordPerfect 6 so this converter should be able to open all four versions.

TABLE 19.2 FEATURES SUPPORTED WHEN CONVERTING BETWEEN WORDPERFECT 5.X AND WORD 2002

FEATURE	EXPORT: WORD 2002 TO WP 5.X	IMPORT: WP 5.X TO WORD 2002
[Center]/ [Flsh Rgt] codes		X (convert to center and right tabs)
Alignment	X (center codes may change a little)	X
All Caps	X (becomes capital letters)	
Comments	X	
Condensed/ Expanded Spacing		
Date/Time Stamps	X (default formats only)	X (default formats only)
Decimal Tab Alignment		X (converted to right alignment)
Default Tab Stops		X
Document Titles/ Descriptive Names	X (document title property convert to descriptive name)	X (descriptive name is converted to document title property)
Endnotes At End Of Section	X (put at end of document) X	X
Equations		
Extended Characters	X	X (not all characters)
First Line Indents	X (created with tabs)	X (created with tabs)
Footnotes	X (separators and restarted numbers are not, custom footnote marks are converted to numbering in WP)	X
Gutter Margins	X	X
Hidden	X (becomes comment text)	
Kerning	X	X
Leading/baselines, lines/baselines		
Line Draw	X	X (spacing may be off)
Macros		
Margins	X (measured area is different between programs so this may be off a little)	X (measured area is different between programs so this may be off a little)
Newspaper Columns	X	X

TABLE 19.2 FEATURES SUPPORTED WHEN CONVERTING BETWEEN WORDPERFECT 5.X AND WORD 2002 (CONTINUED)

FEATURE	EXPORT: WORD 2002 TO WP 5.X	IMPORT: WP 5.X TO WORD 2002
Outline/Paragraph Numbering/ Word 7.0 Lists	X	X (using listnum fields)
Page Break Before	X (page break is inserted)	
Paper Size	X	
Parallel Columns		X (becomes a table)
Print Merge	X	X
Private Field Codes		X
Space Before/After	X (Blank lines used in WordPerfect)	
Strikethrough	X	X
Styles	X	X
Subdocuments (INCLUDE filed)	X	X
Tab Leaders	X	X (all leaders convert to the same character in Word, if available; otherwise, the dot leader is used)
Table Formulas/Math		
Tables	X (not vertical cell merge)	X (not vertical cell merge)
Text Boxes/Lines	X	X
Track Changes	X (becomes redlining)	X
Underlining	X (type of underline may change)	X (type of underline may change)
Widow Control	X	X

TIP

If the WordPerfect file will not open in Word 2002, try using WordPerfect to save it as WordPerfect 6.x format.

Table 19.3 lists the features supported when a WordPerfect 6.x file is imported into Word 2002.

TABLE 19.3 SUPPORTED FEATURES OF WORDPERFECT 6.X

FEATURE	WP 6.X TO WORD 2002
[Center]/[Flsh Rgt] codes	X (convert to center and right tabs)
Advance	X
Back Tabs	X (if not preceded by text)
Bookmarks	X
Captions	
Chapter and Volume Numbers	
Comments	X (except if located in header, footer, footnotes, or endnotes)
Condensed/Expanded Spacing	
Cross-References and Hypertext Links	Plain text in Word
Default Tab Stops	X (trailing tabs at end of line are not converted)
Drop Caps	
Equations	X (convert to editable object)
Equation Field	
Footnotes	X (custom marks are converted to numbered marks)
Hidden	X
Indexes and Lists	Plain text in Word
Insert Filename	X
Keep Text Together Properties	X
Kerning	X
Labels and Barcodes	Only text of labels is retained
Leading adjustment between lines/baselines	
Line Numbers	
Macros	
Margins	X
Merge Codes	
Outline/Paragraph Numbering	X
Page Features	X
Paragraph Margins	X (changed to indents)

TABLE 19.3 SUPPORTED FEATURES OF WORDPERFECT 6.X (CONTINUED)

FEATURE	WP 6.X TO WORD 2002
Parallel Columns	X (becomes a table)
Private Field Codes	
Space Before/After	X
Strikethrough	X
Styles	X
Tab Leaders	X (unrecognized types of leaders convert to the dot leaders in Word)
Tables	X
Text Boxes/Lines	X
Track Changes	X
Watermarks	X
Widow Control	
WordPerfect Characters	X (only if WordPerfect fonts are available)

WORD TO WORDPERFECT

Most firms these days have been converting from WordPerfect to Word; however, there may be a need to go the other way and convert a Word document to WordPerfect.

Based on the list of converters already discussed, the only export converters Word offers are WordPerfect 5.x and previous. Given the differences between the 5.x version of the software and the newer versions, quite a bit of formatting may be lost. So it may be easier to convert the Word file using WordPerfect's built-in converter.

WordPerfect 8 and higher can open Word documents without any difficulty.

WordPerfect 6 and 7 users may need to download a free conversion utility to open these documents. The WP_CONVERT_UTILITY.EXE converter can be found at www.corel.com/support/ftpsite/pub/wordperfect/wpwin/70/cwps7.htm.

This utility requires a 32-bit operating system. Corel does not offer support for the WP Convert Utility.

DOESN'T WORD CONVERT ON THE FLY?

When you choose to open a non-Word document, the applicable converter begins to work. A message on the status bar at the bottom of the screen tells you to wait while Word converts the document, so it would be reasonable to think Word was actually doing the conversion. Unfortunately, this message is absolutely, positively one of the most misleading and infuriating things in the whole application. It gives the false impression that the document is being converted when it's really just being made *viewable* in Word. Although the document may look just fine onscreen, without further cleanup, you are faced with increased odds of document corruption.

CONVERT A DOCUMENT

1. From the File menu, choose Open.
2. Select a non-Word 2002 document. You can also use a file on the CD-ROM named Convert for this exercise.

TIP

To see which converter is being used to convert a document, from the Tools menu, choose Options and select the General tab. Enable the Confirm Conversion At Open option and click OK.

3. Click Open. Notice the "converting" message on the status bar at the bottom of the screen.

NOTE

You may be prompted to install the converter if it is not yet installed. Click OK to do so.

4. The converted file opens.
5. Leave this document open for the next exercise.

The document looks good on the screen, but it is still not a converted document. This will become more obvious in the course of the next few exercises, which go through additional steps required to clean up the document. The converters are merely a set of instructions on how to display text from a non-Word format in Word.

SAVING A CONVERTED DOCUMENT

It doesn't take long to see some of the signs that the document onscreen has not been converted. If you attempt to save the document, the default file type is that

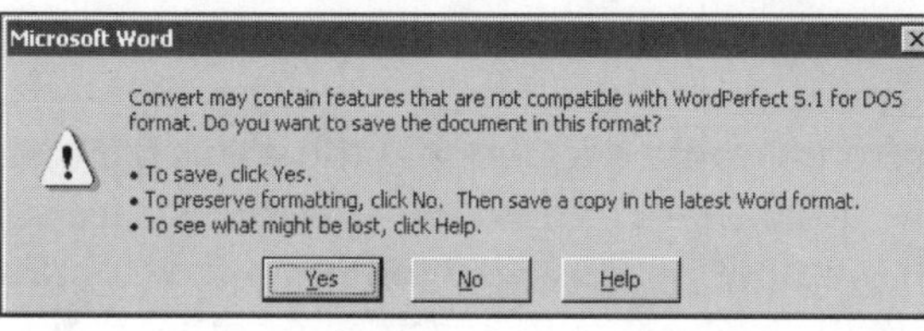

FIGURE 19.4

A warning appears when trying to save changes to a non-Word document.

of the original application used to created the document. Since the original format and Word are different, a dialog box will open to inform you that you may lose some of your changes if you save the changes back to the original format, as shown in Figure 19.4.

MAKING EDITS TO AN ALLEGEDLY CONVERTED DOCUMENT

1. The document from the preceding exercise should still be open.
2. Make a few changes to the document.
3. Click Save. The dialog box shown in Figure 19.4 opens.
4. Click No to preserve the formatting. The Save As dialog box opens.
5. Word Document should be listed under Save As Type.
6. Click Save.

TIP

Enter a new name to eliminate the confusion of having two documents with the same name but different file formats.

TIP

To preserve the file name and to keep the file in the original format, enclose the complete file name in quote marks. For example, if a file is being saved to WordPerfect file format and should not have the .doc (Word) file extension, type **"FileName.wpd"** and click Save.

HIDDEN CODES

Even if you choose Save As and select Word Document from the Save As Type drop-down list, the conversion is still not complete. You won't get any more prompts regarding the file format, but look a little closer and you will discover many items in your document that aren't quite right.

Look on the ruler and you will probably see an abundance of tabs. Some even appear in a negative position on the ruler. This is a sign that the document contains codes left over from WordPerfect. Look at the status bar and see how many sections are in the document. When Word detects any change in page formatting—which includes headers and footers—it automatically inserts a section break. There can also be strange spacing and other seemingly unneeded formats, as shown in Figure 19.5.

Other oddities show up only when you print. Some appear both in print and onscreen as with the top of the text being cut off in some areas throughout the document. Many of these oddities may seem harmless—but they are actually deadly document assassins. They are indicators that leftover formatting codes remain from the original word processing program.

Not only will these excess codes convert each time the document is opened and edited, they will interfere with Word's formatting codes in the document. With this constant battle over which codes to use and which to disregard, it is only a matter of time until the document becomes corrupt.

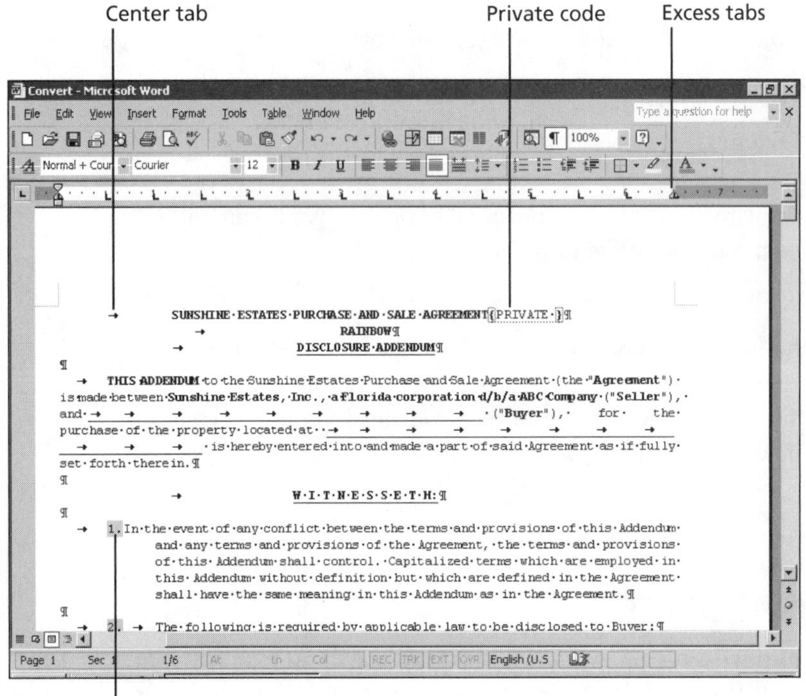

FIGURE 19.5

One sign of a converted document is a ruler filled with extra tabs. Some tabs may even appear in a negative position on the ruler. Other signs of a document being converted are embedded {PRIVATE} codes.

COMPATIBILITY SETTINGS

Text, alignment, spacing, and tables are just a few of the things that are often incompatible when converting documents. Word offers some help for manually tweaking this setting—just choose Tools, Options and select the Compatibility tab.

Think of compatibility settings as a set of rules on how Word should handle certain aspects of the format and display of the document. The set of rules selected by default depends on which software originally created the document. Even after a document has been converted and saved into Word 2002 format, the compatibility settings still remember the document's original format and treat it as such.

Here is an example: A document converted from WordPerfect to Word contains a large table (over 100 pages). The text is being cut off on the right side of each cell. If you didn't know about compatibility, you would most likely adjust the right indent for each cell, which would be time consuming. If you set the compatibility settings correctly, this problem will fix itself automatically.

CHANGE THE COMPATIBILITY SETTINGS

1. Open the document you converted earlier in this chapter.
2. From the Tools menu, choose Options.
3. Choose the Compatibility tab, as shown in Figure 19.6.

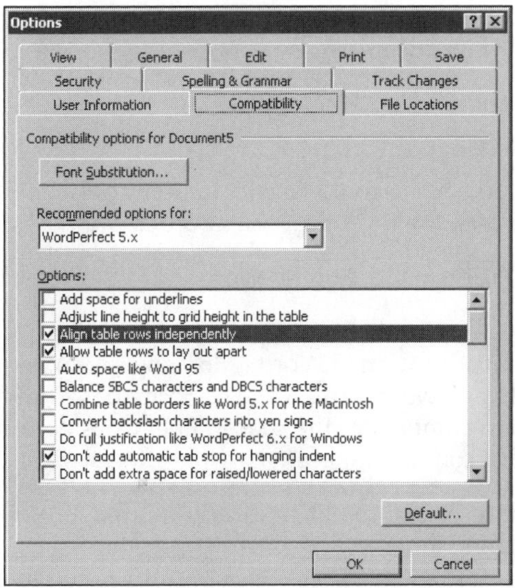

FIGURE 19.6

Options available on the Compatibility tab are designed to handle different formatting and settings similar to the original word processing application.

4. Choose Word 2002 from the Recommended Options For drop-down list.
5. Click OK. Can you see a difference in the document?

The list of compatibility settings is extensive, and it varies depending on which document format is chosen. You can also choose your own custom settings. Table 19.4 lists a brief description for each setting on the Compatibility tab.

TABLE 19.4 COMPATIBILITY SETTINGS

OPTION	RESULT
Add Space For Underlines	Word adds extra space for underlines.
Adjust Line Height To Grid Height In Table	Determines whether text within table cells is snapped to the document grid. Used in East Asian text.
Align Table Rows Independently	For centered or right-aligned, non-wrapped tables: When this option is not checked, different size rows will not move when the table is being aligned; when it is checked, the rows will align independently to match the table alignment.
Allow Table Rows Lay To Out Apart	When a non-wrapped table is positioned to the right of a wrapped object and extends past the object, this option keeps the table on the right. If it is not checked, the table will move back to the left.
Auto Space Like Word 95	This option determines how lines wrap in an East Asian Word 95 document.
Balance SBCS Characters And DBCS Characters	Not used in U.S. English Word.
Combine Table Borders Like Word 5.X For The Macintosh	When a table contains two adjacent cells with different borders, the rightmost cell's border width applies.
Convert Backslash Characters Into Yen Signs	Not used in U.S. English Word.
Do Full Justification Like WordPerfect 6.X For Windows	Full justification in Word is done by expanding the space between words. This is the opposite of WordPerfect, which compresses the spaces. Check this option to have Word compress spaces.
Don't Add Automatic Tab Stop For Hanging Indent	Ignores the automatic tab stop created in Word 6.0 for a hanging indent.

Table 19.4 Compatibility Settings (continued)

Option	Result
Don't Add Extra Space For Raised/ Lowered Characters	Prevents Word from inserting additional space between lines to adjust for raised or lowered characters.
Don't Add Leading (Extra Space) Between Rows Of Text	Displays text without leading between the lines as in Word versions 5.x for the Macintosh.
Don't Allow Hanging Punctuation With Character Grid	This option is for use with Asian text.
Don't Balance Columns For Continuous Section Starts	When this is not checked, Word balances a column when followed by a section break or the end of document.
Don't Blank The Area Behind Metafile Pictures	When this option is selected, it decreases editing speed as it prevents Word from blocking out text or graphics that may surround an inserted metafile.
Don't Break Wrapped Tables Across Page	If the table has text wrapping set, this option prevents the table from breaking across pages. When wrapping is set, it overrides Allow Row To Break Across Pages.
Don't Center "Exact Line Height" Lines	If the text is formatted with exact line spacing, the vertical position of the text will either be split between the ascender and descender or the extra space goes to the descender. When this option is checked, the space goes to the descender.
Don't Expand Character Spaces On The Line Ending Shift-Return	When you use Shift+Enter on a justified paragraph, large gaps of space could appear between the words of the paragraph. Turn this option on to have Word switch to left alignment under these circumstances.
Don't Snap Text To Grid Inside Table With Inline Objects	If a table cell includes an inline with text object and East Asian text, this option prevents the text from snapping to the character grid.
Don't Use Asian Rules For Line Breaks With Character Grid	Controls the line-break of East Asian text in relation to the character grid as in earlier versions of Word.
Don't Use HTML Paragraph Auto Spacing	When turned off, and there is both a Space Before and After spacing amount, Word will use the greater value. If this option is on, it can affect two items: (1) If Auto is set in the Space Before/After field, Word adjusts it to 5pt. (2) If there are values in both Spacing Before and After, both values are used.
Draw Underline On Trailing Spaces	Not used in U.S. English Word.
Expand/Condense By Whole Number Of Points	Condensed or expanded spacing is rounded to the nearest whole number.

TABLE 19.4 COMPATIBILITY SETTINGS (CONTINUED)

OPTION	RESULT
Forget Last Tab Alignment	Sets tab alignment at the end of a line to behave the same as in Word 97.
Lay Out AutoShapes Like Word 97	In Word 97, an AutoShape would be forced behind the text if it appeared at the bottom of the document and wrapping was set to Top & Bottom.
Lay Out Footnotes Like Word 6.0/95/97	Causes footnotes to position the same as they did in earlier versions of Word.
Lay Out Tables With Raw Width	Word determines the width of a table (table width plus table indent) and prevents a table from being cut off or pushed off the page when aligned with a floating object.
Lines Wrap Like Word 6.0	Not used in U.S. English Word.
Print Body Text Before Header/Footer	To allow for the process of PostScript codes in the text layer, this option prints the main text layer before the Header/Footer layer. (This is the reverse of the default method but the same as Word 5.x for the Macintosh.)
Print Colors As Black On Non-Color Printers	This option is used to print colored text on a non-color printer. Instead of getting lighter (gray) text, it will print colors as black.
Select Entire Field With First Or Last Character	Similar to Automatically Select Entire Word but in relation to fields. It does not work when field codes are visible.
Set The Width Of A Space Like WordPerfect 5.X	The Word 97 text converters can use the WordPerfect calculation for the spacing in a proportional font. This type of spacing is called WordPerfect Optimal.
Show Hard Page Or Column Breaks In Frames	Word displays hard page or column breaks, if contained in a frame.
Substitute Fonts Based On Font Size	Option used by the WordPerfect 6.x converter to substitute fonts. The substitution will look at font size first and, if a match is not found, it will actually map the font.
Suppress Extra Line Spacing At Bottom Of Page	Select this option to suppress extra line spacing from the last line on a page. This is how WordPerfect treats spacing.
Suppress Extra Line Spacing At Top Of Page	Select this option to suppress extra line spacing at the top a page. For example, if the paragraph has space before and it appears at the top of the page, the extra space will be ignored so the top margin is not increased.

TABLE 19.4 COMPATIBILITY SETTINGS (CONTINUED)

OPTION	RESULT
Suppress Extra Line Spacing At The Top Of Page Like Word 5.X For The Mac	Select this option to suppress extra line spacing at the top of a page. For example, if the paragraph has space before and it appears at the top of the page, the extra space will be ignored so the top margin is not increased.
Suppress Extra Line Spacing Like WordPerfect 5.X	This ensures that the layout of converted WordPerfect documents formatted with Automatic line height closely matches that of the original document.
Suppress Space Before After A Hard Page Or Column Break	When a paragraph is followed by a hard page/column break and contains Space Before formatting, Word suppresses the Space Before.
Swap Left And Right Borders On Odd Facing Pages	When using a left border on a paragraph and the document is formatted with "Different Odd/Even Headers" or "Mirror Margins," Word prints the border on the right side for odd-numbered pages.
Treat \" As " " In Mail Merge Data Sources	Converts a delimiter composed of a backslash and quotation mark (\") to two quotation marks (" ") when used in a data source. This way Word can recognize quotation marks.
Truncate Font Height	Word rounds the font size up or down as in WordPerfect 6.x for Windows.
Use Line Breaking Rules	This controls line breaks in Thai documents.
Use Larger Small Caps Like Word 5.X For The Macintosh	This option, when used in Word 6.0 for the Mac, will produce slightly larger capital letters the same way as Word 5.x for the Mac.
Use Printer Metrics To Lay Out Document	Select this option to remember the printer driver of the printer currently installed. This way the document looks the same no matter what printer driver is installed.
Use Word 6.x/95 Border Rules	Suppresses paragraph borders when paragraph is intersected by frames or wrapped drawing objects.
Use Word 97 Line Breaking Rules For Asian Text	With the introduction of the language pack in Word 2000, there are many options now available for Asian text. This option changes the word wrap rule to act like Word 97.
Wrap Trailing Spaces To Next Line	Spaces that trail into the margin after a word at the end of a line are moved to the beginning of the next line.

THE RIGHT WAY TO CLEAN UP A DOCUMENT

There are two steps to correctly converting a document. The first is fairly easy—open the document and save it in the format you want. The second is cleanup. The cleanup process is the most important since this is where you take control over the document to get rid of formatting and codes that can otherwise lead to document corruption. Taking shortcuts during the document cleanup process is a bad idea.

The level of cleanup required varies depending on the amount of time you have and the importance of the document. For example, do you base other documents on this one, or is this a one-time document?

There are three levels of cleanup:

- **Insert File**. A quickie: 5 minutes or less.
- **Top 12**. Expect to spend 15 to 30 minutes fixing the main potential trouble spots—and to find hidden problems later, at least some of the time.
- **Reformat from Scratch**. The time required varies with the size and complexity of the document but this method is the best way to convert a document when not using a third-party conversion utility. To be sure you have a sound file, strip out the formatting, recover the text, and reapply the formatting.

INSERT FILE

You have five minutes to open and print a file but it's in WordPerfect and, when you open it, the formatting is not right. What can you do? In this circumstance, by inserting the file instead of opening it, you can achieve better results.

When a file must be viewed and printed, but not edited, from the Insert menu, choose File, navigate to the document, and insert it into a blank Word file. This method is by no means a permanent solution, but it will serve the purpose of allowing you to see or print the document quickly—without having to do a lot of cleanup. This method does not clean any excess codes within the document but offers a few benefits. First, the text is inserted into a new Word document so the compatibility settings are set correctly to Word 2002. Second, and most important, the binary file header (where file information is stored) from the original file is not inserted into the document.

The end result of using the Insert, File command is that the text of the document is inserted into Word and will, in most cases, print fairly well. The document will need cleanup if you intend to make any changes, especially to remove WordPerfect codes.

USE INSERT FILE

1. Create a new blank document.
2. From the Insert menu, choose File.
3. Select the file named Convert From The CD-ROM and click Insert. If you do not have access to the CD-ROM, select any non-Word document such as a file created in WordPerfect and click Insert.
4. From the File menu, choose Save As and name the file **Converted Document**.
5. Leave this document open for the next exercise.

Think of Insert File as the quick-fix solution. It offers the bare minimum conversion and cleanup to get a document out the door. Once the immediate need is satisfied, revisit the document and ask the following questions:

- Will this document require more edits?
- Will this document be used as a precedent document?
- Will text from this document be copied into other documents?

If you answered yes to any of these questions, the document will need to undergo a more thorough cleaning.

THE TOP 12 MUST-DO CLEANUP CHORES

There are some things that you can do to clean up a converted document which are not too time consuming:

- Set the file type.
- Check compatibility options.
- Reset language.
- Fix quotation marks and apostrophes.
- Adjust table borders.
- Remove excess tabs.
- Adjust for Widow/Orphan text flow.
- Remove extraneous section breaks.
- Adjust header and footer margins.
- Check numbering.
- Delete legacy table of contents and generate a new one.
- Remove residual field codes.

CUT DOWN ON CLEANUP

Microsoft has definitely stepped up to the plate with conversion issues in Word 2002 by adding registry settings to control many of the items that needed to be cleaned up such as negative tabs, compatibility, and much more.

Since editing the registry can be dangerous and is not supported by Microsoft, the process of editing the registry is not covered in this book. To learn how to set registry keys, consider taking an installation and configuration class offered by Payne Consulting Group.

Microsoft plans to release a macro to make changing these settings easier. At the time of publication, however, this macro has not yet been released.

If you touch all these bases, you are taking the middle ground for document cleanup; you will be better off than just opening or inserting the file, but not entirely safe. You can use Find And Replace to perform much of this level of cleanup.

FILE TYPE

Before the cleanup process begins, it is essential that the converted document be saved in the correct file format—Word 2002. Converting a document does not guarantee that the file type has been changed, which was evident earlier in the chapter when a prompt appeared while trying to save a change to a newly converted WordPerfect file. The prompt warned that saving in a different format may result in edits not being retained.

To check the document's file type, choose Save As from the File menu. Under Save As Type, select Word Document if it is not highlighted already.

NOTE

If you have used the Insert, File command, the file type will be set to Word 2002 already.

CHECK COMPATIBILITY

The Recommended Options For setting in the Compatibility tab of Tools, Options definitely plays a big role in how the document will look on the screen and when printed. This setting is discussed in detail in the "Compatibility Settings" section earlier in this chapter.

It is good practice to set the Compatibility to the version of Word that you are using; for example, Word 2002.

LANGUAGE SETTINGS

A common occurrence with converted documents is that proofing language is turned off during the conversion process. This can lead to spelling errors being overlooked and embarrassing mistakes being made when these errors are not detected. In Word, language is considered a character format, which means it is attached to each individual character. This setting determines the way Word checks the spelling in the document. If the language is not set for certain characters in the document or a different language is selected for certain words, those characters and words will be skipped when the Spelling Checker runs.

SETTING THE LANGUAGE

1. The converted document from the preceding exercise should be open.
2. Press Ctrl+A to select the entire document.
3. From the Tools menu, choose Language, Set Language. The Language dialog box opens, as shown in Figure 19.7.
4. Select English (U.S.), if using this version of the software; otherwise, select the appropriate language.
5. Make sure the Do Not Check Spelling And Grammar option is not checked. Click OK.
6. Leave this document open for the next exercise.

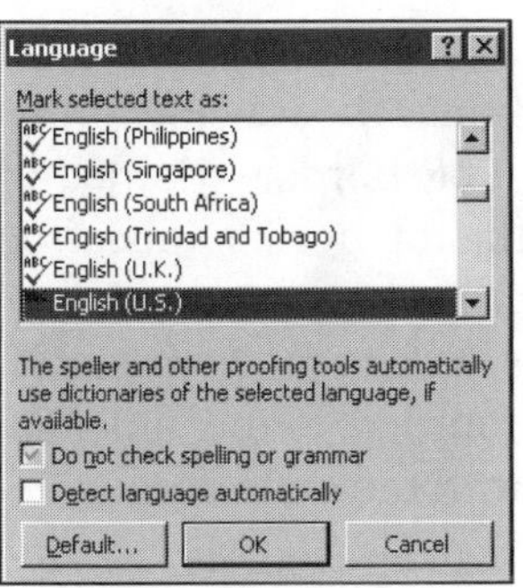

FIGURE 19.7

Multiple languages can be selected from the Language dialog box.

QUOTATIONS AND APOSTROPHES

A converted WordPerfect document often contains straight quotation marks. Most firms are now using the smart (curly) quotation marks. If you continue to work in the document and add quotation marks, the new text formatting by default is to add smart quotes. The combination of quote styles makes the document look unprofessional. You can quickly find and replace all straight quotes with smart quotes using Word's Find And Replace feature.

NOTE

If your firm uses straight quotes, you will not need to complete this step.

CONVERTING STRAIGHT QUOTES TO CURLY QUOTES

1. The document from the preceding exercise should still be open.
2. From the Tools menu, choose AutoCorrect Options.
3. In the AutoFormat As You Type tab, make sure that the "Straight Quotes" With “Smart Quotes” option is selected.
4. Click OK.
5. From the Edit menu, choose Replace.
6. Type “ in both the Find What and Replace With boxes.
7. Click Replace All.
8. Repeat steps 5 through 7 for single quotes.

CAUTION

This method will replace all quotations and apostrophes. If your document contains any inch and foot marks, these will need to be restored to straight quotes, as curly quotes are not used for these symbols.

TABLE BORDERS

Tables convert fairly well but one frustration is the way the format of tables convert. In most examples, it has to do with table borders where the bottom border disappears at the bottom of the page or the top border appears at the top of the page. This is due to the fact that WordPerfect sets top and bottom borders differently than Word. This can be fixed by selecting the entire table, turning off all borders, and then using Word to reapply borders to the table. These three steps should prevent any strange occurrences with the table borders.

EXCESS TABS

As noted earlier, the excessive number of tab stops that appear on the ruler of a converted document is a good indicator that the paragraph or document has been converted (or copied and pasted) from a WordPerfect document. The tab stops crowd the ruler, even appearing at negative positions outside the margins, as shown in Figure 19.8.

Select the entire document. From the Format menu, choose Tabs and click Clear All. The excess tab stops are removed and Word's defaults are restored.

NOTE

Signature blocks and other items that may have been aligned using tabs will need to be reformatted.

TEXT FLOW

The way text flow is controlled in WordPerfect is completely different from the way it is set and controlled in Word. Therefore, Widow/Orphan control is not always retained. There may also be additional Keep With Next and Keep Lines Together formatting applied that is not needed in Word.

Negative tabs

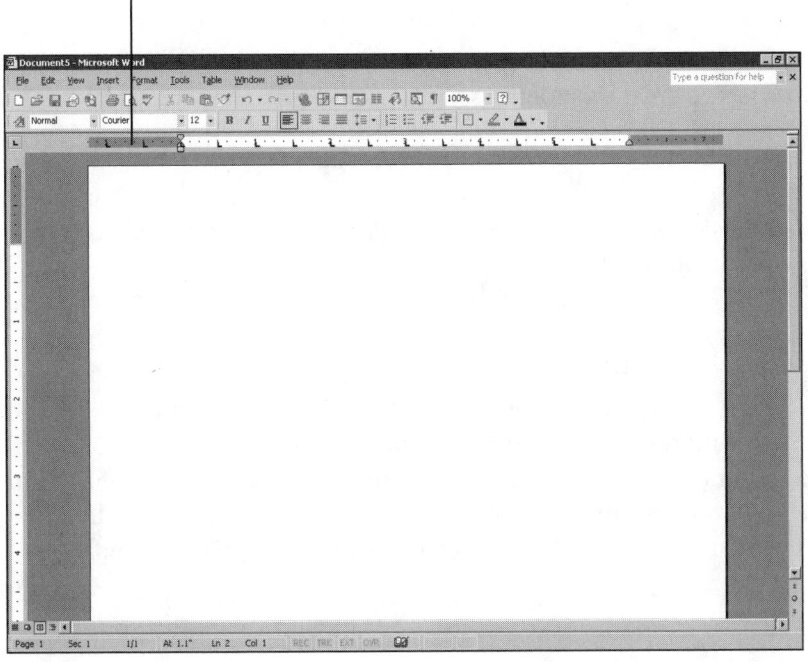

FIGURE 19.8

Many people think that copying paragraphs from a WordPerfect document and pasting them into Word will avoid the problems involved with converting a document. However, copying and pasting even a paragraph from WordPerfect brings over unwanted formats.

To check the text flow formatting in the converted document, first select the entire document, and then from the Format menu, choose Paragraph. On the Line And Page Breaks tab, check Widow/Orphan Control and uncheck Keep Lines Together and Keep With Next. Click OK to close the Paragraph dialog box and apply the changes.

Certain document types, such as pleadings, have Widow/Orphan control turned off to help text line up with the line numbers on the pleading paper. This step is not required for these types of documents.

SECTION BREAKS

There is no greater difference between Word and WordPerfect than the way page formatting is handled. In the converted document, each time Word encounters a change in formatting such as Header A, Header B, or different page formatting, it inserts a section break. The result is that a simple document can develop tens, even hundreds of section breaks. Unneeded section breaks in Word can make working with headers and footers difficult and, therefore, it is a good idea to search for and delete all section breaks that are unnecessary to the structure of the document.

Since section breaks are used to control page formats, you must go to each section break and determine if it is needed or not. If it is unnecessary, delete the section break.

The Object Browser is a great tool for this since it includes an option to search by section.

It's often easier to delete section breaks when working in Normal view. Click on the section break and press Delete.

HEADER AND FOOTER

Many times when a document is converted from WordPerfect to Word, the header and footer margins get set to 1" instead of Word's default of 0.5". Also, headers and footers are directly connected to section breaks. So, if the section breaks were adjusted, attention must be given to the corresponding headers and footers to ensure the information is correctly inserted and formatted.

If the Insert, File command was not used to convert the file, be sure to check the header and footer margin settings.

PARAGRAPH NUMBERING

Paragraph numbering is used extensively in legal documents. How numbering is retained during conversion depends on which converter is being used. If the WordPerfect 5.x converter is used, the numbering is converted to sequence codes, which produce similar results to automated lists but work quite differently behind the scenes. With the WordPerfect 6.x converter, there is a greater chance the numbering will convert into an automatic Word numbered list format (although some levels work better than others). Other converters often change the number to plain text. Table 19.5 describes how each of the converters treats bullets and numbering.

Outline numbering should be linked to styles when working in Microsoft Word. This will take a bit more work since you will need to visit each paragraph and apply the appropriate heading style; however, in the long run, the extra effort is worth it. Ease of sharing the document or generating the table of contents are just two benefits of using numbering that is linked to a style. For more information, see Chapter 9, "Styles," and Chapter 8, "Bullets and Numbering."

CONVERSION IMPROVEMENT

In previous versions of Word, the converters for WordPerfect documents did a poor job of converting paragraph numbering. The numbering in a WordPerfect 5.x document, would convert to sequence codes, which were difficult for even the more advanced Word user to use. WordPerfect 6.x would attempt to convert to outline numbering or sequence codes. The outline numbering format usually became unstable.

In Word 2002, the conversion of paragraph numbering from all WordPerfect documents has been improved with the use of Listnum fields. Listnum paragraph numbering provides an automated numbering feature that is easier to use in Word than sequence codes and translates to Word's outline numbering feature, which is the preferred method in Word.

TABLE 19.5 HOW BULLETED AND NUMBERED LISTS CONVERT

TYPE OF CONVERTER	RESULT
WordPerfect 6.x (Windows or MS-DOS)	Numbered and Outline Numbered lists convert.
Word 6.0/95	Bulleted, Numbered, and Outline Numbered lists convert.
AmiPro 3.x Text Only	Bullets and numbering are converted to plain text.
MS-DOS Text Only	Bullets and numbering are converted to plain text. Indents do not convert.
Text w/Line Breaks	Bullets and numbering are converted to plain text.
MS-DOS Text w/ Line Breaks	Bullets and numbering are converted to plain text. Indents do not convert.
MS-DOS Word 3–6	Bullets and numbering are converted to plain text.
RTF-DCA	Bullets and numbering are converted to plain text. Tabs are used to indicate indents.
Text with Layout	Bullets and numbering are converted to plain text.
MS-DOS Text with Layout	Bullets and numbering are converted to plain text. Spaces are used to indicate indents.
Rich Text Format (RTF)	Bulleted, Numbered, and Outline Numbered lists convert.
Mac Word 4.0, 5.0, 5.1	Bullets and numbering are converted to plain text. Tabs are used to indicate indents.
Word for Windows 2.0	Bulleted, Numbered, and Outline Numbered lists convert.
HTML Document	Bulleted, Numbered, and Outline Numbered lists convert.
Unicode Text	Bullets and numbering are converted to plain text. Tabs are used to indicate indents.
Windows Write 3.0	Bullets and numbering are converted to plain text. Tabs are used to indicate indents.
WordPad	Bullets are converted correctly. Numbered lists are converted to plain text. Tabs are used to indicate indents.
Works 3.0 for Windows	Bullets and numbering are converted to plain text.
Works 4.0 for Windows	Bullets and numbering are converted to plain text. Tabs are used to indicate indents.
WordStar 4.0	Bullets and numbering are converted to plain text.
WordStar 7.0	Bullets do not convert. Numbered lists are converted to plain text. Tabs are used to indicate indents.
WordPerfect 5.0, 5.1, 5.2, 6.x	Numbering is converted to Word listnum codes.

TABLE OF CONTENTS

Since Word and WordPerfect lay out pages differently, the table of contents in a converted document will need to be regenerated to reflect the correct page numbers. Select and delete the converted table of contents and let Word create a new one for you. To generate a table of contents, from the Insert menu, choose Reference, then Index And Tables. Select the Table Of Contents tab and click OK.

UNWANTED CODES

When a document is converted, many codes are converted and embedded into the Word document. Codes flagged as "{PRIVATE }" hold information necessary to convert the document back to WordPerfect—but, if the document will remain in Word, it's a good idea to delete these extraneous codes.

Some of these codes are easy to see when you first glance at the document. The {PRIVATE } code is a good example. Other codes are harder to detect because the result of the code is showing and not the code itself. For example, with the SEQ code, the resulting number is displayed and not the field itself.

To clean these codes from the document, first turn on Show/Hide and then press Alt+F9. This keystroke displays the field codes in the document to ensure that Word will find them.

From the Edit menu, choose Replace. Click More to expand the dialog box, if necessary. Click Special and select Field. Make sure the Replace With box is empty. Since you may have fields that belong in the document and should not be deleted, use Find Next and click Replace repeatedly until you find and delete all unwanted field codes.

Do not use Replace All if you did not remove the SEQ fields for numbering or the TC codes for table of contents. There is no easy way to strip out a specific type of code so you will need to visit each code to make your decision.

CODE-FREE CLEANUP

The best method for converting a document is to strip away the formatting and reapply new formats (using styles) to the text. There are two ways to do this. You can choose File, Open and use the Recover Text From Any File import converter, or you can use Word's Paste Special, Unformatted Text commands. Both extract just the text from the document, but the Recover Text From Any File method also recovers footnotes and endnotes.

Both methods require additional time to reformat the document, but once this is complete, the document is stable and has less chance of corruption because it is a true Word document with no residual codes or formatting left over from WordPerfect.

Here are a few tricks to make this process easier:

- Retain a copy of the original file so that you can refer to it, if necessary.
- Consider printing a copy of the original document to use as reference when reapplying the formats.
- Paste the unformatted text into a document based on a similar document's template. The template will already be set up with the styles and page formats to make formatting easier.
- Use Find And Replace to help fix straight quotation marks and apostrophes as well as extraneous tabs.

USE PASTE SPECIAL

1. Open the document you wish to convert.
2. Select the entire document and, from the Edit menu, choose Copy.
3. Create a new document.
4. From the Edit menu, choose Paste Special. The Paste Special dialog box opens, as shown in Figure 19.9.
5. Select Unformatted Text and click OK. All formatting is removed.
6. From the Edit menu, choose Replace.
7. Type " in both the Find What and Replace With boxes. This instructs Word to find all instances of quotes and replace them with the same quote character, but using Word's curly quote format.

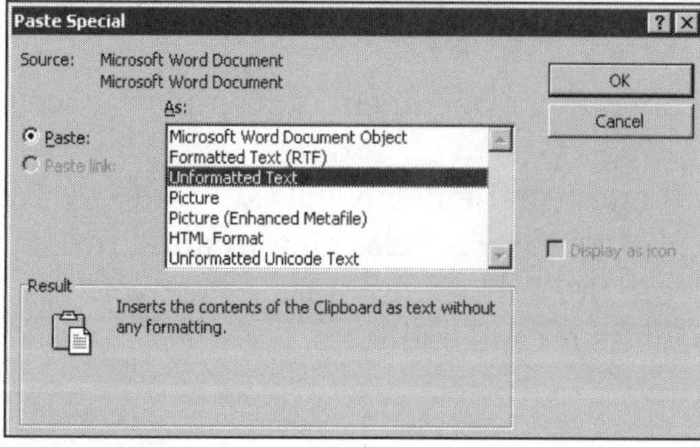

FIGURE 19.9

Although the Paste Special dialog box contains multiple formats and the ability to create a link, when converting documents, always select Unformatted Text.

8. Click Replace All.
9. Repeat steps 8 and 9 for apostrophes.
10. Type **^t** in the Find What field and delete anything in the Replace With field.
11. Click Replace All. This will remove tab characters in the document.
12. Save the new document.
13. Leave this document open for the next exercise.

REFORMATTING

Now that the document is clean and code free, it's time to apply formatting. By using styles, you can reformat most documents quickly. If you copied the text into a document based on a template, the styles should be there and just need to be applied. If not, you can easily copy the needed styles using the Organizer.

USING THE ORGANIZER

The Organizer quickly moves styles from one document to another.

USE THE ORGANIZER TO COPY STYLES INTO A NEW DOCUMENT

1. The document from the preceding exercise should still be open.
2. From the Tools menu, choose Templates And Add-Ins.
3. Click Organizer. The Organizer dialog box opens, as shown in Figure 19.10.

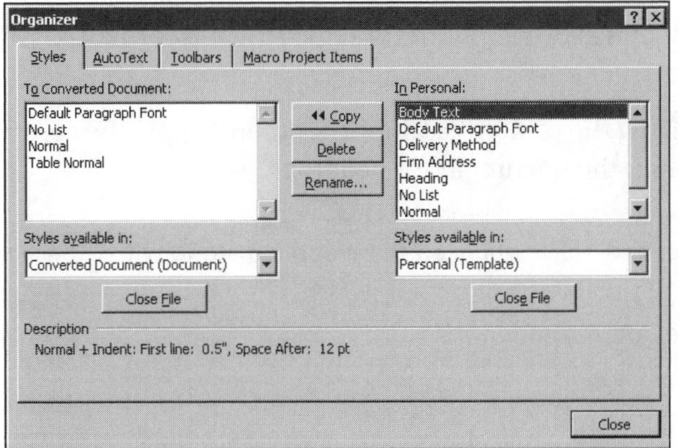

FIGURE 19.10

The Organizer can be used to copy, move, and rename styles.

4. Click Close File on the right side of the window. Notice the button changes to Open File.
5. Click Open File to access the Open dialog box.
6. Navigate to where your exercise files are stored. Select Personal.dot and click Open. The styles from this template are now listed.

NOTE

When working with your documents, select the applicable template in place of Personal.dot.

7. Select Body Text and click Copy.

NOTE

If the style name that you are trying to copy already exists in the document, you will see a prompt to overwrite the existing style.

8. Select Heading and click Copy.
9. Copy other styles, if applicable.
10. Click Close to close the Organizer.

APPLYING STYLES

Once the styles have been copied into the document, reformatting can begin. A tip for applying styles to a document that has no formats is to apply a base style to the entire document and then apply specific styles thereafter.

APPLY STYLES

1. Press Ctrl+A to select the entire document.
2. Apply Body Text style. The entire document is formatted with the style Body Text.
3. Referencing the printed original document, apply the correct formatting throughout the document for headings.

NOTE

Bold, underline, and italics will need to be applied along with other formats.

4. Save the document.

THIRD-PARTY UTILITIES

How many documents does your firm create daily, monthly, within six months? Probably more than you want to clean up yourself using any of the methods described in this chapter. So many law firms have chosen to switch from WordPerfect to Word using products that third-party conversion vendors are entering the market to offer assistance. There are two primary companies that law firms turn to for their conversion needs—Levit & James (www.levitjames.com) and Microsystems (www.microsystems.com). These companies offer products that do the conversion for you and will assist with some of the cleanup.

Each company's product has been developed specifically for the conversion between Word and WordPerfect. Both products can be integrated with document management systems or can be used in a stand-alone mode for firms that do not have a document management system. Also, the cleanup components that both companies offer integrate with most third-party numbering packages including Payne's Numbering Assistant.

CROSSWORDS BY LEVIT & JAMES

CrossWords automates the conversion process of WordPerfect documents into Word. The product can be accessed by alternate-clicking on the target document and choosing CrossWords. A batch file conversion option is also available when you need to convert many documents at once.

Each document converted is put through a three-step process by CrossWords: Preprocessor, Word Import, and Post Processing Reformatting. The CrossWords Preprocessor is not a simple WordPerfect macro but an ActiveX Control, which reads through every binary character in a WordPerfect document, creating a new pre-coded document that is then converted into Word. In the final Post Conversion processor, the Word document is reformatted, based on a set of user-defined and user-modifiable settings. One of the most favorable features of CrossWords is the ability to convert paragraph numbering into Word's Heading styles during the Post Conversion stage.

Levit & James also offers a product to help with formatting documents. Stylizer is used for reformatting Word documents through the application of styles and the automation of many routine reformatting tasks. Stylizer applies styles to paragraphs, using a technique called paragraph "Search By Example," which makes the application of styles as simple as using Word's built-in Find And Replace dialog box.

For more information, visit the company's Web site at www.levitjames.com.

DOCXCHANGE BY MICROSYSTEMS

The Microsystems DocXChange tool provides conversion automation for documents going from WordPerfect to Word, as well as Word to Word conversions.

DocXChange commences the conversion process by opening the document in WordPerfect and stripping out unnecessary codes. The document is then opened in Word and a series of commands rebuild the Word document closely matching the original WordPerfect file. This can include applying firm styles, if desired.

This product is most commonly run in a batch mode where multiple documents are converted at the same time. Microsystems also offers the option to convert your documents at their site. A new addition, DocXSubmit, offers users the ability to submit individual documents to a conversion server from their desktop.

DocXTools is a toolbar that contains handy tools to clean up documents after DocXChange has converted them. For example, once the document has been converted, DocXNumbering helps apply automatic paragraph numbering. Other tools help with troubleshooting documents. A particularly useful feature is the Am I A Bad Document button, which analyzes troublesome documents and offers solutions.

For more information, visit the company's Web site at www.microsystems.com.

CONVERSIONS PLUS BY DATAVIZ

Conversions Plus is a utility that has been around law firms for quite some time because it offers the ability to view and convert documents from a wide range of formats (67 of them, all told). This is done without needing the format's original program installed on the computer.

Although Payne Consulting has not had much experience with Conversions Plus, some of our law firm clients have had success with it for individual document conversion.

For more information visit the company's Web site at www.dataviz.com.

SCANNING A DOCUMENT

With the increase in electronic document sharing, document scanning is not as popular as it used to be. But it is far from becoming obsolete! Like any non-native method of inserting text into a word processing program, it deals with some type of conversion.

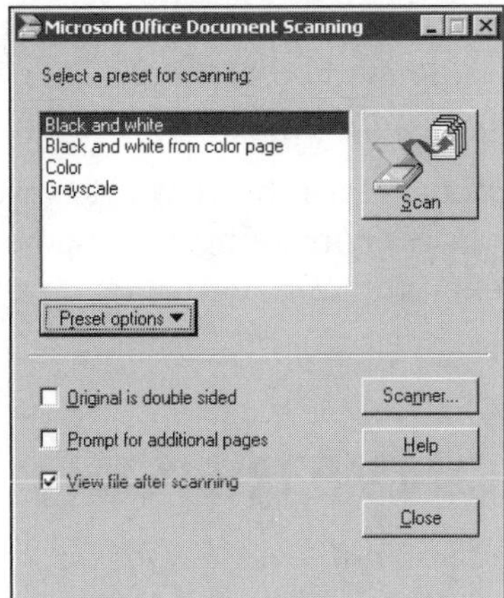

FIGURE 19.11

Select a preset list of scanning options or choose custom settings for document and image scanning.

Office XP includes the Microsoft Office Document Scanning tool. To access this tool, click Start and choose Programs, Microsoft Office Tools, Microsoft Document Scanning. The Microsoft Office Document Scanning dialog box appears, as shown in Figure 19.11. This dialog box allows access to a number of features that control interpretation of the scanned document, from what size paper to where the file should be stored and how the text should be handled.

Microsoft Office Document Scanning offers Optical Character Recognition (OCR) technology, which translates text images into text characters that can be edited. With this translation, some characters may not come over exactly as expected and formats may be applied incorrectly—especially in the case of headers, footers, and numbers. These are a few of the reasons why it is a good idea to follow the same cleanup practices with a scanned document as you would if the document was converted, then read through it to spot scanning glitches that duplicate real but incorrect words.

SUMMARY

As shown in this chapter, there are many ways to convert a document. If you need a document immediately and only need to view or print, you can use Insert, File to place the document within a new Word document. The middle ground is to run through a dozen steps for cleaning the document, bearing in mind that many residual items may remain in the document, which can lead to corruption. The best method for converting a document is to open the document with the Recover Text From Any File import converter or copy the text and choose Edit, Paste Special, Unformatted Text (into a new document) and reapply the formatting using styles.

You can use third-party products to do much of the conversion and cleanup for you. Nonetheless, it's important to understand that there will be some cleanup required even after running the document through the converter.

Conversion is not easy and it's tempting to take shortcuts. However, if you want a stable document that runs a lower risk of corrupting, it's important to take the time and effort to clean the document right. And remember—say no to round-tripping!

TROUBLESHOOTING CONVERSION

When I open a WordPerfect document in Word, it doesn't look right on the screen.

Word has a set of compatibility options for each document that determines how the document is viewed while it is in Word. This setting is probably still set to WordPerfect, which is causing some differences on the screen. From the Tools menu, choose Options. Choose the recommended options for Word 2002 under Compatibility.

I am trying to insert another table into my existing table but the table button is grayed out.

Check Tools, Options, Save to see if the Disable Features Introduced After Word 97 option is turned on. This feature prevents the use of items that will not be supported in previous versions of Word.

A client sent me an old AmiPro document. I do not see an option in File, Open to convert AmiPro.

The Office Converter Pack does contain a converter for AmiPro 3.x documents. You can access this converter through Microsoft's Web site.

My converted document has a combination of smart (curly) quotes and straight quotes.

When a document is converted from WordPerfect, the quotes come over as straight. If you then add more quotes, they will take on the format set in Word's settings, which is Smart Quotes. To correct this, choose AutoCorrect Options from the Tools menu. In the AutoFormat As You Type tab, make sure that the Smart Quotes option is checked (or uncheck it if you want straight quotes). Then use Find And Replace, finding " and replacing with “. Word will insert the correct format of quotes as it replaces them. You will probably want to do this for apostrophes as well, but be careful to make sure that leading apostrophes and single quotes get differentiated properly.

CHAPTER 20

DOCUMENT FORENSICS

IN THIS CHAPTER

- When good documents go bad
- Detecting corruption
- Fixing damaged files
- Using Word's Detect and Repair feature
- Metadata risks
- Viruses
- Microsoft Support10.dot macros
- Application and document recovery
- Tips from the experts

We've all been there. It's four in the afternoon, and the document that needs to be out the door by 4:30 P.M. won't open. Or perhaps (as we've found in writing some of our books), a document is nearly complete and then corrupts and is nonrecoverable. When this happens, it takes every ounce of restraint not to open the window and chuck the computer out of it.

This chapter is dedicated to anyone who has felt the frustration of documents and applications behaving badly, who has missed a filing deadline due to corruption, and to everyone who has lost hours of productivity recreating documents.

WHEN GOOD DOCUMENTS GO BAD

Let's get something out of the way up front. A document that originated in Word, that has proper formatting, and that is saved in the same version of Word as it is edited has little chance of corruption in Word 2002. It's not impossible for the document to become corrupt; however, chances are slimmer than ever that this will happen.

Corruption occurs for a variety of reasons, but the number one culprit seems to be improper conversion and cleanup. Documents that are not cleaned properly continue to have embedded codes and fields that eventually lead to corruption. Documents converted from WordPerfect to Word have the most difficulty. WordPerfect and Word both produce a document—but the way they go about doing this is very different.

Chapter 19, "Document Conversion," goes into the topic of protecting your firm and your files by using proper cleanup techniques in great detail. The fast and dirty way is to insert the file into a new Word document. This method is good for printing and viewing a document, but this method will not create a stable version of the file. The intermediate step is to perform a set of cleanup steps, but this still doesn't guarantee a document free from residual code and problems. The only way to get a truly clean document is to strip all codes and formatting from the document and then reformat it using Word styles.

Several companies offer conversion services and automated document cleanup—but you can also produce clean documents in-house if you take the necessary precautions. This is so important that it's worth restating the techniques in this chapter.

CONVERTING WITH PASTE SPECIAL

By selecting the content of the file, copying it to the Clipboard, and using the Paste Special, Unformatted Text command, you can achieve a code-free document quickly. You will, however, need to reapply formatting to the document—this technique transfers only the text, none of the formatting to the new document. There are some pros and cons to using this method. Pros include easy-to-follow steps and a clean and unformatted result document. Experts typically agree that this is a great method for converting documents. The con is that if you use this method, you will lose formatting and must re-create all footnotes and endnotes the document may contain.

CONVERT DOCUMENTS USING PASTE SPECIAL

1. From the File menu, choose Open (using the native Word Open dialog box, not one from a document management system), select the file you plan to convert, and click Open.
2. Select and copy all the text in the document, except the last paragraph mark.
3. Press Ctrl+N to create a new Word document or create a new Word document based on an appropriate template.
4. From the Edit menu, choose Paste Special, Unformatted Text. Figure 20.1 shows the Paste Special dialog box.
5. Click OK.
6. Reapply formatting using styles.

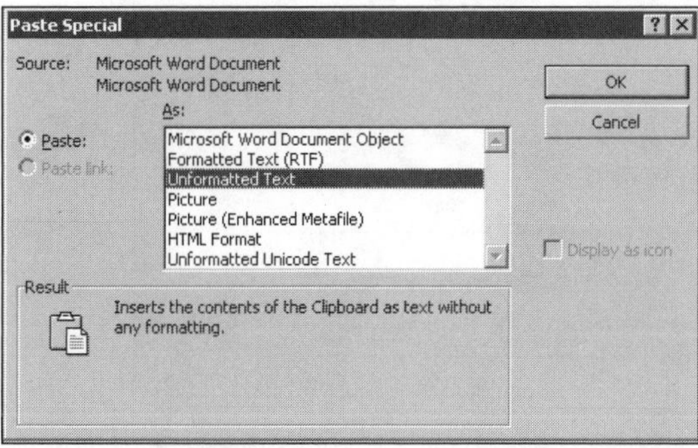

FIGURE 20.1

When you select Paste Special, Unformatted Text, all residual codes and formatting are cleared.

CONVERTING WITH RECOVER TEXT FROM ANY FILE

If a document contains numerous footnotes and endnotes, using the Recover Text From Any File import converter is probably the best solution for you. This method strips all formatting and codes while retaining all notes in the document. The drawback, however, is that much more information from the Word binary file is extracted and included in the recovered document text. This information is referred to as *metadata* and will be covered in detail later in this chapter.

CONVERT DOCUMENTS WITH RECOVER TEXT FROM ANY FILE

1. From the File menu, choose Open (using the native Word Open dialog box).
2. Click the drop-down arrow and change Files Of Type to Recover Text From Any File. Figure 20.2 shows the Recover Text From Any File option.
3. Locate and select the file to be opened.
4. Click Open.
5. Scroll to the end of the file and delete any text that is not a part of the document.
6. Return to the top of the document and begin reformatting by applying styles.

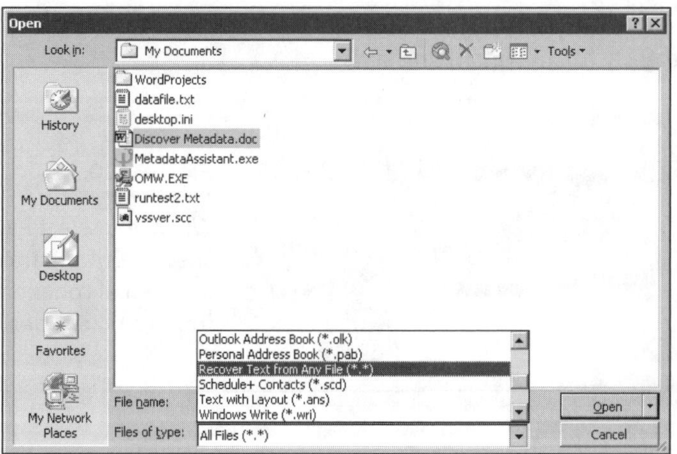

FIGURE 20.2

Recover Text From Any File can usually recover the text even if the file is corrupt.

IDENTIFYING CORRUPT DOCUMENTS

If you open a Word document and strange things happen with the formatting as you type, there are several possible causes: You might have a virus, the document may contain corruption, or an option may be turned on that causes the document to exhibit unwanted behavior. The issue becomes how to quickly identify the exact problem and implement the resolution.

Answering questions like "Does it happen in other documents, other applications, on other machines?" helps to narrow down the problem as to whether something is occurring within the operating system, Word, or the document itself. Before giving up and starting a new document, the following areas should be checked to make sure everything is working properly:

- Windows
- Word
- Document
- Template

RATTLING WINDOWS

Sometimes Windows itself becomes unstable. Rather than looking for specific problems, you'll often find that it's simplest to close all the programs you have running and reboot your system. The file may well behave normally next time you open it after restarting Windows.

PROBLEMS WITH WORD

If things seem to work properly in Windows or other Windows applications and you've already closed Word and reopened it in the course of checking on Windows, try to reproduce the behavior in a blank Word document. Copy all text except for the last paragraph mark and paste it into a new document. If that document works properly, you can delete the original and rename this one with the old name. Be sure that all the header and footer information is included in the new document as well.

UNUSUAL FORMATTING

Sometimes people apply a format such as Keep Lines Together or Framing to a paragraph without realizing it. If the situation is unique to the document, look for some of the following items:

FORMATTING

If a blank document from the original template doesn't have the problem, look for modified styles and other styles in use.

STYLES

Look for poorly designed styles. A common occurrence is building a style based on another style, which was based on another style, and so on. This can lead to problems with document formatting. Also, if a style is based on a style that has been removed from the template, the basis reverts to Normal style—which may not include everything needed at that point.

SECTION FORMATTING

Look for unusual settings that are part of section formatting. A common situation is that section break starts on the wrong page.

LAST PARAGRAPH MARK

Look for fonts that may not exist on the current default printer. Copy everything but the last paragraph mark to a new document. This may remove bad printer information and incorrect section formatting.

NUMBERING

If numbering is not correct, click the Numbering button once to turn off numbering, and then click the button again. Or from the Format menu, choose Bullets And Numbering and click Customize to see specific settings that may affect numbering. The best practice is to link numbering to styles.

AUTOCORRECT

Check for unusual settings in AutoCorrect. You may have some odd rules set in AutoCorrect that replace or insert text when certain characters are typed in sequence. For example, "*s" might be set to insert a section symbol. To check existing AutoCorrect settings, from the Tools menu, choose AutoCorrect Options and select the AutoCorrect tab. The AutoCorrect dialog box is shown in Figure 20.3.

Sometimes the AutoCorrect's AutoFormat As You Type can produce some unexpected results. Perhaps you've typed a numbered paragraph and when you pressed the Enter key, the entire paragraph reformatted itself. To view these settings, from the Tools menu, choose AutoCorrect Options and select the AutoFormat As You Type tab.

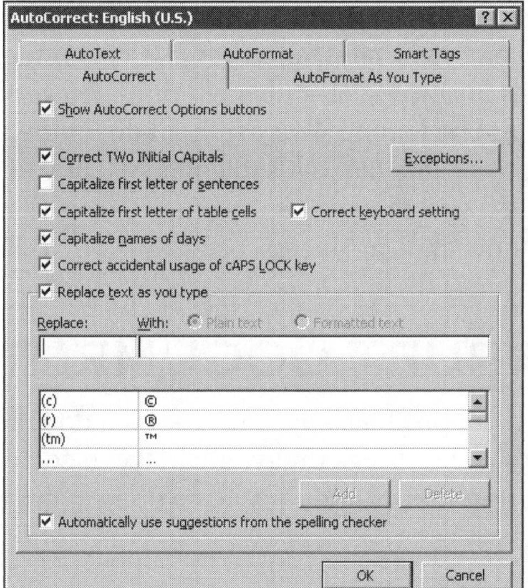

FIGURE 20.3

If the text you type is mysteriously replaced by something else, check to see if an AutoCorrect entry has been activated.

MACROS AND ADD-INS

Watch for macros that run automatically when the application is started or closed. Firm custom macros are often designed to run automatically—but virus writers sometimes embed their viruses in macros as well.

To see what macros are in your templates or documents, from the Tools menu, choose Macro, Macros. This opens the Macros dialog box, as shown in Figure 20.4.

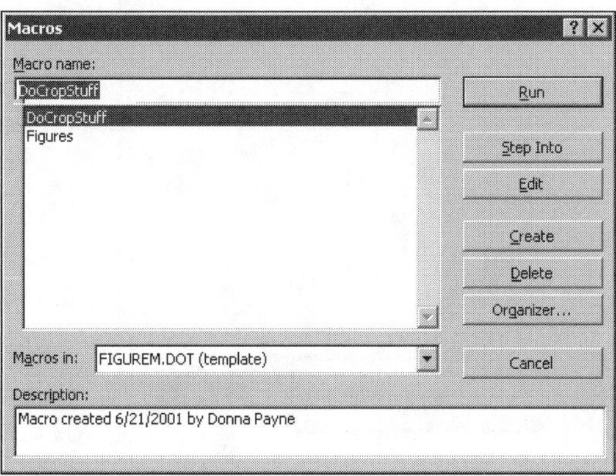

FIGURE 20.4

If you see macros listed here, it is possible that one or more of them are part of a macro virus that has infected your system. Some examples of these types of macro names: AAAZAO, AAAZFS, FileSaveAs, and PayLoad.

Click the drop-down arrow next to Macros In and switch the Macros In box to Normal.dot, then the current document, and then the current template. If you do discover a macro in this location, don't delete it until you verify that it is not a firm macro and should not be loaded. You can hold down the Shift key when starting Word or opening a specific file to disable macros, or you can set macro security to high, which will disable macros unless they have a signed digital certificate. From the Tools menu, choose Macros, Security.

CORRECTING CORRUPT DOCUMENTS

If checking formatting did not produce any leads—or if a document cannot be opened at all—there are several things that you can try to correct a corrupted document, depending on the severity and the nature of the corruption.

OPEN AND REPAIR

Word 2002 includes a new Open and Repair feature, shown in Figure 20.5, which attempts to open an otherwise unrecoverable file and correct the detected problem.

This is the easiest method to recover a damaged file. If a problem is detected upon opening the file, a dialog box will appear stating that the problem was located and repaired. Once the file is open, you may need to search for the cause of the problem—but getting the file open with the formatting intact is a good first step.

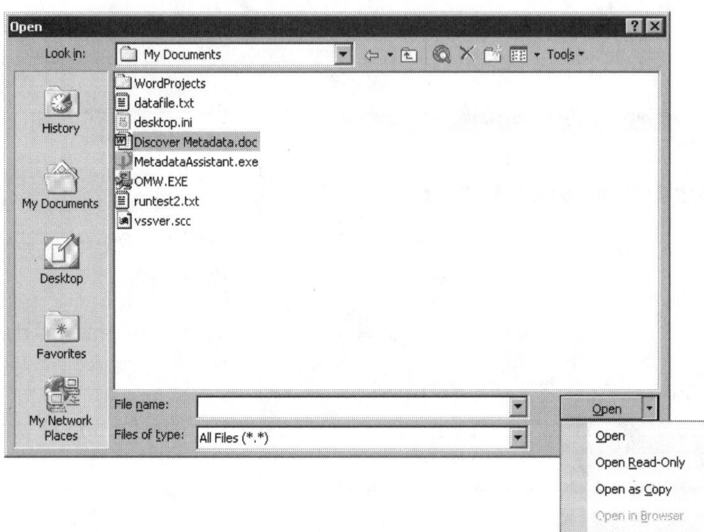

FIGURE 20.5

Open and Repair allows you to prompt Word to force a document open and attempt to fix its problems.

USE OPEN AND REPAIR

1. From the File menu, choose Open (using the native Word Open dialog box).
2. Locate and select the file to be opened.
3. Click the drop-down arrow on the Open button and choose Open And Repair. If Word detects errors in the file, the Show Repairs dialog box shown in Figure 20.6 opens.

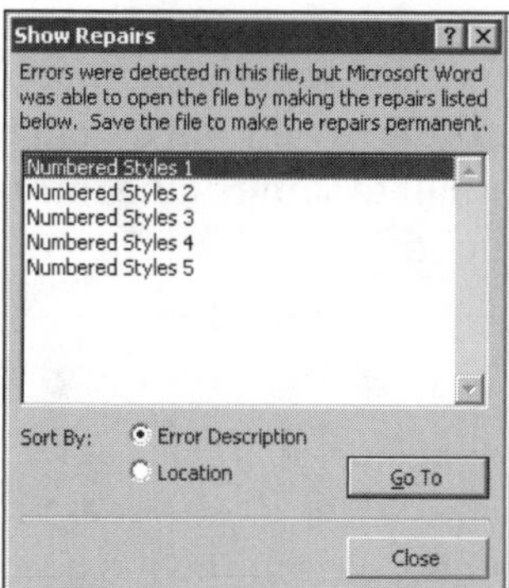

FIGURE 20.6

The file being opened in this figure is one that consistently caused previous versions of Word to crash. Word 2002 opens the 65-page file without difficulty.

NOTE

In an attempt to find items that were unrecoverable, we inserted graphics, macros, page numbers within frames, text boxes, and more, then used the Open And Repair feature. All such information was recoverable in our tests.

RECOVER TEXT FROM ANY FILE

If the document cannot be opened by any other means, you can recover the text from the file and then use styles to reapply formatting. When a file is opened with this method, Word is actually using an import converter file to extract everything in the document that can be read as text. Besides the intended text, additional information saved as metadata with the document is also visible when opening the document using Recover Text From Any File.

RECOVER TEXT FROM ANY FILE

1. From the File menu, choose Open (using the native Word Open dialog box).
2. Click the drop-down arrow and change Files Of Type to Recover Text From Any File.
3. Locate and select the file to be opened.
4. Click Open.
5. Scroll to the end of the file and delete anything that is not a part of the document.
6. Return to the top of the document and begin reformatting by applying styles. You may want to copy the text into a new document based on the appropriate template if that will eliminate some of the formatting that needs to be reapplied to the document.

In previous versions of Word, once Recover Text From Any File was selected, the setting stuck and all subsequent Word documents would recover as text only—even when opened via a document management system. This has been fixed in Word 2002. If Recover Text From Any File is selected, the drop-down arrow resets to All Files or Word Documents (the previous state of the drop-down list) after the immediate use. Thank you, Microsoft!

SAVE AS A PREVIOUS VERSION OF WORD

If the document can be opened, one way to remove corruption is to save the document in the file format of an earlier version of the software. Many people find success by first trying to save the file as a Word 6.0 document. If that doesn't do the job, save it as a Word 2.0 document.

SAVE AS RICH TEXT FORMAT

The file can be saved in Rich Text Format. RTF is a tagged language, much like PostScript, where all font, style, and property information is stored at the beginning of the file and, therefore, may help stabilize an otherwise unstable Word document.

SAVE AS TEXT ONLY

If saving as RTF doesn't work, try saving as Text Only, or in another word-processing format. If the document is simple, save it as a WordPad or Write file. Letters and one- to two-page memos may not require any fixing after going through the Write filter.

COPY TO A NEW FILE

Another trick is to copy portions of the document to a new file. Select one or two paragraphs at a time and copy them in. Often you can locate the exact location of the corruption in the document, delete it, change the style to Normal, and then retype or use Paste Special to solve the problem. This strips out potentially damaging formatting that has been applied to the text.

If the document is long, rather than starting at one end and moving a couple of paragraphs at a time to a new file, split the original in half. If (as usually happens) one half is okay and the other is corrupt, save the good half and split the corrupt one again. Repeat this process until you've narrowed the problem down to the paragraph with the corrupt code, and retype or use Paste Special, Unformatted Text to fix it.

PASTE SPECIAL DIALOG BOX

As noted earlier, a popular method for removing codes and formatting from text is to copy the text, switch to a new blank document, and from the Edit menu, choose Paste Special, Unformatted Text.

PASTE SPECIAL UNFORMATTED TEXT

1. Copy text that has formatting applied.
2. Create a new blank document.
3. From the Edit menu, choose Paste Special, Unformatted Text. The Paste Special dialog box was shown previously in Figure 20.1.
4. Click OK.

PASTE OPTIONS BUTTON

Word 2002 has added a Paste Options button that provides functionality at your fingertips. The Paste Options button makes Paste Special, Unformatted Text easy. When information is pasted, a Paste Options button appears with options for how to format the information.

PASTE OPTIONS BUTTON

1. Create a new blank document.
2. Type your name and format it as red, bold, and 20-point type.
3. Create a new style named **BigRed** and apply it to your name text.
4. Select and copy the text.
5. Create a new blank document.
6. From the Edit menu, choose Paste (or press Ctrl+V).
7. Click the Paste Options button that appears with the pasted text. The Paste Option button is shown in Figure 20.7.
8. Choose Keep Text Only. The text is pasted, but the formatting and style are removed.

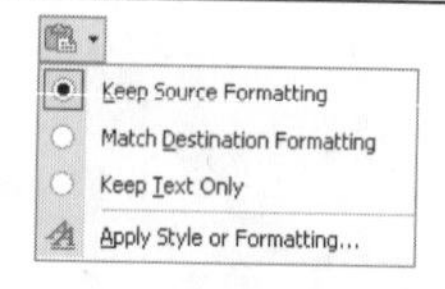

FIGURE 20.7

One of Microsoft's goals in this version was to bring features buried in menus and toolbars to the forefront, making them available for everyone to easily and quickly access.

DETECT AND REPAIR

The Word application itself can experience problems—as is the case with any software. Microsoft Office includes a feature called Detect And Repair that makes diagnosing and fixing problems easy—for anyone.

To run properly, Word needs certain files. To check spelling, it needs specific files. When one or more of these files becomes unstable or deleted, Detect And Repair may kick in automatically when Word is started, or you can initiate the action by choosing Detect And Repair from the Help menu. The Detect And Repair dialog box is shown in Figure 20.8.

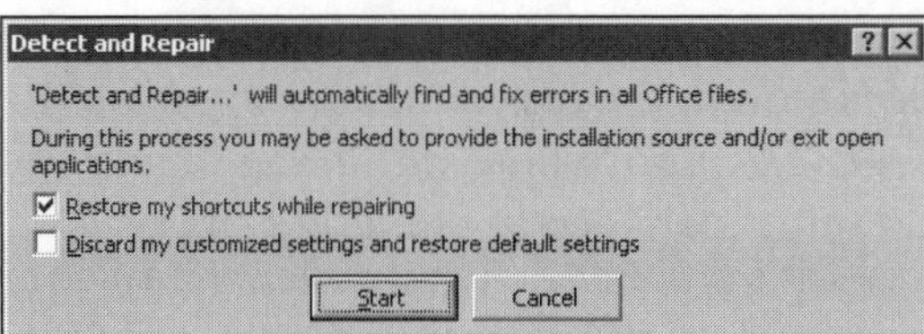

FIGURE 20.8

Detect and Repair searches through files on the computer to make sure all necessary files are present and in good working order. If a problem is found, the feature fixes it, if possible.

Word includes more invasive Detect and Repair methods that are designed for high-end technical staff. This chapter covers the method of invoking Detect and Repair from the Help menu only. For more information on the advanced methods, consider taking the Payne Consulting Group Word 2002 Master Series class. Information on training is available at www.payneconsulting.com.

DETECT AND REPAIR

1. From the Help menu, choose Detect And Repair.
2. Select Restore My Shortcuts When Repairing and click Start. This initiates what can sometimes be a lengthy process of searching for any problems within the application; fixing the problems discovered automatically.

THE RISK OF METADATA

A few years back, a law firm sent us a document that contained tracked changes. Upon unveiling these changes, we could see that a document written for another company had been used as the basis for our document, and some of the differences were very interesting—not to mention revealing—indeed. This law firm has since changed its policy for working with electronic documents, but many firms continue to send documents that include hidden text, changes, and comments—without even knowing about it.

True metadata is information saved with a file that aids in the process of searching and retrieving documents. Some of this information is stored in Word's underlying binary file, and it's necessary to write advanced macros to modify or remove it while leaving the rest of the Word file intact. While it may be difficult to modify or remove this information, it certainly isn't difficult to review it, since anyone can use Recover Text From Any File to reveal this type of information.

Metadata includes up to the previous 10 authors of a document, the full name and path where the file is stored, the template used to create the file, and even deleted text that no longer exists anywhere within the visible body of the document. These items, and more, can lead to embarrassing situations and potentially damaging discovery.

NEW SECURITY AND METADATA REMOVAL IN WORD

In Word 2002, Microsoft has taken steps to eliminate, or at least substantially reduce, the amount of metadata contained in documents. Personal information can be removed from the document before it is saved, and a warning can appear before a document containing tracked changes or comments is sent electronically or printed.

VIEW NEW SECURITY IN WORD

1. From the Tools menu, choose Options.
2. Select the Security tab, which is shown in Figure 20.9.
3. Under Privacy Options, check the Remove Personal Information From This File On Save option.

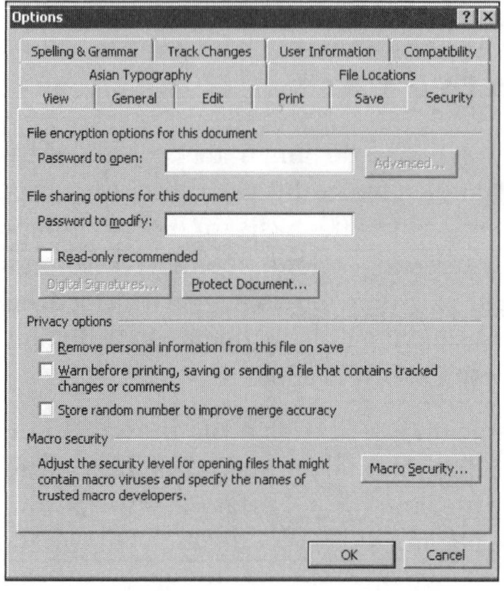

FIGURE 20.9

The Security tab—new in Word—places most of the security measures in one location. It enables the user to assign passwords, specify whether personal information should be stored, and whether or not to display a warning when a file is about to be printed, saved, or sent via e-mail.

4. Check the Warn Before Printing, Saving Or Sending A File That Contains Tracked Changes Or Comments option. This directs Word to open a message box with a warning if the file being printed, saved, or sent contains tracked changes or comments.
5. Click OK to close the Options dialog box.

Not all metadata is removed by checking the option to remove personal information, but at least some of the information—specifically information that appears in the Properties dialog box (File, Properties)—is removed. File properties that are removed when this option is checked include Author, Manager, Company, and Last Saved By. From the binary file, the option removes the names of the last 10 authors, path to printer, any e-mail header, and routing slip information.

The Remove Personal Information From This File On Save option is unchecked by default for every file. You can't turn it on and forget it—when it is checked, it applies only to the active document and not all or new documents.

ANALYZING METADATA

So what does metadata actually look like and can it really be all that harmful? The answer to both questions may surprise you. How many times have you rushed a document out the door electronically to meet a closing deadline or client request? Did you check to make sure that all the comments had been removed? Was the Allow Fast Saves option accidentally turned on? Was the document actually a copy of a master template? Did it contain hidden text or were Track Changes used? These questions are designed to illustrate just how easily discoverable metadata can build up in your documents without your knowledge. And although the security tools available in Office XP are definitely an improvement over past versions, they only go so far. It's still possible for interested parties to discover confidential information stored within your documents.

USE RECOVER TEXT FROM ANY FILE TO VIEW METADATA

1. Start Word
2. From the File menu, choose Open.
3. Locate a file to open (files worked on by multiple reviewers are the most interesting, as are files with Fast Saves enabled, Track Changes, versions and routing slips).
4. At the bottom of the Open dialog box, change the setting for Files Of Type to Recover Text From Any File and open the document.
5. Scroll down through the document—notice that toward the bottom of the document you can view Author information, file location, attached template information, and more.
6. This is just one simple way to quickly discover or uncover metadata.

PROTECT YOURSELF AND YOUR FIRM

So what can you do to protect yourself and your firm from unknowingly sending out confidential or potentially embarrassing information? The first step is to use the built-in security features that come with Word 2002. These will not only provide a valuable first line of defense but will also prompt you and others within your firm to think about the risks of metadata. But, unfortunately, these security tools alone will not remove all the metadata Word adds to your documents.

At Payne we've been talking about metadata for quite some time. In fact, we were recently featured on the front page of the *Wall Street Journal* in an article that talked exclusively about the origins and risks of metadata. In 1998, we developed a product that would later become known as the Metadata Assistant to help some of our clients deal with problems they were having related to metadata. As the product grew in popularity, we made it available on our Web site as a free download. Today, the Metadata Assistant, Enterprise edition, is more popular than ever.

The Enterprise edition, which integrates with Outlook 2000 and higher, can be purchased by firms that want full protection from the risks of metadata. The Enterprise edition can scan entire directories, work with both .doc and .dot files, remove the last 10 authors, and best of all, prompt users to analyze and clean attachments for metadata before sending them from Outlook. The utility also provides analysis and reporting functionality.

In addition to the features described in the preceding paragraph, the Metadata Assistant Enterprise edition, (shown in Figure 20.10) removes metadata by performing the following actions:

- Deletes all comments
- Deletes hidden text
- Deletes last 10 authors
- Accepts all tracked changes
- Deletes all versions (does not affect versions stored on a document management system—only Word's native Versions feature, which gangs versions in the same file)
- Turns off Fast Save
- Converts graphics to pictures
- Removes built-in document properties
- Removes custom document properties
- Deletes all document variables
- Deletes all hyperlinks
- Changes attached template to Normal.dot
- Removes routing slip entries

For more information about the Enterprise edition, contact metadataassistant@payneconsulting.com.

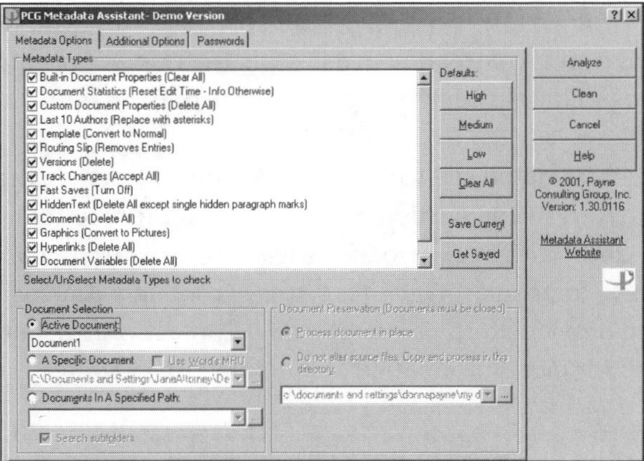

FIGURE 20.10

The Metadata Assistant provides a wide range of security settings for eliminating metadata from your documents.

With the Metadata Assistant, you can analyze and process a single document or an entire directory. If you're concerned about removing information from a master document, no problem. You can selectively choose each of the options you wish to use or even process a copy of the document so the original remains intact. The Metadata Assistant also comes with an online help file.

VIRUSES

Computer viruses, the modern-day equivalent of the plague, are the scourge and bane of office workers everywhere. Whether it's the notorious Melissa, I Love You, or Anna Kournikova virus, most computer users have fallen victim or have been affected by some type of virus at one time or another. Computer viruses often strike with little or no warning, spread quickly, and wreak havoc on files, hard drives, and entire networks. Where do viruses come from? How do they spread—and what can you do to protect yourself and your firm from the potentially devastating effects they often bring?

Viruses come in many different shapes and sizes. Some are malicious and destructive, others are simply annoying. A *virus* is a program that infects a specific file or program and propagates itself. Viruses can be picked up and spread through e-mail attachments, files downloaded from the Internet, and documents shared on floppy disks. Some viruses are date-specific—triggered to execute on a certain day of a month or year—while others do their damage instantly.

For Word users, the most common type of virus is the macro virus. A *macro virus* is a type of virus that is stored in a macro within a .doc or .dot file. Macro viruses are typically designed to attack and infect Word's Normal.dot. Since every new Word document is based on the Normal template, what easier way could there be to quickly spread a virus? Microsoft does provide a few built-in security measures to help protect you and your firm from being sabotaged.

New viruses are being created every day. For maximum protection, use third-party antivirus software in conjunction with Word's built-in security features. Norton/Symantec and McAfee sell two of the leading antivirus products on the market today. These companies' Web sites typically contain a running list of all known viruses and provide up-to-date protection. Contact your system administrator or help desk for more information about antivirus software.

MACRO SECURITY

Macro viruses are spread through the use of macros, and macros are stored in documents and templates. Word contains three levels of security for filtering

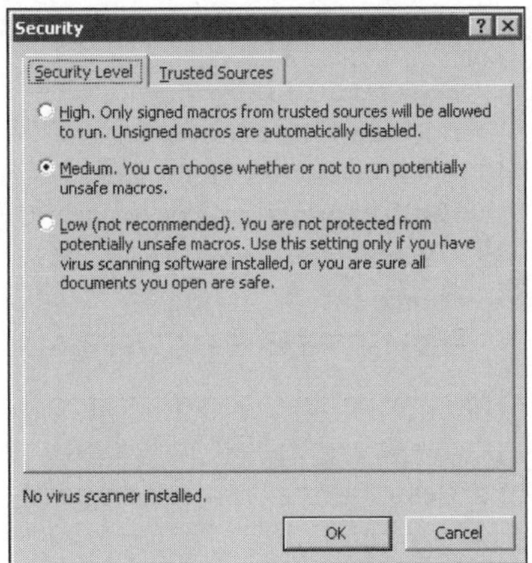

FIGURE 20.11

From the Tools menu, choose Macro, Security to open the Macro Security dialog box.

unknown or potentially harmful macros—High, Medium, and Low—as shown in Figure 20.11.

Each of the macro security settings is explained in greater detail in the following list. Choose the setting most appropriate for your environment.

- **High**. This setting provides the maximum amount of protection against macro viruses. Only digitally signed and accepted macros (explained in the next section) will be enabled. All others will be automatically disabled.
- **Medium**. Provides a warning when documents containing macros are opened. You have the option to enable or disable the macros. If you receive a document from an unknown (or, for that matter, known) source that contains a macro you weren't expecting, it's best to have Word disable it.
- **Low**. Provides no protection and no warning. Any macros in documents you open will be automatically enabled. Unless you work in a network environment where incoming documents are scanned by antivirus software, this option should never be used.

DIGITAL SIGNATURES

Another protection method from harmful macro viruses is through the use of digital signatures. A digital signature acts as a calling card of sorts, identifying the sender of a macro or executable program. A digitally signed macro names the macro's source and also provides information regarding the identity and validity of that source. Digital signatures help users distinguish valid code from dangerous and viral code.

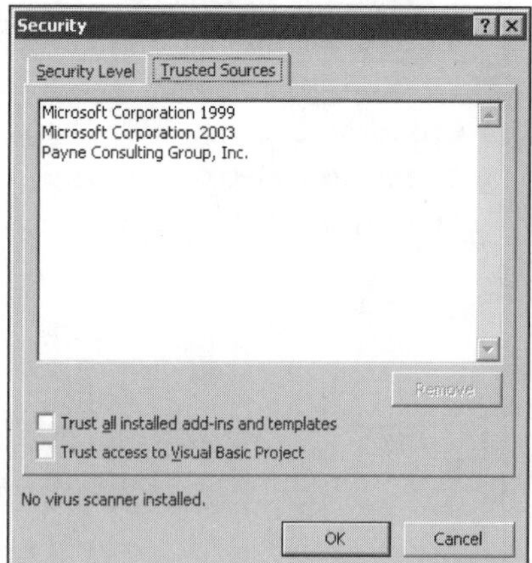

FIGURE 20.12

Digital certificates do not guarantee that the file is virus free, but they do guarantee that the file came from the source listed.

Digital signatures (often referred to as certificates) can be purchased from a commercial vendor such as VeriSign, or they can be created by a system administrator. Figure 20.12 shows installed digital certificates.

For more information regarding digital certificates, contact your system administrator or go to www.verisign.com.

The most important thing to keep in mind regarding macro viruses is this—never open a document containing macros unless you're sure that the macros are valid and the source is legitimate. Word allows you to open the document without activating the macros, and it's always best to err on the side of caution.

MORE USEFUL INFORMATION

This section includes the limitations of Word, such as the maximum number of smart tags you can place in a document, as well as tips and tricks from some industry experts.

WORD LIMITS

Word will work on some things right up to the extent of your computer's memory, but in other areas, it has limits that you should know. Table 20.1 lists the relevant features and the limitation of each.

TABLE 20.1 WORD LIMITATIONS AND SIZE DEFAULTS

FEATURE	DESCRIPTION
Amount of space between characters	1,584 points
Default bitmap memory	1MB
Default cache size	64KB
Distance text can be raised or lowered	1,584 points
Length of AutoText entry names including spaces	32 characters
Length of bookmark names	40 characters
Length of style names	255 characters
Maximum custom dictionary file size	65,593 bytes
Maximum file size	32MB
Maximum font size	1,638 points (22 inches)
Maximum number of cascading style sheets linked together	11
Maximum number of colors in color palette	256
Maximum page height	22 inches
Maximum page width and table width	22 inches
Minimum font size	1 point
Minimum page height	0.1 inch
Minimum page width	0.1 inch
Number of bookmarks in a document	16,379
Number of characters per line	768
Number of columns in a table	63
Number of custom toolbar buttons	Limited by available memory
Number of custom toolbars	Limited by available memory
Number of fields in a document	32,000
Number of field-specific switches in a field	10
Number of fonts in a document	32,767
Number of general switches in a field	10
Number of global AutoText entries	Limited by available memory and template file size
Number of nesting levels for fields	20
Number of newspaper columns	45
Number of open windows	Limited by available memory
Number of smart tags	32,752
Number of styles in a document or template	10,000
Number of subdocuments in a master document	255
Number of tab stops set in a paragraph	64
Number of words in custom dictionaries	5,000

MICROSOFT SUPPORT10.DOT MACROS

Word 2002 includes a set of macros developed by Microsoft Product Support Services that help you troubleshoot and resolve issues with the software. Support10.dot is located by default at C:\Program Files\Microsoft Office\Office10\Macros. Included are Troubleshoot Utility, Registry Options, and AutoCorrect Backup.

BEWARE! Editing the Registry is not supported by Microsoft (or this book). You should never make changes to the Registry unless you are expert at doing so. Altering or deleting Registry keys can render your computer useless.

This section of the chapter discusses the Registry only where it is accessible from Support10.dot.

TROUBLESHOOT UTILITY

This macro may well become your best friend in troubleshooting problems with Word. Click Troubleshoot Utility and the Microsoft Word Troubleshoot Utility box appears, as shown in Figure 20.13.

The options listed under Select An Item include.

- **Introduction**. This item introduces the utility and provides useful information on using Startup switches when starting Word.
- **Data Registry Key**. Going into the Windows Registry and editing data keys can be dangerous if you don't know what you are doing. However, at times you may need to delete or restore information stored there to reset options in Word. The Data Registry Key option in Support10.dot allows you click Restore or Delete to make adjustments to the Registry.
- **Normal.dot Global Template**. When Word starts, it loads the Normal.dot file. If the file becomes corrupt or damaged, Word may run incorrectly. This

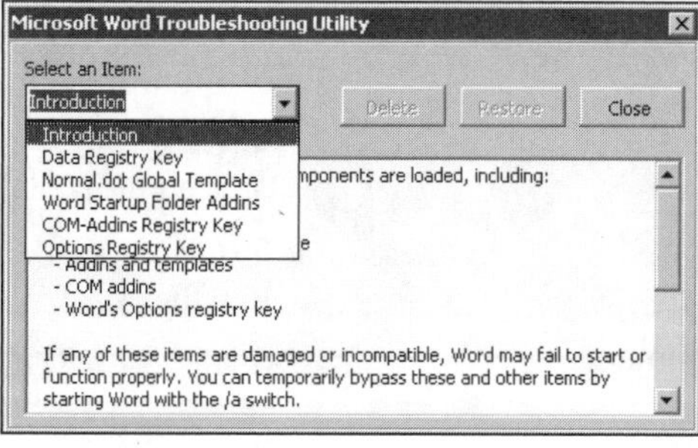

FIGURE 20.13

The Troubleshoot Utility is a user-friendly interface for restoring configurations that could be causing Word to malfunction.

option includes buttons to Rename and Restore as well as descriptive help text for each option.

- **Word Startup Folder Add-ins**. Helps troubleshoot files that load when Word starts.
- **COM Add-Ins Registry Key**. Isolates whether a problem is occurring when loading COM add-ins. If files are damaged or incompatible, it can cause errors when starting or working with Word.
- **Options Registry Key**. Deletes and restores registry settings that may be damaged, and therefore affecting Word.

REGISTRY OPTIONS

The Registry stores information about your computer, preferences for each user who logs on to the computer, and software installed. Some Registry keys are specific to Word and can affect how Word runs. As noted previously, Microsoft does not support your editing the Registry but realizes that at times, doing so can be useful for troubleshooting serious issues that occur with the software. Therefore, they have included a utility in Support10.dot that provides a user-friendly interface for doing so. Remember however that by changing or deleting the wrong Registry key, you can cause permanent damage to your computer.

The two tabs in the Registry Options dialog box are: Word Options (Figure 20.14) and Equation Editor Options (Figure 20.15).

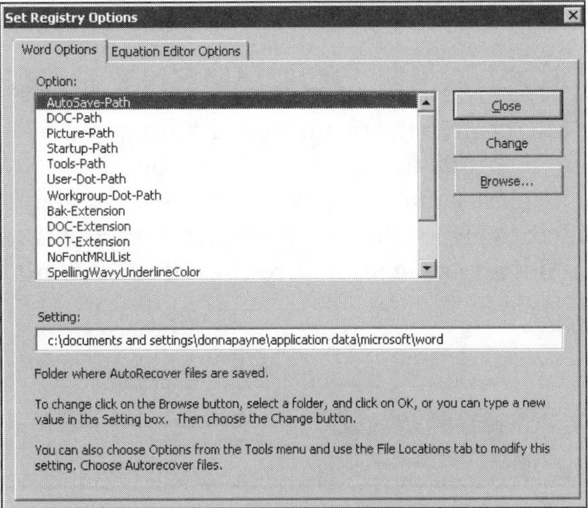

FIGURE 20.14

Word Options that can be set in the Registry include AutoSavePath, DOC Path, Picture Path, Smart Tag, Underline Color, and more.

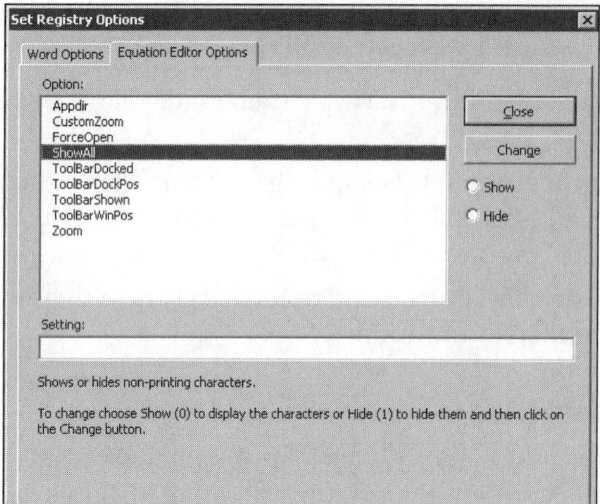

FIGURE 20.15

Equation Editor Options that can be set include Appdir, CustomZoom, ForceOpen, ShowAll, and more.

AUTOCORRECT BACKUP

AutoCorrect entries are stored on the computer and include all of the words found under Tools, AutoCorrect Options, AutoCorrect. This includes frequently misspelled words as well as words that you manually add to AutoCorrect.

The AutoCorrect Backup macro creates a backup file named AutoCorrect Backup Document.doc that includes a table with all existing AutoCorrect entries. If your AutoCorrect file becomes corrupt, or if you move to a new computer, you can take this file with you. Figure 20.16 shows the AutoCorrect Utility dialog box and Figure 20.17 shows the resulting backup document created.

APPLICATION AND DOCUMENT RECOVERY

A top priority for Microsoft in the planning and subsequent release of Office XP was to reduce general protection faults and document loss. In Word 2002, if a gpf occurs, Word displays a message box letting you know about the discovered problem—and apologizing for the inconvenience. Figure 20.18 shows the message box displayed if an application error has occurred and Word needs to restart.

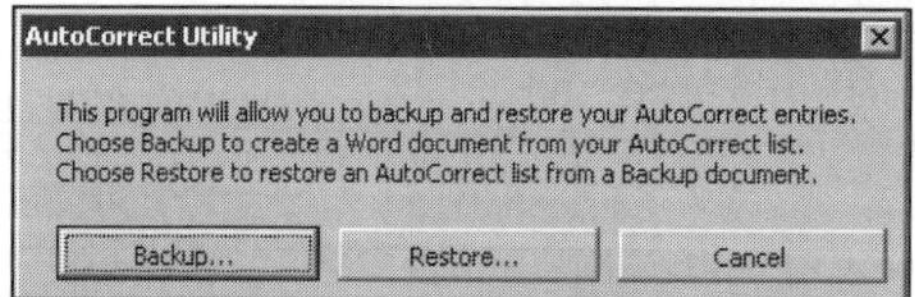

FIGURE 20.16

Click Backup to create a file with all of your existing AutoCorrect entries.

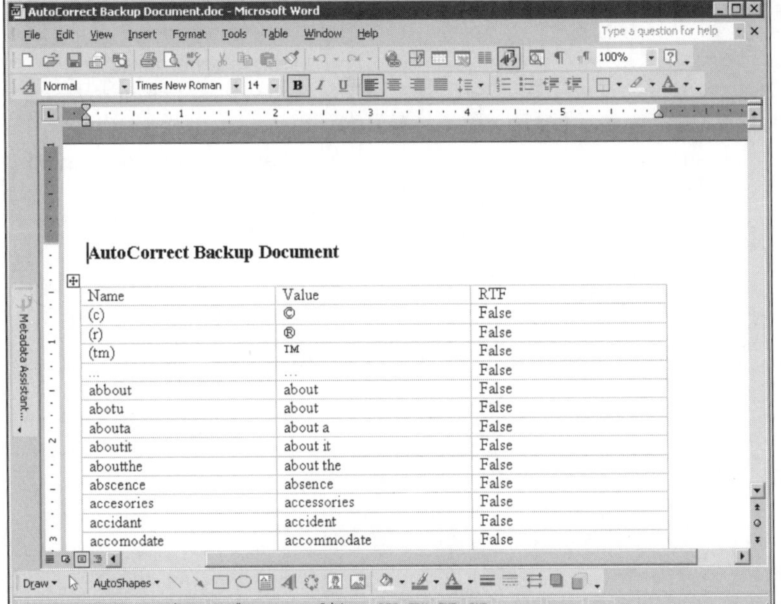

FIGURE 20.17

The backup AutoCorrect entries file includes a table with all existing entries. Click Restore and select the backup AutoCorrect file to be used for the current computer.

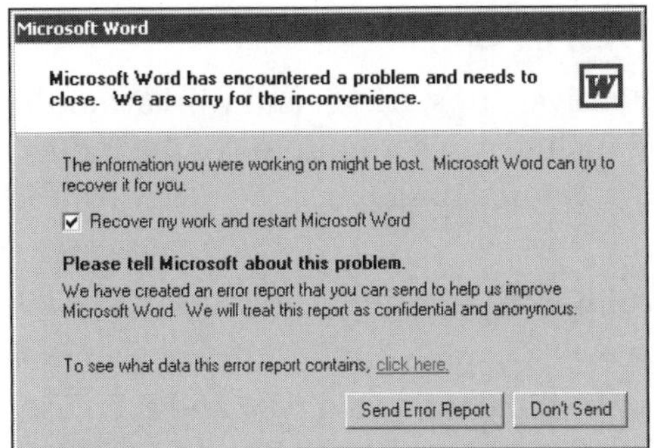

FIGURE 20.18

The apology on the message box is a nice touch.

You can choose to send a report to Microsoft that includes the specific error number and cause of the problem, or not send the information. Sending the report typically only takes a few moments. Internet access is required. Once Microsoft receives the information, it is entered into a database. If a resolution is known, you may be contacted with information on how to acquire the fix immediately.

After choosing whether or not to send a report to Microsoft, Word shuts down gently and restarts. Documents open at the time of the crash are most often recovered and displayed on the left side of the screen in a Document Recovery pane, as shown in Figure 20.19.

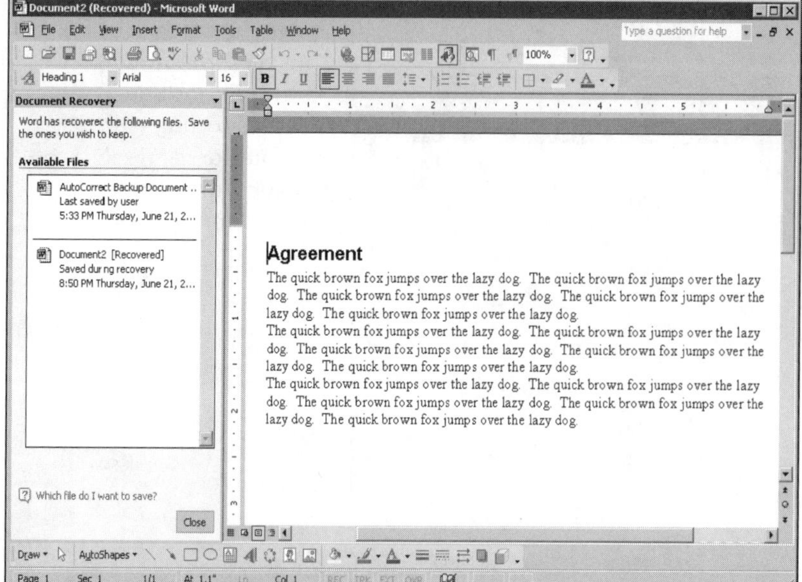

FIGURE 20.19

Most documents are recoverable when Word restarts—even if they have not yet been saved.

ADVICE FROM THE EXPERTS

Anyone who works in Word for a while discovers tips, tricks, and workarounds for using the software better. This section includes tips from some of the industry experts whom we asked to see what they wanted to share.

SCOTT HARRIS, LATHAM & WATKINS

The best advice I've received regarding Word is to plan out the structure of the document before hitting the keyboard. In the old days, you'd type and then use the format-as-you-go method. If you follow this approach with Word for a complex document, you will likely spend a great deal of time replacing manual formatting with automatic formatting and troubleshooting page and paragraph numbering issues.

The better approach is to first think about the overall look of the document. For example, when you're creating a corporate agreement, you might know that you'll need a title page with the main body, a table of contents, and an "Exhibit A" page. The pages in each section will be numbered differently, so you know that you'll need section breaks. You also know that you'll need Article/Section style paragraph headings and you'd like them to be numbered.

Before typing the first word in your document, set up your section breaks and your headers and footers. Then create your numbering scheme using heading styles. Now that you've got the framework in place, you can build your masterpiece.

ROBYN W. PASCALE, BALLARD SPAHR, ANDREWS, & INGERSOLL

This is better than "Shrink to Fit"! Shrink to Fit, a feature tucked away in Print Preview, can be helpful when a short document such as a letter extends to a second page by only a few lines of text. Shrink to Fit reduces the font size to keep the document to one page. However, changing font size is an obvious change.

I have a tip that will accomplish the same feat, but will not change the size of the font and is very inconspicuous. The information can be formatted directly to text or applied in a style (such as Body Text).

FIT WITHOUT SHRINKING

1. Select the paragraph to be affected.
2. From the Format menu, choose Paragraph.
3. Select the Indents And Spacing tab.
4. Set Line Spacing to Multiple, and At to .91. Line spacing at .91 is slightly less than single spacing, so it is barely noticeable to the eye. Yet it may allow at least one more paragraph to fit on the page.

BRUCE LEWIS, PAYNE CONSULTING GROUP

If you've used outline numbering linked to heading styles, you may already know that the shortcut keys Ctrl+Alt+1, Ctrl+Alt+2, and Ctrl+Alt+3 apply levels 1–3 of the outline. But legal documents often contain outlines that are more than three levels deep. For keyboard users, applying levels 4–9 can be time consuming and inefficient—it takes a while to select the appropriate heading style from the Styles list. Luckily, Word provides a way around this. You can create shortcut keys for Headings 4–9 using the same keystroke combination as Headings 1–3 by modifying the style for Headings 4–9. Once the shortcut keys are set, applying any of the outline levels is a snap—and best of all, your fingers won't have to leave the keyboard!

CREATE SHORTCUT KEYS FOR HEADINGS 4–9

1. From the Format menu, choose Styles and Formatting.
2. At the bottom of the task pane, change the Show list to All Styles.
3. Choose Heading 4 from the list, click the drop-down arrow next to it, and select Modify.
4. Once the Modify Style dialog box opens, click Format and select Shortcut Key from the drop-down list.
5. Place your insertion point in the Press New Shortcut Key box and press Ctrl+Alt+4. Click Assign and Close.
6. Do the same for headings 5–9, using Ctrl+Alt+5, Ctrl+Alt+6, and so on for each corresponding heading.

CYNTHIA A. AYLSWORTH, CUMMINGS & LOCKWOOD

Select any paragraph, bullet point, heading, or whatever, and press Alt+ Shift+up-arrow (or down-arrow) to reposition the text anywhere in the document. Works with table rows too! Also—if you replace the up- and down-arrows with left- and right-arrows, you can demote and promote numbered or listed items.

This is even easier to use than Outline view since you don't have to change the view at all.

MICHELE ROLLINS, TRAINER

When it is necessary to replace one style with another in a large document, Find and Replace can make the procedure more efficient. Users often are unaware of the many ways Find and Replace can help when editing large documents.

FIND AND REPLACE STYLES

1. Position the insertion point at the appropriate starting location.
2. From the Edit menu, choose Replace, or press Ctrl+H, to open the Replace tab on the Find And Replace dialog box.
3. Click the More button to expand the dialog box, if necessary.

4. Click Format and select the Style command. The Find Style dialog box opens.
5. Select the appropriate style name and click OK.
6. Click in the Replace With dialog box and repeat steps 4 and 5.
7. Click Replace or Replace All to find information formatted with the Find What style and then replace it with the defined Replace With style.

DORA PONTOW, MICROLAW

If you need more space on the Desktop for your document and you really don't use the ruler very often, why not turn off the ruler? To turn off the ruler, from the View menu, choose Ruler. If there is a check mark beside the item, it means the ruler is visible. To turn it off, click Ruler and the ruler will disappear.

But what if you need to use the ruler to set a tab or an indent? It isn't necessary to turn the ruler back on. Simply move the mouse pointer to the narrow border at the top of the document area, let the tip of the pointer hover for just a second or two, and the ruler will appear. Keeping the pointer on the ruler, make the necessary change to a tab or indent or margin. Move the pointer away from the ruler and the ruler disappears.

Visit MicroLaw's Web site at www.microlaw.com.

SANDY HAGMAN, WOMBLE CARLYLE SANDRIDGE & RICE, PLLC

One benefit to using the Microsoft Office Suite is how well the software applications work together. For example, you can add a button to a toolbar in Word and automatically insert names and addresses stored in Outlook Contacts into the active document. The only problem with this is that the default way the information is inserted does not include company name. This can be quickly fixed, however, with the following steps.

MODIFY ADDRESS LAYOUT

1. From the View menu, choose Toolbars, and click Customize.
2. Select the Commands tab.
3. Under Categories, select Insert. Select Address Book under Commands, drag the button to any toolbar, and release the mouse.

4. Close the Customize dialog box.
5. Click the Insert Address button and change Show Names From The to Contacts.
6. Select a name with an address and click OK. The name and address appear in your document, but without the company name.
7. In a blank document, type the following:

   {<PR_GIVEN_NAME>} {<PR_SURNAME>}{<PR_COMPANY_NAME>}
   {<PR_STREET_ADDRESS>}
   {<PR_LOCALITY>}, {<PR_STATE_OR_PROVINCE>},
   {<PR_POSTAL_CODE>}

8. Select the text that you just typed.
9. From the Insert menu, choose AutoText, AutoText.
10. In the Enter AutoText Entries Here box, type **AddressLayout** and click Add.
11. Insert an address using the Insert Address button again. This time, the company name will be inserted along with the name and address.

One more quick favorite trick—if you need to repeat a paragraph that you just typed (or copied), press Alt+Enter right after you finish typing or copying the material. Alt+Enter functions the same as pressing the F4 key to repeat the last action.

Sherry Kappel, Microsystems

NOTE

It's safe to say that no one knows Word better than Sherry Kappel at Microsystems. Sherry is passionate about the software, and doesn't rest until she has an answer to even the most obscure problem. This is a good thing!

When we decided to include a section for expert tips and advice, there was no question that Sherry had to be in it.

I know that pressing Ctrl+A and then Ctrl+Spacebar strips Font formatting from the content of my document, but all of my character (bold, underline, engraved) attributes go right along with it. Isn't there another way?

Yes, but it requires that you think like Word! Keep in mind that a directly applied attribute is anything *contrary* to the underlying style. Which means that if you change the *style* to match the *content,* it won't be contrary any longer, now, will it? These steps will guide you:

1. Determine the predominant font of the document.
2. Modify the governing style (most often Normal) such that its font matches the content's predominant font.
3. From the File menu, choose Close and save the document—this refreshes the content so that formerly contrary attributes become merged with properties of your styles. (In previous versions of Word, have you ever seen the "What's This?" box misreport the status of a directly applied attribute? That's because the content's formatting and the styles had been completely reconciled....)
4. Reopen the document. Now, when you modify your document's governing style to be the desired font, the whole document responds as it should!

Incidentally, if you're lucky enough to encounter this problem but the font applied doesn't even exist on your system, don't worry! Word's Font dialog box and its Font drop-down accepts font names other than those in the list: just type in the missing font name, making sure you spell and capitalize it exactly—which means that this trick works even when the content exhibits such font relics as "Tms Rmn" or "Times"!

Recently, I've seen documents where multiple paragraphs are selected as I click on the style name in the Style Area. Why is this happening, and how can I make it stop?

While we are currently unclear of the root cause, we do know how to discover it—and fix it! The following steps will tell you if the issue exists in your document:

1. From the Edit menu, choose Replace.
2. Type **^13** in the Find What box.
3. Type **^p** in the Replace With box.
4. Click Replace All.

"^13" in the Find What? box represents the ASCII character code for the carriage return. These not-quite-Word-like paragraphs can cause one or more of the following "upstream" document issues: loss of formatting, formatting applied to more than selected paragraphs, comparison failures, automation errors on routines which select elements of the paragraphs collection, odd behaviors while applying or modifying styles, unsynchronized display of the Style Area Width to your document content, etc.

TARA BYERS, PAYNE CONSULTING GROUP

When it comes to Word knowledge, again, no one surpasses Tara Byers. She is vice president of training here at Payne and is expert at being able to solve problems in a way that anyone can understand. The following are two tips from Tara.

CONVERT A LIST OF LABELS INTO A MAIL MERGE DATA FILE (TABLE)

There are probably a lot of documents floating around your firm that contain pages and pages of names and addresses, one right after another. This tip will show you how to use Find and Replace to convert the list of addresses into a table format that can be used as a data source for Mail Merge.

To start, ensure that your addresses are separated by one or more empty paragraph marks. This example assumes that there are two paragraph marks after each address—one on the last line, and one empty one after it. You will need to adjust Step 3 to match the number of paragraph marks in your address list.

REPLACING FIELDS

1. Open a document that contains a list of addresses.
2. From the Edit menu, choose Replace.
3. In the Find What field, type **^p^p**. You can also select Paragraph Mark twice from the Special button to get the same result.
4. In the Replace With field, type * (an asterisk).
5. Click Replace All. All the paragraph marks separating the addresses have now been replaced with asterisks.
6. The Find And Replace dialog box should still be open. If not, press Ctrl+H to open it.
7. In the Find What field, type **^p**.
8. In the Replace With field, type **^t**.

9. Click Replace All. This step inserts a tab character after all but the last field of each address.
10. In the Find What field, type *.
11. In the Replace With field, type **^p**.
12. Click Replace All. All the asterisks are replaced with paragraph marks separating the addresses.
13. Select the entire list.
14. From the Table menu, choose Convert, Text To Table.
15. Select Tabs under Separate Text At and click OK.
16. Insert a row at the top of the table and type headings to match the contents of each column. For example, Name, Street, City, and so on.

Note: You may need to do a little cleanup (move or format contents) of the resulting table, depending on the individual address list.

RESTORING FIELDS FROM A RECOVER TEXT FROM ANY FILE DOCUMENT

When you open a troublesome document using Recover Text From Any File, you may be happy to see the text of the document that you couldn't open—but a little surprised at the extra information that shows up in the file. Some of this information you will want to delete, but you can salvage some of the fields quite easily. For example, if there was a date code in the original document, you will see the field code in the Recover Text document. Rather than delete out the codes, you can restore them to working fields. This can be especially handy for dates, tables of authorities, manually marked tables of contents, and indexes.

RESTORING FIELDS

1. From the File menu, choose Open.
2. From Files Of Type, choose Recover Text From Any File.
3. Navigate to and select a file that you know contains field codes.
4. Click Open.
5. Scroll through your document for a date code. It will look similar to this: DATE \@ "MMMM d, yyyy."

6. Select the entire entry and press Ctrl+F9. This keyboard command converts the text to a field code.
7. Press F9 to update the field. You should now see the original date result instead of the field code.
8. Try the same thing with a Table of Authorities Marked Citation field. Here is a sample of what one would look like:
   TA \l "Home Improvement v. Average Household Contractors, 94 Wn.2d 255, 261 n.4, 616 P.2d 644 (1980)" \s "Home Improvement v. Average Household Contractors" \c 1
9. Select the entire field and press Ctrl+F9, then F9.
10. Continue repeating steps 6 and 7 for other fields in your document.

Other types of field codes common in a legal document include:

SAMPLE RECOVERED FIELD	PURPOSE
INDEX \e " " \c "2" \z "1033"	Index
SEQ Table * ARABIC	Caption for tTables
TC "B. Definitions" \f C \l "4"	Table of contents marked entry
TOA \h \c "1" \p	Table of authorities
TOC \h \z \c "Table"	Table of tables, figures, etc.
TOC \o "4-4" \f \t "Heading 1,1,Heading 2,2"	Table of contents
XE "estoppel"	Marked index entry

DONNA PAYNE, PAYNE CONSULTING GROUP

WordPerfect has the built-in ability to save a document as a .pdf file. Many Word users wish this same functionality was built into Word. Although Word doesn't have Save As .PDF as an export converter or option, you can use a combination of protection and forms to get similar results.

PROTECT A DOCUMENT FOR VIEW AND PRINT ONLY

1. Open the document to be protected.
2. From the Tools menu, choose Protect Document.
3. Click Forms and type a password. It's important to remember this password so you can remove protection later. Also, it's a good idea to apply the protection to a backup document and not the original file stored in the firm document management system.
4. Reapply the password when prompted. (Remember that passwords are case-sensitive.)
5. Try to select information in the document. The protection does not allow any information to be selected.
6. Attempt to copy text. The Copy and Paste commands are unavailable.
7. From the File menu, choose Save As, and name the file a different name to see if the protection holds. You'll notice that even saving the file under a different name does not alter the protection.

SHIRLEY GORMAN, PAYNE CONSULTING GROUP

CREATING JURY INSTRUCTIONS

When you need to create jury instructions, there is no need to create two separate documents—one for the judge that includes citations at the bottom of the page and another for the jury without the cites. Just type the jury instruction at the top of each page and add the cite information at the bottom of the page. Select the cite information at the bottom of the page and choose Format, Font from the menu and select the Font tab. Under Effects, select Hidden to hide the citation text. When it is time to print a copy of the jury instructions for the judge that includes citation information, choose File, Print from the menu, and click the Options button. From the Print dialog box, select Hidden Text under Include With Document and click OK twice to close the dialog box and print the document with cites.

AUTOMATING A PLEADING TEMPLATE

Let's say that you are creating a pleading template and want to be prompted at document creation for the pleading title and have that information automatically inserted into the caption as well as the pleading footer. One way to do this is to use the Set field to create a bookmark at the very beginning of the document (e.g., SET PLDTitle). This field will also include a Fillin field to prompt for the pleading title information. Since you only want to be prompted for this information once (at document creation), you'll need to include a switch (o). You then reference that bookmark wherever the information should be inserted into the document—pleading caption and footer.

An example of the code at the beginning of the pleading document would look similar to this:

{SET PLDTitle {FILLIN "Enter Abbreviated Pleading Title for Footer" \o}}

An example of the reference field located in the caption and footer, where the pleading title is placed, would look similar to this:

{REF PLDTitle *Upper *MergeFormat}

The switch Upper converts the input text to all caps no matter how the text is input into the message box at the prompt.

SUSAN HORIUCHI, PAYNE CONSULTING GROUP

WHAT VERSION OF THE SOFTWARE ARE YOU USING?

As bugs or "known issues" are uncovered with software, manufacturers release updates or service releases that resolve problems. This is a good thing for consumers because otherwise, we would have to wait for the next full version of the software to come out, which could mean a year or two of working with software that doesn't function as intended. It's not uncommon for numerous service releases to be announced and it's important to know which you have installed on your computer and understand the issues that were resolved in each release.

To see which version of Word you have installed, from the Help menu, choose About Microsoft Word. At the top of the dialog box, Microsoft® Word 2002 appears, followed by a number in parentheses. If the number is followed by an SR number (*e.g.*, SR-1), a service release is installed. If you need to call the Microsoft help desk for support, it's useful to know which version is installed and they will typically ask you for this information.

SUMMARY

The next time you receive a document that is behaving strangely or will not open at all, you can call on the information in this chapter to determine why the problem is occurring—and, more important, to figure out how to rescue the document or at least the text of the document. Since the setup and formatting is unique with each document, there is no perfect solution that will work every time, so try a combination of the options listed. And remember—the first line of defense is to create properly formatted documents that remain in Word.

TROUBLESHOOTING DOCUMENT FORENSICS

I received a document from another law firm, and when I open it, most of the commands on the toolbars are grayed out. How can I edit this document?

It sounds like the document has been protected, which prevents editing and copying the text. You should contact the firm where the document originated and discuss editing alternatives.

I have been editing a document for the last three days. I can make changes to the text just fine, but when I double-click on the footer, the document freezes and Word shuts down.

There is a pretty good chance that your document is starting to corrupt—but since you are still able to edit the text, you should be able to salvage the formatting. Select the entire document except the last paragraph mark and copy it. Create a new blank document and paste the text. Now you can re-create the headers and footers.

I am sending a number of documents to another firm. I selected the Remove Personal Information From This File On Save option, but some of the documents still show my name and the firm name.

This setting is a document setting, which means you need to turn it on for each document where you want it to apply.

CHAPTER 21

MACROS

IN THIS CHAPTER

- An overview of VBA
- Working with objects, properties, and methods
- Where macros live
- Running and recording macros
- Creating code from scratch
- Macro security
- Some sample macros

The components of Microsoft Office make up a very powerful suite of applications. In Word, you can create a mail merge or address envelopes or labels—all without having to write a single line of programming code.

But what happens when these applications, as they come out of the box, do not meet your needs? When this happens, you can use Microsoft Office's built-in programming language, Visual Basic for Applications (VBA), to customize the software and extend Word's capabilities.

AN OVERVIEW OF VBA

The macro language in Word 2002 is called Visual Basic for Applications, or VBA for short. VBA is a robust and easy-to-use programming language based on the programming language Visual Basic. Unlike Visual Basic, however, Visual Basic for Applications runs from within an application such as Word, Excel, or PowerPoint.

Although it helps to be a programmer to write macros, with VBA you can get started right away by recording macros of your own that capture your steps as you work and reproduce them for you on command. To refine your recorded macros—and to add some tricks that you can't do in Word with the keyboard and mouse—you need at least a basic idea of how VBA works.

VBA PARTS OF SPEECH

VBA is a language like any other. Okay, it's not what you would call a "natural" language, but it has spelling, grammar, punctuation, and usage rules just like any other language. Because it's for computers, it's pretty simple. The "parts of speech" in VBA are listed in the following sections.

OBJECTS

Look around the room you're in. There are objects everywhere: desks, chairs, writing boards, computers. All are *objects* that can be described, named, and even moved. Objects can also combine with other objects to be part of a collection of objects that has a name and even a life of its own. A good example of this is a computer, where the keyboard, CPU, monitor, and mouse together make up the computer object.

Software objects—and the way you work with objects in Visual Basic for Applications—resemble the computer example. Some objects in Word include the application itself, a dialog box, a document, a paragraph, a bookmark, and much more. Objects are considered nouns.

You can use *properties, methods,* and *events* to make the objects do what you want.

PROPERTIES

A *property* is an attribute or a characteristic of an object. You might refer to the size of an object, the shape, the position, or a descriptive adjective. If you create a Word document and name it First.doc, the name First.doc is a property of the Document object. You'll find that some objects share a similar set of properties. VBA lets you set properties (as long as they're not read-only), as well as retrieve information on their state. Properties are considered adjectives.

METHODS

A *method* is something that changes an object. Using a document as an example, if you have the document (object) named First.doc (property) and you close it, save it, or open it, you are using a method to make something happen to the object. Methods are considered to be verbs.

EVENTS

An *event* is anything that causes a program to do something. On a dialog box, you may click a button that causes the dialog box to disappear. The click, in this example, is an event. Not all objects have events.

PROCEDURES

The statements in VBA are combined into *procedures,* which is just a fancy term for macros. A procedure is a macro and a macro is a procedure—nothing more or less. The following example is a fully formed macro that displays a message box with the current or active document's name, followed by the application name for the document.

```
Sub TellMe()

    MsgBox Application.ActiveDocument.Name

    MsgBox Application.ActiveDocument.Parent

End Sub
```

Here's a slightly more complex example. This one controls the Font object by changing the selection to the font Arial and setting the font size to 10. Then, if the selection is determined to be Word's Normal style, it uses the Grow method to enlarge the font—which, unless specified otherwise, boosts the font by one point size.

```
Sub ControlFontObject

Selection.Font.Name = "Arial"

    Selection.Font.Size = 10

    If Selection.Style = ActiveDocument.Styles(wdStyleNormal) Then

        Selection.Font.Grow

    End If

End Sub
```

While you may not understand everything you see here, it should be clear already that Visual Basic for Applications is a very readable and user-friendly programming language.

WHERE MACROS LIVE

When you create a macro using VBA, it can be stored in several different places:

- In the file (a document in Word, a workbook in Excel, a presentation in PowerPoint)
- In Normal.dot or a global template
- In an add-in or wizard

How and when you use the macro determines where you should store it. If you want a macro to be available only in the current document, it's simplest to store the macro in the document itself (though that has security implications for shared documents, as discussed in the next section and later in the chapter). If a macro would be useful each time you create a similar type of document, such as a letter or agreement, you might consider storing the macro in the specific document template. For a macro to be available at all times in all Word documents, your options would be to store the macro in the Normal template (Normal.dot), or in a template loaded globally (via the Startup folder), or as an add-in template. Using an add-in template adds further protection to the macro because users cannot delete or edit the macro without first accessing the add-in template. To take this one step further, once you're an advanced programmer, you can also create a wizard to walk users through steps to accomplish a process.

ADVANTAGES AND DISADVANTAGES OF STORING MACROS IN DOCUMENTS

When you store macros in documents, the macro travels with the document. So, if you send the document outside the firm, either through e-mail or by placing the document on a diskette and handing it to someone, every user will have access to the macro. That can be an advantage or a disadvantage, and there are several other disadvantages as well. If the macro is stored only in the document, it is not available to other documents. Further, it may not run automatically unless macro security (touched on later in this chapter) is set to Medium or Low or if the macro is signed with a digital certificate.

ADVANTAGES AND DISADVANTAGES OF STORING MACROS IN REGULAR TEMPLATES

When you create a document based on a template, you have access to all macros, toolbars, styles, menu commands, and macros built into that template. This can be a tremendous time-saver and will allow for greater consistency in documents. Further, it eliminates the need to store everything in a Normal template. The disadvantage to storing macros in standard templates such as Letter.dot, Fax.dot, or Memo.dot occurs when you plan to send the document to someone who does not have access to these templates.

ADVANTAGES AND DISADVANTAGES OF STORING MACROS IN GLOBAL TEMPLATES

Many firms create read-only templates that can either be attached to the document manually or loaded automatically upon starting the application. Templates can be attached or loaded as an add-in by choosing Tools, Templates And Add-Ins. This method is shown in Figure 21.1.

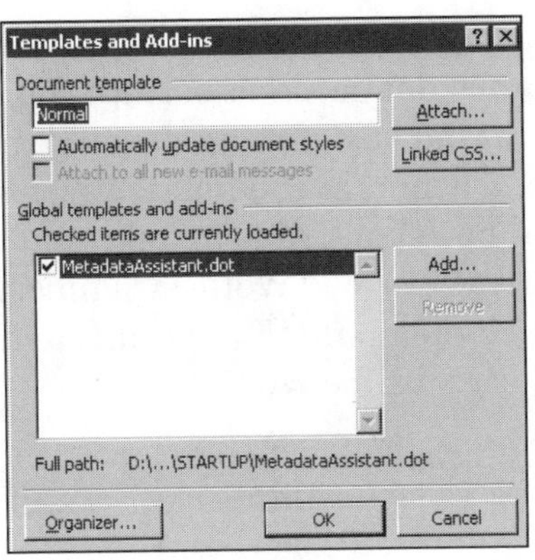

FIGURE 21.1

You can set up global templates via the Templates And Add-Ins dialog box.

Loading a template makes it available as a global template, which allows access to all items stored in the template. Once the template or add-in is loaded, it remains available only while that session of Word is active. If you quit and then restart Word, the template or add-in is not automatically loaded and you'll have to manually add the global template again.

If this sounds like too much work, as an alternative, you can create a template and save it in your Startup folder. This instructs Word to load the template each time the program is started. As with the Normal template, this means that the macro will always be available to you—but it also means that a system with limited resources may run out of memory if you have a lot of items stored in the Startup folder. If system resources are an issue, you may want to add and unload global templates as you need them.

An advantage to storing templates in the Startup folder is that they cannot be edited directly. A good rule is to set protection as read-only on any firmwide global templates so users don't modify them in ways that interfere with other users' work.

Advantages and Disadvantages of Storing Macros in the Normal Template

If you choose File, New and select the blank document icon or click the New button on the Standard toolbar, by default, you get a document based on the Normal template (Normal.dot). The Normal template is so important that, if it gets deleted, Word will automatically create a new one when you restart Word.

A lot of information is stored in the Normal template: keyboard shortcuts, AutoText, toolbar configurations, and more. If you are developing applications for use by others, you should avoid modifying their Normal template. Let people use the Normal template to store their own customizations. It's much safer to create firmwide, read-only templates for enterprise solutions.

Two more reasons for not storing firm customizations in the Normal template are corruption and file size. If Normal.dot becomes corrupt and Word needs to create a new one on the fly, none of your customizations will be recreated in the newly created Normal template. Further, as the file size gets larger with the users' customizations (remember, by default, AutoText is stored in the Normal template), it will take longer and longer to load Word each time the application starts. The users will not know to complain that the Normal template is taking too long to load; instead, they will likely blame Word.

MACRO HIERARCHY

Word follows a strict hierarchy in how it accesses macros. If two macros with the same name exist, Word will look in the following locations (and in the following order) to determine which macro has priority. Whichever macro is encountered first is the one that is activated:

- Document
- Document or attached template
- Normal template
- Add-in or global templates (in alphabetical order by file name)

There is one exception to this rule. If the user has accessed the Macros dialog box (Figure 21.2) and changed the Macros In default to a specific template or add-in, then that template or add-in will take precedence over all others.

RUNNING MACROS

There are several ways in which Word accesses macros. The most common ways are from.

- The Macros dialog box (Tools, Macro, Macros)
- A menu or toolbar assignment
- A keyboard assignment
- A MacroButton field

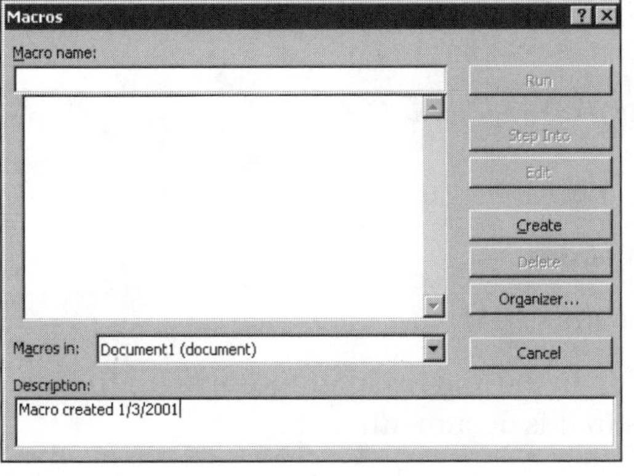

FIGURE 21.2

Macros appearing in the Macros dialog box are listed in alphabetical order.

MACROS DIALOG BOX

The Macros dialog box lists all available macros in each template or document that you have currently open or available. Macros are listed in alphabetical order. To run the macro, first select the macro from the Macro Name list and either double-click on it or click Run. Step Into runs the macro one line at a time while you control when to move to the next step. Table 21.1 shows each element in the Macros dialog box and its function.

TABLE 21.1 MACRO DIALOG BOX ELEMENTS

ELEMENT	FUNCTION
Macro Name	Lists all macros in alphabetical order.
Macros In	Specifies where the macros are stored.
Description	Allows the user to enter text comments. If a macro is recorded, the user name and date of the macro are inserted in this area by default.
Run	Runs active or selected macro.
Step Into	Steps line by line through code.
Edit	Opens the Visual Basic Editor and takes you to a specific macro.
Create	Creates a new macro with the name listed in the Macro name box. Takes you to the Visual Basic Editor interface where you would finish the macro.
Delete	Deletes the selected macro.
Organizer	Displays the Organizer dialog box with the Macro Project Items tab selected.
Cancel	Closes Macros dialog box

USE THE MACRO DIALOG BOX

1. Create a new document.
2. Name the file **First.doc**.
3. From the Tools menu, choose Macro, Macros.
4. Change the option in the Macros In drop-down list to First.doc. This is a list of all macros in this document.
5. Change Macros In to Word Commands. This is a list of all commands built into Word.

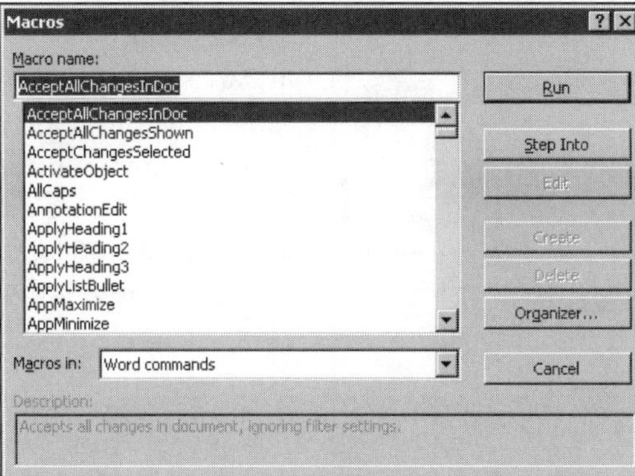

FIGURE 21.3

All of the functionality of Word is actually performed by commands. Word Commands shows a list of tasks, such as displaying a dialog box or inserting a footnote, that are a part of the command.

6. Change Macros In to Normal.dot to view a list of all macros stored in your Normal template. Figure 21.3 shows the Word built-in macros.
7. Click Cancel to close the Macros dialog box.

The keyboard shortcut for displaying the Macros dialog box is ALT+F8.

RUN A BUILT-IN WORD COMMAND

A fun first macro to run is one automatically built into Word. This command lists all the keyboard shortcuts and commands available in Word.

RUN A BUILT-IN WORD MACRO

1. From the Tools menu, choose Macro, Macros.
2. Change the Macros In setting to Word Commands.
3. Type the letter **L**.
4. Locate and select ListCommands under Macro name. The selected ListCommands macro is shown in Figure 21.4.
5. Click Run.
6. Select Current Menu And Keyboard Settings and click OK. A new document is created with assigned keyboard shortcut commands.

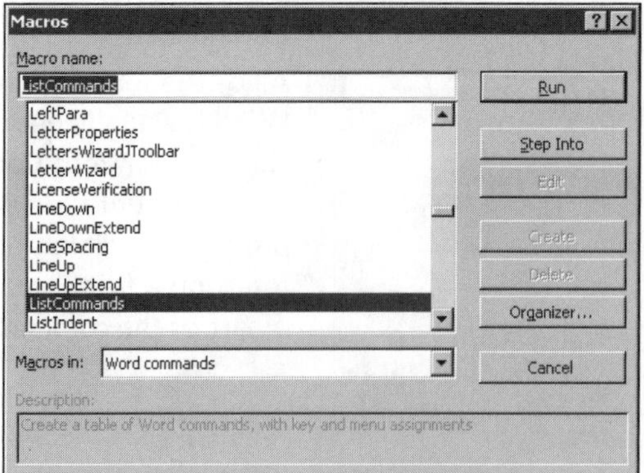

FIGURE 21.4

If you prefer keyboard shortcuts to the mouse, run the ListCommands macro and have Word create a table listing all assigned keyboard shortcut combinations.

RUN A MACRO FROM THE VISUAL BASIC TOOLBAR

Word 2002 has a toolbar named Visual Basic that was designed specifically to work with macros. You will just be using the first button, Run Macro, in this exercise. The Visual Basic toolbar is shown in Figure 21.5.

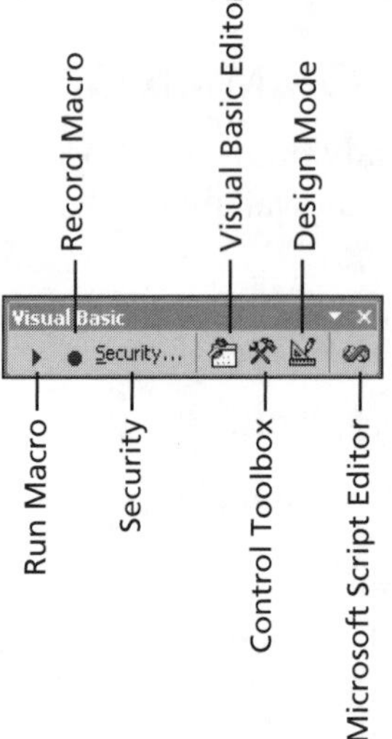

FIGURE 21.5

The Visual Basic toolbar includes shortcuts to running and working with macros.

USE THE VISUAL BASIC TOOLBAR

1. From the View menu, choose Toolbars, and turn on the Visual Basic toolbar (or alternate-click on any toolbar and select Visual Basic).
2. Click the first button on the toolbar, Run Macro, to open the Macros dialog box.
3. Close the Macros dialog box.
4. Turn off the Visual Basic toolbar.

RECORDING MACROS

Word, Excel, and PowerPoint have a built-in Macro Recorder feature that makes creating macros, or at least getting started, relatively easy. Outlook and Access do not include a Macro Recorder.

The Macro Recorder acts like a video recorder, making a record of each action that you perform in the application. Each line of macro code is like a frame in a movie. Once the Macro Recorder is turned off, the macro can be run (or replayed) either line by line or as a whole, as often as you like.

Recording is often sufficient for creating everyday macros. For example, you can record a macro that will update fields and insert text automatically when a new file is created. You might also record macros that run through a series of text replacements and other cleanup tasks when working with converted documents.

WHAT THE MACRO RECORDER IS GOOD FOR

The Macro Recorder is an excellent tool to get you started writing macros. If you can perform an action, the recorder will keep track of that action and allow you to play it back when you're ready.

WHAT THE MACRO RECORDER IS NOT GOOD FOR

The Macro Recorder is not designed for creating advanced or complex macros. It's great for some uses, but it's also important to understand the downside to using the tool.

Many developers frown on using the Macro Recorder for writing code because it records a lot of unnecessary lines of code, which often results in messy, slow, and inelegant macros. Often what could be a single line of code will instead end up having 25 lines. Often VBA developers will edit the macro recorded code to remove unnecessary code.

In addition, some tasks simply can't be recorded. If you want the macro to offer the user a range of choices, for example, or display a message box to tell the user about something, you'll have to dig in and start writing code (or borrowing it from other macros). The Macro Recorder should not be relied upon for macros you plan to distribute for general use without a good deal of editing.

USING THE MACRO RECORDER

To open the Record Macro dialog box, from the Tools menu, choose Macro, then Record New Macro. Alternatively, you can double-click the REC button on the status bar.

The Record Macro dialog box provides a place to name the macro (no spaces), assign the macro to a keyboard shortcut or toolbar button, specify where the macro should be stored, and enter any descriptive text about the macro. This comment area is a great way to provide minimal documentation about what each macro does.

The Record Macro dialog box is shown in Figure 21.6.

STEPS FOR RECORDING MACROS

1. Open the Record Macro dialog box.
2. Name the macro.
3. Assign the macro to a toolbar or keyboard shortcut, if desired.
4. Choose which template or document to store the macro in.
5. Perform the steps required for the task.
6. Click the Stop Recording button on the Stop Recording toolbar, which appears on your screen when you start using the Macro Recorder.

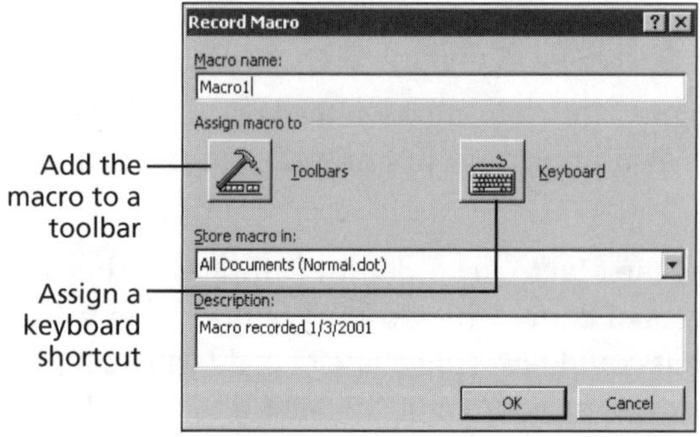

FIGURE 21.6

When naming the macro, remember that macros are listed in alphabetical order once created.

RULES FOR NAMING MACROS

The following rules govern naming a macro:

- The first character must be a letter.
- The name may not include a period, @, &, $, #, or an exclamation point (!).
- The name cannot exceed 255 characters in length.
- The name cannot contain any spaces.

If you don't specify a name, Microsoft will create a name for you while you are recording. The default name is Macro1, Macro2, Macro3, and so on. This technique is fine unless you need to find a specific macro in a hurry but have named your macros Macro1 through Macro99 without any comment or description. It's advisable to use descriptive names for your macros.

RECORD A MACRO

1. Create a new document and name it **Recording Practice**.
2. Double-click the REC button on the status bar to start the Macro Recorder.
3. Type **AddFormatForMemo** as the macro name.
4. Store the macro in Recording Practice.doc.
5. Add a Description for the macro.
6. Click OK.
7. Now that the Macro Recorder is running, from the Insert menu, choose Date And Time, and insert a date format.
8. Press Enter three times and type your name.
9. Press Enter again and type your company or firm name.
10. Click the Stop Recording button shown in Figure 21.7.

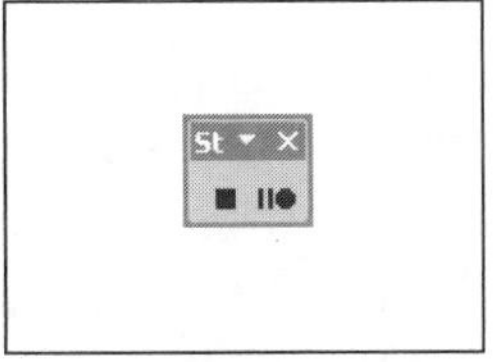

FIGURE 21.7

The Stop Recording button may be a bit difficult to locate—the toolbar is much smaller than most and floats within the document window by default.

NOTE

When you record a macro, Word displays a Stop Recording toolbar on the screen. This toolbar has special buttons that allow you to stop and pause recording. If you accidentally close the Stop Recording toolbar, you can get it back by alternate-clicking any toolbar and selecting the Stop Recording toolbar from the list.

Even if the Stop Recording toolbar is closed while you are recording a macro, the Macro Recorder will still continue to record everything that you do until it is turned off. You can turn it off without the toolbar by double-clicking the REC button on the status bar.

RUN THE RECORDED MACRO

You've just recorded a macro that can be replayed as often as you like—so long as you're in this document.

RUN A MACRO

1. Select and delete all text in the document you just created (press Ctrl+A, then press the Delete key).
2. Choose Tools, Macro, Macros.
3. If necessary, change Macros In to Recording Practice.doc.
4. Select the macro AddFormatForMemo and click Run.

THINGS TO REMEMBER ABOUT THE MACRO RECORDER

- You cannot use your mouse to select text because the Macro Recorder changes your mouse pointer to a pointer with an arrow and cassette tape next to it. This effectively prevents you from clicking on anything or using the mouse to select text. If you must select text when recording a macro, position your insertion point where the text selection needs to start, and then use the left-, right-, up-, and down-arrow in conjunction with the Shift key to select text.
- Not everything can be recorded. You cannot record the action of copying styles with the Organizer or, more simply, the task of choosing File, Open without actually opening a file.
- Each recordable step you perform will be recorded. So work carefully—all your mistakes will also be recorded. If you do make a mistake, it may be better to start over rather than undoing the mistake and continuing on. The code that results from a correction may be difficult to decipher.

- The recorded code can be changed manually. Portions may be deleted or added.
- When the macro is recording, the Stop Recording toolbar will be visible and the mouse pointer will look like it has a miniature cassette next to it.
- To stop recording the macro, click the Stop Recording button, which looks like a blue square. To pause recording, click the Pause Recording button.
- Clicking the "X" on the macro toolbar will not stop the macro from recording. Instead, the macro continues recording but the toolbar disappears. To redisplay the Stop Recording toolbar, from the View menu, choose Toolbars, then Stop Recording. You can also turn off the Macro Recorder by double-clicking the REC button located on Word's status bar. You can easily determine if the Macro Recorder is still running because the letters REC on the status bar appear in black.

DELETING UNWANTED MACROS

It's a good idea to occasionally do a bit of housecleaning to get rid of unwanted or obsolete macros. To delete a macro, open the Macros dialog box, select the macro to be deleted, and then click the Delete button.

SEEING WHAT THE MACRO RECORDER RECORDS

Now that you know how to use the Macro Recorder, it's time to take a quick look at what it does for you behind the scenes.

RECORD AND VIEW A MACRO

1. Double-click the REC button on the status bar.
2. Name the macro **TestMacro** and store it in the Normal template.
3. Click OK to start the Macro Recorder.
4. From the Insert menu, choose Symbol and select the Special Characters tab.
5. Insert a Paragraph symbol and a nonbreaking space after it.
6. Select the text and make it bold.
7. Press Enter three times to add three empty lines after the symbol.
8. Stop the Macro Recorder.
9. Choose Tools, Macro, Macros to open the Macros dialog box.

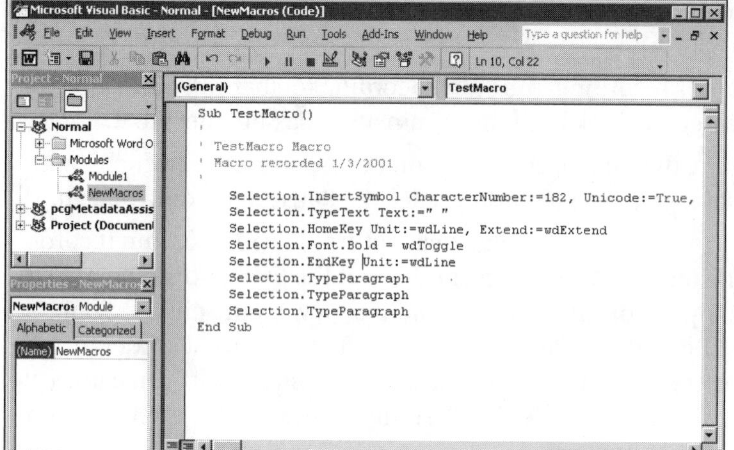

FIGURE 21.8

The Visual Basic Editor is where all macro code can be viewed and edited.

10. Select TestMacro and click Edit. The Visual Basic Editor, shown in Figure 21.8, will open to show the TestMacro code.
11. From the File menu, choose Close And Return To Microsoft Word to close the Visual Basic Editor, or use the keyboard shortcut Alt+Q.

VISUAL BASIC EDITOR

When you create a macro, the code for that macro is stored in a VBA project within the Visual Basic Integrated Development Environment (VB IDE). To modify the code, you must open the project in the Visual Basic Editor (VBE).

NOTE

The VB IDE is a separate application that will show up as a new application in the Windows Taskbar.

ELEMENTS OF THE VBE WINDOW

The VBE window is made up of three smaller windows:

- The Project Explorer window
- The Properties window
- The Code window

The Visual Basic Editor also contains other items, including a menu bar and toolbars, a Procedures list, and an Object list.

The Project, Properties, and other windows can be moved to different positions within the Editor window. They can be increased or decreased in size, as needed.

Additional windows can be displayed, such as the Immediate window, which is used to debug your code. Figure 21.9 shows the components of the Visual Basic Editor.

PROJECT WINDOW

The Project window contains a list of all open or loaded projects. This includes all projects that are stored in the Startup folder, as well as Normal.dot. The elements of a project could include some or all of the following: Microsoft Word objects, references, user forms, modules, and class modules.

PROPERTIES WINDOW

The Properties window lets you change the properties associated with the selected object. For example, if a macro is selected, the Properties window displays its name. If a form or other object were selected, additional properties would be listed.

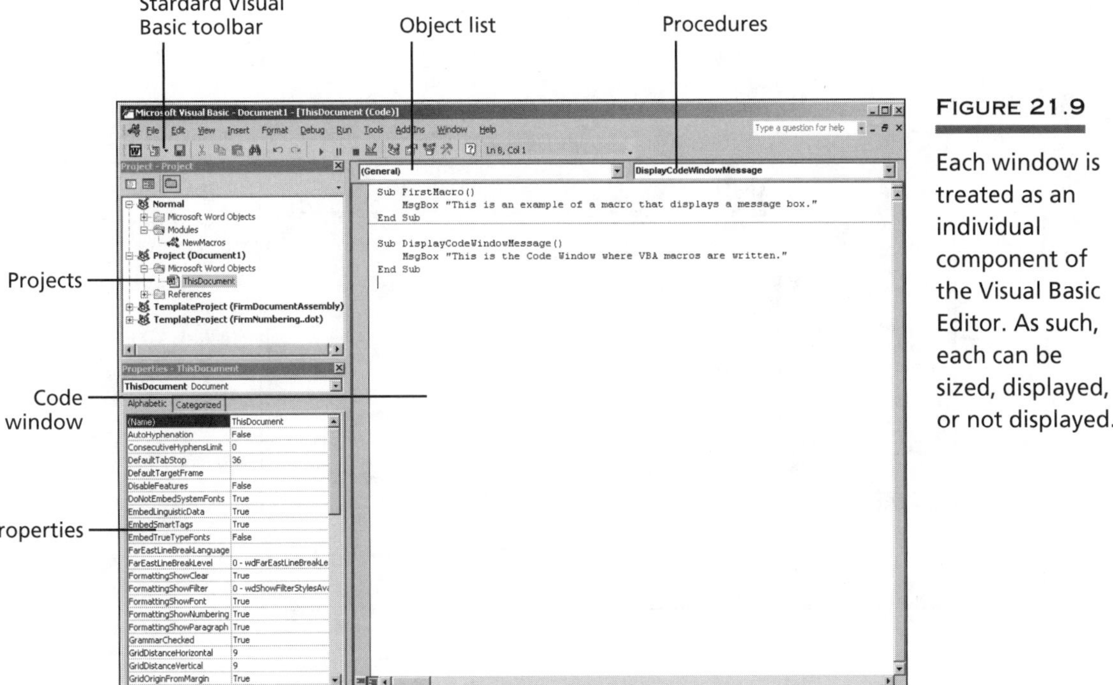

FIGURE 21.9

Each window is treated as an individual component of the Visual Basic Editor. As such, each can be sized, displayed, or not displayed.

The Properties window contains a drop-down list that you can use to switch between objects when a component of the project has multiple objects that can be selected. When the drop-down list is shown, all objects on the form are listed and you can quickly switch to show the properties for each.

CODE WINDOW

The Code window displays code that is stored for the object selected in the Project window. Code previously recorded by the Macro Recorder will appear when its project (Normal.dot) is selected. Figure 21.10 shows code in the Code window of the Visual Basic Editor.

WRITING YOUR OWN CODE

Using the Macro Recorder is a great way to get started. However, you can also create your own macros without the recorder—or use the recorder to record certain portions of a macro then insert them into your custom macro.

To write a new macro, press Alt+F8 or, from the Tools menu, choose Macro, Macros. Choose the location where you would like your macro stored, type in a name for your macro, and then click Create.

The Visual Basic Editor will automatically open up with your new blank macro, ready and waiting for you to enter your code.

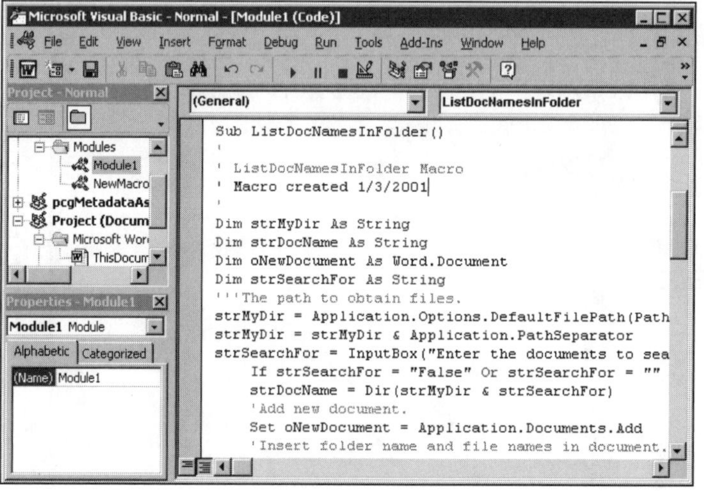

FIGURE 21.10

VBA code ready for editing.

WRITE A MACRO

1. Create a new document.
2. From the Tools menu, choose Macro, Macros.
3. Name the macro **SayHello** (no spaces) and click Create. The Visual Basic Editor opens and the beginning, end, and a comment have been entered for you.
4. After the last comment, type **MsgBox "Hello"**— but make sure you put it before End Sub.

   The macro should look similar to the following:

   ```
   Sub SayHello()

   ' SayHello Macro

   ' Macro created 5/2/2001 by Jane Attorney

   MsgBox "Hello"

   End Sub
   ```
5. Click within the macro and press F5 to run it. A message box with the word "Hello" appears along with an OK button.
6. Click OK, or the (X) Close button in the upper-right corner of the message box, to close it.
7. From the File menu, choose Close And Return To Microsoft Word.

MACRO SECURITY

It seems that as long as there are macros, there will be Word macro viruses. Broadly defined, macro viruses work like conventional computer viruses, but take advantage of Word's structure to replicate and trigger when certain events occur. Many macro viruses are harmless nuisances, but others can damage your sensitive and critical documents. Microsoft and others have responded to the need for macro virus security in Word. In Word 2002, there is a feature built into Word that will help protect you from macro viruses.

While the security in Word 2002 against macro viruses is impressive, it isn't a substitute for good antivirus software. If you haven't already done so, purchase and install a well-known antivirus software package and keep it up to date.

To set security levels for macros, from the Tools menu, choose Macro, then select Security. Select the Security Level tab to see the three options available: High, Medium, and Low, as shown in Figure 21.11. The setting you choose depends on how much protection you desire. For more information on macro protection in Word, click in the Ask A Question box in the upper-right corner of the Word window and type **Security levels in Word** or **Protection from documents that might contain viruses**, and press Enter.

Here is a brief description of what the security levels will do for you:

- **High**. The only macros that will run are those that have a digital certificate (just like the ones you may have seen warnings for while Web-browsing) from a trusted source. Other macros are automatically disabled. This setting is the default in Word 2002.
- **Medium**. Whenever Word encounters a macro that does not have a digital certificate from a trusted source, you will receive a warning and be presented with a choice to enable or disable macros.
- **Low**. All macros are enabled.

For more information on macro viruses and on document corruption and its causes, see Chapter 20, "Document Forensics."

COMMON LEGAL MACROS

Now that you understand some of the fundamentals about Visual Basic for Applications, you can combine everything you learned so far in this chapter to create useful macros for your firm.

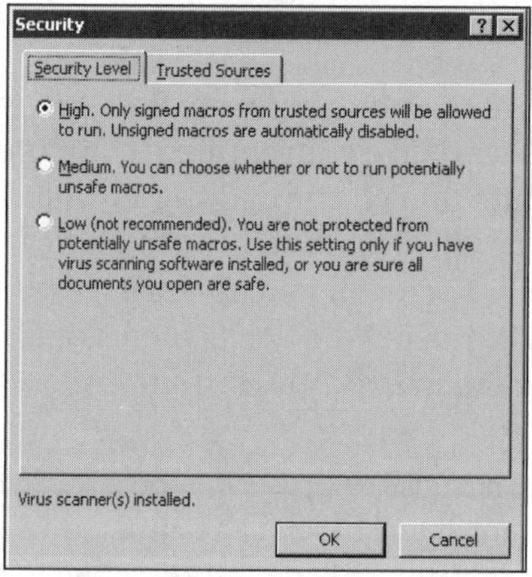

FIGURE 21.11

As a general rule, law firms should not select Low security. This leaves the document vulnerable for becoming infected with a virus.

FULL DOCUMENT PATH ON TITLE BAR

One of the first things that many students in our Introduction to VBA class want to know is how to put the name of the document in the Word title bar.

Write this code and save it in Normal.dot to add this functionality to Word.

```
Sub FileSaveandDisplayPathInTitle()
   With ActiveDocument
      .Save
      .ActiveWindow.Caption = .Path & "\" & .Name
   End With
End Sub
```

NOTE

You'll find this macro and others from this chapter on the accompanying CD-ROM.

LIST ALL WORD DOCUMENTS IN A FOLDER

To create a new document that lists all Word files in a specific folder location, recreate and run the following macro. This macro will list all the Word files in the C:\My Documents folder.

```
Sub ListDocNamesInFolder()
    Dim strMyDir As String
    Dim strDocName As String
    Dim oNewDocument As Word.Document
    Dim strSearchFor As String
        ' The path to obtain files.
    strMyDir = Application.Options.DefaultFilePath(Path:=wdDocumentsPath)
    strMyDir = strMyDir & Application.PathSeparator
    strSearchFor = InputBox("Enter the documents to search for: ", ➥
"Search For", "*.DOC")
        If strSearchFor = "False" Or strSearchFor = "" Then Exit Sub
        strDocName = Dir(strMyDir & strSearchFor)
    ' Add new document.
    Set oNewDocument = Application.Documents.Add
```

```
' Insert folder name  and file names in document.

oNewDocument.Range.InsertAfter strSearchFor & " Documents in ➥
folder " & strMyDir & vbCr & vbCr

    Do While strDocName <> ""

     ' Insert filename in document.

     oNewDocument.Range.InsertAfter strDocName & vbCr

     ' Get next file name.

     strDocName = Dir()

    Loop

End Sub
```

HOW AUTOMATION HELPS

A number of macro packages on the market automate the process of creating common legal documents. Payne Consulting Group has a package called the Forms Assistant for this purpose.

If you give a law firm Word just as it comes out of the box, it's going to take a long time to create documents, especially complex documents such as pleadings or briefs. Also, without some guidelines, each person's documents will be very different. One person may prefer Times New Roman, 10 point; another person may use Courier New, 12 point, for all their documents. If you file documents electronically with the courts, you'll want to make sure that these documents are formatted according to court guidelines and one way to do that is to create a template for documents where users just fill in blanks to insert information.

Automating firm documents also helps with some of the trickier elements such as inserting firm letterhead electronically or looking up bar numbers for signature blocks. Your templates can be integrated with address books or desktop faxing software.

If you plan well and create or purchase a third-party macro package, training time is reduced—users just fill in the blanks and click OK—court rules and firm standards are preserved and using Word will be much easier.

INSTALLING WORD WITHOUT VBA

Many people use Word successfully every day without knowing that VBA even exists. The majority learn about macros for the first time when they receive a macro virus through e-mail or from downloading a file from the Internet. For these individuals, the ability to install Word without VBA is of value.

In Word 2002, the application can be installed without the VBA component. The default configuration is to include VBA when Word and Office are installed.

REMOVING VBA SUPPORT

VBA can be removed during the initial setup, through an installation script, or in Maintenance Mode from Add/Remove Programs in the Control Panel. The Visual Basic for Applications component is under the Office Shared Features category. Figure 21.12 shows the installation option for VBA.

Be careful! If VBA is not installed, some features and functionality of the software will be unavailable. In fact, Microsoft Access will be uninstalled if you choose to remove VBA and the following message box warning will display (Figure 21.13).

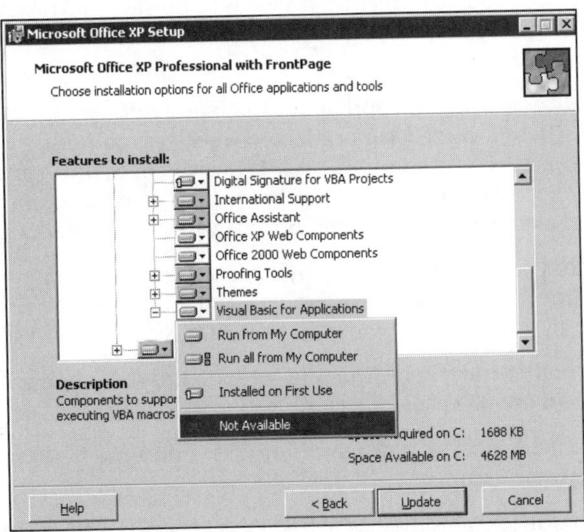

FIGURE 21.12

Word 2002 allows you to choose whether or not to install VBA support.

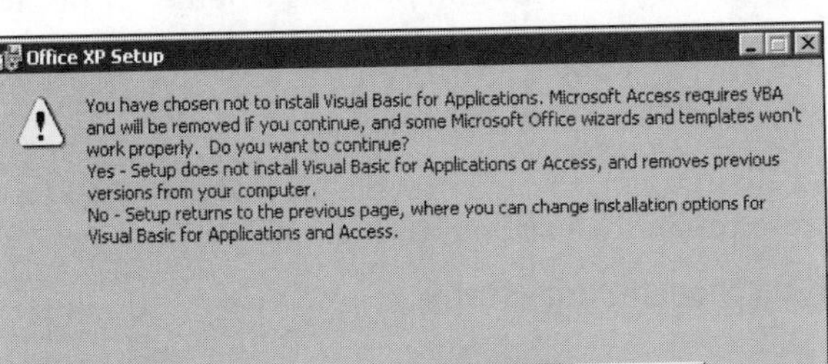

FIGURE 21.13

Many features, templates, and applications require VBA to run correctly, so give considerable thought before removing or not installing the component.

FEATURES DISABLED WITHOUT VBA

Commands that require VBA such as Tools, Macro, Record New Macros still appear in the menu but when chosen, display an alert box stating that the feature is unavailable. If you attempt to open a file that contains a macro, a different alert box opens with information that macros in this application have been disabled and you receive a prompt to either open the file as read-only without any macros, or respond No to not open the file.

NOTE

ADO, DAO, MAPI, ODBC, and OLEDB are not affected when VBA is removed.

Table 21.2 lists many of the features affected when VBA support is not installed.

TABLE 21.2 WORD FEATURES AFFECTED WHEN VBA SUPPORT IS NOT INSTALLED

FEATURE	EFFECT
Add-Ins	Third-party add-ins do not function if VBA is not installed. This can affect the document management system, template and macro packages, and other add-ins used by the firm.
Commands	Several menu commands will appear on the menu but, when chosen, display an alert box. These include Macros, Record New Macro, Visual Basic Editor (or pressing the keyboard shortcut Alt+F11), Web Tools, and Control Toolbox. If a menu command is controlled by a macro such as a document management system taking over File, Open, or File, Save As, this functionality is disabled.
Documents	Documents that contain macros display a dialog box when opened stating that macro language support has been disabled and with the choice to open the file as read-only, and without the macros. Active X controls are disabled as well.
Form fields with Macros attached	Macros attached to form fields that are intended to run when entering or exiting the field are disabled.
Macro button	MacroButton fields such as those used for Click And Type fields in templates and documents are disabled.
Normal.dot	If the Normal.dot contains macros, when Word starts, an alert displays stating that Normal.dot contains macros and prompts whether or not to open a copy of the file. If Yes is clicked, the file and all attributes, except for macros, open. Since a copy is being opened, when Word is closed, a message opens asking if you want to save the file with a different name. If No is clicked when trying to open Normal.dot, a message box displays stating that Word cannot open the existing Normal file.
Object model	The Word Object Model is unavailable.

TABLE 21.2 WORD FEATURES AFFECTED WHEN VBA SUPPORT IS NOT INSTALLED (CONTINUED)

FEATURE	AFFECT
Templates	Many templates contain VBA so, if your firm has developed automated letter, memo, fax, or pleading templates that contain automation, these will likely be unavailable without VBA.
Wizards	Many wizards will not function without VBA. Included are any third-party products that help to build documents and templates, and built-in wizards that come with Word. Included in this list are Fax Wizard, Web Page, Flyer, Letter, Postcard, Envelope, Mailing Label, Memo, Resume, Agenda, Batch Conversion, Calendar, and Pleading.

Removing macro language support doesn't affect disk space considerably. A typical installation without VBA is 229MB. When VBA and VBA help are installed, the difference is only 15MB (243MB).

SUMMARY

Chapter 21 focuses on the Word's macro language, Visual Basic for Application (VBA). The chapter provides an overview of how to use VBA and the different components of the macro languages. It provides information on where macros are stored, as well as useful macros, tips, and tricks for getting started writing and editing your own code. Finally, the chapter covers what happens when VBA is removed or not installed.

Because Microsoft Word built so much functionality into the application, you won't need macros for most things. However, there are times when having a macro to perform specific tasks makes processes much easier.

TROUBLESHOOTING VBA

Is there any VBA help in Word?

To access VBA help, switch to the Visual Basic Editor (Alt+F11). Click in the code window and press F1. If you have a question on a specific command in VBA, first type and then select the command and press F1. For example, to obtain help on InputBox, type the command **InputBox** in the code window, select the text, and then press F1.

Why isn't the Create button available when I type the name for my new macro in the Macros dialog box?

Macro names cannot contain any spaces, a period, @, &, $, #, or an exclamation point (!). Also, the name cannot exceed 255 characters and the first character must be a letter.

What is happening when I type something in the code window and a drop-down list appears?

When VBA recognizes something that is being typed, it tries to help you by letting you know what other VBA commands can be used with the one that you just entered. For example, if you type ActiveDocument. (with a period following the word), VBA tries to locate commands for you to help finish the statement. Accept the suggestion by pressing the Tab key. If you prefer seeing all of the objects, properties, and methods at once, you can click the Object Browser button.

Where can I learn more about VBA?

Payne Consulting Group has a series of classes on Visual Basic for Applications. A great class for beginner programmers is the three-day Introduction to Word VBA course. This class teaches the basics and gives you hands-on projects that are useful immediately within your firm. Watch for a book on VBA from Payne Consulting Group as well.

Other resources include the Microsoft Office Developer Web site at www.microsoft.com/office/developer/.

How long will it take for me to become an expert at VBA?

There is no hard and fast rule on how long it will take to be a proficient or expert programmer. VBA is a powerful programming language and you won't learn to become a good programmer overnight, in a week, a month, perhaps even a year. No matter what your experience, you need to practice and continually take on new programming challenges to become a proficient developer. If you use VBA every day for six months, you will probably become a decent intermediate developer.

Will macros that I created in Word 2000 work in Word 2002?

Most macros between these versions should work fine.

Why are some features such as Record New Macro and MacroButton fields not functioning properly?

In Word 2002, VBA can be removed or not installed, which causes some features to be unavailable.

APPENDIX A

RESOURCES

IN THIS APPENDIX

- Additional resources
- Web sites
- Available services

WEB SITES

A number of excellent Web sites stand ready to provide help for using Word. Many of these offer support, tips, and tricks at no cost.

WWW.MICROSOFT.COM

This Web site offers help and information on all Microsoft products. One of the most useful resources on the site is the searchable Microsoft Knowledge Base (Figure A.1), which contains literally thousands of articles on known problems and workarounds with the product. To access the Knowledge Base, go to Microsoft.com and click Support, Knowledge Base.

Also on the Microsoft Web site you will find a list of frequently asked questions and reliable answers, a number of articles and case studies for different products, and the *Microsoft Word Legal User's Guide*. Currently the location for this guide is http://officeupdate.microsoft.com/2000/articles/wdlegaluserguide.htm. Article links on the Web site often get moved around, however. If you have difficulty locating a resource, try searching for it by typing **Legal User** as the search criterion.

WWW.PAYNECONSULTING.COM

The Payne Web site provides tips, tricks, articles, and free macros for working with software. The Web site also provides links to other Web pages developed by industry experts.

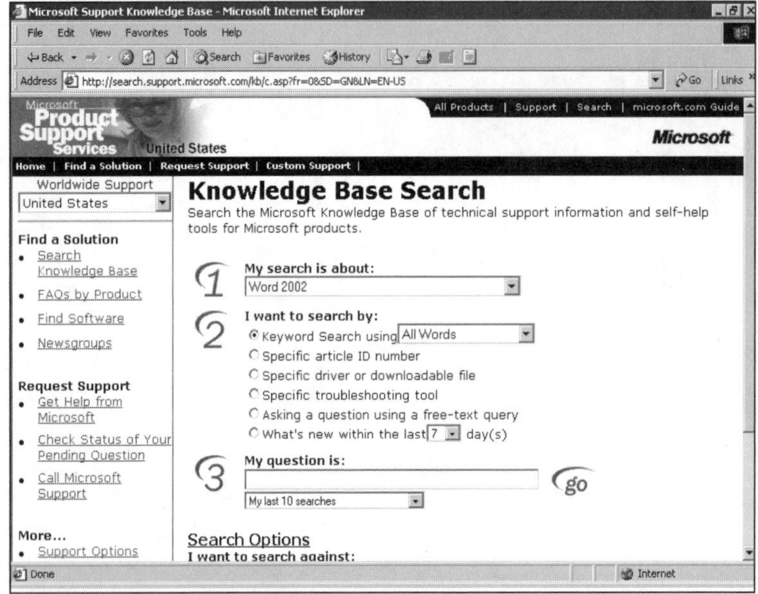

FIGURE A.1

Search through new and archived articles in the Microsoft Knowledge Base.

WWW.MICROSYSTEMS.COM

Microsystems is best known for being document conversion specialists, however they have added tips, tricks, and expert advice to their Web site. For more information visit the company Web site at www.microsystems.com.

WWW.EDITORIUM.COM

The Editorium Web site offers Word add-ins, a useful newsletter, and tools for helping to work successfully with Microsoft Word. Some of the tools available for purchase are an Editor's ToolKit; File Cleaner, which cleans up multiple spaces; multiple returns; unnecessary tabs; improperly typed ellipses; and more.

WWW.ALKI.COM

Alki Software has been providing Word tools and assistance for 10 years. It offers proofing tools (for a fee) that integrate with and expand Word's capabilities. Proofing tools include a legal and medical dictionary.

WWW.WOPR (WOODY'S OFFICE PORTAL)

Woody Leonard's Web site includes a support center, an Ask Woody section, as well as software downloads. Sign up for Woody's Office Watch, an excellent newsletter that is currently distributed free through e-mail. The information is presented in a straightforward, no holds barred approach; always with a sense of humor.

WWW.PEERTOPEER.ORG (LAWNET)

Corporate legal departments and law firms have issues regarding technology that are different from those encountered by general businesses. Even in those cases in which common software is used, the practical application of the software can vary markedly. LawNet provides a forum—the only one of its kind—for those involved in technology for corporate legal departments and law firms to share experiences and gain knowledge from each other.

LawNet generally, and the Microsoft Special Interest Group specifically, provides many resources to LawNet members (law firms and legal departments) who utilize Microsoft's product offerings.

NEWSGROUPS

The Microsoft newsgroups are peer-to-peer areas where questions and answers are posted and where information is exchanged among members of the technical community. A group of individuals who are Microsoft Most Valuable Professional (MVP) award recipients volunteer and monitor the newsgroup postings, offering assistance as often as possible.

The newsgroups are an excellent place to get an answer fast, as well as a place to lurk and learn how to master the software.

Before you can access the newsgroups, you will need a newsreader that gives you the ability to read and post messages. If you do not have a newsreader installed on your computer, you may want to consider downloading one from www.forteinc.com.

There are currently 20 newsgroups devoted to using Microsoft Word, including Invalid Page Faults and Application Errors, Mail Merge, and Programming with Visual Basic for Applications. For a list and access to these newsgroups, visit Microsoft.com and search for the keyword Newsgroup.

TRAINING

Although reading a book often provides an answer, a training class geared to what you need to learn and to your current level of proficiency can accelerate the process. Several companies specialize in providing training to the legal industry, and many more provide excellent classes on using and mastering Microsoft Word. This section cannot list all training companies, but here are some of the companies that provide training services to law firms and legal corporate counsel.

PAYNE CONSULTING GROUP

Part of our job at Payne Consulting Group is to work with you and your firm to find just the right amount and method of training required. Learning may occur in the form of classroom instruction, self-study, e-learning, or blended learning, where different methods are combined. Whichever method you choose, Payne can assist in taking the "pain" out of the learning experience.

Training is available for all levels—from the beginner who just wants to get started to the IT professional who needs to know the software inside and out. We also offer Word VBA training for beginners through expert level programmers. The next sections list two of our most popular offerings.

MASTER SERIES FOR IT PROFESSIONALS

This intensive class is the best way to prepare for training or supporting Microsoft Word. Master Series training is available for Word 2002, 2000, or 97. The class takes five days and can be held at our facilities or yours.

MASTER SERIES FOR WORD PROCESSORS

The fact is, word processing staff have one of the toughest jobs in a law firm. They receive dirty, and often corrupt, documents and are required to turn them around and fix any problems quickly. Not being able to do so can cause missed filing deadlines and a lot of frustration for everyone. This three-day class is designed for document production specialists and digs deep into the DNA of the document.

For more information on Payne training services, visit www.payne consulting.com or call 1-888-GOPAYNE.

COMPUTER TRAINING PROFESSIONALS

Computer Training Professionals (CT Pros) located in Gaithersburg, Maryland, specializes in software training, help desk, and floor support for the legal environment in the greater Washington, D.C., area. For information on the company and services, e-mail ctpros@ureach.com.

COMPUWORKS SYSTEMS

For 11 years, CompuWorks has provided excellent training and support services to their Northeastern clientele, which includes New England's legal, government, financial, and high-tech communities. In addition to classroom instruction, CompuWorks offers E-Learning; contact CompuWorks at www.compuworks.com.

HALPERN & HOLT

Halpern & Holt has been providing training to law firms, businesses, and governmental organizations in the San Francisco Bay Area for over fourteen years. Visit the company Web site at www.halpernandholt.com.

KING, HERPEL AND ASSOCIATES

King, Herpel and Associates, located in Los Angeles, provides software training and support services for the legal and corporate environment and has been doing so since 1988. Visit the company Web site at www.king-herpel.com.

KRAFT KENNEDY & LESSER

Kraft Kennedy & Lesser, based in New York, Texas, and California, offer training, consulting, network design and management, and system support to law firms. For more information, visit the company Web site at www.kkl.com.

MAROE TECHNOLOGY

Jim Maroe has been training in the legal industry for years. He now heads a company of his own that specializes in software training and support for law firms. Visit the company Web site at www.maroe.com/.

MICROLAW

Ross Kodner and the folks at MicroLaw specialize in offering training and consulting services to lawyers. Many of their sessions are CLE-approved, and their Web site contains many technical papers and presentations that are useful for everyone. Visit the company at www.microlaw.com.

PERFECT ACCESS SPEER

The staff of Perfect Access Speer have been providing training to law firms and financial institutions for years. They offer blended learning solutions, onsite training, and more. The company also offers briefings on legal software. Visit the company Web site at www.perfectaccess.com.

PROMPT CONSULTING

PROMPT Consulting, based in San Francisco, offers customized computer training and consulting to law firms and corporations. Visit the company Web site at www.promptconsulting.com.

TIGER INFORMATION SYSTEMS

Tiger Information Systems provides a complete range of consulting, IT staffing, desktop staffing, training, development, and assessment products and services. Visit the company Web site at www.tigerinfo.com/.

TRAVELING COACHES

Traveling Coaches is located in Dallas, Texas, and offers training, support, and consulting and specializes in working with the legal industry. Visit the company at www.travelingcoaches.com.

CERTIFICATION

The MOUS (Microsoft Office User Specialist) program allows those with proficient and expert knowledge of Microsoft Office products to obtain certification. The tests are hands-on—you must demonstrate your working knowledge of the product. Tests are offered at many computer stores, technical colleges, and universities. For more information, visit www.microsoft.com/trainingandservices.

MACROS

Word out of the box isn't always the best solution. Sometimes it's better to provide a customized and automated approach to creating complex and firm-standard documents. Imagine being able to create a complex agreement with a cover page, table of contents, schedules, exhibits, and appendices in a matter of seconds. This is just an example of how macro automation can help raise the level of your firm's productivity.

PAYNE LEGAL TOOLS

To simplify often complex tasks in Word, Payne Consulting Group offers robust products and add-ins that make using Microsoft Word and Office easier.

FORMS ASSISTANT

Our Forms Assistant automates and simplifies the process of creating new documents based on templates. The Forms Assistant includes letter, memo, fax, pleadings, agreements, and address tools, illustrated in Figures A.2 through A.4.

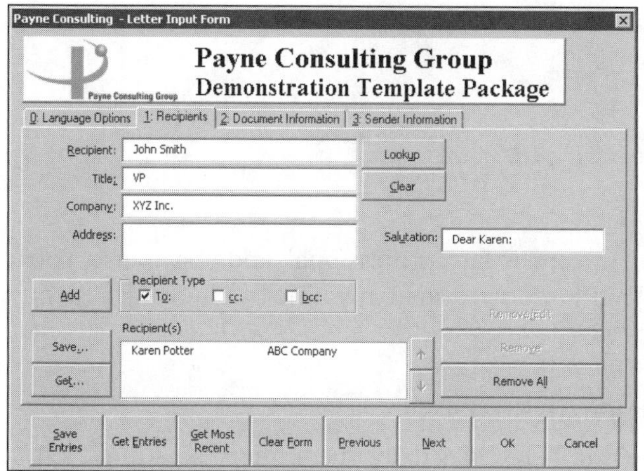

FIGURE A.2

Create a letter, fax, or memo in seconds. Include letterhead and signature options with a mouse click.

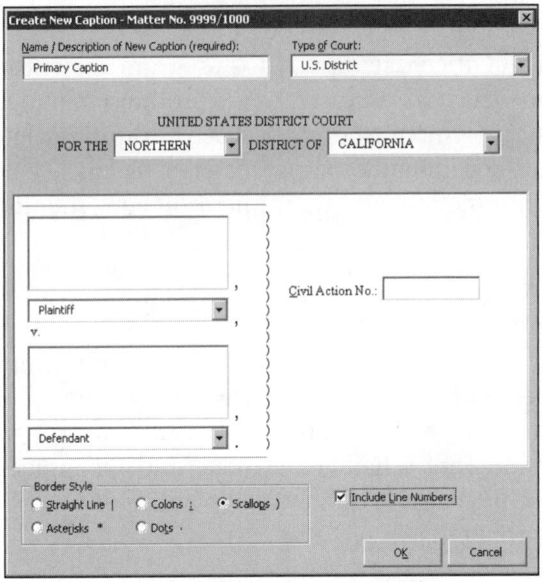

FIGURE A.3

The pleading templates include a caption bank to avoid rekeying information.

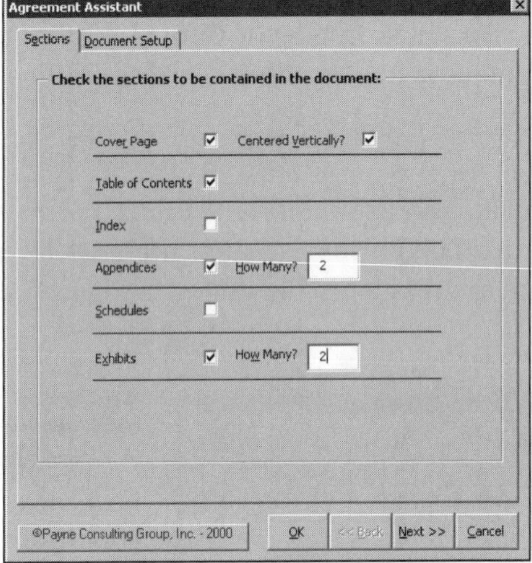

FIGURE A.4

Create and format complex, multiple-section agreements in seconds!

All macros are extremely fast, professional, and easy to use. You can reopen dialog boxes and edit information at any time by choosing a menu command that we create for you.

NUMBERING ASSISTANT

Law firms use numbered lists daily in contracts, pleadings, letters, and memos. Most firms have developed specific numbering styles for general use, as well as additional styles for each practice group. That's why we developed the legal numbering utility shown in Figure A.5, which makes applying and changing legal numbering a breeze.

We use all native Word features so you can seamlessly share documents with clients.

METADATA ASSISTANT

This product was written about on the front page of the *Wall Street Journal.* The Payne Metadata Assistant Enterprise product (Figure A.6) strips extraneous and often confidential information from Word documents including the last 10 authors, file paths where the document was saved, comments, tracked changes, and more.

For information on all Payne Consulting Group products and services, visit the company Web page at www.payneconsulting.com or send an e-mail to info@payneconsulting.com.

OTHER MACRO VENDORS

Other macro and template companies also provide excellent products. The following is a list of some of the other companies that provide quality template and macro development specifically for law firms.

- **KI Systems** (www.kisys.com)
- **Kraft Kennedy & Lesser** (www.kkl.com)

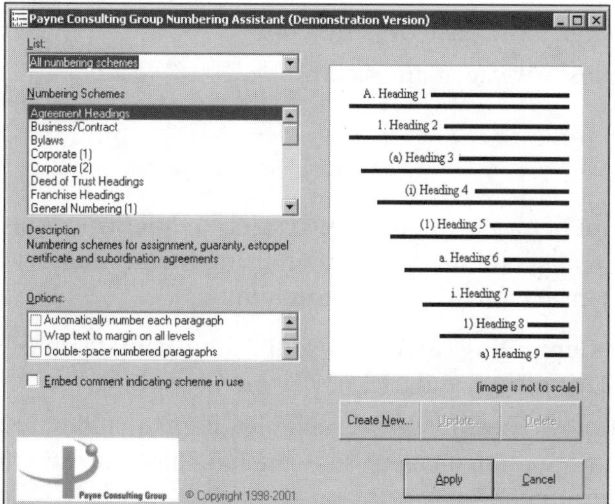

FIGURE A.5

To create robust legal numbering, use numbering linked to heading styles.

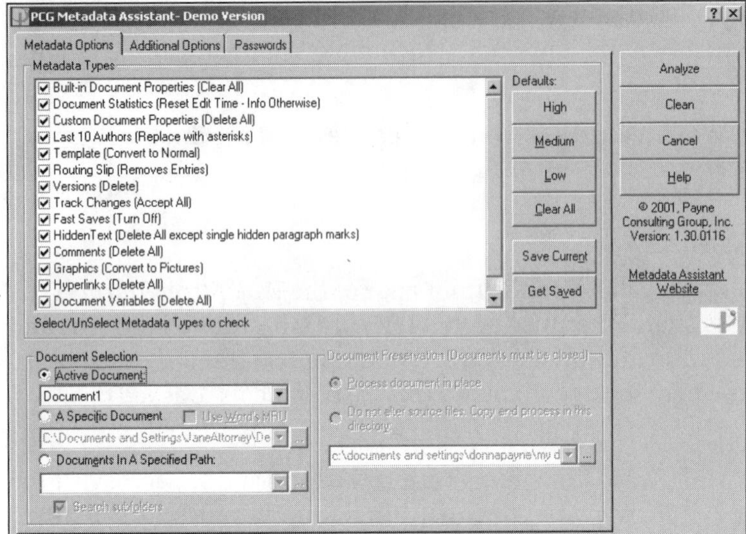

FIGURE A.6

Don't let others uncover your firm's secrets.

- **Legal MacPac** (www.legalmacpac.com)
- **SoftWise** (wrobertson@softwise.net)
- **TechLaw - iCreate** (www.techlawinc.com)

DOCUMENT CONVERSION

There are two primary companies that specialize in document conversion. Both are reputable and offer a good set of products and expertise.

- **Microsystems** (www.microsystems.com)
- **Levit & James** (www.levitjames.com)

MAGAZINES

There aren't a lot of magazines dedicated solely to Microsoft Word for law firms, but two do provide good information on using the products—along with the use of software in general in the legal community.

- **Law Office Computing** (www.jamespublishing.com) features a regular column on Microsoft tips and tricks by Payne Consulting.
- **Law Technology News** (www.lawtechnews.com) includes up-to-the-minute news and information on using software (and hardware, for that matter) in a legal environment.

APPENDIX B

Available Settings in the Options Dialog Box

Word gives you hundreds of options to control how the application works with your documents. These settings are accessed by choosing Options from the Tools menu. In fact, there are so many options in the dialog box that it takes 11 tabs to display them all. Tabs include View, General, Edit, Print, Save, User Information, Compatibility, File Locations, Track Changes, Spelling & Grammar, and Security.

This appendix is made up of tables that include each option name and description for a typical installation of Word 2002.

TABLE B.1 VIEW TAB

OPTION	DEFINITION
Startup Task Pane	Displays the New Document Task Pane when Word is opened.
Highlight	Shows any area of the document that contains highlight formatting.
Bookmarks	Displays brackets or an I-bar around bookmarked text in the document. The brackets display but do not print.
Status Bar	Shows the status bar at the bottom of the Word window. The status bar provides useful information about the document such as the current page number, section, number of pages, and position of the mouse cursor within the document.
ScreenTips	Displays a box with explanatory information above a reference. For example, toolbar buttons, footnotes, and comments include a ScreenTip when the mouse pointer is hovered over each element.
Smart Tags	New! A dotted line automatically appears beneath text to assist with certain tasks.
Animated Text	Displays animated text effects applied under the Format, Font menu.
Horizontal Scroll Bar	Displays the horizontal scroll bar above the status bar.
Vertical Scroll Bar	Displays the vertical scroll bar on the right side of the window.
Picture Placeholders	Displays the frame only of an inserted graphic in place of the actual object. This can speed up navigation through documents that contain numerous graphics.
Windows In Taskbar	Toggles the display of individual icons on the Taskbar for each open Word document. This behavior is known as *Single Document Interface* (SDI). Uncheck the option to revert to Word 97 behavior and show only one Word icon on the Taskbar and all other documents under the Window menu.
Field Codes	Displays field codes rather than results.
Field Shading:	Controls the visibility of fields in a document by shading them either all the time or when you select them, depending on the option selected (Always or When Selected)—or not at all, if you prefer.
Tab Characters	Displays nonprinting arrow characters for tabs when viewing a document onscreen.
Spaces	Displays a dot where there is a space between words or characters.

TABLE B.1 VIEW TAB (CONTINUED)

OPTION	DEFINITION
Paragraph Marks	Displays paragraph marks onscreen to reference each paragraph in the document.
Hidden Text	Displays text that is formatted as hidden. This text is marked with a nonprinting dotted underline.
Optional Hyphens	Displays an optional hyphen character when applied. The optional hyphen character does not print. It will print as a regular hyphen if the word appears at the end of a line.
All	Displays all the nonprinting formatting marks onscreen. This option is toggled on and off with the Show/Hide button.
Drawings	Displays Word objects created with the Drawing tools when working in Print Layout and Web Layout view.
Object Anchors	Displays an anchor to specify which paragraph an object is anchored to in Print Layout and Web Layout view.
Text Boundaries	Display dotted lines around the document at the margins in Print Layout and Web Layout view.
White Space Between Pages (Print View Only)	Displays the white space between the bottom on one page and the top of the next. When deselected, the area is separated by lines in the document.
Vertical Ruler (Print View Only)	Displays the vertical ruler on the left side of the window.
Wrap To Window	The text will wrap according to the zoom so that it fits horizontally in the window. This avoids needing to use the horizontal ruler. This affects Outline and Normal views only.
Draft Font	Used in Outline and Normal view to speed up screen display in documents with extensive formatting. Select a generic font and size and that font will be displayed throughout the document. Most character formatting such as bold and underline will still appear, but not font type or size. Graphics appear as empty boxes.
Style Area Width	Enter the measurement for the Style Area. This pane displays applied paragraph style names on the left side of the document window in Normal and Outline view.

TABLE B.2 GENERAL TAB

OPTION	DEFINITION
Background Repagination	Repaginates the document and page numbers automatically while you work in a document. This option cannot be disabled in Print Layout view.
Blue Background, White Text	Changes the white default background and black text to a blue background with white text. This option is used by people who enjoyed DOS screen formatting.
Provide Feedback With Sound	Plays a sound when applying certain tasks in Office.
Provide Feedback With Animation	Animates the mouse pointer when applying certain tasks in Office.
Confirm Conversion At Open	Displays a dialog box with a list of converters when opening a non-Word document.
Update Automatic Links At Open	Updates any links to other files in a document every time you open it.
Mail As Attachment	Makes the option to send the current document as an attachment available when you choose File, Send To.
Recently Used File List	Makes a list of the recently used files appear at the bottom of the File menu or in the New Document Task Pane, allowing you to open these files without going through the Open dialog box. You can include up to nine files.
Help For WordPerfect Users	Presents a WordPerfect Help dialog box when the user types WordPerfect for DOS keystroke combinations, providing the Word equivalent.
Navigation Keys For WordPerfect Users	Changes the navigation key commands Page Up, Page Down, Home, End, and Esc to function as they do in WordPerfect.
Allow Background Open Of Web Pages	Opens Web pages in the background while still working in Word.
Automatically Create Drawing Canvas When Inserting AutoShapes	Creates the drawing canvas when an object is inserted into the document. The canvas offers the ability to manipulate multiple objects at once.
Measurement Units	Allows you to choose your preferred measurement unit when working with the ruler, margins, indents and more. Select from inches, centimeters, millimeters, points, and picas.
Show Pixels For HTML Features	Directs Word to use pixels instead of the default measurement chosen in the Measurement Units option when working with HTML.

TABLE B.2 GENERAL TAB (CONTINUED)

OPTION	DEFINITION
Web Options	Opens a dialog box containing many options for displaying and viewing Web pages. Choose what Web browser will be used, where supporting files are stored, and font options.
E-Mail Options	Displays the E-Mail Options dialog box offering choices for e-mail signatures, stationery, font, and more.

TABLE B.3 EDIT TAB

OPTION	DEFINITION
Typing Replaces Selection	Typing over selected text erases the selection and replaces it with new text.
Drag-And-Drop Text Editing	Allows you to use the mouse to move and copy text by dragging and dropping.
Use The INS Key For Paste	Activates the Insert key to be used to paste items saved to the Office Clipboard.
Overtype Mode	Toggles the way newly typed text affects existing material. Word's default method for typing inserts the text where needed and moves existing material to the right. When Overtype mode is active, new material overwrites existing material and replaces it.
Picture Editor	Allows you to select which application to use to edit pictures.
Insert/Paste Pictures As	Specifies the default wrapping for inserting or pasting pictures.
Allow Accented Uppercase In French	Allows accent marks to be included with uppercase text formatted as French.
Use Smart Paragraph Selection	Makes sure that the paragraph mark is selected when you select a paragraph. This retains paragraph formatting for moved or copied paragraphs and ensures that no empty paragraph marks are left behind.
Use Ctrl+Click To Follow Hyperlink	Toggles the way hyperlinks function. Word's default is to follow hyperlinks on a simple click, but this option requires the user to press Ctrl+Click to follow the hyperlink.
When Selecting, Automatically Select Entire Word	Expands the selection to include the entire word when you start to select any part of the word with the mouse.

TABLE B.3 EDIT TAB (CONTINUED)

OPTION	DEFINITION
Prompt To Update Style	Controls the behavior of reapplied styles. If a paragraph is formatted with a style and direct formatting and you click on the style name in the Styles And Formatting Task Pane, Word 2002 defaults to reapply original formatting. With this option selected, Word behaves as it did in previous versions and offers the option to update the style.
Keep Track Of Formatting	Keeps track of formatting as it is used in the document and displays it in the Styles and Formatting Task Pane.
Mark Formatting Inconsistencies	Marks inconsistent formatting with a blue wavy underline. Alternate-clicking underlined text will display formatting options. (This option becomes available when Keep Track of Formatting is selected.)
Show Paste Options Buttons	Displays a Paste Options button when information is copied and pasted into the document. The button includes options for formatting the pasted item. Options include Keep Source Formatting, Match Destination Formatting, Keep Text Only, and Apply Style Or Formatting. Pasting items from different applications provides additional options.
Smart Cut And Paste	Word will automatically adjust spaces when cutting and pasting words and sentences (extra spaces are removed). The Settings button also offers other Smart Cut And Paste choices when working with styles, tables, and lists, as well as with PowerPoint and Excel data.
Enable Click And Type	Allows you to click anywhere in the document and start typing. Word will apply the correct formatting to make text appear at that position on the page. For example, if you click in the center of the page, Word will apply center formatting and extra spaces to insert the text at that location. Available in Print Layout and Web Layout view only.
Default Paragraph Style	Allows you to select which style should be applied when using Enable Click And Type.

Table B.4 Print Tab

Option	Definition
Draft Output	Prints the document with minimal formatting, making the print process faster.
Update Fields	Updates all fields in the document before printing.
Update Links	Updates all links in the document before printing.
Allow A-4/Letter Paper Resizing	Adjusts the page layout on the fly to print A4 documents on letter paper. The original document is not affected, just the printed version.
Background Printing	Prints the document in the background and allows you to continue working on other documents or applications.
Print PostScript Over Text	Prints PostScript code in a converted Word for the Macintosh document on top of document text instead of underneath it. An example would be a document that contains a watermark. This option has no effect if the document does not contain print codes.
Reverse Print Order	Prints the document in reverse order, beginning with the last page, so documents come out in the correct order from printers that use separate sheets of paper instead of fanfold paper.
Document Properties	Prints the document summary information stored on the Summary tab. Choose Properties from the File menu and select the Summary tab to see what information is stored and can be printed.
Field Codes	Prints field codes residing in the document rather than the field results.
Hidden Text	Prints text formatted as hidden in the document. Does not print the dotted line Word uses to indicate hidden formatting.
Drawing Objects	Directs Word to print the objects created with the Drawing toolbar. When the option is deselected, Word prints blank boxes in the document as a placeholder for the object.
Print Data Only For Forms	Prints the data contained in an online form, not the form itself.
Default Tray	Indicates the printer tray to use each time a document is printed.
Front Of The Sheet	Prints the front of the page only for those who do not have a copier or printer with a duplex option.
Back Of The Sheet	Prints the back of the page only for those who do not have a copier or printer with a duplex option.

TABLE B.5 SAVE TAB

OPTION	DEFINITION
Always Create Backup Copy	Saves the previous version each time the document is saved.
Allow Fast Saves	Speeds up saving by recording only the changes made as the document is edited. Does not perform a full save of the document.
Allow Background Saves	Saves the document in the background, which allows the user to continue working in Word.
Embed True Type Fonts	Stores the True Type fonts used to create the document with the document. This allows others who open the document and do not have the same True Type fonts to print the document as created, rather than using alternative fonts on their own machines.
Embed Characters In Use Only	Directs Word to embed only those characters of the True Type font that actually appear in the document. This option becomes active if Embed True Type Fonts is selected.
Do Not Embed Common System Fonts	Directs Word not to embed True Type fonts that are likely to be installed on another computer already—the ones that come with Word or Windows, for example. This option becomes active if Embed True Type Fonts is selected.
Prompt For Document Properties	Opens the Document Property dialog box when the document is saved for the first time. Displays a message each time you exit Word if changes have been made to the default settings. If this option is not checked, the changes are saved automatically.
Prompt To Save Normal Template	Displays a message each time you close Word if changes have been made to the default settings. If the option is not checked, the changes are automatically saved.
Save Data Only For Forms	Saves data entered in an online form as a single tab-delimited record so you can use it as a database.
Embed Linguistic Data	Embeds speech and handwritten data in the document, which allows users to edit and share the information.
Make Local Copy Of Files Stored On Network Or Removable Drives	Directs Word to make a temporary local copy while a document stored on a network or removable drive is in use. On Save, if the network copy is not available, Word will prompt the user to save the document in another location.
Save AutoRecover Info Every X Minutes	Directs Word to automatically save to the document recovery file at the interval you indicate in the Minutes box.
Embed Smart Tags	Saves smart tags with the document.

TABLE B.5 SAVE TAB (CONTINUED)

OPTION	DEFINITION
Save Smart Tags As XML Properties In Web Pages	Saves all smart tags in one place in an HTML file.
Save Word Files As	Sets the default application in which the documents will be saved.
Disable Features Introduced After	Turns off features that became available in recent versions of Word. This is useful when sharing files with users of an older version of the product. If a document contains features that are not supported, Word displays a list of those items and number of occurrences in the document.

TABLE B.6 USER INFORMATION TAB

OPTION	DEFINITION
Name	Stores the user's name. This option typically represents the name of the person using the computer. Some firms have entered the firm name in this field to reduce personal metadata stored within their files. When a name is entered into this box, it is used in the Document Properties dialog box, in letters, envelopes, tracked changes, and to label comments when they are inserted.
Initials	Stores the user's initials for identifying comment marks and for several elements in letters and envelopes.
Mailing Address	Sets the default mailing address used for return addresses on envelopes and letters.

TABLE B.7 USER COMPATIBILITY TAB

OPTION	DEFINITION
Font Substitution	Substitutes fonts that are available on your system for those specified but not included in the document, if you don't have the fonts the document calls for.
Recommended Options For	Selects the word processing application and version for which you want to be compatible.
Options	Presents different sets of options depending on what is chosen in Recommended Options For. Uncheck or check any options to create custom display choices for working in Word. This is document-specific.
Default	Sets the options selected on this tab as the default compatibility for the Normal template.

TABLE B.8 FILE LOCATIONS TAB

OPTION	DEFINITION
File Types	Lists the file location and path for documents, templates, and other elements while working in Word.
Modify	Allows you to change the default file location and to browse the path for the item selected.

TABLE B.9 SECURITY TAB

OPTION	DEFINITION
Password To Open	Allows you to assign a password in order to open the document. When the document is opened, a message box is displayed where the password must be entered.
Advanced	Opens the Encryption Type dialog box to select specific information for the encryption including the type, key length, and encryption document properties.
Password To Modify	Allows you to assign a password to limit who can make changes to the document.
Read-Only Recommended	Displays a message box stating that the document should be opened as read-only. The user then has a choice of creating a copy of the document, or opening the document with the ability to make changes.
Digital Signatures	Opens the Digital Signature dialog box to attach and remove signatures as well as view certificates.
Protect Document	Displays the Protect Document dialog box to select which part of the document should be protected—track changes, comments, or sections.
Remove Personal Information From This File On Save	Removes some personal information stored as metadata in the file when the file is being saved.
Warn Before Printing, Saving Or Sending A File That Contains Tracked Changes Or Comments	Provides a warning message when a document that contains tracked changes or comments is about to be printed, saved, or sent.
Store Random Number To Improve Merge Accuracy	Stores the random number generated to help keep track of related merge documents.
Macro Security	Displays the Security dialog box, where you can set the security level for macros to High, Medium, or Low. In the Trusted Sources tab, you can set up the sources to trust for templates, macros, and add-ins as well as which warnings will occur for each source.

Table B.10 Spelling & Grammar Tab

Option	Definition
Check Spelling As You Type	Checks spelling and marks potential errors with red wavy underlines.
Hide Spelling Errors In This Document	Hides the wavy red line indicating potential spelling errors.
Always Suggest Corrections	Instructs Word to present a list of suggested spellings for misspelled words detected during a spelling check.
Suggest From Main Dictionary Only	Uses only the main dictionary and not any installed custom dictionaries for spelling suggestions. Clear the option to use both the main dictionary and custom dictionary.
Ignore Words In UPPERCASE	Instructs Word not to check the spelling of words that are formatted as uppercase.
Ignore Words With Numbers	Instructs Word to skip words with numbers when checking spelling.
Ignore Internet And File Addresses	Instructs Word to skip Internet addresses, file names, and e-mail addresses when checking spelling.
Custom Dictionaries	Displays a list of available custom dictionaries as well as options to Modify, Change Default, Create New, Add, and Remove.
Check Grammar As You Type	Checks grammar automatically as you type and marks potential errors with a green wavy underline.
Hide Grammatical Errors In This Document	Hides the wavy green line under potential grammar errors in the document.
Check Grammar With Spelling	Instructs Word to check grammar along with spelling each time the Spelling Checker is run. Clear this option to tell Word to check spelling but not grammar.
Show Readability Statistics	After checking grammar, Word opens the Readability Statistics dialog box that includes information about how well the document is constructed and the reading level for comprehending the document.
Writing Style	Choose from predefined or custom writing style rules that instruct Word what to mark as a grammatical error.
Settings Button	Opens the Grammar Settings dialog box, where you can select individual items that the Grammar Checker should check or pick a preset Writing Style for different sets of items.
Check Document (sometimes Recheck Document)	Resets the Ignore All list for this document so that Word will check all words for which the user previously clicked Ignore All. Also checks spelling and grammar again after the spelling and grammar options are changed or a custom or special dictionary is opened.

TABLE B.11 TRACK CHANGES TAB

OPTION	DEFINITION
Insertions	Controls how inserted text is marked when Track Changes is enabled.
Formatting	Determines the way formatting changes are shown when Track Changes is enabled.
Color	Provides a choice of color to be used to identify changed items such as comments and tracked changes. By default, Word uses a different color for each reviewer. To restore this functionality, click By Author.
Use Balloons In Print And Web Layout	Instructs Word to show changes and comments in balloons appearing in the margin of the document when in Print Layout and Web Layout view.
Preferred Width	Set the preferred width of the balloon containing the tracked change or markup.
Measure In	Select the measurement type for the balloon width.
Margin	Select which margin to place the balloons in (left or right).
Show Lines Connecting To Text	Displays a line connecting each balloon to the place in the document where a change has occurred or comment inserted.
Paper Orientation	Controls the orientation in which the marked-up document should print. Auto lets Word pick the best layout. Preserve uses the orientation from Page Setup, and Force Landscape allows the most room for the balloons.
Mark	Places a line mark in the left or right margin (as selected) indicating where a change has been made.
Color	Specifies which color to use for the Mark lines. By default, the color is set to Auto.

APPENDIX C

KEYBOARD SHORTCUTS

KEYBOARD SHORTCUTS

FORMATTING	CHANGE VIEWS
Bold	Ctrl+B
Normal View	Ctrl+Alt+N
Italic	Ctrl+I
Underline	Ctrl+U
Hidden	Ctrl+Shift+H
Center Alignment	Ctrl+E
Left Alignment	Ctrl+L
Right Alignment	Ctrl+R
Change the font	Ctrl+Shift+F
Change the font size	Ctrl+Shift+P
Increase the font size	Ctrl+Shift+>
Decrease the font size	Ctrl+Shift+<
Indent from left	Ctrl+M
Decrease indent	Ctrl+Shift+M
Hanging indent	Ctrl+T
Reduce a hanging indent	Ctrl+Shift+T
Single-space	Ctrl+1
Double-space	Ctrl+2
1.5–line spacing	Ctrl+5
(Toggle) Space Before 12pt.	Ctrl+0 (zero)
Remove paragraph formatting	Ctrl+Q
Remove character formatting	Ctrl+Spacebar
What's This	Shift+F1

Working with Documents

Create a new document	Ctrl+N
Open a document	Ctrl+O
Close a document	Ctrl+W
Save a document	Ctrl+S
Save As	F12
Print Layout View	Ctrl+Alt+P
Outline View	Ctrl+Alt+O

KEYBOARD SHORTCUTS

FORMATTING	CHANGE VIEWS
Navigation	
Top of Document	Ctrl+Home Key
End of Document	Ctrl+End Key
Character Left	Arrow Key Left
Character Right	Arrow Key
One Word Left	Ctrl+Left Arrow
One Word Right	Ctrl+Right Arrow
Beginning of Line	Home Key
End of Line	End Key
Top of Previous Page	Ctrl+Page Up
Top of Next Page	Ctrl+Page Down
Next Cell in a table	Tab
Previous Cell in a table	Shift+Tab
Selecting Text	
One Character Right	Shift+Right Arrow
One Character Left	Shift+Left Arrow
Beginning of One Word	Ctrl+Shift+Left Arrow
End of One Word	Ctrl+Shift+Right Arrow
One Line Up	Shift+Up Arrow
One Line Down	Shift+Down Arrow
One Paragraph Up	Ctrl+Shift+Up Arrow
One Paragraph Down	Ctrl+Shift+Down Arrow
Entire Table	Alt+5 (Numeric Keypad with Numlock off)
Apply Paragraph Styles	
Apply a style	Ctrl+Shift+S
Print	Ctrl+P
Spellcheck	F7
Thesaurus	Shift+F7
Cut	Ctrl+X

KEYBOARD SHORTCUTS

FORMATTING	CHANGE VIEWS
Copy	Ctrl+C
Paste	Ctrl+V
Undo an action	Ctrl+Z
Redo an action	Ctrl+Y
Repeat an action	F4
Find	Ctrl+F
Replace	Ctrl+H
Go To	Ctrl+G
Apply the Normal style	Ctrl+Shift+N
Apply the Heading 1 style	Ctrl+Alt+1
Apply the Heading 2 style	Ctrl+Alt+2
Apply the Heading 3 style	Ctrl+Alt+3
Apply the List style	Ctrl+Shift+L

Symbols and Special Characters

Soft Line Break	Shift+Enter
Page Break	Ctrl+Enter
Column Break	Ctrl+Shift+Enter
Nonbreaking Hyphen	Ctrl+Shift+Hyphen
Copyright Symbol	Ctrl+Alt+C
Registered Trademark Symbol	Ctrl+Alt+R
Trademark Symbol	Ctrl+Alt+T
Last Edit	Shift+F5
Ellipsis	Ctrl+Alt+Period
Footnote	Ctrl+Alt+F
Euro Symbol	Ctrl+Alt+E
Endnote	Ctrl+Alt+D
Tab in a Cell	Ctrl+Tab
Show/Hide	Ctrl+Shift+*

GLOSSARY

Address Assistant: An add-in available from Payne Consulting Group, Inc., that simplifies the creation of envelopes and labels. *See* Add-In.

Add-In: A program or template that enhances an application, such as Word, with additional functionality. Add-ins are designed to assist users with some of the more difficult functions and features associated with a given application. The Payne Numbering Assistant is an example of an add-in.

Alt+Ctrl+Delete: This combination of keystrokes is used to break into a program that is not responding.

Alternate-Click: This describes pressing and quickly releasing the right mouse button (unless the mouse buttons have been reconfigured via the Control Panel). Alternate-clicking produces a shortcut menu with options specific to the object that was alternate-clicked.

Applet: A mini application that inserts different objects into Word with various formatting choices available. Applets commonly used in law firms include Organization Chart and Equation Editor.

Arrange All: Command that arranges open documents in the active window so they are all visible.

Ask A Question: If the user does not want to activate the Office Assistant, there is a new feature located at the upper-right-hand of the screen called Ask A Question. Type a question into the available box and an answer will be returned.

Attached Template: A template attached to a document. All the macros, toolbars, shortcut keys, AutoText entries, and styles in the attached template are made available to the document whenever it is open. If the document was created based on the template, any boilerplate text contained in the template also appears in the document; however, the text can be edited or removed. Boilerplate text does not transfer from a template to a document when the template is attached to the document after the document is created. *See* Global Template.

AutoComplete: A built-in Word feature that will offer ScreenTips to automatically complete what the user has begun to type. Some of the more common AutoComplete entries appear when a user begins to type the month, date, or year. A ScreenTip will appear offering the completed word. To accept the AutoComplete prompt, press the Enter key at the appearance of the identifying ScreenTip. If you do not want to accept the suggested AutoComplete entry, just keep typing and it will not be inserted into your document.

AutoCorrect: A feature designed to automatically correct misspelled words and other common typing mistakes as well as expand shortcuts while you type. Word has an extensive built-in list of AutoCorrect entries. Users can create additional AutoCorrect entries whenever needed.

AutoFit: Used with tables, AutoFit allows users to set a fixed column width, automatically fit columns to match their contents, and automatically adjust the table to match the width of the document.

AutoFormat: Located under the Format menu, AutoFormat automatically applies formatting to documents based on the options set in the AutoFormat dialog box. When selected, AutoFormat analyzes the contents of the document and applies the specified formatting.

AutoFormat As You Type: This feature will allow the user to choose default-formatting settings to be applied as the document is created. For example, the user has the option to select the default type of quotation marks used in their documents (curly or straight). There are many formatting options available in this dialog box, including styles, borders, and shading. The most important thing to remember with this feature is that these option settings will affect documents as you work on them.

AutoText: Saved text or graphics that you can use repeatedly. AutoText entries that have a name length of four characters or more can be inserted by using AutoComplete. Entries with a name of less than four characters can be inserted by typing the name of the AutoText entry and pressing F3.

Background: Primarily used when designing Web pages in Word, backgrounds can also be used in documents. Adding a background to a document can change the color of the page onscreen; however, the background will not print (except when inserting a Watermark from the Background menu).

Bar Code: A bar code or field placed in an address block of an envelope or label used to speed up delivery of documents; similar to a ZIP code.

Bitmap: A graphics file format identified by the file extension .bmp.

Boilerplate Text: Text in a document or template that is used repeatedly as the basis for creating new documents.

Bookmark: A method for identifying a location in a document. Bookmarks can be inserted into a document for the purpose of marking or cross-referencing. Bookmark names cannot start with a number and cannot contain spaces.

Branding: The term used to designate a unique image for the firm that includes firm logo, mission statement, standardized formats, and much more. This is also referred to as *branding an image*.

Browse Object: This feature is a shortcut to move the insertion point or find specific items in a document. It is located on the vertical scrollbar at the bottom right-hand side of the screen. Click on the circle between the double arrows and a grid will display showing the available items to browse from, such as footnotes, graphics, section breaks, and more.

Cache: (Pronounced *cash*.) Storage area used to speed up the retrieval of data by holding the most recently used data in memory or on a network or local storage medium. Web cache retains the most recently updated contents of a visited Web site by creating a cached collection of graphics and images on the PC's hard disk or in memory.

Caption: Identifying text and numbers that appear above or below items such as tables or graphics.

Cell: The intersection of a row and a column in a table.

Cell Reference: The code identifying a cell's position within a table. Each cell reference contains a letter (A, B, C) to identify the column and a number (1, 2, 3) to identify the row.

Changed Lines: To make it easy to find tracked changes, Word can add vertical bars in the margins next to the lines of edited text.

Character Style: A saved collection of font attributes that can be applied to words or characters within a paragraph or document.

Click And Type: Double-click anywhere in the Word document, and begin typing. A special cursor appears when using this feature, allowing you to see the formatting associated with the placement of your cursor. A small icon is added below your cursor to indicate centered, left-aligned, or right-aligned text. These icons are identical to the alignment toolbar buttons found on the Formatting toolbar. This feature must be activated through the Tools, Options menu and the document must be in either Print Layout or Web Layout view for this feature to work.

Client: When using computer equipment, the requesting entity in a client/server environment. Most often, this is a workstation. *See* Client/Server.

Client/Server: A network architecture where the client (workstation) requests information from the server. A good example of a client/server relationship would be with a document management system. The workstation requests a document from the server and the server sends the document to the client/workstation.

Clipboard: A temporary storage area for cut or copied items. The Office XP clipboard can hold up to 24 items and can be used to copy items within a given application or between Office applications. A new Clipboard Task Pane has been added to Word 2002, which will allow users to easily identify items on the Clipboard and paste them into a document.

Column: A vertical collection of cells within a table or spreadsheet.

Columns: A Word feature for inserting newspaper-like columns into a document.

Comment: Usually nonprinting text that appears in balloons while in Print Layout or Web Layout view. Comments are less visible in Normal view but can be viewed using ScreenTips or opening the Reviewing Pane from the Reviewing toolbar.

Compare And Merge: A feature used to analyze the differences between two documents by merging them together and producing a marked-up output file. If the Legal Blackline option is selected, the output file is a separate document.

Conversions Plus: A third-party document conversion utility. More information can be found at www.dataviz.com.

CPU (Central Processing Unit): Also referred to as the *processor*, the CPU is the brains of the computer and performs all the computations that make a computer operate.

Cross Reference: A statement in a document that refers the reader to another part of the document. Cross references can be used with headings, bookmarks, numbers, footnotes, endnotes, tables, and figures.

CrossWords: A third-party utility used to convert documents from WordPerfect to Microsoft Word. More information can be found at www.levitjames.com

Data Source: A document that contains variable information for use with Word's Mail Merge feature. Valid data sources include a Word table, an Excel worksheet, an Access database file, or any MAPI-compliant database.

DeltaView: A third-party utility used to run document comparisons. More information can be found at www.workshare.net.

Detect And Repair: A feature included in the Office installation program that automatically looks for missing or damaged files and replaces or repairs them as needed.

Diagram: A feature in Word 2002 used to quickly create and insert Organizational, Venn, Pyramid, and other types of charts directly into the active document.

Direct Formatting: Any formatting that you manually apply to the text in the document, such as font style, size, bold, underline, or other formatting, rather than modifying the text style.

DMS (Document Management System): An enterprise-wide system used to store, protect, retrieve, share, and distribute documents and other files within the confines of a network.

DOCS Open: A third-party document management system. More information can be found at www.hummingbird.com.

Document Grid: A feature that allows users to turn on a nonprinting grid that appears in the Word document.

Document Map: A feature designed to allow users to quickly navigate through long documents formatted with heading styles. The Document Map opens as a separate pane and displays the headings in a document as links. Click on a link to jump to that part of the document.

Document Properties: Details about a document that include file location, author, date created, date modified, editing time, the number of revisions made, and the number of words in the document.

DocXChange: A third-party utility used for converting WordPerfect documents to Microsoft Word documents. More information can be found at www.microsystems.com.

Drag And Drop: A visual method used to drag objects from one location to another. The user selects text or clicks on an object, holds down the left mouse button, and drags the selected text or object to another location. While the mouse button is held down, the item travels with the cursor until the left mouse button is released. Once released, the item is dropped into the new location.

Drawing Canvas: New toolbar available in Word 2002 that offers the ability to manipulate multiple graphics at one time.

Drawing Object: The user can access different types of drawing objects from the Drawing toolbar. Includes free-form tools as well as predefined drawing shapes and text boxes. To display the Drawing toolbar, alternate-click on the toolbars and choose Drawing from the menu.

Drop Cap: Used often in novels or newsletters, this feature enlarges the first letter of a paragraph so that it spans two or more lines.

Embedded Object: An object created and edited in a non-Word program; the object is inserted into and stored as part of the document.

Endnote: A note placed at the end of a document, or section, which describes or provides additional information about a referenced piece of text within the document. *See* Footnote.

Equation Editor: An Office add-in used to create complex or scientific equations. *See* Add-In.

Extend: Extends the current selection to the next place you click within the document. Pressing the F8 key activates extended selection mode.

Field: A code that provides variable information within a document or directs Word to take a certain action. For example, a document containing a date field, with the Update Automatically option selected, will always show the current date every time the document is opened. Fields are often shaded in gray.

Field Code: The actual code associated with a field. The field code acts as a placeholder for variable information. To view the field code rather than the field, place the insertion point in the field and press Alt+F9.

Field Label: A word or phrase that identifies the information users should enter for a particular field.

File Properties: This feature lists the attributes associated with the current document; to view the file properties in Word, from the File menu, choose Properties. This dialog box contains five tabs: General, Summary, Statistics, Contents, and Custom. Among other things, document properties stores information such as author, title, file size, and how many pages, words, and characters are contained in the document.

Firewall: A system designed to maintain network security. Firewalls are intended to prevent unwanted external access to an internal network. They also provide secure access to the Internet for users within a network.

First Line Indent: This feature only affects the first line of a paragraph. Rather than pressing Tab at the beginning of every paragraph, this feature will automatically indent the first line by the amount of space designated. The first line indentation amount can be set by using the ruler or by choosing Indentation Special from the Paragraph dialog box located under the Format menu.

Font: A typeface used in documents. Every font is a combination of different qualities such as height, width, and spacing. Times New Roman and Arial are examples of fonts.

Footer: Repeating text that appears at the bottom of each page in a document.

Footnote: A note at the bottom of a page that describes or provides additional information about a referenced piece of text on that same page. *See* Endnote.

Format Painter: A feature that allows you to copy character or paragraph formatting from one part of a document to another.

Formatting Toolbar: The toolbar that usually appears beneath the Standard toolbar and contains a set of buttons used for applying the most common formatting commands.

Forms Assistant: An add-in available from Payne Consulting Group, Inc., that simplifies the creation of complex legal documents. *See* Add-In.

Frames: Used in Web design, frames allow Web pages to have different windows as opposed to one long, continuous page.

Freeware: Software that is distributed free of charge via the Internet. *See* Shareware.

Front End Profiling: When working with a document management system, you will be prompted to fill out a profile when first creating a new document rather than the first time you click Save.

Full Screen: A view option that allows you to see more of a document by temporarily hiding the menu bar, toolbars, ruler, and scrollbars.

Global Template: A template activated either via Word's Startup folder or from the Templates And Add-Ins dialog box, but not attached to a given file. Any macros, toolbars, or AutoText entries stored in a global template are available to any document open while the template is active, but disappear when the template is deactivated. Normal.dot acts like a global template when it is not attached to the current file. *See* Attached Template.

Gridlines: Nonprinting horizontal and vertical lines that are used to provide assistance when lining up graphics on the page.

Hanging Indent: Sets a left indentation for all lines in the paragraph except for the first line. Used to make the first line of a paragraph more prominent. Similar to the first line indentation option, the user can set the hanging indent using the ruler or by choosing Indentation Special from the Paragraph dialog box located under the Format menu.

Header: Repeating text that appears at the top of each page in a document.

Header And Footer: A separate layer of the Word document that can contain repetitive information, such as letterhead, document ID, and page number information.

Hidden Paragraph Mark: A paragraph mark with the hidden font attribute applied.

Horizontal Scrollbar: The scrollbar located at the bottom of the document window used to move from one side of the document to the other. This scrollbar is extremely helpful with documents using a landscape orientation.

HTML (HyperText Markup Language): A language that uses *tags* (beginning and ending codes) to format text so that regular documents can be displayed in Web browsers.

Hyperlink: A word or phrase, usually underlined, used to transport you to another point in the current document, an outside document, a location on a file server, or even a Web site when clicked.

iManage: A third-party document management system. More information can be found at www.imanage.com.

Insertion Point: The short blinking vertical line used to indicate where text will be inserted when you type in the current document.

Install On First: An option that can be set during the installation process to load specific files or features the first time you attempt to use them.

Intranet: An internal version of the Internet. An intranet is typically used by companies to display and communicate internal information critical to the operation of the company. Intranets use the same technology as the Internet but are geared for a much more limited audience.

Jason Tab: This is an unsolicited tab stop named after the horror movie character (because it just keeps coming back), positioned .25" after the left indent. This tab setting will occur on any level where numbering is defined to be followed by a tab character. Naming credit to Microsystems.

Keep Lines Together: A paragraph format that keeps all the lines in a paragraph on the same page.

Keep With Next: A paragraph format that prevents a page break from occurring between two paragraphs.

Kerning: A type of character formatting that allows the user to adjust the spacing between characters where the width of each character varies. Kerning is a font-formatting attribute used in conjunction with True Type Fonts.

Knowledge Base: Microsoft provides a searchable database at their Web site for all Microsoft products. This helpful database contains troubleshooting information on known problems and issues with Microsoft software. More information can be found at www.microsoft.com.

LAN (Local Area Network): A network that serves users within a confined geographical area such as an office building or college campus. A LAN is used to connect workstations and servers using data lines. *See* WAN.

Legal Blackline: This option can be found by choosing Compare And Merge from the Tools menu. Legal Blackline opens a separate document showing the comparison results from merging two documents together.

Line Spacing: A button on the Formatting toolbar that includes a drop-down arrow that, when clicked, reveals options for 1.0, 1.5, 2.0, 3.0, and More line spacing. When More is chosen, the Paragraph dialog box opens.

Link: A connection between an object and the source file.

List Style: Preset options for outline numbering. You can use one of Word's built-in list styles or create your own.

Macro: A collection of commands and keystrokes that can be recorded, named, and saved to perform repetitive tasks. Rather than record a macro, they can also be created from scratch with the programming language called Visual Basic for Applications (VBA).

Macro Virus: A dangerous routine that is written in a macro language and placed within a file or a template. Macro viruses can be very destructive due in part to the rapid manner in which they propagate. *See* Word Macro Virus.

Mail Merge: A feature used to merge a main document with a data source to quickly create large sets of letters, labels, envelopes, e-mail messages, or catalogs.

Main Document: The document in a Mail Merge that contains the standard, boilerplate text and includes the merge fields that pull information from the data source to create the individualized merge documents.

Markup Balloon: New to Word 2002, Markup balloons appear in the margin of documents when working in Print Layout and Web Layout view. These Markup balloons provide information about changes made to the text of the document while using Track Changes. They also include comments inserted by the user.

Media Gallery: The Media Gallery is the library that holds all the media clips found on your computer.

Menu Bar: A set of menu items usually located at the top of the application window, directly below the title bar. Each menu item contains related commands that appear in a drop-down list. The menu bar can either be docked or floating.

Merge Fields: Placeholders located in the main document for the variable information contained in a data source. These fields are inserted in the main document during a Mail Merge operation. *See* Main Document, Data Source.

Merge Pasted Lists With Surrounding Lists: Allows you to combine numbered lists from two separate documents into one continuous list, even if the numbering is formatted differently. To ensure that this option is turned on, from the Tools menu, choose Options, select the Edit tab, and click Settings.

Metadata: Hidden information that is attached to and travels with every Word document. Metadata includes data such as the last 10 authors, tracked changes, hidden text, file locations, and file properties.

Metadata Assistant: A utility available from Payne Consulting Group, Inc., that analyzes and strips metadata from Word documents. This utility was written about on the front page of the *Wall Street Journal* on October 20, 2000.

Mouse Pointer: The onscreen element that indicates what text, button, or other item will be affected by the next mouse click. The appearance of the pointer changes according to where it is and what it is able to do—for example, it looks like an I-beam when in a text passage and a pointing hand on a hyperlink.

Nested Table: This feature allows the user to create a table within an existing table.

Normal.dot (Pronounced Normal dot-dot): A Word template that loads every time the application is launched and serves as the basis for every new document unless another template is specifically designated during the creation process. The Normal.dot can be modified to include custom toolbars, macros, AutoText entries, styles, and boilerplate text. *See* Attached Template, Global Template.

Normal View: The view most commonly used to quickly input text into a document. Headers, footers, footnotes, endnotes, and graphics do not appear in Normal view, allowing for faster scrolling.

Numbering Assistant: An add-in available from Payne Consulting Group, Inc., that simplifies the process of applying multilevel numbering schemes in a document and also is used to quickly generate a table of contents. *See* Add-In.

Object: A non–text-based item in a document. Objects can include pictures, sound files, movie files, or clip art.

ODMA (Open Document Management API [application programming interface]): A standard allowing desktop applications, such as Word and Excel, to communicate with document management systems located on a server.

Office Assistant: An animated character that automatically provides tips while you work. Some users find the Office Assistant intrusive, so this feature can be turned off or limited.

Office Clipboard: A tool that allows you to cut, copy, and paste up to 24 objects or sections of text at a time. The Office Clipboard can be used to copy, cut, and paste items within or between Office applications. A new Clipboard Task Pane has been added to Word 2002, which allows you to identify items on the Clipboard and paste them into a document.

Open And Repair: An option that attempts to repair a damaged or corrupt file prior to opening it.

Organization Chart: The user can create different types of organizational and flowcharts directly from the Drawing toolbar. When clicking on the organizational chart icon on the toolbar, different formatting options for the organizational chart will appear.

Organizer: A Word utility used to quickly copy styles, macros, AutoText entries, and toolbars from one template or document to another.

Outline View: The view used for creating outlines using Word's heading styles. Also used when working with Word's Master Document feature. You can see more or less of the document in Outline view by expanding or collapsing each of the heading items.

Overtype Mode: A feature that automatically replaces existing text as you type. Overtype mode can be turned on by pressing the Insert key, or by double-clicking OVR on the Status bar.

Page Break: A break that occurs between pages within a document. A soft page break occurs naturally when the text from one page flows onto the next page. A hard page break is used to manually force Word to start a new page.

Paragraph: A block of text ending with a hard carriage return, represented in Word by the ¶ symbol. This symbol also indicates where all of the formatting for each paragraph is stored. Each paragraph in Word can have its own set of formatting without affecting other paragraphs within the document. Pressing the Enter key creates a new paragraph.

Paragraph Position Mark: An identifying mark to the left of a paragraph to indicate that the paragraph format Keep With Next or Keep Lines Together has been applied.

Paragraph Spacing: The amount of space between paragraphs and typically measured in points. In a single-spaced document, paragraph spacing should be set to 12 points of space after, or one line between paragraphs, thus eliminating the need to press Enter twice at the end of a paragraph to create the space needed between paragraphs.

Paragraph Style: A named, saved collection of character and paragraph formats that can be applied to one or more paragraphs within a document. Styles help to reduce or eliminate unnecessary manual or direct formatting. *See* Direct Formatting.

Paste Options: Word has a feature called Smart Cut and Paste. This feature will automatically adjust the spacing when deleting or inserting text. To turn on this feature, click the Tools menu, choose Options, select the Edit tab, and place a check next to Smart Cut And Paste.

Paste Special: A command found on the Edit menu used to paste text from a different document or word processing program into a Word document. Use Paste Special As Unformatted Text to reduce the risk of document corruption when working with converted documents, since none of the formatting codes are inserted along with the text.

Pixel: The smallest addressable unit on a display screen. Pixels form the bitmapped graphic images you see onscreen and are made up of one or more dots of color.

Point: A measurement of type size, based on 72 points per inch. The measurement describes the height rather than the width of the letters, so the same point size can designate type that occupies very different amounts of space on a line.

Print Layout View: The view that provides the most accurate representation of how your document will appear on the printed page.

RAM (Random Access Memory): The chips (memory storage devices) in a computer that determine how much the system can do at one time. The more RAM, the more programs that can run at the same time.

Reveal Formatting: Located under the Format menu, this feature allows you to see the font, paragraph, and section formatting for the active document and selected text within it by opening up the Reveal Formatting Task Pane.

Reviewing Toolbar: This toolbar is used to view, accept, and reject Track Changes, including comments, in a document.

Round-Tripping: This term is used to describe when a document is created in one word processing program, then opened (not converted and cleaned) in another, and then reopened back in its original word processing program (also not converted and cleaned up). Round-tripping is very dangerous and can lead to document corruption.

Row: A horizontal collection of cells within a table or spreadsheet.

Sans Serif Font: A font that does not contain the small stroke at the bottom of each character (e.g., Arial). These fonts are frequently used for headings in a document, book, or other publication.

Section Break: Inserted into a Word document when different page formats are needed in the same document. Section breaks are commonly seen when creating different numbering formats for different areas of a document.

Selection Bar: An unmarked area located in the left section of the Word screen and used for selecting text. When the cursor is positioned in the selection area, the mouse pointer changes into a northeasterly pointing arrow and can be used to quickly select lines, paragraphs, and the whole document.

Serif Font: A font that contains the small stroke at the bottom of each character (e.g., Times New Roman). Serif fonts are used most often in business documents and as the body text font in books and publications.

Server: A computer on a network shared by multiple users. In a client/server environment, the server typically stores files or data that can be retrieved or shared by the workstation clients. *See* Client/Server.

Shareware: Programs distributed on a trial basis usually via the Internet. It is assumed that the person downloading the software will pay for the product once the trial period ends; however, this is usually left to the honor system. *See* Freeware.

Shortcut Menu: A context-specific menu that displays a list of commands. Shortcut menus can be accessed by alternate-clicking or pressing the Shift+F10 key. These menus are available for many items such as text, graphics, tables, and misspelled words, just to name a few.

Show/Hide White Space: Used to save screen space while in Print Layout view by hiding the unused white space at the top and bottom of each page. You can hide the white space by default by choosing Options from the Tools menu, and clearing the White Space Between Pages box on the View tab.

Single Document Interface (SDI): Each document resides within its own window and can be accessed directly from the Windows Taskbar.

Sizing Handles: A table can be resized by dragging the table resize handle located in the bottom-right corner of the table. When doing this, the point size of the text remains the same and just the table structure is resized.

Smart Tag: Data that is labeled as a particular type and recognized by Word. Names, addresses, and even telephone numbers can be labeled with Smart Tags. Data labeled with Smart Tags can have certain actions performed automatically, like inserting the name of an Outlook contact into a Word document.

Soft Page Break: Word automatically creates a soft page break as text reaches the end of one page and flows onto the next. This is also known as a *natural page break*.

Spinner: The control most often found in dialog boxes with double-arrows that can be clicked in the up or down direction to set an increment value.

Split: Located on the Window menu, the Split command allows you to split one document into two parts. This command is useful for cutting or copying text between parts of a lengthy document. Each split part has its own set of scrollbars and can be accessed and manipulated independently.

Standard Toolbar: The toolbar usually located at the top of the Word window directly below the menu bar. The Standard toolbar contains buttons for those most frequently used Word commands, such as Save, Print, Copy, Paste, and much more.

Startup Folder: The folder location specified in the File Locations dialog box. The Startup folder is used to load custom global templates and add-ins, which can override or supplement Word's existing settings, toolbars, and macros.

Status Bar: The bar located at the bottom of the document window. It displays information about the active document including the current page number, number of sections, number of pages, and the vertical position of the insertion point. The status bar also displays information regarding the status of the Macro Recorder, Track Changes, Extended Selection, and Overtype mode.

Style: A named collection of formats used to quickly apply formatting to one or more paragraphs within a document. *See* Paragraph Style.

Style Alias: A nickname for a style. Aliases appear after the style name and are separated by a comma.

Style Gallery: This is a collection of templates that allows you to take all the styles from one template and add them to your document.

Styles And Formatting: The Styles And Formatting Task Pane can be used to view and apply styles, analyze current styles, and even create new styles.

Style Area: When activated, an area to the left of the document appears while in Normal and Outline view. The Style Area provides a list of styles associated with each of the paragraphs in the active document.

Style Area Width: Used to set the size of the Style Area. This option can be turned on by choosing Tools, Options, View and then using the spinner controls to set the size in the Style Area Width box.

Style Separator: This feature allows the user to have two different styles existing in the same paragraph; for example, a heading style at the beginning of the paragraph and the normal style for the remainder of the paragraph.

Symbol Dialog Box: A feature that provides access to a large number of common and not-so-common symbols. The section § and paragraph ¶ symbols are frequently used in legal documents and can be found, along with other symbols, by choosing Insert, Symbol, Special Characters, or by pressing Ctrl+W.

Table Styles: Built-in styles that allow users to quickly format a table. Each table style has preset options for color, lines, shading, and font.

Tabs: Settings used to line up text in a document, as with the tab stops on a typewriter. By default, Word tabs are set at .5" increments, but you can place them wherever they are needed. Tabs can be set using the ruler, or the Tabs dialog box. Word has left, centered, right, decimal, and bar tabs.

Task Pane: A window that opens on the right side of the document window and provides task- and document-specific information. There are several different task panes and each varies according to the command or function being performed.

Template: A Word file that can contain boilerplate text, custom toolbars, menus, shortcut keys, styles, and macros. Templates are identified by the file extension .dot. *See* Normal.dot.

Text Box: Text boxes are drawing objects found on the Drawing toolbar that allow you to place text anywhere in the document without the requirement of complex formatting.

Text Flow: Refers to the manner in which text flows or breaks across pages. Widow/Orphan Control, Keep With Next, and Keep Lines Together are examples of commands that control text flow.

Thesaurus: A Word feature used to look up synonyms and antonyms.

Title Bar: The bar at the top of the application window that displays the name of the document or file and the name of the application.

Track Changes: A feature that allows you to see the changes made to a document. Additions and deletions are marked in a specific manner. Changes can be accepted or rejected one by one or all at once. *See* Metadata.

True Type Font: A scalable font that looks the same on the screen as it does on the printed page. True Type fonts are typically used in the word processing environment.

Versions: This feature allows Word to save separate versions of a document within the same file and is accessed by choosing Versions from the File menu. The document Compare and Merge feature will not work with this version feature. *See* Compare And Merge.

Vertical Scrollbar: The scrollbar located on the right side of the document window that allows you to move forward or backward in the document one line, screen, or page at a time.

Visual Basic For Applications (VBA): Microsoft's built-in programming language, which is used to write macros.

Visual Basic Editor: Opened by pressing Alt+F11, the Visual Basic Editor is the primary workspace for writing or editing VBA macros.

WAN (Wide Area Network): A network that covers a large geographic area. WANs are typically used to connect multiple offices or organizations in different locales (cities, states, or even countries) through the use of high-speed data lines.

Watermark: Text, picture, or other graphic that resides in the Header/Footer layer that often appears grayed out behind the text on every page of a document.

Web Browser: A software application used to access and display Web pages. Internet Explorer and Netscape are examples of browsers.

Web Layout View: Word view particularly useful when creating Web pages. Text is wrapped to fit the document window, and graphics that appear in the document will be positioned as they would online.

Web Page: A document constructed with HTML that can be viewed through a Web browser. Web pages typically reside on Web servers and are accessible with an Internet connection.

Web Site: A group of associated Web pages joined together by hyperlinks.

Widow/Orphan Control: The definition of *widow* is when the last line of a paragraph is left by itself at the top of a page. An *orphan* is the first line of a paragraph left by itself at the bottom of a page. The Widow/Orphan control prevents occurrences, as defined above, from happening. The option can be found by choosing Paragraph from the Format menu and clicking on the Line And Page Breaks tab.

Word Macro Virus: A macro virus written specifically for Word documents or templates. When an infected document or template is opened, the macro runs and often infects Normal.dot so that every document created thereafter becomes infected.

Wizard: An interactive set of dialog boxes that step you through the process of installing an application, creating a document, or performing some process or action.

WORLDOX®: A third-party document management system. For more information, visit www.worlddox.com.

WordArt: This feature can be found on the Drawing toolbar and is a gallery of text that already has all of the formatting applied.

Zoom: Located on the Standard toolbar, use the Zoom box to enlarge or shrink the onscreen image so you can see more or less of the active document.

INDEX

NUMBERS/SYMBOLS

A

B

D

E

F

G

H

I

L

N

P

Q

R

T

U

V

W

License Agreement/Notice of Limited Warranty

By opening the sealed disc container in this book, you agree to the following terms and conditions. If, upon reading the following license agreement and notice of limited warranty, you cannot agree to the terms and conditions set forth, return the unused book with unopened disc to the place where you purchased it for a refund.

License:
The enclosed software is copyrighted by the copyright holder(s) indicated on the software disk. You are licensed to copy the software onto a single computer for use by a single concurrent user and to a backup disk. You may not reproduce, make copies, or distribute copies or rent or lease the software in whole or in part, except with written permission of the copyright holder(s). You may transfer the enclosed disc only together with this license, and only if you destroy all other copies of the software and the transferee agrees to the terms of the license. You may not decompile, reverse assemble, or reverse engineer the software.

Notice of Limited Warranty:
The enclosed disc is warranted by Prima Publishing to be free of physical defects in materials and workmanship for a period of sixty (60) days from end user's purchase of the book/disc combination. During the sixty-day term of the limited warranty, Prima will provide a replacement disc upon the return of a defective disc.

Limited Liability:
THE SOLE REMEDY FOR BREACH OF THIS LIMITED WARRANTY SHALL CONSIST ENTIRELY OF REPLACEMENT OF THE DEFECTIVE DISC. IN NO EVENT SHALL PRIMA OR THE AUTHORS BE LIABLE FOR ANY OTHER DAMAGES, INCLUDING LOSS OR CORRUPTION OF DATA, CHANGES IN THE FUNCTIONAL CHARACTERISTICS OF THE HARDWARE OR OPERATING SYSTEM, DELETERIOUS INTERACTION WITH OTHER SOFTWARE, OR ANY OTHER SPECIAL, INCIDENTAL, OR CONSEQUENTIAL DAMAGES THAT MAY ARISE, EVEN IF PRIMA AND/OR THE AUTHOR HAVE PREVIOUSLY BEEN NOTIFIED THAT THE POSSIBILITY OF SUCH DAMAGES EXISTS.

Disclaimer of Warranties:
PRIMA AND THE AUTHORS SPECIFICALLY DISCLAIM ANY AND ALL OTHER WARRANTIES, EITHER EXPRESS OR IMPLIED, INCLUDING WARRANTIES OF MERCHANTABILITY, SUITABILITY TO A PARTICULAR TASK OR PURPOSE, OR FREEDOM FROM ERRORS. SOME STATES DO NOT ALLOW FOR EXCLUSION OF IMPLIED WARRANTIES OR LIMITATION OF INCIDENTAL OR CONSEQUENTIAL DAMAGES, SO THESE LIMITATIONS MAY NOT APPLY TO YOU.

Other:
This Agreement is governed by the laws of the State of California without regard to choice of law principles. The United Convention of Contracts for the International Sale of Goods is specifically disclaimed. This Agreement constitutes the entire agreement between you and Prima Publishing regarding use of the software.